ARISTOPHANES

III

LCL 180

ARISTOPHANES

WITH AN ENGLISH TRANSLATION BY

BENJAMIN BICKLEY ROGERS

THE LYSISTRATA
THE THESMOPHORIAZUSAE
THE ECCLESIAZUSAE   THE PLUTUS

HARVARD UNIVERSITY PRESS
CAMBRIDGE, MASSACHUSETTS
LONDON, ENGLAND

First published 1924
Reprinted 1927, 1931, 1946, 1955, 1963, 1972, 1979,
1991, 1996

ISBN 0-674-99199-0

Printed in Great Britain by St Edmundsbury Press Ltd,
Bury St Edmunds, Suffolk, on acid-free paper.
Bound by Hunter & Foulis Ltd, Edinburgh, Scotland.

CONTENTS

BIBLIOGRAPHICAL NOTE (1979)

Editions :

Lysistrata : U. von Wilamowitz-Moellendorff (introduction, text, apparatus, commentary, excursus on
Ecclesiazusae), Berlin, 1927 (repr. 1958).

Ecclesiazusae : R. G. Ussher (introduction, text, apparatus, commentary), Oxford, 1973.

Plutus : K. Holzinger (commentary), Vienna, 1940.

Other :

C. W. Dearden, *The Stage of Aristophanes*, London, 1976.

K. J. Dover, *Aristophanic Comedy*, London, 1972.

Victor Ehrenberg, *The People of Aristophanes*, Oxford,
1951².

Gilbert Murray, *Aristophanes : A Study*, Oxford, 1933,

O. J. Todd, *Index Aristophaneus*, Cambridge, Mass.
1932.

T. B. L. Webster, *Greek Theatre Production*, London,
1970².

Cedric H. Whitman, *Aristophanes and the Comic Hero*,
Cambridge, Mass., 1964.

THE LYSISTRATA

INTRODUCTION

" In the autumn of 413 B.C. the news of the over-whelming catastrophe in Sicily reached Athens, and the *Lysistrata* was written in the year 412, at the very darkest period of the Peloponnesian War, the darkest, that is to say, before the ultimate disaster of Aegospotami, and the consequent fall of Athens. It was produced at the commencement of the year 411 B.C., but whether at the Lenaea or at the Great Dionysia, and with what success, the scanty record which has come down to us contains nothing to show." [a]

In spite, however, of their difficulties, the Athenians determined that they would not give in ; they would build a new navy in place of the fleets they had lost. The sum of 1000 talents, held in reserve, was voted to build the new fleet, timber and oar-spars being amongst the articles most sorely needed, and amongst other measures, " they appointed a Board of Ten Probuli, a sort of Committee of Public Safety." [b] (In the play the Probulus commands the Scythian archers, whom elsewhere we find attending upon the βουλή; he comes to the Acropolis to obtain the means of rebuilding the fleet ; he directs the βουλή to send plenipotentiaries to treat with the Spartans.) " It was in a period of hopeless despond-ency that Lysistrata developed her own original scheme for a general pacification of the warring Hellenic states." [c]

[a] Rogers, Introduction, p. x.   [b] *Ib.* p. xi.   [c] *Ib.* p. xviii.

2

INTRODUCTION

The Acropolis is an isolated rock, rising to a height of about 500 feet above the level of the sea ; the levelled top measures some 1000 feet by 450 at the widest part. This plateau the Pelasgians " surrounded by a wall (τὸ Πελασγικόν), which lasted, apparently unaltered, till the time of the Persian invasion." [a] Then the wall was thrown down, and it was rebuilt by Cimon ; the southern part is called Cimonian, the rest Pelasgian. " The entire Acropolis was holy ground ; and the numerous temples which crowded it were all dominated by the triple presentment of Athens as the Πολιάς, the Παρθένος, and the Πρόμαχος." [b] The Erechtheum was the most ancient temple in Athens, and it contained the sacred serpent and the ancient wooden statue of Athene, to which the Peplus used to be offered at the Great Panathenaea. The Parthenon contained the famous gold-ivory statue of Athena, by Pheidias. In the hinder cell of this temple was the Athenian treasury. The Promachus was a colossal image of bronze, which stood in the open air, representing Athene armed and holding a spear. There were many other temples and shrines in the precinct.

The Acropolis was approached by a sloping road, which led to the Propylaea, or entry, of five gates. Near this, outside the wall, was an intermittent spring known as the Clepsydra and the grotto of Pan. The statues of Harmodius and Aristogeiton stood near the foot of the slope.

In this play Mr. Rogers prints text and translation not side by side but separately, the translation for obvious reasons being in many places only a paraphrase.

[a] *Ib.* p. xix.   [b] *Ib.* p. xx.

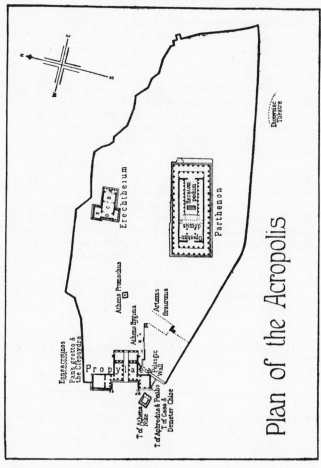

Plan of the Acropolis

ΤΑ ΤΟΥ ΔΡΑΜΑΤΟΣ ΠΡΟΣΩΠΑ

ΛΥΣΙΣΤΡΑΤΗ

ΚΑΛΟΝΙΚΗ

ΜΥΡΡΙΝΗ

ΛΑΜΠΙΤΩ

ΧΟΡΟΣ ΓΕΡΟΝΤΩΝ

ΧΟΡΟΣ ΠΡΕΣΒΥΤΑΤΩΝ ΓΥΝΑΙΚΩΝ

ΠΡΟΒΟΥΛΟΣ

ΣΤΡΑΤΥΛΛΙΣ

ΓΥΝΑΙΚΕΣ ΤΙΝΕΣ

ΚΙΝΗΣΙΑΣ

ΠΑΙΣ

ΚΗΡΥΞ ΛΑΚΕΔΑΙΜΟΝΙΩΝ

ΠΡΕΣΒΕΙΣ ΛΑΚΕΔΑΙΜΟΝΙΩΝ

ΠΡΕΣΒΕΙΣ ΑΘΗΝΑΙΩΝ

ΑΓΟΡΑΙΟΙ ΤΙΝΕΣ

ΘΥΡΩΡΟΣ

ΑΘΗΝΑΙΟΙ ΤΙΝΕΣ

ΛΑΚΩΝ

ΤΟΞΟΤΑΙ

5

ΛΥΣΙΣΤΡΑΤΗ

ΛΥΣΙΣΤΡΑΤΗ. Ἀλλ' εἴ τις εἰς Βακχεῖον αὐτὰς ἐκάλεσεν,
ἢ 's Πανός, ἢ 'πὶ Κωλιάδ', ἢ 's Γενετυλλίδος,
οὐδ' ἂν διελθεῖν ἦν ἂν ὑπὸ τῶν τυμπάνων.
νῦν δ' οὐδεμία πάρεστιν ἐνταυθοῖ γυνή,
πλὴν ἥ γ' ἐμὴ κωμῆτις ἥδ' ἐξέρχεται.   5
χαῖρ', ὦ Καλονίκη.

ΚΑΛΟΝΙΚΗ.   καὶ σύ γ', ὦ Λυσιστράτη.
τί συντετάραξαι; μὴ σκυθρώπαζ', ὦ τέκνον.
οὐ γὰρ πρέπει σοι τοξοποιεῖν τὰς ὀφρῦς.

ΛΤ. ἀλλ', ὦ Καλονίκη, κάομαι τὴν καρδίαν,
καὶ πόλλ' ὑπὲρ ἡμῶν τῶν γυναικῶν ἄχθομαι,   10
ὁτιὴ παρὰ μὲν τοῖς ἀνδράσιν νενομίσμεθα
εἶναι πανοῦργοι,

ΚΑ.   καὶ γάρ ἐσμεν νὴ Δία.

ΛΤ. εἰρημένον δ' αὐταῖς ἀπαντᾶν ἐνθάδε
βουλευσομέναισιν οὐ περὶ φαύλου πράγματος,
εὕδουσι κοὐχ ἥκουσιν.

ΚΑ.   ἀλλ', ὦ φιλτάτη,   15
ἥξουσι· χαλεπή τοι γυναικῶν ἔξοδος.

---

^a It is daybreak at *Athens*; and *Lysistrata*, a young and
beautiful woman, is standing alone, with marks of evident anxiety
in her countenance and demeanour. The scene represents the
sloping hill which rises from the Lower to the Upper City. In the
background are the Propylaea, the splendid portals of the *Athenian*

6

THE LYSISTRATA [a]

LYSISTRATA. Now were they summoned to some shrine of
        Bacchus,
    Pan, Colias, Genetyllis,[b] there had been
    No room to stir, so thick the crowd of timbrels.
    And NOW !—there's not one woman to be seen.
    Stay, here comes one, my neighbour Calonice.
    Good morning, friend.
CALONICE.   Good morn, Lysistrata.
    Why, what's the matter ? don't look gloomy, child.
    It don't become you to knit-knot [c] your eyebrows.
LY. My heart is hot within me, Calonice,
    And sore I grieve for sake of womankind,
    Because the men account us all to be
    Sly, shifty rogues,
CA.   And so, by Zeus, we are.
LY. Yet though I told them to be here betimes,
    To talk on weighty business, they don't come,
    They're fast asleep.
CA.   They'll come, dear heart, they'll come.
    'Tis hard, you know, for women to get out.

*Acropolis. Lysistrata is on the look-out for persons who do not
come, and after exhibiting various symptoms of impatience, she
suddenly begins to speak with abrupt and indignant emphasis.*

  [b] " All Gods of Wine and Love, the chief pleasures, according
to Aristophanes, of the Athenian women ": R.

  [c] The knit brows, two curves with a line between, are compared
to the double-curved bow with a hand-piece connecting them.

7

ἡ μὲν γὰρ ἡμῶν περὶ τὸν ἄνδρ' ἐκύπτασεν,
ἡ δ' οἰκέτην ἤγειρεν, ἡ δὲ παιδίον
κατέκλινεν, ἡ δ' ἔλουσεν, ἡ δ' ἐψώμισεν.

ΛΥ. ἀλλ' ἦν γὰρ ἔτερα τῶνδε προὐργιαίτερα   20
αὐταῖς.

ΚΑ.   τί δ' ἐστίν, ὦ φίλη Λυσιστράτη,
ἐφ' ὅ τι ποθ' ἡμᾶς τὰς γυναῖκας συγκαλεῖς;
τί τὸ πρᾶγμα; πηλίκον τι;

ΛΥ.   μέγα.

ΚΑ.   μῶν καὶ παχύ;

ΛΥ. καὶ νὴ Δία παχύ.

ΚΑ.   κᾆτα πῶς οὐχ ἥκομεν;

ΛΥ. οὐχ οὗτος ὁ τρόπος· ταχὺ γὰρ ἂν ξυνήλθομεν.   25
ἀλλ' ἔστιν ὑπ' ἐμοῦ πρᾶγμ' ἀνεζητημένον,
πολλαῖσί τ' ἀγρυπνίαισιν ἐρριπτασμένον.

ΚΑ. ἦ πού τι λεπτόν ἐστι τοὐρριπτασμένον.

ΛΥ. οὕτω γε λεπτὸν ὥσθ' ὅλης τῆς Ἑλλάδος
ἐν ταῖς γυναιξίν ἐστιν ἡ σωτηρία.   30

ΚΑ. ἐν ταῖς γυναιξίν; ἐπ' ὀλίγου γ' ᾠχεῖτ' ἄρα.

ΛΥ. ὡς ἔστ' ἐν ἡμῖν τῆς πόλεως τὰ πράγματα,
ἢ μηκέτ' εἶναι μήτε Πελοποννησίους,

ΚΑ. βέλτιστα τοίνυν μηκέτ' εἶναι νὴ Δία.

ΛΥ. Βοιωτίους τε πάντας ἐξολωλέναι.   35

ΚΑ. μὴ δῆτα πάντας, ἀλλ' ἄφελε τὰς ἐγχέλεις.

ΛΥ. περὶ τῶν Ἀθηνῶν δ' οὐκ ἐπιγλωττήσομαι
τοιοῦτον οὐδέν· ἀλλ' ὑπόνοησον σύ μοι.
ἢν δὲ ξυνέλθωσ' αἱ γυναῖκες ἐνθάδε,
αἵ τ' ἐκ Βοιωτῶν αἵ τε Πελοποννησίων   40
ἡμεῖς τε, κοινῇ σώσομεν τὴν Ἑλλάδα.

ΚΑ. τί δ' ἂν γυναῖκες φρόνιμον ἐργασαίατο
ἢ λαμπρόν, αἳ καθήμεθ' ἐξηνθισμέναι,

---

[a] The terms μέγα and παχύ are used πρὸς τὸ αἰδοῖον: Schol.

One has to mind her husband : one, to rouse
Her servant : one, to put the child to sleep :
One, has to wash him : one, to give him pap.

LY. Ah ! but they've other duties still more pressing
Than such as these.

CA.   Well but, Lysistrata,
Why have you, dear, convoked us ?   Is the matter
A weighty subject ?

LY.   Weighty ? yes.

CA.   And pregnant ? [a]

LY. Pregnant, by Zeus.

CA.   Why ever don't we come, then ?

LY. No, it's not that : we'd have come fast enough
For such-like nonsense. 'Tis a scheme I've hit on,
Tossing it over many a sleepless night.

CA. Tossing it over ? then 'tis light, I fancy.

LY. Light ? ay, so light, my dear, that all the hopes
Of all the States are anchored on us women.

CA. Anchored on us ! a slender stay to lean on.

LY. Ay, all depends on us : whether as well the
Peloponnesians all shall cease to be—

CA. Sure and 'tis better they should cease to be.

LY. And all the dwellers in Boeotia perish—

CA. Except the eels ; do pray except the eels.[b]

LY. But about Athens, mark you, I won't utter
Such words as these : you must supply my meaning.
But if the women will but meet here now,
Boeotian girls, Peloponnesian girls,
And we ourselves, we'll save the States between us.

CA. What can we women do ? What brilliant scheme
Can we, poor souls, accomplish ? we who sit

λεπτὸν (28) is the natural opposite to παχύ. The allusion in 29 is
to the proverbial saying ἐπὶ λεπτῆς ἐλπίδος ὀχεῖσθαι ; *K.* 1244.
  [b] The eels of Lake Copaïs.

κροκωτὰ φοροῦσαι καὶ κεκαλλωπισμέναι
καὶ Κιμβερίκ' ὀρθοστάδια καὶ περιβαρίδας;   45
ΛΥ. ταῦτ' αὐτὰ γάρ τοι κᾆσθ' ἃ σώσειν προσδοκῶ,
τὰ κροκωτίδια καὶ τὰ μύρα χαί περιβαρίδες
χἠ 'γχουσα καὶ τὰ διαφανῆ χιτώνια.
ΚΑ. τίνα δὴ τρόπον ποθ';
ΛΥ.   ὥστε τῶν νῦν μηδένα
ἀνδρῶν ἐπ' ἀλλήλοισιν αἴρεσθαι δόρυ,   50
ΚΑ. κροκωτὸν ἄρα νὴ τὼ θεὼ 'γὼ βάψομαι.
ΛΥ. μήτ' ἀσπίδα λαβεῖν
ΚΑ.   Κιμβερικὸν ἐνδύσομαι.
ΛΥ. μήτε ξιφίδιον.
ΚΑ.   κτήσομαι περιβαρίδας.
ΛΥ. ἆρ' οὐ παρεῖναι τὰς γυναῖκας δῆτ' ἐχρῆν;
ΚΑ. οὐ γὰρ μὰ Δί' ἀλλὰ πετομένας ἥκειν πάλαι.   55
ΛΥ. ἀλλ', ὦ μέλ', ὄψει τοι σφόδρ' αὐτὰς Ἀττικάς,
ἅπαντα δρώσας τοῦ δέοντος ὕστερον.
ἀλλ' οὐδὲ Παράλων οὐδεμία γυνὴ πάρα,
οὐδ' ἐκ Σαλαμῖνος.
ΚΑ.   ἀλλ' ἐκεῖναί γ' οἶδ' ὅτι
ἐπὶ τῶν κελήτων διαβεβήκασ' ὄρθριαι.   60
ΛΥ. οὐδ' ἃς προσεδόκων κἀλογιζόμην ἐγὼ
πρώτας παρέσεσθαι δεῦρο, τὰς Ἀχαρνέων
γυναῖκας, οὐχ ἥκουσιν.
ΚΑ.   ἡ γοῦν Θεαγένους
ὡς δεῦρ' ἰοῦσα θοὐκάτειον ἤρετο.
ἀτὰρ αἵδε καὶ δή σοι προσέρχονταί τινες·   65
αἱ δ' αὖθ' ἕτεραι χωροῦσί τινες. ἰοὺ ἰού,

---

[a] The ἄνθη referred to in ἐξηνθισμέναι are cosmetics. ἄγχουσα
(48) is rouge.
[b] Demeter and Persephone.
[c] An obscene jest on another sense of κέλης, σχῆμα συνουσίας.

Trimmed and bedizened [a] in our saffron silks,
Our cambric robes, and little finical shoes.

LY. Why, they're the very things I hope will save us,
Your saffron dresses, and your finical shoes,
Your paints, and perfumes, and your robes of gauze.

CA. How mean you, save us ?

LY.   So that nevermore
Men in our day shall lift the hostile spear—

CA. O, by the Twain,[b] I'll use the saffron dye.

LY. Or grasp the shield—

CA.   I'll don the cambric robe.

LY. Or draw the sword.

CA.   I'll wear the finical shoes.

LY. Should not the women, then, have come betimes ?

CA. Come? no, by Zeus; they should have flown with wings.

LY. Ah, friend, you'll find them Attic to the core :
Always too late in everything they do.
Not even one woman from the coast has come,
Not one from Salamis.

CA.   O they, no doubt,
Will cross this morning, early, in their boats.[c]

LY. And those I counted sure to come the first,
My staunch Acharnian damsels, they're not here—
Not they.

CA.   And yet Theagenes's wife
Consulted Hecate,[d] as if to come.[e]
Hi ! but they're coming now : here they all are :
First one, and then another.   Hoity toity !

Such jests seem to have had some special connexion with Salamis ;
cf. 411, E. 38.

[d] T. used never to leave home without consulting the shrine of
Hecate at his house door.   Here his superstition is transferred to
his wife ; see W. 804.

[e] *Several women enter, headed by Myrrhina, from the village of
Anagyrus.   Others soon follow.*

πόθεν εἰσίν;

ΛΥ.   Ἀναγυρουντόθεν.

ΚΑ.   νὴ τὸν Δία
ὁ γοῦν ἀνάγυρός μοι κεκινῆσθαι δοκεῖ.

ΜΥΡΡΙΝΗ. μῶν ὕστεραι πάρεσμεν, ὦ Λυσιστράτη;
τί φής; τί σιγᾷς;

ΛΥ.   οὐκ ἐπαινῶ, Μυρρίνη,   70
ἤκουσαν ἄρτι περὶ τοιούτου πράγματος.

ΜΥ. μόλις γὰρ εὗρον ἐν σκότῳ τὸ ζώνιον.
ἀλλ' εἴ τι πάνυ δεῖ, ταῖς παρούσαισιν λέγε.

ΛΥ. μὰ Δί', ἀλλ' ἐπαναμείνωμεν ὀλίγου γ' εἵνεκα
τάς τ' ἐκ Βοιωτῶν τάς τε Πελοποννησίων   75
γυναῖκας ἐλθεῖν.

ΜΥ.   πολὺ σὺ κάλλιον λέγεις.
ἡδὶ δὲ καὶ δὴ Λαμπιτὼ προσέρχεται.

ΛΥ. ὦ φιλτάτη Λάκαινα, χαῖρε, Λαμπιτοῖ.
οἷον τὸ κάλλος, γλυκυτάτη, σου φαίνεται.
ὡς δ' εὐχροεῖς, ὡς δὲ σφριγᾷ τὸ σῶμά σου.   80
κἂν ταῦρον ἄγχοις.

ΛΑΜΠΙΤΩ.   μάλα γὰρ οἰῶ ναὶ σιώ·
γυμνάδδομαί γε καὶ ποτὶ πυγὰν ἅλλομαι.

ΛΥ. ὡς δὴ καλὸν τὸ χρῆμα τιτθίων ἔχεις.

ΛΑ. ἇπερ ἱερεῖόν τοί μ' ὑποψαλάσσετε.

ΛΥ. ἡδὶ δὲ ποδαπή 'σθ' ἡ νεᾶνις ἡτέρα;   85

ΛΑ. πρέσβειρά τοι ναὶ τὼ σιὼ Βοιωτία
ἵκει ποθ' ἡμέ.

ΛΥ.   νὴ Δί', ὦ Βοιωτία,
καλόν γ' ἔχουσα τὸ πεδίον.

---

^a " To stir up Anagyre (meaning the nauseous smelling shrub
Anagyris foetida) was a proverb, used of persons who brought
some unpleasantness on themselves. Calonice applies the proverb

Whence come all these ?

LY. From Ánagyre.

CA. Aha !

We've stirred up Anagyre [a] at all events.

MYRRHINA. Are we too late, Lysistrata ? Well ? What ?
Why don't you speak ?

LY. I'm sorry, Myrrhina,
That you should come so late on such a business.

MY. I scarce could find my girdle in the dark.
But if the thing's so pressing, tell us now.

LY. No, no, let's wait a little, till the women
Of Peloponnesus and Boeotia come
To join our congress.

MY. O yes, better so.
And here, good chance, is Lampito approaching.[b]

LY. O welcome, welcome, Lampito, my love.
O the sweet girl ! how hale and bright she looks !
Here's nerve ! here's muscle ! here's an arm could
  fairly
Throttle a bull !

LAMPITO. Weel, by the Twa,[c] I think sae.
An' I can loup an' fling an' kick my hurdies.[d]

LY. See here's a neck and breast ; how firm and lusty !

LA. Wow, but ye pradd me like a fatted calf.

LY. And who's this other damsel ? whence comes she ?

LA. Ane deputation frae Boeoty, comin'
To sit amang you.

LY. Ah, from fair Boeotia,
The land of plains !

to the deme, meaning that the influx of Anagyrasian women
proved that the deme Anagyre was thoroughly stirred up " : R.

  [b] *Lampito, a Spartan woman, enters, accompanied by her friends.*
  [c] Castor and Pollux, the Dioscuri. σιώ=θεώ.
  [d] πηδᾶν εἰώθασι, καὶ οἱ πόδες ἅπτονται τῆς πυγῆς τοῦ πηδῶντος :
Schol.

ΚΑ.   καὶ νὴ Δία
κομψότατα τὴν βληχώ γε παρατετιλμένη.

ΛΥ. τίς δ' ἡτέρα παῖς;

ΛΑ.   χαΐα ναὶ τὼ σιώ,   **90**
Κορινθία δ' αὖ.

ΛΥ.   χαΐα νὴ τὸν Δία
δήλη 'στὶν οὖσα ταυταγὶ τἀντευθενί.

ΛΑ. τίς δ' αὖ συναλίαξε τόνδε τὸν στόλον
τὸν τᾶν γυναικῶν;

ΛΥ.   ἥδ' ἐγώ.

ΛΑ.   μύσιδδέ τοι
ὅ τι λῇς ποθ' ἁμέ.

ΜΥ.   νὴ Δί', ὦ φίλη γύναι,   **95**
λέγε δῆτα τὸ σπουδαῖον ὅ τι τοῦτ' ἐστί σοι.

ΛΥ. λέγοιμ' ἂν ἤδη. πρὶν λέγειν δ', ὑμᾶς τοδὶ
ἐπερήσομαί τι μικρόν.

ΜΥ.   ὅ τι βούλει γε σύ.

ΛΥ. τοὺς πατέρας οὐ ποθεῖτε τοὺς τῶν παιδίων
ἐπὶ στρατιᾶς ἀπόντας; εὖ γὰρ οἶδ' ὅτι   **100**
πάσαισιν ὑμῖν ἐστιν ἀποδημῶν ἀνήρ.

ΚΑ. ὁ γοῦν ἐμὸς ἀνὴρ πέντε μῆνας, ὦ τάλαν,
ἄπεστιν ἐπὶ Θράκης, φυλάττων Εὐκράτην.

ΜΥ. ὁ δ' ἐμός γε τελέους ἑπτὰ μῆνας ἐν Πύλῳ.

ΛΑ. ὁ δ' ἐμός γα, κἂν ἐκ τᾶς ταγᾶς ἔλσῃ ποκά,   **105**
πορπακισάμενος φροῦδος ἀμπτάμενος ἔβα.

ΛΥ. ἀλλ' οὐδὲ μοιχοῦ καταλέλειπται φεψάλυξ.
ἐξ οὗ γὰρ ἡμᾶς προὔδοσαν Μιλήσιοι,
οὐκ εἶδον οὐδ' ὄλισβον ὀκτωδάκτυλον,

ᵃ The words apply in a secondary sense to a woman; πεδίον =
the groin, βληχώ = τὴν τρίχα, the hair being plucked out. βληχώ
or βλήχων also means pennyroyal, a common product of the
Boeotian plain.   ᵇ χαΐα = ἀγαθή: Schol.
ᶜ The last two words in the Greek are accompanied by touches.

CA.   A very lovely land,
Well cropped, and trimmed, and spruce with penny
    royal.[a]

LY. And who's the next ?

LA.   A bonnie burdie[b] she,
She's a Corinthian lassie.

LY.   Ay, by Zeus,
And so she is. A bonnie lass, indeed.[c]

LA. But wha ha' ca'ed thegither[d] a' thae thrangs
O' wenches ?

LY.   I did.

LA.   Did ye noo ? then tell[e] us
What 'tis a' for.

LY.   O yes, my dear, I will.

MY. Ay, surely : tell us all this urgent business.

LY. O yes, I'll tell you now ; but first I'd ask you
One simple question.

MY.   Ask it, dear, and welcome.

LY. Do ye not miss the fathers of your babes,
Always on service ? well I wot ye all
Have got a husband absent at the wars.

CA. Ay, mine, worse luck, has been five months away
In Thracian quarters, watching Eucrates.[f]

MY. And mine's been stationed seven whole months at Pylus.

LA. An' my gude mon nae suner comes[g] frae war
Than he straps targe an' gangs awa' again.

LY. No husbands now, no sparks, no anything.
For ever since Miletus played us false,[h]
We've had no joy, no solace, none at all.[i]

---

[d] συναλλαξε=συνηλιασε.   [e] μύσιδδε=μύθιζε : δδ=ζ.
[f] Circumstances unknown.   [g] ἔλσῃ=ἔλθῃ.
[h] " Miletus had fallen away from Athens in the preceding
summer (Thuc. viii. 17) " : R.
[i] A play on συκίνη ἐπικουρία, a useless support, and the αἰδοῖα
δερμάτινα.

15

ὃς ἦν ἂν ἡμῖν σκυτίνη 'πικουρία.　　　110
ἐθέλοιτ' ἂν οὖν, εἰ μηχανὴν εὕροιμ' ἐγώ,
μετ' ἐμοῦ καταλῦσαι τὸν πόλεμον;
ΜΥ.　　　　　　　　νὴ τὼ θεώ·
ἐγὼ μὲν ἂν κἂν εἴ με χρείη τοὐγκυκλον
τουτὶ καταθεῖσαν ἐκπιεῖν αὐθημερόν.
ΚΑ. ἐγὼ δέ γ' ἂν κἂν ὡσπερεὶ ψῆτταν δοκῶ　　115
δοῦνἂν ἐμαυτῆς παρταμοῦσα θἤμισυ.
ΛΑ. ἐγὼ δὲ καί κα ποττὸ Ταΰγετόν γ' ἄνω
ἔλσοιμ', ὅπα μέλλοιμί γ' εἰράναν ἰδεῖν.
ΛΥ. λέγοιμ' ἄν· οὐ δεῖ γὰρ κεκρύφθαι τὸν λόγον.
ἡμῖν γάρ, ὦ γυναῖκες, εἴπερ μέλλομεν　　　120
ἀναγκάσειν τοὺς ἄνδρας εἰρήνην ἄγειν,
ἀφεκτέ' ἐστὶ—
ΚΑ.　　　　τοῦ; φράσον.
ΛΥ.　　　　　　ποιήσετ' οὖν;
ΚΑ. ποιήσομεν, κἂν ἀποθανεῖν ἡμᾶς δέῃ.
ΛΥ. ἀφεκτέα τοίνυν ἐστὶν ἡμῖν τοῦ πέους.
τί μοι μεταστρέφεσθε; ποῖ βαδίζετε;　　　125
αὗται, τί μοι μυᾶτε κἀνανεύετε;
τί χρὼς τέτραπται; τί δάκρυον κατείβεται;
ποιήσετ', ἢ οὐ ποιήσετ'; ἢ τί μέλλετε;
ΜΥ. οὐκ ἂν ποιήσαιμ', ἀλλ' ὁ πόλεμος ἑρπέτω.
ΚΑ. μὰ Δί' οὐδ' ἐγὼ γάρ, ἀλλ' ὁ πόλεμος ἑρπέτω. 130
ΛΥ. ταυτὶ σὺ λέγεις, ὦ ψῆττα; καὶ μὴν ἄρτι γε
ἔφησθα σαυτῆς κἂν παρατεμεῖν θἤμισυ.
ΚΑ. ἄλλ' ἄλλ' ὅ τι βούλει· κἂν με χρῇ, διὰ τοῦ πυρὸς
ἐθέλω βαδίζειν· τοῦτο μᾶλλον τοῦ πέους.
οὐδὲν γὰρ οἷον, ὦ φίλη Λυσιστράτη.　　　135
ΛΥ. τί δαὶ σύ;

So will you, will you, if I find a way,
Help me to end the war ?

MY.   Ay, that we will.
I will, be sure, though I'd to fling me down
This mantling shawl, and have a bout of—drinking.[a]

CA. And I would cleave my very self in twain
Like a cleft turbot,[b] and give half for Peace.

LA. An' I, to glint at Peace again, wad speel
Up to the tap rig o' Taygety.

LY. I'll tell you now : 'tis meet ye all should know.
O ladies ! sisters ! if we really mean
To make the men make Peace, there's but one way,
We must abstain—

MY.   Well ! tell us.

LY.   Will ye do it ?

MY. Do it ? ay, surely, though it cost our lives.

LY. We must abstain—each—from the joys of Love.
How ! what ! why turn away ? where are ye going ?
What makes you pout your lips, and shake your heads ?
What brings this falling tear, that changing colour ?
Will ye, or will ye not ? What mean ye, eh ?

MY. I'll never do it. Let the war go on.

CA. Zeus ! nor I either. Let the war go on.

LY. You, too, Miss Turbot ? you who said just now
You'd cleave, for Peace, your very self in twain ?

CA. Ask anything but this. Why, if needs be,
I'd walk through fire : only, not give up Love.
There's nothing like it, dear Lysistrata.

LY. And what say you ?

---

[a] " ' Fighting ' was the word expected ; but Aristophanes is, throughout this scene, playing upon the alleged bibulous propensities of Athenian women " : R.

[b] Alluding to the belief that two flat fishes were really but one, cut in halves.

ARISTOPHANES

ΜΥ.   κἀγὼ βούλομαι διὰ τοῦ πυρός.

ΛΥ. ὦ παγκατάπυγον θἠμέτερον ἅπαν γένος.
  οὐκ ἐτὸς ἀφ' ἡμῶν εἰσιν αἱ τραγῳδίαι.
  οὐδὲν γάρ ἐσμεν πλὴν Ποσειδῶν καὶ σκάφη.
  ἀλλ', ὦ φίλη Λάκαινα, σὺ γὰρ ἐὰν γένῃ   140
  μόνη μετ' ἐμοῦ, τὸ πρᾶγμ' ἀνασωσαίμεσθ' ἔτ' ἄν,
  ξυμψηφίσαί μοι.

ΛΑ.   χαλεπὰ μὲν ναὶ τὼ σιὼ
  γυναῖκας ὑπνῶν ἔστ' ἄνευ ψωλᾶς, μόνας.
  ὅμως γα μάν· δεῖ τᾶς γὰρ εἰράνας μάλ' αὖ.

ΛΥ. ὦ φιλτάτη σὺ καὶ μόνη τούτων γυνή.   145

ΚΑ. εἰ δ' ὡς μάλιστ' ἀπεχοίμεθ' οὗ σὺ δὴ λέγεις,
  ὃ μὴ γένοιτο, μᾶλλον ἂν διὰ τουτογὶ
  γένοιτ' ἂν εἰρήνη;

ΛΥ.   πολύ γε νὴ τὼ θεώ.
  εἰ γὰρ καθοίμεθ' ἔνδον ἐντετριμμέναι
  κἂν τοῖς χιτωνίοισι τοῖς ἀμοργίνοις   150
  γυμναὶ παρίοιμεν, δέλτα παρατετιλμέναι,
  στύοιντο δ' ἄνδρες κἀπιθυμοῖεν πλεκοῦν,
  ἡμεῖς δὲ μὴ προσίοιμεν, ἀλλ' ἀπεχοίμεθα,
  σπονδὰς ποιήσαιντ' ἂν ταχέως, εὖ οἶδ' ὅτι.

ΛΑ. ὁ γῶν Μενέλαος τᾶς Ἑλένας τὰ μᾶλά πα 155
  γυμνᾶς παρενιδὼν ἐξέβαλ', οἰῶ, τὸ ξίφος.

ΚΑ. τί δ', ἢν ἀφίωσ' ἄνδρες ἡμᾶς, ὦ μέλε;

ΛΥ. τὸ τοῦ Φερεκράτους, κύνα δέρειν δεδαρμένην.

ΚΑ. φλυαρία ταῦτ' ἐστὶ τὰ μεμιμημένα.
  ἐὰν λαβόντες δ' ἐς τὸ δωμάτιον βίᾳ   160
  ἕλκωσιν ἡμᾶς;

ΛΥ.   ἀντέχου σὺ τῶν θυρῶν.

 ᵃ Alluding to the *Tyro* of Sophocles, lately acted : Tyro, daughter of Salmoneus, bore twin sons to Poseidon, and then exposed them in a σκάφη.

18

MY.   I'd liefer walk through fire.

LY. O women ! women ! O our frail, frail sex !
No wonder tragedies are made from us.
Always the same : nothing but loves and cradles.[a]
O friend ! O Lampito ! if you and I
Are of one mind, we yet may pull things through ;
Won't *you* vote with me, dear ?

LA.   Haith, by the Twa',
'Tis sair to bide your lane, withouten men.
Still it maun be : we maun hae Peace, at a' risks.

LY. O dearest friend ; my one true friend of all.

CA. Well, but suppose we do the things you say,
Pray Heaven avert it, but put case we do,
Shall we be nearer Peace ?

LY.   Much, much, much nearer.
For if we women will but sit at home,
Powdered and trimmed, clad in our daintiest lawn,
Employing all our charms, and all our arts
To win men's love, and when we've won it, then
Repel them, firmly, till they end the war,
We'll soon get Peace again, be sure of that.

LA. Sae Menelaus, when he glowered, I ween,
At Helen's breastie, coost his glaive awa'.[b]

CA. Eh, but suppose they leave us altogether ?

LY. O, faddle ! then we'll find some substitute.[c]

---

[b] After the fall of Troy, Menelaus, about to slay Helen, was softened by the sight of her beauty. See Tennyson's *Lucretius*.

[c] Lines 158–163 are: "Then, as P. said, canem excoriatum excoriare." "Those imitations are rubbish. But what if they drag us into the room by force ? " " Cling to the door." " What if they beat us ? " " Yield with a bad grace, for there is no pleasure in what is taken by force."—Pherecrates is unknown. The words κύνα δ. δ. were used as a proverb ἐπὶ τῶν μάτην πονούντων, but there is a reference to the *penis coriaceus* of 109.

ARISTOPHANES

ΚΑ. ἐὰν δὲ τύπτωσιν, τί;

ΛΥ.   παρέχειν χρὴ κακῶς.
οὐ γὰρ ἔνι τούτοις ἡδονὴ τοῖς πρὸς βίαν.
κἄλλως ὀδυνᾶν χρή· κἀμέλει ταχέως πάνυ
ἀπεροῦσιν. οὐ γὰρ οὐδέποτ᾽ εὐφρανθήσεται   165
ἀνήρ, ἐὰν μὴ τῇ γυναικὶ συμφέρῃ.

ΚΑ. εἴ τοι δοκεῖ σφῷν ταῦτα, χἠμῖν ξυνδοκεῖ.

ΛΑ. καὶ τὼς μὲν ἁμῶν ἄνδρας ἁμὲς πείσομες
παντᾷ δικαίως ἄδολον εἰράναν ἄγειν·
τὸν τῶν Ἀσαναίων γα μὰν ῥυάχετον   170
πᾷ καί τις ἂν πείσειεν αὖ μὴ πλαδδίην;

ΛΥ. ἡμεῖς ἀμέλει σοι τά γε παρ᾽ ἡμῖν πείσομεν.

ΛΑ. οὐχ ἇς πόδας κ᾽ ἔχωντι ταὶ τριήρεες
καὶ τἀργύριον τὤβυσσον ᾖ παρὰ τᾷ σιῷ.

ΛΥ. ἀλλ᾽ ἔστι καὶ τοῦτ᾽ εὖ παρεσκευασμένον·   175
καταληψόμεθα γὰρ τὴν ἀκρόπολιν τήμερον.
ταῖς πρεσβυτάταις γὰρ προστέτακται τοῦτο δρᾶν,
ἕως ἂν ἡμεῖς ταῦτα συντιθώμεθα,
θύειν δοκούσαις καταλαβεῖν τὴν ἀκρόπολιν.

ΛΑ. πάντ᾽ εὖ κ᾽ ἔχοι, καὶ τᾷδε γὰρ λέγεις καλῶς.   180

ΛΥ. τί δῆτα ταῦτ᾽ οὐχ ὡς τάχιστα, Λαμπιτοῖ,
ξυνωμόσαμεν, ὅπως ἂν ἀρρήκτως ἔχῃ;

ΛΑ. πάρφαινε μὰν τὸν ὅρκον, ὡς ὀμιώμεθα.

ΛΥ. καλῶς λέγεις. ποῦ ᾽σθ᾽ ἡ Σκύθαινα; ποῖ βλέπεις;
θὲς ἐς τὸ πρόσθεν ὑπτίαν τὴν ἀσπίδα,   185
καί μοι δότω τὰ τόμιά τις.

ΚΑ.   Λυσιστράτη,
τίν᾽ ὅρκον ὁρκώσεις ποθ᾽ ἡμᾶς;

ΛΥ.   ὅντινα;

CA. If they try force?

LY. They'll soon get tired of that
If we keep firm. Scant joy a husband gets
Who finds himself at discord with his wife.

CA. Well, then, if so you wish it, so we'll have it.

LA. An' our gude folk we'se easily persuade
To keep the Peace wi' never a thocht o' guile:
But your Athanian hairumscairum callants
Wha sall persuade *them* no to play the fule?

LY. O we'll persuade our people, never fear.

LA. Not while ye've gat thae gallies rigged sae trim,
An' a' that rowth o' siller nigh the Goddess.[a]

LY. O but, my dear, we've taken thought for that:
This very morn we seize the Acropolis.
Now, whilst we're planning and conspiring here,
The elder women have the task assigned them,
Under pretence of sacrifice, to seize it.

LA. A' will gae finely, an' ye talk like that.

LY. Then why not, Lampito, at once combine
All in one oath, and clench the plot securely?

LA. Weel, you propound the aith, an' we'se a' tak' it.

LY. Good; now then, Scythianess,[b] don't stand there
gaping.
Quick, set a great black shield here, hollow
upwards,
And bring the sacrificial bits.

CA. And how
Are we to swear, Lysistrata?

LY. We'll slay

[a] A reserve of 1000 talents set aside for pressing emergency (Thuc. ii. 24). It was now proposed (Thuc. viii. 15) to use this in building a fleet to replace the ships lost at Syracuse.

[b] Scythian archers were employed in Athens as police; the women have therefore a Scythianess.

εἰς ἀσπίδ᾽, ὥσπερ, φάσ᾽, ἐν Αἰσχύλῳ ποτέ,
μηλοσφαγούσας.

ΚΑ.   μὴ σύ γ᾽, ὦ Λυσιστράτη,
εἰς ἀσπίδ᾽ ὀμόσῃς μηδὲν εἰρήνης πέρι.   **190**

ΛΥ. τίς ἂν οὖν γένοιτ᾽ ἂν ὅρκος;

ΚΑ.   εἰ λευκόν ποθεν
ἵππον λαβοῦσαι τόμιον ἐκτεμοίμεθα.

ΛΥ. ποῖ λευκὸν ἵππον;

ΚΑ.   ἀλλὰ πῶς ὀμούμεθα
ἡμεῖς;

ΜΥ.   ἐγώ σοι νὴ Δί᾽, ἢν βούλῃ, φράσω.
θεῖσαι μέλαιναν κύλικα μεγάλην ὑπτίαν,   **195**
μηλοσφαγοῦσαι Θάσιον οἴνου σταμνίον,
ὀμόσωμεν ἐς τὴν κύλικα μὴ 'πιχεῖν ὕδωρ.

ΛΑ. φεῦ δᾶ, τὸν ὅρκον ἄφατον ὡς ἐπαινίω.

ΛΥ. φερέτω κύλικά τις ἔνδοθεν καὶ σταμνίον.

ΚΑ. ὦ φίλταται γυναῖκες, ὁ κεραμὼν ὅσος.   **200**
ταύτην μὲν ἄν τις εὐθὺς ἡσθείη λαβών.

ΛΥ. καταθεῖσα ταύτην προσλαβοῦ μοι τοῦ κάπρου.
δέσποινα Πειθοῖ καὶ κύλιξ φιλοτησία,
τὰ σφάγια δέξαι ταῖς γυναιξὶν εὐμενής.

ΚΑ. εὔχρων γε θαῖμα κἀποπυτίζει καλῶς.   **205**

ΛΑ. καὶ μὰν ποτόδδει γ᾽ ἁδὺ ναὶ τὸν Κάστορα.

ΜΥ. ἐᾶτε πρώτην μ᾽, ὦ γυναῖκες, ὀμνύναι.

ΚΑ. μὰ τὴν Ἀφροδίτην οὔκ, ἐάν γε μὴ λάχῃς.

---

[a] Aesch. *Septem* 42 ταυροσφαγοῦντες ἐς μελάνδετον σάκος. "The substitution of μηλοσφαγοῦντες for ταυροσφαγοῦντες, if not a mere inadvertence, is probably due to the double meaning of ταῦρος (217) and μῆλον (155)."   [b] See note on 59.

[c] The Scythians used a large cup, mingling wine and blood: Herod. iv. 70. The end of the oath is a surprise for their especial purpose ἀπέχεσθαι, etc.

[d] *A maiden brings out a jar of wine and an immense cup.*

(Like those Seven Chiefs in Aeschylus)^a a lamb
Over a shield.

CA.   Nay, when our object's Peace,
Don't use a shield, Lysistrata, my dear.

LY. Then what shall be the oath ?

CA.   Could we not somehow
Get a grey mare,^b and cut her up to bits ?

LY. Grey mare, indeed !

CA.   Well, what's the oath will suit
Us women best ?

MY.   I'll tell you what I think.
Let's set a great black CUP here, hollow upwards :^c
Then for a lamb we'll slay a Thasian wine-jar,
And firmly swear to—pour no water in.

LA. Hech, the braw aith ! my certie, hoo I like it.

LY. O yes, bring out the wine-jar and the cup.^d

CA. La ! here's a splendid piece of ware, my dears.
Now that's a cup 'twill cheer one's heart to take.

LY. (to the servant) Set down the cup, and take the victim
   boar.^e

O Queen Persuasion, and O Loving Cup,
Accept our offerings, and maintain our cause !^f

CA. 'Tis jolly coloured blood, and spirts out bravely ^g

LA. Ay, an' by Castor, vera fragrant too !

MY. Let me swear first, my sisters ?

CA.   Yes, if you
Draw the first lot ; not else, by Aphrodite.^h

---

^e " She means the Wine-jar, but she speaks of it as a victim
whose blood is about to be shed " : R.

^f The servant pours the wine into the cup, the women all pressing
round to see.

^g She uses a sacrificial formula : Schol. $\pi o\tau \acute{o}\delta\delta\epsilon\iota = \pi\rho o\sigma \acute{o}\zeta\epsilon\iota.$

^h " Since the first to swear would have the first drink " : Schol.
At a symposium, the president was determined by lot, and sometimes the order of drinking.

ARISTOPHANES

ΛΥ. λάζυσθε πᾶσαι τῆς κύλικος, ὦ Λαμπιτοῖ·
  λεγέτω δ᾽ ὑπὲρ ὑμῶν μί᾽ ἅπερ ἂν κἀγὼ λέγω· 210
  ὑμεῖς δ᾽ ἐπομεῖσθε ταὐτὰ κἀμπεδώσετε.

  Οὐκ ἔστιν οὐδεὶς οὐδὲ μοιχὸς οὐδ᾽ ἀνὴρ
ΚΑ. οὐκ ἔστιν οὐδεὶς οὐδὲ μοιχὸς οὐδ᾽ ἀνὴρ
ΛΥ. ὅστις πρὸς ἐμὲ πρόσεισιν ἐστυκώς. λέγε.
ΚΑ. ὅστις πρὸς ἐμὲ πρόσεισιν ἐστυκώς. παπαῖ, 215
  ὑπολύεταί μου τὰ γόνατ᾽, ὦ Λυσιστράτη.
ΛΥ. οἴκοι δ᾽ ἀταυρώτη διάξω τὸν βίον
ΚΑ. οἴκοι δ᾽ ἀταυρώτη διάξω τὸν βίον
ΛΥ. κροκωτοφοροῦσα καὶ κεκαλλωπισμένη, 220
ΚΑ. κροκωτοφοροῦσα καὶ κεκαλλωπισμένη,
ΛΥ. ὅπως ἂν ἁνὴρ ἐπιτυφῇ μάλιστά μου·
ΚΑ. ὅπως ἂν ἁνὴρ ἐπιτυφῇ μάλιστά μου·
ΛΥ. κοὐδέποθ᾽ ἑκοῦσα τἀνδρὶ τὠμῷ πείσομαι.
ΚΑ. κοὐδέποθ᾽ ἑκοῦσα τἀνδρὶ τὠμῷ πείσομαι.
ΛΥ. ἐὰν δέ μ᾽ ἄκουσαν βιάζηται βίᾳ, 225
ΚΑ. ἐὰν δέ μ᾽ ἄκουσαν βιάζηται βίᾳ,
ΛΥ. κακῶς παρέξω κοὐχὶ προσκινήσομαι.
ΚΑ. κακῶς παρέξω κοὐχὶ προσκινήσομαι.
ΛΥ. οὐ πρὸς τὸν ὄροφον ἀνατενῶ τὼ Περσικά.
ΚΑ. οὐ πρὸς τὸν ὄροφον ἀνατενῶ τὼ Περσικά. 230
ΛΥ. οὐ στήσομαι λέαιν᾽ ἐπὶ τυροκνήστιδος.
ΚΑ. οὐ στήσομαι λέαιν᾽ ἐπὶ τυροκνήστιδος.
ΛΥ. ταῦτ᾽ ἐμπεδοῦσα μὲν πίοιμ᾽ ἐντευθενί·
ΚΑ. ταῦτ᾽ ἐμπεδοῦσα μὲν πίοιμ᾽ ἐντευθενί·
ΛΥ. εἰ δὲ παραβαίην, ὕδατος ἐμπλῇθ᾽ ἡ κύλιξ. 235
ΚΑ. εἰ δὲ παραβαίην, ὕδατος ἐμπλῇθ᾽ ἡ κύλιξ.

ΛΥ. ξυνεπόμνυθ᾽ ὑμεῖς ταῦτα πᾶσαι;
ΜΥ.   νὴ Δία.
ΛΥ. φέρ᾽ ἐγὼ καθαγίσω τήνδε.

LY. All place your hands upon the wine-cup : so.
One, speak the words, repeating after me.
Then all the rest confirm it.   Now begin.

I will abstain from Love and Love's delights.[a]

CA. *I will abstain from Love and Love's delights.*

LY. And take no pleasure though my lord invites.

CA. *And take no pleasure though my lord invites.*

LY. And sleep a vestal all alone at nights.

CA. *And sleep a vestal all alone at nights.*

LY. And live a stranger to all nuptial rites.

CA. *And live a stranger to all nuptial rites.*
I don't half like it though, Lysistrata.

LY. I will abjure the very name of Love.

CA. *I will abjure the very name of Love.*

LY. So help me Zeus, and all the Powers above.

CA. *So help me Zeus, and all the Powers above.*

LY. If I do this, my cup be filled with wine.

CA. *If I do this, my cup be filled with wine.*

LY. But if I fail, a water draught be mine.

CA. *But if I fail, a water draught be mine.*

LY. You all swear this ?

MY.   O yes, my dear, we do.

LY. I'll now consume these fragments.[b]

    [a] 212-233 Nemo est sive adulter sive vir qui mihi ad amorem
paratus appropringuabit: (—papae, genua mihi solvuntur,
Lysistrata !)—et domi casta vitam degam, croceum gerens
vestimentum et ornatissima, ut vir meus quam maxime ardeat, et
numquam libens morem viro geram, et si invitae vim adhibebit,
vix dabo et motu non subsequar : non ad tectum crepidulas
extendam, non stabo ut leaena supra radulam [σχῆμα συνουσίας,
τετραποδηδόν P. 896. τυρόκνηστις is a "cheese-grater," but these
were very dissimilar to our "graters," being a sort of knife
with a bronze or ivory handle, and it was common to carve
figures of animals on such handles].
    [b] *Lysistrata takes the wine-cup in her hand.*

ΚΑ.   τὸ μέρος γ᾽, ὦ φίλη,
ὅπως ἂν ὦμεν εὐθὺς ἀλλήλων φίλαι.
ΛΑ. τίς ὠλολυγά;
ΛΥ.   τοῦτ᾽ ἐκεῖν᾽ οὑγὼ ᾽λεγον·   240
αἱ γὰρ γυναῖκες τὴν ἀκρόπολιν τῆς θεοῦ
ἤδη κατειλήφασιν. ἀλλ᾽, ὦ Λαμπιτοῖ,
σὺ μὲν βάδιζε καὶ τὰ παρ᾽ ὑμῶν εὖ τίθει,
τασδὶ δ᾽ ὁμήρους κατάλιφ᾽ ἡμῖν ἐνθάδε·
ἡμεῖς δὲ ταῖς ἄλλαισι ταῖσιν ἐν πόλει   245
ξυνεμβάλωμεν εἰσιοῦσαι τοὺς μοχλούς.
ΚΑ. οὔκουν ἐφ᾽ ἡμᾶς ξυμβοηθήσειν οἴει
τοὺς ἄνδρας εὐθύς;
ΛΥ.   ὀλίγον αὐτῶν μοι μέλει.
οὐ γὰρ τοσαύτας οὐδ᾽ ἀπειλὰς οὐδὲ πῦρ
ἥξουσ᾽ ἔχοντες ὥστ᾽ ἀνοῖξαι τὰς πύλας   250
ταύτας, ἐὰν μὴ ᾽φ᾽ οἷσιν ἡμεῖς εἴπομεν.
ΚΑ. μὰ τὴν Ἀφροδίτην οὐδέποτέ γ᾽· ἄλλως γὰρ ἂν
ἄμαχοι γυναῖκες καὶ μιαραὶ κεκλήμεθ᾽ ἄν.

ΧΟΡΟΣ ΓΕΡΟΝΤΩΝ.

χώρει, Δράκης, ἡγοῦ βάδην, εἰ καὶ τὸν ὦμον ἀλγεῖς
κορμοῦ τοσουτονὶ βάρος χλωρᾶς φέρων ἐλάας.   255
ἦ πόλλ᾽ ἄελπτ᾽ ἔνεστιν ἐν τῷ μακρῷ βίῳ, φεῦ,
ἐπεὶ τίς ἄν ποτ᾽ ἤλπισ᾽, ὦ Στρυμόδωρ᾽, ἀκοῦσαι
          γυναῖκας, ἃς ἐβόσκομεν   260
          κατ᾽ οἶκον ἐμφανὲς κακόν,
          κατὰ μὲν ἅγιον ἔχειν βρέτας,

---

[a] *A sound of persons cheering is heard in the distance.*
[b] *The crowd now disperses : Lampito leaving for her homeward journey, and the others disappearing through the gates of the Propylaea. After a pause the Chorus of Men are seen slowly approaching from the Lower City. They are carrying heavy*

CA.   Shares, my friend,
Now at first starting let us show we're friends.

LA. Hark ! what's yon skirlin' ? [a]

LY.   That's the thing I said.
They've seized the Acropolis, Athene's castle,
Our comrades have. Now, Lampito, be off :
You, go to Sparta, and arrange things there,
Leaving us here these girls as hostages.
And We will pass inside the castle walls,
And help the women there to close the bars.

CA. But don't you think that very soon the Men
Will come, in arms, against us ?

LY.   Let them come !
They will not bring or threats or fire enough
To awe our woman hearts, and make us open
These gates again, save on the terms we mentioned.

CA. By Aphrodite, no ! else 'twere for nought
That people call us bold, resistless jades.[b]

CHORUS OF MEN.

     On, sure and slow, my Draces, go :
                though that great log you're bringing
Of olive green, is sore, I ween,
                your poor old shoulder wringing.
O dear, how many things in life
                belie one's expectations !
Since who'd have thought, my Strymodore,
                that these abominations,
Who would have thought that sluts like these,
Our household pests, would have waxed so bold,
As the Holy Image [c] by fraud to seize,

*logs of firewood, and a jar of lighted cinders ; and as they move,
they sing their entrance song.*

    [c] The sacrosanct image of Athene Polias, which fell from
heaven.

κατά τ' ἀκρόπολιν ἐμὰν λαβεῖν,
μοχλοῖς δὲ καὶ κλήθροισιν
τὰ προπύλαια πακτοῦν;
ἀλλ' ὡς τάχιστα πρὸς πόλιν σπεύσωμεν, ὦ Φιλοῦργε, 265
ὅπως ἂν αὐταῖς ἐν κύκλῳ θέντες τὰ πρέμνα ταυτί,
ὅσαι τὸ πρᾶγμα τοῦτ' ἐνεστήσαντο καὶ μετῆλθον,
μίαν πυρὰν νήσαντες ἐμπρήσωμεν αὐτόχειρες
πάσας ὑπὸ ψήφου μιᾶς, πρώτην δὲ τὴν Λύκωνος.   270
οὐ γὰρ μὰ τὴν Δήμητρ' ἐμοῦ ζῶντος ἐγχανοῦνται·
ἐπεὶ οὐδὲ Κλεομένης, ὃς αὐτὴν κατέσχε πρῶτος,
          ἀπῆλθεν ἀψάλακτος, ἀλλ'   275
          ὅμως Λακωνικὸν πνέων
          ᾤχετο θὤπλα παραδοὺς ἐμοί,
          σμικρὸν ἔχων πάνυ τριβώνιον,
          πινῶν, ῥυπῶν, ἀπαράτιλτος,
          ἒξ ἐτῶν ἄλουτος.   280
οὕτως ἐπολιόρκησ' ἐγὼ τὸν ἄνδρ' ἐκεῖνον ὠμῶς
ἐφ' ἑπτακαίδεκ' ἀσπίδων πρὸς ταῖς πύλαις καθεύδων.
τασδὶ δὲ τὰς Εὐριπίδῃ θεοῖς τε πᾶσιν ἐχθρὰς
ἐγὼ οὐκ ἄρα σχήσω παρὼν τολμήματος τοσούτου;
μὴ νῦν ἔτ' ἐν τῇ τετραπόλει τοὐμὸν τροπαῖον εἴη.   285

          ἀλλ' αὐτὸ γάρ μοι τῆς ὁδοῦ   [στρ.

---

a Rhodia (Schol.), an infamous woman.
b The story is told by Herodotus, v. 72. He had been invited to Athens to resist the reforms of Cleisthenes, and took refuge on the Acropolis. The " six years " is a comic exaggeration for two days.
28

As the City Castle by force to hold,
With block and bolt and barrier vast,
Making the Propylaea fast.
Press on, Philurgus, towards the heights ;
            we'll pile a great amazing
Array of logs around the walls,
            and set them all a-blazing :
And as for these conspirators,
            a bonfire huge we'll make them,
One vote shall doom the whole to death,
            one funeral pyre shall take them,
And thus we'll burn the brood accurst,
            but Lycon's wife [a] we'll burn the first.
No, never, never, whilst I live,
            shall woman-folk deride me :
Not scatheless went Cleomenes,[b]
            when he like this defied me,
And dared my castle to seize : yet He,
A Spartan breathing contempt and pride,
Full soon surrendered his arms to me,
And a scanty coat round his loins he tied,
And with unwashed limbs, and with unkempt head,
And with six years' dirt, the intruder fled ;
So strict and stern a watch around
            my mates and I were keeping,
In seventeen rows of serried shields
            before the fortress sleeping.
And THESE, whom both Euripides
            and all the Powers on high
Alike detest, shall these, shall these,
            my manly rage defy ?
Then never be my Trophy shown,
            on those red plains of Marathon !

But over this snubby protruding steep

λοιπόν ἐστι χωρίον
τὸ πρὸς πόλιν, τὸ σιμόν, οἷ σπουδὴν ἔχω·
χώπως ποτ' ἐξαμπρεύσομεν
τοῦτ' ἄνευ κανθηλίου.　　　　　　　　　　　290
ὡς ἐμοῦ γε τὼ ξύλω τὸν ὦμον ἐξιπώκατον·
ἀλλ' ὅμως βαδιστέον,
καὶ τὸ πῦρ φυσητέον,
μή μ' ἀποσβεσθὲν λάθῃ πρὸς τῇ τελευτῇ τῆς ὁδοῦ.
(φυσᾷ τῷ στόματι.)
　　　φῦ φῦ.
　　　ἰοὺ ἰοὺ τοῦ καπνοῦ.　　　　　　　　　295

　　　ὡς δεινόν, ὦναξ Ἡράκλεις,　　　　　　[ἀντ.
　　　προσπεσόν μ' ἐκ τῆς χύτρας
ὥσπερ κύων λυττῶσα τὠφθαλμὼ δάκνει·
　　　κἄστιν γε Λήμνιον τὸ πῦρ
　　　τοῦτο πάσῃ μηχανῇ.　　　　　　　　300
οὐ γὰρ ἄν ποθ' ὧδ' ὀδὰξ ἔβρυκε τὰς λήμας ἐμοῦ.
　　　σπεῦδε πρόσθεν ἐς πόλιν,
　　　καὶ βοήθει τῇ θεῷ,
ἢ πότ' αὐτῇ μᾶλλον ἢ νῦν, ὦ Λάχης, ἀρήξομεν;
　　　φῦ φῦ.
　　　ἰοὺ ἰοὺ τοῦ καπνοῦ.　　　　　　　　305

τουτὶ τὸ πῦρ ἐγρήγορεν θεῶν ἕκατι καὶ ζῇ.
οὔκουν ἄν, εἰ τὼ μὲν ξύλω θείμεσθα πρῶτον αὐτοῦ,
τῆς ἀμπέλου δ' ἐς τὴν χύτραν τὸν φανὸν ἐγκαθέντες
ἅψαντες εἶτ' ἐς τὴν θύραν κριηδὸν ἐμπέσοιμεν;

　　ᵃ Lemnian fire is mentioned to make a play upon λῆμαι.
"The fire has bitten my λήμας (eyesores). It must be a Lemnian
fire." The phrase Lemnian fire is supposed to have arisen from
the volcano which once was active in the island.
30

Ere we reach our goal at the Castle keep,
We've still, with our burdensome load, to creep.
  And how to manage that blunt incline
  Without a donkey, I can't divine.
Dear, how these two great firelogs make
          my wearied shoulders toil and ache.
  But still right onward we needs must go,
  And still the cinders we needs must blow,
Else we'll find the fire extinguished,
            ere we reach our journey's end.
    Puff! Puff! Puff!
    O the smoke! the smoke!

  O royal Heracles! what a lot
  Of fire came raging out of the pot,
And flew, like a dog, at my eyes, red hot.
  'Twas a jet from the Lemnian *a* mines, I ween,
  It came so fierce, and it bit so keen,
And worried, with persistence sore,
          my two poor eyes, inflamed before.
  On, Laches, on! to the castle press,
  And aid the God in her dire distress;
Surely, if we e'er would help her,
          now's the very time, my friend.
    Puff! Puff! Puff!
    O the smoke! the smoke!

Thank heaven the fire is still alight,
          and burning beautifully bright.
So here we'll lay our burdens down,
          with eager hearts delighted,
And dip the vine-torch in the pot,
          and get it there ignited.
Then all together at the gates
          like battering rams we'll butt.

31

κἂν μὴ καλούντων τοὺς μοχλοὺς χαλῶσιν αἱ γυναῖκες, 310
ἐμπιπράναι χρὴ τὰς θύρας καὶ τῷ καπνῷ πιέζειν.
θώμεσθα δὴ τὸ φορτίον. φεῦ τοῦ καπνοῦ, βαβαιάξ.
τίς ξυλλάβοιτ᾽ ἂν τοῦ ξύλου τῶν ἐν Σάμῳ στρατηγῶν;
ταυτὶ μὲν ἤδη τὴν ῥάχιν θλίβοντά μου πέπαυται.
σὸν δ᾽ ἐστὶν ἔργον, ὦ χύτρα, τὸν ἄνθρακ᾽ ἐξεγείρειν, 315
τὴν λαμπάδ᾽ ἡμμένην ὅπως πρώτιστ᾽ ἐμοὶ προσοίσεις.
δέσποινα Νίκη ξυγγενοῦ, τῶν τ᾽ ἐν πόλει γυναικῶν
τοῦ νῦν παρεστῶτος θράσους θέσθαι τροπαῖον ἡμᾶς.

ΧΟΡΟΣ ΓΥΝΑΙΚΩΝ.

λιγνὺν δοκῶ μοι καθορᾶν καὶ καπνόν, ὦ γυναῖκες,
ὥσπερ πυρὸς καομένου· σπευστέον ἐστὶ θᾶττον.   320

       πέτου πέτου, Νικοδίκη,   [στρ.
       πρὶν ἐμπεπρῆσθαι Καλύκην
       τε καὶ Κρίτυλλαν περιφυσήτω
       ὑπό τε νόμων ἀργαλέων
       ὑπό τε γερόντων ὀλέθρων.   325
ἀλλὰ φοβοῦμαι τόδε. μῶν ὑστερόπους βοηθῶ;
νῦν δὴ γὰρ ἐμπλησαμένη τὴν ὑδρίαν κνεφαία
μόγις ἀπὸ κρήνης ὑπ᾽ ὄχλου καὶ θορύβου καὶ πατά-
γου χυτρείου,

---

    a Samos was the Athenian headquarters at this time.
    b " As they approach the Acropolis they have full in view the
Temple of the Wingless Victory, otherwise Athene Nike ": R.
    *c During the last few lines the Men have been completing their
preparations, and the air above them is now growing lurid with
the smoke and the flame of their torches. As the Men relapse into
silence, the voices of Women are heard in the distance. They come
sweeping round from the north side of the Acropolis, carrying their
pitchers of water, and singing, in turn, their entrance song. The
two Choruses are for the present concealed from each other by the
north-western angle of the Acropolis.*

And if our summons they reject,
     and keep the barriers shut,
We'll burn the very doors with fire,
     and them with smoke we'll smother.
So lay the burdens down.   Pheugh !   Pheugh !
     O how this smoke does bother !
What general from the Samian *a* lines
     an active hand will lend us ?
Well, well, I'm glad my back is freed
     from all that weight tremendous.
O pot, 'tis now your turn to help :
     O send a livelier jet
Of flame this way, that I to-day
     the earliest light may get.
O Victory, immortal Queen,*b*
     assist us Thou in rearing
A trophy o'er these woman-hosts,
     so bold and domineering.*c*

CHORUS OF WOMEN.

Redly up in the sky
     the flames are beginning to flicker,
Smoke and vapour of fire !
     come quicker, my friends, come quicker.

  Fly, Nicodice, fly,
  Else will Calyce burn,
  Else Critylla will die,
  Slain by the laws so stern,
  Slain by the old men's hate.
Ah, but I fear ! I fear !
     can it chance that I come too late ?
Trouble it was, forsooth, before my jug I could fill,
All in the dusk of the morn,
     at the spring by the side of the hill,*d*

   d The Enneacrounos.

33

ARISTOPHANES

δούλησιν ὠστιζομένη 330
στιγματίαις θ᾽, ἁρπαλέως
ἀραμένη, ταῖσιν ἐμαῖς
δημότισιν καομέναις
φέρουσ᾽ ὕδωρ βοηθῶ.

ἤκουσα γὰρ τυφογέρον-   [ἀντ. 335
τας ἄνδρας ἔρρειν, στελέχη
φέροντας, ὥσπερ βαλανεύσοντας,
ὡς τριταλανταῖα βάρος,
δεινά τ᾽ ἀπειλοῦντας ἐπῶν,
ὡς πυρὶ χρὴ τὰς μυσαρὰς γυναῖκας ἀνθρακεύειν. 340
ἅς, ὦ θεά, μή ποτ᾽ ἐγὼ πιμπραμένας ἴδοιμι,
ἀλλὰ πολέμου καὶ μανιῶν ῥυσαμένας Ἑλλάδα
καὶ πολίτας,
ἐφ᾽ οἷσπερ, ὦ χρυσολόφα,
σάς, πολιοῦχ᾽, ἔσχον ἕδρας. 345
καί σε καλῶ ξύμμαχον, ὦ
Τριτογένει᾽, ἤν τις ἐκεί-
νας ὑποπίμπρησιν ἀνὴρ
φέρειν ὕδωρ μεθ᾽ ἡμῶν.

ἔασον ὦ. τουτὶ τί ἦν; ὦνδρες πόνῳ πονηροί· 350
οὐ γάρ ποτ᾽ ἂν χρηστοί γ᾽ ἔδρων, οὐδ᾽ εὐσεβεῖς
τάδ᾽ ἄνδρες.

ΧΟ. ΓΕ. τουτὶ τὸ πρᾶγμ᾽ ἡμῖν ἰδεῖν ἀπροσδόκητον ἥκει·
ἑσμὸς γυναικῶν οὑτοσὶ θύρασιν αὖ βοηθεῖ.

ΧΟ. ΓΤ. τί βδύλλεθ᾽ ἡμᾶς; οὔ τί που πολλαὶ δοκοῦμεν
εἶναι;

---

[a] A title of Athena.
[b] *At this juncture the Women wheel round the corner of the Acropolis, and the two Choruses suddenly meet face to face.*

What with the clatter of pitchers,
The noise and press of the throng,
Jostling with knaves and slaves,
Till at last I snatched it along,
Abundance of water supplying
To friends who are burning and dying.

Yea, for hither, they state,
Dotards are dragging, to burn us,
Logs of enormous weight,
Fit for a bath-room furnace,
Vowing to roast and to slay
Sternly the reprobate women.
O Lady, O Goddess, I pray,
Ne'er may I see them in flames !
I hope to behold them with gladness,
Hellas and Athens redeeming
from battle and murder and madness.
This is the cause why they venture,
Lady, thy mansions to hold,
Tritogeneia,[a] Eternal
Champion with helmet of gold !
And O, if with fire men invade them,
O help us with water to aid them.[b]
Stop ! easy all ! what have we here ?
(*To the men*) You vile, abandoned crew,
No good and virtuous men, I'm sure,
would act in the way you do.
M. CH. Hey, here's an unexpected sight !
hey, here's a demonstration !
A swarm of women issuing out
with warlike preparation !
W. CH. Hallo, you seem a little moved !
does this one troop affright you ?

35

καὶ μὴν μέρος γ' ἡμῶν ὁρᾶτ' οὔπω τὸ μυριοστόν. 355

ΧΟ. ΓΕ. ὦ Φαιδρία, ταύτας λαλεῖν ἐάσομεν τοσαυτί;
οὐ περικατᾶξαι τὸ ξύλον τύπτοντ' ἐχρῆν τιν'
αὐτάς;

ΧΟ. ΓΥ. θώμεσθα δὴ τὰς κάλπιδας χἠμεῖς χαμᾶζ',
ὅπως ἄν,
ἢν προσφέρῃ τὴν χεῖρά τις, μὴ τοῦτό μ'
ἐμποδίζῃ.

ΧΟ. ΓΕ. εἰ νὴ Δί' ἤδη τὰς γνάθους τούτων τις ἢ δὶς
ἢ τρὶς   360
ἔκοψεν ὥσπερ Βουπάλου, φωνὴν ἂν οὐκ ἂν
εἶχον.

ΧΟ. ΓΥ. καὶ μὴν ἰδού· παταξάτω· καὶ στᾶσ' ἐγὼ παρέξω,
κοὐ μή ποτ' ἄλλη σου κύων τῶν ὄρχεων
λάβηται.

ΧΟ. ΓΕ. εἰ μὴ σιωπήσει, θενών σου 'κκοκκιῶ τὸ γῆρας.

ΧΟ. ΓΥ. ἅπτου μόνον Στρατυλλίδος τῷ δακτύλῳ προσ-
ελθών.   365

ΧΟ. ΓΕ. τί δ', ἢν σποδῶ τοῖς κονδύλοις, τί μ' ἐργάσει
τὸ δεινόν;

ΧΟ. ΓΥ. βρύκουσά σου τοὺς πλεύμονας καὶ τἄντερ'
ἐξαμήσω.

ΧΟ. ΓΕ. οὐκ ἔστ' ἀνὴρ Εὐριπίδου σοφώτερος ποιητής·
οὐδὲν γὰρ ὡδὶ θρέμμ' ἀναιδές ἐστιν ὡς γυναῖκες.

ΧΟ. ΓΥ. αἱρώμεθ' ἡμεῖς θοὔδατος τὴν κάλπιν, ὦ
Ῥοδίππη.   370

ΧΟ. ΓΕ. τί δ', ὦ θεοῖς ἐχθρά, σὺ δεῦρ' ὕδωρ ἔχουσ'
ἀφίκου;

---

[a] " If we smite them on the cheek, as the iambic poet
Hipponax, that *acer hostis Bupalo* (Hor. *Epod.* 6. 14), threatened
in his lampoons to smite his unhappy antagonist ": R.

[b] The words are not found in the extant plays of Euripides,
but the sentiment is thoroughly Euripidean.

36

You see not yet the myriadth part
of those prepared to fight you

M. CH. Now, really, Phaedrias, shall we stop
to hear such odious treason ?
Let's break our sticks about their backs,
let's beat the jades to reason.

W. CH. Hi, sisters, set the pitchers down,
and then they won't embarrass
Our nimble fingers, if the rogues
attempt our ranks to harass.

M. CH. I warrant, now, if twice or thrice
we slap their faces neatly,
That they will learn, like Bupalus,[a]
to hold their tongues discreetly.

W. CH. Well, here's my face : I won't draw back :
now slap it if you dare,
And I won't leave one ounce of you
for other dogs to tear.

M. CH. Keep still, or else your musty Age
to very shreds I'll batter.

W. CH. Now only touch Stratyllis, sir ;
just lift one finger at her !

M. CH. And what if with these fists, my love,
I pound the wench to shivers ?

W. CH. By Heaven, we'll gnaw your entrails out,
and rip away your livers.

M. CH. There is not than Euripides
a bard more wise and knowing,
For women ARE a shameless set,
the vilest creatures going.[b]

W. CH. Pick up again, Rhodippe dear,
your jug with water brimming.

M. CH. What made you bring that water here,
you God-detested women ?

ΧΟ. ΓΥ. τί δαὶ σὺ πῦρ, ὦ τύμβ᾿, ἔχων; ὡς σαυτὸν
    ἐμπυρεύσων;

ΧΟ. ΓΕ. ἐγὼ μέν, ἵνα νήσας πυρὰν τὰς σὰς φίλας
    ὑφάψω.

ΧΟ. ΓΥ. ἐγὼ δέ γ᾿, ἵνα τὴν σὴν πυρὰν τούτῳ κατα-
    σβέσαιμι.

ΧΟ. ΓΕ. τοὐμὸν σὺ πῦρ κατασβέσεις;

ΧΟ. ΓΥ.   τοὔργον τάχ᾿ αὐτὸ δείξει. 375

ΧΟ. ΓΕ. οὐκ οἶδά σ᾿ εἰ τῇδ᾿ ὡς ἔχω τῇ λαμπάδι σταθεύσω.

ΧΟ. ΓΥ. εἰ ῥύμμα τυγχάνεις ἔχων, λουτρόν γ᾿ ἐγὼ
    παρέξω.

ΧΟ. ΓΕ. ἐμοὶ σὺ λουτρόν, ὦ σαπρά;

ΧΟ. ΓΥ.   καὶ ταῦτα νυμφικόν γε.

ΧΟ. ΓΕ. ἤκουσας αὐτῆς τοῦ θράσους;

ΧΟ. ΓΥ.   ἐλευθέρα γάρ εἰμι

ΧΟ. ΓΕ. σχήσω σ᾿ ἐγὼ τῆς νῦν βοῆς.

ΧΟ. ΓΥ.   ἀλλ᾿ οὐκ ἔθ᾿ ἡλιάξεις. 380

ΧΟ. ΓΕ. ἔμπρησον αὐτῆς τὰς κόμας.

ΧΟ. ΓΥ.   σὸν ἔργον, ὦ ᾿χελῷε.

ΧΟ. ΓΕ. οἴμοι τάλας.

ΧΟ. ΓΥ.   μῶν θερμὸν ἦν;

ΧΟ. ΓΕ. ποῖ θερμόν; οὐ παύσει; τί δρᾷς;

ΧΟ. ΓΥ. ἄρδω σ᾿, ὅπως ἂν βλαστάνῃς.

ΧΟ. ΓΕ. ἀλλ᾿ αὖός εἰμ᾿ ἤδη τρέμων. 385

ΧΟ. ΓΥ. οὐκοῦν, ἐπειδὴ πῦρ ἔχεις,
    σὺ χλιανεῖς σεαυτόν.

ΠΡΟΒΟΥΛΟΣ. ἆρ᾿ ἐξέλαμψε τῶν γυναικῶν ἡ τρυφὴ

ª "The name Achelous was used to denote *water* generally. The women are deluging their opponents with cold water from their pitchers ": R.

w. ch. What made you bring that light, old Tomb ?
　　　　　　　　　　to set *yourselves* afire ?

m. ch. No, but to kindle for your friends
　　　　　　　　　　a mighty funeral pyre.

w. ch. Well, then, we brought this water here
　　　　　　　　　　to put your bonfire out, sirs.

m. ch. *You* put our bonfire out, indeed !

w. ch. 　　　　　　You'll see, beyond a doubt, sirs.

m. ch. I swear that with this torch, offhand,
　　　　　　　　　　I've half a mind to fry you.

w. ch. Got any soap, my lad ? if so,
　　　　　　　　　　a bath I'll soon supply you.

m. ch. A bath for me, you mouldy hag !

w. ch. 　　　　　　And that a bride-bath, too.

m. ch. Zounds, did you hear her impudence ?

w. ch. 　　　　　　Ain't I freeborn as you ?

m. ch. I'll quickly put a stop to this.

w. ch. 　　　　　　You'll judge no more, I vow !

m. ch. Hi ! set the vixen's hair on fire.

w. ch. 　　　　　　Now, Achelous,[a] now !

m. ch. 　Good gracious !

w. ch. 　　　　　　What ! you find it hot ?

m. ch. Hot ? murder ! stop ! be quiet !

w. ch. I'm watering you, to make you grow.

m. ch. I wither up from shivering so.

w. ch. I tell you what : a fire you've got,
So warm your members by it.[b]

magistrate. Has then the women's wantonness blazed
　　　out,

[b] *At this crisis the tumult is stayed for an instant by the appearance on the stage of a venerable official personage, one of the Magistrates who, after the Sicilian catastrophe, were appointed, under the name of Probuli, to form a Directory or Committee of Public Safety. He is attended by four Scythian archers, part of the ordinary police of the Athenian Republic. The Women retire into the background.*

χὠ τυμπανισμὸς χοἰ πυκινοὶ Σαβάζιοι,
ὅ τ' Ἀδωνιασμὸς οὗτος οὑπὶ τῶν τεγῶν,
οὗ 'γώ ποτ' ὢν ἤκουον ἐν τἠκκλησίᾳ;   390
ἔλεγεν δ' ὁ μὴ ὥρασι μὲν Δημόστρατος
πλεῖν εἰς Σικελίαν, ἡ γυνὴ δ' ὀρχουμένη,
" αἰαῖ Ἄδωνιν," φησίν, ὁ δὲ Δημόστρατος
ἔλεγεν ὁπλίτας καταλέγειν Ζακυνθίων·
ἡ δ' ὑποπεπωκυῖ', ἡ γυνὴ 'πὶ τοῦ τέγους,   395
" κόπτεσθ' Ἄδωνιν," φησίν· ὁ δ' ἐβιάζετο
ὁ θεοῖσιν ἐχθρὸς καὶ μιαρὸς Χολοζύγης.
τοιαῦτ' ἀπ' αὐτῶν ἐστιν ἀκολαστάσματα.

ΧΟ.ΓΕ. τί δῆτ' ἄν, εἰ πύθοιο καὶ τὴν τῶνδ' ὕβριν;
αἳ τἄλλα θ' ὑβρίκασι κἀκ τῶν καλπίδων   400
ἔλουσαν ἡμᾶς, ὥστε θαἰμάτίδια
σείειν πάρεστιν ὥσπερ ἐνεουρηκότας.

ΠΡΟ. νὴ τὸν Ποσειδῶ τὸν ἁλυκόν, δίκαιά γε.
ὅταν γὰρ αὐτοὶ ξυμπονηρευώμεθα
ταῖσιν γυναιξὶ καὶ διδάσκωμεν τρυφᾶν,   405
τοιαῦτ' ἀπ' αὐτῶν βλαστάνει βουλεύματα.
οἳ λέγομεν ἐν τῶν δημιουργῶν τοιαδί·
ὦ χρυσοχόε, τὸν ὅρμον ὃν ἐπεσκεύασας,
ὀρχουμένης μου τῆς γυναικὸς ἑσπέρας
ἡ βάλανος ἐκπέπτωκεν ἐκ τοῦ τρήματος.   410
ἐμοὶ μὲν οὖν ἔστ' ἐς Σαλαμῖνα πλευστέα·
σὺ δ' ἢν σχολάσῃς, πάσῃ τέχνῃ πρὸς ἑσπέραν
ἐλθὼν ἐκείνῃ τὴν βάλανον ἐνάρμοσον.
ἕτερος δέ τις πρὸς σκυτοτόμον ταδὶ λέγει
νεανίαν καὶ πέος ἔχοντ' οὐ παιδικόν·   415

ᵃ Plutarch, in his *Life of Nicias* (chap. xiii.), describes these and
similar omens of ill which preceded the Athenian expedition to

Their constant timbrels and Sabaziuses,
And that Adonis-dirge *a* upon the roof
Which once I heard in full Assembly-time.
'Twas when Demostratus (beshrew him) moved
To sail to Sicily : and from the roof
A woman, dancing, shrieked *Woe, woe, Adonis !*
And *he* proposed to enrol Zacynthian hoplites ;
And *she* upon the roof, the maudlin woman,
Cried *Wail Adonis !* yet he forced it through,
That God-detested, vile Ill-temprian.*b*
Such are the wanton follies of the sex.

M. CH.   What if you heard their insolence to-day,
Their vile, outrageous goings on ? And look,
See how they've drenched and soused us from
    their pitchers,
Till we can wring out water from our clothes.*c*

MAG.   Ay, by Poseidon,*d* and it serves us right.
'Tis all our fault : they'll never know their place,
These pampered women, whilst we spoil them so.
Hear how we talk in every workman's shop.
Goldsmith, says one, *this necklace that you made,*
My gay young wife was dancing yester-eve,
And lost, sweet soul, the fastening of the clasp;
*Do please reset it, Goldsmith.*e* Or, again,
O Shoemaker, my wife's new sandal pinches

Sicily. And he also (chap. xii.) tells us that the orator Demostratus took a leading part in recommending that fatal measure.

b Demostratus was nicknamed Βουζύγης and A. alters this to
Χολοζύγης because of his gloomy temper (διὰ τὸ μελαγχολᾶν): Schol.

c ὥσπερ ἐν. = tamquam si in ea minxissemus.

d τὸν ἁλυκόν, the sea-god; the Magistrate emphasizes this
" because he is engaged in refitting the Navy and his mind is full
of ships and seas": R.

e Here follow ll. 411–13: " I have to sail to Salamis ; if you
have leisure, do not fail to visit her this evening and fit in the
peg." A play on the two senses of βάλανος.

41

ὦ σκυτοτόμε, τοῦ τῆς γυναικός μου ποδὸς
τὸ δακτυλίδιον ἐμπιέζει τὸ ζυγόν,
ἄθ᾽ ἁπαλὸν ὄν· τοῦτ᾽ οὖν σὺ τῆς μεσημβρίας
ἐλθὼν χάλασον, ὅπως ἂν εὐρυτέρως ἔχῃ.
τοιαῦτ᾽ ἀπήντηκ᾽ εἰς τοιαυτὶ πράγματα,   420
ὅτε γ᾽ ὢν ἐγὼ πρόβουλος, ἐκπορίσας ὅπως
κωπῆς ἔσονται, τἀργυρίου νυνὶ δέον,
ὑπὸ τῶν γυναικῶν ἀποκέκλεισμαι τῶν πυλῶν.
ἀλλ᾽ οὐδὲν ἔργον ἑστάναι. φέρε τοὺς μοχλοὺς
ὅπως ἂν αὐτὰς τῆς ὕβρεως ἐγὼ σχέθω.   425
τί κέχηνας, ὦ δύστηνε; ποῖ δ᾽ αὖ σὺ βλέπεις,
οὐδὲν ποιῶν ἀλλ᾽ ἢ καπηλεῖον σκοπῶν;
οὐχ ὑποβαλόντες τοὺς μοχλοὺς ὑπὸ τὰς πύλας
ἐντεῦθεν ἐκμοχλεύσετ᾽; ἐνθενδὶ δ᾽ ἐγὼ
συνεκμοχλεύσω.

ΛΥ.   μηδὲν ἐκμοχλεύετε·   430
ἐξέρχομαι γὰρ αὐτομάτη. τί δεῖ μοχλῶν;
οὐ γὰρ μοχλῶν δεῖ μᾶλλον ἢ νοῦ καὶ φρενῶν.

ΠΡΟ. ἄληθες, ὦ μιαρὰ σύ; ποῦ ᾽σθ᾽ ὁ τοξότης;
ξυλλάμβαν᾽ αὐτὴν κὠπίσω τὼ χεῖρε δεῖ.

ΛΥ. εἴ τἄρα νὴ τὴν Ἄρτεμιν τὴν χεῖρά μοι   435
ἄκραν προσοίσει, δημόσιος ὢν κλαύσεται.

ΠΡΟ. ἔδεισας, οὗτος; οὐ ξυναρπάσει μέσην,
καὶ σὺ μετὰ τούτου, κἀνύσαντε δήσετον;

ΚΑ. εἴ τἄρα νὴ τὴν Πάνδροσον ταύτῃ μόνον
τὴν χεῖρ᾽ ἐπιβαλεῖς, ἐπιχεσεῖ πατούμενος.   440

ΠΡΟ. ἰδού γ᾽ ἐπιχεσεῖ. ποῦ ᾽στιν ἕτερος τοξότης;
ταύτην προτέραν ξύνδησον, ὁτιὴ καὶ λαλεῖ.

ΜΥ. εἴ τἄρα νὴ τὴν Φωσφόρον τὴν χεῖρ᾽ ἄκραν

---

[a] He turns to the Scythians, who, instead of setting to work, are
poking idly around them.
[b] The gates are thrown open, and Lysistrata comes out.

Her little toe, the tender, delicate child,
Make it fit easier, please.——Hence all this nonsense !
Yea, things have reached a pretty pass, indeed,
When I, the State's Director, wanting money
To purchase oar-blades, find the Treasury gates
Shut in my face by these preposterous women.
Nay, but no dallying now : bring up the crowbars,
And I'll soon stop *your* insolence, my dears.[a]
What ! gaping, fool ? and *you*, can *you* do nothing
But stare about with tavern-squinting eye ?
Push in the crowbars underneath the gates,
You, stand that side and heave them : I'll stop here
And heave them here.[b]

LY.   O let your crowbars be.
      Lo, I come out unfetched ! What need of crowbars ?
      'Tis wits, not crowbars, that ye need to-day.

MAG.   Ay, truly, traitress, say you so ? Here, Archer !
      Arrest her, tie her hands behind her back.

LY.   And if he touch me with his finger-tip,
      The public scum ! 'fore Artemis, he'll rue it.

MAG.   What, man, afeared ? why, catch her round the waist.
      And *you* go with him, quick, and bind her fast.

CA. (*coming out*) And if you do but lay one hand upon her,
      'Fore Pandrosus,[c] I'll stamp your vitals out.

MAG.   Vitals, ye hag ? Another Archer, ho !
      Seize this one first, because she chatters so.

MY. (*coming out*) And if you touch her with your finger-tip,

---

[c] Pandrosus and Agraulus, sisters of Cecrops. "Since throughout this short altercation the women invoke Artemis in one or other of her characters, I cannot but believe, that in this invocation also, the name of Πάνδροσος, the All-bedewer, is intended to apply to Artemis as identical with Hecate or the moon" : R.

43

ταύτῃ προσοίσεις, κύαθον αἰτήσεις τάχα.
ΠΡΟ. τουτὶ τί ἦν; ποῦ τοξότης; ταύτης ἔχου.   445
παύσω τιν' ὑμῶν τῆσδ' ἐγὼ τῆς ἐξόδου.
ΣΤΡΑΤΤΛΛΙΣ. εἴ τἄρα νὴ τὴν Ταυροπόλον ταύτῃ πρόσει,
ἐκκοκκιῶ σου τὰς στενοκωκύτους τρίχας.
ΠΡΟ. οἴμοι κακοδαίμων· ἐπιλέλοιφ' ὁ τοξότης.
ἀτὰρ οὐ γυναικῶν οὐδέποτ' ἔσθ' ἡττητέα   450
ἡμῖν· ὁμόσε χωρῶμεν αὐταῖς, ὦ Σκύθαι,
ξυνταξάμενοι.
ΛΥ.   νὴ τὼ θεὼ γνώσεσθ' ἄρα
ὅτι καὶ παρ' ἡμῖν εἰσι τέτταρες λόχοι
μαχίμων γυναικῶν ἔνδον ἐξωπλισμένων.
ΠΡΟ. ἀποστρέφετε τὰς χεῖρας αὐτῶν, ὦ Σκύθαι.   455
ΛΥ. ὦ ξύμμαχοι γυναῖκες, ἐκθεῖτ' ἔνδοθεν,
ὦ σπερμαγοραιολεκιθολαχανοπώλιδες,
ὦ σκοροδοπανδοκευτριαρτοπώλιδες,
οὐχ ἕλξετ', οὐ παιήσετ', οὐκ ἀρήξετε;
οὐ λοιδορήσετ', οὐκ ἀναισχυντήσετε;   460
παύσασθ', ἐπαναχωρεῖτε, μὴ σκυλεύετε.
ΠΡΟ. οἴμ' ὡς κακῶς πέπραγέ μου τὸ τοξικόν.
ΛΥ. ἀλλὰ τί γὰρ ᾤου; πότερον ἐπὶ δούλας τινὰς
ἥκειν ἐνόμισας, ἢ γυναιξὶν οὐκ οἴει
χολὴν ἐνεῖναι;
ΠΡΟ.   μὰ τὸν Ἀπόλλω καὶ μάλα   465
πολλήν γ', ἐάνπερ πλησίον κάπηλος ᾖ.

ΧΟ.ΓΕ. ὦ πόλλ' ἀναλώσας ἔπη, πρόβουλε τῆσδε τῆς γῆς,
τί τοῖσδε σαυτὸν εἰς λόγον τοῖς θηρίοις συν-
άπτεις;

ᵃ The Women come forward. After a short struggle the archers
are routed.

'Fore Phosphorus, you'll need a cupping shortly.

MAG. Tcha! what's all this? lay hold of this one, Archer!
I'll stop this sallying out, depend upon it.

STRATYLLIS. And if he touch her, 'fore the Queen of Tauris,
I'll pull his squealing hairs out, one by one.

MAG. O dear! all's up! I've never an archer left.
Nay, but I swear we won't be done by women.
Come, Scythians, close your ranks, and all together
Charge!

LY. Charge away, my hearties, and you'll soon
Know that we've here, impatient for the fight,
Four woman-squadrons, armed from top to toe.

MAG. Attack them, Scythians, twist their hands behind them.

LY. Forth to the fray, dear sisters, bold allies!
O egg-and-seed-and-potherb-market-girls,
O garlic-selling-barmaid-baking-girls,
Charge to the rescue, smack and whack, and thwack them,
Slang them, I say: show them what jades ye be.[a]
Fall back! retire! forbear to strip the slain.

MAG. Hillo! my archers got the worst of that.

LY. What did the fool expect? Was it to fight
With SLAVES you came? Think you we Women feel
No thirst for glory?

MAG. Thirst enough, I trow;
No doubt of that, when there's a tavern handy.

M. CH. O thou who wastest many words,
Director of this nation,
Why wilt thou with such brutes as these
thus hold negotiation?

οὐκ οἶσθα λουτρὸν οἷον αἵδ᾽ ἡμᾶς ἔλουσαν ἄρτι
ἐν τοῖσιν ἱματιδίοις, καὶ ταῦτ᾽ ἄνευ κονίας; 470
ΧΟ. ΓΥ. ἀλλ᾽, ὦ μέλ᾽, οὐ χρὴ προσφέρειν τοῖς πλη-
σίοισιν εἰκῆ
τὴν χεῖρ᾽· ἐὰν δὲ τοῦτο δρᾷς, κυλοιδιᾶν ἀνάγκη.
ἐπεὶ θέλω ᾽γὼ σωφρόνως ὥσπερ κόρη καθῆσθαι,
λυποῦσα μηδέν᾽ ἐνθαδί, κινοῦσα μηδὲ κάρφος,
ἢν μή τις ὥσπερ σφηκιὰν βλίττῃ με κἀρεθίζῃ. 475

ΧΟ. ΓΕ. ὦ Ζεῦ, τί ποτε χρησόμεθα τοῖσδε τοῖς κνωδά-
λοις;   [στρ.
οὐ γὰρ ἔτ᾽ ἀνεκτέα τάδ᾽, ἀλλὰ βασανιστέον
τόδε σοι τὸ πάθος μετ᾽ ἐμοῦ
ὅ τι βουλόμεναί ποτε τὴν   480
Κραναὰν κατέλαβον, ἐφ᾽ ὅ τι τε
μεγαλόπετρον, ἄβατον ἀκρόπολιν,
ἱερὸν τέμενος.

ἀλλ᾽ ἀνερώτα, καὶ μὴ πείθου, καὶ πρόσφερε
πάντας ἐλέγχους.
ὡς αἰσχρὸν ἀκωδώνιστον ἐᾶν τὸ τοιοῦτον
πρᾶγμα μεθέντας.   485
ΠΡΟ. καὶ μὴν αὐτῶν τοῦτ᾽ ἐπιθυμῶ νὴ τὸν Δία πρῶτα
πυθέσθαι,
ὅ τι βουλόμεναι τὴν πόλιν ἡμῶν ἀπεκλείσατε
τοῖσι μοχλοῖσιν.

---

[a] σφηκιάν, wasps' nest, "not a very desirable place to rifle for
honey ; and I suspect that A. is mocking the line of Sophocles
about taking honey from a wasps' nest, while the women may be
wishing to let their opponents know that if they try to rifle their
sweets, they will bring a swarm of hornets about their ears."   R.
The line is ἢ σφηκιὰν βλίττουσιν εὑρόντες τινά: Schol.

Dost thou not see the bath wherewith
>the sluts have dared to lave me,
Whilst all my clothes were on, and ne'er
>a bit of soap they gave me ?

W. CH. For 'tis not right, nor yet polite,
>to strike a harmless neighbour,
And if you do, 'tis needful too
>that she your eyes belabour.
Full fain would I, a maiden shy,
>in maiden peace be resting,
Not making here the slightest stir,
>nor any soul molesting,
Unless indeed some rogue should strive
>to rifle and despoil my hive.[a]

M. CH. O how shall we treat, Lord Zeus, such creatures
>as these ?
Let us ask the cause for which they have dared to
>seize,
To seize this fortress of ancient and high renown,
This shrine where never a foot profane hath trod,
The lofty-rocked, inaccessible Cranaan town,
>The holy Temple of God.

Now to examine them closely and narrowly,
>probing them here and sounding them there,
Shame if we fail to completely unravel
>the intricate web of this tangled affair.

MAG. Foremost and first I would wish to inquire of them,
>what is this silly disturbance about ?
Why have ye ventured to seize the Acropolis,
>locking the gates and barring us out ?

The field is now open for a suspension of hostilities, and a parley
takes place between the leaders of the two contending factions.

47

ΛΥ. ἵνα τἀργύριον σῶν παρέχοιμεν καὶ μὴ πολε-
     μοῖτε δι᾿ αὐτό.
ΠΡΟ. διὰ τἀργύριον πολεμοῦμεν γάρ;
ΛΥ.   καὶ τἆλλα γε πάντ᾿ ἐκυκήθη.
     ἵνα γὰρ Πείσανδρος ἔχοι κλέπτειν χοἰ ταῖς
     ἀρχαῖς ἐπέχοντες,   490
     ἀεί τινα κορκορυγὴν ἐκύκων. οἱ δ᾿ οὖν τοῦδ᾿
     εἵνεκα δρώντων
     ὅ τι βούλονται· τὸ γὰρ ἀργύριον τοῦτ᾿ οὐκέτι μὴ
     καθέλωσιν.
ΠΡΟ. ἀλλὰ τί δράσεις;
ΛΥ.   τοῦτό μ᾿ ἐρωτᾷς; ἡμεῖς ταμιεύσομεν αὐτό.
ΠΡΟ. ὑμεῖς ταμιεύσετε τἀργύριον;
ΛΥ.   τί δὲ δεινὸν τοῦτο νομίζεις;
     οὐ καὶ τἄνδον χρήματα πάντως ἡμεῖς ταμιεύομεν
     ὑμῖν;   495
ΠΡΟ. ἀλλ᾿ οὐ ταὐτόν.
ΛΥ.   πῶς οὐ ταὐτόν;
ΠΡΟ.   πολεμητέον ἔστ᾿ ἀπὸ τούτου.
ΛΥ. ἀλλ᾿ οὐδὲν δεῖ πρῶτον πολεμεῖν.
ΠΡΟ.   πῶς γὰρ σωθησόμεθ᾿ ἄλλως;
ΛΥ. ἡμεῖς ὑμᾶς σώσομεν.
ΠΡΟ.   ὑμεῖς;
ΛΥ.   ἡμεῖς μέντοι.
ΠΡΟ.   σχέτλιόν γε.
[ΛΥ. ὡς σωθήσει, κἂν μὴ βούλῃ.
ΠΡΟ.   δεινόν γε λέγεις.
ΛΥ.   ἀγανακτεῖς·]
     ἀλλὰ ποιητέα ταῦτ᾿ ἐστὶν ὅμως.
ΠΡΟ.   νὴ τὴν Δήμητρ᾿ ἄδικόν γε. 500
ΛΥ. σωστέον, ὦ τᾶν.

LY. Keeping the silver securely in custody,
     lest for its sake ye continue the war.

MAG. What, is the war for the sake of the silver, then ?

LY.   Yes ; and all other disputes that there are.
Why is Peisander [a] for ever embroiling us,
    why do the rest of our officers feel
Always a pleasure in strife and disturbances ?
     Simply to gain an occasion to steal.
Act as they please for the future, the treasury
    never a penny shall yield them, I vow.

MAG. How, may I ask, will you hinder their getting it ?

LY.   We will ourselves be the Treasurers now.

MAG. You, woman, you be the treasurers ?

LY.   Certainly.
    Ah, you esteem us unable, perchance !
Are we not skilled in domestic economy,
    do we not manage the household finance ?

MAG. O, that is different.

LY.   Why is it different ?

MAG.   This is required for the fighting, my dear.

LY. Well, but the fighting itself isn't requisite.

MAG.   Only, without it, we're ruined, I fear.

LY. WE will deliver you.

MAG.   You will deliver us !

LY.   Truly we will.

MAG.   What a capital notion !

LY. Whether you like it or not, we'll deliver you.

MAG.   Impudent hussy !

LY.   You seem in commotion.
Nevertheless we will do as we promise you.

MAG.   That were a terrible shame, by Demeter.

LY. Friend, we must save you.

---

[a] A politician who advocated war for his own private gain. He was at the time scheming to overthrow the democracy. *P.* 394.

ARISTOPHANES

ΠΡΟ.   κεἰ μὴ δέομαι;

ΛΥ.   τοῦδ' εἵνεκα καὶ πολὺ μᾶλλον.

ΠΡΟ. ὑμῖν δὲ πόθεν περὶ τοῦ πολέμου τῆς τ' εἰρήνης
     ἐμέλησεν;

ΛΥ. ἡμεῖς φράσομεν.

ΠΡΟ.   λέγε δὴ ταχέως, ἵνα μὴ κλάῃς.

ΛΥ.   ἀκροῶ δή,
     καὶ τὰς χεῖρας πειρῶ κατέχειν.

ΠΡΟ.   ἀλλ' οὐ δύναμαι· χαλεπὸν γὰρ
     ὑπὸ τῆς ὀργῆς αὐτὰς ἴσχειν.

ΣΤ.   κλαύσει τοίνυν πολὺ μᾶλλον.   505

ΠΡΟ. τοῦτο μέν, ὦ γραῦ, σαυτῇ κρώξαις· σὺ δέ μοι λέγε.

ΛΥ.   ταῦτα ποιήσω.
     ἡμεῖς τοῦ μὲν προτέρου πολέμου κατὰ τὸν χρόνον
       ἠνεχόμεσθα
     ὑπὸ σωφροσύνης τῆς ἡμετέρας, τῶν ἀνδρῶν, ἅττ'
       ἐποιεῖτε.
     οὐ γὰρ γρύζειν εἰᾶθ' ἡμᾶς. καίτοὐκ ἠρέσκετέ
       γ' ἡμᾶς.
     ἀλλ' ᾐσθανόμεσθα καλῶς ὑμῶν· καὶ πολλάκις
       ἔνδον ἂν οὖσαι   510
     ἠκούσαμεν ἄν τι κακῶς ὑμᾶς βουλευσαμένους
       μέγα πρᾶγμα·
     εἶτ' ἀλγοῦσαι τἄνδοθεν ὑμᾶς ἐπανηρόμεθ' ἂν
       γελάσασαι,
     " τί βεβούλευται περὶ τῶν σπονδῶν ἐν τῇ στήλῃ
       παραγράψαι
     ἐν τῷ δήμῳ τήμερον ὑμῖν;" " τί δέ σοι ταῦτ' ;"
       ἦ δ' ὃς ἂν ἀνήρ,

---

a The pillar containing the Peace of Nicias (Thuc. v. 18). Three years later, the Athenians added beneath it, that the Lacedaemonians had failed to abide by their oaths (Thuc. v. 56).

MAG.   But how if I wish it not ?

LY.   That will but make our resolve the completer.

MAG.   Fools! what on earth can possess you to meddle with
            matters of war, and matters of peace ?

LY.   Well, I will tell you the reason.

MAG.   And speedily,
     else you will rue it.

LY.   Then listen, and cease
Clutching and clenching your fingers so angrily ;
       keep yourself peaceable.

MAG.   Hanged if I can ;
Such is the rage that I feel at your impudence.

ST.   Then it is *you* that will rue it, my man.

MAG.   Croak your own fate, you ill-omened antiquity.
    (*To Lysistrata*)   *You* be the spokeswoman, lady.

LY.   I will.
Think of our old moderation and gentleness,
     think how we bore with your pranks, and were
         still,
All through the days of your former pugnacity,
     all through the war that is over and spent :
Not that (be sure) we approved of your policy ;
     never our griefs you allowed us to vent.
Well we perceived your mistakes and mismanage-
     ment.
     Often at home on our housekeeping cares,
Often we heard of some foolish proposal you
     made for conducting the public affairs.
Then would we question you mildly and pleasantly,
     inwardly grieving, but outwardly gay ;
Husband, how goes it abroad ? we would ask of him ?
     what have ye done in Assembly to-day ?
What would ye write on the side of the Treaty stone [a] *?*
     Husband says angrily, *What's that to you ?*

"οὐ σιγήσει;" κἀγὼ 'σίγων.

ΣΤ.   ἀλλ' οὐκ ἂν ἐγώ ποτ' ἐσίγων. 515

ΠΡΟ. κἂν ᾤμωξάς γ', εἰ μὴ 'σίγας.

ΛΥ.   τοιγὰρ ἔγωγ' ἔνδον ἐσίγων.
εὐθὺς δ' ἕτερόν τι πονηρότερον βούλευμ' ἐπεπύ-
    σμεθ' ἂν ὑμῶν·
εἶτ' ἠρόμεθ' ἄν· "πῶς ταῦτ', ὦνερ, διαπράττεσθ'
    ὧδ' ἀνοήτως;"
ὁ δέ μ' εὐθὺς ὑποβλέψας ἂν ἔφασκ', εἰ μὴ τὸν
    στήμονα νήσω,
ὀτοτύξεσθαι μακρὰ τὴν κεφαλήν· "πόλεμος δ'
    ἄνδρεσσι μελήσει."   520

ΠΡΟ. ὀρθῶς γε λέγων νὴ Δί' ἐκεῖνος.

ΛΥ.   πῶς ὀρθῶς, ὦ κακόδαιμον,
εἰ μηδὲ κακῶς βουλευομένοις ἐξῆν ὑμῖν ὑποθέσθαι;
ὅτε δὴ δ' ὑμῶν ἐν ταῖσιν ὁδοῖς φανερῶς ἠκούομεν
    ἤδη,
"οὐκ ἔστιν ἀνὴρ ἐν τῇ χώρᾳ;" "μὰ Δί' οὐ δῆτ'
    ἔσθ' " ἕτερός τις·
μετὰ ταῦθ' ἡμῖν εὐθὺς ἔδοξεν σῶσαι τὴν Ἑλλάδα
    κοινῇ   525
ταῖσι γυναιξὶν συλλεχθείσαις. ποῖ γὰρ καὶ χρῆν
    ἀναμεῖναι;
ἢν οὖν ἡμῶν χρηστὰ λεγουσῶν ἐθελήσητ' ἀντ-
    ακροᾶσθαι
κἀντισιωπᾶν ὥσπερ χἠμεῖς, ἐπανορθώσαιμεν ἂν
    ὑμᾶς.

ΠΡΟ. ὑμεῖς ἡμᾶς; δεινόν γε λέγεις κοὐ τλητὸν ἔμοιγε.

ΛΥ.   σιώπα.

---

[a] Homer, *Iliad*, vi. 492.

[b] "Lysistrata is putting her system into immediate practice,
and therefore addresses the same language and assigns the same

You, hold your tongue ! And I held it accordingly.

ST.   That is a thing which I NEVER would do !

MAG.   Ma'am, if you hadn't, you'd soon have repented it.

LY.   Therefore I held it, and spake not a word.
Soon of another tremendous absurdity,
        wilder and worse than the former we heard.
Husband, I say, with a tender solicitude,
        Why have ye passed such a foolish decree ?
Vicious, moodily, glaring askance at me,
      Stick to your spinning, my mistress, says he,
Else you will speedily find it the worse for you,
   WAR IS THE CARE AND THE BUSINESS OF MEN !*[a]*

MAG.   Zeus ! 'twas a worthy reply, and an excellent !

LY.   What ! you unfortunate, shall we not then,
Then, when we see you perplexed and incompetent,
        shall we not tender advice to the State ?
So when aloud in the streets and the thoroughfares
        sadly we heard you bewailing of late,
Is there a Man to defend and deliver us ?
        No, says another, *there's none in the land ;*
Then by the Women assembled in conference
        jointly a great Revolution was planned,
Hellas to save from her grief and perplexity.
        Where is the use of a longer delay ?
Shift for the future our parts and our characters ;
        you, as the women, in silence obey ;
We, as the men, will harangue and provide for you ;
        then shall the State be triumphant again,
Then shall we do what is best for the citizens.

MAG.   Women to do what is best for the men !
That were a shameful reproach and unbearable !

LY.   Silence,*[b]* old gentleman.

duties to the Magistrate, as the Men had been accustomed aforetime to address and assign to the Women " : R.

ΠΡΟ. σοί γ’, ὦ κατάρατε, σιωπῶ ’γώ, καὶ ταῦτα
     κάλυμμα φορούσῃ   530
     περὶ τὴν κεφαλήν; μή νυν ζῴην.
ΛΥ.   ἀλλ’ εἰ τοῦτ’ ἐμπόδιόν σοι,
     παρ’ ἐμοῦ τουτὶ τὸ κάλυμμα λαβὼν
     ἔχε καὶ περίθου περὶ τὴν κεφαλήν,
     κᾆτα σιώπα,
ΚΑ. . . . .
ΜΥ. καὶ τοῦτον δὴ τὸν καλαθίσκον·   535
ΛΥ. κᾆτα ξαίνειν συζωσάμενος,
     κυάμους τρώγων·
     πόλεμος δὲ γυναιξὶ μελήσει.

ΧΟ. ΓΥ. ἀπαίρετ’, ὦ γυναῖκες, ἀπὸ τῶν καλπίδων,
     ὅπως ἂν
  ἐν τῷ μέρει χἠμεῖς τι ταῖς φίλαισι συλλάβωμεν. 540
                [ἀντ.
  ἔγωγε γὰρ ἂν οὔποτε κάμοιμ’ ἂν ὀρχουμένη,
  οὐδὲ γόνατ’ ἂν κόπος ἕλοι με καματηρὸς ἄν.
     ἐθέλω δ’ ἐπὶ πᾶν ἰέναι
     μετὰ τῶνδ’ ἀρετῆς ἕνεχ’, αἷς
     ἔνι φύσις, ἔνι χάρις, ἔνι θράσος,   545
     ἔνι δὲ σοφόν, ἔνι δὲ φιλόπολις
     ἀρετὴ φρόνιμος.

     ἀλλ’, ὦ τηθῶν ἀνδρειοτάτων καὶ μητριδίων
     ἀκαληφῶν,

---

[a] A line, to some such effect, has fallen out.
[b] " Women were in the habit of chewing some eatable as they
wove or spun ": R.
[c] *During the foregoing lines the Women have been arraying the
Magistrate in the garb and with the apparatus of a spinning-*

MAG.   Silence for YOU ?
        Stop for a wench with a wimple enfolding her ?
           No, by the Powers, may I DIE if I do !

LY.   Do not, my pretty one, do not, I pray,
        Suffer my wimple to stand in the way.
        Here, take it, and wear it, and gracefully tie it,
        Enfolding it over your head, and be quiet.
          Now to your task.

CA.   Here is an excellent spindle to pull.[a]

MY.   Here is a basket for carding the wool.

LY.   Now to your task.
        Haricots chawing up,[b] petticoats drawing up,
        Off to your carding, your combing, your trimming,
        WAR IS THE CARE AND THE BUSINESS OF WOMEN.[c]

W. CH. Up, up, and leave the pitchers there,
                      and on, resolved and eager,
       Our own allotted part to bear
                      in this illustrious leaguer.

       I will dance with resolute, tireless feet all day ;
       My limbs shall never grow faint, my strength give
            way ;
       I will march all lengths with the noble hearts and
            the true,
       For theirs is the ready wit and the patriot hand,
       And womanly grace, and courage to dare and do,
           And Love of our own bright land.

       Children of stiff and intractable grandmothers,
           heirs of the stinging viragoes that bore you,[d]

*woman : just as in the corresponding system, below, they bedeck
him in the habiliments of a corpse.*

  [d] μητριδίων is a diminutive of μήτηρ, but μητριδίων ἀκαληφῶν
means " seedling nettles."

χωρεῖτ' ὀργῇ καὶ μὴ τέγγεσθ'· ἔτι γὰρ νῦν
οὔρια θεῖτε.   550

ΛΥ. ἀλλ' ἤνπερ γ' ὁ γλυκύθυμος "Ερως χἠ Κυπρογένει'
'Αφροδίτη
ἵμερον ἡμῶν κατὰ τῶν κόλπων καὶ τῶν μηρῶν
καταπνεύσῃ,
κᾆτ' ἐντέξῃ τέτανον τερπνὸν τοῖς ἀνδράσι καὶ
ῥοπαλισμούς,
οἶμαί ποτε Λυσιμάχας ἡμᾶς ἐν τοῖς "Ελλησι
καλεῖσθαι.

ΠΡΟ. τί ποιησάσας;

ΛΥ.   ἢν παύσωμεν πρώτιστον μὲν ξὺν ὅπλοισιν 555
ἀγοράζοντας καὶ μαινομένους.

ΣΤ.   νὴ τὴν Παφίαν 'Αφροδίτην.

ΛΥ. νῦν μὲν γὰρ δὴ κἂν ταῖσι χύτραις κἂν τοῖς λα-
χάνοισιν ὁμοίως
περιέρχονται κατὰ τὴν ἀγορὰν ξὺν ὅπλοις, ὥσπερ
Κορύβαντες.

ΠΡΟ. νὴ Δία· χρὴ γὰρ τοὺς ἀνδρείους.

ΛΥ.   καὶ μὴν τό γε πρᾶγμα γέλοιον,
ὅταν ἀσπίδ' ἔχων καὶ Γοργόνα τις κᾆτ' ὠνῆται
κορακίνους.   560

ΣΤ. νὴ Δί' ἐγὼ γοῦν ἄνδρα κομήτην φυλαρχοῦντ'
εἶδον ἐφ' ἵππου
ἐς τὸν χαλκοῦν ἐμβαλλόμενον πῖλον λέκιθον παρὰ
γραός·
ἕτερος δ' αὖ Θρᾷξ πέλτην σείων κἀκόντιον, ὥσπερ
ὁ Τηρεύς,

ᵃ Lysimacha, "she who ends the battle," is an equivalent of
Lysistrata, "she who dismisses the army." The chief character's
name is chosen, of course, to indicate the aim of the proceedings.

On, with an eager, unyielding tenacity,
      wind in your sails, and the haven before you.

LY. Only let Love, the entrancing, the fanciful,
      only let Queen Aphrodite to-day
Breathe on our persons a charm and a tenderness,
      lend us their own irresistible sway,
Drawing the men to admire us and long for us ;
      then shall the war everlastingly cease,
Then shall the people revere us and honour us,
      givers of Joy, and givers of Peace.*a*

MAG. Tell us the mode and the means of your doing it.

LY.   First we will stop the disorderly crew,
Soldiers in arms promenading and marketing.

ST.   Yea, by divine Aphrodite, 'tis true.

LY. Now in the market *b* you see them like Corybants,*c*
      jangling about with their armour of mail.
Fiercely they stalk in the midst of the crockery,
      sternly parade by the cabbage and kail.

MAG. Right, for a soldier should always be soldierly !

LY.   Troth, 'tis a mighty ridiculous jest,
Watching them haggle for shrimps in the market-
    place,
      grimly accoutred with shield and with crest.

ST. Lately I witnessed a captain of cavalry,
      proudly the while on his charger he sat,
Witnessed him, soldierly, buying an omelet,
      stowing it all in his cavalry hat.
Comes, like a Tereus, a Thracian irregular,*d*
      shaking his dart and his target to boot ;

---

b The crockery and vegetable stalls: Schol.

c Phrygian priests of Cybele, who went armed. The Gorgon head (560) was a device on the shield.

d Tereus, the fabulous king of Thrace. The Thracians were engaged as mercenaries.

    ἐδεδίσκετο τὴν ἰσχαδόπωλιν καὶ τὰς δρυπεπεῖς
      κατέπινε.

ΠΡΟ. πῶς οὖν ὑμεῖς πράγματα παῦσαι τεταραγμένα
      πολλὰ δύνασθε   565
      ἐν ταῖς χώραις καὶ διαλῦσαι;

ΛΥ.   φαύλως πάνυ.

ΠΡΟ.   πῶς; ἀπόδειξον.

ΛΥ. ὥσπερ κλωστῆρ᾽, ὅταν ἡμῖν ᾖ τεταραγμένος, ὧδε
      λαβοῦσαι,
      ὑπενεγκοῦσαι τοῖσιν ἀτράκτοις τὸ μὲν ἐνταυθί, τὸ
      δ᾽ ἐκεῖσε,
      οὕτως καὶ τὸν πόλεμον τοῦτον διαλύσομεν, ἤν τις
      ἐάσῃ,
      διενεγκοῦσαι διὰ πρεσβειῶν τὸ μὲν ἐνταυθί, τὸ δ᾽
      ἐκεῖσε.   570

ΠΡΟ. ἐξ ἐρίων δὴ καὶ κλωστήρων καὶ ἀτράκτων πράγ-
      ματα δεινὰ
      παύσειν οἴεσθ᾽, ὦ ἀνόητοι;

ΛΥ.   κἂν ὑμῖν γ᾽ εἴ τις ἐνῆν νοῦς,
      ἐκ τῶν ἐρίων τῶν ἡμετέρων ἐπολιτεύεσθ᾽ ἂν
      ἅπαντα.

ΠΡΟ. πῶς δή; φέρ᾽ ἴδω.

ΛΥ. πρῶτον μὲν ἐχρῆν, ὥσπερ πόκον ἐν βαλανείῳ,
      ἐκπλύναντας τὴν οἰσπώτην ἐκ τῆς πόλεως, ἐπὶ
      κλίνης   575
      ἐκραβδίζειν τοὺς μοχθηροὺς καὶ τοὺς τριβόλους
      ἀπολέξαι,
      καὶ τούς γε συνισταμένους τούτους καὶ τοὺς
      πιλοῦντας ἑαυτοὺς

---

[a] The words that follow are terms used in wool-working:
οἰσπώτη is the dirt and grease in the wool (Schol.); the fleece is
stretched on a bench, and the burrs picked out (ἀπολέξαι) or

> Off runs a shop-girl, appalled at the sight of him,
> > down he sits soldierly, gobbles her fruit.

MAG. You, I presume, could adroitly and gingerly
> > settle this intricate, tangled concern :
> You in a trice could relieve our perplexities.

LY. > > > Certainly.

MAG. > > > > How ? permit me to learn.

LY. Just as a woman, with nimble dexterity,
> > thus with her hands disentangles a skein,
> Hither and thither her spindles unravel it,
> > drawing it out, and pulling it plain.
> So would this weary Hellenic entanglement
> > soon be resolved by our womanly care,
> So would our embassies neatly unravel it,
> > drawing it here and pulling it there.

MAG. Wonderful, marvellous feats, not a doubt of it,
> you with your skeins and your spindles can show ;
> Fools ! do you really expect to unravel a
> > terrible war like a bundle of tow ?

LY. Ah, if you only could manage your politics
> just in the way that we deal with a fleece !ᵃ

MAG. Tell us the recipe.

LY. > > > First, in the washing-tub
> plunge it, and scour it, and cleanse it from grease,
> Purging away all the filth and the nastiness ;
> > then on the table expand it and lay,
> Beating out all that is worthless and mischievous,
> > picking the burrs and the thistles away.
> Next, for the clubs, the cabals, and the coteries,
> > banding unrighteously, office to win,

struck off with sticks (ἐκραβδίζειν). It is then washed, clots and
knots carded out with combs (διαξῆναι), and the nuclei (κεφαλάς)
plucked out. It is now carded into the basket (καλαθίσκος,
represented in the state by κοινὴ εὔνοια), and all the wool drawn
out (κάταγμα, from κατάγω) rolled into a ball ready for use (τολύπη).

ἐπὶ ταῖς ἀρχαῖσι διαξῆναι καὶ τὰς κεφαλὰς ἀπο-
τῖλαι·
εἶτα ξαίνειν εἰς καλαθίσκον, κοινὴν εὔνοιαν, ἅπαντας,
καταμιγνύντας τούς τε μετοίκους κεἴ τις ξένος ἢ
φίλος ὑμῖν,   580
κεἴ τις ὀφείλει τῷ δημοσίῳ, καὶ τούτους ἐγκατα-
μῖξαι·
καὶ νὴ Δία τάς γε πόλεις, ὁπόσαι τῆς γῆς τῆσδ'
εἰσὶν ἄποικοι,
διαγιγνώσκειν ὅτι ταῦθ' ἡμῖν ὥσπερ τὰ κατ-
άγματα κεῖται
χωρὶς ἕκαστον· κᾆτ' ἀπὸ τούτων πάντων τὸ
κάταγμα λαβόντας
δεῦρο ξυνάγειν καὶ συναθροίζειν εἰς ἕν, κἄπειτα
ποιῆσαι   585
τολύπην μεγάλην, κᾆτ' ἐκ ταύτης τῷ δήμῳ
χλαῖναν ὑφῆναι.

ΠΡΟ. οὔκουν δεινὸν ταυτὶ ταύτας ῥαβδίζειν καὶ τολυ-
πεύειν,
αἷς οὐδὲ μετῆν πάνυ τοῦ πολέμου;

ΛΤ.   καὶ μήν, ὦ παγκατάρατε,
πλεῖν ἤ γε διπλοῦν αὐτὸν φέρομεν. πρώτιστον μέν
γε τεκοῦσαι
κἀκπέμψασαι παῖδας ὁπλίτας.

ΠΡΟ.   σίγα, μὴ μνησικακήσῃς. 590
ΛΤ. εἶθ' ἡνίκ' ἐχρῆν εὐφρανθῆναι καὶ τῆς ἥβης ἀπο-
λαῦσαι,
μονοκοιτοῦμεν διὰ τὰς στρατιάς. καὶ θἠμέτερον
μὲν ἐᾶτε,
περὶ τῶν δὲ κορῶν ἐν τοῖς θαλάμοις γηρασκουσῶν
ἀνιῶμαι.

Treat them as clots in the wool, and dissever them,
        lopping the heads that are forming therein.
Then you should card it, and comb it, and mingle it,
        all in one Basket of love and of unity,
Citizens, visitors, strangers, and sojourners,
        all the entire, undivided community.
Know you a fellow in debt to the Treasury ?
        Mingle him merrily in with the rest.
Also remember the cities, our colonies,
        outlying states in the east and the west,
Scattered about to a distance surrounding us,
        these are our shreds and our fragments of wool ;
These to one mighty political aggregate
        tenderly, carefully, gather and pull,
Twining them all in one thread of good fellowship ;
        thence a magnificent bobbin to spin,
Weaving a garment of comfort and dignity,
        worthily wrapping the People therein.
MAG. Heard any ever the like of their impudence,
        these who have nothing to do with the war,
Preaching of bobbins, and beatings, and washing-tubs?
LY.   Nothing to do with it, wretch that you are !
We are the people who feel it the keenliest,
        doubly on us the affliction is cast ;
Where are the sons that we sent to your battle-fields?
MAG.   Silence ! a truce to the ills that are past.
LY. Then in the glory and grace of our womanhood,
        all in the May and the morning of life,
Lo, we are sitting forlorn and disconsolate,
        what has a soldier to do with a wife ?
We might endure it, but ah ! for the younger ones,
        still in their maiden apartments they stay,
Waiting the husband that never approaches them,
        watching the years that are gliding away.

ΠΡΟ. οὔκουν κἄνδρες γηράσκουσιν;

ΛΥ.   μὰ Δί᾽, ἀλλ᾽ οὐκ εἶπας ὅμοιον.
ὁ μὲν ἥκων γάρ, κἂν ᾖ πολιός, ταχὺ παῖδα κόρην
    γεγάμηκεν·   595
τῆς δὲ γυναικὸς μικρὸς ὁ καιρός, κἂν τούτου μὴ
    ᾽πιλάβηται,
οὐδεὶς ἐθέλει γῆμαι ταύτην, ὀττευομένη δὲ κάθ-
    ηται.

ΠΡΟ.   ἀλλ᾽ ὅστις ἔτι στῦσαι δυνατὸς

ΛΥ.   σὺ δὲ δὴ τί μαθὼν οὐκ ἀποθνήσκεις;
χοιρίον ἔσται· σορὸν ὠνήσει·   600
μελιτοῦτταν ἐγὼ καὶ δὴ μάξω·
λαβὲ ταυτί· καὶ στεφάνωσαι.

ΚΑ.   καὶ ταυτασὶ δέξαι παρ᾽ ἐμοῦ.

ΜΥ.   καὶ τοῦτον δὴ λαβὲ τὸν στέφανον.

ΛΥ.   τοῦ δεῖ; τί ποθεῖς, χώρει ᾽ς τὴν ναῦν· 605
ὁ Χάρων σε καλεῖ,
σὺ δὲ κωλύεις ἀνάγεσθαι.

ΠΡΟ.   εἶτ᾽ οὐχὶ ταῦτα δεινὰ πάσχειν ἔστ᾽ ἐμέ;
νὴ τὸν Δί᾽ ἀλλὰ τοῖς προβούλοις ἄντικρυς
ἐμαυτὸν ἐπιδείξω βαδίζων ὡς ἔχω.   610

ΛΥ.   μῶν ἐγκαλεῖς ὅτι οὐχὶ προὐθέμεσθά σε;
ἀλλ᾽ ἐς τρίτην γοῦν ἡμέραν σοὶ πρῲ πάνυ
ἥξει παρ᾽ ἡμῶν τὰ τρίτ᾽ ἐπεσκευασμένα.

---

^a Apparently he was about to add " will soon find a wife," but
Lysistrata interrupts him, and she and her companions dress him
up like a corpse.

^b The "honeyed cake" (μελιτοῦττα) is for Cerberus.   In his
note R. explains ταυτί in the next line as "the small change" with
which to pay Charon's fare.   ταυτί in 603 = ταινίας "ribands"
commonly sent by friends."   For "crowning a corpse with flowers"
cf. E. 537, 538.

MAG.   Men, I suppose, have their youth everlastingly.
LY.   Nay, but it isn't the same with a man :
       Grey though he be when he comes from the battle-
              field,   still if he wishes to marry, he can.
       Brief is the spring and the flower of our womanhood,
                     once let it slip, and it comes not again ;
       Sit as we may with our spells and our auguries,
                     never a husband will marry us then.
MAG.   Truly whoever is able to wed—[a]
LY.   Truly, old fellow, 'tis time you were dead.
       So a pig shall be sought, and an urn shall be bought,
       And I'll bake you and make you a funeral cake.[b]
       Take it and go.
CA.   Here are the fillets all ready to wear.
MY.   Here is the chaplet to bind in your hair.
LY.   Take it and go.
       What are you prating for ?
                     What are you waiting for ?
       Charon is staying, delaying his crew,
       Charon is calling and bawling for you.[c]

MAG.   See, here's an outrage ! here's a scandalous shame !
       I'll run and show my fellow magistrates
       The woeful, horrid, dismal plight I'm in.
LY.   Grumbling because we have not laid you out ?
       Wait for three days, and then with dawn will come,
       All in good time, the third-day [d] funeral rites.[e]

---

   [c] Probably a reminiscence of Eur. *Alc.* 260 ff.
   [d] The body was laid out, and ceremonies performed on the
third and ninth days (τρίτα, ἔνατα).
   [e] *The Magistrate runs off in his grave-clothes to complain of and
exhibit the treatment he has received. Lysistrata and her friends
withdraw into the Acropolis. The two Choruses remain without,
and relieve the tedium of the siege with a little banter*

63

ARISTOPHANES

ΧΟ. ΓΕ. οὐκ ἔτ' ἔργον ἐγκαθεύδειν, ὅστις ἔστ' ἐλεύθερος· [στρ
    ἀλλ' ἐπαποδυώμεθ', ἄνδρες, τουτῳὶ τῷ πράγματι.   615
    ἤδη γὰρ ὄζειν ταδὶ πλειόνων καὶ μειζόνων
      πραγμάτων μοι δοκεῖ·
    καὶ μάλιστ' ὀσφραίνομαι τῆς Ἱππίου τυραννίδος·
      καὶ πάνυ δέδοικα μὴ
      τῶν Λακώνων τινὲς   620
      δεῦρο συνεληλυθότες
      ἄνδρες ἐς Κλεισθένους
    τὰς θεοῖς ἐχθρὰς γυναῖκας ἐξεπαίρωσιν δόλῳ
      καταλαβεῖν τὰ χρήμαθ' ἡμῶν
      τόν τε μισθὸν
      ἔνθεν ἔζων ἐγώ.   625
    δεινὰ γάρ τοι τάσδε γ' ἤδη τοὺς πολίτας νουθετεῖν,
    καὶ λαλεῖν γυναῖκας οὔσας ἀσπίδος χαλκῆς πέρι,
    καὶ διαλλάττειν πρὸς ἡμᾶς ἀνδράσιν Λακωνικοῖς,
    οἷσι πιστὸν οὐδέν, εἰ μή περ λύκῳ κεχηνότι.
    ἀλλὰ ταῦθ' ὕφηναν ἡμῖν, ἄνδρες, ἐπὶ τυραννίδι.   630
    ἀλλ' ἐμοῦ μὲν οὐ τυραννεύσουσ', ἐπεὶ φυλάξομαι,
    καὶ φορήσω τὸ ξίφος τὸ λοιπὸν ἐν μύρτου κλαδί,
    ἀγοράσω τ' ἐν τοῖς ὅπλοις ἑξῆς Ἀριστονείτονι,
    ὧδέ θ' ἑστήξω παρ' αὐτόν· αὐτόθεν μοι γίγνεται

---

a Men of this class were always ready to suspect a conspiracy for setting up a tyranny. Hippias, the last tyrant, after his brother Hipparchus had been killed by Harmodius and Aristogeiton, was expelled by the Alcmaeonidae with the help of Cleomenes, king of Sparta. Cleisthenes is " a fitting intermediary between the Athenian *women* and the Laconian *men*, as partaking of the nature of both " : R. See *Thesm.* 576.

b The words of the scolium or drinking-song : ἐν μύρτου κλαδὶ τὸ ξίφος φορήσω | ὥσπερ Ἁρμόδιος κ' Ἀριστογείτων. Their statues, attacking the tyrant, stood in the Agora ; *E.* 682. At 634, the actor assumes the pose of Aristogeiton striking the tyrant.

м. ch. This is not a time for slumber ;
                    now let all the bold and free,
Strip to meet the great occasion,
                    vindicate our rights with me.
I can smell a deep, surprising
Tide of Revolution rising,
Odour as of folk devising
                    Hippias's tyranny.[a]
And I feel a dire misgiving,
Lest some false Laconians, meeting
                    in the house of Cleisthenes,
Have inspired these wretched women
                    all our wealth and pay to seize,
Pay from whence I get my living.
Gods ! to hear these shallow wenches
                    taking citizens to task,
Prattling of a brassy buckler,
                    jabbering of a martial casque !
Gods ! to think that they have ventured
                    with Laconian men to deal,
Men of just the faith and honour
                    that a ravening wolf might feel !
Plots they're hatching, plots contriving,
                    plots of rampant Tyranny ;
But o'er us they shan't be Tyrants,
                    no, for on my guard I'll be,
And I'll dress my sword in myrtle,[b]
                    and with firm and dauntless hand,
Here beside Aristogeiton
                    resolutely take my stand,
Marketing in arms beside him.
                    This the time and this the place

τῆς θεοῖς ἐχθρᾶς πατάξαι τῆσδε γραὸς τὴν γνάθον. 635

χο. γγ. οὐκ ἄρ' εἰσιόντα σ' οἴκαδ' ἡ τεκοῦσα γνώσεται. [ἀντ.
ἀλλὰ θώμεσθ', ὦ φίλαι γρᾶες, ταδὶ πρῶτον χαμαί.
ἡμεῖς γάρ, ὦ πάντες ἀστοί, λόγων κατάρχομεν
τῇ πόλει χρησίμων·
εἰκότως, ἐπεὶ χλιδῶσαν ἀγλαῶς ἔθρεψέ με.   640
ἑπτὰ μὲν ἔτη γεγῶσ'
εὐθὺς ἠρρηφόρουν·
εἶτ' ἀλετρὶς ἦ, δεκέτις
οὖσα, τἀρχηγέτι·
κᾆτ' ἔχουσα τὸν κροκωτὸν ἄρκτος ἦ Βραυρωνίοις· 645
κἀκανηφόρουν ποτ' οὖσα
παῖς καλὴ 'χουσ'
ἰσχάδων ὁρμαθόν.
ἆρα προὐφείλω τι χρηστὸν τῇ πόλει παραινέσαι;
εἰ δ' ἐγὼ γυνὴ πέφυκα, τοῦτο μὴ φθονεῖτέ μοι,
ἢν ἀμείνω γ' εἰσενέγκω τῶν παρόντων πραγμάτων. 650
τοὐράνου γάρ μοι μέτεστι· καὶ γὰρ ἄνδρας εἰσφέρω.
τοῖς δὲ δυστήνοις γέρουσιν οὐ μέτεσθ' ὑμῖν, ἐπεὶ
τὸν ἔρανον τὸν λεγόμενον παππῷον ἐκ τῶν Μηδικῶν

---

a Unexpectedly suits the action to the word. A similar result takes place at the end of the three succeeding speeches.

b These are the distinctions which a young Athenian girl might hope to attain. Four girls, between the ages of seven and eleven, were chosen yearly from those of noble birth to serve Athene for a year in the Erechtheum; they were called ἀρρηφόροι because they carried certain mysterious objects in caskets. The ἀλετρίδες were of ten years and upwards, also of noble birth, selected to grind on the holy mills (ἱεροὶ μυλῶνες) grain for the sacred cakes. The crowning honour was to carry a basket in the great Panathenaic procession; *A.* 242, *B.* 1551, *E.* 730. Each Athenian girl, before marriage, had to "play the bear" at the festival of Brauronian Artemis, wearing a yellow robe in place of the ancient bearskin:

When my patriot arm must deal a
>—blow [a] upon that woman's face.

w. ch. Ah, your mother shall not know you,
>impudent ! when home you go.
Strip, my sisters, strip for action,
>on the ground your garments throw.
>Right it is that I my slender
>Tribute to the state should render,
>I, who to her thoughtful tender
>>care my happiest memories owe ; [b]
Bore, at seven, the mystic casket ;
Was, at ten, our Lady's miller ;
>then the yellow Brauron bear ;
Next (a maiden tall and stately
>with a string of figs to wear)
>Bore in pomp the holy Basket.
Well may such a gracious City
>all my filial duty claim.
What though I was born a woman,
>comrades, count it not for blame
If I bring the wiser counsels ;
>I an equal share confer
Towards the common stock of Athens,
>I contribute men to her.
But the noble contribution,
>but the olden tribute-pay,
Which your fathers' fathers left you,
>relic of the Median fray, [c]

Brauron, a place on the coast of Attica, claimed to possess the statue of A. which fell from heaven. Archegetis (644) is probably Athene.

[c] The contribution paid by the allies to the treasury at Delos, for war against the Persian king. Since its transfer to Athens the allies were falling away.

εἶτ' ἀναλώσαντες οὐκ ἀντεισφέρετε τὰς εἰσφοράς,
ἀλλ' ὑφ' ὑμῶν διαλυθῆναι προσέτι κινδυνεύομεν.   655
ἆρα γρυκτόν ἐστιν ὑμῖν; εἰ δὲ λυπήσεις τί με,
τῷδέ γ' ἀψήκτῳ πατάξω τῷ κοθόρνῳ τὴν γνάθον.

ΧΟ. ΓΕ.   ταῦτ' οὖν οὐχ ὕβρις τὰ πράγματ'   [στρ.
          ἐστὶ πολλή; κἀπιδώσειν
          μοι δοκεῖ τὸ χρῆμα μᾶλλον.   660
ἀλλ' ἀμυντέον τὸ πρᾶγμ' ὅστις γ' ἐνόρχης ἔστ' ἀνήρ.
ἀλλὰ τὴν ἐξωμίδ' ἐκδυώμεθ', ὡς τὸν ἄνδρα δεῖ
ἀνδρὸς ὄζειν εὐθύς, ἀλλ' οὐκ ἐντεθριῶσθαι πρέπει.

          ἀλλ' ἄγετε, λευκόποδες,
          οἵπερ ἐπὶ Λειψύδριον   665
          ἤλθομεν, ὅτ' ἦμεν ἔτι,
              νῦν δεῖ,
          νῦν ἀνηβῆσαι πάλιν, κἀν-
              απτερῶσαι
          πᾶν τὸ σῶμα κἀποσείσασ-   670
          θαι τὸ γῆρας τοδί.

εἰ γὰρ ἐνδώσει τις ἡμῶν ταῖσδε κἂν σμικρὰν λαβήν,
οὐδὲν ἐλλείψουσιν αὗται λιπαροῦς χειρουργίας.
ἀλλὰ καὶ ναῦς τεκτανοῦνται, κἀπιχειρήσουσ' ἔτι
ναυμαχεῖν καὶ πλεῖν ἐφ' ἡμᾶς, ὥσπερ Ἀρτεμισία·   675
ἢν δ' ἐφ' ἱππικὴν τράπωνται, διαγράφω τοὺς ἱππέας,

---

[a] " λευκόποδες, with a play on λυκόποδες, the name given to
the outlawed Alcmaeonids when they returned to Attica and
established themselves on Leipsydrium, in their first fruitless
attempt to overthrow the tyranny of Hippias " : R.
[b] She fought against the Greeks at Salamis ; Herod. viii. **93**.

Dotards, ye have lost and wasted !
> nothing in its stead ye bring,
Nay ourselves ye're like to ruin,
> spend and waste by blundering.
Murmuring are ye ?   Let me hear you,
> only let me hear you speak,
And from this unpolished slipper
> comes a—slap upon your cheek !

M CH.   Is not this an outrage sore ?
And methinks it blows not o'er,
But increases more and more.
Come, my comrades, hale and hearty,
> on the ground your mantles throw,
In the odour of their manhood
> men to meet the fight should go,
Not in these ungodly wrappers
> swaddled up from top to toe.

On, then on, my white-foot[a] veterans,
> ye who thronged Leipsydrium's height
In the days when we were Men !
Shake this chill old Age from off you,
Spread the wings of youth again.

O these women ! give them once a
> handle howsoever small,
And they'll soon be nought behind us
> in the manliest feats of all.
Yea, they'll build them fleets and navies
> and they'll come across the sea,
Come like Carian Artemisia,[b]
> fighting in their ships with me.
Or they'll turn their first attention,
> haply, to equestrian fights,

69

ἱππικώτατον γάρ ἐστι χρῆμα κἄποχον γυνή,
κοὐκ ἂν ἀπολίσθοι τρέχοντος· τὰς δ᾽ Ἀμαζόνας
σκόπει,
ἃς Μίκων ἔγραψ᾽ ἐφ᾽ ἵππων μαχομένας τοῖς ἀνδράσιν.
ἀλλὰ τούτων χρῆν ἁπασῶν ἐς τετρημένον ξύλον
ἐγκαθαρμόσαι λαβόντας τουτονὶ τὸν αὐχένα. 680

χο. ΓΓ.   εἰ νὴ τὼ θεώ με ζωπυ-   [ἀντ.
ρήσεις, λύσω τὴν ἐμαυτῆς
ὗν ἐγὼ δή, καὶ ποιήσω
τήμερον τοὺς δημότας βωστρεῖν σ᾽ ἐγὼ πεκτούμε-
νον.
ἀλλὰ χἠμεῖς, ὦ γυναῖκες, θᾶττον ἐκδυώμεθα,   685
ὡς ἂν ὄζωμεν γυναικῶν αὐτοδὰξ ὠργισμένων.
νῦν πρὸς ἔμ᾽ ἴτω τις, ἵνα
μή ποτε φάγῃ σκόροδα
μηδὲ κυάμους μέλανας,
ὡς εἰ   690
καὶ μόνον κακῶς μ᾽ ἐρεῖς, ὑ-
περχολῶ γάρ,
αἰετὸν τίκτοντα κάνθα-
ρός σε μαιεύσομαι.
οὐ γὰρ ὑμῶν φροντίσαιμ᾽ ἄν, ἢν ἐμοὶ ζῇ Λαμπιτὼ 695
ἥ τε Θηβαία φίλη παῖς εὐγενὴς Ἰσμηνία.
οὐ γὰρ ἔσται δύναμις, οὐδ᾽ ἢν ἑπτάκις σὺ ψηφίσῃ,
ὅστις, ὦ δύστην᾽, ἀπήχθου πᾶσι καὶ τοῖς γείτοσιν.

---

^a One in the Poecile Stoa, one in the Theseum.
^b *He seizes the neck of Stratyllis.*
^c Alluding to the soldier's garlic, and the voter's beans ; 537.
^d In Aesop's fable (No. 223), the beetle, to revenge itself on the
eagle, contrived to break its eggs, even when they were laid in
the bosom of Zeus; W. 1442, P. 129.

If they do, I know the issue,
     there's an end of all the knights !
Well a woman sticks on horseback :
      look around you, see, behold,
Where on Micon's living frescoes ^a
       fight the Amazons of old !
Shall we let these wilful women,
      O my brothers, do the same ?
Rather first their necks we'll rivet
      tightly in the pillory frame.^b

W. CH.   If our smouldering fires ye wake,
      Soon our wildbeast wrath will break
      Out against you, and we'll make,
Make you howl to all your neighbours,
     currycombed, poor soul, and tanned.
Throw aside your mantles, sisters,
     come, a firm determined band,
In the odour of your wrathful
      snappish womanhood to stand.
Who'll come forth and fight me ? garlic,
     nevermore, nor beans ^c for him.
Nay, if one sour word ye say,
I'll be like the midwife beetle,
Following till the eagle lay.^d
Yea, for you and yours I reck not
     whilst my Lampito survives,
And my noble, dear Ismenia,
     loveliest of the Theban wives.
Keep decreeing seven times over,
     not a bit of good you'll do,
Wretch abhorred of all the people
     and of all our neighbours too.

71

ὥστε κἀχθὲς θἠκάτῃ ποιοῦσα παιγνίαν ἐγὼ   700
τοῖσι παισὶ τὴν ἑταίραν ἐκάλεσ' ἐκ τῶν γειτόνων,
παῖδα χρηστὴν κἀγαπητὴν ἐκ Βοιωτῶν ἔγχελυν·
οἱ δὲ πέμψειν οὐκ ἔφασκον διὰ τὰ σὰ ψηφίσματα.
κοὐχὶ μὴ παύσησθε τῶν ψηφισμάτων τούτων, πρὶν ἂν
τοῦ σκέλους λαβών τις ὑμᾶς ἐκτραχηλίσῃ φέρων.   705

χο.γγ. ἄνασσα πράγους τοῦδε καὶ βουλεύματος,
    τί μοι σκυθρωπὸς ἐξελήλυθας δόμων;
λτ. κακῶν γυναικῶν ἔργα καὶ θήλεια φρὴν
    ποιεῖ μ' ἄθυμον περιπατεῖν ἄνω κάτω.
χο.γγ. τί φῄς; τί φῄς;   710
λτ. ἀληθῆ, ἀληθῆ.
χο.γγ. τί δ' ἐστὶ δεινόν; φράζε ταῖς σαυτῆς φίλαις.
λτ. ἀλλ' αἰσχρὸν εἰπεῖν καὶ σιωπῆσαι βαρύ.
χο.γγ. μή νύν με κρύψῃς ὅ τι πεπόνθαμεν κακόν.
λτ. βινητιῶμεν, ἦ βράχιστον τοῦ λόγου.   715
χο.γγ. ἰὼ Ζεῦ.
λτ. τί Ζῆν' ἀϋτεῖς; ταῦτα δ' οὖν οὕτως ἔχει.
    ἐγὼ μὲν οὖν αὐτὰς ἀποσχεῖν οὐκέτι
    οἵα τ' ἀπὸ τῶν ἀνδρῶν· ἀποδιδράσκουσι γάρ.
    τὴν μέν γε πρώτην διαλέγουσαν τὴν ὀπὴν   720
    κατέλαβον ᾗ τοῦ Πανός ἐστι ταὐλίον,
    τὴν δ' ἐκ τροχιλίας αὖ κατειλυσπωμένην,
    τὴν δ' αὐτομολοῦσαν, τὴν δ' ἐπὶ στρουθοῦ μίαν

---

[a] The eels from Lake Copaïs in Boeotia were famous.

[b] *An interval of several days must here be supposed to elapse. The separation of the sexes has now become insupportable to both parties, and the only question is which side will hold out the longest. The Chorus of Women are alarmed at seeing Lysistrata come on the stage, and walk up and down with an anxious and troubled air. The first twelve lines of the dialogue which ensues are borrowed and burlesqued from Euripides.*

[c] From the *Telephus* of Euripides : Schol.

So that when in Hecate's honour
                              yesterday I sent to get
From our neighbours in Boeotia
                              such a dainty darling pet,
Just a lovely, graceful, slender,
                              white-fleshed eel divinely tender,[a]
Thanks to your decrees, confound them,
                              one and all refused to send her.
And you'll never stop from making
                              these absurd decrees I know,
Till I catch your leg and toss you
                              —Zeus-ha'-mercy, there you go![b]

W. CH. Illustrious leader of this bold emprize,[c]
        What brings thee forth, with trouble in thine eyes?
LY.   Vile women's works: the feminine hearts they show:
        These make me pace, dejected, to and fro.
W. CH. O what! and O what!
LY.   'Tis true! 'tis true!
W. CH. O to your friends, great queen, the tale unfold.
LY.   'Tis sad to tell, and sore to leave untold.
W. CH. What, what has happened? tell us, tell us quick.
LY.   Aye, in one word. The girls are—husband-sick.
W. CH. O Zeus! Zeus! O!
LY.   Why call on Zeus? the fact is surely so.
        I can no longer keep the minxes in.
        They slip out everywhere.   One I discovered
        Down by Pan's grotto, burrowing through the
            loophole:[d]
        Another, wriggling down by crane and pulley[e]:
        A third deserts outright: a fourth I dragged

---

[d] The grotto is in the north-west face of the Acropolis rock, and
a path now leads down to it through a closed doorway.
  [e] These belonged to the well: Schol.

ἤδη πέτεσθαι διανοουμένην κάτω
εἰς Ὀρσιλόχου χθὲς τῶν τριχῶν κατέσπασα.　725
πάσας τε προφάσεις ὥστ' ἀπελθεῖν οἴκαδε
ἕλκουσιν. ἡδὶ γοῦν τις αὐτῶν ἔρχεται.
αὕτη σὺ ποῖ θεῖς;

ΓΥ.Α.　　　　　　οἴκαδ' ἐλθεῖν βούλομαι.
οἴκοι γάρ ἐστιν ἔριά μοι Μιλήσια
ὑπὸ τῶν σέων κατακοπτόμενα.

ΛΥ.　　　　　　　　　ποίων σέων;　　730
οὐκ εἶ πάλιν;

ΓΥ.Α.　　　　ἀλλ' ἥξω ταχέως νὴ τὼ θεώ,
ὅσον διαπετάσασ' ἐπὶ τῆς κλίνης μόνον.

ΛΥ. μὴ διαπετάννυ, μηδ' ἀπέλθῃς μηδαμῇ.

ΓΥ.Α. ἀλλ' ἐῶ 'πολέσθαι τἄρι';

ΛΥ.　　　　　　　ἢν τούτου δέῃ.

ΓΥ.Β. τάλαιν' ἐγώ, τάλαινα τῆς ἀμοργίδος,　　735
ἢν ἄλοπον οἴκοι καταλέλοιφ'.

ΛΥ.　　　　　　　　αὕτη 'τέρα
ἐπὶ τὴν ἄμοργιν τὴν ἄλοπον ἐξέρχεται.
χώρει πάλιν δεῦρ'.

ΓΥ.Β.　　　　ἀλλὰ νὴ τὴν Φωσφόρον
ἔγωγ' ἀποδείρασ' αὐτίκα μάλ' ἀπέρχομαι.

ΛΥ. μὴ μἀποδείρῃς. ἢν γὰρ ἄρξῃ τοῦτο σύ,　　740
ἑτέρα γυνὴ ταὐτὸν ποιεῖν βουλήσεται.

ΓΥ.Γ. ὦ πότνι' Εἰλείθυι', ἐπίσχες τοῦ τόκου,
ἕως ἂν εἰς ὅσιον μόλω 'γὼ χωρίον.

ΛΥ. τί ταῦτα ληρεῖς;

ΓΥ.Γ.　　　　αὐτίκα μάλα τέξομαι.

ΛΥ. ἀλλ' οὐκ ἐκύεις σύ γ' ἐχθές.

ᵃ A comic exaggeration, the sparrow being an amorous bird
(Schol.), and harnessed to Aphrodite's car (Sappho, i. 10).
ᵇ *A woman is seen attempting to cross the stage.*

Back by the hair, yestreen, just as she started
On sparrow's back,[a] straight for Orsilochus's :
They make all sorts of shifts to get away.[b]
Ha ! here comes one, deserting.   Hi there, Hi !
Where are you off to ?

FIRST WOMAN (*hurriedly*)   I must just run home.
I left some fine Milesian wools about,
I'm sure the moths are at them.

LY.   Moths indeed !
Get back.

F.W.   But really I'll return directly,
I only want to spread them on the couch.

LY.   No spreadings out, no running home to-day.

F.W.   What ! leave my wools to perish ?

LY.   If need be.[c]

SECOND W. O goodness gracious ! O that lovely flax
I left at home unhackled !

LY.   Here's another !
She's stealing off to hackle flax forsooth.[d]
Come, come, get back.

S.W.   O yes, and so I will,
I'll comb it out and come again directly.

LY.   Nay, nay, no combing : once begin with that
And other girls are sure to want the same.[e]

THIRD W. O holy Eileithyia, stay my labour
Till I can reach some lawful travail-place.[f]

LY.   How now !

T.W.   My pains are come.

LY.   Why, yesterday
You were not pregnant.

---

[c] *A second woman now attempts to cross the stage.*

[d] *To the second woman.*

[e] *Several women enter one after the other.*

[f] The Acropolis was holy ground, not " lawful for childbirth " :
Schol.

ARISTOPHANES

ΓΥ.Γ.   ἀλλὰ τήμερον.   745
ἀλλ' οἴκαδέ μ' ὡς τὴν μαῖαν, ὦ Λυσιστράτη,
ἀπόπεμψον ὡς τάχιστα.
ΛΥ.   τίνα λόγον λέγεις;
τί τοῦτ' ἔχεις τὸ σκληρόν;
ΓΥ.Γ.   ἄρρεν παιδίον.
ΛΥ. μὰ τὴν Ἀφροδίτην οὐ σύ γ', ἀλλ' ἢ χαλκίον
ἔχειν τι φαίνει κοῖλον· εἴσομαι δ' ἐγώ.   750
ὦ καταγέλαστ', ἔχουσα τὴν ἱερὰν κυνῆν
κυεῖν ἔφασκες;
ΓΥ.Γ.   καὶ κυῶ γε νὴ Δία.
ΛΥ. τί δῆτα ταύτην εἶχες;
ΓΥ.Γ.   ἵνα μ' εἰ καταλάβοι
ὁ τόκος ἔτ' ἐν πόλει, τέκοιμ' ἐς τὴν κυνῆν
ἐσβᾶσα ταύτην, ὥσπερ αἱ περιστεραί.   755
ΛΥ. τί λέγεις; προφασίζει· περιφανῆ τὰ πράγματα.
οὐ τἀμφιδρόμια τῆς κυνῆς αὐτοῦ μενεῖς;
ΓΥ.Δ. ἀλλ' οὐ δύναμαι 'γωγ' οὐδὲ κοιμᾶσθ' ἐν πόλει,
ἐξ οὗ τὸν ὄφιν εἶδον τὸν οἰκουρόν ποτε.
ΓΥ.Ε. ἐγὼ δ' ὑπὸ τῶν γλαυκῶν γε τάλαιν' ἀπόλλυμαι   760
ταῖς ἀγρυπνίαισι κακκαβιζουσῶν ἀεί.
ΛΥ. ὦ δαιμόνιαι, παύσασθε τῶν τερατευμάτων.
ποθεῖτ' ἴσως τοὺς ἄνδρας· ἡμᾶς δ' οὐκ οἴει
ποθεῖν ἐκείνους; ἀργαλέας γ' εὖ οἶδ' ὅτι
ἄγουσι νύκτας. ἀλλ' ἀνάσχεσθ', ὦγαθαί,   765
καὶ προσταλαιπωρῆσατ' ἔτ' ὀλίγον χρόνον,
ὡς χρησμὸς ἡμῖν ἐστιν ἐπικρατεῖν, ἐὰν
μὴ στασιάσωμεν· ἔστι δ' ὁ χρησμὸς οὑτοσί.
ΓΥ. λέγ' αὐτὸν ἡμῖν ὅ τι λέγει.
ΛΥ.   σιγᾶτε δή.

---

[a] " In my opinion, the great bronze helmet of Athene Promachos ": R.

76

T.W.   But to-day I am
        Quick, let me pass, Lysistrata, at once
        To find a midwife.

LY.   What's it all about ?
        What's this hard lump ?

T.W.   That's a male child.

LY.   Not it.
        It's something made of brass, and hollow too.
        Come, come, out with it.   O you silly woman,
        What ! cuddling up the sacred helmet *a* there
        And say you're pregnant ?

T.W.   Well, and so I am.

LY.   What's this for then ?

T.W.   Why, if my pains o'ertake me
        In the Acropolis, I'd creep inside
        And sit and hatch there as the pigeons do.

LY.   Nonsense and stuff : the thing's as plain as can be
        Stay and keep here the name-day of your—helmet.

FOURTH W. But I can't sleep a single wink up here,
        So scared I was to see the holy serpent.*b*

FIFTH W. And I shall die for lack of rest, I know,
        With this perpetual hooting of the owls.

LY.   O ladies, ladies, cease these tricks, I pray.
        Ye want your husbands.   And do you suppose
        They don't want *us* ? Full wearisome, I know,
        Their nights without us.   O bear up, dear friends,
        Be firm, be patient, yet one little while,
        For I've an oracle (here 'tis) which says
        We're sure to conquer if we hold together.

WOMEN. O read us what it says.

LY.   Then all keep silence.*c*

---

b The sacred serpent dwelt in the Erechtheum.
c *Lysistrata reads out the oracle.*

ἀλλ' ὁπόταν πτήξωσι χελιδόνες εἰς ἕνα χῶρον, 770
τοὺς ἔποπας φεύγουσαι, ἀπόσχωνταί τε φα-
λήτων,
παῦλα κακῶν ἔσται, τὰ δ' ὑπέρτερα νέρτερα
θήσει
Ζεὺς ὑψιβρεμέτης,

ΓΥ. .   ἐπάνω κατακεισόμεθ' ἡμεῖς;

ΛΥ. ἢν δὲ διαστῶσιν καὶ ἀναπτῶνται πτερύγεσσιν
ἐξ ἱεροῦ ναοῖο χελιδόνες, οὐκέτι δόξει 775
ὄρνεον οὐδ' ὁτιοῦν καταπυγωνέστερον εἶναι.

ΙΤ. σαφής γ' ὁ χρησμὸς νὴ Δί'. ὦ πάντες θεοί,
μή νυν ἀπείπωμεν ταλαιπωρούμεναι,
ἀλλ' εἰσίωμεν. καὶ γὰρ αἰσχρὸν τουτογί,
ὦ φίλταται, τὸν χρησμὸν εἰ προδώσομεν. 780

ΧΟ. ΓΕ. μῦθον   [στρ.
βούλομαι λέξαι τιν' ὑμῖν, ὅν ποτ' ἤκουσ'
αὐτὸς ἔτι παῖς ὤν.
οὕτως
ἦν ποτε νέος Μελανίων τις, ὃς 785
φεύγων γάμον ἀφίκετ' ἐς ἐρημίαν,
κἀν τοῖς ὄρεσιν ᾤκει·
κᾆτ' ἐλαγοθήρει
πλεξάμενος ἄρκυς, 790
καὶ κύνα τιν' εἶχεν,
κοὐκέτι κατῆλθε πάλιν οἴκαδ' ὑπὸ μίσους.

---

^a φαλῆς, the φαλλός personified, A. 263, with an allusion to the
φαληρίς or coot.

^b καταπυγωνέστερον is explained by the Scholiast as μαλακώτερον
καὶ πορνικώτερον.

^c The women, with Lysistrata, re-enter the Acropolis. The two
Choruses again indulge in an interchange of banter. The Men
begin.

Soon as the swallows are seen
                collecting and crouching together,
Shunning the hoopoes' flight
                and keeping aloof from the Love-birds,[a]
Cometh a rest from ill,
                and Zeus the Lord of the Thunder
Changeth the upper to under.

w.   Preserve us, shall *we* be the upper?

LY. *Nay, but if once they wrangle,*
                and flutter away in dissension
Out of the Temple of God,
                then all shall see and acknowledge,
Never a bird of the air
                so perjured and frail[b] as the swallow.

w. Wow, but that's plain enough! O all ye Gods,
Let us not falter in our efforts now.
Come along in. O friends, O dearest friends,
'Twere sin and shame to fail the oracle.[c]

M. CH.   Now to tell a little story
           Fain, fain I grow,
      One I heard when quite an urchin
           Long, long ago.[d]
          How that once
      All to shun the nuptial bed
      From his home Melanion fled,
      To the hills and deserts sped,
          Kept his dog,
          Wove his snares,
          Set his nets,
          Trapped his hares;
      Home he nevermore would go,

[d] The Men reverse the story, in which Atalanta fled from wedlock, and Melanion won her by the golden apples (so Schol.); Apollodorus iii. 9. 6.

οὕτω
τὰς γυναῖκας ἐβδελύχθη
κεῖνος, ἡμεῖς τ' οὐδὲν ἧττον   795
τοῦ Μελανίωνος οἱ σώφρονες.

ΓΕΡΩΝ. βούλομαί σε, γραῦ, κύσαι,
ΓΥΝΗ. κρόμμυόν τἄρ' οὐκ ἔδει.
ΓΕ. κἀνατείνας λακτίσαι.
ΓΥ. τὴν λόχμην πολλὴν φορεῖς.   800
ΓΕ. καὶ Μυρωνίδης γὰρ ἦν
τραχὺς ἐντεῦθεν μελάμπυ-
γός τε τοῖς ἐχθροῖς ἅπασιν,
ὡς δὲ καὶ Φορμίων.

ΧΟ. ΓΥ. κἀγὼ   [ἀντ. 805
βούλομαι μῦθόν τιν' ὑμῖν ἀντιλέξαι
τῷ Μελανίωνι.
Τίμων
ἦν τις ἀίδρυτος ἀβάτοισιν ἐν
σκώλοισι τὰ πρόσωπα περιειργμένος,   810
Ἐρινύος ἀπορρώξ.
οὗτος ἄρ' ὁ Τίμων
[ἄθλιος ἀφ' ὑμῶν]
ᾤχεθ' ὑπὸ μίσους
πολλὰ καταρασάμενος ἀνδράσι πονηροῖς.   815
οὕτω
κεῖνος ὑμᾶς ἀντεμίσει
τοὺς πονηροὺς ἄνδρας ἀεί,
ταῖσι δὲ γυναιξὶν ἦν φίλτατος.   820

ᵃ The version given requires the reading κρομμύου, and ἔδει to
be taken as from δέω "to be in want of"; the meaning being,
"you shall weep real tears" (κλαύσει χωρὶς κρομμύων Schol.).

	He detested women so.
	We are of Melanion's mind,
	We detest the womankind.
MAN.	May I, mother, kiss your cheek ?
WOMAN.	Then you won't require a leek.[a]
M.	Hoist my leg, and kick you, so ?
W.	Fie ! what stalwart legs you show !
M.	Just such stalwart legs and strong,
	Just such stalwart legs as these,
	To the noble chiefs belong,
	Phormio[b] and Myronides.[c]

W. CH.	Now to tell a little story
	Fain, fain am I,
	To your tale about Melanion
	Take this reply.
	How that once
	Savage Timon, all forlorn,
	Dwelt amongst the prickly thorn
	Visage-shrouded, Fury-born.
	Dwelt alone,
	Far away,
	Cursing men
	Day by day ;
	Never saw his home again,
	Kept aloof from haunts of men ;
	Hating men of evil mind,
	Dear to all the womankind.

Others render " Then you shall never eat onions again," a threat like that of 689 (Schol. : οὐ πολεμήσεις).

  [b] Phormio, a naval hero of the Peloponnesian war ; Myronides, victor over the Corinthians and the Boeotians, 459-6 B.C. See K. 562, P. 348, E. 304.

  [c] *It is now the women's turn. The two systems are of course antistrophical.*

ΓΥ. τὴν γνάθον βούλει θένω;
ΓΕ. μηδαμῶς· ἔδεισά γε.
ΓΥ. ἀλλὰ κρούσω τῷ σκέλει;
ΓΕ. τὸν σάκανδρον ἐκφανεῖς.
ΓΥ. ἀλλ' ὅμως ἂν οὐκ ἴδοις   825
    καίπερ οὔσης γραὸς ὄντ' αὐ-
    τὸν κομήτην, ἀλλ' ἀπεψι-
    λωμένον τῷ λύχνῳ.

ΛΥ. ἰοὺ ἰού, γυναῖκες, ἴτε δεῦρ' ὡς ἐμὲ
    ταχέως.
ΓΥ.Α.   τί δ' ἔστιν; εἰπέ μοι, τίς ἡ βοή;   830
ΛΥ. ἄνδρ' ἄνδρ' ὁρῶ προσιόντα παραπεπληγμένον,
    τοῖς τῆς Ἀφροδίτης ὀργίοις εἰλημμένον.
ΓΥ.Α. ὦ πότνια, Κύπρου καὶ Κυθήρων καὶ Πάφου
    μεδέουσ', ἴθ' ὀρθὴν ἥνπερ ἔρχει τὴν ὁδόν.
    ποῦ δ' ἐστίν, ὅστις ἐστί;
ΛΥ.   παρὰ τὸ τῆς Χλόης. 835
ΓΥ.Α. ὦ νὴ Δί' ἐστὶ δῆτα. τίς κἀστίν ποτε;
ΛΥ. ὁρᾶτε· γιγνώσκει τις ὑμῶν;
ΜΥ.   νὴ Δία,
    ἔγωγε· κἀστὶν οὑμὸς ἀνὴρ Κινησίας.
ΛΥ. σὸν ἔργον εἴη τοῦτον ὀπτᾶν καὶ στρέφειν,
    κἀξηπεροπεύειν, καὶ φιλεῖν καὶ μὴ φιλεῖν,   840
    καὶ πάνθ' ὑπέχειν πλὴν ὧν σύνοιδεν ἡ κύλιξ.
ΜΥ. ἀμέλει, ποιήσω ταῦτ' ἐγώ.
ΛΥ.   καὶ μὴν ἐγὼ
    συνηπεροπεύσω παραμένουσά γ' ἐνθαδί,
    καὶ ξυσταθεύσω τοῦτον. ἀλλ' ἀπέλθετε.
ΚΙΝΗΣΙΑΣ. οἴμοι κακοδαίμων, οἷος ὁ σπασμός μ' ἔχει 845

---

^a τὸν σάκανδρον· τὸ γυναικεῖον αἰδοῖον : Schol.
^b *The two Choruses now retire into the background : and there*

w.   Shall I give your cheek a blow ?

m.   No, I thank you, no, no, no !

w.   Hoist my foot and kick you too ?

m.   Fie ! what vulgar feet [a] I view.

w.   Vulgar feet ! absurd, absurd,
         Don't such foolish things repeat ;
      Never were, upon my word,
         Tinier, tidier little feet.[b]

ly.   Ho, ladies ! ladies ! quick, this way, this way !

f.w. O what's the matter and what means that cry ?

ly.   A man ! a man ! I see a man approaching
      Wild with desire, beside himself with love.

f.w. O lady of Cyprus, Paphos, and Cythera,
      Keep on, straight on, the way you are going now !
      But where's the man ?

ly. (*pointing*)   Down there, by Chloë's chapel.[c]

f.w. O so he is : whoever can he be !

ly.   Know you him, anyone ?

my.   O yes, my dear,
      I know him. That's Cinesias, my husband.

ly.   O then 'tis yours to roast and bother him well ;
      Coaxing, yet coy : enticing, fooling him,
      Going all lengths, save what our Oath forbids.

my. Ay, ay, trust *me*.

ly.   And I'll assist you, dear ;
      I'll take my station here, and help befool
      And roast our victim.   All the rest, retire.[d]

cinesias. O me ! these pangs and paroxysms of love,

*is again a short pause. Suddenly the voice of Lysistrata is heard
calling eagerly to her friends.*

   [c] Near the Acropolis. Demeter was called Chloë after the first
green corn-shoots (χλόη).

   [d] *The others withdraw, leaving Lysistrata alone upon the wall.
Cinesias approaches underneath.*

83

χὠ τέτανος ὥσπερ ἐπὶ τροχοῦ στρεβλούμενον.
ΛΥ. τίς οὗτος οὑντὸς τῶν φυλάκων ἑστώς;
ΚΙ.   ἐγώ.
ΛΥ. ἀνήρ;
ΚΙ.   ἀνὴρ δῆτ᾽.
ΛΥ.   οὐκ ἄπει δῆτ᾽ ἐκποδών;
ΚΙ. σὺ δ᾽ εἶ τίς ἢ ᾽κβάλλουσά μ᾽;
ΛΥ.   ἡμεροσκόπος.
ΚΙ. πρὸς τῶν θεῶν νυν ἐκκάλεσόν μοι Μυρρίνην.   850
ΛΥ. ἰδού, καλέσω ᾽γὼ Μυρρίνην σοι· σὺ δὲ τίς εἶ;
ΚΙ. ἀνὴρ ἐκείνης, Παιονίδης Κινησίας.
ΛΥ. ὦ χαῖρε φίλτατ᾽· οὐ γὰρ ἀκλεὲς τοὔνομα
τὸ σὸν παρ᾽ ἡμῖν ἐστιν οὐδ᾽ ἀνώνυμον.
ἀεὶ γὰρ ἡ γυνή σ᾽ ἔχει διὰ στόμα,   855
κἂν ᾠὸν ἢ μῆλον λάβῃ, "Κινησίᾳ
τουτὶ γένοιτο," φησίν.
ΚΙ.   ὦ πρὸς τῶν θεῶν.
ΛΥ. νὴ τὴν Ἀφροδίτην· κἂν περὶ ἀνδρῶν γ᾽ ἐμπέσῃ
λόγος τις, εἴρηκ᾽ εὐθέως ἡ σὴ γυνὴ
ὅτι λῆρός ἐστι τἆλλα πρὸς Κινησίαν.   860
ΚΙ. ἴθι νυν, κάλεσον αὐτήν.
ΛΥ.   τί οὖν; δώσεις τί μοι;
ΚΙ. ἔγωγέ σοι νὴ τὸν Δί᾽, ἢν βούλῃ γε σύ·
ἔχω δὲ τοῦθ᾽· ὅπερ οὖν ἔχω, δίδωμί σοι.
ΛΥ. φέρε νυν καλέσω καταβᾶσά σοι.
ΚΙ.   ταχύ νυν πάνυ,
ὡς οὐδεμίαν ἔχω γε τῷ βίῳ χάριν,   865
ἐξ οὗπερ αὕτη ᾽ξῆλθεν ἐκ τῆς οἰκίας·
ἀλλ᾽ ἄχθομαι μὲν εἰσιών, ἔρημα δὲ
εἶναι δοκεῖ μοι πάντα, τοῖς δὲ σιτίοις
χάριν οὐδεμίαν οἶδ᾽ ἐσθίων· ἔστυκα γάρ.

	Riving my heart, keen as a torturer's wheel !
LY.	Who's this within the line of sentries ?
CI.	I.
LY.	A man ?
CI.	A man, no doubt.
LY.	Then get you gone.
CI.	Who bids me go ?
LY.	I, guard on outpost duty.
CI.	O call me out, I pray you, Myrrhina.
LY.	Call you out Myrrhina ! And who are you ?
CI.	Why, I'm her husband, I'm Cinesias.[a]
LY.	O welcome, welcome, dearest man ; your name

LY. Is not unknown nor yet unhonoured here.
Your wife for ever has it on her lips.
She eats no egg, no apple, but she says
This to Cinesias !

CI. O, good heaven ! good heaven !

LY. She does, indeed : and if we ever chance
To talk of men, she vows that all the rest
Are veriest trash beside Cinesias.

CI. Ah ! call her out.

LY. And will you give me aught ?

CI. O yes, I'll give you anything I've got.[b]

LY. Then I'll go down and call her.[c]

CI. Pray be quick.
I have no joy, no happiness in life,
Since she, my darling, left me.   When I enter
My vacant home I weep ;   and all the world
Seems desolate and bare :   my very meals
Give me no joy, now Myrrhina is gone.

[a] There was an Attic deme Παιονίδαι, but Παιονίδης is intended to suggest παίειν as Κινησίας does κινεῖν, a verb of the same signification.

[b] *Gives money.*

[c] *Descends from the wall into the Acropolis.*

85

ΜΥ. φιλῶ φιλῶ 'γὼ τοῦτον· ἀλλ' οὐ βούλεται   870
    ὑπ' ἐμοῦ φιλεῖσθαι. σὺ δ' ἐμὲ τούτῳ μὴ κάλει.

ΚΙ. ὦ γλυκύτατον Μυρρινίδιον, τί ταῦτα δρᾷς;
    κατάβηθι δεῦρο.

ΜΥ.   μὰ Δί' ἐγὼ μὲν αὐτόσ' οὔ.

ΚΙ. ἐμοῦ καλοῦντος οὐ καταβήσει, Μυρρίνη;

ΜΥ. οὐ γὰρ δεόμενος οὐδὲν ἐκκαλεῖς ἐμέ.   875

ΚΙ. ἐγὼ οὐ δεόμενος; ἐπιτετριμμένος μὲν οὖν.

ΜΥ. ἄπειμι.

ΚΙ.   μὴ δῆτ', ἀλλὰ τῷ γοῦν παιδίῳ
    ὑπάκουσον· οὗτος, οὐ καλεῖς τὴν μαμμίαν;

ΠΑΙΣ. μαμμία, μαμμία, μαμμία.

ΚΙ. αὕτη, τί πάσχεις; οὐδ' ἐλεεῖς τὸ παιδίον   880
    ἄλουτον ὂν κἄθηλον ἕκτην ἡμέραν;

ΜΥ. ἔγωγ' ἐλεῶ δῆτ'· ἀλλ' ἀμελὴς αὐτῷ πατὴρ
    ἔστιν.

ΚΙ.   κατάβηθ', ὦ δαιμονία, τῷ παιδίῳ.

ΜΥ. οἷον τὸ τεκεῖν· καταβατέον. τί γὰρ πάθω;

ΚΙ. ἐμοὶ γὰρ αὕτη καὶ νεωτέρα δοκεῖ   885
    πολλῷ γεγενῆσθαι κἀγανώτερον βλέπειν·
    χἂ δυσκολαίνει πρὸς ἐμὲ καὶ βρενθύεται,
    ταῦτ' αὐτὰ δή 'σθ' ἃ κἄμ' ἐπιτρίβει τῷ πόθῳ.

ΜΥ. ὦ γλυκύτατον σὺ τεκνίδιον κακοῦ πατρός,
    φέρε σε φιλήσω γλυκύτατον τῇ μαμμίᾳ.   890

ΚΙ. τί, ὦ πονηρά, ταῦτα ποιεῖς χἀτέραις
    πείθει γυναιξί, κἀμέ τ' ἄχθεσθαι ποιεῖς
    αὐτή τε λυπεῖ;

ΜΥ.   μὴ πρόσαγε τὴν χεῖρά μοι.

ΚΙ. τὰ δ' ἔνδον ὄντα τἀμὰ καὶ σά χρήματα
    χεῖρον διατιθεῖς.

ΜΥ.   ὀλίγον αὐτῶν μοι μέλει.   895

_____

^a As she speaks, she appears on the wall.

MY. (*within*) Ay, ay, I love, I love him, but he won't
    Be loved by me : call me not out to him.[a]

CI. What mean you, Myrrhina, my sweet, sweet love ?
    Do, do come down.

MY.   No, no, sir, not to you.

CI. What, won't you when I call you, Myrrhina ?

MY. Why, though you call me, yet you want me not.

CI. Not want you, Myrrhina ! I'm dying for you.

MY. Good-bye.

CI.   Nay, nay, but listen to the child
    At all events : speak to Mama, my child.

CHILD. Mama ! Mama ! Mama !

CI. Have you no feeling, mother, for your child,
    Six days unwashed, unsuckled ?

MY.   Ay, 'tis I
    That feel for baby, 'tis Papa neglects him.

CI. Come down and take him, then ?

MY.   O what it is
    To be a mother ! I must needs go down.[b]

CI. She looks, methinks, more youthful than she did,
    More gentle-loving, and more sweet by far.
    Her very airs, her petulant, saucy ways,
    They do but make me love her, love her more.

MY. O my sweet child, a naughty father's child,
    Mama's own darling, let me kiss you, pet.

CI. Why treat me thus, you baggage, letting others
    Lead you astray : making me miserable
    And yourself too ?

MY.   Hands off ! don't touch me, sir.

CI. And all our household treasures, yours and mine,
    Are gone to wrack and ruin.

MY.   I don't care.

  [b] *She descends from the wall, and four lines below reappears through the gate. While she is gone Cinesias speaks.*

ΚΙ. ὀλίγον μέλει σοι τῆς κρόκης φορουμένης
ὑπὸ τῶν ἀλεκτρυόνων;

ΜΥ.   ἔμοιγε νὴ Δία.

ΚΙ. τὰ τῆς Ἀφροδίτης ἱέρ᾽ ἀνοργίαστά σοι
χρόνον τοσοῦτόν ἐστιν. οὐ βαδιεῖ πάλιν;

ΜΥ. μὰ Δί᾽ οὐκ ἔγωγ᾽, ἢν μὴ διαλλαχθῆτέ γε   900
καὶ τοῦ πολέμου παύσησθε.

ΚΙ.   τοιγάρ, ἢν δοκῇ,
ποιήσομεν καὶ ταῦτα.

ΜΥ.   τοιγάρ, ἢν δοκῇ,
κἄγωγ᾽ ἄπειμ᾽ ἐκεῖσε· νῦν δ᾽ ἀπομώμοκα.

ΚΙ. σὺ δ᾽ ἀλλὰ κατακλίθητι μετ᾽ ἐμοῦ διὰ χρόνου.

ΜΥ. οὐ δῆτα· καίτοι σ᾽ οὐκ ἐρῶ γ᾽ ὡς οὐ φιλῶ.   905

ΚΙ. φιλεῖς; τί οὖν οὐ κατεκλίνης, ὦ Μυρρίνιον;

ΜΥ. ὦ καταγέλαστ᾽, ἐναντίον τοῦ παιδίου;

ΚΙ. μὰ Δί᾽, ἀλλὰ τοῦτό γ᾽ οἴκαδ᾽, ὦ Μανῆ, φέρε.
ἰδού, τὸ μέν σοι παιδίον καὶ δὴ ᾽κποδών·
σὺ δ᾽ οὐ κατακλίνει;

ΜΥ.   ποῦ γὰρ ἄν τις καί, τάλαν, 910
δράσειε τοῦθ᾽;

ΚΙ.   ὅπου τὸ τοῦ Πανός, καλόν.

ΜΥ. καὶ πῶς ἔθ᾽ ἁγνὴ δῆτ᾽ ἂν ἔλθοιμ᾽ ἐς πόλιν;

ΚΙ. κάλλιστα δήπου, λουσαμένη τῇ Κλεψύδρα.

ΜΥ. ἔπειτ᾽ ὀμόσασα δῆτ᾽ ἐπιορκήσω, τάλαν;

ΚΙ. εἰς ἐμὲ τράποιτο· μηδὲν ὅρκου φροντίσῃς.   915

ΜΥ. φέρε νυν ἐνέγκω κλινίδιον νῷν.

ΚΙ.   μηδαμῶς.
ἀρκεῖ χαμαὶ νῷν.

ΜΥ.   μὰ τὸν Ἀπόλλω μή σ᾽ ἐγώ,
καίπερ τοιοῦτον ὄντα, κατακλινῶ χαμαί.

---

        a Lines 904 to 979 were omitted in R.'s translation, 968-978
are taken from his note.

88

CI.   Not care, although the fowls are in the house
      Pulling your threads to pieces ?

MY.   Not a bit.

CI.   Nor though the sacred rites of wedded love
      Have been so long neglected ? won't you come ?

MY.   No, no, I won't, unless you stop the war,
      And all make friends.

CI.   Well, then, if such your will,
      We'll e'en do this.

MY.   Well, then, if such your will,
      I'll e'en come home : but now I've sworn I won't.

CI.[a] Come to my arms, do, after all this time !

MY.   No, no—and yet I won't say I don't love you.

CI.   You love me ? then come to my arms, my dearie !

MY.   You silly fellow, and the baby here ?

CI.   O, not at all—(to slave) here, take the baby home.
      There now : the baby's gone out of the way ;
      Come to my arms !

MY.   Good heavens, where, I ask you !

CI.   Pan's grotto[b] will do nicely.

MY.   Oh, indeed !
      How shall I make me pure to ascend the Mount[c] ?

CI.   Easy enough : bathe in the Clepsydra.

MY.   I've sworn an oath, and shall I break it, man ?

CI.   On my head be it : never mind the oath.

MY.   Well, let me bring a pallet.

CI.   Not at all ;
      The ground will do.

MY.   What—one so much to me ?
      I swear I'll never let you lie o' the ground.[d]

----

[b] " Pan's grotto was to be the nuptial chamber, and she was
to purify herself in the adjoining spring, the Clepsydra " : R.
  [c] *i.e.* the Acropolis.
  [d] *Exit M.*

ΚΙ. ἦ τοι γυνὴ φιλεῖ με, δήλη 'στὶν καλῶς.

ΜΥ. ἰδού, κατάκεισ' ἀνύσας τι· κἀγὼ 'κδύομαι   920
   καίτοι, τὸ δεῖνα, ψίαθός ἐστ' ἐξοιστέα.

ΚΙ. ποία ψίαθος; μή μοί γε.

ΜΥ.   νὴ τὴν Ἄρτεμιν,
   αἰσχρὸν γὰρ ἐπὶ τόνου γε.

ΚΙ.   δός μοί νυν κύσαι.

ΜΥ. ἰδού.

ΚΙ.   παπαιάξ. ἧκέ νυν ταχέως πάνυ.

ΜΥ. ἰδοὺ ψίαθος· κατάκεισο, καὶ δὴ 'κδύομαι.   925
   καίτοι, τὸ δεῖνα, προσκεφάλαιον οὐκ ἔχεις.

ΚΙ. ἀλλ' οὐ δέομ' οὐδὲν ἔγωγε.

ΜΥ.   νὴ Δί' ἀλλ' ἐγώ.

ΚΙ. ἀλλ' ἦ τὸ πέος τόδ' Ἡρακλῆς ξενίζεται.

ΜΥ. ἀνίστασ', ἀναπήδησον.

ΚΙ.   ἤδη πάντ' ἔχω.

ΜΥ. ἅπαντα δῆτα;

ΚΙ.   δεῦρό νυν, ὦ χρύσιον.   930

ΜΥ. τὸ στρόφιον ἤδη λύομαι. μέμνησό νυν·
   μή μ' ἐξαπατήσῃς τὰ περὶ τῶν διαλλαγῶν.

ΚΙ. νὴ Δί' ἀπολοίμην ἄρα.

ΜΥ.   σισύραν οὐκ ἔχεις.

ΚΙ. μὰ Δί' οὐδὲ δέομαί γ', ἀλλὰ βινεῖν βούλομαι.

ΜΥ. ἀμέλει, ποιήσεις τοῦτο· ταχὺ γὰρ ἔρχομαι.   935

ΚΙ. ἅνθρωπος ἐπιτρίψει με διὰ τὰ στρώματα.

ΜΥ. ἔπαιρε σαυτόν.

ΚΙ.   ἀλλ' ἐπῆρται τοῦτό γε.

ΜΥ. βούλει μυρίσω σε;

ΚΙ.   μὰ τὸν Ἀπόλλω μή μέ γε.

---

      [a] Enter M. with pallet.
   [b] Exit M. and returns with mattress.

CI. The woman loves me, plain enough, you see.

MY.[a] There, lie down, do make haste; I'll take my things off
But wait a minute, I must find a mattress.

CI. Bother the mattress, not for me.

MY.   Why yes,
It's nasty on the cords.

CI.   Give me a kiss.

MY. There then.

CI.   Smack, smack. Come back, look sharp about it.[b]

MY. There now, lie down, see, I take off my things—
But wait a minute—what about a pillow?

CI. But I don't want a pillow.

MY.   I do, though.[c]

CI. A veritable feast of Barmecides [d] ! [e]

MY. Up with your head, hop up !

CI.   I've all I want.

MY. What, *all* ?

CI.   Yes, all but you ; come here, my precious !

MY. There goes the girdle. But remember now,
You must not play me false about the peace.

CI. God damn me if I do !

MY.   You have no rug.

CI. I want no rug, I want you in my arms.

MY. Oh, all right, you shall have me, I'll be quick.[f]

CI. She'll be the death of me with all these bedclothes![g]

MY. Up now !

CI.   I'm up enough, be sure of that.

MY. Some nice sweet ointment ?

CI.   By Apollo, no !

   [c] *Exit M.*

   [d] "Ἡρακλῆς ξενίζεται, is having the entertainment of Heracles, that is, is kept waiting for his supper ; *cf. W.* 60 ": R.

   [e] *M. returns with pillow.*

   [f] *Exit M.*

   [g] *Enter M. with rug.*

ΜΥ. νὴ τὴν Ἀφροδίτην, ἤν τε βούλῃ γ᾽ ἤν τε μή.
ΚΙ. εἴθ᾽ ἐκχυθείη τὸ μύρον, ὦ Ζεῦ δέσποτα.   940
ΜΥ. πρότεινε δὴ τὴν χεῖρα κἀλείφου λαβών.
ΚΙ. οὐχ ἡδὺ τὸ μύρον μὰ τὸν Ἀπόλλω τουτογί,
    εἰ μὴ διατριπτικόν γε, κοὐκ ὄζον γάμων.
ΜΥ. τάλαιν᾽ ἐγώ, τὸ Ῥόδιον ἤνεγκον μύρον.
ΚΙ. ἀγαθόν· ἔα αὔτ᾽, ὦ δαιμονία.
ΜΥ.   λῃρεῖς ἔχων.   945
ΚΙ. κάκιστ᾽ ἀπόλοιθ᾽ ὁ πρῶτος ἑψήσας μύρον.
ΜΥ. λαβὲ τόνδε τὸν ἀλάβαστον.
ΚΙ.   ἀλλ᾽ ἕτερον ἔχω.
    ἀλλ᾽ ὠζυρὰ κατάκεισο καὶ μή μοι φέρε
    μηδέν.
ΜΥ.   ποιήσω ταῦτα νὴ τὴν Ἄρτεμιν.
    ὑπολύομαι γοῦν. ἀλλ᾽ ὅπως, ὦ φίλτατε,   950
    σπονδὰς ποιεῖσθαι ψηφιεῖ.
ΚΙ.   βουλεύσομαι—
    ἀπολώλεκέν με κἀπιτέτριφεν ἡ γυνή,
    τά τ᾽ ἄλλα πάντα κἀποδείρασ᾽ οἴχεται.
    οἴμοι τί πάθω; τίνα βινήσω;   [στρ
    τῆς καλλίστης πασῶν ψευσθείς;   955
    πῶς ταυτηνὶ παιδοτροφήσω;
    ποῦ Κυναλώπηξ;
    μίσθωσόν μοι τὴν τιτθήν.
ΧΟ. ΓΕ. ἐν δεινῷ γ᾽, ὦ δύστηνε, κακῷ
    τείρει ψυχὴν ἐξαπατηθείς.   960
    κἄγωγ᾽ οἰκτείρω σ᾽ αἶ, αἶ, αἶ.
    ποῖος γὰρ ἂν ἢ νέφρος ἀντίσχοι,
    ποία ψυχή, ποῖοι δ᾽ ὄρχεις,
    ποία δ᾽ ὀσφύς; ποῖος δ᾽ ὄρρος

    ᵃ Exit M.   ᵇ Enter M. with ointment.
    ᶜ Exit M.   ᵈ Enter M. with a flask.

MY. By Aphrodite, yes ! say what you like.[a]

CI. Lord Zeus, I pray the ointment may be spilt ![b]

MY. Put out your hand, take some, anoint yourself.

CI. I swear this stuff is anything but sweet,
The brand is Wait-and-see, no marriage smell !

MY. How stupid ! here I've brought the Rhodian kind.

CI. It's good enough, my dear.

MY.   Rubbish, good man ![c]

CI. Perdition take the man that first made ointment ![d]

MY. Here, take this flask.

CI.   I've all the flask I want.
Come to my arms, you wretched creature you !
No more things, please !

MY.   I will, by Artemis.
There go my shoes, at least.   Now don't forget,
You'll vote for peace, my dearest.

CI.   Oh, I'll see.[e]
The creature's done for me, bamboozled me,
Gone off and left me in this wretched state.
  What will become of me ? whom shall I fondle
   Robbed of the fairest fair ?
  Who will be ready this orphan to dandle ?
   Where's Cynalopex[f] ? where ?
    Find me a nurse !

M. CH.   She's left you a curse.
  Oh I'm so sorry, O I grieve for ye,
   Tis more than a man can bear :
  Not a soul, not a loin, not a heart, not a groin,

---

[e] " But what he means we cannot say, for before he has gone further Myrrhina disappears into the Acropolis, and he finds that she has been playing him false throughout " : R.

[f] " He speaks of his ψωλήν (*inf.* 979) as if it were a motherless daughter. Its own mother has deserted it; he must hire a nurse for it from the πορνοβοσκός, Philostratus, who was nicknamed Κυναλώπηξ. See *K.* 1069 " : R.

965

κατατεινόμενος,
καὶ μὴ βινῶν τοὺς ὄρθρους.

ΚΙ. ὦ Ζεῦ, δεινῶν ἀντισπασμῶν. ⌈ἀντ.

ΧΟ. ΓΕ. ταυτὶ μέντοι νυνί σ' ἐποίησ'
ἡ παμβδελυρὰ καὶ παμμυσαρά.

ΧΟ. ΓΥ. μὰ Δί' ἀλλὰ φίλη καὶ παγγλυκερά. 970

ΧΟ. ΓΕ. ποία γλυκερά;
μιαρὰ μιαρὰ δῆτ'. ὦ Ζεῦ Ζεῦ,
εἴθ' αὐτήν, ὥσπερ τοὺς θωμούς,
μεγάλῳ τυφῷ καὶ πρηστῆρι
ξυστρέψας καὶ ξυγγογγυλίσας 975
οἴχοιο φέρων, εἶτα μεθείης,
ἡ δὲ φέροιτ' αὖ πάλιν εἰς τὴν γῆν,
κᾆτ' ἐξαίφνης
περὶ τὴν ψωλὴν περιβαίη.

ΚΗΡΥΞ. πᾶ τᾶν 'Ασανᾶν ἐστιν ἁ γερωχία 980
ἢ τοὶ πρυτάνιες; λῶ τι μυσίξαι νέον.

ΠΡΟ. σὺ δὲ τίς; πότερον ἄνθρωπος, ἢ Κονίσαλος;

ΚΗ. κᾶρυξ ἐγών, ὦ κυρσάνιε, ναὶ τὼ σιὼ
ἔμολον ἀπὸ Σπάρτας περὶ τᾶν διαλλαγᾶν.

ΠΡΟ. κἄπειτα δόρυ δῆθ' ὑπὸ μάλης ἥκεις ἔχων; 985

ΚΗ. οὐ τὸν Δί' οὐκ ἐγώνγα.

ΠΡΟ.   ποῖ μεταστρέφει;
τί δὴ προβάλλει τὴν χλαμύδ'; ἢ βουβωνιᾶς
ὑπὸ τῆς ὁδοῦ;

ΚΗ.   παλαιόρ γα ναὶ τὸν Κάστορα
ἄνθρωπος.

ΠΡΟ.   ἀλλ' ἔστυκας, ὦ μιαρώτατε.

---

^a 'Αθηνῶν, γερουσία, and λῶ = ἐθέλω.
^b "Are you a man or Conisalus?" the latter being a local
Priapus.

94

       Can endure such pangs of despair.

CI.   O Zeus, what pangs and throes I bear !

M. CH. All this woe she has wrought you, she only, the
        Utterly hateful, the utterly vile.

W. CH. Not so ; but the darling, the utterly sweet.

M. CH. Sweet, sweet, do you call her ?   Vile, vile, I repeat.
       Zeus, send me a storm and a whirlwind, I pray,
       To whisk her away, like a bundle of hay,
          Up, up, to the infinite spaces,
       And toss her and swirl her, and twist her, and twirl
          her,
       Till, tattered and torn, to the earth she is borne,
       To be crushed—in my ardent embraces.

(Enter Herald)

HERALD. Whaur sall a body fin' the Athanian senate,
    Or the gran' lairds ? Ha' gotten news to tell.*[a]*

MAG. News have you, friend ?
              And what in the world are you ? *[b]*

HER. A heralt, billie ! *[c]* jist a Spartian heralt,
    Come, by the Twa', anent a Peace, ye ken.

MAG. And so you come with a spear beneath your armpit!*[d]*

HER. Na, na, not I.

MAG.   Why do you turn away ?
    Why cast your cloak before you ? Is your groin
    A trifle swollen from the march ?

HER.   By Castor
    This loon's a rogue.

MAG.   Look at yourself, you brute !

---

  [c] ὦ κυρσάνιε = " my lad ": κυρσανίους καλοῦσιν οἱ Λάκωνες τὰ
μειράκια (Schol.). Compare 1248.

  [d] He is trying to hide the φαλλὸς δερμάτινος, but " armpit " is
a comic turn, alluding to conspirators who hide a dagger there.
Lines 985 to 992 are not in R.'s translation.

ΚΗ. οὐ τὸν Δί᾽ οὐκ ἐγώνγα· μηδ᾽ αὖ πλαδδίη. 990

ΠΡΟ. τί δ᾽ ἐστί σοι τοδί;

ΚΗ.   σκυτάλα Λακωνικά.

ΠΡΟ. εἴπερ γε χαύτη ᾽στὶ σκυτάλη Λακωνική.
ἀλλ᾽ ὡς πρὸς εἰδότ᾽ ἐμὲ σὺ τἀληθῆ λέγε.
τί τὰ πράγμαθ᾽ ὑμῖν ἐστι τὰν Λακεδαίμονι;

ΚΗ. ὀρσὰ Λακεδαίμων πᾶα, καὶ τοὶ σύμμαχοι 995
ἅπαντες ἐστύκαντι· Πελλάνας δὲ δεῖ.

ΠΡΟ. ἀπὸ τοῦ δὲ τουτὶ τὸ κακὸν ὑμῖν ἐνέπεσεν;
ἀπὸ Πανός;

ΚΗ.   οὔκ, ἀλλ᾽ ἆρχε μέν, οἰῶ, Λαμπιτώ,
ἔπειτα τἄλλαι ταὶ κατὰ Σπάρταν ἅμα
γυναῖκες ᾇπερ ἀπὸ μιᾶς ὑσπλαγίδος 1000
ἀπήλαον τὼς ἄνδρας ἀπὸ τῶν ὑσσάκων.

ΠΡΟ. πῶς οὖν ἔχετε;

ΚΗ.   μογίομες. ἂν γὰρ τὰν πόλιν
ᾇπερ λυχνοφορίοντες ἀποκεκύφαμες.
ταὶ γὰρ γυναῖκες οὐδὲ τῶ μύρτω σιγῆν
ἐῶντι, πρίν χ᾽ ἄπαντες ἐξ ἑνὸς λόγω 1005
σπονδὰς ποιησώμεσθα ποττὰν Ἑλλάδα.

ΠΡΟ. τουτὶ τὸ πρᾶγμα πανταχόθεν ξυνομώμοται
ὑπὸ τῶν γυναικῶν· ἄρτι νυνὶ μανθάνω.
ἀλλ᾽ ὡς τάχιστα φράζε περὶ διαλλαγῶν
αὐτοκράτορας πρέσβεις ἀποπέμπειν ἐνθαδί. 1010
ἐγὼ δ᾽ ἑτέρους ἐνθένδε τῇ βουλῇ φράσω
πρέσβεις ἑλέσθαι, τὸ πέος ἐπιδείξας τοδί.

ΚΗ. πωτάομαι· κράτιστα γὰρ παντᾶ λέγεις.

ΧΟ. ΓΕ. οὐδέν ἐστι θηρίον γυναικὸς ἀμαχώτερον,

---

^a ὀρθή, πᾶσα.
^b Pan causes all sudden commotions and " panics."
^c ἀπήλαυνον τοὺς ἄνδρας ἀπὸ τῶν γυναικείων αἰδοίων.

HER. There's naught amiss wi' me, don't play the fule.

MAG. Why then, what's this ?

HER. A Spartan letter-staff.

MAG. (*pointing to himself*)
Yes, if *this* is a Spartan letter-staff !
Well, and how fare the Spartans ? tell me that :
And tell me truly, for I know the fact.

HER. They're bad eneugh, they canna weel be waur ;
They're sair bested, Spartans, allies, an' a'.*a*

MAG. And how and whence arose this trouble first ?
From Pan *b* ?

HER. Na, na, 'twer' Lampito, I ween,
First set it gangin' : then our hizzies, a'
Risin' like rinners at ane signal word,
Loupit, an' jibbed, an' dang the men awa'.*c*

MAG. How like ye that ?

HER. Och, we're in waefu' case.
They stan' abeigh, the lassies do, an' vow
They'll no be couthie wi' the laddies mair
Till a' mak' Peace, and throughly en' the War.*d*

MAG. This is a plot they have everywhere been hatching,
These villainous women : now I see it all.
Run home, my man, and bid your people send
Envoys with absolute powers to treat for peace,
And I will off with all the speed I can,
And get our Council here to do the same.

HER. Nebbut, I'se fly, ye rede me weel, I'm thinkin'.*e*

M. CH. There is nothing so resistless
as a woman in her ire,

---

d μογοῦμεν, λυχνοφοροῦντες, θιγεῖν, ἑῶσι, πρὸς τήν. μύρτος is αἰδοῖον γυναικεῖον: Schol.

e *The Herald leaves for Sparta ; the Magistrate returns to the Senate ; and the two Choruses now advance for a final skirmish.*

οὐδὲ πῦρ, οὐδ' ὧδ' ἀναιδὴς οὐδεμία πόρδαλις. 1015

ΧΟ. ΓΥ. ταῦτα μέντοι σὺ ξυνιεὶς εἶτα πολεμεῖς ἐμοί,
ἐξόν, ὦ πόνηρε, σοὶ βέβαιον ἔμ' ἔχειν φίλην;

ΧΟ. ΓΕ. ὡς ἐγὼ μισῶν γυναῖκας οὐδέποτε παύσομαι.

ΧΟ. ΓΥ. ἀλλ' ὅταν βούλῃ σύ· νυνὶ δ' οὔ σε περιόψομαι
γυμνὸν ὄνθ' οὕτως. ὁρῶ γὰρ ὡς καταγέλαστος
εἶ. 1020
ἀλλὰ τὴν ἐξωμίδ' ἐνδύσω σε προσιοῦσ' ἐγώ.

ΧΟ. ΓΕ. τοῦτο μὲν μὰ τὸν Δί' οὐ πονηρὸν ἐποιήσατε·
ἀλλ' ὑπ' ὀργῆς γὰρ πονηρᾶς καὶ τότ' ἀπέδυν
ἐγώ.

ΧΟ. ΓΥ. πρῶτα μὲν φαίνει γ' ἀνήρ· εἶτ' οὐ καταγέλαστος εἶ.
κἄν με μὴ λυπῇς, ἐγὼ σοῦ κἄν τόδε τὸ θηρίον 1025
τοὐπὶ τὠφθαλμῷ λαβοῦσ' ἐξεῖλον ἄν, ὃ νῦν ἔνι.

ΧΟ. ΓΕ. τοῦτ' ἄρ' ἦν με τοὐπιτρῖβον, δακτύλιος οὑτοσί·
ἐκσκάλευσον αὐτό, κᾆτα δεῖξον ἀφελοῦσά μοι·
ὡς τὸν ὀφθαλμόν γέ μου νὴ τὸν Δία πάλαι
δάκνει.

ΧΟ. ΓΥ. ἀλλὰ δράσω ταῦτα· καίτοι δύσκολος ἔφυς ἀνήρ. 1030
ἦ μέγ', ὦ Ζεῦ, χρῆμ' ἰδεῖν τῆς ἐμπίδος ἔνεστί
σοι.

---

[a] " The Scholiast's explanation that the speaker is giving
Stratyllis a ring wherewith to scoop out . . . the insect from his
eye . . . seems to me foreign to the ordinary style and phraseo-
logy of Aristophanes. And I entirely agree with Bergler and
Brunck that the name δακτύλιος, with a play on δάκνειν, is given
to the gnat itself " : R.

She is wilder than a leopard,
     she is fiercer than a fire.
w. ch. And yet you're so daft
     as with women to contend,
When 'tis in your power to win me
     and have me as a friend.
m. ch. I'll never, never cease
     all women to detest.
w. ch. That's as you please hereafter :
     meanwhile you're all undressed.
I really can't allow it,
     you are getting quite a joke ;
Permit me to approach you
     and to put you on this cloak.
m. ch. Now that's not so bad
     or unfriendly I declare ;
It was only from bad temper
     that I stripped myself so bare.
w. ch. There, now you look a man :
     and none will joke and jeer you :
And if you weren't so spiteful
     that no one can come near you,
I'd have pulled out the insect
     that is sticking in your eye.
m. ch. Ay, that is what's consuming me,
     that little biter-fly.[a]
Yes, scoop it out and show me,
     when you've got him safe away :
The plaguy little brute,
     he's been biting me all day.
w. ch. I'll do it, sir, I'll do it :
     but you're a cross one, you.
O Zeus ! here's a monster
     I am pulling forth to view.

οὐχ ὁρᾷς; οὐκ ἐμπίς ἐστιν ἥδε Τρικορυσία;

ΧΟ. ΓΕ. νὴ Δί᾿ ὤνησάς γέ μ᾿, ὡς πάλαι γέ μ᾿ ἐφρεω
ρύχει,
ὥστ᾿ ἐπειδὴ 'ξηρέθη, ῥεῖ μου τὸ δάκρυον πολύ.

ΧΟ. ΓΥ. ἀλλ᾿ ἀποψήσω σ᾿ ἐγώ, καίτοι πάνυ πονηρὸς εἶ, 1035
καὶ φιλήσω.

ΧΟ. ΓΕ. μὴ φιλήσῃς.

ΧΟ. ΓΥ. ἤν τε βούλῃ γ᾿ ἤν τε μή.

ΧΟ. ΓΕ. ἀλλὰ μὴ ὥρασ᾿ ἵκοισθ᾿· ὡς ἐστὲ θωπικαὶ φύσει,
κἄστ᾿ ἐκεῖνο τοὔπος ὀρθῶς κοὐ κακῶς εἰρη
μένον,
οὔτε σὺν πανωλέθροισιν οὔτ᾿ ἄνευ πανωλέθρων.
ἀλλὰ νυνὶ σπένδομαί σοι, καὶ τὸ λοιπὸν οὐκέτι 1040
οὔτε δράσω φλαῦρον οὐδὲν οὔθ᾿ ὑφ᾿ ὑμῶν
πείσομαι.
ἀλλὰ κοινῇ συσταλέντες τοῦ μέλους ἀρξώμεθα.

ΧΟ. οὐ παρασκευαζόμεσθα [στρ.
τῶν πολιτῶν οὐδέν᾿, ὦνδρες,
φλαῦρον εἰπεῖν οὐδὲ ἕν·
ἀλλὰ πολὺ τοὔμπαλιν   1045
πάντ᾿ ἀγαθὰ καὶ λέγειν
καὶ δρᾶν· ἱκανὰ γὰρ τὰ κακὰ
καὶ τὰ παρακείμενα.
ἀλλ᾿ ἐπαγγελλέτω
πᾶς ἀνὴρ καὶ γυνή,   1050
εἴ τις ἀργυρίδιον δεῖ
ται λαβεῖν, μνᾶς ἢ δύ᾿ ἢ τρεῖς,

---

[a] Tricorythus, near Marathon, a marshy district full of gnats.
[b] " These little twin songs, and the similar pair which will be
found a few pages further on, are all fashioned in the same vein

Just look ! don't you think

'tis a Tricorysian ^{a} gnat ?

M. CH. And he's been dig, dig, digging

(so I thank you much for that)

Till the water, now he's gone,

keeps running from my eye

W. CH. But although you've been so naughty,

I'll come and wipe it dry,

And I'll kiss you.

M. CH.　　　　No, not kiss me !

W. CH.　　　　　　　Will you, nill you, it must be.

M. CH. Get along, a murrain on you.

Tcha ! what coaxing rogues are ye !

That was quite a true opinion

which a wise man gave about you,

We can't live with such tormentors,

no, by Zeus, nor yet without you.

Now we'll make a faithful treaty,

and for evermore agree,

I will do no harm to women,

they shall do no harm to me.

Join our forces, come along :

one and all commence the song

JOINT CH.^{b} Not to objurgate and scold you,

Not unpleasant truths to say,

But with words and deeds of bounty

Come we here to-day.

Ah, enough of idle quarrels,

Now attend, I pray.

Now whoever wants some money,

Minas two or minas three,

of pleasantry ; consisting of large and liberal offers made by the Chorus, but with an intimation at the end that they have no means or intention of performing them " : R.

πόλλ᾽ ἔσω γὰρ
κέν᾽ ἔχομεν βαλλάντια.
κἂν ποτ᾽ εἰρήνη φανῇ,　　　　　　　　1055
ὅστις ἂν νυνὶ δανείση-
ται παρ᾽ ἡμῶν,
ἂν λάβῃ μηκέτ᾽ ἀποδῷ.

ἑστιᾶν δὲ μέλλομεν ξέ-　　　　　　　[ἀντ.
νους τινὰς Καρυστίους, ἄνδρας καλούς τε κἀγαθούς.
κᾄστιν ἔτ᾽ ἔτνος τι, καὶ　　　　　　　1060
δελφάκιον ἦν τί μοι,
καὶ τοῦτο τέθυχ᾽, ὥστε κρέ᾽ ἔ-
δεσθ᾽ ἁπαλὰ καὶ καλά.
ἥκετ᾽ οὖν εἰς ἐμοῦ
τήμερον· πρῲ δὲ χρὴ　　　　　　　　1065
τοῦτο δρᾶν λελουμένους, αὐτούς τε καὶ τὰ παιδί᾽, εἶτ᾽ ἔ-
σω βαδίζειν,
μηδ᾽ ἐρέσθαι μηδένα,
ἀλλὰ χωρεῖν ἄντικρυς,
ὥσπερ οἴκαδ᾽ εἰς ἑαυτῶν,　　　　　　1070
γεννικῶς, ὡς
ἡ θύρα κεκλείσεται.

καὶ μὴν ἀπὸ τῆς Σπάρτης οἱδὶ πρέσβεις ἕλκοντες ὑπήνας
χωροῦσ᾽, ὥσπερ χοιροκομεῖον περὶ τοῖς μηροῖσιν ἔχοντες.
ἄνδρες Λάκωνες πρῶτα μέν μοι χαίρετε,
εἶτ᾽ εἴπαθ᾽ ἡμῖν πῶς ἔχοντες ἥκετε.　　　　　1075

---

[a] Carystus in Euboea was supposed to contain a remnant of
the old pre-Hellenic population. See 1181 n.

Let them say so, man and woman,
      Let them come with me.
Many purses, large and—empty,
      In my house they'll see.
Only you must strictly promise,
Only you indeed must say
That whenever Peace re-greet us,
      You will—not repay.

SOME Carystian [a] friends are coming,
Pleasant gentlemen, to dine ;
And I've made some soup, and slaughtered
      Such a lovely swine ;
Luscious meat ye'll have and tender
      At this feast of mine.
Come along, yourselves and children,
Come to grace my board to-day ;
Take an early bath, and deck you
      In your best array ;
Then walk in and ask no questions,
      Take the readiest way.
Come along, like men of mettle ;
Come as though 'twere all for you :
Come, you'll find my only entrance
      Locked and bolted too. [b]

Lo here from Sparta the envoys come :
            in a pitiful plight they are hobbling in. [c]
Heavily hangs each reverend beard ;
            heavily droops and trails from the chin.
Laconian envoys ! first I bid you welcome,
And next I ask how goes the world with *you* ?

[b] *The Laconian ambassadors are seen approaching.*
[c] *Quasi porcorum caveam ante femora habent.*

103

ARISTOPHANES

ΛΑΚΩΝ. τί δεῖ ποθ' ὑμὲ πολλὰ μυσίδδειν ἔπη;
    ὁρῆν γὰρ ἔξεσθ' ὡς ἔχοντες ἥκομες.

ΧΟ. βαβαί· νενεύρωται μὲν ἥδε συμφορὰ
    δεινῶς· τεθερμῶσθαί γε χεῖρον φαίνεται.

ΛΑΚ. ἄφατα. τί κα λέγοι τις; ἀλλ' ὅπᾳ σέλει   1080
    παντᾶ τις ἐλσὼν ἀμὶν εἰράναν σέτω.

ΧΟ. καὶ μὴν ὁρῶ γε τούσδε τοὺς αὐτόχθονας
    ὥσπερ παλαιστὰς ἄνδρας ἀπὸ τῶν γαστέρων
    θαἰμάτι' ἀποστέλλοντας· ὥστε φαίνεται
    ἀσκητικὸν τὸ χρῆμα τοῦ νοσήματος.   1085

ΑΘΗΝΑΙΟΣ. τίς ἂν φράσειε ποῦ 'στιν ἡ Λυσιστράτη;
    ὡς ἄνδρες ἡμεῖς οὑτοιὶ τοιουτοί.

ΧΟ. χαὕτη ξυνᾴδει χἀτέρα ταύτῃ νόσῳ.
    ἦ που πρὸς ὄρθρον σπασμὸς ὑμᾶς λαμβάνει;

ΑΘ. μὰ Δί', ἀλλὰ ταυτὶ δρῶντες ἐπιτετρίμμεθα.   1090
    ὥστ' εἴ τις ἡμᾶς μὴ διαλλάξει ταχύ,
    οὐκ ἔσθ' ὅπως οὐ Κλεισθένη βινήσομεν.

ΧΟ. εἰ σωφρονεῖτε, θαἰμάτια λήψεσθ', ὅπως
    τῶν Ἑρμοκοπιδῶν μή τις ὑμᾶς ὄψεται.

ΑΘ. νὴ τὸν Δί' εὖ μέντοι λέγεις.

ΛΑΚ.   ναὶ τὼ σιὼ   1095
    παντᾶ γα. φέρε τὸ ἔσθος ἀμβαλώμεθα.

ΑΘ. ὦ χαίρετ', ὦ Λάκωνες· αἰσχρά γ' ἐπάθομεν.

ΛΑΚ. ὦ πουλυχαρίδα, δεινὰ τἂν πεπόνθεμες,
    αἴ κ' εἶδον ἀμὲ τὤνδρες ἀναπεφλασμένως.

ΑΘ. ἄγε δή, Λάκωνες, αὔθ' ἕκαστα χρὴ λέγειν.   1100
    ἐπὶ τί πάρεστε δεῦρο;

ΛΑΚ.   περὶ διαλλαγᾶν
    πρέσβεις.

  ᵃ νενεύρωται, "is high-strung."   τὴν ἔντασιν τοῦ αἰδοίου λέγει:
Schol.

  ᵇ θέλει, ἐλθών, θέτω.

104

LACONIAN. I needna mony words to answer that !
'Tis unco plain hoo the warld gangs wi' us.

CH. Dear, dear, this trouble grows from bad to worse.[a]

LAC. 'Tis awfu' bad : 'tis nae gude talkin', cummer.
We maun hae peace whatever gaet we gang till't.[b]

CH. And here, good faith, I see our own Autochthons
Bustling along. They seem in trouble [c] too.[d]

ATHENIAN. Can some good soul inform me where to find
Lysistrata ? our men are (*shrugging his shoulders*) as
you see.[e]

CH. Sure, we are smitten with the same complaint.
Say, don't you get a fit i' the early morning ?

ATH. Why, we are all worn out with doing this :
So Cleisthenes will have to serve our turn
Unless we can procure a speedy peace.

CH. If you are wise, wrap up, unless you wish
One of those Hermes-choppers[f] to catch sight o' you.

ATH. Prudent advice, by Zeus.

LAC.   Aye, by the Twa :
Gie us the clout to cover up oorsels.

ATH. Aha, Laconians ! a bad business this.

LAC. 'Deed is it, lovey ; though it grow nae waur,
Gin they see us too all agog like this.[g]

ATH. Well, well, Laconians, come to facts at once.
What brings you here ?

LAC.   We're envoys sent to claver
Anent a Peace.

---

[c] ἀσκητικόν, " a trouble such as an athlete in training might
have," with a play on ἀσκίτης νόσος, " dropsy."

[d] *The Athenian ambassadors enter.*

[e] *He perceives the Laconian ambassadors.* Lines 1086 to 1096,
and 1099, are omitted in R.'s version.

[f] See Thuc. vi. 27. They knocked off the phalli of the
figures of Hermes which stood at the doors.

[g] ἐκδεδαρμένους, τὰ αἰδοῖα ἀνατεταμένους: Schol. ἀμέ = ἡμᾶς.

ΑΘ.   καλῶς δὴ λέγετε· χἠμεῖς ταυτογί.
          τί οὐ καλοῦμεν δῆτα τὴν Λυσιστράτην,
          ἥπερ διαλλάξειεν ἡμᾶς ἂν μόνη;
ΛΑΚ. ναὶ τὼ σιώ, κἂν λῆτε, τὸν Λυσίστρατον.   1105
ΑΘ. ἀλλ' οὐδὲν ἡμᾶς, ὡς ἔοικε, δεῖ καλεῖν·
          αὐτὴ γάρ, ὡς ἤκουσεν, ἥδ' ἐξέρχεται.

ΧΟ. χαῖρ', ὦ πασῶν ἀνδρειοτάτη· δεῖ δὴ νυνί σε
              γενέσθαι
          δεινήν, ἀγαθήν, φαύλην, σεμνήν, [χαλεπήν,]
              ἀγανήν, πολύπειρον·
          ὡς οἱ πρῶτοι τῶν Ἑλλήνων τῇ σῇ ληφθέντες ἴυγγι 1110
          συνεχώρησάν σοι καὶ κοινῇ τἀγκλήματα πάντ'
              ἐπέτρεψαν.

ΛΥ. ἀλλ' οὐχὶ χαλεπὸν τοὖργον, εἰ λάβοι γέ τις
          ὀργῶντας ἀλλήλων τε μὴ 'κπειρωμένους.
          τάχα δ' εἴσομαι 'γώ. ποῦ 'στιν ἡ Διαλλαγή;
          πρόσαγε λαβοῦσα πρῶτα τοὺς Λακωνικούς,   1115
          καὶ μὴ χαλεπῇ τῇ χειρὶ μηδ' αὐθαδικῇ,
          μηδ' ὥσπερ ἡμῶν ἄνδρες ἀμαθῶς τοῦτ' ἔδρων,
          ἀλλ' ὡς γυναῖκας εἰκός, οἰκείως πάνυ.
          ἢν μὴ διδῷ τὴν χεῖρα, τῆς σάθης ἄγε.
          ἴθι καὶ σὺ τούτους τοὺς Ἀθηναίους ἄγε·   1120
          οὗ δ' ἂν διδῶσι, πρόσαγε τούτου λαβομένη.
          ἄνδρες Λάκωνες, στῆτε παρ' ἐμὲ πλησίον,
          ἐνθένδε θ' ὑμεῖς, καὶ λόγων ἀκούσατε.
          ἐγὼ γυνὴ μέν εἰμι, νοῦς δ' ἔνεστί μοι·

ᵃ The text has *Lysistratus*, *i.e.* anyone, man or woman, who
will " disband armies."

ATH.   Ah, just the same as we.
Then let's call out Lysistrata at once,
There's none but she can make us friends again.
LAC. Ay, by the Twa, ca' oot Lysistrata.*a*
ATH. Nay, here she is ! no need, it seems, to call.
She heard your voices, and she comes uncalled.*b*

CH. O Lady, noblest and best of all !
                    arise, arise, and thyself reveal,
Gentle, severe, attractive, harsh,
          well skilled with all our complaints to deal,
The first and foremost of Hellas come,
     they are caught by the charm of thy spell-drawn
          wheel,*c*
They come to Thee to adjust their claims,
                    disputes to settle, and strifes to heal.

LY. And no such mighty matter, if you take them
In Love's first passion, still unsatisfied.
I'll try them now. Go, RECONCILIATION,
Bring those Laconians hither, not with rude
Ungenial harshness hurrying them along,
Not in the awkward style our husbands used,
But with all tact, as only women can.
So ; so : now bring me those Athenians too.*d*
Now then, Laconians, stand beside me here,
And you stand there, and listen to my words.
I am a woman, but I don't lack sense ;

     b *Lysistrata comes forward attended by her handmaid Reconciliation.*
     c Properly the wryneck, which was used in working charms ;
hence, a charm, or the wheel to which the bird was tied. See
Theocritus, *Idylls*, ii.
     d Line 1119 (omitted by R.): "If he won't give his hand,
mentula prehensum duc." Line 1121 (also omitted) : "Take
hold of whatever they offer."

ARISTOPHANES

αὐτὴ δ' ἐμαυτῆς οὐ κακῶς γνώμης ἔχω·   1125
τοὺς δ' ἐκ πατρός τε καὶ γεραιτέρων λόγους
πολλοὺς ἀκούσασ' οὐ μεμούσωμαι κακῶς.
λαβοῦσα δ' ὑμᾶς λοιδορῆσαι βούλομαι
κοινῇ δικαίως, οἳ μιᾶς ἐκ χέρνιβος
βωμοὺς περιρραίνοντες, ὥσπερ ξυγγενεῖς,   1130
'Ολυμπίασιν, ἐν Πύλαις, Πυθοῖ—πόσους
εἴποιμ' ἂν ἄλλους, εἴ με μηκύνειν δέοι;—
ἐχθρῶν παρόντων βαρβάρων στρατεύματι
Ἕλληνας ἄνδρας καὶ πόλεις ἀπόλλυτε.
εἷς μὲν λόγος μοι δεῦρ' ἀεὶ περαίνεται.   1135
ΑΘ. ἐγὼ δ' ἀπόλλυμαί γ' ἀπεψωλημένος.
ΛΥ. εἶτ', ὦ Λάκωνες, πρὸς γὰρ ὑμᾶς τρέψομαι,
οὐκ ἴσθ', ὅτ' ἐλθὼν δεῦρο Περικλείδας ποτὲ
ὁ Λάκων 'Αθηναίων ἱκέτης καθέζετο
ἐπὶ τοῖσι βωμοῖς ὠχρὸς ἐν φοινικίδι,   1140
στρατιὰν προσαιτῶν; ἡ δὲ Μεσσήνη τότε
ὑμῖν ἐπέκειτο, χὠ θεὸς σείων ἅμα.
ἐλθὼν δὲ σὺν ὁπλίταισι τετρακισχιλίοις
Κίμων ὅλην ἔσωσε τὴν Λακεδαίμονα.
ταυτὶ παθόντες τῶν 'Αθηναίων ὕπο   1145
δῃοῦτε χώραν, ἧς ὕπ' εὖ πεπόνθατε;
ΑΘ. ἀδικοῦσιν οὗτοι νὴ Δί', ὦ Λυσιστράτη.
ΛΑΚ. ἀδικοῦμες· ἀλλ' ὁ πρωκτὸς ἄφατον ὡς καλός.
ΛΥ. ὑμᾶς δ' ἀφήσειν τοὺς 'Αθηναίους μ' οἴει;
οὐκ ἴσθ' ὅθ' ὑμᾶς οἱ Λάκωνες αὖθις αὖ   1150

---

[a] From Euripides' *Melanippe Sapiens* : Schol.
[b] The games near Thermopylae (*Pylaea*), Delphi, and Olympia.
Line 1131 is from Eur. *Erechtheus* : Schol. The whole speech
is in tragic style and probably echoes Euripides.
108

I'm of myself not badly off for brains,[a]
And often listening to my father's words
And old men's talk, I've not been badly schooled.
And now, dear friends, I wish to chide you both,
That ye, all of one blood, all brethren sprinkling
The selfsame altars from the selfsame laver,
At Pylae, Pytho, and Olympia,[b] ay
And many others which 'twere long to name,
That ye, Hellenes—with barbarian foes
Armed, looking on—fight and destroy Hellenes!
So far one reprimand includes you both.

ATH. And I, I'm dying all for love, sweetheart.

LY. And ye, Laconians, for I'll turn to you,
Do ye not mind how Pericleidas [c] came,
(His coat was scarlet but his cheeks were white),
And sat a suppliant at Athenian altars
And begged for help ? 'Twas when Messene pressed
Weighing you down, and God's great earthquake too.
And Cimon went, Athenian Cimon went
With his four thousand men, and saved your State.
And ye, whom Athens aided, now in turn
Ravage the land which erst befriended you.

ATH. 'Fore Zeus they're wrong, they're wrong, Lysistrata.

LAC. O ay, we're wrang, but she's a braw ane, she.

LY. And you, Athenians, think ye that I mean
To let You off ? Do *ye* not mind, when ye
Wore skirts of hide, how these Laconians [d] came

[c] See Plutarch, *Cimon*, chap. xvi.; Thuc. i. 102, iii. 54. In 464 B.C. an earthquake devastated Sparta, and the Helots revolted and took refuge in the fortress of Ithome. P. was sent to Athens for help and received it.

[d] See Hdt. v. 64, 65. They sent help to expel the tyrants from Athens. Under the tyrants, certain returned exiles had been allowed to stay in Attica but not to enter Athens, and compelled to wear the rough dress bordered with sheepskin (κατωνάκη) of slaves or labourers, so as to identify them.

κατωνάκας φοροῦντας ἐλθόντες δορὶ
πολλοὺς μὲν ἄνδρας Θετταλῶν ἀπώλεσαν,
πολλοὺς δ' ἑταίρους Ἱππίου καὶ ξυμμάχους,
ξυνεκμαχοῦντες τῇ τόθ' ἡμέρᾳ μόνοι,
κἀλευθέρωσαν, κἀντὶ τῆς κατωνάκης   1155
τὸν δῆμον ὑμῶν χλαῖναν ἤμπισχον πάλιν;

ΛΑΚ. οὔπα γυναῖκ' ὄπωπα χαϊωτέραν.

ΑΘ. ἐγὼ δὲ κύσθον γ' οὐδέπω καλλίονα.

ΛΥ. τί δῆθ' ὑπηργμένων γε πολλῶν κἀγαθῶν
μάχεσθε κοὐ παύεσθε τῆς μοχθηρίας;   1160
τί δ' οὐ διηλλάγητε; φέρε, τί τοὐμποδών;

ΛΑΚ. ἁμές γε λῶμες, αἴ τις ἁμὶν τοὔγκυκλον
λῇ τοῦτ' ἀποδόμεν.

ΛΥ.   ποῖον, ὦ τᾶν;

ΛΑΚ.   τὰν Πύλον,
ᾆσπερ πάλαι δεόμεθα καὶ βλιμάττομες.

ΑΘ. μὰ τὸν Ποσειδῶ, τοῦτο μέν γ' οὐ δράσετε.   1165

ΛΥ. ἄφετ', ὦγάθ', αὐτοῖς.

ΑΘ.   κᾆτα τίνα κινήσομεν;

ΛΥ. ἕτερόν γ' ἀπαιτεῖτ' ἀντὶ τούτου χωρίον.

ΑΘ. τὸ δεῖνα τοίνυν, παράδοθ' ἡμῖν τουτονὶ
πρώτιστα τὸν Ἐχινοῦντα καὶ τὸν Μηλιᾶ
κόλπον τὸν ὄπισθεν καὶ τὰ Μεγαρικὰ σκέλη.   1170

ΛΑΚ. οὐ τὼ σιώ, οὐχὶ πάντα γ', ὦ λυσσάνιε.

ΛΥ. ἐᾶτε, μηδὲν διαφέρου περὶ τοῖν σκελοῖν.

ΑΘ. ἤδη γεωργεῖν γυμνὸς ἀποδὺς βούλομαι.

ΛΑΚ. ἐγὼ δὲ κοπραγωγῆν γα πρῶ ναὶ τὼ σιώ.

ΛΥ. ἐπὴν διαλλαγῆτε, ταῦτα δράσετε.   1175

---

^a " The desire of recovering their lost possessions is for the
moment merged in their love for Lysistrata, and their reciprocal
demands are throughout worded with reference to her dress and

And stood beside you in the fight alone,
And slew full many a stout Thessalian trooper,
Full many of Hippias's friends and helpers,
And freed the State, and gave your people back
The civic mantle for the servile skirt ?

LAC. Danged, an' there ever waur a bonnier lassie !

ATH. Hanged if I ever saw so sweet a creature !

LY. Such friends aforetime, helping each the other,
What is it makes you fight and bicker now?
Why can't ye come to terms ?   Why can't ye, hey ?

LAC. Troth an' we're willin', gin they gie us back
Yon girdled neuk.ᵃ

ATH.   What's that ?

LAC.   Pylus, ye ninny,
Whilk we've been aye langin' an' graipin' for.

ATH. No, by Poseidon, but you won't get that.

LY. O let them have it, man.

ATH.   How can we stir
Without it ?

LY.   Ask for something else instead.

ATH. Hum ! haw ! let's see ; suppose they give us back
Echinus first, then the full-bosomed gulf
Of Melis, then the straight Megaric limbs.

LAC. Eh, mon, ye're daft ; ye'll no hae everything.

LY. O let it be : don't wrangle about the limbs.

ATH. I'fecks, I'd like to strip, and plough my field.ᵇ

LAC. An' I to bring the midden, by the Twa.

LY. All this ye'll do, when once ye come to terms.

---

person " : R. τοῦτο τοὔγκυκλον is her mantle ; Echinus 1169 = τὸ
γυναικεῖον αἰδοῖον ; κόλπον Μηλιᾶ = *sinum pomis simillimum,* or the
whole phrase τὸν Μ. κόλπον τὸν ὄπισθεν = πρωκτόν ; Μεγαρικὰ σκέλη
= the Long Walls, but σκέλη also alludes to Lysistrata.
   ᵇ *Cf. nudus ara, sere nudus,* Virg. *Georg.* i. 299, from Hesiod,
Works and Days, p. 391 ; there is also a sexual allusion, *cf.*
Soph. *Antig.* 569 ἀρώσιμοι γύαι.

ἀλλ' εἰ δοκεῖ δρᾶν ταῦτα, βουλεύσασθε καὶ
τοῖς ξυμμάχοις ἐλθόντες ἀνακοινώσατε.

ΑΘ. ποίοισιν, ὦ τᾶν, ξυμμάχοις; ἐστύκαμεν.
οὐ ταὐτὰ δόξει τοῖσι συμμάχοισι νῷν,
βινεῖν ἅπασιν;

ΛΑΚ.   τοῖσι γοῦν ναὶ τὼ σιώ 1180
ἁμοῖσι.

ΑΘ. καὶ γὰρ ναὶ μὰ Δία Καρυστίοις.

ΛΥ. καλῶς λέγετε. νῦν οὖν ὅπως ἁγνεύσετε,
ὅπως ἂν αἱ γυναῖκες ὑμᾶς ἐν πόλει
ξενίσωμεν ὧν ἐν ταῖσι κίσταις εἴχομεν.
ὅρκους δ' ἐκεῖ καὶ πίστιν ἀλλήλοις δότε. 1185
κἄπειτα τὴν αὑτοῦ γυναῖχ' ὑμῶν λαβὼν
ἄπεισ' ἕκαστος.

ΑΘ.   ἀλλ' ἴωμεν ὡς τάχος.

ΛΑΚ. ἄγ' ὅπᾳ τυ λῇς.

ΑΘ.   νὴ τὸν Δί' ὡς τάχιστά γε.

ΧΟ. στρωμάτων δὲ ποικίλων καὶ   [στρ.
 χλανιδίων καὶ ξυστίδων καὶ
 χρυσίων, ὅσ' ἐστί μοι,   1190
 οὐ φθόνος ἔνεστί μοι
 πᾶσι παρέχειν φέρειν
 τοῖς παισίν, ὁπόταν τε θυγά-
 τηρ τινὶ κανηφορῇ.
 πᾶσιν ὑμῖν λέγω   1195
 λαμβάνειν τῶν ἐμῶν
 χρημάτων νῦν ἔνδοθεν, καὶ
 μηδὲν οὕτως εὖ σεσημάν-
 θαι τὸ μὴ οὐχὶ
 τοὺς ῥύπους ἀνασπάσαι, 1200

---

^a Cf. 1058. The people of Carystus in Euboea were supposed

112

So if ye would, go and consult together
And talk it over, each with your allies.

ATH. Allies, says she ! Now my good soul consider :
What *do* they want, what *can* they want, but this,
Their wives again ?

LAC.   The fient anither wiss
Ha' mine, I ween.

ATH.   Nor my Carystians [a] either.

LY. O that is well : so purify yourselves ;
And in the Acropolis we'll feast you all
On what our cupboards still retain in store.
There, each to other, plight your oath and troth,
Then every man receive his wife again,
And hie off homeward

ATH.   That we will, and quickly.

LAC. Gae on : we'se follow.[b]

ATH.   Ay, as quick as quick.[c]

CH.   Gorgeous robes and golden trinkets,
     Shawls and mantles rich and rare,
     I will lend to all who need them,
         Lend for youths to wear,
     Or if any comrade's daughter
         Would the Basket bear.[d]
     One and all I here invite you,
     Freely of my goods partake,
     Nought is sealed so well, but boldly
         Ye the seals may break,
     And of all that lurks behind them,

to be one of the pre-Hellenic populations, Thuc. vii. 57. Three
hundred of them were in the service of the Four Hundred at Athens,
Thuc. viii. 69. Probably they were of savage manners.

[b] ὅπῃ σὺ θέλεις.

[c] *Lysistrata and the ambassadors go in.*

[d] As κανηφόρος in the Panathenaic procession.

χἄττ' ἂν ἔνδον ᾖ φορεῖν.
ὄψεται δ' οὐδὲν σκοπῶν, εἰ
μή τις ὑμῶν
ὀξύτερον ἐμοῦ βλέπει.

εἰ δέ τῳ μὴ σῖτος ὑμῶν   [ἀντ.
ἔστι, βόσκει δ' οἰκέτας καὶ
σμικρὰ πολλὰ παιδία,   1205
ἔστι παρ' ἐμοῦ λαβεῖν
πυρίδια λεπτὰ μέν,
ὁ δ' ἄρτος ἀπὸ χοίνικος ἰ-
δεῖν μάλα νεανίας.
ὅστις οὖν βούλεται
τῶν πενήτων ἴτω   1210
εἰς ἐμοῦ σάκους ἔχων καὶ
κωρύκους, ὡς λήψεται πυ-
ρούς· ὁ Μανῆς δ'
οὑμὸς αὐτοῖς ἐμβαλεῖ.
πρός γε μέντοι τὴν θύραν
προαγορεύω μὴ βαδίζειν
τὴν ἐμήν, ἀλλ'
εὐλαβεῖσθαι τὴν κύνα.   1215

ΑΓΟΡΑΙΟΣ Α. ἄνοιγε τὴν θύραν.
ΘΥΡΩΡΟΣ.   παραχωρεῖν οὐ θέλεις;
ΑΓ.Α. ὑμεῖς τί κάθησθε; μῶν ἐγὼ τῇ λαμπάδι
     ὑμᾶς κατακαύσω; φορτικὸν τὸ χωρίον.
     οὐκ ἂν ποιήσαιμ'. εἰ δὲ πάνυ δεῖ τοῦτο δρᾶν,
     ὑμῖν χαρίσασθαι, προσταλαιπωρήσομεν.   1220
ΑΓ.Β. χἠμεῖς γε μετὰ σοῦ ξυνταλαιπωρήσομεν.
ΘΥ.   οὐκ ἄπιτε; κωκύσεσθε τὰς τρίχας μακρά.

114

Quick partition make.
Only, if you find the treasures,
Only, if the stores you spy,
You must have, I tell you plainly,
    Keener sight than I.

Is THERE any man among you,
With a lot of children small,
With a crowd of hungry servants,
    Starving in his hall ?
I have wheat to spare in plenty,
    I will feed them all.
Loaves, a quart apiece, I'll give them,
Come along, whoever will,
Bring your bags, and bring your wallets
    For my slave to fill ;
Manes, he's the boy to pack them
    Tight and tighter still.
Only you must keep your distance,
Only you must needs take care,
Only—don't approach my doorway,
    Ware the watch-dog, ware ! [a]

IDLER. Open the door there, ho !
PORTER.   Be off, you rascal !
ID. What, won't you stir ? I've half a mind to roast you
    All with this torch. No, that's a vulgar trick.
    I won't do that. Still if the audience wish it,
    To please their tastes we'll undertake the task.
SECOND IDLER. And we, with you, will undertake the task.
POR. Hang you, be off ! what are you at ? you'll catch it. [b]

[a] *Some idlers come in from the market-place, and attempt to enter the house in which the ambassadors are feasting.*

[b] " Ye shall wail for your hair, which I will pull out by the handful " : R.

οὐκ ἄπιθ᾽, ὅπως ἂν οἱ Λάκωνες ἔνδοθεν
καθ᾽ ἡσυχίαν ἀπίωσιν εὐωχημένοι;

ΑΘ. Α. οὔπω τοιοῦτον συμπόσιον ὄπωπ᾽ ἐγώ.   1225
ἦ καὶ χαρίεντες ἦσαν οἱ Λακωνικοί·
ἡμεῖς δ᾽ ἐν οἴνῳ ξυμπόται σοφώτατοι.

ΑΘ. Β. ὀρθῶς γ᾽, ὁτιὴ νήφοντες οὐχ ὑγιαίνομεν·
ἢν τοὺς Ἀθηναίους ἐγὼ πείσω λέγων,
μεθύοντες ἀεὶ πανταχοῦ πρεσβεύσομεν.   1230
νῦν μὲν γὰρ ὅταν ἔλθωμεν ἐς Λακεδαίμονα
νήφοντες, εὐθὺς βλέπομεν ὅ τι ταράξομεν·
ὥσθ᾽ ὅ τι μὲν ἂν λέγωσιν οὐκ ἀκούομεν,
ἃ δ᾽ οὐ λέγουσι, ταῦθ᾽ ὑπονενοήκαμεν.
ἀγγέλλομεν δ᾽ οὐ ταὐτὰ τῶν αὐτῶν πέρι.   1235
νυνὶ δ᾽ ἅπαντ᾽ ἤρεσκεν· ὥστ᾽ εἰ μέν γέ τις
ᾄδοι Τελαμῶνος, Κλειταγόρας ᾄδειν δέον,
ἐπῃνέσαμεν ἂν καὶ πρὸς ἐπιωρκήσαμεν.

ΘΥ. ἀλλ᾽ οὑτοιὶ γὰρ αὖθις ἔρχονται πάλιν
ἐς ταὐτόν. οὐκ ἐρρήσετ᾽, ὦ μαστιγίαι;   1240

ΑΓ. νὴ τὸν Δί᾽, ὡς ἤδη γε χωροῦσ᾽ ἔνδοθεν.

ΛΑΚ. ὦ πουλυχαρίδα, λαβὲ τὰ φυσατήρια,
ἵν᾽ ἐγὼ διποδιάξω γε κἀείσω καλὸν
ἐς τοὺς Ἀσαναίους τε κῄς ἡμᾶς ἅμα.

ΑΘ. λαβὲ δῆτα τὰς φυσαλλίδας πρὸς τῶν θεῶν,   1245
ὡς ἥδομαί γ᾽ ὑμᾶς ὁρῶν ὀρχουμένους.

---

[a] The banqueters begin to come out.
[b] As the lyre, sprig of myrtle, or other badge of minstrelsy
was passed from one to another, the recipient was supposed to
cap the scolium sung just before, echoing it by some catch-

Come, come, begone ; that these Laconians here,
The banquet ended, may depart in peace.[a]

F.ATH. Well, if I ever saw a feast like this !
What cheery fellows those Laconians were,
And we were wondrous witty in our cups.

SEC.ATH. Ay, ay, 'tis when we're sober, we're so daft.
Now if the State would take a friend's advice,
'Twould make its envoys always all get drunk.
When we go dry to Sparta, all our aim
Is just to see what mischief we can do.
We don't hear aught they say ; and we infer
A heap of things they never said at all.
Then we bring home all sorts of differing tales.
Now everything gives pleasure : if a man,
When he should sing Cleitagora, strike up
With Telamon's song,[b] we'd clap him on the back,
And say 'twas excellent ; ay, and swear it too.[c]

POR. Why, bless the fellows, here they come again,
Crowding along. Be off, you scoundrels, will you ?

ID. By Zeus, we must : the guests are coming out.[d]

LAC. O lovey mine, tak' up the pipes an' blaw.
An' I'se jist dance [e] an' sing a canty sang
Anent the Athanians an' our ainsells too.

ATH. Ay, by the Powers, take up the pipes and blow.
Eh, but I dearly love to see you dance.

word or similar thought. If the singer blundered, he would
be ridiculous ; but at this feast it merely evokes a kindly
approval. Part of the Cleitagora scolium is given in *W.* 1245
χρήματα καὶ βίαν | Κλειταγόρᾳ τε κἀμοὶ μετὰ Θετταλῶν. The
Telamon catch is given in Athenaeus xv. 50 παῖ Τελαμῶνος, Αἶαν
αἰχμητά, λέγουσί σε | ἐς Τροίαν ἄριστον ἐλθεῖν Δαναῶν μετ' Ἀχιλλέα.

^c *The idlers again approach.*

^d *The ambassadors come out from the banquet.*

^e Dance a reel. διποδία, a stately Spartan dance.

ARISTOPHANES

ΛΑΚ. ὅρμαον
τὼς κυρσανίως, ὦ Μναμόνα,
τὰν τεὰν μῶαν, ἅτις
οἶδεν ἀμὲ τούς τ' Ἀσαναίους, 1250
ὅκα τοὶ μὲν ἐπ' Ἀρταμιτίῳ
πρόκροον θείκελοι
ποττὰ κᾶλα, τοὺς Μήδους τ' ἐνίκων,
ἀμὲ δ' αὖ Λεωνίδας
ἆγεν ᾇπερ τὼς κάπρως 1255
θάγοντας, οἰῶ, τὸν ὀδόντα·
πολὺς δ' ἀμφὶ τὰς γέννας ἀφρὸς ἤνσει,
πολὺς δ' ἅμα καττῶν σκελῶν ἀφρὸς ἵετο.
ἦν γὰρ τὤνδρες οὐκ ἐλάσσως 1260
τᾶς ψάμμας, τοὶ Πέρσαι.
Ἀγρότερ' Ἄρτεμι σηροκτόνε
μόλε δεῦρο, παρσένε σιά,
ποττὰς σπονδάς,
ὡς συνέχῃς πολὺν ἀμὲ χρόνον. 1265
νῦν δ' αὖ
φιλία τ' αἰὲς εὔπορος εἴη
ταῖς συνθήκαις,
καὶ τᾶν αἱμυλᾶν ἀλωπέκων
παυσαίμεθ'· ὢ 1270
δεῦρ' ἴθι, δεῦρ', ὦ
κυναγὲ παρσένε.

ΛΥ. ἄγε νυν, ἐπειδὴ τἆλλα πεποίηται καλῶς,
ἀπάγεσθε ταύτας, ὦ Λάκωνες, τάσδε τε

---

[a] The songs with which the Play concludes are, in the original, representatives of two widely differing styles of minstrelsy : the light and airy measures of the Ionians, and the " Dorian movement, bold or grave." ὅρμησον τοὺς κυρσανίους, ὦ Μνημοσύνη, τὴν

LAC.[a] Stir, Memory, stir the chiels
Wi' that auld sang o' thine,
Whilk kens what we an' Attics did
In the gran' fechts lang syne.

At Artemisium They
A' resolute an' strang
Rushed daurly to the fray,
Hurtlin' like Gudes amang
The timmered ships, an' put the Medes to rout.
An' Us Leonidas led out
Like gruesome boars, I ween,
Whettin' our tuskies keen.
Muckle around the chaps was the white freath gleamin',
Muckle adoon the legs was the white freath streamin',
For a' unnumbered as the sands
Were they, thae Persian bands.

O Artemis, the pure, the chaste,
The virgin Queller o' the beasties,
O come wi' power an' come wi' haste,
An' come to join our friendly feasties.
Come wi' thy stoutest tether,
To knit our sauls thegither,
An' gie us Peace in store,
An' Luve for evermore.
Far hence, far hence depart
The tod's deceitfu' heart!
O virgin huntress, pure an' chaste,
O come wi' power, an' come wi' haste.

LY. There, all is settled, all arranged at last.
Now, take your ladies; you, Laconians, those,

σὴν Μοῦσαν . . . ὅτε οἱ μὲν (1251), προὔκρουον θεοείκελοι πρὸς τὰ πλοῖα
. . . ἤνθει (1257), κατὰ τῶν σκελῶν (1259), θηροκτόνε (1262), παρθένε
θεά (1264).

119

ὑμεῖς· ἀνὴρ δὲ παρὰ γυναῖκα καὶ γυνὴ
στήτω παρ' ἄνδρα, κᾆτ' ἐπ' ἀγαθαῖς συμφοραῖς   1275
ὀρχησάμενοι θεοῖσιν εὐλαβώμεθα
τὸ λοιπὸν αὖθις μὴ 'ξαμαρτάνειν ἔτι.

ΧΟ.   πρόσαγε δὴ χορόν, ἔπαγε Χάριτας,
        ἐπὶ δὲ κάλεσον Ἄρτεμιν·   1280
        ἐπὶ δὲ δίδυμον [ἀγέχορον] εὔφρον' ἰήιον
        ἐπὶ δὲ Νύσιον ὃς μετὰ Μαινάσι
        Βάκχιος ὄμμασι δαίεται,
        Δία τε πυρὶ φλεγόμενον,   1285
        ἐπί τε πότνιαν ἄλοχον ὀλβίαν,
        εἶτα δὲ δαίμονας, οἷς ἐπιμάρτυσι
        χρησόμεθ' οὐκ ἐπιλήσμοσιν
        Ἡσυχίας πέρι τῆς μεγαλόφρονος,
        ἣν ἐποίησε θεὰ Κύπρις.   1290
        ἀλαλαὶ ἰὴ παιήων·
        αἴρεσθ' ἄνω, ἰαί,
        ὡς ἐπὶ νίκῃ, ἰαί.
        εὐοῖ εὐοῖ, εὐαὶ εὐαί.

        πρόφαινε δὴ σὺ μοῦσαν ἐπὶ νέᾳ νέαν.   1295

ΛΑΚ.   Ταΰγετον αὖτ' ἐραννὸν ἐκλιπῶα,
        Μῶα μόλε Λάκαινα πρεπτὸν ἁμὶν
        κλέωα τὸν Ἀμύκλαις ['Απόλλω] σιὸν
        καὶ χαλκίοικον Ἀσάναν·   1300
        Τυνδαρίδας τ' ἀγασώς,
        τοὶ δὴ παρ' Εὐρώταν ψιάδδοντι.
        εἶα μάλ' ἔμβη,

---

a "The δαίμονες or " secondary powers, whose especial business
it is to witness the conclusion of a treaty and to punish its in-
fraction " : R.   See *Iliad.* iii. 276-80.

And you, take these ; then standing side by side,
Each by his partner, lead your dances out
In grateful honour to the Gods, and O
Be sure you nevermore offend again.

CH.   Now for the Chorus, the Graces, the minstrelsy.
Call upon Artemis, queen of the glade ;
Call on her brother, the Lord of festivity,
Holy and gentle one, mighty to aid.
Call upon Bacchus, afire with his Maenades ;
Call upon Zeus, in the lightning arrayed ;
Call on his queen, ever blessed, adorable ;
Call on the holy, infallible Witnesses,[a]
Call them to witness the peace and the harmony,
This which divine Aphrodite has made.
Allala ! Lallala ! Lallala, Lallala !
Whoop for victory, Lallalalae !
Evoi ! Evoi ! Lallala, Lallala !
Evae ! Evae ! Lallalalae.

Our excellent new song is done ;
Do you, Laconian, give us one.

LAC.[b]   Leave Taygety, an' quickly
Hither, Muse Laconian, come.
Hymn the Gude o' braw Amyclae,
Hymn Athana, Brassin-dome.
Hymn the Tyndarids, for ever
Sportin' by Eurotas river.
Noo then, noo the step begin,

---

[b] ἐκλιποῦσα, Μοῦσα, κλείουσα, θεόν, χαλκέοικον ᾿Αθηνᾶν, ἀγαθούς,
παίζουσιν, ὑμνέωμεν, μέλουσι, ἀνακονέουσαι, θυρσαζουσῶν, παιζουσῶν,
παραμπύκιζε, πήδα.

ὦια κοῦφα πάλλων,
ὡς Σπάρταν ὑμνίωμες,   1305
τᾷ σιῶν χοροὶ μέλοντι
καὶ ποδῶν κτύπος.
ᾇ τε πῶλοι ταὶ κόραι
πὰρ τὸν Εὐρώταν
ἀμπάλλοντι πυκνὰ ποδοῖν   1310
ἀγκονίωαι,
ταὶ δὲ κόμαι σείονθ' ᾇπερ Βακχᾶν
θυρσαδδοᾶν καὶ παιδδωᾶν.
ἁγῆται δ' ἁ Λήδας παῖς
ἁγνὰ χοραγὸς εὐπρεπής.   1315
ἀλλ' ἄγε, κόμαν παραμπύκιδδε
χερί, ποδοῖν τε πάδη,
ᾇ τις ἔλαφος· κρότον δ' ἁμᾶ ποί-
η χορωφελήταν.
καὶ τὰν σιὰν δ' αὖ τὰν κρατίσταν   1320
χαλκίοικον ὕμνη
τὰν πάμμαχον.

Twirlin' licht the fleecy skin ;
Sae we'se join our blithesome voices,
Praisin' Sparta, loud an' lang,
Sparta wha of auld rejoices
In the Choral dance an' sang.
O to watch her bonnie dochters
Sport alang Eurotas' waters !
Winsome feet for ever plyin',
Fleet as fillies, wild an' gay,
Winsome tresses tossin', flyin',
As o' Bacchanals at play.
Leda's dochter, on before us,
Pure an' sprety, guides the Chorus.

    Onward go,
Whilst your eager hand represses
A' the glory o' your tresses ;
Whilst your eager foot is springin'
    Like the roe ;
Whilst your eager voice is singin'
Praise to Her in might excellin'
Goddess o' the Brassin Dwellin'.

THE THESMOPHORIAZUSAE

INTRODUCTION

THE Greeks celebrated two great festivals in honour of Demeter and Persephone. " In the Eleusinia were unfolded the Mysteries of the Four Last Things —Death, Judgement, the Reward of the Good, and the Punishment of the Wicked—mysteries which were naturally open to the queen of the unseen world below. In the Thesmophoria, the Mother and Daughter were worshipped under quite a different aspect, as the Civilizers of the visible world above." [a] They were the Θεσμοφόροι, the givers and guardians of Home, of the social laws (θεσμά), the rights of property, the laws of wedlock, and the family.

The festival was held " at the fall of the year, when the Daughter once more descended into the lower world, to return four months later in all the freshness of immortal youth to greet the Mother again." [b] Only women took part in this festival. At Athens it occupied four days towards the end of October, Pyanepsia 10th to 13th. The days were named (10) Thesmophoria, (11) Κάθοδος, (12) Νηστεία, (13) Καλλιγένεια.

On the first, the women went up to the Thesmophorion, which stood on an eminence (hence the title ἄνοδος, and ἀναπέμψαι, T. 585), and there made the necessary preparations.

[a] Rogers, Introduction, p. x.   [b] *Ib.* p. xi.

THE THESMOPHORIAZUSAE

The second commemorated the Descent of the Maid into Hades.

The third was given to fasting and mourning, with torchlight ceremonials. Being placed between the Descent and the New Birth, it was also called ἡ Μέση, "not the *Middle* Day of the festival, but the *Intermediate* Day," between these two.[a]

The fourth day was the New Birth or Resurrection.

It is the third day, the Fast, on which the events of this play occur.

The comedy has no didascalia ; hence the date is not known for certain. But it seems clearly to belong to the year 410, after the disappearance of the Four Hundred.[b] The happier tone of this play, as compared with the *Lysistrata* (411 B.C.), supports this view : constitutional government had been restored, and Alcibiades was once more serving his country ; the Peloponnesian fleet had been defeated in a great battle at Cynossema, and a greater still at Abydos. The allusion also in ll. 808-9 speaks of the oligarchical revolution of 411 as " last year " ; and there are other indications pointing the same way.

Whether the comedy won the prize we do not know.

The plot is as follows. The women are to hold an assembly, in which they will debate what punishment is to be inflicted on Euripides for his slanders made against their sex. Euripides, accompanied by Mnesilochus, a connexion by marriage, visits the poet Agathon, to induce him, being a man of effeminate appearance and manners, to attend disguised as a woman, and to defend Euripides. Agathon declines, but lends a selection of women's garments from his wardrobe for the disguise of Mnesilochus, who is shaved and sent off. While he makes his attempt, the effeminate Cleisthenes appears, and warns them that a traitor is amongst them. Mnesilochus is discovered and bound to a plank. Various schemes, based on certain incidents in the tragedies of Euripides, the " schemer," are tried for his rescue. Euripides himself appears, and with Mnesilochus makes his escape. Three tragedies in particular are drawn on: the *Palamede*, the *Helen*, and the *Andromeda*.

(1) The *Palamede* suggests, that as Palamede's story was carved on oar-blades, which were cast into the sea, so the present victim's plight may be carved on the votive tablets which are to hand.

(2) Mnesilochus, lamenting over his sad case, wittily parodies (855 ff.) the Prologue to the *Helen*, in which Helen, sitting on the tomb of Proteus, explains the state of affairs. When Menelaus enters himself and tries to persuade an old woman, who kept the doors of the palace of Proteus, to let him in, he gives a model for the dialogue between Euripides and Mnesilochus, with the woman-guardian intervening (874 ff.). The meeting of Menelaus and Helen is used later in the same dialogue (905 ff.). Details are given in the notes.

(3) Andromeda bound to the rock, and lamenting her coming fate, sings a hymn to Night, and is softly answered by Echo; presently a chorus of maidens enters, and sorrows with her. This scene is parodied by Mnesilochus (1015-1055), bound to his plank, and Echo's part becomes highly ludicrous. So Euripides to the rescue plays on the part of Perseus (1105 ff.).

ΤΑ ΤΟΥ ΔΡΑΜΑΤΟΣ ΠΡΟΣΩΠΑ

ΜΝΗΣΙΛΟΧΟΣ

ΕΥΡΙΠΙΔΗΣ

ΘΕΡΑΠΩΝ Ἀγάθωνος

ΑΓΑΘΩΝ

ΚΗΡΥΚΑΙΝΑ

ΧΟΡΟΣ ΘΕΣΜΟΦΟΡΙΑΖΟΥΣΩΝ

ΓΥΝΗ Α

ΓΥΝΗ Β

ΚΛΕΙΣΘΕΝΗΣ

ΚΡΙΤΥΛΛΑ

ΠΡΥΤΑΝΙΣ

ΣΚΥΘΗΣ

ΗΧΩ

ΕΛΑΦΙΟΝ

ΘΕΣΜΟΦΟΡΙΑΖΟΥΣΑΙ

ΜΝΗΣΙΛΟΧΟΣ. Ὦ Ζεῦ, χελιδὼν ἆρά ποτε φανήσεται;
    ἀπολεῖ μ' ἀλοῶν ἄνθρωπος ἐξ ἑωθινοῦ.
    οἷόν τε, πρὶν τὸν σπλῆνα κομιδῇ μ' ἐκβαλεῖν,
    παρὰ σοῦ πυθέσθαι ποῖ μ' ἄγεις, ὦυριπίδη;
ΕΥΡΙΠΙΔΗΣ. ἀλλ' οὐκ ἀκούειν δεῖ σε πάνθ' ὅσ' αὐτίκα 5
    ὄψει παρεστώς.
ΜΝ.   πῶς λέγεις; αὖθις φράσον.
    οὐ δεῖ μ' ἀκούειν;
ΕΥ.   οὐχ ἅ γ' ἂν μέλλῃς ὁρᾶν.
ΜΝ. οὐδ' ἆρ' ὁρᾶν δεῖ μ';
ΕΥ.   οὐχ ἅ γ' ἂν ἀκούειν δέῃ.
ΜΝ. πῶς μοι παραινεῖς; δεξιῶς μέντοι λέγεις.
    οὐ φῂς σὺ χρῆναί μ' οὔτ' ἀκούειν οὔθ' ὁρᾶν. 10
ΕΥ. χωρὶς γὰρ αὐτοῖν ἑκατέρου 'στὶν ἡ φύσις.
ΜΝ. τοῦ μήτ' ἀκούειν μήθ' ὁρᾶν;
ΕΥ.   εὖ ἴσθ' ὅτι.
ΜΝ. πῶς χωρίς;

---

[a] *Two elderly men are discovered, when the Play opens, pacing along an Athenian street. In one, both by his gait and by his language, we at once recognize a Philosopher and a Genius. His companion is a garrulous and cheery old man, evidently tired out by a long promenade. They prove to be the poet Euripides, and Mnesilochus, his connexion by marriage, in the translation inaccurately styled his cousin. The latter is the first to speak.*

THE THESMOPHORIAZUSAE[a]

MNESILOCHUS. Zeus! is the swallow NEVER going to come?
    Tramped up and down[b] since daybreak! I can't
      stand it.
    Might I, before my wind's ENTIRELY gone,
    Ask where you're taking me, Euripides?
EURIPIDES.[c] You're not to hear the things which face
    to face
    You're going to see.
MN.   What!   Please say that again.
    I'm not to hear?
EU.   The things which you shall see.
MN. And not to see?
EU.   The things which you shall hear.
MN. A pleasant jest! a mighty pleasant jest!
    I'm not to hear or see at all, I see.
EU. (*in high philosophic rhapsody*)
    To hear! to see! full different things, I ween;
    Yea verily, generically diverse.[d]
MN. What's "diverse"?

    [b] Lit. "the fellow will destroy me, driving me round and
round," as they do on the threshing-floor.
    [c] He "talks in a high philosophic strain, quite above the
comprehension of his simple though shrewd companion": R.
    [d] The Greek text gives τοῦ . . . ὁρᾶν to M.—E. Yea, the
nature of the two is diverse. M. Of hearing and seeing?
E. Be sure of it. M. How diverse? E. This is how they
were separated at the time when, etc.

131

ΕΥ.   οὕτω ταῦτα διεκρίθη τότε.
Αἰθὴρ γὰρ ὅτε τὰ πρῶτα διεχωρίζετο,
καὶ ζῷ᾽ ἐν αὑτῷ ξυνετέκνου κινούμενα,   15
ᾧ μὲν βλέπειν χρή, πρῶτ᾽ ἐμηχανήσατο
ὀφθαλμόν, ἀντίμιμον ἡλίου τροχῷ,
ἀκοῇ δὲ χοάνην, ὦτα διετετρήνατο.

ΜΝ. διὰ τὴν χοάνην οὖν μήτ᾽ ἀκούω μήθ᾽ ὁρῶ;
νὴ τὸν Δί᾽ ἥδομαί γε τουτὶ προσμαθών.   20
οἷόν γέ πού ᾽στιν αἱ σοφαὶ ξυνουσίαι.

ΕΥ. πόλλ᾽ ἂν μάθοις τοιαῦτα παρ᾽ ἐμοῦ.

ΜΝ.   πῶς ἂν οὖν
πρὸς τοῖς ἀγαθοῖς τούτοισιν ἐξεύροις ὅπως
ἔτι προσμάθοιμι χωλὸς εἶναι τὼ σκέλη;

ΕΥ. βάδιζε δευρὶ καὶ πρόσεχε τὸν νοῦν.

ΜΝ.   ἰδού.   25

ΕΥ. ὁρᾷς τὸ θύριον τοῦτο;

ΜΝ.   νὴ τὸν Ἡρακλέα
οἶμαί γε.

ΕΥ.   σιώπα νυν.

ΜΝ.   σιωπῶ τὸ θύριον;

ΕΥ. ἄκου᾽.

ΜΝ.   ἀκούω καὶ σιωπῶ τὸ θύριον;

ΕΥ. ἐνταῦθ᾽ Ἀγάθων ὁ κλεινὸς οἰκῶν τυγχάνει
ὁ τραγῳδοποιός.

ΜΝ.   ποῖος οὗτος Ἀγάθων;   30

ΕΥ. ἔστιν τις Ἀγάθων—

---

[a] " In the original, Ether is the creative agent throughout;
she parcels herself out ; she herself gives birth to the breathing and moving creatures. She is always put forward by
A. as the chief Euripidean deity ; see *F. 892* " : R.

[b] Alluding to a line of E. quoted by Schol., σοφοὶ τύραννοι
τῶν σοφῶν συνουσίᾳ. It appeared originally in the *Locrian
Aias* of Sophocles.

EU.   I will explicate my meaning.
When Ether *a* first was mapped and parcelled out,
And living creatures breathed and moved in her,
She, to give sight, implanted in their heads
The Eye, a mimic circlet of the Sun,
And bored the funnel of the Ear, to hear with.

MN. DID SHE ! That's why I'm not to hear or see !
I'm very glad to get that information !
O, what a thing it is to talk with Poets ! *b*

EU. Much of such knowledge I shall give you.

MN. (*involuntarily*)   O !
Then p'raps (excuse me) you will tell me how
Not to be lame to-morrow, after this.*c*

EU. (*loftily disregarding the innuendo*)
Come here and listen.

MN. (*courteously*)   Certainly I will.

EU. See you that wicket ? *d*

MN.   Why, by Heracles,
Of course I do.

EU.   Be still.

MN.   Be still the wicket ?

EU. And most attentive.

MN.   Still attentive wicket ? *e*

EU. There dwells, observe, the famous Agathon,
The Tragic Poet.

MN. (*considering*)   Agathon.   Don't know him.

EU. He is that Agathon—

---

c The translation implies προσμάθω μή ; another reading
for MS. προσμάθοι μή. Either reading is a gird at E. as the
great χωλοποιός or introducer of lame heroes ; *A.* 411, *P.* 147,
F. 846.

d He points to the house of Agathon in the background.
Cf. C. 92.

e The answers appear to be nonsense, like 19, the old
man being dazed by the philosophical talk.

ARISTOPHANES

ΜΝ.   μῶν ὁ μέλας, ὁ καρτερός;
ΕΥ. οὔκ, ἀλλ᾽ ἕτερός τις· οὐχ ἑόρακας πώποτε;
ΜΝ. μῶν ὁ δασυπώγων;
ΕΥ.   οὐχ ἑόρακας πώποτε;
ΜΝ. μὰ τὸν Δί᾽ οὗτοί γ᾽, ὥστε κἀμέ γ᾽ εἰδέναι.
ΕΥ. καὶ μὴν βεβίνηκας σύ γ᾽, ἀλλ᾽ οὐκ οἶσθ᾽ ἴσως. 35
  ἀλλ᾽ ἐκποδὼν πτήξωμεν, ὡς ἐξέρχεται
  θεράπων τις αὐτοῦ πῦρ ἔχων καὶ μυρρίνας,
  προθυσόμενος, ἔοικε, τῆς ποιήσεως.
ΘΕΡΑΠΩΝ. εὔφημος πᾶς ἔστω λαός,
  στόμα συγκλείσας· ἐπιδημεῖ γὰρ   40
  θίασος Μουσῶν ἔνδον μελάθρων
   τῶν δεσποσύνων μελοποιῶν.
  ἐχέτω δὲ πνοὰς νήνεμος αἰθήρ,
  κῦμα δὲ πόντου μὴ κελαδείτω
  γλαυκόν·
ΜΝ.   βομβάξ.
ΕΥ.   σίγα. τί λέγεις;   45
ΘΕ. πτηνῶν τε γένη κατακοιμάσθω,
  θηρῶν τ᾽ ἀγρίων πόδες ὑλοδρόμων
  μὴ λυέσθων.
ΜΝ.   βομβαλοβομβάξ.
ΘΕ. μέλλει γὰρ ὁ καλλιεπὴς Ἀγάθων
  πρόμος ἡμέτερος—
ΜΝ.   μῶν βινεῖσθαι;   50
ΘΕ. τίς ὁ φωνήσας;
ΜΝ.   νήνεμος αἰθήρ.

---

[a] Contrast his real description in 191.
[b] Atqui paedicasti tu eum : sed non noveras fortasse.
[c] As about to offer a solemn prayer or sacrifice; cf. W.
860, F. 871, B. 43.

MN. (*interrupting*)   Dark, brawny fellow ? [a]

EU. O no, quite different ; don't you know him really?

MN. Big-whiskered fellow ?

EU.   Don't you know him really ?

MN. No. (*Thinks again*) No, I don't ; at least I don't
       remember.

EU. (*severely*) I fear there's much you don't remem-
       ber, sir.[b]

       But step aside : I see his servant coming.

       See, he has myrtles and a pan of coals [c]

       To pray, methinks, for favourable rhymes.[d]

SERVANT. All people be still !

       Allow not a word from your lips to be heard,

       For the Muses are here, and are making their odes

          In my Master's abodes.

       Let Ether be lulled, and forgetful to blow,

       And the blue sea-waves, let them cease to flow,

       And be noiseless.

MN.   Fudge !

EU.   Hush, hush, if you please.

SER. Sleep, birds of the air, with your pinions at ease ;

       Sleep, beasts of the field, with entranquillized
          feet ;

       Sleep, sleep, and be still.

MN.   Fudge, fudge, I repeat.

SER. For the soft and the terse professor of verse,

       Our Agathon now is about to—

MN. (*scandalized*) [e]   No, no !

SER. What's that ?

MN.   'Twas the ETHER, FORGETTING TO BLOW !

---

   [d] *The two retire into the background. Agathon's servant
enters from the house.*

   [e] " He is scandalized at what he expects is coming (for
Agathon was suspected of great immorality), but apparently
the word was only *rehearse* " : R.

ΘΕ. δρυόχους τιθέναι δράματος ἀρχάς.
κάμπτει δὲ νέας ἀψῖδας ἐπῶν,
τὰ δὲ τορνεύει, τὰ δὲ κολλομελεῖ,
καὶ γνωμοτυπεῖ κἀντονομάζει   55
καὶ κηροχυτεῖ καὶ γογγύλλει
καὶ χοανεύει.

ΜΝ.   καὶ λαικάζει.

ΘΕ. τίς ἀγροιώτας πελάθει θριγκοῖς;

ΜΝ. ὃς ἕτοιμος σοῦ τοῦ τε ποιητοῦ
τοῦ καλλιεποῦς κατὰ τοῦ θριγκοῦ   60
συγγογγυλίσας καὶ συστρέψας
τουτὶ τὸ πέος χοανεῦσαι.

ΘΕ. ἦ που νέος γ᾽ ὢν ἦσθ᾽ ὑβριστής, ὦ γέρον.

ΕΥ. ὦ δαιμόνιε τοῦτον μὲν ἔα χαίρειν, σὺ δὲ
Ἀγάθωνά μοι δεῦρ᾽ ἐκκάλεσον πάσῃ τέχνῃ. 65

ΘΕ. μηδὲν ἱκέτευ᾽· αὐτὸς γὰρ ἔξεισιν τάχα.
καὶ γὰρ μελοποιεῖν ἄρχεται· χειμῶνος οὖν
ὄντος, κατακάμπτειν τὰς στροφὰς οὐ ῥᾴδιον,
ἢν μὴ προΐῃ θύρασι πρὸς τὸν ἥλιον.

ΜΝ. τί οὖν ἐγὼ δρῶ;

ΕΥ.   περίμεν᾽, ὡς ἐξέρχεται.   70
ὦ Ζεῦ τί δρᾶσαι διανοεῖ με τήμερον;

ΜΝ. νὴ τοὺς θεοὺς ἐγὼ πυθέσθαι βούλομαι
τί τὸ πρᾶγμα τουτί. τί στένεις; τί δυσφορεῖς;
οὐ χρῆν σε κρύπτειν, ὄντα κηδεστὴν ἐμόν.

---

^a Mn. uses the servant's words in a perverted sense:
θριγκοῦ = πρωκτοῦ.—ἦ που (63) is a favourite phrase with
Euripides.
^b The servant goes back into the house.
^c Lines 70-72 are literally: " E. Wait, for he is coming

SER. (*beginning pettishly, but soon falling back into his
former tone*)

I was going to say he is going to lay
The stocks and the scaffolds for building a play.
And neatly he hews them, and sweetly he glues
them,
And a proverb he takes, and an epithet makes,
And he moulds a most waxen and delicate song,
And he tunnels, and funnels, and—

MN.   Does what is wrong.

SER. What clown have we here, so close to our eaves?

MN. Why, one who will take you and him, by your
leaves,
Both you and your terse professor of verse,
And with blows and with knocks set you both on
the stocks,
And tunnel and funnel, and pummel, and worse.[a]

SER. Old man, you must have been a rare pert
youngster.

EU. O, heed not *him*; but quickly call me out
Your master Agathon; do pray make haste.

SER. No need of prayer: he's coming forth directly.
He's moulding odes; and in the cold hard winter
He cannot turn, and twist, and shape his strophes
Until they are warmed and softened in the sun.[b]

MN. And what am I to do?

EU.   You're to keep quiet.
O Zeus! the Hour is come, and so's the Man![c]

MN. O, what's the matter? what disturbs you so?
O, tell me what: I really want to know.
Come, I'm your cousin; won't you tell your cousin?

out. O Zeus, what do you mean to do to me this day!
M. Yes, by the Gods, that's what I want to ask, what means
this business."

ARISTOPHANES

ΕΥ. ἔστιν κακόν μοι μέγα τι προπεφυραμένον.[a]   75
ΜΝ. ποῖόν τι;
ΕΥ.   τῇδε θἠμέρᾳ κριθήσεται
εἴτ' ἔστ' ἔτι ζῶν εἴτ' ἀπόλωλ' Εὐριπίδης.
ΜΝ. καὶ πῶς; ἐπεὶ νῦν γ' οὔτε τὰ δικαστήρια
μέλλει δικάζειν οὔτε βουλῆς ἐσθ' ἕδρα,
ἐπεὶ τρίτη 'στὶ Θεσμοφορίων, ἡ Μέση.[b]   80
ΕΥ. τοῦτ' αὐτὸ γάρ τοι κἀπολεῖν με προσδοκῶ.[c]
αἱ γὰρ γυναῖκες ἐπιβεβουλεύκασί μοι,
κἂν Θεσμοφόροιν[d] μέλλουσι περί μου τήμερον
ἐκκλησιάζειν ἐπ' ὀλέθρῳ.
ΜΝ.   τιὴ τί δή;
ΕΥ. ὁτιὴ τραγῳδῶ, καὶ κακῶς αὐτὰς λέγω.   85
ΜΝ. νὴ τὸν Ποσειδῶ, καὶ δίκαιά γ' ἂν πάθοις.
ἀτὰρ τίν' ἐκ ταύτης σὺ μηχανὴν ἔχεις;
ΕΥ. Ἀγάθωνα πεῖσαι τὸν τραγῳδοδιδάσκαλον
ἐς Θεσμοφόροιν ἐλθεῖν.
ΜΝ.   τί δράσοντ'; εἰπέ μοι.
ΕΥ. ἐκκλησιάσοντ' ἐν ταῖς γυναιξί, κἂν δέῃ,   90
λέξονθ' ὑπὲρ ἐμοῦ.
ΜΝ.   πότερα φανερὸν ἢ λάθρᾳ;
ΕΥ. λάθρᾳ, στολὴν γυναικὸς ἠμφιεσμένον.
ΜΝ. τὸ πρᾶγμα κομψὸν καὶ σφόδρ' ἐκ τοῦ σοῦ
τρόπου·
τοῦ γὰρ τεχνάζειν ἡμέτερος ὁ πυραμοῦς.
ΕΥ. σίγα.

---

[a] Lit. "kneaded beforehand."
[b] "The day between the Κάθοδος, or Descent into Hades, and the Καλλιγένεια, or fair new birth of the Resurrection Morning": R. See Introduction.
[c] Lit. "that very thing I fear will be my ruin."
[d] ἐν Θεσμ., "(in the temple) of the goddesses."

138

EU. There's a great danger brewing for my life.*

MN. O, tell your cousin what.

EU.   This hour decides
Whether Euripides shall live or die.

MN. Why, how is that ? There's no tribunal sitting.
No Court, no Council, will be held to-day.
'Tis the Mid-Fast, the third Home-Festival.*

EU. It is ! it is ! I wish enough it wasn't.*
For on this day the womankind have sworn
To hold a great assembly,* to discuss
How best to serve me out.

MN.   Good gracious ! Why ?

EU. (*with the mild surprise of injured innocence*)
Because, they say, I write lampoons upon them.

MN. Zeus and Poseidon ! they may well say that.
But tell your cousin what you mean to do

EU. I want to get the poet Agathon
To go among them.

MN.   Tell your cousin why.

EU. To mingle in the Assembly, perhaps to speak
On my behalf.

MN.   What, openly, do you mean ?

EU. O no, disguised : dressed up in women's clothes.

MN. A bright idea that, and worthy you :
For in all craftiness we take the cake.*

EU. O, hush !

* The cake was the prize for the man who kept awake
until sunrise in a drinking bout. A proverb. *Cf. F.* 1214,
K. 277.

*By a contrivance very common in ancient theatres, a
portion of Agathon's house is here wheeled forward, turning
on a pivot, so as to disclose the interior of an apartment.
The poet is discovered, surrounded by the most effeminate
luxuries, and in the act of writing a tragic play. He has
just composed, and is now about to recite, a little lyrical
dialogue between his Chorus and one of his actors.*

MN.　　　τί δ' ἔστιν;

ΕΤ.　　　　　　Ἀγάθων ἐξέρχεται.　　　95

MN. καὶ ποῖός ἐστιν;

ΕΤ.　　　　　οὗτος· οὐκκυκλούμενος.

MN. ἀλλ' ἢ τυφλὸς μέν εἰμ'· ἐγὼ γὰρ οὐχ ὁρῶ
　　　ἄνδρ' οὐδέν' ἐνθάδ' ὄντα, Κυρήνην δ' ὁρῶ.

ΕΤ. σίγα· μελῳδεῖν νῦν παρασκευάζεται.
　　　　　(μινύρισμός)

MN. μύρμηκος ἀτραπούς, ἢ τί διαμινύρεται;　　　100

ΑΓΑΘΩΝ. (ὡς ὑποκριτής) Ἱερὰν Χθονίαις δεξάμεναι
　　　λαμπάδα, κοῦραι, ξὺν ἐλευθέρᾳ
　　　πατρίδι χορεύσασθε βοᾷ.

(ὡς χορός) τίνι δὲ δαιμόνων ὁ κῶμος;
　　　λέγε νυν· εὐπίστως δὲ τοὐμὸν　　　105
　　　δαίμονας ἔχει σεβίσαι.

(ὡς ὑπ.) ἄγε νυν ὄλβιζε, Μοῦσα,
　　　χρυσέων ῥύτορα τόξων
　　　Φοῖβον, ὃς ἱδρύσατο χώρας
　　　γύαλα Σιμουντίδι γᾷ.　　　110

(ὡς χορ.) χαῖρε καλλίσταις ἀοιδαῖς,

---

[a] " This is, of course, a hit at Agathon's effeminacy.
Cyrene was a dissolute woman of the day " : R.

[b] *Agathon gives a fantastic little trill.*

[c] " He compares the intricate notes to the tiny and in-
numerable galleries in an ant-hill " : R.

[d] *Agathon now sings his little dialogue in a soft womanly
voice and with pretty effeminate gestures.*

[e] Lit. " Receive, O damsels, the torch holy to the nether-
world goddesses, and dance the choral dance with the free
song of your fatherland. For which of the deities is this
revel ? Tell me now, my mind is easily swayed to worship the
deities. Come then, O Muse, and bless the god who draws
the golden bow, Phoebus, who settled in the country's
glades in the land of the river Simoïs. We greet thee with

MN.   What now ?

EU.   Here's Agathon himself.

MN. Where ?   Which ?

EU.   Why there : the man in the machine.

MN. O dear, what ails me ?   Am I growing blind ?
I see Cyrene ^{a} ; but I see no man.

EU. Do, pray, be silent ; he's just going to sing.^{b}

MN. Is it " the Pathway of the Ants," ^{c} or what ? ^{d}

AGATHON. (*As actor*) *Move ye slowly, with the holy*
                    Torchlight dear to Awful Shades,
                    Singing sweetly, dancing featly,
                    Yes, and neatly, freeborn maids.^{e}

(*As Chorus*) *Whose the song of festal praise ?*
                    Only tell us, we are zealous
                    Evermore our hymns to raise.

(*As actor*) *Sing of Leto,^{f} sing of Thee too,*
                    Archer of the golden bow,
                    Bright Apollo, in the hollow
                    Glades where Ilian rivers flow,
                    Building buildings, long ago.

(*As Chorus*) *Raise the music, softly swelling*
                    To the fame of Leto's name,

our loveliest hymns, O Phoebus, who awardest the sacred
guerdon in our fair musical celebrations. Sing too the
Maiden in the oak-bearing mountains, the huntress Artemis.
I follow on with songs of praise, blessing the exalted child
of Leto, the stainless virgin Artemis. Sing too of Leto,
and the smiting of the Asian lyre, keeping time with the
dance of the Graces, the whirling dance rhythmical to the
Phrygian style. I worship Leto the Queen, and the lyre
the mother of hymns, with notable masculine song : by
which, and by means of our suddenly raised voices, light
flashes from eyes divine. For this cause magnify King
Phoebus. Hail to thee, Leto's blessed son " : R.

^{f} " Leto does not, in the original, assume this prominent
position ; she is here, as elsewhere, placed in the background,
as subordinate to her own children " : R.

Φοῖβ', ἐν εὐμούσαισι τιμαῖς
γέρας ἱερὸν προφέρων.
(ὡς ὑπ.) τάν τ' ἐν ὄρεσι δρυογόνοισι
. . . κόραν ἀείσατ'   115
"Αρτεμιν 'Αγροτέραν.
(ὡς χορ.) ἕπομαι κλῄζουσα σεμνὸν
γόνον ὀλβίζουσα Λατοῦς,
"Αρτεμιν ἀπειρολεχῆ.
(ὡς ὑπ.) Λατώ τε, κρούματά τ' 'Ασιάδος   120
ποδὶ παρ' εὔρυθμα Φρυγίῳ
δινεύματα Χαρίτων.
(ὡς χορ.) σέβομαι Λατώ τ' ἄνασσαν,
κιθαρίν τε ματέρ' ὕμνων,
ἄρσενι βοᾷ δοκίμῳ·   125
τᾷ φῶς ἔσσυτο δαιμονίοις ὄμμασιν,
ἡμετέρας τε δι' αἰφνιδίου ὀπός·
ὦν χάριν ἄνακτ' ἄγαλλε Φοῖβον τιμᾷ.
χαῖρ', ὄλβιε παῖ Λατοῦς.
(ὀλολύζει ὁ γέρων.)

MN. ὡς ἡδὺ τὸ μέλος, ὦ πότνιαι Γενετυλλίδες,   130
καὶ θηλυδριῶδες καὶ κατεγλωττισμένον
καὶ μανδαλωτόν, ὥστ' ἐμοῦ γ' ἀκρωμένου
ὑπὸ τὴν ἕδραν αὐτὴν ὑπῆλθε γάργαλος.
καί σ', ὦ νεανίσχ', ὅστις εἶ, κατ' Αἰσχύλον
ἐκ τῆς Λυκουργίας ἐρέσθαι βούλομαι.   135
ποδαπὸς ὁ γύννις; τίς πάτρα, τίς ἡ στολή;
τίς ἡ τάραξις τοῦ βίου; τί βάρβιτος

---

^a Podicem ipsum subiit titillatio. The epithets κατ. and
μαν. suggest lascivious kisses.
^b From the *Edonians* of Aeschylus, where it is said to
Dionysus (γύννις, a wench, or womanish fellow). Λυκουργία
is the tetralogy of which this play was a part.

        To the God in song excelling,
        Brightest he, of all there be,
        Giving gifts of minstrelsy.
(As actor)   *Sing the maiden, quiver-laden,*
        From the woodland oaks emerging,
        Haunted shades of mountain glades,
        Artemis, the ever Virgin.
(As Chorus) *We rejoice, heart and voice,*
        Hymning, praising, gently phrasing,
        Her, the maiden quiver-laden.
(As actor)   *Soft pulsation of the Asian*
        Lyre, to which the dancers go,
        When the high and holy Graces
        Weave their swiftly whirling paces,
        Phrygian measure, to and fro.
(As Chorus) *Lyre Elysian, heavenly vision,*
        When thy witching tones arise,
        Comes the light of joy and gladness
        Flashing from immortal eyes.
        Eyes will glisten, ears will listen,
        When our manful numbers ring.
        Mighty master, Son of Leto,
        Thine the glory, Thou the King.

               (Mnesilochus utters a cry of delight.)

MN. Wonderful ! Wonderful !
How sweet, how soft, how ravishing the strain !
What melting words ! and as I heard them sung,
Ye amorous Powers, there crept upon my soul
A pleasant, dreamy, rapturous titillation.[a]
And now, dear youth, for I would question thee
And sift thee with the words of Aeschylus,
Whence art thou, what thy country, what thy
    garb ? [b]
Why all this wondrous medley ? Lyre and silks,

λαλεῖ κροκωτῷ; τί δὲ λύρα κεκρυφάλῳ;
τί λήκυθος καὶ στρόφιον; ὡς οὐ ξύμφορον.
τίς δαὶ κατόπτρου καὶ ξίφους κοινωνία;   140
τίς δ' αὐτός, ὦ παῖ; πότερον ὡς ἀνὴρ τρέφει;
καὶ ποῦ πέος; ποῦ χλαῖνα; ποῦ Λακωνικαί;
ἀλλ' ὡς γυνὴ δῆτ'· εἶτα ποῦ τὰ τιτθία;
τί φῄς; τί σιγᾷς; ἀλλὰ δῆτ' ἐκ τοῦ μέλους
ζητῶ σ', ἐπειδή γ' αὐτὸς οὐ βούλει φράσαι; 145

ΑΓ. ὦ πρέσβυ πρέσβυ, τοῦ φθόνου μὲν τὸν ψόγον
ἤκουσα, τὴν δ' ἄλγησιν οὐ παρεσχόμην·
ἐγὼ δὲ τὴν ἐσθῆθ' ἅμα γνώμῃ φορῶ.
χρὴ γὰρ ποιητὴν ἄνδρα πρὸς τὰ δράματα
ἃ δεῖ ποιεῖν, πρὸς ταῦτα τοὺς τρόπους ἔχειν. 150
αὐτίκα γυναικεῖ' ἢν ποιῇ τις δράματα,
μετουσίαν δεῖ τῶν τρόπων τὸ σῶμ' ἔχειν.

ΜΝ. οὐκοῦν κελητίζεις, ὅταν Φαίδραν ποιῇς;

ΑΓ. ἀνδρεῖα δ' ἢν ποιῇ τις, ἐν τῷ σώματι
ἔνεσθ' ὑπάρχον τοῦθ'. ἃ δ' οὐ κεκτήμεθα,   155
μίμησις ἤδη ταῦτα συνθηρεύεται.

ΜΝ. ὅταν σατύρους τοίνυν ποιῇς, καλεῖν ἐμέ,
ἵνα συμποιῶ σοὔπισθεν ἐστυκὼς ἐγώ.

ΑΓ. ἄλλως τ' ἄμουσόν ἐστι ποιητὴν ἰδεῖν
ἀγρεῖον ὄντα καὶ δασύν· σκέψαι δ' ὅτι   160
Ἴβυκος ἐκεῖνος κ'Ἀνακρέων ὁ Τήιος
κ'Ἀλκαῖος, οἵπερ ἁρμονίαν ἐχύμισαν,
ἐμιτροφόρουν τε καὶ διεκινοῦνθ' ὡδέ πως,
καὶ Φρύνιχος, τοῦτον γὰρ οὖν ἀκήκοας,
αὐτός τε καλὸς ἦν καὶ καλῶς ἠμπίσχετο·   165

---

[a] Red Laconian shoes were men's wear; see W. 1158,
E. 345.
[b] " By ' Phaedra' he means the *Hippolytus* ; by ' the

144

A minstrel's lute, a maiden's netted hair,
Girdle and wrestler's oil ! a strange conjunction.
How comes a sword beside a looking-glass ?
What art thou, man or woman ?   If a man,
Where are his clothes ? his red Laconian shoes *a ?*
If woman, 'tis not like a woman's shape.
What art thou, speak ; or if thou tell me not,
Myself must guess thy gender from thy song.

AG. Old man, old man, my ears receive the words
Of your tongue's utterance, yet I heed them not.
I choose my dress to suit my poesy.
A poet, sir, must needs adapt his ways
To the high thoughts which animate his soul.
And when he sings of women, he assumes
A woman's garb, and dons a woman's habits.

MN. (*aside to Eu.*) When you wrote Phaedra,*b* did you
take her habits ?

AG. But when he sings of men, his whole appearance
Conforms to man.   What nature gives us not,
The human soul aspires to imitate.

MN. (*as before*) Zounds, if I'd seen you when you
wrote the Satyrs ! *c*

AG. Besides, a poet never should be rough,
Or harsh, or rugged.   Witness to my words
Anacreon, Alcaeus, Ibycus,
Who when they filtered and diluted song,
Wore soft Ionian manners and attire.*d*
And Phrynichus, perhaps you have seen him, sir,
How fair he was, and beautifully dressed ;

Satyrs,' the *Cyclops* of Euripides " : R.   κελητίζω is σχῆμα
συνουσίας, cf. W. 501.

c Ergo cum Satyros facies, voca me, ut opera mea te
adiuvem pone stans arrecto veretro.

d Lit. "they wore the headband, and moved as I do,"
giving a specimen of the *motus Ionicos,* Hor. *Odes,* iii. 6. 21.

145

δια τοῦτ' ἄρ' αὐτοῦ καὶ κάλ' ἦν τὰ δράματα.
ὅμοια γὰρ ποιεῖν ἀνάγκη τῇ φύσει.

ΜΝ. ταῦτ' ἄρ' ὁ Φιλοκλέης αἰσχρὸς ὢν αἰσχρῶς
ποιεῖ,
ὁ δ' αὖ Ξενοκλέης ὢν κακὸς κακῶς ποιεῖ,
ὁ δ' αὖ Θέογνις ψυχρὸς ὢν ψυχρῶς ποιεῖ. 170

ΑΓ. ἅπασ' ἀνάγκη· ταῦτα γάρ τοι γνοὺς ἐγὼ
ἐμαυτὸν ἐθεράπευσα.

ΜΝ.   πῶς πρὸς τῶν θεῶν;

ΕΤ. παῦσαι βαΰζων· καὶ γὰρ ἐγὼ τοιοῦτος ἦν
ὢν τηλικοῦτος, ἡνίκ' ἠρχόμην ποιεῖν.

ΜΝ. μὰ τὸν Δί' οὐ ζηλῶ σε τῆς παιδεύσεως. 175

ΕΤ. ἀλλ' ὧνπερ οὕνεκ' ἦλθον, ἔα μ' εἰπεῖν.

ΑΓ.   λέγε.

ΕΤ. Ἀγάθων, σοφοῦ πρὸς ἀνδρός, ὅστις ἐν βραχεῖ
πολλοὺς καλῶς οἷός τε συντέμνειν λόγους.
ἐγὼ δὲ καινῇ ξυμφορᾷ πεπληγμένος
ἱκέτης ἀφῖγμαι πρὸς σέ.

ΑΓ.   τοῦ χρείαν ἔχων; 180

ΕΤ. μέλλουσί μ' αἱ γυναῖκες ἀπολεῖν τήμερον
τοῖς Θεσμοφορίοις, ὅτι κακῶς αὐτὰς λέγω.

ΑΓ. τίς οὖν παρ' ἡμῶν ἐστιν ὠφέλειά σοι;

ΕΤ. ἡ πᾶσ'· ἐὰν γὰρ ἐγκαθεζόμενος λάθρᾳ
ἐν ταῖς γυναιξίν, ὡς δοκῶν εἶναι γυνή, 185
ὑπεραποκρίνῃ μου, σαφῶς σώσεις ἐμέ.
μόνος γὰρ ἂν λέξειας ἀξίως ἐμοῦ.

ΑΓ. ἔπειτα πῶς οὐκ αὐτὸς ἀπολογεῖ παρών;

ΕΤ. ἐγὼ φράσω σοι. πρῶτα μὲν γιγνώσκομαι·
ἔπειτα πολιός εἰμι καὶ πώγων' ἔχω, 190
σὺ δ' εὐπρόσωπος, λευκός, ἐξυρημένος,

ᵃ "The waspish composer of waspish tragedies," W.
462 : R.

Therefore his plays were beautifully fair.
For as the Worker, so the Work will be.

MN. Then that is why harsh Philocles [a] writes harshly,
And that is why vile Xenocles writes vilely,
And cold Theognis writes such frigid plays.

AG. Yes, that is why. And I perceiving this
Made myself womanlike.

MN.   My goodness, how ?

EU. O, stop that yapping : in my youthful days
I too was such another one as he.

MN. Good gracious ! I don't envy you your schooling.

EU. (sharply) Pray, let us come to business, sir.

MN.   Say on.

EU. A wise man, Agathon, compacts his words,
And many thoughts compresses into few.[b]
So, I in my extremity am come
To ask a favour of you.

AG.   Tell me what.

EU. The womankind at their Home-feast to-day
Are going to pay me out for my lampoons.

AG. That's bad indeed, but how can I assist you ?

EU. Why, every way. If you'll disguise yourself,
And sit among them like a woman born,
And plead my cause, you'll surely get me off.
There's none but you to whom I dare entrust it.[c]

AG. Why don't you go yourself, and plead your cause ?

EU. I'll tell you why. They know me well by sight ;
And I am grey, you see, and bearded too,
But you've a baby face, a treble voice,

[b] These two lines come from the *Aeolus* of Euripides, with
" Agathon " for Παῖδες. Line 179 is from *Alcestis* 856 καίπερ
βαρεία συμφορᾷ πεπληγμένος.

[c] Lit. " for you alone could speak in a manner worthy
of me."

γυναικόφωνος, ἁπαλός, εὐπρεπὴς ἰδεῖν.

ΑΓ. Εὐριπίδη—

ΕΥ.   τί ἔστιν;

ΑΓ.   ἐποίησάς ποτε,
"χαίρεις ὁρῶν φῶς, πατέρα δ' οὐ χαίρειν
    δοκεῖς;"

ΕΥ. ἔγωγε.

ΑΓ.   μή νυν ἐλπίσῃς τὸ σὸν κακὸν   195
ἡμᾶς ὑφέξειν. καὶ γὰρ ἂν μαινοίμεθ' ἄν.
ἀλλ' αὐτὸς ὅ γε σόν ἐστιν οἰκείως φέρε.
τὰς συμφορὰς γὰρ οὐχὶ τοῖς τεχνάσμασιν
φέρειν δίκαιον, ἀλλὰ τοῖς παθήμασιν.

ΜΝ. καὶ μὴν σύ γ', ὦ κατάπυγον, εὐρύπρωκτος εἶ   200
οὐ τοῖς λόγοισιν, ἀλλὰ τοῖς παθήμασιν.

ΕΥ. τί δ' ἔστιν ὅτι δέδοικας ἐλθεῖν αὐτόσε;

ΑΓ. κάκιον ἀπολοίμην ἂν ἢ σύ.

ΕΥ.   πῶς;

ΑΓ.   ὅπως;
δοκῶν γυναικῶν ἔργα νυκτερείσια
κλέπτειν, ὑφαρπάζειν τε θήλειαν Κύπριν.   205

ΜΝ. ἰδού γε κλέπτειν· νὴ Δία βινεῖσθαι μὲν οὖν.
ἀτὰρ ἡ πρόφασίς γε νὴ Δί' εἰκότως ἔχει.

ΕΥ. τί οὖν; ποιήσεις ταῦτα;

ΑΓ.   μὴ δόκει γε σύ.

ΕΥ. ὦ τρισκακοδαίμων, ὡς ἀπόλωλ' Εὐριπίδης.

ΜΝ. ὦ φίλτατ', ὦ κηδεστά, μὴ σαυτὸν προδῷς.   210

ΕΥ. πῶς οὖν ποιήσω δῆτα;

ΜΝ.   τοῦτον μὲν μακρὰ
κλαίειν κέλευ', ἐμοὶ δ' ὅ τι βούλει χρῶ λαβών.

ᵃ From *Alcestis*, 691. "The question is put by Pheres to his son Admetus, who expects his father to die as a substitute

148

A fair complexion, pretty, smooth, and soft.

AG. Euripides !

EU.   Yes.

AG.   Wasn't it you who wrote

You value life ; do you think your father
   doesn't ? [a]

EU. It was : what then ?

AG.   Expect not me to bear

Your burdens ; that were foolishness indeed.
Each man must bear his sorrows for himself.
And troubles, when they come, must needs be met
By manful acts,[b] and not by shifty tricks.

MN. Aye, true for you, your wicked ways are shown
By sinful acts, and not by words alone.[c]

EU. But tell me really why you fear to go.

AG. They'd serve me worse than you.

EU   How so ?

AG.   How so ?

I'm too much like a woman, and they'd think
That I was come to poach on their preserves.[d]

MN. Well, I must say that's not a bad excuse.

EU. Then won't you really help ?

AG.   I really won't.

EU. Thrice luckless I ! Euripides is done for !

MN. O friend ! O cousin ! don't lose heart like this.

EU. Whatever can I do ?

MN.   Bid *him* go hang !

See, here am I ; deal with me as you please.

for himself " : R. See *C.* 1415. There is probably much of
Euripides in Agathon's next speech.

  [b] Lit. " by endurance," with a hint at the pathic vice.

  [c] Enimvero tu, impudice, latiorem culum habes, non
dicendo sed patiendo.

  [d] AG. Quia viderer mulierum opera nocturna furari, et
surripere muliebrem Venerem. MN. Vah, furari ! immo vero
paedicari.

ΕΥ. ἄγε νυν ἐπειδὴ σαυτὸν ἐπιδίδως ἐμοί,
    ἀπόδυθι τουτὶ θοἰμάτιον.

ΜΝ.   καὶ δὴ χαμαί.
    ἀτὰρ τί μέλλεις δρᾶν μ';

ΕΥ.   ἀποξυρεῖν ταδί,   215
    τὰ κάτω δ' ἀφεύειν.

ΜΝ.   ἀλλὰ πρᾶττ', εἴ σοι δοκεῖ.
    ἢ μὴ διδόναι γ' ἐμαυτὸν ὤφελόν ποτε.

ΕΥ. Ἀγάθων σὺ μέντοι ξυροφορεῖς ἑκάστοτε,
    χρῆσόν τί νυν ἡμῖν ξυρόν.

ΑΓ.   αὐτὸς λάμβανε
    ἐντεῦθεν ἐκ τῆς ξυροδόκης.

ΕΥ.   γενναῖος εἶ.   220
    κάθιζε· φύσα τὴν γνάθον τὴν δεξιάν.

ΜΝ. ὤμοι.

ΕΥ.   τί κέκραγας; ἐμβαλῶ σοι πάτταλον,
    ἢν μὴ σιωπᾷς.

ΜΝ.   ἀτταταῖ ἰατταταῖ.

ΕΥ. οὗτος σὺ ποῖ θεῖς;

ΜΝ.   ἐς τὸ τῶν σεμνῶν θεῶν·
    οὐ γὰρ μὰ τὴν Δήμητρά γ' ἐνταυθοῖ μενῶ   225
    τεμνόμενος.

ΕΥ.   οὔκουν καταγέλαστος δῆτ' ἔσει
    τὴν ἡμίκραιραν τὴν ἑτέραν ψιλὴν ἔχων;

ΜΝ. ὀλίγον μέλει μοι.

ΕΥ.   μηδαμῶς πρὸς τῶν θεῶν
    προδῷς με· χώρει δεῦρο.

ΜΝ.   κακοδαίμων ἐγώ.

---

^a The idea of this depilation scene seems to have been
borrowed from a play by Cratinus, the *Idaeans*, where the

EU. (*striking while the iron is hot*)
Well, if you'll really give yourself to me,
First throw aside this overcloak.

MN. 'Tis done.
But how are you going to treat me?

EU. Shave you here,
And singe you down below.[a]

MN. (*magnanimously*) Well, do your worst;
I've said you may, and I'll go through with it.

EU. You've always, Agathon, got a razor handy;
Lend us one, will you?

AG. Take one for yourself
Out of the razor-case.

EU. Obliging youth!
(*To Mn.*) Now sit you down,[b] and puff your right
cheek out.

MN. Oh!

EU. What's the matter? Shut your mouth, or else
I'll clap a gag in.

MN. Lackalackaday![c]

EU. Where are you fleeing?

MN. To sanctuary I.
Shall I sit quiet to be hacked like that?
Demeter, no!

EU. Think how absurd you'll look,
With one cheek shaven, and the other not.

MN. (*doggedly*) Well, I don't care.

EU. O, by the Gods, come back.
Pray don't forsake me.

MN. Miserable me![d]

chorus were probably Idaean Dactyls, the effeminate
ministers of Cybele.
  [b] *Mnesilochus seats himself in a chair.*
  [c] *He jumps up, and runs away.*
  [d] *He resumes his seat. Euripides goes on with the shaving.*

ΕΥ. ἔχ᾽ ἀτρέμα σαυτὸν κἀνάκυπτε· ποῖ στρέφει; 230
ΜΝ. μῦ μῦ.
ΕΥ.　　　　τί μύζεις; πάντα πεποίηται καλῶς.
ΜΝ. οἴμοι κακοδαίμων, ψιλὸς αὖ στρατεύσομαι.
ΕΥ. μὴ φροντίσῃς· ὡς εὐπρεπὴς φανεῖ πάνυ.
βούλει θεᾶσθαι σαυτόν;
ΜΝ.　　　　　　　εἰ δοκεῖ, φέρε.
ΕΥ. ὁρᾷς σεαυτόν;
ΜΝ.　　　　οὐ μὰ Δί᾽ ἀλλὰ Κλεισθένην. 235
ΕΥ. ἀνίστασ᾽, ἵν᾽ ἀφεύσω σε, κἀγκύψας ἔχε.
ΜΝ. οἴμοι κακοδαίμων, δελφάκιον γενήσομαι.
ΕΥ. ἐνεγκάτω τις ἔνδοθεν δᾷδ᾽ ἢ λύχνον.
ἐπίκυπτε· τὴν κέρκον φυλάττου νυν ἄκραν.
ΜΝ. ἐμοὶ μελήσει νὴ Δία, πλήν γ᾽ ὅτι κάομαι. 240
οἴμοι τάλας. ὕδωρ ὕδωρ ὦ γείτονες.
πρὶν ἀντιλαβέσθαι τόν γε πρωκτὸν τῆς φλογός.
ΕΥ. θάρρει.
ΜΝ.　　τί θαρρῶ καταπεπυρπολημένος;
ΕΥ. ἀλλ᾽ οὐκ ἔτ᾽ οὐδὲν πρᾶγμά σοι· τὰ πλεῖστα γὰρ
ἀποπεπόνηκας.
ΜΝ.　　　　φῦ· ἰοὺ τῆς ἀσβόλου. 245
αἰθὸς γεγένημαι πάντα τὰ περὶ τὴν τράμιν.
ΕΥ. μὴ φροντίσῃς· ἕτερος γὰρ αὐτὰ σπογγιεῖ.
ΜΝ. οἰμώξετἄρ᾽ εἴ τις τὸν ἐμὸν πρωκτὸν πλυνεῖ.
ΕΥ. Ἀγάθων, ἐπειδὴ σαυτὸν ἐπιδοῦναι φθονεῖς,
ἀλλ᾽ ἱμάτιον γοῦν χρῆσον ἡμῖν τουτωὶ 250
καὶ στρόφιον· οὐ γὰρ ταῦτά γ᾽ ὡς οὐκ ἔστ᾽
ἐρεῖς.
ΑΓ. λαμβάνετε καὶ χρῆσθ᾽· οὐ φθονῶ.
ΜΝ.　　　　　　　τί οὖν λάβω;
ΕΥ. ὅ τι; τὸν κροκωτὸν πρῶτον ἐνδύου λαβών.

EU. Sit steady ; raise your chin ; don't wriggle so.

MN. (*wincing*) O tchi, tchi, tchi !

EU.   There, there, it's over now.

MN. And I'm, worse luck, a Rifled Volunteer.[a]

EU. Well, never mind ; you're looking beautiful.
    Glance in this mirror.

MN.   Well then, hand it here.

EU. What see you there ?

MN. (*in disgust*)   Not me, but Cleisthenes.[b]

EU. Get up : bend forward.   I've to singe you now.

MN. O me, you'll scald me like a sucking-pig.

EU. Someone within there, bring me out a torch.
    Now then, stoop forward : gently ; mind yourself.[c]

MN. I'll see to that. Hey ! I've caught fire there. Hey !
    O, water ! water ! neighbours, bring your buckets.
    Fire ! Fire ! I tell you ; I'm on fire, I am !

EU. There, it's all right.

MN.   All right, when I'm a cinder ?

EU. Well, well, the worst is over ; 'tis indeed.
    It won't pain now.

MN.   Faugh, here's a smell of burning !
    Drat it, I'm roasted all about the stern.

EU. Nay, heed it not.   I'll have it sponged directly.

MN. I'd like to catch a fellow sponging *me*.

EU. Though you begrudge your active personal aid,
    Yet, Agathon, you won't refuse to lend us
    A dress and sash : you can't deny you've got them.

AG. Take them, and welcome.   I begrudge them not.

MN. What's first to do ?

EU.   Put on this yellow silk.

[a] A play on ψιλός, light-armed, and smooth-shaven.

[b] " Cleisthenes was the most effeminate man in Athens;
he comes on the stage by-and-by " : R.

[c] Caudae cave extremae.   " M. has to be singed fore and
aft " : R.

ΜΝ. νὴ τὴν Ἀφροδίτην ἡδύ γ' ὄζει ποσθίου.

ΕΥ. σύζωσον ἀνύσας.

ΜΝ.   αἶρε νῦν στρόφιον.

ΕΥ.   ἰδού.   255

ΜΝ. ἴθι νυν κατάστειλόν με τὰ περὶ τὼ σκέλη.

ΕΥ. κεκρυφάλου δεῖ καὶ μίτρας.

ΑΓ.   ἡδὶ μὲν οὖν
κεφαλὴ περίθετος, ἣν ἐγὼ νύκτωρ φορῶ.

ΕΥ. νὴ τὸν Δί', ἀλλὰ κἀπιτηδεία πάνυ.

ΜΝ. ἆρ' ἁρμόσει μοι;

ΕΥ.   νὴ Δί' ἀλλ' ἄριστ' ἔχει.   260
φέρ' ἔγκυκλον.

ΑΓ.   τουτὶ λάβ' ἀπὸ τῆς κλινίδος.

ΕΥ. ὑποδημάτων δεῖ.

ΑΓ.   τἀμὰ ταυτὶ λάμβανε.

ΜΝ. ἆρ' ἁρμόσει μοι;

ΕΥ. χαλαρὰ γοῦν χαίρεις φορῶν.

ΑΓ. σὺ τοῦτο γίγνωσκ'· ἀλλ' ἔχεις γὰρ ὧν δέει,
εἴσω τις ὡς τάχιστά μ' εἰσκυκλησάτω.   265

ΕΥ. ἁνὴρ μὲν ἡμῖν οὑτοσὶ καὶ δὴ γυνὴ
τό γ' εἶδος· ἢν λαλῇς δ', ὅπως τῷ φθέγματι
γυναικιεῖς εὖ καὶ πιθανῶς.

ΜΝ.   πειράσομαι.

ΕΥ. βάδιζε τοίνυν.

ΜΝ.   μὰ τὸν Ἀπόλλω οὔκ, ἤν γε μὴ
ὀμόσῃς ἐμοί—

ΕΥ.   τί χρῆμα;

ΜΝ.   συσσώσειν ἐμὲ   270
πάσαις τέχναις, ἤν μοί τι περιπίπτῃ κακόν.

ΕΥ. ὄμνυμι τοίνυν αἰθέρ' οἴκησιν Διός.

---

^a δέον εἰπεῖν μύρου, εἶπε ποσθίου: Schol. (π.=αἰδοῖον τοῦ ἀνδρός). It has been worn by a man.

MN. By Aphrodite, but 'tis wondrous nice.[a]

EU. Gird it up tighter.

MN.   Where's the girdle ?

EU.   Here.

MN. Make it sit neatly there about the legs.

EU. Now for a snood and hair-net.

AG.   Will this do ?
It's quite a natty hairdress ; it's my nightcap.

EU. The very thing : i'faith, the very thing.

MN. Does it look well ?

EU.   Zeus ! I should think it did !
Now for a mantle.

AG.   Take one from the couch.

EU. A pair of woman's shoes.

AG.   Well, here are mine.

MN. Do they look well ?

EU.   They are loose enough, I trow

AG. You see to that ; I've lent you all you need.
Will someone kindly wheel me in again ? [b]

EU. There then, the man's a regular woman now,
At least to look at ; and if you've to speak,
Put on a feminine mincing voice.

MN. (*in a shrill treble*)   I'll try.

EU. And now begone, and prosper.

MN.   Wait a bit.
Not till you've sworn—

EU.   Sworn what ?

MN.   That if I get
In any scrape, you'll surely see me through.

EU. I swear by Ether, Zeus's dwelling-place.[c]

[b] *Agathon's apartment, with A. in it, is wheeled back into
the house ; E. and Mn. are left standing on the stage.
E. turns Mn. round, and surveys him with complacency.*

[c] From *the Melanippe Sapiens* of Euripides (fr. 487 Nauck),
with τοίνυν for δ᾽ ἱερόν.

ΜΝ. τί μᾶλλον ἢ τὴν Ἱπποκράτους ξυνοικίαν;
ΕΥ. ὄμνυμι τοίνυν πάντας ἄρδην τοὺς θεούς.
ΜΝ. μέμνησο τοίνυν ταῦθ', ὅτι ἡ φρὴν ὤμοσεν,   275
 ἡ γλῶττα δ' οὐκ ὀμώμοκ'· οὐδ' ὥρκωσ' ἐγώ.
   (ὀλολύζουσι. τὸ ἱερὸν ὠθεῖται.)
ΕΥ. ἔκσπευδε ταχέως· ὡς τὸ τῆς ἐκκλησίας
 σημεῖον ἐν τῷ Θεσμοφορίῳ φαίνεται.
 ἐγὼ δ' ἄπειμι.
ΜΝ.   δεῦρό νυν ὦ Θρᾷτθ' ἕπου.
 ὦ Θρᾷττα, θέασαι, καομένων τῶν λαμπάδων,   280
 ὅσον τὸ χρῆμ' ἀνέρχεθ' ὑπὸ τῆς λιγνύος.
 ἀλλ' ὦ περικαλλῆ Θεσμοφόρω δέξασθέ με
 ἀγαθῇ τύχῃ καὶ δεῦρο καὶ πάλιν οἴκαδε.
 ὦ Θρᾷττα, τὴν κίστην κάθελε, κᾆτ' ἔξελε
 τὸ πόπανον, ὡς λαβοῦσα θύσω ταῖν θεαῖν.   285
 δέσποινα πολυτίμητε Δήμητερ φίλη
 καὶ Φερσέφαττα, πολλὰ πολλάκις μέ σοι
 θύειν ἔχουσαν, εἰ δὲ μή, ἀλλὰ νῦν λαθεῖν.
 καὶ τὴν θυγατέρα, Χοιρίον, ἀνδρός μοι τυχεῖν
 πλουτοῦντος, ἄλλως τ' ἠλιθίου κἀβελτέρου,   290
 καὶ Ποσθαλήκον νοῦν ἔχειν μοι καὶ φρένας.
 ποῦ ποῦ καθίζωμ' ἐν καλῷ, τῶν ῥητόρων
 ἵν' ἐξακούω; σὺ δ' ἄπιθ', ὦ Θρᾷττ', ἐκποδών.
 δούλοις γὰρ οὐκ ἔξεστ' ἀκούειν τῶν λόγων.

 ᵃ An Athenian general, whose sons were " priggish and
ill-bred " : Schol. to C. 1001.

 ᵇ He quotes a famous line in the *Hippolytus* of Euripides :
ἡ γλῶσσ' ὀμώμοχ', ἡ δὲ φρὴν ἀνώμοτος. *Cf. F.* 1471.

 ᶜ Lit. "nor did I so put the oath." Thratta (279) is a
servant.

 *The background of the scene opens and a large building
is pushed forward upon the stage, representing the Thesmo-
phorium or Temple of the Home-givers. The Athenian
ladies, who form the Chorus of the Play, are seen, a few*

MN. As well by vile Hippocrates's [a] cabin.

EU. Well, then, I swear by every blessèd God.

MN. And please remember 'twas your MIND that
swore,[b]
Not your tongue only ; please remember that.[c]

EU. O, get you gone : for there's the signal hoisted
Over the Temple ; they are assembling now.
I think I'll leave you.

MN.   Thratta, come along.
O Thratta, Thratta, here's a lot of women
Coming up here ! O, what a flare of torches !
O sweet Twain-goddesses, vouchsafe me now
A pleasant day, and eke a safe return.
Set down the basket, Thratta ; give me out
The sacred cake to offer to the Twain.
O dread Demeter, high unearthly one,
O Persephassa, grant your votaress grace
To join in many festivals like this,
Or if not so, at least escape this once.
And may my daughter, by your leaves, pick up
A wealthy husband, and a fool to boot ;
And little Bull-calf have his share of brains.[d]
Now, then, I wonder which is the best place
To hear the speeches ? Thratta, you may go.
These are not things for servant-girls to hear.[e]

lines later, thronging into the orchestra, to assist in the
solemnities of the festival, and to take part in the Assembly
they are about to hold. The air above them is thick with
the smoke of the torches they are bearing in their hands.
Euripides thinks it time to make himself scarce. Mnesilochus
assumes the fussy airs and treble voice of an Athenian
matron, talking to an imaginary maid-servant.

[d] Χοιρίον and Ποσθάληκος are comic names from χοῖρος
(γυναικεῖον αἰδοῖον) and πόσθη.

[e] The officials now take their places, and the Assembly at
once begins.

ΚΗΡΤΚΑΙΝΑ.   εὐφημία "στω,   295
                εὐφημία "στω.
                εὔχεσθε ταῖν Θεσμοφόροιν,
                τῇ Δήμητρι καὶ τῇ Κόρῃ,
                καὶ τῷ Πλούτῳ, καὶ τῇ Καλλιγενείᾳ,
                καὶ τῇ Κουροτρόφῳ τῇ Γῇ,   300
                καὶ τῷ Ἑρμῇ, καὶ Χάρισιν,
      ἐκκλησίαν τήνδε καὶ ξύνοδον τὴν νῦν
      κάλλιστα κἄριστα ποιῆσαι,
    πολυωφελῶς μὲν πόλει τῇ Ἀθηναίων,
      τυχηρῶς δ' ἡμῖν αὐταῖς·   305
    καὶ τὴν δρῶσαν καὶ τὴν ἀγορεύουσαν
    τὰ βέλτιστα περὶ τὸν δῆμον τῶν Ἀθηναίων,
        καὶ τὸν τῶν γυναικῶν,
             ταύτην νικᾶν.
    ταῦτ' εὔχεσθε, καὶ ὑμῖν αὐταῖς τἀγαθά.   310
    ἰὴ παιών, ἰὴ παιών, χαίρωμεν.

ΧΟΡΟΣ.   δεχόμεθα καὶ θεῶν γένος
             λιτόμεθα ταῖσδ' ἐπ' εὐχαῖς
             φανέντας ἐπιχαρῆναι.
             Ζεῦ μεγαλώνυμε, Χρυσολύρα τε   315
             Δῆλον ὃς ἔχεις ἱεράν, καὶ σὺ
             παγκρατὲς κόρα, γλαυκῶπι,
             χρυσόλογχε, πόλιν ἔχουσα
             περιμάχητον, ἐλθὲ δεῦρο.
             καὶ πολυώνυμε, θηροφόνη παῖ,   320
             Λατοῦς χρυσώπιδος ἔρνος·
             σύ τε, πόντιε σεμνὲ Πόσειδον,

---

   ^a The Bidding Prayer (295-311) is in prose in the original.
   ^b Athena and Poseidon had contended for the possession
of Athens.

CRIERESS.[a]

> Worldly clamour
> Pass away !
> Silence, Silence,
> While we pray ;
> To the Twain, the Home-bestowers,
> Holy Parent, holy Daughter,
> And to Wealth, and Heavenly Beauty,
> And to Earth the foster-mother,
> And to Hermes and the Graces,
> That they to this important high debate
> Grant favour and success,
> Making it useful to the Athenian State,
> And to ourselves no less.
> And O, that she who counsels best to-day
> About the Athenian nation,
> And our own commonwealth of women, may
> Succeed by acclamation.
> These things we pray, and blessings on our cause.
> Sing Paean, Paean, ho ! with merry loud applause.

CHORUS.

> We in thy prayers combine,
> And we trust the Powers Divine
> Will on these their suppliants smile,
> Both Zeus the high and awful,
> And the golden-lyred Apollo
> From the holy Delian isle.
> And thou, our Mighty Maiden,
> Lance of gold, and eye of blue,
> Of the God-contested city,[b]
> Help us too :
> And the many-named, the Huntress,
> Gold-fronted Leto's daughter ;
> And the dread Poseidon ruling

ἁλιμέδον, προλιπὼν
μυχὸν ἰχθυόεντ᾽ οἰστροδόνητον·
Νηρέος εἰναλίου τε κόραι,
Νύμφαι τ᾽ ὀρείπλαγκτοι.   325
χρυσέα τε Φόρμιγξ
ἰαχήσειεν ἐπ᾽ εὐχαῖς
ἡμετέραις· τελέως δ᾽ ἐκ-
κλησιάσαιμεν, ᾽Αθηνῶν
εὐγενεῖς γυναῖκες.

                                              330

ΚΗ. εὔχεσθε τοῖς θεοῖσι τοῖς ᾽Ολυμπίοις
καὶ ταῖς ᾽Ολυμπίαισι, καὶ τοῖς Πυθίοις
καὶ ταῖσι Πυθίαισι, καὶ τοῖς Δηλίοις
καὶ ταῖσι Δηλίαισι, τοῖς τ᾽ ἄλλοις θεοῖς,
εἴ τις ἐπιβουλεύει τι τῷ δήμῳ κακὸν
τῷ τῶν γυναικῶν, ἢ ᾽πικηρυκεύεται   335
Εὐριπίδῃ Μήδοις τ᾽ ἐπὶ βλάβῃ τινὶ
τῇ τῶν γυναικῶν, ἢ τυραννεῖν ἐπινοεῖ
ἢ τὸν τύραννον συγκατάγειν, ἢ παιδίον
ὑποβαλλομένης κατεῖπεν, ἢ δούλη τινὸς
προαγωγὸς οὖσ᾽ ἐνετρύλλισεν τῷ δεσπότῃ,   340
ἢ πεμπομένη τις ἀγγελίας ψευδεῖς φέρει,
ἢ μοιχὸς εἴ τις ἐξαπατᾷ ψευδῆ λέγων
καὶ μὴ δίδωσιν ἃν ὑπόσχηταί ποτε,
ἢ δῶρά τις δίδωσι μοιχῷ γραῦς γυνή,
ἢ καὶ δέχεται προδιδοῦσ᾽ ἑταίρα τὸν φίλον,   345
κεἴ τις κάπηλος ἢ καπηλὶς τοῦ χοὸς
ἢ τῶν κοτυλῶν τὸ νόμισμα διαλυμαίνεται,

ᵃ The following passage is modelled on the ᾽Αρά, one of
the ceremonies preliminary to a meeting of the Athenian
Assembly. It included a curse on those who would wish to
subvert the Constitution.

Over Ocean's stormy water ;
Come from the deep where fishes
Swarm, and the whirlwinds rave ;
And the Oreads of the mountain,
And the Nereids of the wave.
Let the Golden Harp sound o'er us
And the Gods with favour crown
This Parliament of Women,
The free and noble matrons
Of the old Athenian town.

CRI.*a* O yes ! O yes !
Pray ye the Olympian Gods—and Goddesses,
And all the Pythian Gods—and Goddesses,
And all the Delian Gods—and Goddesses,
And all the other Gods—and Goddesses,
Whoso is disaffected, ill-disposed
Towards this commonwealth of womankind,
Or with Euripides, or with the Medes
Deals to the common hurt of womankind,
Or aims at tyranny, or fain would bring
The Tyrant back ; or dares betray a wife
For palming off a baby as her own ;
Or tells her master tales against her mistress ;
Or does not bear a message faithfully ;
Or, being a suitor, makes a vow, and then
Fails to perform ; or, being a rich old woman,
Hires for herself a lover with her wealth ;
Or, being a girl, takes gifts and cheats the giver ;
Or, being a trading man or trading woman,
Gives us short measure in our drinking-cups ;—

---

a Passages concerning the tyrants and the Medes were part of it, with denunciations of those who brought false news, or deceived the people. In the parody, men only are denounced (349), women blessed (350).

κακῶς ἀπολέσθαι τοῦτον αὐτὸν κᾠκίαν
ἀρᾶσθε, ταῖς δ' ἄλλαισιν ὑμῖν τοὺς θεοὺς   350
εὔχεσθε πάσαις πολλὰ δοῦναι κἀγαθά.

ΧΟ.   ξυνευχόμεσθα τέλεα μὲν
πόλει, τέλεά τε δήμῳ
τάδ' εὔγματα γενέσθαι,
τὰ δ' ἄρισθ' ὅσαις προσήκει   355
νικᾶν λεγού-
σαις· ὁπόσαι δ' ἐξαπατῶ-
σιν, παραβαίνουσί τε τοὺς
ὅρκους τοὺς νενομισμένους
κερδῶν οὕνεκ' ἐπὶ βλάβῃ,   360
ἢ ψηφίσματα καὶ νόμον
ζητοῦσ' ἀντιμεθιστάναι,
τἀπόρρητά τε τοῖσιν ἐχ-
θροῖς τοῖς ἡμετέροις λέγουσ',
ἢ Μήδους ἐπάγουσι γῇ,   365
κερδῶν οὕνεκ' ἐπὶ βλάβῃ,
ἀσεβοῦσί τε τοὺς θεούς,
ἀδικοῦσί τε τὴν πόλιν.
ἀλλ' ὦ παγκρατὲς [εὐμενὲς]
Ζεῦ, ταῦτα κυρώσειας, ὥσθ'
ἡμῖν θεοὺς παραστατεῖν   370
καίπερ γυναιξὶν οὔσαις.

ΚΗ.   ἄκουε πᾶς. ἔδοξε τῇ βουλῇ τάδε
τῇ τῶν γυναικῶν· Τιμόκλει' ἐπεστάτει,
Λύσιλλ' ἐγραμμάτευεν, εἶπε Σωστράτη·
ἐκκλησίαν ποιεῖν ἕωθεν τῇ Μέσῃ   375
τῶν Θεσμοφορίων, ᾗ μάλισθ' ἡμῖν σχολή,

---

[a] The curse against those who export contraband of war
(τἀπόρρητα) to the enemy is diverted to women who divulge
the secrets of the festival. See F. 362, E. 442.

Perish that man, himself and all his house ;
But pray the Gods—and Goddesses—to order
To all the women always all things well.

CH.   We also pray,
             And trust it may
Be done as thou premisest,
             And hope that they
             Will win the day
Whose words are best and wisest.
             But they who fain
             Would cheat for gain,
Their solemn oaths forgetting,
             Our ancient laws
             And noble cause
And mystic rites upsetting ; [a]
             Who plot for greed,
             Who call the Mede
With secret invitation,
             I say that these
             The Gods displease,
And wrong the Athenian nation.
             O Zeus most high
             In earth and sky,
All-powerful, all-commanding,
             We pray to Thee,
             Weak women we,
But help us notwithstanding.

CRI.[b] O yes ! O yes !   The Women's Council-Board
    Hath thus enacted (moved by Sostrata,
    President Timocleia, clerk Lysilla),
    To hold a morning Parliament to-day
    When women most have leisure ; to discuss

    [b] The crier uses the terms customary in public proclamations.

163

καὶ χρηματίζειν πρῶτα περὶ Εὐριπίδου,
ὅ τι χρὴ παθεῖν ἐκεῖνον· ἀδικεῖν γὰρ δοκεῖ
ἡμῖν ἁπάσαις. τίς ἀγορεύειν βούλεται;

ΓΥ.Α. ἐγώ.

ΚΗ. περίθου νυν τόνδε πρῶτον πρὶν λέγειν. 380
σίγα, σιώπα, πρόσεχε τὸν νοῦν· χρέμπτεται
  γὰρ ἤδη
ὅπερ ποιοῦσ᾽ οἱ ῥήτορες. μακρὰν ἔοικε λέξειν.

ΓΥ.Α. φιλοτιμίᾳ μὲν οὐδεμιᾷ μὰ τὼ θεώ
λέξουσ᾽ ἀνέστην, ὦ γυναῖκες· ἀλλὰ γὰρ
βαρέως φέρω τάλαινα, πολὺν ἤδη χρόνον 385
προπηλακιζομένας ὁρῶσ᾽ ὑμᾶς ὑπὸ
Εὐριπίδου τοῦ τῆς λαχανοπωλητρίας,
καὶ πολλὰ καὶ παντοῖ᾽ ἀκουούσας κακά.
τί γὰρ οὗτος ἡμᾶς οὐκ ἐπισμῇ τῶν κακῶν;
ποῦ δ᾽ οὐχὶ διαβέβληχ᾽, ὅπουπερ ἐμβραχὺ 390
εἰσὶν θεαταὶ καὶ τραγῳδοὶ καὶ χοροί,
τὰς μυχοτρόπους, τὰς ἀνδρεραστρίας καλῶν,
τὰς οἰνοπότιδας, τὰς προδότιδας, τὰς λάλους,
τὰς οὐδὲν ὑγιές, τὰς μέγ᾽ ἀνδράσιν κακόν·
ὥστ᾽ εὐθὺς εἰσιόντες ἀπὸ τῶν ἰκρίων 395
ὑποβλέπουσ᾽ ἡμᾶς σκοποῦνταί τ᾽ εὐθέως
μὴ μοιχὸς ἔνδον ᾖ τις ἀποκεκρυμμένος.
δρᾶσαι δ᾽ ἔθ᾽ ἡμῖν οὐδὲν ὥσπερ καὶ πρὸ τοῦ
ἔξεστι· τοιαῦθ᾽ οὗτος ἐδίδαξεν κακὰ
τοὺς ἄνδρας ἡμῶν· ὥστ᾽ ἐάν τις νῦν πλέκῃ 400
γυνὴ στέφανον, ἐρᾶν δοκεῖ· κἂν ἐκβάλῃ
σκεῦός τι κατὰ τὴν οἰκίαν πλανωμένη,

---

 a It was customary for speakers to put on a garland before
beginning: Schol.

 b The common gibe against Cleito, his mother. See *F.* 840.

What shall be done about Euripides,
How best to serve him out ; for that he's guilty
We all admit.   Who will address the meeting ?

F.W. I wish to, I.

CRI.   Put on this chaplet first.[a]
Order ! order !   Silence, ladies, if you please.
She's learnt the trick ; she hems and haws ;
                                    she coughs in preparation ;
I know the signs ; my soul divines
                                    a mighty long oration.

F.W. 'Tis not from any feeling of ambition
I rise to address you, ladies, but because
I long have seen, and inly burned to see
The way Euripides insults us all,
The really quite interminable scoffs
This market-gardener's son[b] pours out against us.
I don't believe that there's a single fault
He's not accused us of[c] ; I don't believe
That there's a single theatre or stage,
But there is he, calling us double-dealers,
False, faithless, tippling, mischief-making gossips,
A rotten set, a misery to men.
Well, what's the consequence ?

                                    The men come home[d]
Looking so sour—O, *we* can see them peeping
In every closet, thinking friends are there.
Upon my word we can't do ANYTHING
We used to do ; he has made the men so silly
Suppose I'm hard at work upon a chaplet,
Hey, she's in love with somebody ; suppose
I chance to drop a pitcher on the floor,

[c] Lit. " he does not besmear us with."
[d] From the benches of the theatre.

ἀνὴρ ἐρωτᾷ, " τῷ κατέαγεν ἡ χύτρα;
οὐκ ἔσθ' ὅπως οὐ τῷ Κορινθίῳ ξένῳ."
κάμνει κόρη τις; εὐθὺς ἀδελφὸς λέγει, 405
" τὸ χρῶμα τοῦτό μ' οὐκ ἀρέσκει τῆς κόρης."
εἶεν, γυνή τις ὑποβαλέσθαι βούλεται
ἀποροῦσα παίδων, οὐδὲ τοῦτ' ἔστιν λαθεῖν,
ἄνδρες γὰρ ἤδη παρακάθηνται πλησίον.
πρὸς τοὺς γέροντάς θ', οἳ πρὸ τοῦ τὰς μείρακας 410
ἤγοντο, διαβέβληκεν, ὥστ' οὐδεὶς γέρων
γαμεῖν θέλει γυναῖκα διὰ τοὔπος τοδί,
" δέσποινα γὰρ γέροντι νυμφίῳ γυνή."
εἶτα διὰ τοῦτον ταῖς γυναικωνίτισιν
σφραγῖδας ἐπιβάλλουσιν ἤδη καὶ μοχλούς, 415
τηροῦντες ἡμᾶς, καὶ προσέτι Μολοττικοὺς
τρέφουσι, μορμολυκεῖα τοῖς μοιχοῖς, κύνας.
καὶ ταῦτα μὲν ξυγγνώσθ'. ἃ δ' ἦν ἡμῖν πρὸ τοῦ
αὐταῖς ταμιεῦσαι καὶ προαιρούσαις λαβεῖν
ἄλφιτον, ἔλαιον, οἶνον, οὐδὲ ταῦτ' ἔτι 420
ἔξεστιν. οἱ γὰρ ἄνδρες ἤδη κλειδία
αὐτοὶ φοροῦσι, κρυπτά, κακοηθέστατα,
Λακωνίκ' ἄττα, τρεῖς ἔχοντα γομφίους.
πρὸ τοῦ μὲν οὐκ ἦν ἀλλ' ὑποῖξαι τὴν θύραν
ποιησαμέναισι δακτύλιον τριωβόλου, 425
νῦν δ' οὗτος αὐτοὺς ὡκότριψ Εὐριπίδης
ἐδίδαξε θριπήδεστ' ἔχειν σφραγίδια
ἐξαψαμένους. νῦν οὖν ἐμοὶ τούτῳ δοκεῖ
ὄλεθρόν τιν' ἡμᾶς κυρκανᾶν ἀμωσγέπως,

ᵃ " These are all references to actual plays of Euripides.
This is from the *Stheneboea*, the ' Corinthian friend ' being
Bellerophon ": R. The words are: πεσὸν δέ νιν λέληθεν οὐδὲν
ἐκ χερός, ἀλλ' εὐθὺς αὐδᾷ Τῷ Κορινθίῳ ξένῳ. Lovers were apt

And straightway 'tis, *For whom was that intended?*
I warrant now, for our Corinthian ᵃ friend.
Is a girl ill?   Her brother shakes his head;
The girl's complexion is not to my taste.
Why, if you merely want to hire a baby,
And palm it off as yours, you've got no chance,
They sit beside our very beds, they do.ᵇ
Then there's another thing; the rich old men
Who used to marry us, are grown so shy
We never catch them now; and all because
Euripides declares, the scandal-monger,
An old man weds a tyrant, not a wife.ᶜ
You know, my sisters, how they mew us up,
Guarding our women's rooms with bolts and seals
And fierce Molossian dogs.ᵈ That's all his doing.
We might put up with that; but, O my friends,
Our little special perquisites,ᵉ the corn,
The wine, the oil, gone, gone, all gone for ever.
They've got such keys, our husbands have, such brutes,ᶠ
Laconian-made, with triple rows of teeth.
Then in old times we only had to buy
A farthing ring, and pantry-doors flew open.
But now this wretch Euripides has made them
Wear such worm-eaten perforated seals,
'Tis hopeless now to try it.   Therefore, ladies,
What I propose is that we slay the man,
Either by poison or some other way;

to connect all they did with absent lovers; *cf. L.* 856. The
dropped pot gives a comic turn to this custom.
    ᵇ " She is really making the very charges which cause
such indignation when Mnesilochus makes them " : R.
    ᶜ From the *Phoenix* of Euripides.
    ᵈ To terrify gallants.
    ᵉ Lit. " the things which we would cater for ourselves and
pick out and take."
    ᶠ Lit. " secret and most malignant."

167

ἢ φαρμάκοισιν ἢ μιᾷ γέ τῳ τέχνῃ,　430
ὅπως ἀπολεῖται. ταῦτ᾽ ἐγὼ φανερῶς λέγω,
τὰ δ᾽ ἄλλα μετὰ τῆς γραμματέως συγγράψομαι.

ΧΟ.　οὔποτε ταύτης ἤκουσα
πολυπλοκωτέρας γυναικὸς
οὐδὲ δεινότερον λεγούσης.　435
πάντα γὰρ λέγει δίκαια,
πάσας δ᾽ ἰδέας ἐξετάζει,
πάντα δ᾽ ἐβάστασεν, πυκνῶς τε
ποικίλους λόγους ἀνεῦρεν
εὖ διεζητημένους·
ὥστ᾽ ἂν εἰ λέγοι παρ᾽ αὐτὴν　440
Ξενοκλέης ὁ Καρκίνου, δο-
κεῖν ἂν αὐτόν, ὡς ἐγῷμαι,
πᾶσιν ὑμῖν
ἄντικρυς μηδὲν λέγειν.

ΓΡ.Β. ὀλίγων μὲν ἕνεκ᾽ αὐτὴ παρῆλθον ῥημάτων.
τὰ μὲν γὰρ ἄλλ᾽ αὕτη κατηγόρηκεν εὖ·
ἃ δ᾽ ἐγὼ πέπονθα, ταῦτα λέξαι βούλομαι.　445
ἐμοὶ γὰρ ἀνὴρ ἀπέθανεν μὲν ἐν Κύπρῳ,
παιδάρια πέντε καταλιπών, ἁγὼ μόλις
στεφανηπλοκοῦσ᾽ ἔβοσκον ἐν ταῖς μυρρίναις.
τέως μὲν οὖν ἀλλ᾽ ἡμικάκως ἐβοσκόμην·
νῦν δ᾽ οὗτος ἐν ταῖσιν τραγῳδίαις ποιῶν　450
τοὺς ἄνδρας ἀναπέπεικεν οὐκ εἶναι θεούς·
ὥστ᾽ οὐκέτ᾽ ἐμπολῶμεν οὐδ᾽ εἰς ἥμισυ.
νῦν οὖν ἀπάσαισιν παραινῶ καὶ λέγω
τοῦτον κολάσαι τὸν ἄνδρα πολλῶν οὕνεκα·

---

[a] Lit. " she speaks all fairly, tests all methods, has weighed all, and wisely discovered clever arguments well sought out."

Somehow or other he must die the death.
That's all I'll say in public : I'll write out
A formal motion with the clerkess there.

CH.   Good heavens ! what force and tact combined !
    O, what a many-woven mind !
    A better speech, upon my word,
    I don't believe I ever heard.
    Her thoughts so clean dissected,
    Her words so well selected,
    Such keen discrimination,
    Such power and elevation,
    'Twas really quite a grand, superb,
                    magnificent oration.[a]
    So that if, in opposition,
                  Xenocles came forth to speak,
        Compared with her
        You'd all aver
    All his grandest, happiest efforts
                  are immeasurably weak !

SECOND WOMAN. Ladies, I've only a few words to add.
    I quite agree with the honourable lady
    Who has just sat down : she has spoken well and
        ably.
    But I can tell you what I've borne myself.
    My husband died in Cyprus, leaving me
    Five little chicks to work and labour for.
    I've done my best, and bad's the best, but still
    I've fed them, weaving chaplets for the Gods.[b]
    But now this fellow writes his plays, and says
    There are no Gods ; and so, you may depend,
    My trade is fallen to half ; men won't buy chaplets.
    So then for many reasons he must die ;

    [b] Lit. " in the myrtle-market. Up to this time I maintained
myself, though in a very poor way."

ἄγρια γὰρ ἡμᾶς, ὦ γυναῖκες, δρᾷ κακά,   455
ἅτ' ἐν ἀγρίοισι τοῖς λαχάνοις αὐτὸς τραφείς.
ἀλλ' εἰς ἀγορὰν ἄπειμι· δεῖ γὰρ ἀνδράσιν
πλέξαι στεφάνους συνθηματιαίους εἴκοσιν.

ΧΟ.   ἕτερον αὖ τι λῆμα τοῦτο,
         κομψότερον ἔτ' ἢ τὸ πρότερον,   460
         ἀναπέφηνεν.
       οἷα κατεστωμύλατο
       οὐκ ἄκαιρα, φρένας ἔχουσα
       καὶ πολύπλοκον αὖ νόημ', οὐδ'
       ἀσύνετ', ἀλλὰ πιθανὰ πάντα.
         δεῖ δὲ ταύτης
       τῆς ὕβρεως ἡμῖν τὸν ἄνδρα
       περιφανῶς δοῦναι δίκην.   465

ΜΝ.   τὸ μέν, ὦ γυναῖκες, ὀξυθυμεῖσθαι σφόδρα
         Εὐριπίδῃ, τοιαῦτ' ἀκουούσας κακά,
         οὐ θαυμάσιόν ἐστ', οὐδ' ἐπιζεῖν τὴν χολήν.
         καὐτὴ γὰρ ἔγωγ', οὕτως ὀναίμην τῶν τέκνων,   470
         μισῶ τὸν ἄνδρ' ἐκεῖνον, εἰ μὴ μαίνομαι.
         ὅμως δ' ἐν ἀλλήλαισι χρὴ δοῦναι λόγον·
         αὐταὶ γάρ ἐσμεν, κοὐδεμί' ἔκφορος λόγου.
         τί ταῦτ' ἔχουσαι 'κεῖνον αἰτιώμεθα
         βαρέως τε φέρομεν, εἰ δύ' ἡμῶν ἢ τρία   475
         κακὰ ξυνειδὼς εἶπε, δρώσας μυρία;
         ἐγὼ γὰρ αὐτὴ πρῶτον, ἵνα μὴ ἄλλην λέγω,
         ξύνοιδ' ἐμαυτῇ πολλὰ δείν'· ἐκεῖνο δ' οὖν

---

[a] Lit. "he does savage injuries, as one reared amidst his mother's wild potherbs."

[b] Lit. "how neatly she has spoken, all to the point, having wit and a subtle mind, nothing foolish, but all persuasive."

[c] *The motion for putting Euripides to death having, so*

The man is bitterer than his mother's potherbs.[a]
I leave my cause with you, my sisters : I
Am called away on urgent private business,
An order, just received, for twenty chaplets.

CH.　　　　Better and better still.
　　A subtler intellect, a daintier skill.
　　　　Wise are her words, and few ;
　　　　　Well timed and spoken too.
　　A many-woven mind she too has got, I find.[b]
　　　　　And he must clearly,
　　This rascal man, be punished most severely.[c]

MN. Mrs. Speaker and ladies,
I'm not surprised, of course I'm not surprised,
To find you all so angry and aggrieved
At what Euripides has said against us.
For I myself—or slay my babies else—[d]
Hate him like poison, to be sure I do,[e]
He's most provoking, I admit he is.
But now we're all alone, there's no reporter,
All among friends, why not be fair and candid ? [f]
Grant that the man has really found us out,
And told a thing or two, sure they're all TRUE,
And there's a many thousand still behind.
For I myself, to mention no one else,
Could tell a thousand plaguy tricks I've played
On my poor husband ; I'll just mention one.

*to say, been proposed and seconded, Mnesilochus rises to
speak in opposition.*
　　[d] Lit. "so may I have joy of my children."
　　[e] Lit. " I were mad else."
　　[f] Lit. " discuss the matter together," 473 : " Why being in
this case do we find fault with him and feel annoyance if he
has found out and told two or three things, when we have
done thousands ? "

171

δεινότατον, ὅτε νύμφη μὲν ἦν τρεῖς ἡμέρας,
ὁ δ' ἀνὴρ παρ' ἐμοὶ 'καθεῦδεν· ἦν δ' ἐμοὶ φίλος,
ὅσπερ με διεκόρευσεν οὖσαν ἑπτέτιν.   480
οὗτος πόθῳ μου 'κνυεν ἐλθὼν τὴν θύραν·
κᾆτ' εὐθὺς ἔγνων· εἶτα καταβαίνω λάθρᾳ.
ὁ δ' ἀνὴρ ἐρωτᾷ " ποῖ σὺ καταβαίνεις; " " ὅποι;
στρόφος μ' ἔχει τὴν γαστέρ', ὦνερ, κὠδύνη·
ἐς τὸν κοπρῶν' οὖν ἔρχομαι." " βάδιζέ νυν."   485
κᾆθ' ὁ μὲν ἔτριβε κεδρίδας, ἄννηθον, σφάκον·
ἐγὼ δὲ καταχέασα τοῦ στροφέως ὕδωρ
ἐξῆλθον ὡς τὸν μοιχόν· εἶτ' ἠρειδόμην
παρὰ τὸν Ἀγυιᾶ, κύβδ' ἐχομένη τῆς δάφνης.
ταῦτ' οὐδεπώποτ' εἶφ', ὁρᾶτ', Εὐριπίδης·   490
οὐδ' ὡς ὑπὸ τῶν δούλων τε κὠρεωκόμων
σποδούμεθ', ἢν μὴ 'χωμεν ἕτερον, οὐ λέγει·
οὐδ' ὡς ὅταν μάλισθ' ὑπό του ληκώμεθα
τὴν νύχθ', ἕωθεν σκόροδα διαμασώμεθα,
ἵν' ὀσφρόμενος ἀνὴρ ἀπὸ τείχους εἰσιὼν   495
μηδὲν κακὸν δρᾶν ὑποτοπῆται. ταῦθ', ὁρᾷς,
οὐπώποτ' εἶπεν. εἰ δὲ Φαίδραν λοιδορεῖ,
ἡμῖν τί τοῦτ' ἔστ'; οὐδ' ἐκεῖν' εἴρηκέ πω,
ὡς ἡ γυνὴ δεικνῦσα τἀνδρὶ τοὔγκυκλον
οἷόν γ' ὑπ' αὐγάς ἐστιν, ἐγκεκαλυμμένον   500
τὸν μοιχὸν ἐξέπεμψεν, οὐκ εἴρηκέ πω.
ἑτέραν δ' ἐγᾦδ' ἣ 'φασκεν ὠδίνειν γυνὴ
δέχ' ἡμέρας, ἕως ἐπρίατο παιδίον·
ὁ δ' ἀνὴρ περιήρχετ' ὠκυτόκι' ὠνούμενος·

---

[a] Septuennem me constupraverat.
[b] Inclinato corpore iuxta signum Apollinis, prehensaque
lauro, subagitata sum.

We'd been but three days married ; I'm abed,
Husband asleep beside me ; when my lover
(I'd been familiar with him from a child) *a*
Came softly scratching at the outer door.
I hear ; I know " the little clinking sound,"
And rise up stealthily, to creep downstairs.
Where go you, pray ? says husband. *Where !* say I,
I've such a dreadful pain in my inside
I must go down this instant. Go, says he.
He pounds his anise, juniper, and sage,
To still my pains : *I* seize the water-jug,
And wet the hinge, to still its creaking noise,
Then open, and go out : and I and lover
Meet by Aguieus and his laurel-shade,
Billing and cooing to our hearts' content.*b*
(*With vivacity*) Euripides has never found out that.
Nor how a wife contrived to smuggle out
Her frightened lover, holding up her shawl
To the sun's rays for husband to admire.*c*
Nor how we grant our favours to bargees
And muleteers, if no one else we've got.
Nor how, arising from a night's debauch,
We chew our garlic, that our husbands, coming
Back from the walls at daybreak, may suspect
Nothing amiss at home. Then what's the odds
If he does rail at Phaedra ? Let him rail.
What's that to us ? Let him rail on, say I.
Phaedra indeed ! He might come nearer home.
I knew a woman, I won't mention names,
Remained ten days in childbirth. Why, do you think ?
Because she couldn't buy a baby sooner.
Her husband runs to every medicine-man

---

a Lines 499-501 are here anticipated.

τὸ δ' εἰσέφερε γραῦς ἐν χύτρᾳ τὸ παιδίον,   505
ἵνα μὴ βοώη, κηρίῳ βεβυσμένον·
εἶθ' ὡς ἔνευσεν ἡ φέρουσ', εὐθὺς βοᾷ,
" ἄπελθ' ἄπελθ', ἤδη γὰρ ὦνέρ μοι δοκῶ
τέξειν·" τὸ γὰρ ἦτρον τῆς χύτρας ἐλάκτισεν.
χὠ μὲν γεγηθὼς ἔτρεχεν, ἡ δ' ἐξέσπασεν   510
ἐκ τοῦ στόματος τοῦ παιδίου, τὸ δ' ἀνέκραγεν.
εἶθ' ἡ μιαρὰ γραῦς, ἣ 'φερεν τὸ παιδίον,
θεῖ μειδιῶσα πρὸς τὸν ἄνδρα καὶ λέγει,
" λέων λέων σοι γέγονεν, αὐτέκμαγμα σόν,
τά τ' ἄλλ' ἁπαξάπαντα καὶ τὸ πόσθιον   515
τῷ σῷ προσόμοιον, στρεβλὸν ὥσπερ κύτταρον."
ταῦτ' οὐ ποιοῦμεν τὰ κακά; νὴ τὴν Ἄρτεμιν
ἡμεῖς γε. κᾆτ' Εὐριπίδῃ θυμούμεθα,
οὐδὲν παθοῦσαι μεῖζον ἢ δεδράκαμεν;

ΧΟ.   τουτὶ μέντοι θαυμαστόν,   520
       ὁπόθεν εὑρέθη τὸ χρῆμα,
       χἥτις ἐξέθρεψε χώρα
       τήνδε τὴν θρασεῖαν οὕτω.
       τάδε γὰρ εἰπεῖν τὴν πανοῦργον
       κατὰ τὸ φανερὸν ὧδ' ἀναιδῶς   525
       οὐκ ἂν ᾠόμην ἐν ἡμῖν
        οὐδὲ τολμῆσαί ποτ' ἄν.
       ἀλλ' ἅπαν γένοιτ' ἂν ἤδη·
       τὴν παροιμίαν δ' ἐπαινῶ

ᵃ ὠκυτόκια ὠνούμενος, " buying helps to labour," amulets
and the like, or potions.
ᵇ Lit. " in a crock, with honeycomb in its mouth."
ᶜ The Greek adds: " for it (the child) kicked at the lining

In dreadful agitation ; *a* while he's out,
They bring a little baby in a basket,*b*
Bunging its mouth up that it mayn't cry out,
And stow it safe away till he comes home.
Then at a given sigh she feebly says,
*My time is come : please, husband, go away.*c
He goes ; they open basket ; *d* baby cries.
O, what delight, surprise, congratulations !
The man runs in ; the nurse comes running out,
(The same that brought the baby in the basket),
A prodigy ! a Lion ! such a boy !
Your form, your features : just the same expression :
Your very image : e *lucky, lucky man !*
Don't we do this ?   By Artemis, we do.
Then wherefore rail we at Euripides ?
We're not one bit more sinned against than sinning.*f*

CH. What a monstrous, strange proceeding !
Whence, I wonder, comes her breeding ?
From what country shall we seek her,
Such a bold, audacious speaker ?
That a woman so should wrong us,
Here among us, here among us,
I could never have believed it ;
         such a thing was never known.
But what *may* be, no man knoweth,
And the wise old proverb showeth,

of the crock," χύτρας being comically substituted for μήτρας.
ἦτρον is the membrane of the womb.
   d Lit. " she pulls out the plug of honeycomb."
   e Expressa tua imago, et cum cetera omnia, tum etiam
mentula tuae similis, tortuosa, instar nucamenti pinei.
   f From the *Telephus* of Euripides : εἶτα δὴ θυμούμεθα,
παθόντες οὐδὲν μᾶλλον ἢ δεδρακότες.

175

τὴν παλαιάν· ὑπὸ λίθῳ γὰρ
παντί που χρὴ
μὴ δάκῃ ῥήτωρ ἀθρεῖν.　　　　　　530

ἀλλ' οὐ γάρ ἐστι τῶν ἀναισχύντων φύσει γυναικῶν
οὐδὲν κάκιον εἰς ἅπαντα πλὴν ἄρ' εἰ γυναῖκες.

ΓΥ.Α. οὔ τοι μὰ τὴν Ἄγραυλον, ὦ γυναῖκες, εὖ
　　　　φρονεῖτε,
　　　ἀλλ' ἢ πεφάρμαχθ', ἢ κακόν τι μέγα πεπόνθατ'
　　　　ἄλλο,
　　　ταύτην ἐῶσαι τὴν φθόρον τοιαῦτα περιυβρίζειν　535
　　　ἡμᾶς ἁπάσας. εἰ μὲν οὖν τις ἔστιν· εἰ δὲ μή,
　　　　ἡμεῖς
　　　αὐταί γε καὶ τὰ δουλάρια τέφραν ποθὲν
　　　　λαβοῦσαι
　　　ταύτης ἀποψιλώσομεν τὸν χοῖρον, ἵνα διδαχθῇ
　　　γυνὴ γυναῖκας οὖσα μὴ κακῶς λέγειν τὸ λοιπόν.

ΜΝ. μὴ δῆτα τόν γε χοῖρον ὦ γυναῖκες. εἰ γὰρ οὔσης　540
　　　παρρησίας κἀξὸν λέγειν ὅσαι πάρεσμεν ἀσταί,
　　　εἶτ' εἶπον ἁγίγνωσκον ὑπὲρ Εὐριπίδου δίκαια,
　　　διὰ τοῦτο τιλλομένην με δεῖ δοῦναι δίκην ὑφ'
　　　　ὑμῶν;

ΓΥ.Α. οὐ γάρ σε δεῖ δοῦναι δίκην; ἥτις μόνη
　　　　τέτληκας
　　　ὑπὲρ ἀνδρὸς ἀντειπεῖν, ὃς ἡμᾶς πολλὰ κακὰ
　　　　δέδρακεν　　　　　　　　　　　　　　　545
　　　ἐπίτηδες εὑρίσκων λόγους, ὅπου γυνὴ πονηρὰ
　　　ἐγένετο, Μελανίππας ποιῶν Φαίδρας τε·
　　　Πηνελόπην δὲ

---

[a] The proverb is ὑπὸ παντὶ λίθῳ σκορπίος.
[b] Eur. *Melanippe Desmotis*, τῆς μὲν κακῆς κάκιον οὐδὲν γίγνεται | γυναικός, with the final words as a surprise.

That perchance a poisonous sophist
               lurketh under every stone.*

O, nothing, nothing in the world
               so hateful you will find
As shameless women, save of course
               the rest of womankind.*b*

F.W. What can possess us, sisters mine ?
               I vow by old Agraulus,
We're all bewitched, or else have had
               some strange mischance befall us,
To let this shameless hussy tell
               her shameful, bold, improper
Unpleasant tales, and we not make
               the least attempt to stop her.
If anyone assist me, good ; if not, alone we'll try,
We'll strip and whip her well, we will,
               my serving-maids and I.*c*

MN. Not strip me, gentle ladies ; sure
               I heard the proclamation,
That every freeborn woman now
               might make a free oration ;
And if I spoke unpleasant truths
               on this your invitation,
Is that a reason why I now
               should suffer castigation ?

F.W. It is, indeed : how dare you plead
               for him who always chooses
Such odious subjects for his plays,
               on purpose to abuse us ?
Phaedras and Melanippes too :
               but ne'er a drama made he

---

c Cinere alicunde sumpto, cunnum eius depilabimus, **ut** discat mulier mulieribus non male dicere.

οὐπώποτ' ἐποίησ', ὅτι γυνὴ σώφρων ἔδοξεν
   εἶναι.

ΜΝ. ἐγὼ γὰρ οἶδα ταἴτιον. μίαν γὰρ οὐκ ἂν εἴποις
   τῶν νῦν γυναικῶν Πηνελόπην, Φαίδρας δ'
   ἀπαξαπάσας.   550

ΓΥ.Α. ἀκούετ', ὦ γυναῖκες, οἷ' εἴρηκεν ἡ πανοῦργος
   ἡμᾶς ἁπάσας αὖθις αὖ.

ΜΝ.   καὶ νὴ Δί' οὐδέπω γε
   εἴρηχ' ὅσα ξύνοιδ'· ἐπεὶ βούλεσθε πλεῖον' εἴπω;

ΓΥ.Α. ἀλλ' οὐκ ἂν ἔτ' ἔχοις· ὅσα γὰρ ᾔδεις ἐξέχεας
   ἅπαντα.

ΜΝ. μὰ Δί' οὐδέπω τὴν μυριοστὴν μοῖραν ὧν
   ποιοῦμεν.   555
   ἐπεὶ τάδ' οὐκ εἴρηχ', ὁρᾷς, ὡς στλεγγίδας
   λαβοῦσαι
   ἔπειτα σιφωνίζομεν τὸν σῖτον.

ΓΥ.Α.   ἐπιτριβείης.

ΜΝ. ὥς τ' αὖ τὰ κρέ' ἐξ Ἀπατουρίων ταῖς μαστρο-
   ποῖς διδοῦσαι
   ἔπειτα τὴν γαλῆν φαμεν—

ΓΥ.Α.   τάλαιν' ἐγώ· φλυαρεῖς.

ΜΝ. οὐδ' ὡς τὸν ἄνδρα τῷ πελέκει γυνὴ κατ-
   εσπόδησεν,   560
   οὐκ εἶπον· οὐδ' ὡς φαρμάκοις ἑτέρα τὸν ἄνδρ'
   ἔμηνεν,
   οὐδ' ὡς ὑπὸ τῇ πυέλῳ κατώρυξέν ποτ'—

ΓΥ.Α.   ἐξόλοιο.

ΜΝ. Ἀχαρνικὴ τὸν πατέρα.

ΓΥ.Α.   ταυτὶ δῆτ' ἀνέκτ' ἀκούειν;

---

^a They use the strigil as a scoop to get out the corn, which
pours down like a stream of liquid.

About the good Penelope,
                            or such-like virtuous lady.
MN. The cause I know ; the cause I'll show :
                            you won't discover any
Penelope alive to-day, but Phaedras very many.
F.W. You will ? you dare ? how *can* we bear
                            to hear such things repeated,
Such horrid, dreadful, odious things ?
MN.   O, I've not near completed
The things I know ; I'll give the whole :
                            I'm not disposed to grudge it.
F.W. You can't, I vow ; you've emptied now
                            your whole disgusting budget.
MN. No, not one thousandth part I've told :
                            not even how we take
The scraper from the bathing-room,
                            and down the corn we rake,[a]
And push it in, and tap the bin.
F.W.   Confound you and your slanders !
MN. Nor how the Apaturian meat [b]
                            we steal to give our panders,
And then declare the cat was there.
F W.   You nasty telltale you !
MN. Nor how with deadly axe a wife
                            her lord and master slew,
Another drove her husband mad
                            with poisonous drugs fallacious,
Nor how beneath the reservoir
                            the Acharnian girl—
F.W.   Good gracious !
MN. Buried her father out of sight.
F.W.   Now really this won't do.

---

[b] The Apaturia, the great festival of the clans, began with
a banquet on the first evening.

ΜΝ. οὐδ' ὡς σὺ τῆς δούλης τεκούσης ἄρρεν εἶτα σαυτῇ
τοῦθ' ὑπεβάλου, τὸ σὸν δὲ θυγάτριον παρῆκας
αὐτῇ. 565

ΓΥ.Α. οὔ τοι μὰ τὼ θεὼ σὺ καταπροίξει λέγουσα
ταυτί,
ἀλλ' ἐκποκιῶ σου τὰς ποκάδας.

ΜΝ. οὐ δὴ μὰ Δία σύ γ' ἅψει.

ΓΥ.Α. καὶ μὴν ἰδού.

ΜΝ. καὶ μὴν ἰδού.

ΓΥ.Α. λαβὲ θοἰμάτιον, Φιλίστη.

ΜΝ. πρόσθες μόνον, κἀγώ σε νὴ τὴν Ἄρτεμιν—

ΓΥ.Α. τί δράσεις;

ΜΝ. τὸν σησαμοῦνθ' ὃν κατέφαγες, τοῦτον χεσεῖν
ποιήσω. 570

ΧΟ. παύσασθε λοιδορούμεναι· καὶ γὰρ γυνή τις ἡμῖν
ἐσπουδακυῖα προστρέχει. πρὶν οὖν ὁμοῦ γενέσθαι,
σιγᾶθ', ἵν' αὐτῆς κοσμίως πυθώμεθ' ἅττα λέξει.

ΚΛΕΙΣΘΕΝΗΣ.φίλαι γυναῖκες, ξυγγενεῖς τοὐμοῦ τρόπου,
ὅτι μὲν φίλος εἴμ' ὑμῖν, ἐπίδηλος ταῖς γνάθοις· 575
γυναικομανῶ γάρ, προξενῶ θ' ὑμῶν ἀεί.
καὶ νῦν ἀκούσας πρᾶγμα περὶ ὑμῶν μέγα
ὀλίγῳ τι πρότερον κατ' ἀγορὰν λαλούμενον,
ἥκω φράσων τοῦτ' ἀγγελῶν θ' ὑμῖν, ἵνα
σκοπῆτε καὶ τηρῆτε καὶ μὴ προσπέσῃ 580
ὑμῖν ἀφράκτοις πρᾶγμα δεινὸν καὶ μέγα.

ΧΟ. τί δ' ἔστιν, ὦ παῖ; παῖδα γάρ σ' εἰκὸς καλεῖν,
ἕως ἂν οὕτως τὰς γνάθους ψιλὰς ἔχῃς.

---

[a] Demeter and Persephone: so in 594.

[b] F.W. Quid facies?

ΜΝ. Efficiam ut caces sesaminam placentam, quam comedisti (in spite of the Fast).

MN. Nor how when late your servant bare
                              a child as well as you,
    You took her boy, and in his stead
                              your puling girl you gave her.
F.W. O, by the Two,[a] this jade shall rue
                              her insolent behaviour.
    I'll comb your fleece, you saucy minx.

MN.   By Zeus, you had best begin it.

F.W. Come on !

MN.   Come on !

F.W.   You will ? you will ?

    (*Flinging her upper mantle to Philista*)
                Hold this, my dear, a minute.

MN. Stand off, or else, by Artemis,
                              I'll give you such a strumming— [b]

CH. For pity's sake, be silent there :
                              I see a woman coming,
    Who looks as if she'd news to tell.
                              Now prithee both be quiet
    And let us hear the tale she brings,
                              without this awful riot.[c]

CLEISTHENES. Dear ladies, I am one with you in heart ;
    My cheeks, unfledged, bear witness to my love,
    I am your patron, aye, and devotee.
    And now, for lately in the market-place
    I heard a rumour touching you and yours,
    I come to warn and put you on your guard,
    Lest this great danger take you unawares.

CH. What now, my child ? for we may call thee child,
    So soft, and smooth, and downy are thy cheeks.

---

[c] The supposed woman turns out to be the notorious Cleisthenes, of whom we have already heard. The reader must imagine the feelings of Mnesilochus during the ensuing dialogue.

ARISTOPHANES

ΚΛ. Εὐριπίδην φάσ' ἄνδρα κηδεστήν τινα
    αὑτοῦ γέροντα δεῦρ' ἀναπέμψαι τήμερον.   585

ΧΟ. πρὸς ποῖον ἔργον ἢ τίνος γνώμης χάριν;

ΚΛ. ἵν' ἄττα βουλεύοισθε καὶ μέλλοιτε δρᾶν,
    ἐκεῖνος εἴη τῶν λόγων κατάσκοπος.

ΧΟ. καὶ πῶς λέληθεν ἐν γυναιξὶν ὢν ἀνήρ;

ΚΛ. ἀφεῦσεν αὐτὸν κἀπέτιλ' Εὐριπίδης,   590
    καὶ τἄλλ' ἅπανθ' ὥσπερ γυναῖκ' ἐσκεύασεν.

ΜΝ. πείθεσθε τούτῳ ταῦτα; τίς δ' οὕτως ἀνὴρ
    ἠλίθιος, ὅστις τιλλόμενος ἠνείχετ' ἄν;
    οὐκ οἴομαι 'γωγ', ὦ πολυτιμήτω θεώ.

ΚΛ. ληρεῖς· ἐγὼ γὰρ οὐκ ἂν ἦλθον ἀγγελῶν,   595
    εἰ μὴ 'πεπύσμην ταῦτα τῶν σάφ' εἰδότων.

ΧΟ. τὸ πρᾶγμα τουτὶ δεινὸν εἰσαγγέλλεται.
    ἀλλ', ὦ γυναῖκες, οὐκ ἐλινύειν ἐχρῆν,
    ἀλλὰ σκοπεῖν τὸν ἄνδρα καὶ ζητεῖν ὅπου
    λέληθεν ἡμᾶς κρυπτὸς ἐγκαθήμενος.   600
    καὶ σὺ ξυνέξευρ' αὐτόν, ὡς ἂν τὴν χάριν
    ταύτην τε κἀκείνην ἔχῃς, ὦ πρόξενε.

ΚΛ. φέρ' ἴδω· τίς εἶ πρώτη σύ;

ΜΝ.   ποῖ τις τρέψεται;

ΚΛ. ζητητέαι γάρ ἐστε.

ΜΝ.   κακοδαίμων ἐγώ.

ΓΥ.Α. ἔμ' ἥτις εἴμ' ἤρου; Κλεωνύμου γυνή.   605

ΚΛ. γιγνώσκεθ' ὑμεῖς ἥτις ἔσθ' ἥδ' ἡ γυνή;

ΧΟ. γιγνώσκομεν δῆτ'. ἀλλὰ τὰς ἄλλας ἄθρει.

ΚΛ. ἡδὶ δὲ δὴ τίς ἐστιν ἡ τὸ παιδίον
    ἔχουσα ;

ΓΥ.Α.   τίτθη νὴ Δί' ἐμή.

ΜΝ.   διοίχομαι.

THE THESMOPHORIAZUSAE, 584-609

CL. Euripides, they say, has sent a cousin,
    A bad old man, amongst you here to-day.
CH. O, why and wherefore, and with what design ?
CL. To be a spy, a horrid, treacherous spy,
    A spy on all your purposes and plans.
CH. O, how should he be here, and we not know it ?
CL. Euripides has tweezered him, and singed him,
    And dressed him up, disguised in women's clothes.
MN. (*stamping about with a lively recollection of his recent
    sufferings*) I don't believe it ; not one word of it ;
    No man would let himself be tweezered so.
    Ye Goddesses, I don't believe there's one.
CL. Nonsense : I never should have come here else,
    I had it on the best authority.
CH. This is a most important piece of news.
    We'll take immediate steps to clear this up.
    We'll search him out : we'll find his lurking-place.
    Zounds, if we catch him ! r-r-r ! the rascal man.
    Will you, kind gentleman, assist the search ?
    Give us fresh cause to thank you, patron mine.
CL. (*to F.W.*) Well, who are you ?
MN. (*aside*)   Wherever can I flee ?
CL. I'll find him, trust me.[a]
MN. (*aside*)   Here's a precious scrape !
F.W. Who ? I ?
CL.   Yes, you.
F.W.   Cleonymus's wife.
CL. Do you know her, ladies ? Is she speaking truth ?
CH. O yes, we know her : pass to someone else.
CL. Who's this young person with the baby here ?
F.W. O, she's my nursemaid.
MN. (*aside*)   Here he comes ; I'm done for.

    [a] Lit. " you must all be searched."

ΚΛ. αὕτη σὺ ποῖ στρέφει; μέν' αὐτοῦ. τί τὸ κακόν; 610
ΜΝ. ἔασον οὐρῆσαί μ'.
ΚΛ.   ἀναίσχυντός τις εἶ.
    σὺ δ' οὖν ποίει τοῦτ'· ἀναμενῶ γὰρ ἐνθάδε.
ΧΟ. ἀνάμενε δῆτα καὶ σκόπει γ' αὐτὴν σφόδρα·
    μόνην γὰρ αὐτήν, ὦνερ, οὐ γιγνώσκομεν.
ΚΛ. πολύν γε χρόνον οὐρεῖς σύ.
ΜΝ.   νὴ Δί', ὦ μέλε·   615
    στραγγουριῶ γάρ· ἐχθὲς ἔφαγον κάρδαμα.
ΚΛ. τί καρδαμίζεις; οὐ βαδιεῖ δεῦρ' ὡς ἐμέ;
ΜΝ. τί δῆτά μ' ἕλκεις ἀσθενοῦσαν;
ΚΛ.   εἰπέ μοι,
    τίς ἔστ' ἀνήρ σοι;
ΜΝ.   τὸν ἐμὸν ἄνδρα πυνθάνει;
    τὸν δεῖνα γιγνώσκεις, τὸν ἐκ Κοθωκιδῶν;   620
ΚΛ. τὸν δεῖνα; ποῖον; ἔσθ' ὁ δεῖν', ὃς καί ποτε—
ΜΝ. τὸν δεῖνα τὸν τοῦ δεῖνα.
ΚΛ.   λῆρεῖν μοι δοκεῖς.
    ἀνῆλθες ἤδη δεῦρο πρότερον;
ΜΝ.   νὴ Δία
    ὅσ' ἔτη γε.
ΚΛ.   καὶ τίς σοῦστὶ συσκηνήτρια;
ΜΝ. ἡ δεῖν' ἔμοιγ'. οἴμοι τάλας.
ΚΛ.   οὐδὲν λέγεις.   625
ΓΥ.Α. ἄπελθ'. ἐγὼ γὰρ βασανιῶ ταύτην καλῶς
    ἐκ τῶν ἱερῶν τῶν πέρυσι· σὺ δ' ἀπόστηθί μοι,
    ἵνα μὴ 'πακούσῃς ὢν ἀνήρ. σὺ δ' εἰπέ μοι
    ὅ τι πρῶτον ἡμῖν τῶν ἱερῶν ἐδείκνυτο.
ΜΝ. φέρ' ἴδω, τί μέντοι πρῶτον ἦν; ἐπίνομεν.   630
ΓΥ.Α. τί δαὶ μετὰ τοῦτο δεύτερον;

---

[a] 611 Sine me mingere.—Impudens es tu quidem: tu

184

CL. Hey! where's she off to? Stop! Why, what
the mischief! [a]

CH. (*aside to Cl.*) Yes, sift her well; discover who she is.
We know the others, but we don't know her.

CL. Come, come, no shuffling, madam, turn this way.

MN. (*fretfully*) Don't pull me, sir, I'm poorly.

CL.   Please to tell me
Your husband's name.

MN.   My husband's name? my husband's?
Why What-d'ye-call-him from Cothocidae.

CL. Eh, what? (*Considers*)
           There was a What-d'ye-call-him once—

MN. He's Who-d'ye-call-it's son.

CL.   You're trifling with me.
Have you been here before?

MN.   O, bless you, yes.
Why, every year.

CL.   And with what tent-companion?

MN. With What's-her-name.

CL.   This is sheer idling, woman.

F.W. (*to Cl.*) Step back, sir, please, and let me question
her
On last year's rites; a little further, please;
No *man* must listen now.
               (*To Mn.*) Now, stranger, tell me
What first we practised on that holy day.

MN. Bless me, what was it? first? why, first we—
drank.

F.W. Right; what was second?

---

autem rem tuam age, ego hic opperiar . . . 615 Heus tu, diu
mingis.—At enim stranguria laboro: heri edi medicinam.
—Quid de medicina garris?

MN.   προὐπίνομεν.

ΓΥ.Α. ταυτὶ μὲν ἤκουσάς τινος· τί δ' αὖ τρίτον;

MN. σκάφιον Ξένυλλ' ᾔτησεν· οὐ γὰρ ἦν ἀμίς.

ΓΥ.Α. οὐδὲν λέγεις. δεῦρ' ἐλθέ, δεῦρ', ὦ Κλείσθενες·
       ὅδ' ἐστὶν ἀνὴρ ὃν λέγεις.

ΚΛ.   τί οὖν ποιῶ;   635

ΓΥ.Α. ἀπόδυσον αὐτόν· οὐδὲν ὑγιὲς γὰρ λέγει.

MN. κἄπειτ' ἀποδύσετ' ἐννέα παίδων μητέρα;

ΚΛ. χάλα ταχέως τὸ στρόφιον, ὦναίσχυντε σύ.

ΓΥ.Α. ὡς καὶ στιβαρά τις φαίνεται καὶ καρτερά·
       καὶ νὴ Δία τιτθούς γ' ὥσπερ ἡμεῖς οὐκ ἔχει. 640

MN. στερίφη γάρ εἰμι κοὐκ ἐκύησα πώποτε.

ΓΥ.Α. νῦν· τότε δὲ μήτηρ ἦσθα παίδων ἐννέα.

ΚΛ. ἀνίστασ' ὀρθός. ποῖ τὸ πέος ὠθεῖς κάτω;

ΓΥ.Α. τοδὶ διέκυψε καὶ μάλ' εὔχρων, ὦ τάλαν.

ΚΛ. καὶ ποῦ 'στιν;

ΓΥ.Α.   αὖθις ἐς τὸ πρόσθεν οἴχεται.   645

ΚΛ. οὐκ ἐνγεταυθί.

ΓΥ.Α.   μὴ ἀλλὰ δεῦρ' ἥκει πάλιν.

ΚΛ. ἰσθμόν τιν' ἔχεις, ὦνθρωπ'· ἄνω τε καὶ κάτω
       τὸ πέος διέλκεις πυκνότερον Κορινθίων.

ΓΥ.Α. ὦ μιαρὸς οὗτος· ταῦτ' ἄρ' ὑπὲρ Εὐριπίδου
       ἡμῖν ἐλοιδορεῖτο.

MN.   κακοδαίμων ἐγώ,   650
       εἰς οἷ' ἐμαυτὸν εἰσεκύλισα πράγματα.

ΓΥ.Α. ἄγε δὴ τί δρῶμεν;

ΚΛ.   τουτονὶ φυλάττετε
       καλῶς, ὅπως μὴ διαφυγὼν οἰχήσεται·
       ἐγὼ δὲ ταῦτα τοῖς πρυτάνεσιν ἀγγελῶ.

---

[a] Scaphium petiit Xenylla, matula enim non aderat.

[b] *Mnesilochus is seized, carried before a jury of matrons, and pronounced a MAN! A general uproar ensues.*

MN.   Second ?   Drank again.

F.W. Somebody's told you this.   But what was third ?

MN. Well, third, Xenylla had a drop too much.[a]

F.W. Ah, that won't do.   Here, Cleisthenes, approach.
       This is the MAN for certain.

CL.   Bring him up.[b]

F.W.[c] Strip off his clothes ! for there's no truth in him.

MN. What ! strip the mother of nine little ones ?

CL. Loosen that belt, look sharp, you shameless thing.

F.W. She does appear a stout and sturdy one :
       Upon my word, she has no breasts like ours.

MN. Because I'm barren, never had a child.

F.W. Yes, *now* ; but *then* you had nine little ones !

CL. Stand up and show yourself.   See ! he's a man !

F.W. O, this is why you mocked and jeered us so !
       And dared defend Euripides like that !
       O, villain, villain.   .   .

MN.   Miserable me !
       I've put my foot in it, and no mistake.

F.W. What shall we do with him ?

CL.   Surround him here,
       And watch him shrewdly that he 'scape you not.
       I'll go at once and summon the police.[d]

                              (*Cleisthenes goes out.*)

---

[c] 635-648 are not in R.'s translation. 643-648 are literally :
   CL. Sta erectus.   Quo phallum trudis deorsum ?
   MU. I. Ecce subit ille quidem, nec mali coloris, eheu.
   CL. Ubi est ? MU. I. Rursus abit in partem anteriorem.
   CL. Non hic quidem est. MU. I. At huc est reversus.
   CL. Habes isthmum tu quidem, trahisque phallum huc
illuc frequentius quam Corinthii.

There was a track (the διολκός) across the Corinthian
isthmus, by which ships were hauled to and fro on trolleys
(ὁλκοί) ; hence διέλκεις here.

[d] It was the duty of the Prytanes, with the Scythian police,
to keep order in the Assembly. See *A*. 54, *K*. 665.

ΧΟ. ἡμᾶς τοίνυν μετὰ τοῦτ᾽ ἤδη τὰς λαμπάδας
    ἀψαμένας χρὴ   655
ξυζωσαμένας εὖ κἀνδρείως τῶν θ᾽ ἱματίων
    ἀποδύσας
ζητεῖν, εἴ που κάλλος τις ἀνὴρ ἐσελήλυθε, καὶ
    περιθρέξαι
τὴν πύκνα πᾶσαν καὶ τὰς σκηνὰς καὶ τὰς
    διόδους διαθρῆσαι.

εἶα δὴ πρώτιστα μὲν χρὴ κοῦφον ἐξορμᾶν πόδα
καὶ διασκοπεῖν σιωπῇ πανταχῇ· μόνον δὲ χρὴ   660
μὴ βραδύνειν, ὡς ὁ καιρός ἐστι μὴ μέλλειν ἔτι,
ἀλλὰ τὴν πρώτην τρέχειν χρῆν ὡς τάχιστ᾽ ἤδη
    κύκλῳ.
εἶά νυν ἴχνευε καὶ μάτευε πάντ᾽ [ἐρρωμένως,]
εἴ τις ἐν τόποις ἑδραῖος ἄλλος αὖ λέληθεν ὤν.
    πανταχῇ δὲ ῥῖψον ὄμμα,   665
    καὶ τὰ τῇδε, καὶ τὰ δεῦρο,
    πάντ᾽ ἀνασκόπει καλῶς.

ἢν γάρ με λάθῃ δράσας ἀνόσια,   [στρ.
δώσει τε δίκην, καὶ πρὸς τούτῳ
    τοῖς ἄλλοις ἀνδράσιν ἔσται   670
παράδειγμ᾽ ὕβρεως ἀδίκων τ᾽ ἔργων
ἀθέων τε τρόπων· ‿‿–‿‿–
φήσει δ᾽ εἶναί τε θεοὺς φανερῶς,
    δείξει τ᾽ ἤδη
πᾶσιν ἀνθρώποις σεβίζειν δαίμονας ‿–‿–   675
δικαίως τ᾽ ἐφέποντας ὅσια, καὶ νόμιμα

CH. Light we our torches, my sisters,
    and manfully girding our robes,
Gather them sternly about us,
    and casting our mantles aside
On through the tents and the gangways,
    and up by the tiers and the rows,
Eyeing, and probing, and trying,
    where men would be likely to hide.

Now 'tis time, 'tis time, my sisters,
    round and round and round to go,
Soft, with light and airy footfall,
    creeping, peeping, high and low.
Look about in each direction,
    make a rigid, close inspection,
Lest in any hole or corner,
    other rogues escape detection.
  Hunt with care, here and there,
Searching, spying, poking, prying,
    up and down, and everywhere.

  For if once the evil-doer we can see,[a]
He shall soon be a prey to our vengeance to-day,
 And to all men a warning he shall be
Of the terrible fate that is sure to await
The guilty sin-schemer and lawless blasphemer.
And then he shall find that the Gods are not blind
  To what passes below ;
  Yea, and all men shall know
It is best to live purely, uprightly, securely,

discover any man, who unperceived by me, has perpetrated this sacrilegious act," or (2) " if we fail to detect him, yet the gods will not leave him unpunished."

μηδομένους, ποιεῖν ὅ τι καλῶς ἔχει.
κἂν μὴ ποιῶσι ταῦτα, τοιάδ' ἔσται·
αὐτῶν ὅταν ληφθῇ τις οὐχ
ὅσιόν τι δρῶν, μανίαις φλέγων,   680
λύσσῃ παράκοπος —◡—,
  εἴ τι δρώῃ,
πᾶσιν ἐμφανὴς ὁρᾶν ἔσ-
ται γυναιξὶ καὶ βροτοῖσιν,
ὅτι τὰ παράνομα τά τ' ἀνόσια θεὸς
παραχρῆμ' ἀποτίνεται.   685

ἀλλ' ἔοιχ' ἡμῖν ἅπαντά πως διεσκέφθαι καλῶς.
οὐχ ὁρῶμεν γοῦν ἔτ' ἄλλον οὐδέν' ἐγκαθήμενον.
ΓΥ.Α. ἆ ἆ.
  ποῖ ποῖ σὺ φεύγεις; οὗτος οὗτος οὐ μενεῖς;   690
τάλαιν' ἐγὼ τάλαινα, καὶ τὸ παιδίον
ἐξαρπάσας μοι φροῦδος ἀπὸ τοῦ τιτθίου.
ΜΝ. κέκραχθι· τοῦτο δ' οὐδέποτε σὺ ψωμιεῖς,
ἢν μή μ' ἀφῆτ'· ἀλλ' ἐνθάδ', ἐπὶ τῶν μηρίων,
πληγὲν μαχαίρᾳ τῇδε φοινίας φλέβας
καθαιματώσει βωμόν.   695
ΓΥ.Α.   ὦ τάλαιν' ἐγώ.
  γυναῖκες, οὐκ ἀρήξετ'; οὐ πολλὴν βοὴν

---

^a Lines 673 to 685 are literally: " He shall show to all
mankind that they should reverence the gods, and following
after what is holy, and studying what is lawful, should do
the thing that is right. And if they do not so, this shall
follow : when one of them is caught doing what is impious,
blazing with madness, distraught with frenzy, if he should
do aught . . . it shall be manifest to all women and mortals
that God suddenly avenges all impious and unlawful acts."
^b *Just as the Chorus are concluding their search, Mnesilochus
snatches the First Woman's baby from her arms, and takes
refuge at the altar.*

It is best to do well,
And to practise day and night
what is orderly and right,
And in virtue and in honesty to dwell.
But if anyone there be who a wicked deed shall do
In his raving, and his raging,
and his madness, and his pride,
Every mortal soon shall see,
aye, and every woman too,
What a doom shall the guilty one betide.
For the wicked evil deed
shall be recompensed with speed,
The Avenger doth not tarry to begin,
Nor delayeth for a time,
but He searcheth out the crime,
And He punisheth the sinner in his sin.[a]

Now we've gone through every corner,
every nook surveyed with care,
And there's not another culprit
skulking, lurking anywhere.[b]

F.W.   Hoy ! Hoy there ! Hoy !
He's got my child, he's got my darling, O !
He's snatched my little baby from my breast.
O, stop him, stop him ! O, he's gone. O ! O !
MN.   Aye, weep ! you ne'er shall dandle him again,[c]
Unless you loose me. Soon shall these small limbs,
Smit with cold edge of sacrificial knife,[d]
Incarnadine this altar.
F.W.   O ! O ! O !
Help, women, help me. Sisters, help, I pray.

  [c] Lit. " feed on sops and morsels."
  [d] Lit. " here over the sacrificial meats, his bleeding veins
smitten by this knife."

στήσεσθε καὶ τροπαῖον, ἀλλὰ τοῦ μόνου
τέκνου με περιόψεσθ' ἀποστερουμένην;

ΧΟ.   ἔα ἔα.
       ὦ πότνιαι Μοῖραι, τί τόδε δέρκομαι   700
          νεοχμὸν αὖ τέρας;
     ὡς ἅπαντ' ἄρ' ἐστὶ τόλμης ἔργα κἀναισχυντίας.
     οἷον αὖ δέδρακεν ἔργον, οἷον αὖ, φίλαι, τόδε.
ΜΝ. οἷον ὑμῶν ἐξαράξει τὴν ἄγαν αὐθαδίαν.
ΧΟ. ταῦτα δῆτ' οὐ δεινὰ πράγματ' ἐστὶ καὶ περαι-
      τέρω;   705
ΓΥ.Α. δεινὰ δῆθ', ὅστις γ' ἔχει μου 'ξαρπάσας τὸ
      παιδίον.
ΧΟ.   τί ἂν οὖν εἴποι πρὸς ταῦτά τις, ὅτε [ἀντ.
      τοιαῦτα ποιῶν ὅδ' ἀναισχυντεῖ;
ΜΝ.   κοὔπω μέντοι γε πέπαυμαι.
ΓΥ.Α.   ἀλλ' οὖν ἥκεις ὅθεν οὐ φεύξει,   710
      φαύλως τ' ἀποδρὰς οὔποτε λέξεις
      οἷον δράσας διέδυς ἔργον,
      λήψει δὲ κακόν.
ΜΝ. τοῦτο μέντοι μὴ γένοιτο μηδαμῶς, ἀπεύχομαι.
ΧΟ. τίς οὖν σοι, τίς ἂν σύμμαχος ἐκ θεῶν   715
     ἀθανάτων ἔλθοι ξὺν ἀδίκοις ἔργοις;
ΜΝ. μάτην λαλεῖτε· τὴν δ' ἐγὼ οὐκ ἀφήσω.
ΧΟ.   ἀλλ' οὐ μὰ τὼ θεὼ τάχ' οὐ
      χαίρων ἴσως ἔμ' ἐνυβρίεις,

Charge to the rescue, shout, and rout, and scout
    him.
Don't see me lose my baby, my one pet.

CH.   Alas!   Alas!
        Mercy o' me! what do I see?
            What can it be?
    What, will deeds of shameless violence
                    never, never, never, end?
        What's the matter, what's he up to,
                    what's he doing now, my friend?
MN. Doing what I hope will crush you
                    out of all your bold assurance.
CH. Zounds, his words are very dreadful;
                more than dreadful, past endurance.
F.W. Yes, indeed, they're very dreadful,
                    and he's got my baby too.
CH.   Impudence rare!   Look at him there,
            Doing such deeds, and I vow and declare
            Never minding or caring—
MN.   Or likely to care.
F.W.   Here you are come : here you shall stay,
        Never again shall you wander away;
        Wander away, glad to display
        All the misdeeds you have done us to-day,
            But dear you shall pay.
MN. There at least I'm hoping, ladies,
                    I shall find your words untrue.
CH.   What God do you think his assistance will lend,
        You wicked old man, to escort you away?
MN.   Aha, but I've captured your baby, my friend,
        And I shan't let her go, for the best you can say.
CH.   But no, by the Goddesses Twain,
            Not long shall our threats be in vain,

λόγους τε λέξεις ἀνοσίους·   720
    ἀθέοις ἔρ-
γοις γὰρ ἀνταμειψόμεσθά σ᾽,
ὥσπερ εἰκός, ἀντὶ τῶνδε.
τάχα δὲ μεταβαλοῦσ᾽ ἐπὶ κακὸν ἑτε-
    ρότροπόν σ᾽ ἐπέχει τύχη.   725
ἀλλὰ τάσδε μὲν λαβεῖν χρῆν σ᾽, ἐκφέρειν τε
    τῶν ξύλων,
καὶ καταίθειν τὸν πανοῦργον, πυρπολεῖν θ᾽
    ὅσον τάχος.

ΓΥ.Α. ἴωμεν ἐπὶ τὰς κληματίδας, ὦ Μανία.
κἀγώ σ᾽ ἀποδείξω θυμάλωπα τήμερον.

ΜΝ. ὕφαπτε καὶ κάταιθε· σὺ δὲ τὸ Κρητικὸν   730
ἀπόδυθι ταχέως· τοῦ θανάτου δ᾽, ὦ παιδίον,
μόνην γυναικῶν αἰτιῶ τὴν μητέρα.
τουτὶ τί ἔστιν; ἀσκὸς ἐγένεθ᾽ ἡ κόρη
οἴνου πλέως, καὶ ταῦτα Περσικὰς ἔχων.
ὦ θερμόταται γυναῖκες, ὦ ποτίσταται,   735
κἀκ παντὸς ὑμεῖς μηχανώμεναι πιεῖν,
ὦ μέγα καπήλοις ἀγαθὸν ἡμῖν δ᾽ αὖ κακόν,
κακὸν δὲ καὶ τοῖς σκευαρίοις καὶ τῇ κρόκῃ.

ΓΥ.Α. παράβαλλε πολλὰς κληματίδας, ὦ Μανία.

ΜΝ. παράβαλλε δῆτα· σὺ δ᾽ ἀπόκριναί μοι τοδί.   740
τουτὶ τεκεῖν φής;

ΓΥ.Α.   καὶ δέκα μῆνας αὔτ᾽ ἐγὼ
ἤνεγκον.

ΜΝ.   ἤνεγκας σύ;

ΓΥ.Α.   νὴ τὴν Ἄρτεμιν.

ΜΝ. τρικότυλον ἢ πῶς; εἰπέ μοι.

ΓΥ.Α.   τί μ᾽ ἠργάσω;

ᵃ Lit. " Yes, and I went with her ten months." " You
did?" " Yes, by Artemis."

Not long shall you flout at our pain.
Unholy your deeds, and you'll find
That WE shall repay you in kind,
And perchance you will alter your mind
When Fate, veering round like the blast,
In its clutches has seized you at last,
   Very fast.
Comrades, haste, collect the brushwood :
     pile it up without delay :
Pile it, heap it, stow it, throw it,
    burn and fire and roast and slay.

F.W. Come, Mania, come ; let's run and fetch the
  fagots.
 (*To Mn.*) Ah, wretch, you'll be a cinder before
  night.

MN. (*Busily engaged in unpacking the baby*)
 With all my heart. Now I'll undo these wrappers,
 These Cretan long clothes ; and remember,
  darling,
 It's all your mother that has served you thus.
 What have we here ? a flask, and not a baby !
 A flask of wine, for all its Persian slippers.
 O ever thirsty, ever tippling women,
 O ever ready with fresh schemes for drink,
 To vintners what a blessing : but to us
 And all our goods and chattels what a curse !

F.W. Drag in the fagots, Mania ; pile them up.

MN. Aye, pile away ; but tell me, is this baby
 Really your own ?

F.W.   My very flesh and blood.[a]

MN. Your flesh and blood ?

F.W.   By Artemis it is.

MN. Is it a pint ?

F.W.   O, what have you been doing ?

ἀπέδυσας, ὦναίσχυντέ, μου τὸ παιδίον
τυννοῦτον ὄν.

ΜΝ.   τυννοῦτο;

ΓΥ.Α.   μικρὸν νὴ Δία.   745

ΜΝ. πόσ᾽ ἔτη δὲ γέγονεν; τρεῖς Χοᾶς ἢ τέτταρας;

ΓΥ.Α. σχεδὸν τοσοῦτον χὥσον ἐκ Διονυσίων.
ἀλλ᾽ ἀπόδος αὐτό.

ΜΝ.   μὰ τὸν Ἀπόλλω τουτογί.

ΓΥ.Α. ἐμπρήσομεν τοίνυν σε.

ΜΝ.   πάνυ γ᾽ ἐμπίμπρατε·
αὕτη δ᾽ ἀποσφαγήσεται μάλ᾽ αὐτίκα.   750

ΓΥ.Α. μὴ δῆθ᾽, ἱκετεύω σ᾽· ἀλλ᾽ ἔμ᾽ ὅ τι χρῄζεις ποίει
ὑπέρ γε τούτου.

ΜΝ.   φιλότεκνός τις εἶ φύσει.
ἀλλ᾽ οὐδὲν ἧττον ἥδ᾽ ἀποσφαγήσεται.

ΓΥ.Α. οἴμοι τέκνον. δός μοι τὸ σφάγιον Μανία,
ἵν᾽ οὖν τό γ᾽ αἷμα τοῦ τέκνου τοὐμοῦ λάβω.   755

ΜΝ. ὕπεχ᾽ αὐτό, χαριοῦμαι γὰρ ἕν γε τοῦτό σοι.

ΓΥ.Α. κακῶς ἀπόλοι᾽, ὡς φθονερὸς εἶ καὶ δυσμενής.

ΜΝ. τουτὶ τὸ δέρμα τῆς ἱερείας γίγνεται.

ΓΥ.Α. τί τῆς ἱερείας γίγνεται;

ΜΝ.   τουτὶ λαβέ.

ΚΡΙΤΥΛΛΑ. ταλαντάτη Μίκα, τίς ἐξεκόρησέ σε;   760
τίς τὴν ἀγαπητὴν παῖδά σοὐξηρήσατο;

ΓΥ.Α. ὁ πανοῦργος οὗτος. ἀλλ᾽ ἐπειδήπερ πάρει,
φύλαξον αὐτόν, ἵνα λαβοῦσα Κλεισθένην
τοῖσιν πρυτάνεσιν ἃ πεποίηχ᾽ οὗτος φράσω.

ΜΝ. ἄγε δὴ τίς ἔσται μηχανὴ σωτηρίας;   765

─────────────

ᵃ Lit. "About that, adding the time since the last
Dionysia," the Pitchers (χοᾶς) being the name of the second
day of the Anthesteria.
ᵇ *Puts the bottle to his lips and drains every drop; taking*
196

O, you have stripped my baby of its clothes.
Poor tiny morsel!

MN. *(holding up a large bottle)* Tiny?

F.W.   Yes, indeed.

MN. What is its age? Three Pitcher-feasts or four?

F.W. Well, thereabouts, a little over now.[a]
Please give it back.

MN.   No thank you, not exactly.

F.W. We'll burn you then.

MN.   O, burn me by all means;
But anyhow I'll sacrifice this victim.

F.W. O! O! O!
Make *me* your victim, anything you like;
But spare the child.

MN.   A loving mother truly.
But this dear child must needs be sacrificed.

F.W. My child! my child! give me the bason, Mania,
I'll catch my darling's blood at any rate.

MN. And so you shall; I'll not deny you that.[b]

F.W. You spiteful man! you most ungenerous man!

MN. This skin, fair priestess, is your perquisite.

F.W. What is my perquisite?

MN.   This skin, fair priestess.[c]

CRITYLLA. O Mica, who has robbed thee of thy flower,
And snatched thy babe, thine only one, away?[d]

F.W. This villain here: but I'm so glad you're come.
You see he doesn't run away, while I
Call the police, with Cleisthenes, to help us.[e]

MN. *(soliloquizes)* O me, what hope of safety still remains?

care that none shall fall into the bason which the F.W. is holding underneath.   [c] *Another woman, Critylla, now enters.*
   [d] ἐξεκόρησε, "swept or cleaned out," with a play on κόρη, as if it meant "robbed you of your child."
   [e] *F.W. goes out.*

197

ARISTOPHANES

τίς πεῖρα, τίς ἐπίνοι'; ὁ μὲν γὰρ αἴτιος
κἄμ' ἐσκυλίσας ἐς τοιαυτὶ πράγματα
οὐ φαίνετ' οὔπω. φέρε τίν' οὖν ἂν ἄγγελον
πέμψαιμ' ἐπ' αὐτόν; οἶδ' ἐγὼ καὶ δὴ πόρον
ἐκ τοῦ Παλαμήδους· ὡς ἐκεῖνος, τὰς πλάτας   770
ῥίψω γράφων. ἀλλ' οὐ πάρεισιν αἱ πλάται.
πόθεν οὖν γένοιντ' ἄν μοι πλάται; πόθεν; πόθεν;
τί δ' ἂν εἰ ταδὶ τἀγάλματ' ἀντὶ τῶν πλατῶν
γράφων διαρρίπτοιμι; βέλτιον πολύ.
ξύλον γέ τοι καὶ ταῦτα, κἀκεῖν' ἦν ξύλον.
    ὦ χεῖρες ἐμαί,   775
ἐγχειρεῖν χρῆν ἔργῳ πορίμῳ.
ἄγε δὴ πινάκων ξεστῶν δέλτοι,
    δέξασθε σμίλης ὁλκούς,
κήρυκας ἐμῶν μόχθων· οἴμοι,
    τουτὶ τὸ ῥῶ μοχθηρόν·   780
χώρει, χώρει. ποίαν αὔλακα;
βάσκετ', ἐπείγετε πάσας καθ' ὁδούς,
    κείνᾳ, ταύτᾳ· ταχέως χρή.

ΧΟ. ἡμεῖς τοίνυν ἡμᾶς αὐτὰς εὖ λέξωμεν παραβᾶσαι. 785
    καίτοι πᾶς τις τὸ γυναικεῖον φῦλον κακὰ πόλλ'
        ἀγορεύει,
    ὡς πᾶν ἐσμὲν κακὸν ἀνθρώποις κἀξ ἡμῶν
        ἐστιν ἅπαντα,
    ἔριδες, νείκη, στάσις ἀργαλέα, λύπη, πόλεμος.
        φέρε δή νυν,

---

^a Palamede was put to death before Troy; and his
brother Oeax, wishing to send the news to his father in
Euboea, wrote it upon oar-blades which he cast into the sea.
The "votive slabs" are tablets with votive inscriptions.

^b *Writes, and sings to himself as he writes.*

^c "He flings the tablets about, in the hope that some or

What plan? what stratagem?   My worthy cousin,
Who first involved me in this dreadful scrape,
" He cometh not."   Suppose I send him word.
But how to send it ?   Hah, I know a trick
Out of his *Palamede*.[a]   I'll send a message
Written on oar-blades.   Tush ! I've got no oar-
 blades.
What shall I do for oar-blades ?   Why not send
These votive slabs instead ?   The very thing.
Oar-blades are wood, and slabs are wood. I'll try.[b]
 Now for the trick ; fingers be quick ;
 Do what you can for my notable plan.
 Slab, have the grace to permit me to trace
 Grooves with my knife on your beautiful face.
 The tale of my woe it is yours for to show.
 O, o, what a furrow ! I never did see
 Such a horrible " R " as I've made it to be.
 Well, that must do ; so fly [c] away you,
 Hither and thither, off, off, and away.
 Do not delay for a moment, I pray.[d]

CH.   Now let us turn to the people,
     our own panegyric to render.
 Men never speak a good word,
     never one, for the feminine gender,
 Every one says we're a Plague,
     the source of all evils to man,
 War, dissension, and strife.
     Come, answer me this, if you can ;

one of them may reach Euripides.   It is, of course, a parody
on that poet's *Palamede* ": R.   χώρει is addressed to the
chisel : " move on."
 [d] *Here follows the* PARABASIS.   *As a rule, all the actors
leave the stage before the Parabasis begins : but Mnesilochus
is unable to leave, and Critylla remains to keep watch.*

εἰ κακόν ἐσμεν, τί γαμεῖθ᾿ ἡμᾶς, εἴπερ ἀληθῶς κακόν
    ἐσμεν,
κἀπαγορεύετε μήτ᾿ ἐξελθεῖν μήτ᾿ ἐκκύψασαν ἁλῶναι, 790
ἀλλ᾿ οὑτωσὶ πολλῇ σπουδῇ τὸ κακὸν βούλεσθε
    φυλάττειν;
κἂν ἐξέλθῃ τὸ γύναιόν ποι, κᾆθ᾿ εὕρητ᾿ αὐτὸ θύρασιν,
μανίας μαίνεσθ᾿, οὓς χρῆν σπένδειν καὶ χαίρειν,
    εἴπερ ἀληθῶς
ἔνδοθεν εὕρετε φροῦδον τὸ κακὸν καὶ μὴ κατελαμ-
    βάνετ᾿ ἔνδον.
κἂν καταδάρθωμεν ἐν ἀλλοτρίων παίζουσαι καὶ
    κοπιῶσαι,   795
πᾶς τις τὸ κακὸν τοῦτο ζητεῖ περὶ τὰς κλίνας
    περινοστῶν.
κἂν ἐκ θυρίδος παρακύπτωμεν, τὸ κακὸν ζητεῖτε
    θεᾶσθαι·
κἂν αἰσχυνθεῖσ᾿ ἀναχωρήσῃ, πολὺ μᾶλλον πᾶς
    ἐπιθυμεῖ
αὖθις τὸ κακὸν παρακύψαν ἰδεῖν. οὕτως ἡμεῖς
    ἐπιδήλως
ὑμῶν ἐσμεν πολὺ βελτίους, βάσανός τε πάρεστιν
    ἰδέσθαι.   800
βάσανον δῶμεν πότεροι χείρους. ἡμεῖς μὲν γάρ
    φαμεν ὑμᾶς,
ὑμεῖς δ᾿ ἡμᾶς. σκεψώμεθα δὴ κἀντιτιθῶμεν πρὸς
    ἕκαστον,
παραβάλλουσαι τῆς τε γυναικὸς καὶ τἀνδρὸς τοὔνομ᾿
    ἑκάστου.
Ναυσιμάχης μέν γ᾿ ἥττων ἐστὶν Χαρμῖνος· δῆλα
    δὲ τἄργα.

ᵃ Charminus a short time before had been defeated by a
Peloponnesian fleet off Tyre : Thuc. viii. 41-42. The name

Why, if we're *really* a Plague,
>   you're so anxious to have us for wives ;
And charge us not to be peeping,
>   nor to stir out of doors for our lives.
Isn't it silly to guard
>   a Plague with such scrupulous care ?
Zounds ! how you rave, coming home,
>   if your poor little wife isn't there.
Should you not rather be glad,
>   and rejoice all the days of your life,
Rid of a *Plague*, you know,
>   the source of dissension and strife ?
If on a visit we sport,
>   and sleep when the sporting is over,
O, how you rummage about ;
>   what a fuss, your lost Plague to discover.
Every one stares at your Plague
>   if she happens to look on the street :
Stares all the more if your Plague
>   thinks proper to blush and retreat.
Is it not plain then, I ask,
>   that Women are really the best ?
What, can you doubt that we are ?
>   I will bring it at once to the test.
We say Women are best ;
>   you men (just like you) deny it,
Nothing on earth is so easy
>   as to come to the test, and to try it.
I'll take the name of a Man,
>   and the name of a Woman, and show it.
Did not Charminus give way
>   to Miss-Fortune ? [a]   Do you not know it ?

N. like the others (except Salabaccho) is chosen for its
meaning.

καὶ μὲν δὴ καὶ Κλεοφῶν χείρων πάντως δήπου
    Σαλαβακχοῦς.   805
πρὸς Ἀριστομάχην δὲ χρόνου πολλοῦ, πρὸς ἐκείνην
    τὴν Μαραθῶνι,
καὶ Στρατονίκην, ὑμῶν οὐδεὶς οὐδ' ἐγχειρεῖ πολεμί-
    ζειν.
ἀλλ' Εὐβούλης τῶν πέρυσίν τις βουλευτής ἐστιν
    ἀμείνων
παραδοὺς ἑτέρῳ τὴν βουλείαν; οὐδ' αὐτὸς τοῦτό γε
    φήσεις.
οὕτως ἡμεῖς πολὺ βελτίους τῶν ἀνδρῶν εὐχόμεθ'
    εἶναι.   810
οὐδ' ἂν κλέψασα γυνὴ ζεύγει κατὰ πεντήκοντα
    τάλαντα
ἐς πόλιν ἔλθοι τῶν δημοσίων· ἀλλ' ἢν τὰ μέγισθ'
    ὑφέληται
φορμὸν πυρῶν τἀνδρὸς κλέψασ', αὐθημερὸν αὖτ'
    ἀπέδωκεν.
    ἀλλ' ἡμεῖς ἂν πολλοὺς τούτων
    ἀποδείξαιμεν ταῦτα ποιοῦντας.
    καὶ πρὸς τούτοις γάστριδας ἡμῶν   815
    ὄντας μᾶλλον καὶ λωποδύτας
    καὶ βωμολόχους κἀνδραποδιστάς.

---

^a The Council of Five Hundred had surrendered their
office to the usurping Four Hundred. Eubule was the name
of one of the three daughters of Leos, who died to save
Athens, to whom the Leocorion was erected; Aelian, *V.H.*
xii. 28. The speaker then cites five names of women which
suggest superiority to men. Charminus, who was defeated
in a naval engagement off Syme about a year before this
play was exhibited (Thuc. viii. 41, 42), is therefore Ναυσιμάχης ἥττων; Cleophon cannot cope with the notorious
Salabaccho in vileness; Ἀριστομάχη, "best in battle," and
Στρατονίκη, "conquering in war," cannot be matched;
Εὐβούλη is "wise in counsel."

Is not Cleophon viler
than vile Salabaccho by far?
Is there a Man who can equal,
in matters of glory and war,
Lady Victoria, Mistress
of Marathon, queen of the Sea?
Is not Prudence a Woman,
and who is so clever as she?
Certainly none of your statesmen,
who only a twelvemonth ago
Gave up their place and their duty.[a]
Would women demean themselves so?
Women don't ride in their coaches,
as Men have been doing of late,
Pockets and purses distended
with cash they have filched from the State.
We, at the very outside,
steal a wee little jorum of corn,
Putting it back in the even,
whatever we took in the morn.[b]

(*The Strophe.*)

But this is a true description of you.[c]

Are ye not gluttonous, vulgar, perverse,

Kidnappers, housebreakers, footpads, and worse?

---

[b] " The passage seems rather to mean, ' A woman does not steal the public money by the fifty talents, and spend it in sumptuous equipages ; however much of the public money she may steal, she replaces it the same day, having (for the purpose of replacing it) purloined a basketful of wheat from her husband " : R.

[c] Lit. " but we could show that many of them do these things."

καὶ μὲν δήπου καὶ τὰ πατρῷά γε
χείρους ἡμῶν εἰσιν σῴζειν·   820
ἡμῖν μὲν γὰρ σῶν ἔτι καὶ νῦν
τἀντίον, ὁ κανών, οἱ καλαθίσκοι,
    τὸ σκιάδειον·
τοῖς δ' ἡμετέροις ἀνδράσι τούτοις
ἀπόλωλεν μὲν πολλοῖς ὁ κανὼν   825
ἐκ τῶν οἴκων αὐτῇ λόγχῃ,
    πολλοῖς δ' ἑτέροις
ἀπὸ τῶν ὤμων ἐν ταῖς στρατιαῖς
    ἔρριπται τὸ σκιάδειον.

πόλλ' ἂν αἱ γυναῖκες ἡμεῖς ἐν δίκῃ μεμψαίμεθ' ἂν   830
τοῖσιν ἀνδράσιν δικαίως, ἓν δ' ὑπερφυέστατον.
χρῆν γάρ, ἡμῶν εἰ τέκοι τις ἄνδρα χρηστὸν τῇ πόλει,
ταξίαρχον ἢ στρατηγόν, λαμβάνειν τιμήν τινα,
προεδρίαν τ' αὐτῇ δίδοσθαι Στηνίοισι καὶ Σκίροις,
ἔν τε ταῖς ἄλλαις ἑορταῖς αἷσιν ἡμεῖς ἤγομεν·   835
εἰ δὲ δειλὸν καὶ πονηρὸν ἄνδρα τις τέκοι γυνή,
ἢ τριήραρχον πονηρόν, ἢ κυβερνήτην κακόν,
ὑστέραν αὐτὴν καθῆσθαι, σκάφιον ἀποκεκαρμένην,

---

[a] The women wish to show their superiority to men by
showing how much more carefully they have preserved
their mothers' belongings, than the men have preserved
what their fathers left them. They are still using the
ἀντίον, or bar at the top of the loom from which the threads
hung; the κανών, or weaving-rod; the καλαθίσκοι, or wool-
baskets; and the σκιάδειον, or sunshade. But with the men,
the κανών is the spearshaft, and the σκιάδειον, under the
shadow of which the warrior fights, is the shield: these the
men have thrown away. The climax of the whole passage
is the σκιάδειον, 823, 828.

[b] Stenia and Scira were women's feasts. See *E.* 18.

And we in domestic economy too
Are thriftier, shiftier, wiser than you.[a]
For the loom which our mothers
    employed with such skill,
With its Shafts and its Thongs,—
    we are working it still.
And the ancient umbrella by no means is done,
We are wielding it yet,
    as our Shield from the Sun.
But O for the Shafts,
    and the Thong of the Shield,
Which your Fathers in fight
    were accustomed to wield.
Where are they to-day ?
    Ye have cast them away
As ye raced, in hot haste,
    and disgraced, from the fray !

(*The Epirrhema.*)

Many things we have against you,
    many rules we justly blame ;
But the one we now will mention
    is the most enormous shame.
What, my masters ! ought a lady,
    who has borne a noble son,
One who in your fleets and armies
    great heroic deeds has done,
Ought she to remain unhonoured ?
    ought she not, I ask you, I,
In our Stenia and our Scira [b]
    still to take precedence high ?
Whoso breeds a cowardly soldier,
    or a seaman cold and tame.
Crop her hair, and seat her lowly ;
    brand her with the marks of shame ;

ARISTOPHANES

τῆς τὸν ἀνδρεῖον τεκούσης. τῷ γὰρ εἰκός, ὦ
    πόλις,
τὴν Ὑπερβόλου καθῆσθαι μητέρ᾽ ἠμφιεσμένην 840
λευκὰ καὶ κόμας καθεῖσαν πλησίον τῆς Λαμά-
    χου,
καὶ δανείζειν χρήμαθ᾽, ᾗ χρῆν, εἰ δανείσειέν τινι
καὶ τόκον πράττοιτο, διδόναι μηδέν᾽ ἀνθρώπων
    τόκον, 845
ἀλλ᾽ ἀφαιρεῖσθαι βίᾳ τὰ χρήματ᾽, εἰπόντας τοδί,
" ἀξία γοῦν εἶ τόκου, τεκοῦσα τοιοῦτον τόκον."

MN. ἰλλὸς γεγένημαι προσδοκῶν· ὁ δ᾽ οὐδέπω.
τί δῆτ᾽ ἂν εἴη τοὐμποδών; οὐκ ἔσθ᾽ ὅπως
οὐ τὸν Παλαμήδην ψυχρὸν ὄντ᾽ αἰσχύνεται.
τῷ δῆτ᾽ ἂν αὐτὸν προσαγαγοίμην δράματι;
ἐγᾦδα· τὴν καινὴν Ἑλένην μιμήσομαι. 850
πάντως ὑπάρχει μοι γυναικεία στολή.

KP. τί αὖ σὺ κυρκανᾷς; τί κοικύλλεις ἔχων;
πικρὰν Ἑλένην ὄψει τάχ᾽, εἰ μὴ κοσμίως
ἕξεις, ἕως ἂν τῶν πρυτάνεών τις φανῇ.

MN. (ὡς Ἑλένη) Νείλου μὲν αἵδε καλλιπάρθενοι ῥοαί, 855

ᵃ Lamachus, the distinguished soldier who fell before
Syracuse.

ᵇ *The close of the Parabasis finds the position of Mnesilochus
unaltered. The dispatch of the tablets has, so far, produced
no result.*

ᶜ Lit. " Why are you so restless? Why are you staring
about ? "

ᵈ " We have had a short caricature of the *Palamede*. We
are about to have a more elaborate caricature of the *Helen*,
which is still extant. Almost all the speeches of Euripides
and Mnesilochus in the ensuing scene are taken, with
occasional comic perversions, from that play : " R. Euripides
followed a version of the story which sent merely a phantom
Helen to Ilium, while the real Helen, a pure and stainless

Set the nobler dame above her.
                  Can it, all ye Powers, be right
That Hyperbolus's mother,
           flowing-haired, and robed in white,
Should in public places sit by
               Lamachus's [a] mother's side,
Hoarding wealth, and lending monies,
                gathering profits far and wide ?
Sure 'twere better every debtor,
                calm, resolving not to pay,
When she comes exacting money,
               with a mild surprise should say,
Keeping principal and income, *You to claim per-
    centage due !*
Sure a son so capital is CAPITAL enough for you. [b]

MN. I've strained my eyes with watching ; but my
        poet,
" He cometh not." Why not ? Belike he feels
Ashamed of his old frigid *Palamede*.
Which is the play to fetch him ? O, I know ;
Which but his brand-new *Helen* ? I'll be Helen.
I've got the woman's clothes, at all events.

CR. What are you plotting ? What is that you're
        muttering ? [c]
I'll Helen you, my master, if you don't
Keep quiet there till the policeman comes.

MN.[d] (*as Helen*) These are the fair-nymphed waters
        of the Nile,

wife, was wafted by Hermes into Egypt and entrusted to the
charge of the good king Proteus. After the king's death,
his son Theoclymenus sought to make Helen his wife ; and
in the play she is discovered sitting upon the tomb of Proteus.
For a detailed analysis of the allusions in this play the reader
is referred to Mr. Rogers's Introduction.

ὅς, ἀντὶ δίας ψακάδος, Αἰγύπτου πέδον
λευκῆς νοτίζει, μελανοσυρμαῖον λεών.

ΚΡ. πανοῦργος εἶ νὴ τὴν Ἑκάτην τὴν φωσφόρον.

ΜΝ. ἐμοὶ δὲ γῆ μὲν πατρὶς οὐκ ἀνώνυμος
Σπάρτη, πατὴρ δὲ Τυνδάρεως.

ΚΡ.   σοί γ', ὦλεθρε, 860
πατὴρ ἐκεῖνός ἐστι; Φρυνώνδας μὲν οὖν.

ΜΝ. Ἑλένη δ' ἐκλήθην.

ΚΡ.   αὖθις αὖ γίγνει γυνή,
πρὶν τῆς ἑτέρας δοῦναι γυναικίσεως δίκην;

ΜΝ. ψυχαὶ δὲ πολλαὶ δι' ἔμ' ἐπὶ Σκαμανδρίαις
ῥοαῖσιν ἔθανον.

ΚΡ.   ὤφελες δὲ καὶ σύ γε.   865

ΜΝ. κἀγὼ μὲν ἐνθάδ' εἴμ'· ὁ δ' ἄθλιος πόσις
οὑμὸς Μενέλαος οὐδέπω προσέρχεται.
τί οὖν ἔτι ζῶ τῶν κοράκων πονηρίᾳ;
ἀλλ' ὥσπερ αἰκάλλει τι καρδίαν ἐμήν.
μὴ ψεῦσον, ὦ Ζεῦ, τῆς ἐπιούσης ἐλπίδος.   870

ΕΥ. (ὡς Μενέλαος) τίς τῶνδ' ἐρυμνῶν δωμάτων ἔχει
κράτος,
ὅστις ξένους δέξαιτο ποντίῳ σάλῳ
κάμνοντας ἐν χειμῶνι καὶ ναυαγίαις;

ΜΝ. Πρωτέως τάδ' ἐστὶ μέλαθρα.

ΕΥ.   ποίου Πρωτέως;

ΚΡ. ὦ τρισκακόδαιμον, ψεύδεται νὴ τὼ θεώ,   875
ἐπεὶ τέθνηκε Πρωτέας ἔτη δέκα.

---

[a] From Eur. *Helen*, 1-3 (as far as λευκῆς). There is a
play upon σύρμα, " a robe," and συρμαία, " an emetic,"
which the Egyptians were notorious for taking ; Herod. i. 71,
P. 1254.

[b] *Helen*, 16-17.

[c] " A rogue of such superior and notable rascality that to

Whose floods bedew, in place of heavenly showers,
Egypt's white plains and black-dosed citizens.[a]

CR. Sweet-shining Hecate, what a rogue it is.

MN. Ah, not unknown my Spartan fatherland,
Nor yet my father Tyndareus.[b]

CR.   My gracious!
Was *he* your father? Sure, Phrynondas[c] was.

MN. And I was Helen.

CR.   What, again a woman?
You've not been punished for your first freak yet.

MN. Full many a soul, by bright Scamander's stream,
Died for my sake.[d]

CR.   Would yours had died among them!

MN. And now I linger here; but Menelaus,
My dear, dear lord, ah wherefore comes he not?
O sluggish crows, to spare my hapless life!
But soft! some hope is busy at my heart,
A laughing hope—O Zeus, deceive me not.[e]

EU. Who is the lord of this stupendous pile?[f]
Will he extend his hospitable care
To some poor storm-tossed, shipwrecked mariners?

MN. These are the halls of Proteus.

EU.   Proteus, are they?

CR. O, by the Twain, he lies like anything.
    I knew old Protteas[g]; he's been dead these
       ten years.

---

call a man a Phrynondas was equivalent to calling him a
cheat:" R.

   [d] *Helen*, 52–53.

   [e] *Euripides enters disguised as Menelaus.*

   [f] *Helen*, 63. The dialogue between Mn. and E. is adopted
from a dialogue in the *Helen* between Menelaus and an old
woman, 441 foll.

   [g] Commonly supposed to be a general mentioned by
Thucydides, i. 45, ii. 23.

ARISTOPHANES

ΕΥ. ποίαν δὲ χώραν εἰσεκέλσαμεν σκάφει;

ΜΝ. Αἴγυπτον.

ΕΥ.   ὦ δύστηνος, οἷ πεπλώκαμεν.

ΚΡ. πείθει τι τούτῳ, τῷ κακῶς ἀπολουμένῳ
λαροῦντι λῆρον; Θεσμοφόριον τουτογί.   880

ΕΥ. αὐτὸς δὲ Πρωτεὺς ἔνδον ἔστ' ἢ 'ξώπιος;

ΚΡ. οὐκ ἔσθ' ὅπως οὐ ναυτιᾷς ἔτ', ὦ ξένε,
ὅστις γ' ἀκούσας ὅτι τέθνηκε Πρωτέας
ἔπειτ' ἐρωτᾷς " ἔνδον ἔστ' ἢ 'ξώπιος; "

ΕΥ. αἰαῖ· τέθνηκε; ποῦ δ' ἐτυμβεύθη τάφῳ;   885

ΜΝ. τόδ' ἐστὶν αὐτοῦ σῆμ', ἐφ' ᾧ καθήμεθα.

ΚΡ. κακῶς ἄρ' ἐξόλοιο κἀξολεῖ γέ τοι,
ὅστις γε τολμᾷς σῆμα τὸν βωμὸν καλεῖν.

ΕΥ. τί δαὶ σὺ θάσσεις τάσδε τυμβήρεις ἕδρας
φάρει καλυπτός, ὦ ξένη;

ΜΝ.   βιάζομαι   890
γάμοισι Πρωτέως παιδὶ συμμῖξαι λέχος.

ΚΡ. τί, ὦ κακόδαιμον, ἐξαπατᾷς αὖ τὸν ξένον;
οὗτος πανουργῶν δεῦρ' ἀνῆλθεν, ὦ ξένε,
ὡς τὰς γυναῖκας ἐπὶ κλοπῇ τοῦ χρυσίου.

ΜΝ. βάϋζε, τοὐμὸν σῶμα βάλλουσα ψόγῳ.   895

ΕΥ. ξένη, τίς ἡ γραῦς ἡ κακορροθοῦσά σε;

ΜΝ. αὕτη Θεονόη Πρωτέως.

ΚΡ.   μὰ τὼ θεώ,
εἰ μὴ Κρίτυλλά γ' Ἀντιθέου Γαργηττόθεν·
σὺ δ' εἶ πανοῦργος.

ΜΝ.   ὁπόσα τοι βούλει λέγε.
οὐ γὰρ γαμοῦμαι σῷ κασιγνήτῳ ποτέ,   900
προδοῦσα Μενέλαον ἐμὸν ἐν Τροίᾳ πόσιν.

ΕΥ. γύναι, τί εἶπας; στρέψον ἀνταυγεῖς κόρας.

ᵃ Cf. Helen, 466.

210

EU. Then whither, whither have we steered our bark?

MN. To Egypt.

EU.   O, the weary, weary way!

CR. Pray don't believe one single word he says.
This is the holy temple of the Twain.

EU. Know you if Proteus be at home or not?

CR. Why, don't I tell you, he's been dead these ten
    years!
You can't have quite got over your sea-sickness,
Asking if Protteas be at home or not.

EU. Woe's me! is Proteus dead? and where's he
    buried?

MN. This is his tomb whereon I'm sitting now.[a]

CR. O, hang the rascal; and he *shall* be hanged!
How dare he say this altar is a tomb?

EU. And wherefore sitt'st thou on this monument,
Veiled in thy mantle, lady?

MN.   They compel me,
A weeping bride, to marry Proteus' son.

CR. Why do you tell the gentleman such fibs?
Good gentleman, he's a bad man; he came
Among the women here, to steal their trinkets.

MN. Aye, aye, rail on: revile me as you list.

EU. Who is the old woman who reviles you, lady?

MN. Theonoë, Proteus' daughter.

CR.   What a story!
Why, I'm Critylla, of Gargettus, sir,
A very honest woman.

MN.   Aye, speak on.
But never will I wed thy brother, no,
I won't be false to absent Menelaus.

EU. What, lady, what?   O, raise those orbs to mine.

ARISTOPHANES

ΜΝ. αἰσχύνομαί σε, τὰς γνάθους ὑβρισμένη.

ΕΤ. τουτὶ τί ἔστιν; ἀφασία τίς τοί μ' ἔχει.
ὦ θεοί, τίν' ὄψιν εἰσορῶ; τίς εἶ, γύναι;   905

ΜΝ. σὺ δ' εἶ τίς; αὐτὸς γὰρ σὲ κἄμ' ἔχει λόγος.

ΕΤ. Ἑλληνὶς εἶ τις ἢ 'πιχωρία γυνή;

ΜΝ. Ἑλληνίς. ἀλλὰ καὶ τὸ σὸν θέλω μαθεῖν.

ΕΤ. Ἑλένῃ σ' ὁμοίαν δὴ μάλιστ' εἶδον, γύναι.

ΜΝ. ἐγὼ δὲ Μενελάῳ σ' ὅσα γ' ἐκ τῶν ἰφύων. 910

ΕΤ. ἔγνως ἄρ' ὀρθῶς ἄνδρα δυστυχέστατον.

ΜΝ. ὦ χρόνιος ἐλθὼν σῆς δάμαρτος ἐς χέρας,
λαβέ με λαβέ με πόσι, περίβαλε δὲ χέρας.
φέρε σὲ κύσω. ἄπαγέ μ' ἄπαγ' ἄπαγ'
ἄπαγέ με   915
λαβὼν ταχὺ πάνυ.

ΚΡ.   κλαύσετ' ἄρα νὴ τὼ θεὼ
ὅστις σ' ἀπάξει, τυπτόμενος τῇ λαμπάδι.

ΕΤ. σὺ τὴν ἐμὴν γυναῖκα κωλύεις ἐμέ,
τὴν Τυνδάρειον παῖδ', ἐπὶ Σπάρτην ἄγειν;

ΚΡ. οἴμ' ὡς πανοῦργος καὐτὸς εἶναί μοι δοκεῖς, 920
καὶ τοῦδέ τις ξύμβουλος. οὐκ ἐτὸς πάλαι
ἠγυπτιάζετ'. ἀλλ' ὅδε μὲν δώσει δίκην.
προσέρχεται γὰρ ὁ πρύτανις χὠ τοξότης.

ΕΤ. τουτὶ πονηρόν· ἀλλ' ὑπαποκινητέον.

ΜΝ. ἐγὼ δ' ὁ κακοδαίμων τί δρῶ;

ΕΤ.   μέν' ἥσυχος. 925
οὐ γὰρ προδώσω σ' οὐδέποτ', ἤνπερ ἐμπνέω,

---

a "He remembers, for the moment, that Helen is the
shaved and singed Mnesilochus, just as he remembers,
seven lines below, that Menelaus is really the market-
gardener's son:" R.

MN. O sir, I blush to raise them, with these cheeks.[a]

EU. O dear, O dear, I cannot speak for trembling.
Ye Gods, is't possible ?   Who art thou, lady ?[b]

MN. O, who art thou ?   I feel the same myself.

EU. Art thou Hellenic, or a born Egyptian ?

MN. Hellenic I : O, tell me what art thou.

EU. O surely, surely, thou art Helen's self.

MN. O, from the greens thou must be Menelaus.

EU. Yes, yes, you see that miserable man.

MN. O, long in coming to these longing arms,
    O, carry me, carry me, from this place,
    O, wrap me in thy close embrace,
  O, carry me, carry me, carry me home,
              by this fond and loving kiss,
  O, take me, take me, take me hence.

CR.   I say now, none of this.
Let go there, or I'll strike you with this link !

EU. Let go my wife, the child of Tyndareus,
Not take her home to Sparta ?   O, what mean
    you ?

CR. O, that's it, is it ?   You're a bad one too !
Both of one gang.   That's what your gipsying
    meant !
But he at any rate shall meet his due.
Here's the policeman, and the Scythian coming.

EU. Ah, this won't do : I must slip off awhile,

MN. And what am I to do ?

EU.   Keep quiet here,
Be sure I'll never fail you while I live ;

[b] Lines 906-912 are from the *Helen* 558 and 561-566, but
Aristophanes substitutes for the end of 564 (ἐγὼ δὲ Μενέλεῳ
γε σέ· οὐδ' ἔχω τί φῶ) the words "to judge from these sprigs
of lavender" to make a hit at the mother of Euripides; *cf.*
387, 456.

ἢν μὴ προλίπωσ' αἱ μυρίαι με μηχαναί.

ΜΝ. αὕτη μὲν ἡ μήρινθος οὐδὲν ἔσπασεν.

ΠΡΥΤΑΝΙΣ. ὅδ' ἔσθ' ὁ πανοῦργος ὃν ἔλεγ' ἡμῖν Κλει-
    σθένης;

οὗτος, τί κύπτεις; δῆσον αὐτὸν εἰσάγων   930
ὦ τοξότ' ἐν τῇ σανίδι, κἄπειτ' ἐνθαδὶ
στήσας φύλαττε καὶ προσιέναι μηδένα
ἔα πρὸς αὐτόν, ἀλλὰ τὴν μάστιγ' ἔχων
παῖ', ἢν προσίῃ τις.

ΚΡ.   νὴ Δί' ὡς νῦν δή γ' ἀνὴρ
ὀλίγου μ' ἀφείλετ' αὐτὸν ἱστιορράφος.   935

ΜΝ. ὦ πρύτανι πρὸς τῆς δεξιᾶς, ἥνπερ φιλεῖς
κοίλην προτείνειν, ἀργύριον ἤν τις διδῷ,
χάρισαι βραχύ τί μοι καίπερ ἀποθανουμένῳ.

ΠΡ. τί σοι χαρίσωμαι;

ΜΝ.   γυμνὸν ἀποδύσαντά με
κέλευε πρὸς τῇ σανίδι δεῖν τὸν τοξότην,   940
ἵνα μὴ 'ν κροκωτοῖς καὶ μίτραις γέρων ἀνὴρ
γέλωτα παρέχω τοῖς κόραξιν ἑστιῶν.

ΠΡ. ἔχοντα ταῦτ' ἔδοξε τῇ βουλῇ σε δεῖν,
ἵνα τοῖς παριοῦσι δῆλος ᾖς πανοῦργος ὤν.

ΜΝ. ἰατταταιάξ· ὦ κροκώθ' οἷ' εἴργασαι·   945
κοὐκ ἔστ' ἔτ' ἐλπὶς οὐδεμία σωτηρίας.

ΧΟ. ἄγε νυν ἡμεῖς παίσωμεν ἅπερ νόμος ἐνθάδε
    ταῖσι γυναιξίν,
ὅταν ὄργια σεμνὰ θεαῖν ἱεραῖς ὥραις ἀνέχωμεν,
ἅπερ καὶ

ᵃ *The high official, who is here inadequately called " a Policeman," now enters upon the stage, attended by one of the Scythian
archers.*

I have ten thousand tricks to save you yet.

MN. Well, you caught nothing by *that* haul, I think.*a*

POLICEMAN. O archer, here's the vagabond, of whom
Cleisthenes told us.

(*To Mn.*) Why do you hang your head ?
(*To Sc.*) Take him within ; there tie him on the
plank ;
Then bring him here and watch him. Let not any
Approach too near him : should they try to, take
The whip, and smite them.

CR.   Aye, one came but now
Spinning his yarns, and all but got him off.

MN. O sir ! policeman ! grant me one request,
O, by that hand I pray you, which you love
To hold out empty, and to draw back full.

PO. What should I grant you ?

MN.   Don't expose me thus ;
Do tell the Scythian he may strip me first ;
Don't let a poor old man, in silks and snoods,
Provoke the laughter of the crows that eat him.

PO. Thus hath the Council ordered it, that so
The passers-by may see the rogue you are.

MN. Alas ! alas !   O yellow silk, I hate ye !
O, I've no hope, no hope of getting free.*b*

CH.*c* Now for the revels, my sisters,
              which we to the great Twain Powers
Prayerfully, carefully raise,
              in the holy festival hours.

*b All the actors leave the stage.   And the Chorus commence
their great ceremonial worship of dance and song.*
    c Lines 947-8 : lit. " come now, let us disport ourselves,
as we women are wont to do, when in the holy seasons we
celebrate the noble solemnities of the Twain."

Παύσων σέβεται καὶ νηστεύει,
πολλάκις αὐταῖν ἐκ τῶν ὡρῶν   950
ἐς τὰς ὥρας ξυνεπευχόμενος
    τοιαῦτα μέλειν θάμ' ἑαυτῷ.

    ὅρμα, χώρει·
κοῦφα ποσὶν ἄγ' ἐς κύκλον,
χειρὶ σύναπτε χεῖρα, ῥυθ-   955
μὸν χορείας ὕπαγε πᾶσα,
βαῖνε καρπαλίμοιν ποδοῖν.
    ἐπισκοπεῖν δέ,
πανταχῇ κυκλοῦσαν ὄμμα, χρὴ Χοροῦ κατάστασιν.

    ἅμα δὲ καὶ   960
    γένος Ὀλυμπίων θεῶν
μέλπε καὶ γέραιρε φωνῇ πᾶσα χορομανεῖ τρόπῳ.

    εἰ δέ τις
    προσδοκᾷ κακῶς ἐρεῖν
ἐν ἱερῷ γυναῖκά μ' οὖσαν ἄνδρας, οὐκ ὀρθῶς φρονεῖ. 965

    ἀλλὰ χρῆν,
[ὡς ἐπ' ἔργον ᾠδικόν,]
πρῶτον εὐκύκλου χορείας εὐφυᾶ στῆσαι βάσιν.

    πρόβαινε ποσὶ τὸν Εὐλύραν   [στρ.
    μέλπουσα καὶ τὴν τοξοφόρον   970
    Ἄρτεμιν ἄνασσαν ἁγνήν.

---

[a] An animal-painter, poor and of bad character. He is
such a devotee of fasting that he will pray for many such
fasts.

[b] Lines 960-8: lit. "at the same time, each sing and
honour the Olympian gods with voice and mad dances.
And if anyone expects me, a woman, to abuse men in the
sanctuary, he is mistaken. But we must needs stay the

And Pauson [a] will join in our worship to-day,
  And Pauson will join in the fasting,
And, keen for the fast, to the Twain he will pray
  For the rite to be made everlasting, I ween,
  For the rite to be made everlasting.

      Now advance
  In the whirling, twirling dance,
With hand linked in hand, as we deftly trip along,
Keeping time to the cadence
                of the swiftly-flowing song ;
      And be sure as we go
That we dart careful glances,
                up and down, and to and fro.

      Now 'tis ours [b]
  To entwine our choicest flowers,
Flowers of song and adoration
            to the great Olympian Powers.

      Nor expect
  That the garland will be flecked
With abuse of mortal men ;
            such a thought is incorrect.

      For with prayer
  And with sacred loving care,
A new and holy measure we will heedfully prepare.

  To the high and holy Minstrel [c]
  Let the dancers onward go,
  And to Artemis, the maiden
  Of the quiver and the bow ;

graceful movement of the prettily circling dance, in preparation for the business of the odes."
  [c] Eulyras = Apollo.

χαῖρ' ὦ Ἑκάεργε,
ὄπαζε δὲ νίκην·
Ἥραν δὲ τὴν τελείαν
μέλψωμεν ὥσπερ εἰκός,
ἣ πᾶσι τοῖς χοροῖσιν ἐμπαίζει τε καὶ   975
κλῇδας γάμου φυλάττει.

Ἑρμῆν τε Νόμιον ἄντομαι   [ἀντ.
καὶ Πᾶνα καὶ Νύμφας φίλας
ἐπιγελάσαι προθύμως
ταῖς ἡμετέραισι   980
χαρέντα χορείαις.
ἔξαιρε δὴ προθύμως
διπλῆν χάριν χορείας.
παίσωμεν ὦ γυναῖκες οἷάπερ νόμος,
πάντως δὲ νηστεύωμεν.

ἀλλ' εἶ' ἐπ' ἄλλ' ἀνάστρεφ' εὐρύθμῳ ποδί,   985
τόρευε πᾶσαν ᾠδήν·
ἡγοῦ δέ γ' ᾠδῆς αὐτός,
σὺ κισσοφόρε Βάκχειε
δέσποτ'· ἐγὼ δὲ κώμοις
σὲ φιλοχόροισι μέλψω.

Εὔιον ὦ Διός τε   [στρ. 990
Βρόμιε καὶ Σεμέλας παῖ,
χοροῖς τερπόμενος
κατ' ὄρεα νυμφᾶν ἐρατοῖς ἐν ὕμνοις,
ὦ Εὔι' Εὔι' εὐοῖ
ὦ Εὔι' ἀναχορεύων.

O, hear us, Far-controller, and the victory bestow.
        And we trust our merry music
        Will the matron Hera please,[a]
        For she loves the pleasant Chorus
        And the dances such as these,
        —Wearing at her girdle
        The holy nuptial keys.

        To Pan and pastoral Hermes
        And the friendly Nymphs we pray,
        That they smile with gracious favour
        On our festival to-day,
With their laughter-loving glances
                beaming brightly on our Play,
        As we dance the Double chorus
        To the old familiar strain,
        As we weave our ancient pastime
        On our holy day again,
        —Keeping fast and vigil
        In the Temple of the Twain.

    Turn the step, and change the measure,
    Raise a loftier music now ;
    Come, the Lord of wine and pleasure,
    Evoi, Bacchus, lead us thou !

        Yea, for Thee we adore !
        Child of Semele, thee
        With thy glittering ivy-wreaths,
        Thee with music and song
        Ever and ever we praise.
Thee with thy wood-nymphs delightedly singing,
        Evoi ! Evoi ! Evoi !

[a] Zeus Teleius and Hera Teleia were patrons of marriage.

219

ARISTOPHANES

ἀμφὶ δὲ σοὶ κτυπεῖται   [ἀντ. 995
Κιθαιρώνιος ἠχώ,
μελάμφυλλά τ' ὄρη
δάσκια πετρώδεις τε νάπαι βρέμονται·
κύκλῳ δὲ περὶ σὲ κισσὸς
εὐπέταλος ἕλικι θάλλει.   1000

ΣΚΥΘΗΣ. ἐνταῦτα νῦν οἰμῶξι πρὸς τὴν αἰτρίαν.
ΜΝ. ὦ τοξόθ' ἱκετεύω σε.
ΣΚ.   μή μ' ἱκετεῦσι σύ.
ΜΝ. χάλασον τὸν ἧλον.
ΣΚ.   ἀλλὰ ταῦτα δρᾶσ' ἐγώ.
ΜΝ. οἴμοι κακοδαίμων, μᾶλλον ἐπικρούεις σύ γε.
ΣΚ. ἔτι μᾶλλο βοῦλις;
ΜΝ.   ἀτταταῖ ἰατταταῖ·   1005
κακῶς ἀπόλοιο.
ΣΚ.   σῖγα κακοδαίμων γέρον.
πέρ', ἐγὼ 'ξενίγκι πορμός, ἵνα πυλάξι σοι.
ΜΝ. ταυτὶ τὰ βέλτιστ' ἀπολέλαυκ' Εὐριπίδου.
ἔα· θεοί, Ζεῦ σῶτερ, εἰσὶν ἐλπίδες.
ἀνὴρ ἔοικεν οὐ προδώσειν, ἀλλά μοι   1010
σημεῖον ὑπεδήλωσε Περσεὺς ἐκδραμών,
ὅτι δεῖ με γίγνεσθ' Ἀνδρομέδαν· πάντως δέ μοι
τὰ δέσμ' ὑπάρχει. δῆλον οὖν ἔτ' ἔσθ' ὅτι
ἥξει με σώσων· οὐ γὰρ ἂν παρέπτατο.

---

[a] The Scythian brings Mnesilochus in, fastened to his plank, and sets it up on the stage.

[b] ἐνταῦθα, οἴμωξε, αἰθρίαν, (1002) ἱκετεύσῃς, (1003) δρῶ, (1005) μᾶλλον βούλη, (1007) φέρε ἐξενέγκω φορμόν, ἵνα φυλάξω σε.

[c] Euripides makes a momentary appearance in the character of Perseus. The third play to be caricatured is the famous

Over the joyous hills
> the sweet strange melody ringing.
Hark ! Cithaeron resounds,
Pleased the notes to prolong ;
Hark ! the bosky ravines
And the wild slopes thunder and roar,
Volleying back the song.
Round thee the ivy fair
With delicate tendril twines.[a]

SCYTHIAN. Dere now bemoany to de ouder air.[b]
MN. O, I entreat you.
SC.   Nod endread me zu.
MN. Slack it a little.
SC.   Dat is vat I does.
MN. O mercy ! mercy ! O, you drive it tighter.
SC. Dighder zu wiss him ?
MN.   Miserable me !
Out on you, villain.
SC.   Zilence, bad ole man.
I'se fetch de mad, an' vatch zu comfibly.
MN. These are the joys Euripides has brought me ![c]
O Gods ! O Saviour Zeus ! there's yet a hope.
Then he won't fail me ! Out he flashed as Perseus.
I understand the signals, I'm to act
The fair Andromeda in chains. Ah, well,
Here are the chains, worse luck, wherewith to
> act her.
He'll come and succour me ; he's in the wings.[d]

Andromeda; see Introduction. Andromeda, bound to the
rock, laments to her friends, who answer her.
  [d] Lit. " or he would not have flitted by." He probably
does not enter until 1098, and the song given to E. in the
translation belongs properly to Mn.
  Euripides enters singing airily.

(ὡς Ἀνδρομέδα)
φίλαι παρθένοι φίλαι,   1015
πῶς ἂν ἀπέλθοιμι, καὶ
τὸν Σκύθην λάθοιμι;
κλύεις, ὦ προσᾴδουσα ταῖς ἐν ἄντροις,
κατάνευσον, ἔασον ὡς   1020
τὴν γυναῖκά μ᾽ ἐλθεῖν.
ἄνοικτος ὅς μ᾽ ἔδησε τὸν
πολυπονώτατον βροτῶν·
μόλις δὲ γραῖαν ἀποφυγὼν
σαπράν, ἀπωλόμην ὅμως.   1025
ὅδε γὰρ ὁ Σκύθης φύλαξ
πάλαι ἐφέστηκ᾽, ὀλοὸν ἄφιλον
ἐκρέμασεν κόρακι δεῖπνον.
ὁρᾷς; οὐ χοροῖσιν, οὐδ᾽ ὑφ᾽   1030
ἡλίκων νεανίδων [κη-
μῷ ᾽φέστηκ᾽] ἔχουσα ψῆφον,
ἀλλ᾽ ἐν πυκνοῖς δεσμοῖσιν ἐμ-
πεπλεγμένη κήτει βορὰ
Γλαυκέτῃ πρόκειμαι.
γαμηλίῳ μὲν οὐ ξὺν
παιῶνι, δεσμίῳ δέ,   1035
γοᾶσθέ μ᾽, ὦ γυναῖκες,—ὡς
μέλεα μὲν πέπονθα μέλεος,
ὦ τάλας ἐγώ, τάλας,
ἀπὸ δὲ συγγόνων ἄλλ᾽ ἄνομα

---

^a ἐξ Ἀνδρομέδας Εὐριπίδου φίλαι παρθένοι, φίλαι μοι: Schol.

^b 1019-21 are taken from the *Andromeda*, but the exact words cannot be restored (fr. 119, Nauck).

Euripides retires, and Mnesilochus commences a Euripidean monody, mostly composed of quotations from the "Andromeda," adapted to his own position.

^c ἄνοικτος ὃς τεκών σε τὴν πολυπονωτάτην βροτῶν μεθῆκεν Ἅιδᾳ πατρὸς ὑπερθανεῖν, Androm. fr. 118.

EU.   Now to peep, now to creep
      Soft and slily through.
    Maidens, pretty maidens,[a]
    Tell me what I am to do.
    Tell me how to glide
    By the Scythian Argus-eyed,
    And to steal away my bride.
   Tell me, tell me, tell me, tell me,
         tell me, tell me, tell,
  Echo, always lurking in the cavern and the dell.[b]

MN.   A cold unpitying heart had he
    Who bound me here in misery.[c]
    Hardly escaped from mouldy dame,
    I'm caught and done for, just the same.
    Lo, the Scythian guard beside me,
    Friendless, helpless, here he tied me ;
    Soon upon these limbs of mine
    Shall the greedy ravens dine.
    Seest thou ? not to me belong
    Youthful pleasures, dance and song,
    Never, never more shall I
    With my friends sweet law-suits try,[d]
  But woven chains with many a link surround me,
  Till Glaucetes,[e] that ravening whale, has found me.
    Home I nevermore shall see ;
    Bridal songs are none for me,
    Nought but potent incantations ;
    Sisters, raise your lamentations,
    Woe, woe, woeful me,
    Sorrow, and trouble, and misery.
    Weeping, weeping, endless weeping,

---

[d] ὁρᾷς . . . νεανίδων, *Androm.* fr. 122. So also 1034, 1039
and probably most of the ode.
 [e] A glutton, *cf. P.* 1008.

πάθεα—φῶτα λιτομέναν, πολυ-   1040
δάκρυτον Ἀίδα γόον φεύζουσαν
  αἶ αἶ αἶ αἶ, ἔ, ἔ,
ὃς ἔμ' ἀπεξύρησε πρῶτον,
ὃς ἐμὲ κροκόεν εἶτ' ἐνέδυσεν,
ἐπὶ δὲ τοῖσδ', ἐς τόδ' ἀνέπεμψεν   1045
  ἱερόν, ἔνθα γυναῖκες.
ἰώ μοι μοίρας ἄτεγκτε δαίμων·
  ὦ κατάρατος ἐγώ.
τίς ἐμὸν οὐκ ἐπόψεται
πάθος ἀμέγαρτον ἐπὶ κακῶν παρουσίᾳ;
εἴθε με πυρφόρος αἰθέρος ἀστὴρ   1050
τὸν βάρβαρον ἐξολέσειεν.
οὐ γὰρ ἔτ' ἀθανάταν φλόγα λεύσσειν
ἐστὶν ἐμοὶ φίλον, ὡς ἐκρεμάσθην,
λαιμότμητ' ἄχη δαιμόνων, αἰόλαν
  νέκυσιν ἔπι πορείαν.   1055

ΗΧΩ. χαῖρ', ὦ φίλη παῖ· τὸν δὲ πατέρα Κηφέα,
  ὅς σ' ἐξέθηκεν, ἀπολέσειαν οἱ θεοί.
ΜΝ. σὺ δ' εἶ τίς, ἥτις τοὐμὸν ᾤκτειρας πάθος;
ΗΧΩ. Ἠχώ, λόγων ἀντῳδὸς ἐπικοκκάστρια,
  ἥπερ πέρυσιν ἐν τῷδε ταὐτῷ χωρίῳ   1060
  Εὐριπίδῃ καὐτὴ ξυνηγωνιζόμην.
  ἀλλ', ὦ τέκνον, σὲ μὲν τὸ σαυτῆς χρὴ ποιεῖν,
  κλαίειν ἐλεινῶς.
ΜΝ.   σὲ δ' ἐπικλαίειν ὕστερον.
ΗΧΩ. ἐμοὶ μελήσει ταῦτά γ'. ἀλλ' ἄρχου λόγων.
ΜΝ.   ὦ νὺξ ἱερὰ   1065

---

[a] The Scythian (βάρβαρον) is a surprise, diverting the curse from the speaker to his jailer.

[b] *A voice is heard from behind the scenes. It is the voice of Echo.*

Far from home and all I know,
Praying him who wronged me so.
　　O ! O ! Woe ! woe !
First with razor keen he hacks me,
Next in yellow silk he packs me,
Sends me then to dangerous dome,
Where the women prowl and roam.
O heavy Fate !　O fatal blow !
O woeful lot ! and lots of woe !
O, how they will chide me,
　　　　　　　and gibe, and deride me !
And O that the flashing, and roaring, and dashing
Red bolt of the thunder
　　　　　　　might smite me in sunder—
The Scythian [a] who lingers beside me !
For where is the joy of the sunshine and glow
To one who is lying, distracted and dying,
With throat-cutting agonies
　　　　　　　riving him, driving him
Down, down to the darkness below.[b]

ECHO. O welcome, daughter ; but the Gods destroy
Thy father Cepheus, who exposed thee thus.

MN. O, who art thou that mournest for my woes ?

EC. Echo, the vocal mocking-bird of song,
I who, last year, in these same lists contended,
A faithful friend, beside Euripides.[c]
And now, my child, for thou must play thy part,
Make dolorous wails.

MN. 　　　　　　　And you wail afterwards ?

EC. I'll see to that ; only begin at once.

MN. 　　[d]O Night most holy,

---

[c] When the *Andromeda* was exhibited. Andromeda in that play addressed her laments to Night (1065), and Echo answered her. Thus she "helped Euripides."

[d] This stanza comes from the *Andromeda*; so 1070.

ARISTOPHANES

ὡς μακρὸν ἵππευμα διώκεις,
ἀστεροειδέα νῶτα διφρεύουσ'
αἰθέρος ἱερᾶς,
τοῦ σεμνοτάτου δι' Ὀλύμπου.

ΗΧΩ.   δι' Ὀλύμπου.

ΜΝ. τί ποτ' Ἀνδρομέδα περίαλλα κακῶν   1070
   μέρος ἐξέλαχον;

ΗΧΩ.   μέρος ἐξέλαχον;

ΜΝ. θανάτου τλήμων.

ΗΧΩ.   θανάτου τλήμων.

ΜΝ. ἀπολεῖς μ', ὦ γραῦ, στωμυλλομένη.

ΗΧΩ. στωμυλλομένη.

ΜΝ. νὴ Δί' ὀχληρά γ' εἰσήρρηκας   1075
   λίαν.

ΗΧΩ.   λίαν.

ΜΝ. ὦγάθ', ἔασόν με μονῳδῆσαι,
   καὶ χαριεῖ μοι. παῦσαι.

ΗΧΩ.   παῦσαι.

ΜΝ. βάλλ' ἐς κόρακας.

ΗΧΩ.   βάλλ' ἐς κόρακας,

ΜΝ τί κακόν;

ΗΧΩ.   τί κακόν;

ΜΝ.   ληρεῖς.

ΗΧΩ.   ληρεῖς.   1080

ΜΝ. οἴμωζ'.

ΗΧΩ.   οἴμωζ'.

ΜΝ.   ὀτότυζ'.

ΗΧΩ.   ὀτότυζ'.

ΣΚ. οὗτος σί λαλῖς;

O'er dread Olympus, vast and far,
In thy dark car
Thou journeyest slowly
Through Ether ridged with many a star.

EC. With many a star.

MN. Why on Andromeda ever must flow
Sorrow and woe?

EC. Sorrow and woe?

MN. Heavy of fate.

EC. Heavy of fate.

MN. Old woman, you'll kill me, I know, with your prate.

EC. Know with your prate.

MN. Why, how tiresome you are: you are going too far.

EC. You are going too far.

MN. Good friend, if you kindly will leave me in peace,[a]
You'll do me a favour, O prithee, cease.

EC. Cease.

MN. O, go to the crows!

EC. O, go to the crows!

MN. Why can't you be still?

EC. Why can't you be still?

MN. (*spitefully*) Old gossip!

EC. (*spitefully*) Old gossip!

MN. Lackaday!

EC. Lackaday!

MN. And alas!

EC. And alas![b]

SC.[c] O, vat does zu say?

---

[a] In the tragedy, Andromeda says: ἔασον, Ἀχοῖ, με σὺν
φίλαις γόου πόθον λαβεῖν.

[b] *The Scythian suddenly awakes to the fact that his prisoner
is taking part in a conversation.*

[c] τί λαλεῖς, 1086 πόθεν ἡ φωνή, 1089 κακκάσκι· καταγελᾷς
(Schol.), 1092 φεύγει χαιρήσεις.

ΗΧΩ.   οὗτος σί λαλῖς;
ΣΚ. πρυτάνεις καλέσω.
ΗΧΩ.   πρυτάνεις καλέσω.
ΣΚ.   σί κακόν;
ΗΧΩ.   σί κακόν; 1085
ΣΚ. πῶτε τὸ πωνή;
ΗΧΩ.   πῶτε τὸ πωνή;
ΣΚ. σὺ λαλῖς;
ΗΧΩ.   σὺ λαλῖς;
ΣΚ.   κλαύσαι.
ΗΧΩ.   κλαύσαι.
ΣΚ. κακκάσκι μοι;
ΗΧΩ.   κακκάσκι μοι;
ΜΝ. μὰ Δί', ἀλλὰ γυνή πλησίον αὕτη.   1090
ΗΧΩ. πλησίον αὕτη.
ΣΚ. ποῦ 'στ' ἡ μιαρά; καὶ δὴ πεύγει.
    ποῖ ποῖ πεύγεις; οὐ καιρήσεις.
ΗΧΩ. οὐ καιρήσεις.
ΣΚ. ἔτι γὰρ γρύζεις;
ΗΧΩ.   ἔτι γὰρ γρύζεις;   1095
ΣΚ. λαβὲ τῇ μιαρά.
ΗΧΩ.   λαβὲ τῇ μιαρά.
ΣΚ. λάλο καὶ κατάρατο γύναικο.
ΕΤ. (ὡς Περσεύς) ὦ θεοὶ τίν' ἐς γῆν βαρβάρων
        ἀφίγμεθα
    ταχεῖ πεδίλῳ; διὰ μέσου γὰρ αἰθέρος
    τέμνων κέλευθον, πόδα τίθημ' ὑπόπτερον,   1100
    Περσεύς, πρὸς Ἄργος ναυστολῶν, τὸ Γοργόνος
    κάρα κομίζων.
ΣΚ.   σί λέγι; τῇ Γόργος πέρι

ᵃ *Euripides enters in the guise of Perseus.*

EC.   O, vat does zu say ?

SC.   I'se calls de police.

EC.   I'se calls de police.

SC.   Vat nosense is dis ?

EC.   Vat nosense is dis ?

SC.   Vy, vere is de voice ?

EC.   Vy, vere is de voice ?

SC. (*to Mn.*) Vos id zu ?

EC.   Vos id zu ?

SC.   Zu'll catch id.

EC.   Zu'll catch id.

SC.   Does zu mocksh ?

EC.   Does zu mocksh ?

MN.   'Tisn't I, I declare : it is that woman there.

EC.   It is that woman there.

SC.   Vy, vere is de wretch ?

                               Me mush catch, me mush catch.
           Her's a gone, her's a fled.

EC.   Her's a gone, her's a fled.

SC.   Zu'll a suffer for dis.

EC.   Zu'll a suffer for dis.

SC.   Vat again ?

EC.   Vat again ?

SC.   Zeege ole o' de mix.

EC.   Zeege ole o' de mix.

SC.   Vat a babbled an' talketing ooman.[a]

EU.   [b]Ah me, what wild and terrible coast is this ?
           Plying the pathless air with wingèd feet,
           Steering for Argos, bearing in my hand
           The Gorgon's head—

SC.   Vat dat zu say o' Gorgo ?

[b] All E.'s speech comes from the *Andromeda*; so 1105
(fr. 124-125). In the *Andromeda*, Perseus sees the maiden
and a dialogue ensues. Doubtless he attempts to loose her
after slaying the monster.

τὸ γραμματέο σὺ τὴ κεπαλή;

ΕΥ.   τὴν Γοργόνος
ἔγωγε φημί.

ΣΚ.   Γοργό τοι κἀγὼ λέγι.

ΕΥ. ἔα· τίν' ὄχθον τόνδ' ὁρῶ καὶ παρθένον   1105
θεαῖς ὁμοίαν ναῦν ὅπως ὡρμισμένην;

ΜΝ. ὦ ξένε, κατοίκτειρόν με τὴν παναθλίαν,
λῦσόν με δεσμῶν.

ΣΚ.   οὐκὶ μὶ λαλῆσι σύ;
κατάρατο τολμᾷς ἀποτανουμένη λαλᾷς;

ΕΥ. ὦ παρθέν' οἰκτείρω σὲ κρεμαμένην ὁρῶν.   1110

ΣΚ. οὐ παρτέν' ἐστίν, ἀλλ' ἁμαρτωλὴ γέρων,
καὶ κλέπτο καὶ πανοῦργο.

ΕΥ.   ληρεῖς ὦ Σκύθα.
αὕτη γάρ ἐστιν Ἀνδρομέδα παῖς Κηφέως.

ΣΚ. σκέψαι τὸ κύστο· μή τι μικτὸν παίνεται;

ΕΥ. φέρε δεῦρό μοι τὴν χεῖρ', ἵν' ἅψωμαι κόρης·1115
φέρε, Σκύθ'· ἀνθρώποισι γὰρ νοσήματα
ἅπασίν ἐστιν· ἐμὲ δὲ καὐτὸν τῆς κόρης
ταύτης ἔρως εἴληφεν.

ΣΚ.   οὐ ζηλῶσί σε·
ἀτὰρ εἰ τὸ πρωκτὸ δεῦρο περιεστραμμένον,
οὐκ ἐπτόνησά σ' αὐτὸ πυγίζεις ἄγων.   1120

ΕΥ. τί δ' οὐκ ἐᾷς λύσαντά μ' αὐτήν, ὦ Σκύθα,
πεσεῖν ἐς εὐνὴν καὶ γαμήλιον λέχος;

ΣΚ. εἰ σπόδρ' ἐπιτυμεῖς τὴ γέροντο πύγισο,
τὴ σανίδο τρήσας ἐξόπιστο πρώκτισον.

ΕΥ. μὰ Δί', ἀλλὰ λύσω δεσμά.

ᵃ τί λέγεις; τοῦ Γόργου φέρεις τοῦ γραμματέως τὴν κεφαλήν.
For Gorgon's head he substitutes "the head of Gorgias the
writer," that is, the famous rhetorician of Leontini, who was
then living at Athens.   Cf. Plato, *Symposium*, ch. xx.

Dat zu has gots de writer Gorgo's head ? [a]

EU. " Gorgon," I say.

SC. An' me says " Gorgo " too.

EU. Alas, what crag is this, and lashed upon it
What maiden, beautiful as shapes divine,
A lovely craft too rudely moored ?

MN. [b] O stranger,
Pity the sorrows of a poor young woman,
And loose my bonds.

SC.[c] Vat, vill zu no be quiet ?
Vat, talkee, talkee, ven zu're goin' to die ?

EU. Fair girl, I weep to see thee hanging there.

SC. Disn't von gal : dis von ole vilain man,
Von vare bad rascal fellow.

EU. Scythian, peace !
This is Andromeda, King Cepheus' daughter.

SC. Von dawder ! Dis ? Vare obvious man, metinks.[d]

EU. O, reach thy hand, and let me clasp my love ;
O Scythian, reach. Ah me, what passionate storms
Toss in men's souls ; and as for mine, O lady,
Thou art my love !

SC.[e] Me nod admire zure dasde.
Sdill zu may tiss her, if zu wiss id, dere.

EU. Hard-hearted Scythian, give me up my love,
And I will take her,—take her aye to wife.

SC.[f] Tiss her, me says ; me nod objex to dat.

EU. Ah me, I'll loose her bonds.

[b] *Andromeda*, fr. 128.

[c] οὐχὶ μὴ λαλήσεις, λαλῆσαι, 1114 τὸν κύσθον, μικρὸν φαίνεται.

[d] Lit. specta penem hunc: num tibi parvus videtur?

[e] εἰ μὴ τὸ νῶτον ἦν πρὸς τῇ σανίδι, ἀλλὰ πρὸς ἡμᾶς ἐτέτραπτο,
οὐκ ἄν σοι ἐφθόνησα ἀπαγαγόντι περανεῖν: Schol. Lines 1119-
20: si podex huc conversus esset, non tibi inviderem, quin
praecideres.

[f] εἰ σφόδρα ἐπιθυμεῖς τὸν γέροντα πυγίσαι, τὴν σανίδα τρήσας
ἐξόπισθε πρώκτισον : tabula perforata a tergo culum divide.

ΣΚ.   μαστιγῶ σ᾽ ἄρα.   1125
ΕΥ. καὶ μὴν ποιήσω τοῦτο.
ΣΚ.   τὸ κεπαλή σ᾽ ἄρα
     τὸ ξιπομάκαιραν ἀποκεκόψω τουτοΐ.
ΕΥ. αἲ αἲ τί δράσω; πρὸς τίνας στρεφθῶ λόγους;
     ἀλλ᾽ οὐκ ἂν ἐνδέξαιτο βάρβαρος φύσις.
     σκαιοῖσι γάρ τοι καινὰ προσφέρων σοφὰ   1130
     μάτην ἀναλίσκοις ἄν, ἀλλ᾽ ἄλλην τινὰ
     τούτῳ πρέπουσαν μηχανὴν προσοιστέον.
ΣΚ. μιαρὸς ἀλώπηξ, οἷον ἐπιτήκιζέ μοι.
ΜΝ. μέμνησο Περσεῦ μ᾽ ὡς καταλείπεις ἀθλίαν.
ΣΚ. ἔτι γὰρ σὺ τῇ μάστιγαν ἐπιτυμεῖς λαβεῖν;   1135

ΧΟ.   Παλλάδα τὴν φιλόχορον ἐμοὶ
        δεῦρο καλεῖν νόμος ἐς χορόν,
           παρθένον ἄζυγα κούρην,
        ἣ πόλιν ἡμετέραν ἔχει   [στρ. α 1140
        καὶ κράτος φανερὸν μόνη
           κλῃδοῦχός τε καλεῖται.
        φάνηθ᾽ ὦ τυράννους
        στυγοῦσ᾽ ὥσπερ εἰκός.
        δῆμός τοί σε καλεῖ γυναι-   [ἀντ. α 1145
        κῶν· ἔχουσα δέ μοι μόλοις
        εἰρήνην φιλέορτον.

        ἥκετέ τ᾽ εὔφρονες ἵλαοι,   [στρ. β
        πότνιαι, ἄλσος ἐς ὑμέτερον,
        οὗ δὴ ἀνδράσιν οὐ θέμις εἰσορᾶν   1150
        ὄργια σεμνὰ θεαῖν, ἵνα λαμπάσι

     ᵃ τὴν κεφαλήν σου τῇ ξιφομαχαίρᾳ ἀποκόψω ταύτῃ.
     ᵇ Line 1130 is from Eur. *Medea*, 299.
     ᶜ ἐπιθήκιζε.

sc.   Zu bedder nod.

eu. Ah me, I will.

sc.[a]   Den, me'se cut off zure head.
Me draw de cudless, and zu die, zu dead.

eu. Ah, what avails me ?   Shall I make a speech ?
His savage nature could not take it in.
True wit and wisdom were but labour lost
On such a rude barbarian.[b]   I must try
Some more appropriate, fitter stratagem.

(He goes out.)

sc. O, de vile vox !   He jocket me vare near.[c]

mn. O, Perseus, Perseus, wilt thou leave me so ?

sc. Vat, does zu askin' for de vip again ?

ch.   Pallas we call upon,
             Chastest and purest one,
             Maiden and Virgin, our
                   Revels to see :
             Guarding our portals
             Alone of Immortals,
             Mightily, potently,
                   Keeping the key.
             Hater of Tyranny,
             Come, for we call thee, we
                   Women in Chorus.
             Bring Peace again with thee,
             Jocundly, merrily,
                   Long to reign o'er us.

             Sacred, unearthly ones,
                   Awfullest Shades,
             Graciously, peacefully,
                   Come to your glades.
             Man must not gaze on the
                   Rites at your shrine,

233

φαίνετον ἄμβροτον ὄψιν.
μόλετον ἔλθετον, ἀντόμεθ᾽ ὦ   [ἀντ. β 1155
Θεσμοφόρω πολυποτνία,
εἰ καὶ πρότερόν ποτ᾽ ἐπηκόω
ἤλθετον, ἔλθετε νῦν, ἀφίκεσθ᾽ ἱκε-
τεύομεν ἐνθάδε χἠμῖν.

ΕΥ. γυναῖκες εἰ βούλεσθε τὸν λοιπὸν χρόνον   1160
σπονδὰς ποιήσασθαι πρὸς ἐμέ, νυνὶ πάρα,
ἐφ᾽ ᾧτ᾽ ἀκοῦσαι μηδὲν ὑπ᾽ ἐμοῦ μηδαμὰ
κακὸν τὸ λοιπόν. ταῦτ᾽ ἐπικηρυκεύομαι.

ΧΟ. χρεία δὲ ποία τόνδ᾽ ἐπεισφέρεις λόγον;

ΕΥ. ὅδ᾽ ἐστίν, οὑν τῇ σανίδι, κηδεστὴς ἐμός.   1165
ἢν οὖν κομίσωμαι τοῦτον, οὐδὲν μού ποτε
κακῶς ἀκούσετ᾽· ἢν δὲ μὴ πίθησθέ μοι,
ἃ νῦν ὑποικουρεῖτε, τοῖσιν ἀνδράσιν
ἀπὸ τῆς στρατιᾶς παροῦσιν ὑμῶν διαβαλῶ.

ΧΟ. τὰ μὲν παρ᾽ ἡμῶν ἴσθι σοι πεπεισμένα·   1170
τὸν βάρβαρον δὲ τοῦτον αὐτὸς πεῖθε σύ.

ΕΥ. ἐμὸν ἔργον ἐστίν· καὶ σόν, ὦλάφιον, ἅ σοι
καθ᾽ ὁδὸν ἔφραζον ταῦτα μεμνῆσθαι ποιεῖν.
πρῶτον μὲν οὖν δίελθε κἀνακόλπασον
σὺ δ᾽, ὦ Τερηδών, ἐπαναφύσα Περσικόν.   1175

ΣΚ. τί τὸ βόμβο τοῦτο; κῶμο τίς ἀνεγείρί μοι;

ΕΥ. ἡ παῖς ἔμελλε προμελετᾶν, ὦ τοξότα.
ὀρχησομένη γὰρ ἔρχεθ᾽ ὡς ἄνδρας τινάς.

ΣΚ. ὄρκησι καὶ μελετῆσι, οὐ κωλύσ᾽ ἐγώ.

---

a *Euripides comes in, dressed as an old music-woman.*
b The name of some piper.   c ὁ βόμβος, κῶμον ἀνεγείρει.
d (1179) ὀρχησάσθω καὶ μελετησάτω· οὐ κωλύσω ἐγώ. ὡς
ἐλαφρά, ὥσπερ ψύλλα κατὰ τὸ κώδιον. (1183) ναιχί, κάθησο
θυγάτριον· ὡς στέριφον τὸ τιτθίον. (1187) κλαύσῃ, ἀνακύπτει

Torch-glimmer flashing o'er
    Features divine.
Come, for we're pouring
Imploring, adoring,
    Intense veneration ;
Dawn on your worshippers,
Givers of Home and our
    Civilization.[a]

EU. Ladies, I offer terms.   If well and truly
Your honourable sex befriend me now,
I won't abuse your honourable sex
From this time forth for ever.   This I offer.

CH. (*suspiciously*) But what's your object in proposing
    this ?

EU. That poor old man there, he's my poor old cousin.
Let him go free, and nevermore will I
Traduce your worthy sex ; but if you won't,
I'll meet your husbands coming from the Wars,
And put them up to all your goings-on.

CH. We take your terms, so far as we're concerned,
But you yourself must manage with the Scythian.

EU. I'll manage *him*.   Now, Hop-o'-my-thumb, come
    forward,

                    (*A dancing-girl enters.*)

And mind the things I taught you on the way.
Hold up your frock : skip lightly through the
    dance.
The Persian air, Teredon,[b] if you please.

SC.[c] Vy, vat dis buzbuz ? revels come dis vay ?

EU. She's going to practise, Scythian, that is all.
She's got to dance in public by-and-by.

SC.[d] Yesh, practish, yesh.   Hoick ! how se bobs about !

καὶ παρακύπτει ἀπεψωλημένον. εἶεν· καλὸν τὸ σχῆμα περὶ τὸ
πόσθιον.

235

ὡς ἐλαπρός, ὥσπερ ψύλλο κατὰ τὸ κώδιο. 1180

ΕΥ. φέρε, θοἰμάτιον κατάθου μέν, ὦ τέκνον, τοδί·
καθιζομένη δ᾽ ἐπὶ τοῖσι γόνασι τοῦ Σκύθου,
τὼ πόδε πρότεινον, ἵν᾽ ὑπολύσω.

ΣΚ.   ναῖκι ναὶ
κάτησο κάτησο, ναῖκι ναί, τυγάτριον.
οἴμ᾽ ὡς στέριπο τὸ τιττί, ὥσπερ γογγύλη. 1185

ΕΥ. αὔλει σὺ θᾶττον· ἔτι δέδοικας τὸν Σκύθην;

ΣΚ. καλό γε τὸ πυγή. κλαῦσί γ᾽ ἂν μὴ ᾽νδον
    μένῃς.
ἀνακύπτι καὶ παρακύπτι ἀπεψωλημένος·
εἶεν· καλὴ τὸ σκῆμα περὶ τὸ πόστιον.

ΕΥ. καλῶς ἔχει. λαβὲ θοἰμάτιον· ὥρα ᾽στὶ νῶν
ἤδη βαδίζειν.

ΣΚ.   οὐκὶ πιλῆσι πρῶτά με; 1190

ΕΥ. πάνυ γε· φίλησον αὐτόν.

ΣΚ.   ὂ ὂ ὂ παπαπαῖ,
ὡς γλυκερὸ τὸ γλῶσσ᾽, ὥσπερ Ἀττικὸς μέλις.
τί οὐ κατεύδει παρ᾽ ἐμέ;

ΕΥ.   χαῖρε τοξότα,
οὐ γὰρ γένοιτ᾽ ἂν τοῦτο.

ΣΚ.   ναὶ ναὶ γράδιο.
ἐμοὶ κάρισο σὺ τοῦτο.

ΕΥ.   δώσεις οὖν δραχμήν; 1195

ΣΚ. ναὶ ναῖκι δῶσι.

ΕΥ.   τἀργύριον τοίνυν φέρε.

ΣΚ. ἀλλ᾽ οὐκ ἔκωδέν· ἀλλὰ τὸ συβήνην λαβέ.
ἔπειτα κομίζις αὖτις; ἀκολούτι, τέκνον.
σὺ δὲ τοῦτο τήρει τὴ γέροντο, γράδιο.
ὄνομα δέ σοι τί ἔστιν;

ΕΥ.   Ἀρτεμισία. 1200

ΣΚ. μεμνῆσι τοίνυν τοὔνομ᾽· Ἀρταμουξία.

  Now here, now dere : von vlea upon de planket.

EU. Just stop a moment ; throw your mantle off ;
  Come, sit you down beside the Scythian here,
  And I'll unloose your slippers. That will do.
  We must be moving homeward.[a]

SC.[b]   May I tiss her ?

EU. Once, only once.

SC. (*kissing her*) O, O, vat vare sweet tiss !
  Dat's vare moche sweeter dan zure Attish honies.
  Dooze let me tiss her tecon time, ole lady.

EU. No, Scythian, no ; we really can't allow it.

SC. O doozy, doozy, dear ole lady, doozy.

EU. Will you give silver for one kiss ?

SC.[c]   Yesh ! yesh !

EU. Well, p'raps on that consideration, Scythian,
  We won't object ; but give the silver first.

SC.[d] Silver ? Vy, vere ? I'se got none. Take dis
   bow-cus.
  Zu, vat I call zu ?

EU.   Artemisia.

SC. Yesh. Hartomixer.

---

 [a] Lines 1183-1189. sc. Nae, sede, sede, nae, filiola. Hei
mihi, quam firmae sunt papillae, instar rapae! EU. Cane
tu ocius. An adhuc Scytham times? sc. Pulchrae hercle
sunt nates. (*Mutonem ipsum allocutus*) Male tibi erit, nisi
sub veste manebis. Sursum deorsum movetur nudatus.
Esto: pulchra est species mentulae. EU. Recte est: cape
vestem, tempus est iam nobis abeundi.
 [b] φιλήσεις.   [c] δώσω.
 [d] ἔχω οὐδέν, σιβύνην "bow-case," κομίζεις, ἀκολούθει, (1201)
μεμνήσομαι.

ΕΥ. Ἑρμῆ δόλιε, ταυτὶ μὲν ἔτι καλῶς ποιεῖς.
σὺ μὲν οὖν ἀπότρεχε, παιδάριον τουτὶ λαβών·
ἐγὼ δὲ λύσω τόνδε. σὺ δ᾽ ὅπως ἀνδρικῶς
ὅταν λυθῇς τάχιστα, φεύξει, καὶ τενεῖς   1205
ὡς τὴν γυναῖκα καὶ τὰ παιδί᾽ οἴκαδε.
ΜΝ. ἐμοὶ μελήσει ταῦτά γ᾽, ἢν ἅπαξ λυθῶ.
ΕΥ. λέλυσο. σὸν ἔργον, φεῦγε πρὶν τὸν τοξότην
ἥκοντα καταλαβεῖν.
ΜΝ.   ἐγὼ δὴ τοῦτο δρῶ.
ΣΚ. ὦ γράδι᾽ ὡς καρίεντό σοι τὸ τυγάτριον,   1210
κοὐ δύσκολ᾽ ἀλλὰ πρᾶο. ποῦ τὸ γράδιο;
οἴμ᾽ ὡς ἀπόλωλο· ποῦ τὸ γέροντ᾽ ἐντευτενί;
ὦ γράδι᾽, ὦ γρᾷ᾽. οὐκ ἐπαινῶ γράδιο.
Ἀρταμουξία.
διέβαλλέ μ᾽ ὁ γραῦς. ἀπότρεκ᾽ ὡς τάκιστα σύ·
ὀρτῶς δὲ συβήνη 'στί· καταβηνῆσι γάρ.   1215
οἴμοι,
τί δρᾶσι; ποῖ τὸ γράδι᾽; Ἀρταμουξία.
ΧΟ. τὴν γραῦν ἐρωτᾷς ἢ 'φερεν τὰς πηκτίδας;
ΣΚ. ναὶ ναῖκι. εἶδες αὐτό;
ΧΟ.   ταύτῃ γ᾽ οἴχεται
αὐτή τ᾽ ἐκείνη καὶ γέρων τις εἵπετο.
ΣΚ. κροκῶτ᾽ ἔκοντο τὴ γέροντο;
ΧΟ.   φήμ᾽ ἐγώ.   1220
ἔτ᾽ ἂν καταλάβοις, εἰ διώκοις ταυτηί.
ΣΚ. ὦ μιαρὸ γρᾶο· πότερα τρέξι τὴν ὁδό;
Ἀρταμουξία.

---

[a] *Hop-o'-my-thumb runs out. The Scythian flings his bow-case to Euripides and runs after her.*

[b] *Euripides and Mnesilochus leave the stage. They are hardly out of sight when the Scythian returns.*

EU.   Hillo, what's that ?   She's off.

SC. I'se fetch her pack ; zu, look to bad ole man.[a]

EU. O tricky Hermes, you befriend me still.
    Good-bye, old Scythian ; catch her if you can.
    Meanwhile I'll free your prisoner : and do you
    (*to Mn.*) Run like a hero, when I've loosed your bonds,
    Straight to the bosom of your family.

MN. Trust me for that, so soon as these are off.

EU. There then, they are off : now run away, before
    The Scythian come and catch you.

MN.   Won't I just ![b]

SC.[c] Ole lady, here's—vy, vere's ole lady fannish ?
    Vere's dat ole man ? O bah, I smells de trick.
    Ole lady, dis vare bad o' zu, ole lady !
    Me nod expex dis of zu.   Bad ole lady.
        Hartomixer !
    Bow-cusses ?   Yesh, zu von big howcus-bowcus.[d]
    Vat sall I does ? vere can ole lady was ?
        Hartomixer !

CH. Mean you the ancient dame who bore the lute ?

SC. Yesh, does zu saw her ?

CH.   Yes, indeed I did.
    She went *that* way : there was an old man with
      her.

SC.[e] Von yellow-shilk ole man ?

CH.   Exactly so.
    I think you'll catch them if you take *that* road.

SC. Vare bad ole lady, did se vich vay run ?
        Hartomixer !

---

[c] χαρίεν, σου, δύσκολον, πρᾷον, ἀπόλωλα, ὁ γέρων ἐντευθενί·
ἀπότρεχε, τάχιστα.
[d] Line 1215 : ὀρθῶς σιβύνη ἐστί, κατεβίνησε γάρ, " well is it
named, for it has played me a foul trick " (σι-βύνη, ἐ-βίνησε).
[e] κροκωτὸν ἔχων ὁ γέρων.

χο. ὀρθὴν ἄνω δίωκε. ποῖ θεῖς; οὐ πάλιν.
    τῃδὶ διώξεις; τοὔμπαλιν τρέχεις σύ γε.
ΣΚ. κακόδαιμον, ἀλλὰ τρέξι Ἀρταμουξία.   1225
χο. τρέχε νυν, τρέχε νυν, κατὰ τοὺς κόρακας,
    ἐπουρίσας.
       ἀλλὰ πέπαισται μετρίως ἡμῖν·
       ὥσθ᾽ ὥρα δῆτ᾽ ἐστὶ βαδίζειν
         οἴκαδ᾽ ἑκάστῃ.
       τὼ Θεσμοφόρω δ᾽ ἡμῖν ἀγαθὴν   1230
       τούτων χάριν ἀνταποδοίτην.

---

[a] *They are of course misdirecting him; notwithstanding which, he seems likely, in his flurry, to stumble on the right road.*

CH. Straight up the hill; no, no, not that direction.[a]
You're going wrong: see, that's the way she went.

SC. O dear, O dear, but Hartomixer runnish.

(*He runs out the wrong way.*)

CH. Merrily, merrily, merrily on
      to your own confusion go.
  But we've ended our say,
      and we're going away,
  Like good honest women,
      straight home from the Play.
  And we trust that the twain-
      Home-givers will deign
  To bless with success our performance to-day.

THE ECCLESIAZUSAE

INTRODUCTION

THERE is no direct evidence of the date of this Comedy; but the allusions made in the play itself, and the Scholiasts' comments, make it clear that it was exhibited in 393 B.C., when Eubulides was archon.

After the Peloponnesian War, Athens remained for about nine years, 404–395 B.C., in a state of humiliation and subjection to Sparta. The Spartans had behaved with great magnanimity, in refusing to destroy Athens utterly; but by so doing, they gave offence to Thebes and Corinth. These states never again supported the Spartan League; they refused to help in opposing Thrasybulus, and later in a war against Elis, nor would they join in the expedition of Agesilaus to Asia Minor; in fact, the Boeotians offered him a direct affront, when he attempted, in remembrance of the Trojan War, to sacrifice at Aulis. Hence in 395, when the Phocians appealed for help against Thebes, Sparta summoned her allies to invade Boeotia: Corinth alone refused. The Boeotians appealed to Athens to form a league against Sparta. "It must have been a time for great searchings of heart amongst the wisest Athenians; and Thrasybulus, then the most eminent leader of the people, seems to have been seriously perplexed and uncertain which course it would be most prudent to adopt. For this was doubtless the occasion on which he first promised the Lacedaemonians to speak in their favour, and then, changing his mind, excused himself on the ground of sudden indisposition" (*Eccl.* 356).[a] However, the League against Sparta was formed, and Athenian troops at once set out for Haliartus ; arriving indeed too late for the battle in which Lysander perished, but in time to aid in driving out the army of Pausanias without another battle.

" Here then we find an alliance which precisely answers to the description given in the speech of Praxagora." [b] At first all went well ; but the great battle of Corinth (394) resulted in the defeat of the League. Agesilaus, returning from Asia, defeated the League again at Coronea. " It was at this juncture, at the commencement of the year 393, that Praxagora comes forward, in the play before us, to condemn the vacillating policy of the men, and to propose that the government of Athens should henceforth be entrusted to the women, as the more stable and conservative sex." [c]

A year later Conon, who had already in 393 won the naval victory of Cnidus, returned to Athens, bringing the Persian fleet and Persian gold ; the Long Walls and the fortifications of the Peiraeus were restored, and Athens was delivered from her anxieties. This is why Conon's name is associated with the League ; and why 392 B.C. is too late a date for the play.

We have yet to discover why Praxagora, the apostle of conservatism, develops in this play " a

---

[a] Rogers, Introduction, p. xiv.
[b] *Ibid.* p. xv.   See 193 and n.   [c] *Ibid.* p. xviii.

scheme so startling and so novel, as to throw into the shade the wildest extravagances of the men. It is a scheme of naked socialism, involving the community of goods, the abolition of marriage, and (what is inaccurately called) the community of women." [a] It seems " impossible to doubt that the cause is to be found in the appearance, whilst Aristophanes was engaged on the *Ecclesiazusae*, of the *Republic* of Plato, or at all events of that part of the work which now constitutes Books II. to V. (inclusive) of the *Republic*." [b] Aristophanes was not the man to let pass such a delightful subject for caricature. Many similarities of thought and diction will be found. At the same time, of course, the comedian alters or exaggerates to suit his purpose ; thus the Platonic communism was confined to the φύλακες, or Guardians of the State, and there is nothing in Plato resembling promiscuous intercourse between the sexes, until the members of this class had passed their prime.

[a] Rogers, Introduction, p. xxii.
[b] *Ibid.* p. xxii.   See notes on 597, 612, 636, 657.

ΤΑ ΤΟΥ ΔΡΑΜΑΤΟΣ ΠΡΟΣΩΠΑ

ΠΡΑΞΑΓΟΡΑ

ΓΥΝΗ Α

ΓΥΝΗ Β

ΧΟΡΟΣ ΓΥΝΑΙΚΩΝ

ΒΛΕΠΥΡΟΣ, ἀνὴρ Πραξαγόρας

ΑΝΗΡ γυναικὸς Β

ΧΡΕΜΗΣ

ΚΗΡΥΞ

ΓΡΑΥΣ Α

ΓΡΑΥΣ Β

ΓΡΑΥΣ Γ

ΜΕΙΡΑΞ

ΝΕΑΝΙΑΣ

ΘΕΡΑΠΑΙΝΑ Πραξαγόρας

ΕΚΚΛΗΣΙΑΖΟΥΣΑΙ

ΠΡΑΞΑΓΟΡΑ. Ὦ λαμπρὸν ὄμμα τοῦ τροχηλάτου λύχνου
κάλλιστ᾿ ἐν εὐσκόποισιν ἐξηρτημένον,
γονάς τε γὰρ σὰς καὶ τύχας δηλώσομεν·
τροχῷ γὰρ ἐλαθεὶς κεραμικῆς ῥύμης ὕπο
μυκτῆρσι λαμπρὰς ἡλίου τιμὰς ἔχεις·   5
ὅρμα φλογὸς σημεῖα τὰ ξυγκείμενα.
σοὶ γὰρ μόνῳ δηλοῦμεν, εἰκότως, ἐπεὶ
κἂν τοῖσι δωματίοισιν Ἀφροδίτης τρόπων
πειρωμέναισι πλησίον παραστατεῖς,
λορδουμένων τε σωμάτων ἐπιστάτην   10
ὀφθαλμὸν οὐδεὶς τὸν σὸν ἐξείργει δόμων.
μόνος δὲ μηρῶν εἰς ἀπορρήτους μυχοὺς
λάμπεις, ἀφεύων τὴν ἐπανθοῦσαν τρίχα·
στοάς τε καρποῦ βακχίου τε νάματος
πλήρεις ὑποιγνύσαισι συμπαραστατεῖς·   15
καὶ ταῦτα συνδρῶν οὐ λαλεῖς τοῖς πλησίον.

ᵃ " The stage represents an Athenian street, with three houses in
the background, the houses of Blepyrus, Chremes, and the husband
of the Second Woman. The hour is 3 ʌ.м. and the stars are still
visible in the sky. A young and delicate woman, clad in masculine
attire, is standing in the street, hanging up a lighted lamp in some
conspicuous place. The woman is Praxagora, the wife of Blepyrus,
who has just left her husband asleep within, and has come out wearing his garments, with his sturdy walking-stick in her hand, and his
red Laconian shoes upon her feet. And the lamp is to serve as a

THE ECCLESIAZUSAE^a

PRAXAGORA. O glowing visage of the earthen lamp,
    On this conspicuous eminence well-hung,—
    (For through thy fates and lineage will we go,
    Thou, who, by whirling wheel of potter moulded,
    Dost with thy nozzle do the sun's bright duty)—
    Awake the appointed signal of the flame!
    Thou only knowest it, and rightly thou,
    For thou alone, within our chambers standing,
    Watchest unblamed the mysteries of love.^b
    Thine eye, inspector of our amorous sports,^c
    Beholdeth all, and no one saith *Begone!*
    Thou comest, singeing, purifying all
    The dim recesses which none else may see;
    And when the garners, stored with corn and wine,
    By stealth we open, thou dost stand beside us.
    And though thou knowest all this, thou dost not peach.

signal to other Athenian women who have agreed to meet her here
before the break of day. No one is yet in sight: and while she is
expecting their arrival, she apostrophizes the lamp in mock-heroic
style, using such language as in tragedy might be addressed to the
sun or moon or to some divine or heroic personage. According to
the Scholiast the poet, in this opening speech, is glancing at some
passage in the tragedies either of Agathon or of Dicaeogenes ": R.
  ^b " The words Ἀφροδίτης τρόποι are equivalent to σχήματα
συνουσίας. In passages like these the translation is not intended
to give the precise sense of the original ": R.
  ^c λοοδουμένων = curvatorum.

ἀνθ' ὧν συνείσει καὶ τὰ νῦν βουλεύματα,
ὅσα Σκίροις ἔδοξε ταῖς ἐμαῖς φίλαις.
ἀλλ' οὐδεμία πάρεστιν ἃς ἥκειν ἐχρῆν.
καίτοι πρὸς ὄρθρον γ' ἐστίν· ἡ δ' ἐκκλησία   20
αὐτίκα μάλ' ἔσται· καταλαβεῖν δ' ἡμᾶς ἕδρας,
ἃς Φυρόμαχός ποτ' εἶπεν, εἰ μέμνησθ' ἔτι,
δεῖ τὰς ἑταίρας κἀγκαθιζομένας λαθεῖν.
τί δῆτ' ἂν εἴη; πότερον οὐκ ἐρραμμένους
ἔχουσι τοὺς πώγωνας, οὓς εἴρητ' ἔχειν;   25
ἢ θαἰμάτια τἀνδρεῖα κλεψάσαις λαθεῖν
ἦν χαλεπὸν αὐταῖς; ἀλλ' ὁρῶ τονδὶ λύχνον
προσιόντα. φέρε νυν ἐπαναχωρήσω πάλιν,
μὴ καί τις ὢν ἀνὴρ ὁ προσιὼν τυγχάνῃ.

ΓΥΝΗ.Α. ὥρα βαδίζειν, ὡς ὁ κῆρυξ ἀρτίως   30
ἡμῶν προσιόντων δεύτερον κεκόκκυκεν.

ΠΡ. ἐγὼ δέ γ' ὑμᾶς προσδοκῶσ' ἐγρηγόρειν
τὴν νύκτα πᾶσαν. ἀλλὰ φέρε, τὴν γείτονα
τήνδ' ἐκκαλέσωμαι, θρυγονῶσα τὴν θύραν.
δεῖ γὰρ τὸν ἄνδρ' αὐτῆς λαθεῖν.

ΓΥ.Β.   ἤκουσά τοι   35
ὑποδουμένη τὸ κνῦμά σου τῶν δακτύλων,
ἅτ' οὐ καταδαρθοῦσ'. ὁ γὰρ ἀνήρ, ὦ φιλτάτη,

ᵃ " The parasol festival ; a festival celebrated by the women
alone, at midsummer, in the month Scirophorion, in honour of
Athene Sciras.   The place of its celebration seems to have been a
spot on the Sacred Way just outside the gates of Athens, where
was the tomb of Scirus, the Dodonaean seer ; and near it a Temple
of Athene Sciras.   It was attended by the priestess of Athene, the
priest of the Sun, and the priest of Erechtheus who came down
from the Acropolis bearing the sacred white parasol, σκιάδειον
λευκὸν ὃ λέγεται Σκῖρον : Scholiast. Cf. T. 834, 835 " : R.
    ᵇ A reference to one of the tragedies spoken of on 1, above, in
which P. seems to have ordered his ἑταίρους to lie in ambush, to

Therefore our plans will we confide to thee,
What at the Scira ^a we resolved to do.
Ah, but there's no one here who should be here.
Yet doth it draw towards daybreak; and the Assembly
Full soon will meet ; and we frail womankind
Must take the seats Phyromachus assigned us
(You don't forget ?) and not attract attention.[b]
What can the matter be ?   Perchance their beards
Are not stitched on, as our decree commanded,
Perchance they found it difficult to steal
Their husband's garments.   Stay !   I see a lamp
Moving this way.   I will retire and watch,
Lest it should haply be some MAN approaching ! [c]

FIRST WOMAN. It is the hour to start.   As I was coming
I heard the herald give his second—crow.[d]

PR. I have been waiting, watching for you all
The whole night long ; and now I'll summon forth
My neighbour here, scratching her door so gently
As not to rouse her husband.

SECOND WOMAN.[e]   Yea, I heard
(For I was up and putting on my shoes)
The stealthy creeping of thy finger-nail.

which Aristophanes gives a new turn by saying ἐταίρας. Probably
εἰ μέμνησθ' ἔτι was part of the speech ; it is not appropriate here.

  [c] *She conceals herself: enter woman with lamp.*

  [d] *Praxagora reappears.*

  [e] " The women who during the next sixteen lines keep drop-
ping in, either singly or in small groups, are in my opinion all
members of the Chorus making their way to the orchestra.   They
are probably twelve in all, forming a semichorus, and representing
that section of Praxagora's followers which dwelt within the city
walls.   The other section, the women from the country, enter in a
body, infra 300, singing their entrance song.   Then the two semi-
choruses coalesce and become the full Chorus of the play.   And
the speaker of lines 54-56, and a few other lines in the conversation,
is in my opinion the Coryphaeus, who enters with the first semichorus " : R.

Σαλαμίνιος γάρ ἐστιν ᾧ ξύνειμ' ἐγώ,
τὴν νύχθ' ὅλην ἤλαυνέ μ' ἐν τοῖς στρώμασιν,
ὥστ' ἄρτι τουτὶ θοἰμάτιον αὐτοῦ λαβεῖν.   40

ΓΥ.Α. καὶ μὴν ὁρῶ καὶ Κλειναρέτην καὶ Σωστράτην
παροῦσαν ἤδη τήνδε καὶ Φιλαινέτην.

ΗΜΙΧΟΡΙΟΝ. οὔκουν ἐπείξεσθ'; ὡς Γλύκη κατώμοσεν
τὴν ὑστάτην ἥκουσαν οἴνου τρεῖς χόας
ἡμῶν ἀποτίσειν κἀρεβίνθων χοίνικα.   45

ΓΥ.Α. τὴν Σμικυθίωνος δ' οὐχ ὁρᾷς Μελιστίχην
σπεύδουσαν ἐν ταῖς ἐμβάσιν; καί μοι δοκεῖ
κατὰ σχολὴν παρὰ τἀνδρὸς ἐξελθεῖν μόνη.

ΓΥ.Β. τὴν τοῦ καπήλου δ' οὐχ ὁρᾷς Γευσιστράτην,
ἔχουσαν ἐν τῇ δεξιᾷ τὴν λαμπάδα;   50

ΠΡ. καὶ τὴν Φιλοδωρήτου τε καὶ Χαιρητάδου
ὁρῶ προσιούσας, χἀτέρας πολλὰς πάνυ
γυναῖκας, ὅ τι πέρ ἐστ' ὄφελος ἐν τῇ πόλει.

ΗΜΙΧ. καὶ πάνυ ταλαιπώρως ἔγωγ', ὦ φιλτάτη,
ἐκδρᾶσα παρέδυν. ὁ γὰρ ἀνὴρ τὴν νύχθ' ὅλην   55
ἔβηττε, τριχίδων ἑσπέρας ἐμπλήμενος.

ΠΡ. κάθησθε τοίνυν, ὡς ἂν ἀνέρωμαι τάδε
ὑμᾶς, ἐπειδὴ συλλελεγμένας ὁρῶ,
ὅσα Σκίροις ἔδοξεν εἰ δεδράκατε.

ΓΥ.Α. ἔγωγε. πρῶτον μέν γ' ἔχω τὰς μασχάλας   60
λόχμης δασυτέρας, καθάπερ ἦν ξυγκείμενον·
ἔπειθ' ὁπόθ' ἁνὴρ εἰς ἀγορὰν οἴχοιτό μου,

---

^a " Now enter, on their way to the orchestra, seven other
women, all distinguished by their own names or by the names of
their husbands. As they are passing in, the actors, standing
on the stage, make their comments about them, exactly as Peisth-
etaerus and the Hoopoe, in the *Birds*, discuss the members of the
Chorus, hurrying in to the orchestra there. These seven women
were probably well known to the audience, and doubtless there
were reasons for their selection with which we are now un-

My husband, dear—a Salaminian he—
Has all night long been tossing in his bed ;
Wherefore I could not steal his garb till now.

F.W. O now they are coming !^a Here's Cleinarete,
Here's Sostrata, and here's Philaenete.

SEMICHORUS. Come, hurry up : for Glyce vowed a vow
That whosoever comes the last shall pay
One quart of chickpeas and nine quarts of wine.

F.W. And look ! Melistiche, Smicythion's wife,
Wearing her husband's shoes.   She, only she,
Has come away, methinks, at ease, unflurried.

S.W. And look ! Geusistrata, the tapster's wife,
In her right hand the torch.
PR.   And now the wives
Of Philodoretus and Chaeretades,
And many another, hurrying on I see,
All that is best and worthiest in the town.

S.CH. O honey, I'd tremendous work to come.
My husband gorged his fill of sprats at supper,
And he's been cough, cough, coughing all night long.

PR. Well, sit ye down, that I may ask you this,
Now that ye're all assembled : have ye done
What at the Scira 'twas resolved to do ?

F.W. I have, for one.   See, underneath my arms
The hair is growing thicker than a copse,^b
As 'twas agreed : and when my husband started

acquainted : but we may conjecture that Smicythion resembled
the ' auld man ' whom Burns's ' young lassie ' married, ' who's
doyl't an' who's dozin', whose bluid it is frozen,' so that Melistiche
found no difficulty in escaping from him unobserved.   And Geusistrata was probably often seen by her customers in the attitude
here depicted, ἔχουσα τὴν λαμπάδα ἐν τῇ δεξιᾷ. Torches would
be frequently blazing in the καπηλεῖον till late at night " : R.

^b ἔθρεψαν γὰρ τρίχας, ἵνα ὅταν χειροτονῶσι, δοκῶσιν ἄνδρες εἶναι :
Scholiast.

253

ἀλειψαμένη τὸ σῶμ’ ὅλον δι’ ἡμέρας
ἐχλιανόμην ἑστῶσα πρὸς τὸν ἥλιον.
ΓΥ.Β. κἄγωγε· τὸ ξυρὸν δέ γ’ ἐκ τῆς οἰκίας 65
ἔρριψα πρῶτον, ἵνα δασυνθείην ὅλη
καὶ μηδὲν εἴην ἔτι γυναικὶ προσφερής.
ΠΡ. ἔχετε δὲ τοὺς πώγωνας, οὓς εἴρηθ’ ἔχειν
πάσαισιν ὑμῖν, ὁπότε συλλεγοίμεθα;
ΓΥ.Α. νὴ τὴν Ἑκάτην, καλόν γ’ ἔγωγε τουτονί. 70
ΓΥ.Β. κἄγωγ’ Ἐπικράτους οὐκ ὀλίγῳ καλλίονα.
ΠΡ. ὑμεῖς δὲ τί φατέ;
ΓΥ.Α.   φασί· κατανεύουσι γοῦν.
ΠΡ. καὶ μὴν τά γ’ ἄλλ’ ὑμῖν ὁρῶ πεπραγμένα.
Λακωνικὰς γὰρ ἔχετε καὶ βακτηρίας
καὶ θαἰμάτια τἀνδρεῖα, καθάπερ εἴπομεν. 75
ΓΥ.Α. ἔγωγέ τοι τὸ σκύταλον ἐξηνεγκάμην
τὸ τοῦ Λαμίου τουτὶ καθεύδοντος λάθρᾳ.
ΠΡ. τοῦτ’ ἔστ’ ἐκεῖνο, “ τῶν σκυτάλων ὧν πέρδεται.”
ΓΥ.Α. νὴ τὸν Δία τὸν σωτῆρ’ ἐπιτήδειός γ’ ἂν ἦν
τὴν τοῦ Πανόπτου διφθέραν ἐνημμένος 80
εἴπερ τις ἄλλος βουκολεῖν τὸν δήμιον.
ΠΡ. ἀλλ’ ἄγεθ’ ὅπως καὶ τἀπὶ τούτοις δράσομεν,
ἕως ἔτ’ ἐστὶν ἄστρα κατὰ τὸν οὐρανόν·
ἡκκλησία δ’, εἰς ἣν παρεσκευάσμεθα
ἡμεῖς βαδίζειν, ἐξ ἕω γενήσεται. 85
ΓΥ.Α. νὴ τὸν Δί’, ὥστε δεῖ σε καταλαβεῖν ἕδρας
ὑπὸ τῷ λίθῳ, τῶν πρυτάνεων καταντικρύ.

---

[a] To make her skin brown; ὥστε μέλαινα γενέσθαι ὡς ἀνήρ :
Scholiast.

[b] Epicrates was dubbed ὁ Σακεσφόρος, "the Beard-bearer"
(σάκος, -ου) in allusion to Αἴας Σ., "the Shield-bearer" (from
σάκος, -ους). The Schol. quotes from Plato Comicus, ἄναξ ὑπήνης,
Ἐπίκρατες σακεσφόρε.

Off to the market-place, I'd oil my body
And stand all day decocting in the sun.[a]

s.w. I too have done it : flinging, first of all,
The razor out of doors, that so my skin
Might grow quite hairy, and unlike a woman.

pr. But have ye got the beards, which, 'twas determined,
Ye all should bring, assembling here to-day ?

f.w. I have, by Hecate ! Look ! a lovely one.

s.w. And I, much lovelier than Epicrates's.[b]

pr. And what say *ye* ?

f.w.   They nod assent : they've got them.

pr. The other matters, I perceive, are done.
Laconian[c] shoes ye've got, and walking-sticks,
And the men's overcloaks, as we desired you

f.w. O I've a splendid club I stole away
(See, here it is) from Lamias as he slept.

pr. O yes, I know : " the clubs he sweltered with." [d]

f.w. By Zeus the Saviour, he's the very man
To don the skins the All-eyed herdsman wore,
And, no man better, tend the — public hangman.

pr. But now to finish what remains to do
While yet the stars are lingering in the sky ;
For this Assembly, as you know, whereto
We all are bound, commences with the dawn.

f.w. And so it does : and we're to seat ourselves
Facing the prytanes, just below the speakers.[e]

[c] Men's shoes : 345, *W*. 1158.

[d] Lamias, her husband, was a jailer; and the mention of
his name and " club " (σκύταλον) suggests a coarse allusion to the
ogress Lamia, of whom Crates wrote in a comedy σκυτάλην ἔχουσα
ἐπέρδετο. See *W*. 1177. In 79–81 the wife emphasizes her clever-
ness in escaping him by saying he was a veritable Argus (ὁ
Πανόπτης); but instead of " keeping watch " (βουκολεῖν) over Io,
she makes him watch over the " public executioner " (τὸν δήμιον).

[e] λίθῳ=βήματι : Schol. See *P*. 680.

ARISTOPHANES

ΓΥ.Β. ταυτί γέ τοι νὴ τὸν Δί' ἐφερόμην, ἵνα
πληρουμένης ξαίνοιμι τῆς ἐκκλησίας.
ΠΡ. πληρουμένης, τάλαινα;
ΓΥ.Β.   νὴ τὴν Ἄρτεμιν,   90
ἔγωγε. τί γὰρ ἂν χεῖρον ἀκροῴμην ἅμα
ξαίνουσα; γυμνὰ δ' ἐστί μοι τὰ παιδία.
ΠΡ. ἰδού γέ σε ξαίνουσαν, ἣν τοῦ σώματος
οὐδὲν παραφῆναι τοῖς καθημένοις ἔδει.
οὐκοῦν καλά γ' ἂν πάθοιμεν, εἰ πλήρης τύχοι   95
ὁ δῆμος ὤν, κἄπειθ' ὑπερβαίνουσά τις
ἀναβαλλομένη δείξειε τὸν Φορμίσιον.
ἢν δ' ἐγκαθιζώμεσθα πρότεραι, λήσομεν
ξυστειλάμεναι θαἰμάτια· τὸν πώγωνά τε
ὅταν καθῶμεν, ὃν περιδησόμεσθ', ἐκεῖ,   100
τίς οὐκ ἂν ἡμᾶς ἄνδρας ἡγήσαιθ' ὁρῶν;
Ἀγύρριος γοῦν τὸν Προνόμου πώγων' ἔχων
λέληθε· καίτοι πρότερον ἦν οὗτος γυνή·
νυνὶ δ', ὁρᾷς, πράττει τὰ μέγιστ' ἐν τῇ πόλει.
τούτου γέ τοι, νὴ τὴν ἐπιοῦσαν ἡμέραν,   105
τόλμημα τολμῶμεν τοσοῦτον οὕνεκα,
ἤν πως παραλαβεῖν τῆς πόλεως τὰ πράγματα
δυνώμεθ', ὥστ' ἀγαθόν τι πρᾶξαι τὴν πόλιν·
νῦν μὲν γὰρ οὔτε θέομεν οὔτ' ἐλαύνομεν.
ΓΥ.Α. καὶ πῶς γυναικῶν θηλύφρων ξυνουσία   110
δημηγορήσει;
ΠΡ.   πολὺ μὲν οὖν ἄριστά που.
λέγουσι γὰρ καὶ τῶν νεανίσκων ὅσοι
πλεῖστα σποδοῦνται, δεινοτάτους εἶναι λέγειν·
ἡμῖν δ' ὑπάρχει τοῦτο κατὰ τύχην τινά.

ᵃ ξαίνουσα, lit. "carding," which would require some exposure of the arms or the like.

s.w.　See what I've brought, dear heart : I mean to do
　　　A little spinning while the Assembly fills.

pr.　Fills ?　miserable woman !

s.w.　　　　　　　　　　　　　Yes, why not ?
　　　O I can spin [a] and listen just as well.
　　　Besides, my little chicks have got no clothes.

pr.　Fancy you SPINNING !　when you must not have
　　　The tiniest morsel of your person seen.
　　　'Twere a fine scrape, if when the Assembly's full,
　　　Some woman clambering o'er the seats, and throwing
　　　Her cloak awry, should show that she's a woman.[b]
　　　No, if we sit in front and gather round us
　　　Our husbands' garments, none will find us out.
　　　Why, when we've got our flowing beards on there,
　　　Who that beholds us will suppose we're women ?
　　　Was not Agyrrhius [c] erst a woman ?　Yet
　　　Now that he wears the beard of Pronomus,
　　　He passes for a man, a statesman too.
　　　O by yon dawning day, 'tis just for that,
　　　We women dare this daring deed to do,
　　　If we can seize upon the helm of state
　　　And trim the ship to weather through the storm ;
　　　For neither sails nor oars avail it now.

f.w.　How can the female soul of womankind [d]
　　　Address the Assembly ?

pr.　　　　　　　　　　　Admirably well.
　　　Youths that are most effeminate, they say,
　　　Are always strongest in the speaking line ;
　　　And we've got that by nature.

---

　[b] Phormisius was a hairy man ; αἰνίττεται δὲ τὸ γυναικεῖον
αἰδοῖον : Schol.

　[c] Agyrrhius was accused of debauchery in his youth ; he had
gained popularity by proposing a fee of three obols for attending
the Assembly.　Both he and Pronomus must have been noted for
their beards.　　　　　　　　　[d] " From a tragedy " : Schol.

ARISTOPHANES

ΓΥ.Α. οὐκ οἶδα· δεινὸν δ' ἐστὶν ἡ μὴ 'μπειρία. 115
ΠΡ. οὐκοῦν ἐπίτηδες ξυνελέγημεν ἐνθάδε,
    ὅπως προμελετήσωμεν ἀκεῖ δεῖ λέγειν.
    οὐκ ἂν φθάνοις τὸ γένειον ἂν περιδουμένη,
    ἄλλαι θ' ὅσαι λαλεῖν μεμελετήκασί που;
ΓΥ.Α. τίς δ', ὦ μέλ', ἡμῶν οὐ λαλεῖν ἐπίσταται; 120
ΠΡ. ἴθι δὴ σὺ περιδοῦ καὶ ταχέως ἀνὴρ γενοῦ·
    ἐγὼ δὲ θεῖσα τοὺς στεφάνους περιδήσομαι
    καὐτὴ μεθ' ὑμῶν, ἤν τί μοι δόξῃ λέγειν.
ΓΥ.Β. δεῦρ', ὦ γλυκυτάτη Πραξαγόρα, σκέψαι, τάλαν,
    ὡς καὶ καταγέλαστον τὸ πρᾶγμα φαίνεται. 125
ΠΡ. πῶς καταγέλαστον;
ΓΥ.Β.   ὥσπερ εἴ τις σηπίαις
    πώγωνα περιδήσειεν ἐσταθευμέναις.
ΠΡ. ὁ περιστίαρχος, περιφέρειν χρὴ τὴν γαλῆν.
    πάριτ' ἐς τὸ πρόσθεν. Ἀρίφραδες, παῦσαι λαλῶν.
    κάθιζε παριών. τίς ἀγορεύειν βούλεται; 130
ΓΥ.Α. ἐγώ.
ΠΡ.   περίθου δὴ τὸν στέφανον τύχἀγαθῇ.
ΓΥ.Α. ἰδού.
ΠΡ.   λέγοις ἄν.
ΓΥ.Α.   εἶτα πρὶν πιεῖν λέγω;
ΠΡ. ἰδοὺ πιεῖν.
ΓΥ.Α.   τί γάρ, ὦ μέλ', ἐστεφανωσάμην;

---

[a] " ἀπρόσλογος ἡ εἰκασία, says the Scholiast. It probably refers to some fanciful similarity between the complexion of the women, lightly bronzed by the sun, and the colour of the white cuttlefish lightly browned by the fire. λευκαὶ γὰρ αἱ σηπίαι, says one Scholiast : ἐσταθευμέναις δὲ, ἐξ ἐπιπολῆς ὀπτηθείσαις· σταθεύειν γὰρ τὸ μὴ λίαν ὀπτῆσαι, adds another " : R.
[b] " The peristiarch was an official who superintended the purification of the place in which an Athenian Assembly was to be held by carrying sacrificed sucking-pigs around its limit. All who took part in the Assembly were required to come within this

F.W.	Maybe so.
	Still inexperience is a serious matter.
PR.	And is not that the very reason why
	We've met together to rehearse the scene ?
	Now do make haste and fasten on your beards,
	And all you others who have practised talking.
F.W.	Practised, indeed ! can't every woman talk ?
PR.	Come, fasten on your beard, and be a man.
	I'll lay these chaplets down, and do the same.
	Maybe I'll make a little speech myself.
S.W.	O, here, sweet love, Praxagora : look, child !
	O what a merry joke this seems to me !
PR.	Joke ! where's the joke ?
S.W.	'Tis just as if we tied
	A shaggy beard to toasting cuttlefish.[a]
PR.	Now, Purifier [b] carry round the — cat.
	Come in ! [c] Ariphrades, don't chatter so.
	Come in, sit down. Who will address the meeting ?[d]
F.W.	I.
PR.	Wear this chaplet then, and luck be with you.
F.W.	There.
PR.	Speak away.
F.W.	What, speak before I drink ?
PR.	Just listen. DRINK !
F.W.	Then what's this chaplet for ?[e]

line of purification. *Cf. Acharnians*, 44. Praxagora substitutes
γαλῆν for χοιρίδιον, not wishing in an assembly of ladies to use
so ambiguous a word as the latter " : R.

[c] " It would seem, from *Acharnians*, 43, 44, that this was the
recognized formula wherewith the κῆρυξ invited the people to
come within the line of lustration " : R.

[d] The recognized formula.

[e] The wreaths being worn both by a speaker in the Assembly,
and by a reveller at a banquet. The speaker betrays her ignorance
of parliamentary customs, and so P. tells her to be gone : " that is
how you would have betrayed us in the Assembly also (κἀκεῖ)."

ΠΡ. ἄπιθ' ἐκποδών· τοιαῦτ' ἂν ἡμᾶς εἰργάσω
κἀκεῖ.

ΓΥ.Α.   τί δ'; οὐ πίνουσι κἂν τἠκκλησίᾳ;   135
ΠΡ. ἰδού γέ σοι πίνουσι.

ΓΥ.Α.   νὴ τὴν Ἄρτεμιν,
καὶ ταῦτά γ' εὔζωρον. τὰ γοῦν βουλεύματα
αὐτῶν ὅσ' ἂν πράξωσιν ἐνθυμουμένοις
ὥσπερ μεθυόντων ἐστὶ παραπεπληγμένα.
καὶ νὴ Δία σπένδουσί γ'· ἢ τίνος χάριν   140
τοσαῦτά γ' εὔχοντ', εἴπερ οἶνος μὴ παρῆν;
καὶ λοιδοροῦνταί γ' ὥσπερ ἐμπεπωκότες,
καὶ τὸν παροινοῦντ' ἐκφέρουσ' οἱ τοξόται.

ΠΡ. σὺ μὲν βάδιζε καὶ κάθησ'· οὐδὲν γὰρ εἶ.

ΓΥ.Α. νὴ τὸν Δί', ἦ μοι μὴ γενειᾶν κρεῖττον ἦν·   145
δίψει γάρ, ὡς ἔοικ', ἀφαυανθήσομαι.

ΠΡ. ἔσθ' ἥτις ἑτέρα βούλεται λέγειν;

ΓΥ.Β.   ἐγώ.

ΠΡ. ἴθι δὴ στεφανοῦ· καὶ γὰρ τὸ χρῆμ' ἐργάζεται.
ἄγε νυν ὅπως ἀνδριστὶ καὶ καλῶς ἐρεῖς,
διερεισαμένη τὸ σχῆμα τῇ βακτηρίᾳ.   150

ΓΥ.Β. ἐβουλόμην μὲν ἕτερον ἂν τῶν ἠθάδων
λέγειν τὰ βέλτισθ', ἵν' ἐκαθήμην ἥσυχος·
νῦν δ' οὐκ ἐάσω, κατά γε τὴν ἐμὴν μίαν,
ἐν τοῖσι καπηλείοισι λάκκους ἐμποιεῖν
ὕδατος. ἐμοὶ μὲν οὐ δοκεῖ μὰ τὼ θεώ.   155

ΠΡ. μὰ τὼ θεώ; τάλαινα, ποῦ τὸν νοῦν ἔχεις;

---

^a " ἐνθυμουμένοις, 'to such as ponder these things in their
minds.' The acts they pass are, if you consider them carefully,
like the mad acts of drunkards ": R.

^b The "tedious prayers" were usually accompanied by
libations.   ^c The Scythian archers, the police; *A.* 54, *K.* 665.

^d " ἀφαυανθήσομαι, ξηρανθήσομαι: Scholiast; *cf. F.* 1089. 'Av
I didn't shave, I wud be torminted wid an outrajis thurrst ; for
there's nothin' so dhryin' to the throat as a big billy-goat beard

PR.   O get away.   Is this what you'd have done
      Amongst the men ?

F.W.   What, don't men drink at meetings ?

PR.   Drink, fool ?

F.W.   By Artemis, I know they do,
      And strong drink too.   Look at the acts they pass.
      Do you mean to tell me that they'd pass such
          nonsense
      If they weren't drunk ?[a] Besides, they pour
         libations.
      Or what's the meaning of those tedious prayers[b]
      Unless they'd got some wine, I'd like to know.
      Besides, they quarrel just like drunken men,
      And when one drinks too much, and gets too noisy,
      In come the Archer-boys,[c] and run him out.

PR.   Begone and sit you down, for you're no good.

F.W.   Good lack, I wish I'd never worn a beard ;[d]
      I'm parched to death with thirst, I really am.

PR.   Would any other like to speak ?

S.W.   Yes, I.

PR.   Put on this chaplet and be quick.   Time presses.
      Now lean your weight upon your walking-stick,
      And speak your words out manfully and well.

S.W.   I could have wished some more experienced man
      Had risen to speak, while I sat still and listened.
      But now I say I'll not permit, for one,[e]
      That in their taverns men should make them tanks
      Of water.[f]   'Tis not proper, by the Twain.[g]

PR.   How ! by the Twain ?   Girl, have you lost your wits ?

waggin' undher the chin,' says Private Mulvaney in one of
Rudyard Kipling's tales " : R.

   [e] μίαν, *sc.* γνώμην or ψῆφον.

   [f] Tanks for storing wine, dishonestly filled with water ; the
bibulous woman protests.

   [g] Demeter and Persephone ; a woman's oath.

ARISTOPHANES

ΓΥ.Β. τί δ' ἔστιν; οὐ γὰρ δὴ πιεῖν γ' ᾔτησά σε.
ΠΡ. μὰ Δί', ἀλλ' ἀνὴρ ὢν τὼ θεὼ κατώμοσας,
    καίτοι τά γ' ἄλλ' εἰποῦσα δεξιώτατα.
ΓΥ.Β. ὦ νὴ τὸν Ἀπόλλω.
ΠΡ.   παῦε τοίνυν, ὡς ἐγὼ   160
    ἐκκλησιάσουσ' οὐκ ἂν προβαίην τὸν πόδα
    τὸν ἕτερον, εἰ μὴ ταῦτ' ἀκριβωθήσεται.
ΓΥ.Β. φέρε τὸν στέφανον· ἐγὼ γὰρ αὖ λέξω πάλιν.
    οἶμαι γὰρ ἤδη μεμελετηκέναι καλῶς.
    ἐμοὶ γάρ, ὦ γυναῖκες αἱ καθήμεναι,   165
ΠΡ. γυναῖκας, ὦ δύστηνε, τοὺς ἄνδρας λέγεις;
ΓΥ.Β. δι' Ἐπίγονόν γ' ἐκεῖνον· ἐπιβλέψασα γὰρ
    ἐκεῖσε πρὸς γυναῖκας ᾠόμην λέγειν.
ΠΡ. ἄπερρε καὶ σὺ καὶ κάθησ' ἐντευθενί.
    αὐτὴ γὰρ ὑμῶν γ' ἕνεκά μοι λέξειν δοκῶ   170
    τονδὶ λαβοῦσα· τοῖς θεοῖς μὲν εὔχομαι
    τυχεῖν κατορθώσασα τὰ βεβουλευμένα.
    ἐμοὶ δ' ἴσον μὲν τῆσδε τῆς χώρας μέτα
    ὅσονπερ ὑμῖν· ἄχθομαι δὲ καὶ φέρω
    τὰ τῆς πόλεως ἅπαντα βαρέως πράγματα.   175
    ὁρῶ γὰρ αὐτὴν προστάταισι χρωμένην
    ἀεὶ πονηροῖς· κἄν τις ἡμέραν μίαν
    χρηστὸς γένηται, δέκα πονηρὸς γίγνεται.
    ἐπέτρεψας ἑτέρῳ· πλείον' ἔτι δράσει κακά.
    χαλεπὸν μὲν οὖν ἄνδρας δυσαρέστους νουθετεῖν,   180
    οἳ τοὺς φιλεῖν μὲν βουλομένους δεδοίκατε,
    τοὺς δ' οὐκ ἐθέλοντας ἀντιβολεῖθ' ἑκάστοτε.
    ἐκκλησίαισιν ἦν ὅτ' οὐκ ἐχρώμεθα
    οὐδὲν τὸ παράπαν· ἀλλὰ τόν γ' Ἀγύρριον
    πονηρὸν ἡγούμεσθα· νῦν δὲ χρωμένων   185
    ὁ μὲν λαβὼν ἀργύριον ὑπερεπῄνεσεν,
    ὁ δ' οὐ λαβὼν εἶναι θανάτου φήσ' ἀξίους

s.w.   Why, what's amiss ?   *I* never asked for drink.

pr.   You are a man, and yet invoked the Twain.
    All else you said was excellently right.

s.w.   O yes, by Apollo !

pr.   Mind then, I won't move
    Another step in this Assembly business,
    Unless you are strict and accurate in this.

s.w.   Give me the chaplet, and I'll try again.
    I've thought of something very good to say.
      In my opinion, O assembled women,

pr.   O monstrous ! women, idiot, when they're men ?

s.w.   'Twas all Epigonus : he caught my eye
    And so, methought 'twas women I harangued.

pr.   You, too, retire and sit you down again,
    For I myself will wear the chaplet now
    Your cause to further : and I pray the gods
    That I may haply prosper our design.

      I have, my friends, an equal stake with you
    In this our country, and I grieve to note
    The sad condition of the State's affairs.
    I see the State employing evermore
    Unworthy ministers ; [a] if one do well
    A single day, he'll act amiss for ten.
    You trust another : he'll be ten times worse.
    Hard, hard it is to counsel wayward men,
    Always mistrusting those who love you best,
    And paying court to those who love you not.
    There was a time, my friends, we never came
    To these Assemblies ; then we knew full well
    Agyrrhius was a rogue : we come here now,
    And he who gets the cash applauds the man,
    And he who gets it not, protests that they

  [a] προστάτης τοῦ δήμου, although not an official title, was used of
the leading demagogue.

ARISTOPHANES

τοὺς μισθοφορεῖν ζητοῦντας ἐν τἠκκλησίᾳ.
ΓΥ.Α. νὴ τὴν Ἀφροδίτην, εὖ γε ταυταγὶ λέγεις.
ΠΡ. τάλαιν᾽, Ἀφροδίτην ὤμοσας. χαρίεντά γ᾽ ἂν 190
ἔδρασας, εἰ τοῦτ᾽ εἶπας ἐν τἠκκλησίᾳ.
ΓΥ.Α. ἀλλ᾽ οὐκ ἂν εἶπον.
ΠΡ.   μηδ᾽ ἐθίζου νυν λέγειν.
τὸ συμμαχικὸν αὖ τοῦθ᾽, ὅτ᾽ ἐσκοπούμεθα,
εἰ μὴ γένοιτ᾽, ἀπολεῖν ἔφασκον τὴν πόλιν·
ὅτε δὴ δ᾽ ἐγένετ᾽, ἤχθοντο, τῶν δὲ ῥητόρων 195
ὁ τοῦτ᾽ ἀναπείσας εὐθὺς ἀποδρὰς ᾤχετο.
ναῦς δεῖ καθέλκειν· τῷ πένητι μὲν δοκεῖ,
τοῖς πλουσίοις δὲ καὶ γεωργοῖς οὐ δοκεῖ.
Κορινθίοις ἤχθεσθε, κἀκεῖνοί γέ σοι·
νῦν εἰσὶ χρηστοί, καὶ σὺ νῦν χρηστὸς γενοῦ. 200
Ἀργεῖος ἀμαθής, ἀλλ᾽ Ἱερώνυμος σοφός·
Σωτηρία παρέκυψεν, ἀλλ᾽ ὀρίζεται
Θρασύβουλος αὐτός, οὐχὶ παρακαλούμενος.
ΓΥ.Α. ὡς ξυνετὸς ἀνήρ.
ΠΡ.   νῦν καλῶς ἐπήνεσας.
ὑμεῖς γάρ ἐστ᾽, ὦ δῆμε, τούτων αἴτιοι. 205
τὰ δημόσια γὰρ μισθοφοροῦντες χρήματα
ἰδίᾳ σκοπεῖσθ᾽ ἕκαστος ὅ τι τις κερδανεῖ.

---

[a] Alluding to Agyrrhius's three-obol fee; see 103 above.

[b] " Praxagora is beyond all doubt referring to the momentous anti-Spartan League of 395 B.C., which was inaugurated by the battle of Haliartus and the death of Lysander, which at once raised Athens from the position of a mere dependency of Sparta into that of a free and leading Hellenic state ; and which in its result altered the whole current of Hellenic history. Originally struck between Thebes and Athens, it was quickly joined by Argos, Corinth, and other important states, and became so powerful that the military leaders proposed at once to march upon Sparta and 'destroy the wasps in their nest.' But in the following summer the great battle of Corinth, ἡ μεγάλη μάχη πρὸς Λακεδαι-

Who come for payment ought to die the death.[a]

F.W. By Aphrodite now, but that's well said !

PR. Heavens ! Aphrodite ! 'Twere a pleasant jest,
If in the Assembly you should praise me so !

F.W. Ah, but I won't.

PR.   Then don't acquire the habit.
This League [b] again, when first we talked it over,
It seemed the only thing to save the State.
Yet when they'd got it, they disliked it. He
Who pushed it through was forced to cut and run.[c]
Ships must be launched ; the poor men all approve,
The wealthy men and farmers disapprove.[d]
You used to hate Corinthians, and they you ;
They are friendly now : do you be friendly too.
Argeius was a fool : now Jerome's wise.[e]
Safety just showed her face : but Thrasybulus,[f]
No more called in, is quite excluded now.

F.W. Here's a shrewd man !

PR.   Ah, now you praise me rightly
Ye are to blame for this, Athenian people,
Ye draw your wages from the public purse,
Yet each man seeks his private gain alone.

μονίους, ἡ ἐν Κορίνθῳ (Demosthenes, *In Lept.* 59), resulted in a Lacedaemonian victory ; and no contingent suffered so severely as the Athenian, which was assailed both in front and on the flank by the Spartan troops. And shortly afterwards Agesilaus won another victory in the well-contested battle of Coronea. No wonder that the Athenians were disgusted, ἤχθοντο, at this discomfiture of the League from which they had expected so much " : R.

   [c] Unknown.

   [d] The wealthy had to fit out the triremes ; the farmers saw their lands ravaged.

   [e] Argeius was a wise man, Hieronymus a fool : Schol. Nothing more is known of them.

   [f] Thrasybulus had brought them safety in darker days than these.

τὸ δὲ κοινὸν ὥσπερ Αἴσιμος κυλίνδεται.
ἢν οὖν ἐμοὶ πείθησθε, σωθήσεσθ᾽ ἔτι.
ταῖς γὰρ γυναιξὶ φημὶ χρῆναι τὴν πόλιν   210
ἡμᾶς παραδοῦναι. καὶ γὰρ ἐν ταῖς οἰκίαις
ταύταις ἐπιτρόποις καὶ ταμίαισι χρώμεθα.
ΓΥ.Α. εὖ γ᾽, εὖ γε νὴ Δί᾽, εὖ γε· λέγε, λέγ᾽, ὦγαθέ.
ΠΡ. ὡς δ᾽ εἰσὶν ἡμῶν τοὺς τρόπους βελτίονες
ἐγὼ διδάξω. πρῶτα μὲν γὰρ τἄρια
βάπτουσι θερμῷ κατὰ τὸν ἀρχαῖον νόμον
ἁπαξάπασαι, κοὐχὶ μεταπειρωμένας
ἴδοις ἂν αὐτάς. ἡ δ᾽ Ἀθηναίων πόλις,
εἴ πού τι χρηστῶς εἶχεν, οὐκ ἂν ἐσῴζετο,
εἰ μή τι καινὸν ἄλλο περιειργάζετο;   220
καθήμεναι φρύγουσιν ὥσπερ καὶ πρὸ τοῦ·
ἐπὶ τῆς κεφαλῆς φέρουσιν ὥσπερ καὶ πρὸ τοῦ·
τὰ Θεσμοφόρι᾽ ἄγουσιν ὥσπερ καὶ πρὸ τοῦ·
πέττουσι τοὺς πλακοῦντας ὥσπερ καὶ πρὸ τοῦ·
τοὺς ἄνδρας ἐπιτρίβουσιν ὥσπερ καὶ πρὸ τοῦ·
μοιχοὺς ἔχουσιν ἔνδον ὥσπερ καὶ πρὸ τοῦ·   225
αὑταῖς παροψωνοῦσιν ὥσπερ καὶ πρὸ τοῦ·
οἶνον φιλοῦσ᾽ εὔζωρον ὥσπερ καὶ πρὸ τοῦ·
βινούμεναι χαίρουσιν ὥσπερ καὶ πρὸ τοῦ.
ταύταισιν οὖν, ὦνδρες, παραδόντες τὴν πόλιν
μὴ περιλαλῶμεν, μηδὲ πυνθανώμεθα   230
τί ποτ᾽ ἄρα δρᾶν μέλλουσιν, ἀλλ᾽ ἁπλῷ τρόπῳ
ἐῶμεν ἄρχειν, σκεψάμενοι ταυτὶ μόνα,
ὡς τοὺς στρατιώτας πρῶτον οὖσαι μητέρες
σῴζειν ἐπιθυμήσουσιν· εἶτα σιτία
τίς τῆς τεκούσης μᾶλλον ἐπιπέμψειεν ἄν;   235
χρήματα πορίζειν εὐπορώτατον γυνή,
ἄρχουσά τ᾽ οὐκ ἂν ἐξαπατηθείη ποτέ,

_____

* χωλός, ἄτιμος, ἀμαθής : Schol.

So the State reels, like any Aesimus.[a]
Still, if ye trust me, ye shall yet be saved.
I move that now the womankind be asked
To rule the State.   In our own homes, ye know,
They are the managers and rule the house.

F.W.   O good, good, good ! speak on, speak on, dear man

PR.   That they are better in their ways than we
I'll soon convince you.   First, they dye their wools
With boiling tinctures, in the ancient style.
You won't find *them*, I warrant, in a hurry
Trying new plans.[b]   And would it not have saved
The Athenian city had she let alone
Things that worked well, nor idly sought things new ?
They roast their barley, sitting, as of old :
They on their heads bear burdens, as of old :
They keep their Thesmophoria, as of old :
They bake their honied cheesecakes, as of old ;
They victimize their husbands, as of old :
They still secrete their lovers, as of old :
They buy themselves sly dainties, as of old :
They love their wine unwatered, as of old :
They like a woman's pleasures, as of old :
Then let us, gentlemen, give up to them
The helm of State, and not concern ourselves,
Nor pry, nor question what they mean to do ;
But let them really govern, knowing this,
The statesman-mothers never will neglect
Their soldier-sons.   And then a soldier's rations,
Who will supply as well as she who bare him ?
For ways and means none can excel a woman.
And there's no fear at all that they'll be cheated

---

[b] " We shall see by-and-by how completely all forecasts of the
conservative policy to be pursued by the women will be falsified
by the event " : R.

αὐταὶ γάρ εἰσιν ἐξαπατᾶν εἰθισμέναι.
τὰ δ' ἄλλ' ἐάσω· ταῦτα κἂν πείθησθέ μοι,
εὐδαιμονοῦντες τὸν βίον διάξετε.   240

ΓΥ.Α. εὖ γ', ὦ γλυκυτάτη Πραξαγόρα, καὶ δεξιῶς.
πόθεν, ὦ τάλαινα, ταῦτ' ἔμαθες οὕτω καλῶς;

ΠΡ. ἐν ταῖς φυγαῖς μετὰ τἀνδρὸς ᾤκησ' ἐν πυκνί·
ἔπειτ' ἀκούουσ' ἐξέμαθον τῶν ῥητόρων.

ΓΥ.Α. οὐκ ἐτὸς ἄρ', ὦ μέλ', ἦσθα δεινὴ καὶ σοφή·   245
καί σε στρατηγὸν αἱ γυναῖκες αὐτόθεν
αἱρούμεθ', ἢν ταῦθ' ἀπινοεῖς κατεργάσῃ.
ἀτὰρ ἢν Κέφαλός σοι λοιδορῆται προσφθαρείς,
πῶς ἀντερεῖς πρὸς αὐτὸν ἐν τἠκκλησίᾳ;

ΠΡ. φήσω παραφρονεῖν αὐτόν.

ΓΥ.Α.   ἀλλὰ τοῦτό γε   250
ἴσασι πάντες.

ΠΡ.   ἀλλὰ καὶ μελαγχολᾶν.

ΓΥ.Α. καὶ τοῦτ' ἴσασιν.

ΠΡ.   ἀλλὰ καὶ τὰ τρύβλια
κακῶς κεραμεύειν, τὴν δὲ πόλιν εὖ καὶ καλῶς.

ΓΥ.Α. τί δ', ἢν Νεοκλείδης ὁ γλάμων σε λοιδορῇ;

ΠΡ. τούτῳ μὲν εἶπον ἐς κυνὸς πυγὴν ὁρᾶν.   255

ΓΥ.Α. τί δ', ἢν ὑποκρούσωσίν σε;

ΠΡ.   προσκινήσομαι,
ἅτ' οὐκ ἄπειρος οὖσα πολλῶν κρουμάτων.

ΓΥ.Α. ἐκεῖνο μόνον ἄσκεπτον, ἢν σ' οἱ τοξόται
ἕλκωσιν, ὅ τι δράσεις ποτ'.

ΠΡ.   ἐξαγκωνιῶ

---

^a " With these words Praxagora lays aside her wreath, the Rehearsal is concluded, and the women relapse into their ordinary style of conversation " : R.

^b " In my opinion the flight to which Praxagora is alluding is the flight of the Athenians from the islands and seaports into the city before the conquering progress of Lysander. We know that

When they're in power, for they're the cheats them-
    selves.
Much I omit.   But if you pass my motion,
You'll lead the happiest lives that e'er you dreamed
    of.[a]

F.W.   O, good ! Praxagora.   Well done, sweet wench.
       However did you learn to speak so finely ?

PR.   I and my husband in the general flight [b]
       Lodged in the Pnyx, and there I heard the speakers.

F.W.   Ah, you were clever to some purpose, dear.
       And if you now succeed in your designs
       We'll then and there proclaim you chieftainess.
       But what if Cephalus, ill fare,[c] insult you,
       How will you answer *him* in full Assembly ?

PR.   I'll say he's frenzied.

F.W.   True enough ; but all
       The world know that.

PR.   I'll say he's moody-mad.

F.W.   They know that too.

PR.   That he's more fit to tinker
       The constitution than his pots and pans.

F.W.   If Neocleides, blear-eyed oaf, insult you ?

PR.   *Peep at a puppy's tail,[d] my lad,* quoth I.

F.W.   What if they interrupt ?

PR.   I'll meet them there,
       I'm quite accustomed to that sort of thing.[e]

F.W.   O but suppose the archers hale you off,
       What will you do ?

PR.   Stick out my elbows, so.

after his great success at Aegospotami, he passed round the coasts
and islands, and compelled all the Athenians he found, whether
garrisons or private individuals, to return to Athens on pain of
death " : R.   [c] Cephalus: a potter and demagogue.
   [d] A proverb said to the short-sighted : Schol.
   [e] Alluding to κρούω *sensu obscoeno.*

ὡδί· μέση γὰρ οὐδέποτε ληφθήσομαι.　　　260
HMIX. ἡμεῖς δέ γ', ἢν αἴρωσ', ἐᾶν κελεύσομεν.
ΓΥ.Α. ταυτὶ μὲν ἡμῖν ἐντεθύμηται καλῶς,
　　ἐκεῖνο δ' οὐ πεφροντίκαμεν, ὅτῳ τρόπῳ
　　τὰς χεῖρας αἴρειν μνημονεύσομεν τότε.
　　εἰθισμέναι γάρ ἐσμεν αἴρειν τὼ σκέλη.　　265
ΠΡ. χαλεπὸν τὸ πρᾶγμ'· ὅμως δὲ χειροτονητέον
　　ἐξωμισάσαις τὸν ἕτερον βραχίονα.
　　　ἄγε νυν ἀναστέλλεσθ' ἄνω τὰ χιτώνια·
　　ὑποδεῖσθε δ' ὡς τάχιστα τὰς Λακωνικάς,
　　ὥσπερ τὸν ἄνδρ' ἐθεᾶσθ', ὅτ' εἰς ἐκκλησίαν　　270
　　μέλλοι βαδίζειν ἢ θύραζ' ἑκάστοτε.
　　ἔπειτ' ἐπειδὰν ταῦτα πάντ' ἔχῃ καλῶς,
　　περιδεῖσθε τοὺς πώγωνας. ἡνίκ' ἂν δέ γε
　　τούτους ἀκριβῶς ἦτε περιηρμοσμέναι,
　　καὶ θαἰμάτια τἀνδρεῖ' ἅπερ γ' ἐκλέψατε　　275
　　ἐπαναβάλεσθε, κᾆτα ταῖς βακτηρίαις
　　ἐπερειδόμεναι βαδίζετ', ᾄδουσαι μέλος
　　πρεσβυτικόν τι, τὸν τρόπον μιμούμεναι
　　τὸν τῶν ἀγροίκων.
ΓΥ.Α.　　　　　　εὖ λέγεις· ἡμεῖς δέ γε
　　προΐωμεν αὐτῶν. καὶ γὰρ ἑτέρας οἴομαι　　280
　　ἐκ τῶν ἀγρῶν ἐς τὴν πύκν' ἥξειν ἄντικρυς
　　γυναῖκας.
ΠΡ.　　　　ἀλλὰ σπεύσαθ', ὡς εἴωθ' ἐκεῖ
　　τοῖς μὴ παροῦσιν ὀρθρίοις ἐς τὴν πύκνα
　　ὑπαποτρέχειν ἔχουσι μηδὲ πάτταλον.
HMIX. ὥρα προβαίνειν, ὦνδρες, ἡμῖν ἐστι· τοῦτο γὰρ χρὴ　285
　　μεμνημένας ἀεὶ λέγειν, ὡς μή ποτ' ἐξολίσθῃ,
　　ἡμᾶς. ὁ κίνδυνος γὰρ οὐχὶ μικρός, ἢν ἁλῶμεν

---

a The formula used by the κῆρυξ was: ἀράτω τὰς χεῖρας, ὅτῳ
ταῦτα δοκεῖ. For αἴρειν τὰ σκέλη cf. L. 229.

They shan't seize *me*, the varlets, round my waist.

S.CH. Aye, and we'll help : we'll bid the men let go.

F.W. Then that we've settled, wonderfully well.
But this we've not considered, how to mind
We lift our hands, and not our feet, in voting.*a*
We're more for lifting feet than lifting hands.

PR. A knotty point. However, we must each
Hold up one arm, bare from the shoulder, so.
   Now then, my dears, tuck up your tunics neatly,
And slip your feet in those Laconian shoes,
Just as ye've seen your husbands do, whene'er
They're going out, mayhap to attend the Assembly.
And next, so soon as everything is right
With shoes and tunics, fasten on your beards,
And when ye've got them neatly fitted on,
Then throw your husbands' mantles over all,
Those which ye stole ; and leaning on your sticks
Off to the Meeting, piping as ye go
Some old man's song, and mimicking the ways
Of country fellows.

F.W.   Good ! but let ourselves
Get on before them : other women soon
Will come I know from all the countryside
Straight for the Pnyx.

PR.   Be quick, for 'tis the rule
That whoso comes not with the early dawn
Must slink abashed, with never a doit,*b* away.

S.CH. Time to be moving, gentlemen !
                 'tis best we keep repeating
This name of ours, lest we forget
                 to use it at the Meeting
For terrible the risk would be, if any man detected

---

b That is, the fee for attendance.

271

ARISTOPHANES

ἐνδυόμεναι κατὰ σκότον τόλμημα τηλικοῦτον.

χωρῶμεν εἰς ἐκκλησίαν, ὦνδρες· ἠπείλησε γὰρ
ὁ θεσμοθέτης, ὃς ἂν
μὴ πρῲ πάνυ τοῦ κνέφους
ἥκῃ κεκονιμένος,
στέργων σκοροδάλμῃ,
βλέπων ὑπότριμμα, μὴ
δώσειν τὸ τριώβολον.
ἀλλ᾽, ὦ Χαριτιμίδη
καὶ Σμίκυθε καὶ Δράκης,
ἕπου κατεπείγων,
σαυτῷ προσέχων, ὅπως
μηδὲν παραχορδιεῖς   295
ὧν δεῖ σ᾽ ἀποδεῖξαι·
ὅπως δὲ τὸ σύμβολον
λαβόντες ἔπειτα πλη-
σίοι καθεδούμεθ᾽, ὡς
ἂν χειροτονῶμεν
ἅπανθ᾽ ὁπόσ᾽ ἂν δέῃ
τὰς ἡμετέρας φίλας.
καίτοι τί λέγω; φίλους
γὰρ χρῆν μ᾽ ὀνομάζειν.

ΗΜΙΧ.Β. ὅρα δ᾽ ὅπως ὠθήσομεν τούσδε τοὺς ἐξ ἄστεως   300
ἥκοντας, ὅσοι πρὸ τοῦ
μέν, ἡνίκ᾽ ἔδει λαβεῖν
ἐλθόντ᾽ ὀβολὸν μόνον,

ᵃ Lit. "satisfied with their garlic pickle, with a vinegar aspect." He is dusty after his hurried journey, and still smells of a rustic breakfast including garlic and vinegar salad.

The great and daring scheme which we
                    in darkness have projected.

Song of the (town) Semichorus.

On to the Meeting, worthy sirs :
                for now the magistrate avers
    That whoever shall fail to
    Arrive while the dusk of the
        Morning is grey,
    All dusty and smacking of
    Pickle and acid,*a* that
    Man shall assuredly
        Forfeit his pay.
    Now Charitimides,
    Draces, and Smicythus,
        Hasten along :
    See that there fall from you
    Never a word or a
        Note that is wrong.
    Get we our tickets, and
    Sit we together, and
        Choose the front rows.
    Vote we whatever our
        Sisters propose.
Our *sisters* !   My wits are gone gleaning !
Our " brothers," of course, was my meaning.

Song of the country Semichorus.[b]

We'll thrust aside this bothering throng
              which from the city crowds along,
    These men, who aforetime
    When only an obol they

---

[b] *Enter band of twelve countrywomen.* " There is not a word
in their song to indicate that they were really women in disguise " : R.

καθῆντο λαλοῦντες
ἐν τοῖς στεφανώμασιν·
νυνὶ δ' ἐνοχλοῦσ' ἄγαν.
ἀλλ' οὐχί, Μυρωνίδης
ὅτ' ἦρχεν ὁ γεννάδας,
οὐδεὶς ἂν ἐτόλμα   305
τὰ τῆς πόλεως διοι-
κεῖν ἀργύριον φέρων·
ἀλλ' ἦκεν ἕκαστος
ἐν ἀσκιδίῳ φέρων
πιεῖν ἅμα τ' ἄρτον αὖ-
ον καὶ δύο κρομμύω
καὶ τρεῖς ἂν ἐλάας.
νυνὶ δὲ τριώβολον
ζητοῦσι λαβεῖν ὅταν
πράττωσί τι κοινὸν ὥσ-
περ πηλοφοροῦντες.   310

ΒΛΕΠΥΡΟΣ. τί τὸ πρᾶγμα; ποῖ ποθ' ἡ γυνὴ φρούδη
            'στί μοι;
ἐπεὶ πρὸς ἕω νῦν γ' ἔστιν, ἡ δ' οὐ φαίνεται.
ἐγὼ δὲ κατάκειμαι πάλαι χεζητιῶν,
τὰς ἐμβάδας ζητῶν λαβεῖν ἐν τῷ σκότῳ
καὶ θοἰμάτιον· ὅτε δὴ δ' ἐκεῖνο ψηλαφῶν   315
οὐκ ἐδυνάμην εὑρεῖν, ὁ δ' ἤδη τὴν θύραν
ἐπεῖχε κρούων ὁ Κοπρεαῖος, λαμβάνω
τουτὶ τὸ τῆς γυναικὸς ἡμιδιπλοίδιον,

---

[a] See 102 and note. Agyrrhius had at first proposed one obol
as fee for attending the Assembly; Heracleides raised it to two;
and shortly before the date of this play, Agyrrhius raised it again
to three.

[b] Myronides, about 457 B.C., with a force of old men and boys,

> Got for their pay [a]
> Would sit in the wreath-market,
> Chatting away.
> Ah well, in the days of our
> Noble Myronides [b]
> None would have stooped
> Money to take for
> Attending the meetings, but
> Hither they trooped,
> Each with his own little
> Goatskin of wine,
> Each with three olives, two
> Onions, one loaf, in his
> Wallet, to dine.
> But now they are set
> The three-obol to get,
> And whene'er the State business engages,
> They clamour, like hodmen, for wages. [c]

BLEPYRUS. What's up? Where's my wife gone? Why,
> bless the woman,
It's almost daybreak and she can't be found.
Here am I, taken with the gripes abed,
Groping about to find my overcloak
And shoes i' the dark; but hang it, they're gone too:
I could not find them anywhere. Meanwhile
Easums kept knocking hard at my back-door; [d]
So on I put this kirtle of my wife's,

---

defeated the Corinthians at Megara; and in the next year defeated the Boeotians at Oenophyta.

[c] *The Chorus leave the orchestra for a time. Enter Blepyrus
in his wife's dress.*

[d] βούλεται εἰπεῖν ὡς ὅτι ἠπειγόμην ἀποπατῆσαι: Schol. He plays
on the name of an Attic deme, οἱ Κόπρειοι.

καὶ τὰς ἐκείνης Περσικὰς ὑφέλκομαι.
ἀλλ' ἐν καθαρῷ ποῦ ποῦ τις ἂν χέσας τύχοι;   320
ἢ πανταχοῦ τοι νυκτός ἐστιν ἐν καλῷ;
οὐ γάρ με νῦν χέζοντά γ' οὐδεὶς ὄψεται.
οἴμοι κακοδαίμων, ὅτι γέρων ὢν ἠγόμην
γυναῖχ'· ὅσας εἴμ' ἄξιος πληγὰς λαβεῖν.
οὐ γάρ ποθ' ὑγιὲς οὐδὲν ἐξελήλυθεν   325
δράσουσ'. ὅμως δ' οὖν ἐστιν ἀποπατητέον.

ΑΝΗΡ. τίς ἐστιν; οὐ δήπου Βλέπυρος ὁ γειτνιῶν;
νὴ τὸν Δί' αὐτὸς δῆτ' ἐκεῖνος. εἰπέ μοι,
τί τοῦτό σοι τὸ πυρρόν ἐστιν; οὔ τί που
Κινησίας σου κατατετίληκέν ποθεν;   330

ΒΛ. οὔκ, ἀλλὰ τῆς γυναικὸς ἐξελήλυθα
τὸ κροκωτίδιον ἀμπισχόμενος, οὐνδύεται.

ΑΝ. τὸ δ' ἱμάτιόν σου ποῦ 'στιν;

ΒΛ.   οὐκ ἔχω φράσαι.
ζητῶν γὰρ αὔτ' οὐχ εὗρον ἐν τοῖς στρώμασιν.

ΑΝ. εἶτ' οὐδὲ τὴν γυναῖκ' ἐκέλευσάς σοι φράσαι;   335

ΒΛ. μὰ τὸν Δί'· οὐ γὰρ ἔνδον οὖσα τυγχάνει,
ἀλλ' ἐκτετρύπηκεν λαθοῦσά μ' ἔνδοθεν·
ὃ καὶ δέδοικα μή τι δρᾷ νεώτερον.

ΑΝ. νὴ τὸν Ποσειδῶ, ταὐτὰ τοίνυν ἄντικρυς
ἐμοὶ πέπονθας. καὶ γὰρ ᾗ ξύνειμ' ἐγὼ   340
φρούδη 'στ', ἔχουσα θοἰμάτιον οὑγὼ 'φόρουν.
κοὐ τοῦτο λυπεῖ μ', ἀλλὰ καὶ τὰς ἐμβάδας.
οὔκουν λαβεῖν γ' αὐτὰς ἐδυνάμην οὐδαμοῦ.

ΒΛ. μὰ τὸν Διόνυσον, οὐδ' ἐγὼ γὰρ τὰς ἐμὰς
Λακωνικάς, ἀλλ' ὡς ἔτυχον χεζητιῶν,   345
ἐς τὼ κοθόρνω τὼ πόδ' ἐνθεὶς ἱέμην,
ἵνα μὴ 'γχέσαιμ' ἐς τὴν σισύραν· φανὴ γὰρ ἦν.

ΑΝ. τί δῆτ' ἂν εἴη; μῶν ἐπ' ἄριστον γυνὴ

ᵃ Women's slippers ; C. 151, L. 229, T. 734.

And shove my feet into her Persian slippers.[a]
Where's a convenient place ? or shall I say
All are alike convenient in the dark ?
No man can see me here, I am sure of that.
Fool that I was, worse luck, to take a wife
In my old age. Ought to be thrashed, I ought !
'Tis for no good, I warrant, that she's out
This time of night. However, I can't wait.[b]

CITIZEN. Hey-day ! who's this ? Not neighbour Blepyrus ?
Sure and it's he himself. Why, tell me, man,
What's all that yellow ? Do you mean to say
You've had Cinesias at his tricks again ?[c]

BL. No, no ; I wanted to come out, and took
This little yellow kirtle of my wife's.

CIT. But where's your cloak ?

BL.   I've not the least idea.
I searched amongst the clothes, and 'twasn't there.

CIT. Did you not ask your wife to find the thing ?

BL. I didn't. No. For why ? SHE wasn't there.
She's wormed herself away out of the house ;
Some revolution in the wind, I fear.

CIT. O by Poseidon, but your case is just
The same as mine. *My* wife has stolen away,
And carried off my cloak. And that's not all,
Hang her, she's carried off my shoes as well :
At least I could not find them anywhere.

BL. No more can I : I could not anywhere
Find my Laconians : so, my case being urgent,
I shove her slippers on, and out I bolt
For fear I soil my blanket ; 'twas a clean one.

CIT. What can it be ? can any of her gossips

[b] *Enter another husband.*
[c] C. was notorious for having defiled a shrine of Hecate ;
F. 366.

κέκληκεν αὐτὴν τῶν φίλων;

ΒΛ. γνώμην γ' ἐμήν.
οὔκουν πονηρά γ' ἐστὶν ὅ τι κἄμ' εἰδέναι. 350

ΑΝ. ἀλλὰ σὺ μὲν ἱμονιάν τιν' ἀποπατεῖς· ἐμοὶ δ'
ὥρα βαδίζειν ἐστὶν εἰς ἐκκλησίαν,
ἤνπερ λάβω θοἰμάτιον, ὅπερ ἦν μοι μόνον.

ΒΛ. κἄγωγ', ἐπειδὰν ἀποπατήσω· νῦν δέ μοι
ἀχράς τις ἐγκλείσασ' ἔχει τὰ σιτία. 355

ΑΝ. μῶν ἣν Θρασύβουλος εἶπε τοῖς Λακωνικοῖς;

ΒΛ. νὴ τὸν Διόνυσον, ἐνέχεται γοῦν μοι σφόδρα.
ἀτὰρ τί δράσω; καὶ γὰρ οὐδὲ τοῦτό με
μόνον τὸ λυποῦν ἐστιν, ἀλλ' ὅταν φάγω,
ὅποι βαδιεῖταί μοι τὸ λοιπὸν ἡ κόπρος. 360
νῦν μὲν γὰρ οὗτος βεβαλάνωκε τὴν θύραν,
ὅστις ποτ' ἔστ', ἄνθρωπος Ἀχραδούσιος.
τίς ἂν οὖν ἰατρόν μοι μετέλθοι καὶ τίνα;
τίς τῶν καταπρώκτων δεινός ἐστι τὴν τέχνην;
ἆρ' οἶδ' Ἀμύνων; ἀλλ' ἴσως ἀρνήσεται. 365
Ἀντισθένην τις καλεσάτω πάσῃ τέχνῃ.
οὗτος γὰρ ἀνὴρ ἕνεκά γε στεναγμάτων
οἶδεν τί πρωκτὸς βούλεται χεζητιῶν.
ὦ πότνι' Εἰλείθυια, μή με περίδῃς
διαρραγέντα μηδὲ βεβαλανωμένον, 370
ἵνα μὴ γένωμαι σκωραμὶς κωμῳδική.

ΧΡΕΜΗΣ. οὗτος, τί ποιεῖς; οὔ τί που χέζεις;

ΒΛ. ἐγώ;
οὐ δῆτ' ἔτι γε μὰ τὸν Δί', ἀλλ' ἀνίσταμαι.

---

[a] Funem cacas.
[b] T. seems to have promised the Spartans to speak on their
behalf, probably against the Anti-Spartan league, and to have
reconsidered the matter, and excused himself to them ; alleging

Have asked her out to breakfast ?

BL.   I expect so.
She's not a bad one : I don't *think* she is.

CIT. Why, man, you are paying out a cable *a* : I
Must to the Assembly, when I've found my cloak,
My missing cloak : the only one I've got.

BL. I too, when eased ; but now an acrid pear
Is blocking up the passage of my food.

CIT. As Thrasybulus told the Spartans, eh ? *b*

BL. By Dionysus, but it grips me tight,
And that's not all : whatever shall I do ?
For how the food I am going to eat hereafter
Will find a passage out, I can't imagine ;
So firm and close this Acridusian chap *c*
Has fastened up its pathway to the door.
Who'll fetch a doctor, and what doctor, here ?
Which of the pathicks knows this business best ?
Amynon knows : but perhaps he won't admit it.
Fetch, fetch Antisthenes, by all means fetch him. *d*
He's just the man (to judge from his complaints) *e*
To know the pangs from which I'm suffering now.
Great Eileithyia, let me not remain
Thus plugged and barricaded, nor become
A public nightstool for the comic stage. *f*

CHREMES. Taking your ease, good neighbour ?

BL.   No, I'm not.
'Tis true I have been, but I've finished now.

illness brought on by eating wild pears, according to Schol. *Exit second husband.*

  c That is, the 'acrid pear' (ἀχράς) which stopped up the bowels (355), with a play on the name of a deme, Ἀχερδούσιος.

  d Ἀμύνων, ῥήτωρ ἡταιρηκώς, Ἀντισθένης, ἰατρὸς θηλυδριώδης: Schol.

  e Quia nimirum inter cacandum difficulter egerat: Bergler.

  f The σκωραμίς, a vessel ἐν ᾧ ἀποπατοῦσι (Schol.), doubtless had a plug. *Enter Chremes, the other neighbour.*

ARISTOPHANES

ΧΡ. τὸ τῆς γυναικὸς δ' ἀμπέχει χιτώνιον;

ΒΛ. ἐν τῷ σκότῳ γὰρ τοῦτ' ἔτυχον ἔνδον λαβών.   375
ἀτὰρ πόθεν ἥκεις ἐτεόν;

ΧΡ.   ἐξ ἐκκλησίας.

ΒΛ. ἤδη λέλυται γάρ;

ΧΡ.   νὴ Δί', ὄρθριον μὲν οὖν.
καὶ δῆτα πολὺν ἡ μίλτος, ὦ Ζεῦ φίλτατε,
γέλων παρέσχεν, ἣν προσέρραινον κύκλῳ.

ΒΛ. τὸ τριώβολον δῆτ' ἔλαβες;

ΧΡ.   εἰ γὰρ ὤφελον.   380
ἀλλ' ὕστερος νῦν ἦλθον, ὥστ' αἰσχύνομαι,
μὰ τὸν Δί' οὐδὲν ἄλλο γ' ἢ τονδὶ φέρων.

ΒΛ. τὸ δ' αἴτιον τί;

ΧΡ.   πλεῖστος ἀνθρώπων ὄχλος,
ὅσος οὐδεπώποτ', ἦλθ' ἀθρόος ἐς τὴν πύκνα.
καὶ δῆτα πάντας σκυτοτόμοις ἠκάζομεν   385
ὁρῶντες αὐτούς. οὐ γὰρ ἀλλ' ὑπερφυῶς
ὡς λευκοπληθὴς ἦν ἰδεῖν ἡκκλησία·
ὥστ' οὐκ ἔλαβον οὔτ' αὐτὸς οὔτ' ἄλλοι συχνοί.

ΒΛ. οὐδ' ἄρ' ἂν ἐγὼ λάβοιμι νῦν ἐλθών;

ΧΡ.   πόθεν;
οὐδ' εἰ μὰ Δία τότ' ἦλθες, ὅτε τὸ δεύτερον   390
ἀλεκτρυὼν ἐφθέγγετ'.

ΒΛ.   οἴμοι δείλαιος.
'Αντίλοχ', ἀποίμωξόν με τοῦ τριωβόλου
τὸν ζῶντα μᾶλλον. τἀμὰ γὰρ διοίχεται.

---

[a] The ληξίαρχοι, or Registrars, used to send in Scythians with
a rope smeared with ruddle, with which they roped into the
Assembly those who stood in the agora; cf. A. 21.

[b] "τονδὶ φέρων. He points to his empty θύλακον. I have
substituted these words for the τὸν θύλακον of the MSS. and
editions, which in my opinion was originally a gloss on τονδὶ, and

280

CHR. O, and you've got your lady's kirtle on !

BL. 'Twas dark indoors : I caught it up by chance
But whence come *you* ?

CHR. I'm coming from the Assembly.

BL. What, is it over ?

CHR. Aye, betimes to-day.
And O, dear Zeus, the fun it was to see
The way they spattered the vermilion round.[a]

BL. Got your three-obol ?

CHR. No, not I, worse luck.
I was too late : I'm carrying home, ashamed,
This empty wallet :[b] nothing else at all.

BL. Why, how was that ?

CHR. There gathered such a crowd
About the Pnyx, you never saw the like ;
Such pale-faced fellows ; just like shoemakers
We all declared ; and strange it was to see
How pallid-packed the whole Assembly looked.
So I and lots of us could get no pay.

BL. Shall I get any if I run ?

CHR. Not you !
Not had you been there when the cock was giving
Its second crow.

BL. O weep, Antilochus,
Rather for me, the living, than for him,
The loved and lost—three-obol.[c] All is gone !

has crept into the text, usurping the place of τονδὶ φέρων, and destroying the sense of the passage. Bergler refers to *Wasps*, 300-315 " : R.

[c] From Aesch. *Myrmidons* fragm. :

> Ἀντίλοχ᾽, ἀποίμωξόν με τοῦ τεθνηκότος
> τὸν ζῶντα μᾶλλον.

> Weep, Antilochus,
> Rather for me, the living, than for him,
> The loved and lost Patroclus.

ἀτὰρ τί τὸ πρᾶγμ᾽ ἦν, ὅτι τοσοῦτον χρῆμ᾽ ὄχλου
οὕτως ἐν ὥρᾳ ξυνελέγη;

XP.   τί δ᾽ ἄλλο γ᾽ ἢ   395
ἔδοξε τοῖς πρυτάνεσι περὶ σωτηρίας
γνώμας καθεῖναι τῆς πόλεως; κᾆτ᾽ εὐθέως
πρῶτος Νεοκλείδης ὁ γλάμων παρείρπυσεν.
κᾆπειθ᾽ ὁ δῆμος ἀναβοᾷ πόσον δοκεῖς,
οὐ δεινὰ τολμᾶν τουτονὶ δημηγορεῖν,   400
καὶ ταῦτα περὶ σωτηρίας προκειμένου,
ὃς αὐτὸς αὑτῷ βλεφαρίδ᾽ οὐκ ἐσώσατο;
ὁ δ᾽ ἀναβοήσας καὶ περιβλέψας ἔφη·
τί δαί μ᾽ ἐχρῆν δρᾶν;

BΛ.   σκόροδ᾽ ὁμοῦ τρίψαντ᾽ ὀπῷ
τιθύμαλλον ἐμβαλόντα τοῦ Λακωνικοῦ   405
σαυτοῦ παραλείφειν τὰ βλέφαρα τῆς ἑσπέρας,
ἔγωγ᾽ ἂν εἶπον, εἰ παρὼν ἐτύγχανον.

XP. μετὰ τοῦτον Εὐαίων ὁ δεξιώτατος
παρῆλθε γυμνός, ὡς ἐδόκει τοῖς πλείοσιν·
αὐτός γε μέντοὔφασκεν ἱμάτιον ἔχειν,   410
κᾆπειτ᾽ ἔλεξε δημοτικωτάτους λόγους·
ὁρᾶτε μέν με δεόμενον σωτηρίας
τετραστατήρου καὐτοῦ· ἀλλ᾽ ὅμως ἐρῶ
ὡς τὴν πόλιν καὶ τοὺς πολίτας σώσετε.
ἢν γὰρ παρέχωσι τοῖς δεομένοις οἱ κναφῆς   415
χλαίνας, ἐπειδὰν πρῶτον ἥλιος τραπῇ,
πλευρῖτις ἡμῶν οὐδέν᾽ ἂν λάβοι ποτέ.
ὅσοις δὲ κλίνη μή ᾽στι μηδὲ στρώματα,
ἰέναι καθευδήσοντας ἀπονενιμμένους
ἐς τῶν σκυλοδεψῶν· ἢν δ᾽ ἀποκλείῃ τῇ θύρᾳ   420

ᵃ Cf. Pl. 718, 719.

Whatever was it though that brought together
So vast a crowd so early ?

CHR.   'Twas determined
To put this question to the assembled people,
" How best to save the State." So first and foremost
Came Neocleides, groping up to speak.
And all the people shouted out aloud,
What scandal that this blear-eyed oaf, who cannot
Save his own eyesight for himself, should dare
To come and teach us how to save the State.
But he cried out, and leered around, and said,
What's to be done ?

BL.   *Pound garlic up with verjuice,*[a]
Throw in some spurge of the Laconian sort,
And rub it on your eyelids every night.
That's what, had I been present, I'd have said.

CHR. Next came Evaeon,[b] smart accomplished chap,
With nothing on, as most of us supposed,
But he himself insisted he was clothed.
He made a popular democratic speech.
Behold, says he, *I am myself in want*
Of cash to save me ;[c] *yet I know the way*
To save the citizens, and save the State.
Let every clothier give to all that ask
Warm woollen robes, when first the sun turns back.
No more will pleurisy attack us then.
Let such as own no bedclothes and no bed,
After they've dined,[d] *seek out the furriers, there*
To sleep ; and whoso shuts the door against them

---

[b] " A pauper, whose clothes are so scanty and threadbare that
people cannot perceive that he has any on : " R.

[c] " A half-guinea salvation," here as the price of a new suit
of clothes, which he obviously needs.

[d] ἀπονίψασθαι applies specially to the after-dinner wash ; W.
1216.

χειμῶνος ὄντος, τρεῖς σισύρας ὀφειλέτω.

ΒΛ. νὴ τὸν Διόνυσον, χρηστά γ'· εἰ δ' ἐκεῖνά γε
προσέθηκεν, οὐδεὶς ἀντεχειροτόνησεν ἄν,
τοὺς ἀλφιταμοιβοὺς τοῖς ἀπόροις τρεῖς χοίνικας
δεῖπνον παρέχειν ἅπασιν, ἢ κλάειν μακρά.   425
ἵνα τοῦτ' ἀπέλαυσαν Ναυσικύδους τἀγαθόν.

ΧΡ. μετὰ τοῦτο τοίνυν εὐπρεπὴς νεανίας
λευκός τις ἀνεπήδησ', ὅμοιος Νικίᾳ,
δημηγορήσων, κἀπεχείρησεν λέγειν
ὡς χρὴ παραδοῦναι ταῖς γυναιξὶ τὴν πόλιν.   430
εἶτ' ἐθορύβησαν κἀνέκραγον ὡς εὖ λέγοι,
τὸ σκυτοτομικὸν πλῆθος· οἱ δ' ἐκ τῶν ἀγρῶν
ἀνεβορβόρυξαν.

ΒΛ.   νοῦν γὰρ εἶχον νὴ Δία.

ΧΡ. ἀλλ' ἦσαν ἥττους· ὁ δὲ κατεῖχε τῇ βοῇ,
τὰς μὲν γυναῖκας πόλλ' ἀγαθὰ λέγων, σὲ δὲ   435
πολλὰ κακά.

ΒΛ.   καὶ τί εἶπε;

ΧΡ.   πρῶτον μέν σ' ἔφη
εἶναι πανοῦργον.

ΒΛ.   καὶ σέ;

ΧΡ.   μή πω τοῦτ' ἔρῃ.
κἄπειτα κλέπτην.

ΒΛ.   ἐμὲ μόνον;

ΧΡ.   καὶ νὴ Δία
καὶ συκοφάντην.

ΒΛ.   ἐμὲ μόνον;

ΧΡ.   καὶ νὴ Δία
τωνδὶ τὸ πλῆθος.

ΒΛ.   τίς δὲ τοῦτ' ἄλλως λέγει;   440

ΧΡ. γυναῖκα δ' εἶναι πρᾶγμ' ἔφη νουβυστικὸν
καὶ χρηματοποιόν· κοὔτε τἀπόρρητ' ἔφη

In wintry weather, shall be fined three blankets.

BL. Well said indeed ; and never a man would dare
To vote against him, had he added this :
That all who deal in grain shall freely give
Three quarts to every pauper, or be hanged.
That good, at least, they'd gain from Nausicydes.[a]

CHR. Then, after him, there bounded up to speak
A spruce and pale-faced youth, like Nicias.
And *he* declared we ought to place the State
Into the hands of (whom do you think ?) the women !
Then the whole mob of shoemakers [b] began
To cheer like mad ; whilst all the country folk
Hooted and hissed.

BL.   They showed their sense, by Zeus.

CHR. But less their numbers ; so the lad went on,
Speaking all good of women, but of you
Everything bad.

BL.   What ?

CHR.   First of all he called you
An arrant rogue.

BL.   And you ?

CHR.   Let be, awhile.
Also a thief.

BL.   Me only ?

CHR.   And by Zeus,
A sycophant.

BL.   Me only ?

CHR.   And by Zeus,
All our friends here.[c]

BL.   Well, who says nay to that ?

CHR. And then the woman is, he said, a thing
Stuffed full of wit and moneymaking ways.

[a] N. made a fortune from dealing in grain ; Xen. *Mem.* ii. 7.
[b] The disguised women : Schol.
[c] Pointing to the audience.

285

ἐκ Θεσμοφόροιν ἑκάστοτ' αὐτὰς ἐκφέρειν,
σὲ δὲ κἀμὲ βουλεύοντε τοῦτο δρᾶν ἀεί.

ΒΛ. καὶ νὴ τὸν Ἑρμῆν τοῦτό γ' οὐκ ἐψεύσατο.   445

ΧΡ. ἔπειτα συμβάλλειν πρὸς ἀλλήλας ἔφη
ἱμάτια, χρυσί', ἀργύριον, ἐκπώματα,
μόνας μόναις οὐ μαρτύρων γ' ἐναντίον·
καὶ ταῦτ' ἀποφέρειν πάντα κοὐκ ἀποστερεῖν·
ἡμῶν δὲ τοὺς πολλοὺς ἔφασκε τοῦτο δρᾶν.   450

ΒΛ. νὴ τὸν Ποσειδῶ, μαρτύρων τ' ἐναντίον.

ΧΡ. οὐ συκοφαντεῖν, οὐ διώκειν, οὐδὲ τὸν
δῆμον καταλύειν, ἀλλὰ πολλὰ κἀγαθά.
ἔτερά τε πλεῖστα τὰς γυναῖκας εὐλόγει.

ΒΛ. τί δῆτ' ἔδοξεν;

ΧΡ.   ἐπιτρέπειν σὲ τὴν πόλιν   455
ταύταις. ἐδόκει γὰρ τοῦτο μόνον ἐν τῇ πόλει
οὔπω γεγενῆσθαι.

ΒΛ.   καὶ δέδοκται;

ΧΡ.   φήμ' ἐγώ.

ΒΛ. ἅπαντά τ' αὐταῖς ἐστι προστεταγμένα
ἃ τοῖσιν ἀστοῖς ἔμελεν;

ΧΡ.   οὕτω ταῦτ' ἔχει.

ΒΛ. οὐδ' εἰς δικαστήριον ἄρ' εἶμ', ἀλλ' ἢ γυνή;   460

ΧΡ. οὐδ' ἔτι σὺ θρέψεις οὓς ἔχεις, ἀλλ' ἢ γυνή.

ΒΛ. οὐδὲ στένειν τὸν ὄρθρον ἔτι πρᾶγμ' ἆρά μοι;

ΧΡ. μὰ Δί', ἀλλὰ ταῖς γυναιξὶ ταῦτ' ἤδη μέλει·
σὺ δ' ἀστενακτὶ περδόμενος οἴκοι μενεῖς.

ΒΛ. ἐκεῖνο δεινὸν τοῖσιν ἡλίκοισι νῷν,   465
μὴ παραλαβοῦσαι τῆς πόλεως τὰς ἡνίας
ἔπειτ' ἀναγκάζωσι πρὸς βίαν

ΧΡ.   τί δρᾶν;

ΒΛ. κινεῖν ἑαυτάς.

ΧΡ.   ἢν δὲ μὴ δυνώμεθα;

They don't betray their Thesmophorian secrets,
But you and I blab all State secrets out.

BL. By Hermes, there at least he told no lie.

CHR. And women lend each other, said the lad,
Their dresses, trinkets, money, drinking-cups,
Though quite alone, with never a witness there.
And all restore the loan, and none withhold it.
But men, he said, are always doing this.

BL. Aye to be sure : though witnesses were there.

CHR. *They* don't inform, or prosecute, or put
The people down : but everything that's right.
And much, besides, he praised the womankind.

BL. What was determined ?

CHR.   You're to put the State
Into their hands.   This was the one reform
Not yet attempted.

BL.   'Twas decreed ?

CHR.   It was.

BL. So then the women now must undertake
All manly duties ?

CHR.   So I understand.

BL. Then I shan't be a dicast, but my wife ?

CHR. Nor you support your household, but your wife.

BL. Nor I get grumbling up in early morn ?

CHR. No : for the future that's your wife's affair.
You'll lie abed : no grumbling any more.

BL. But hark ye, 'twould be rough on us old men
If, when the women hold the reins of State,
They should perforce compel us to—

CHR.   Do what ?

BL. Make love to them.

CHR.   But if we're not prepared ?

ARISTOPHANES

ΒΛ. ἄριστον οὐ δώσουσι.

ΧΡ.   σὺ δέ γε νὴ Δία
δρᾶ ταῦθ', ἵν' ἀριστᾷς τε καὶ κινῇς ἅμα.   470

ΒΛ. τὸ πρὸς βίαν δεινότατον.

ΧΡ.   ἀλλ' εἰ τῇ πόλει
τοῦτο ξυνοίσει, ταῦτα χρὴ πάντ' ἄνδρα δρᾶν.
λόγος τέ τοί τις ἔστι τῶν γεραιτέρων,
ὅσ' ἂν ἀνόητ' ἢ μῶρα βουλευσώμεθα,
ἅπαντ' ἐπὶ τὸ βέλτιον ἡμῖν ξυμφέρειν.   475
καὶ ξυμφέροι γ', ὦ πότνια Παλλὰς καὶ θεοί.
ἀλλ' εἶμι· σὺ δ' ὑγίαινε.

ΒΛ.   καὶ σύ γ', ὦ Χρέμης.

ΧΟΡΟΣ. ἔμβα, χώρει.
ἆρ' ἔστι τῶν ἀνδρῶν τις ἡμῖν ὅστις ἐπακολουθεῖ;
στρέφου, σκόπει,   480
φύλαττε σαυτὴν ἀσφαλῶς, πολλοὶ γὰρ οἱ πανοῦργοι,
μή πού τις ἐκ τοὔπισθεν ὢν τὸ σχῆμα καταφυλάξῃ·
ἀλλ' ὡς μάλιστα τοῖν ποδοῖν ἐπικτυπῶν βάδιζε.
ἡμῖν δ' ἂν αἰσχύνην φέροι
πάσαισι παρὰ τοῖς ἀνδράσιν τὸ πρᾶγμα τοῦτ'
    ἐλεγχθέν.   485
πρὸς ταῦτα συστέλλου σεαυ-
τήν, πανταχῇ σκοπουμένη
τἀκεῖσε καὶ τὰ τῇδε καὶ

ᵃ " When the contention between Poseidon and Athene for the patronage of Athens was decided in favour of the latter, Poseidon in anger imprecated perpetual δυσβουλία on the new city. Now the decrees of deities were, like those of the Medes and Persians, supposed to be irreversible, even by themselves : what one god had done, no other, not even himself, could undo ; but he could virtually nullify the effect by a subsequent decree. And so in the instance before us, Athene could not change the curse of perpetual

BL.　They'll dock our breakfasts.

CHR.　　　　　　　　　　Therefore learn the way
How to make love, and eat your breakfast too.

BL.　Upon compulsion !　Faugh !

CHR.　　　　　　　　　　If that is for
The public good, we needs must all obey.
There is a legend of the olden time,
That all our foolish plans and vain conceits
Are overruled to work the public good.[a]
So be it now, high Pallas and ye gods !
But I must go.　Farewell.

BL.　　　　　　　　　　And farewell, Chremes.[b]

CHORUS.　　Step strong !　March along !
But search and scan if any man
　　　　　　　be somewhere following in our rear.
　　　Look out !　Wheel about !
And O be sure that all's secure ;
　　　　　　　for many are the rogues, I fear.
Lest someone, coming up behind us,
　　　　　　　in this ungodly guise should find us.
BE SURE you make a clattering sound
　　　　with both your feet against the ground.
For dismal shame and scandal great
Will everywhere upon us wait,
　　　　　　　if our disguise they penetrate.
So wrap your garments round you tight,
And peep about with all your might,
Both here and there and on your right,

δυσβουλία, but she could and did nullify its effect by causing it always to have a successful issue.　And this is why Chremes, in his prayer three lines below, whilst invoking generally all the gods, makes a special appeal to Pallas " : R.

　[b] *Exeunt.*

τἀκ δεξιᾶς, μὴ ξυμφορὰ γενήσεται τὸ πρᾶγμα.
ἀλλ' ἐγκονῶμεν· τοῦ τόπου γὰρ ἐγγύς ἐσμεν ἤδη
ὅθενπερ εἰς ἐκκλησίαν ὡρμώμεθ' ἡνίκ' ἦμεν·   490
τὴν δ' οἰκίαν ἕξεσθ' ὁρᾶν ὅθενπερ ἡ στρατηγὸς
ἔσθ', ἡ τὸ πρᾶγμ' εὑροῦσ' ὃ νῦν ἔδοξε τοῖς πολίταις.
ὥστ' εἰκὸς ἡμᾶς μὴ βραδύνειν ἔστ' ἐπαναμενούσας,
πώγωνας ἐξηρτημένας,
μὴ καί τις ἡμᾶς ὄψεται χἠμῶν ἴσως κατείπῃ.   495
ἀλλ' εἶα δεῦρ' ἐπὶ σκιᾶς
ἐλθοῦσα πρὸς τὸ τειχίον,
παραβλέπουσα θατέρῳ,
πάλιν μετασκεύαζε σαυτὴν αὖθις ἥπερ ἦσθα.
καὶ μὴ βράδυν'· ὡς τήνδε καὶ δὴ τὴν στρατηγὸν
    ἡμῶν   500
χωροῦσαν ἐξ ἐκκλησίας ὁρῶμεν. ἀλλ' ἐπείγου
ἅπασα καὶ μίσει σάκον πρὸς ταῖν γνάθοιν ἔχουσα·
χαὗται γὰρ ἀλγοῦσιν πάλαι τὸ σχῆμα τοῦτ'
    ἔχουσαι.

ΠΡ. ταυτὶ μὲν ἡμῖν, ὦ γυναῖκες, εὐτυχῶς
τὰ πράγματ' ἐκβέβηκεν ἀβουλεύσαμεν.   505
ἀλλ' ὡς τάχιστα, πρίν τιν' ἀνθρώπων ἰδεῖν,
ῥιπτεῖτε χλαίνας, ἐμβὰς ἐκποδὼν ἴτω,
χάλα συναπτοὺς ἡνίας Λακωνικάς,
βακτηρίας ἄφεσθε· καὶ μέντοι σὺ μὲν

---

a "Praxagora is seen returning from the Assembly. She is
still wearing her husband's garments, and enters the stage alone.
We hear no more of the two women who had been her companions
there before. And nobody else comes on the stage until Blepyrus
and Chremes emerge from their respective houses, twenty lines
below. The Chorus fulfil the promise made supra 246": R.

b Line 508 is probably quoted from some tragic poet, which
would explain the singular χάλα.

Or this our plot to save the State
                    will in disaster terminate.
MOVE ON, dear friends, move on apace,
                    for now we're very near the place
From whence we started, when we went
                    to join the men in Parliament.
And there's the mansion, full in view,
                    where dwells our lady chieftain, who
The wise and noble scheme invented
                    to which the State has just assented.
So NOW no longer must we stay,
                    no longer while the time away,
    False-bearded with this bristly hair,
Lest someone see us and declare
                    our hidden secret everywhere.
    So draw ye closer, at my call,
    Beneath the shadow of the wall,
    And glancing sideways, one and all,
Adjust and change your dresses there,
                    and bear the form which erst ye bare.
FOR SEE the noble lady fair,
                    our chieftainess, approaching there.
She's coming home with eager speed
                    from yon Assembly ; take ye heed,
And loathe upon your chins to wear
                    that monstrous equipage of hair ;
For 'neath its tickling mass, I know,
                    they've all been smarting long ago.[a]

PR. So far, dear sisters, these our bold designs
Have all gone off successfully and well.
But now at once, or e'er some wight perceive us,
Off with your woollens ; cast your shoes ; unloose
The jointed clasp of thy Laconian reins : [b]
Discard your staves ;—Nay, but do *you*, my dear,

ταύτας κατευτρέπιζ'· ἐγὼ δὲ βούλομαι   510
εἴσω παρερπύσασα, πρὶν τὸν ἄνδρα με
ἰδεῖν, καταθέσθαι θοἰμάτιον αὐτοῦ πάλιν
ὅθενπερ ἔλαβον τἄλλα θ' ἀξηνεγκάμην.

ΧΟ. κεῖται δ' ἤδη πάνθ' ἅπερ εἶπας· σὸν δ' ἔργον τἄλλα
   διδάσκειν,
ὅ τι σοι δρῶσαι ξύμφορον ἡμεῖς δόξομεν ὀρθῶς
   ὑπακούειν.
οὐδεμιᾷ γὰρ δεινοτέρᾳ σου ξυμμίξασ' οἶδα γυναικί.   515

ΠΡ. περιμείνατέ νυν, ἵνα τῆς ἀρχῆς, ἣν ἄρτι κεχειρο-
   τόνημαι,
ξυμβούλοισιν πάσαις ὑμῖν χρήσωμαι. καὶ γὰρ ἐκεῖ
   μοι
ἐν τῷ θορύβῳ καὶ τοῖς δεινοῖς ἀνδρειόταται γεγέ-
   νησθε.

ΒΛ. αὕτη, πόθεν ἥκεις, Πραξαγόρα;
ΠΡ.   τί δ', ὦ μέλε,   520
σοὶ τοῦθ';
ΒΛ.   ὅ τί μοι τοῦτ' ἐστίν; ὡς εὐηθικῶς.
ΠΡ. οὔ τοι παρὰ τοῦ μοιχοῦ γε φήσεις.
ΒΛ.   οὐκ ἴσως
ἑνός γε.
ΠΡ.   καὶ μὴν βασανίσαι τουτί γέ σοι
ἔξεστι.
ΒΛ.   πῶς;
ΠΡ.   εἰ τῆς κεφαλῆς ὄζω μύρου.
ΒΛ. τί δ'; οὐχὶ βινεῖται γυνὴ κἄνευ μύρου;   525
ΠΡ. οὐ δὴ τάλαιν' ἔγωγε.
ΒΛ.   πῶς οὖν ὄρθριον
ᾤχου σιωπῇ θοἰμάτιον λαβοῦσά μου;

Get these in order : I myself will steal
Into the house, and ere my husband see me,
Put back his overcloak, unnoticed, where
I found it, and whatever else I took.[a]

CH.   We have done your behest, and as touching the rest,
We will do whatsoever you tell us is best.
For truly I ween that a woman so keen,
Resourceful and subtle we never have seen.

PR.   Then all by my side, as the councillors tried
Of the office I hold, be content to abide ;
For *there*, in the fuss and the hullabaloo,
Ye proved yourselves women most manly and true.[b]

BL.   Hallo, Praxagora, whence come you ?

PR.   What's that
To you, my man ?

BL.   What's that to me ? That's cool.

PR.   Not from a lover ; *that* you know.

BL.   Perchance
From more than one.

PR.   That you can test, directly.

BL.   Marry and how ?

PR.   Smell if my hair is perfumed.

BL.   Does not a woman sin unless she's perfumed ?

PR.   *I* don't, at all events.

BL.   What made you steal
Away so early with my overcloak ?

---

  [a] " *Praxagora retires into her house* (*the house of Blepyrus*) *to change her dress, whilst the Chorus change theirs in the orchestra. She almost immediately returns, and henceforth all the women are clothed in their proper habiliments* " : R.

  [b] *Enter Blepyrus and Chremes from their respective houses.*

ΠΡ. γυνή μέ τις νύκτωρ ἑταίρα καὶ φίλη
μετεπέμψατ' ὠδίνουσα.

ΒΛ.   κᾆτ' οὐκ ἦν ἐμοὶ
φράσασαν ἰέναι;

ΠΡ.   τῆς λεχοῦς δ' οὐ φροντίσαι,   **530**
οὕτως ἐχούσης, ὦνερ;

ΒΛ.   εἰποῦσάν γέ μοι.
ἀλλ' ἔστιν ἐνταῦθά τι κακόν.

ΠΡ.   μὰ τὼ θεώ,
ἀλλ' ὥσπερ εἶχον ᾠχόμην· ἐδεῖτο δὲ
ἥπερ μεθῆκέ μ', ἐξιέναι πάσῃ τέχνῃ.

ΒΛ. εἶτ' οὐ τὸ σαυτῆς ἱμάτιον ἐχρῆν σ' ἔχειν;   **535**
ἀλλ' ἔμ' ἀποδύσασ', ἐπιβαλοῦσα τοὐγκυκλον,
ᾤχου καταλιποῦσ' ὡσπερεὶ προκείμενον,
μόνον οὐ στεφανώσασ' οὐδ' ἐπιθεῖσα λήκυθον.

ΠΡ. ψῦχος γὰρ ἦν, ἐγὼ δὲ λεπτὴ κἀσθενής·
ἔπειθ' ἵν' ἀλεαίνοιμι, τοῦτ' ἠμπισχόμην·   **540**
σὲ δ' ἐν ἀλέᾳ κατακείμενον καὶ στρώμασιν
κατέλιπον, ὦνερ.

ΒΛ.   αἱ δὲ δὴ Λακωνικαὶ
ᾤχοντο μετὰ σοῦ κατὰ τί χἠ βακτηρία;

ΠΡ. ἵνα θοἰμάτιον σώσαιμι, μεθυπεδησάμην
μιμουμένη σε καὶ κτυποῦσα τοῖν ποδοῖν   **545**
καὶ τοὺς λίθους παίουσα τῇ βακτηρίᾳ.

ΒΛ. οἶσθ' οὖν ἀπολωλεκυῖα πυρῶν ἑκτέα,
ὃν χρῆν ἔμ' ἐξ ἐκκλησίας εἰληφέναι;

ΠΡ. μὴ φροντίσῃς· ἄρρεν γὰρ ἔτεκε παιδίον.

ΒΛ. ἡκκλησία;

ΠΡ.   μὰ Δί', ἀλλ' ἐφ' ἣν ἐγὼ 'χόμην.   **550**
ἀτὰρ γεγένηται;

---

a The body was placed on a bier or bed, clothed in white, and crowned with wreaths : beside it were flasks of oil.

PR.   I was called out ere daybreak, to a friend
     In pangs of childbirth.

BL.   Why not tell me first,
     Before you went ?

PR.   Not haste to help her in
     Such straits, my husband ?

BL.   After telling me.
     Something's wrong there.

PR.   Nay, by the Twain, I went
     Just as I was ; the wench who came besought me
     To lose no time.

BL.   Is that the reason why
     You did not put your mantle on ?   You threw it
     Over my bed and took my overcloak,
     And left me lying like a corpse laid out ; [a]
     Only I'd never a wreath, or bottle of oil.

PR.   The night was cold, and I'm so slight and fragile,
     I took your overcloak to keep me warm.
     And you I left well snuggled up in warmth
     And rugs, my husband.

BL.   How came my staff to form
     One of your party, and my red Laconians ?

PR.   I took your shoes to save your overcloak ; [b]
     Aping your walk, stumping with both my feet,
     And striking down your staff against the stones.

BL.   You've lost eight quarts of wheat, I'd have you know,
     Which the Assembly would have brought me in.[c]

PR.   Well, never mind ; she's got a bonny boy.

BL.   Who ? the Assembly has ?

PR.   No, fool, the woman.
     But has it met ?

---

   [b] That she might look like a man, and so save the cloak from
thieves who would snatch it off, λωποδύται.
   [c] Bought with the three obols.

ΒΛ.   ναὶ μὰ Δί'. οὐκ ᾔδεισθά με
φράσαντά σοι χθές;

ΠΡ.   ἄρτι γ' ἀναμιμνήσκομαι.

ΒΛ. οὐδ' ἄρα τὰ δόξαντ' οἶσθα;

ΠΡ.   μὰ Δί' ἐγὼ μὲν οὔ.

ΒΛ. κάθησο τοίνυν σηπίας μασωμένη.
ὑμῖν δέ φασι παραδεδόσθαι τὴν πόλιν.   555

ΠΡ. τί δρᾶν; ὑφαίνειν;

ΒΛ.   οὐ μὰ Δί', ἀλλ' ἄρχειν.

ΠΡ.   τίνων;

ΒΛ. ἀπαξαπάντων τῶν κατὰ πόλιν πραγμάτων.

ΠΡ. νὴ τὴν Ἀφροδίτην, μακαρία γ' ἄρ' ἡ πόλις
ἔσται τὸ λοιπόν.

ΒΛ.   κατὰ τί;

ΠΡ.   πολλῶν οὕνεκα.
οὐ γὰρ ἔτι τοῖς τολμῶσιν αὐτὴν αἰσχρὰ δρᾶν   560
ἔσται τὸ λοιπόν, οὐδαμοῦ δὲ μαρτυρεῖν,
οὐ συκοφαντεῖν.

ΒΛ.   μηδαμῶς πρὸς τῶν θεῶν
τουτὶ ποιήσῃς μηδ' ἀφέλῃ μου τὸν βίον.[a]

ΧΡ. ὦ δαιμόνι' ἀνδρῶν, τὴν γυναῖκ' ἔα λέγειν.

ΠΡ. μὴ λωποδυτῆσαι, μὴ φθονεῖν τοῖς πλησίον,   565
μὴ γυμνὸν εἶναι, μὴ πένητα μηδένα,
μὴ λοιδορεῖσθαι, μὴ 'νεχυραζόμενον φέρειν.

ΧΡ. νὴ τὸν Ποσειδῶ, μεγάλα γ', εἰ μὴ ψεύσεται.

ΠΡ. ἀλλ' ἀποφανῶ τοῦθ', ὥστε σέ γέ μοι μαρτυρεῖν,
καὶ τοῦτον αὐτὸν μηδὲν ἀντειπεῖν ἐμοί.[b]   570

ΧΟ. νῦν δὴ δεῖ σε πυκνὴν ἐγείρειν

---

[a] In Sophocles, *Philoct.* 933, Philoctetes thus prays to keep
the bow of Heracles, πρὸς θεῶν πατρῴων, τὸν βίον μή μου 'φέλῃς.

[b] Soph. *Trach.* 899 πεύσει δ' ὥστε μαρτυρεῖν ἐμοί. "He himself"
is Chremes, whom she points at.

BL.   I told you yesterday
'Twas going to meet.

PR.   O yes, I now remember.

BL. Have you not heard then what's decreed ?

PR.   No, dear

BL. Then sit you down and chew your cuttlefish.
The State, they say, is handed over to you !

PR. What for ?   To weave ?

BL.   No, govern.

PR.   Govern what ?

BL. All the whole work and business of the State.

PR. O here's a lucky State, by Aphrodite,
We're going to have !

BL.   How so ?

PR.   For many reasons.
For now no longer shall bold men be free
To shame the city : no more witnessing,
No false informing—

BL.   Hang it, don't do that.
Don't take away my only means of living ! [a]

CHR. Pray, sir, be still, and let the lady speak.

PR. No thefts of overcloaks, no envyings now,
None to be poor and naked any more.
No wranglings, no distraining on your goods.

CHR. Now, by Poseidon, wondrous news if true.

PR. Aye and I'll prove it, so that you'll support me,[b]
And he himself have nought to say against it.

CH.[c]   Now waken your intellect bright,

---

[a] " The first line appears in the mss. as νῦν δὴ δεῖ σε πυκνὴν
φρένα καὶ φιλόσοφον ἐγείρειν, but I have struck out the words
φρένα καὶ φιλόσοφον, which are useless to the sense, and destructive
to the metre, and have plainly crept into the text from some gloss
on the words πυκνὴν φροντίδα. They are, however, retained in
the translation " : R.

φροντίδ᾿ ἐπισταμένην
ταῖσι φίλαισιν ἀμύνειν.
κοινῇ γὰρ ἐπ᾿ εὐτυχίαισιν
ἔρχεται γλώττ-
ης ἐπίνοια, πολίτην
δῆμον ἐπαγλαϊοῦσα   575
μυρίαισιν
ὠφελίαισι βίου. δη-
λοῦν ὅ τί περ δύνασαι. καιρὸς δέ· δεῖται
γάρ τι σοφοῦ τινος ἐξευ-
ρήματος ἡ πόλις ἡμῶν.
ἀλλὰ πέραινε μόνον
μήτε δεδραμένα μήτ᾿ εἰ-
ρημένα πω πρότερον· μι-
σοῦσι γὰρ ἢν τὰ παλαιὰ   580
πολλάκις θεῶνται.
ἀλλ᾿ οὐ μέλλειν, ἀλλ᾿ ἅπτεσθαι καὶ δὴ χρὴ ταῖς δια-
        νοίαις,
ὡς τὸ ταχύνειν χαρίτων μετέχει πλεῖστον παρὰ τοῖσι
        θεαταῖς.

ΠΡ. καὶ μὴν ὅτι μὲν χρηστὰ διδάξω πιστεύω· τοὺς δὲ
        θεατάς,
εἰ καινοτομεῖν ἐθελήσουσιν καὶ μὴ τοῖς ἤθάσι λίαν
τοῖς τ᾿ ἀρχαίοις ἐνδιατρίβειν, τοῦτ᾿ ἔσθ᾿ ὃ μάλιστα
        δέδοικα.   585
ΒΛ. περὶ μὲν τοίνυν τοῦ καινοτομεῖν μὴ δείσῃς· τοῦτο γὰρ
        ἡμῖν
δρᾶν ἀντ᾿ ἄλλης ἀρχῆς ἐστιν, τῶν δ᾿ ἀρχαίων ἀμελῆσαι.
ΠΡ. μή νυν πρότερον μηδεὶς ὑμῶν ἀντείπῃ μηδ᾿ ὑπο-
        κρούσῃ,
298

Your soul philosophic, that knows
So well for your comrades to fight.
For all to our happiness goes
The project your tongue will disclose,
As with thousands of joys you propose
The citizen life to endow.
Now show us what things you can do !
It is time ; for the populace now
Requires an original new
Experiment ; only do you
Some novelty bring from your store
Never spoken or done heretofore.
The audience don't like to be cheated
With humours too often repeated.
So come to the point, and at once ; for delay
Is a thing the spectators detest in a play.

PR. I've an excellent scheme, if you will but believe it ;
But I cannot be sure how our friends will receive it ;
Or what they will do, if the old I eschew,
And propound them a system erratic and new.
This makes me a trifle alarmed and faint-hearted.
BL. As to that, you may safely be fearless and bold :
We adore what is new, and abhor what is old.
This rule we retain when all else has departed.[a]
PR.[b] Then all to the speaker in silence attend,
And don't interrupt till I come to the end,

[a] He plays on ἀρχή and ἀρχαῖα: they have lost their fair empire, and all that is left is to seek novelty, and to keep clear of both " old ways " and " empire."
[b] " Throughout the ensuing discussion, the long Aristophanics of the text are in the translation unworthily represented by anapaestic dimeters, in which many lines are omitted, and a few added, and which generally aim at giving rather the spirit of the argument than a literal rendering of the words " : R.

πρὶν ἐπίστασθαι τὴν ἐπίνοιαν καὶ τοῦ φράζοντος
  ἀκοῦσαι.
Κοινωνεῖν γὰρ πάντας φήσω χρῆναι πάντων
  μετέχοντας,   590
κἀκ ταὐτοῦ ζῆν, καὶ μὴ τὸν μὲν πλουτεῖν, τὸν δ᾽
  ἄθλιον εἶναι,
μηδὲ γεωργεῖν τὸν μὲν πολλήν, τῷ δ᾽ εἶναι μηδὲ
  ταφῆναι·
μηδ᾽ ἀνδραπόδοις τὸν μὲν χρῆσθαι πολλοῖς, τὸν
  δ᾽ οὐδ᾽ ἀκολούθῳ·
ἀλλ᾽ ἕνα ποιῶ κοινὸν πᾶσιν βίοτον καὶ τοῦτον ὅμοιον.
ΒΛ. πῶς οὖν ἔσται κοινὸς ἅπασιν;
ΠΡ.   κατέδει σπέλεθον πρότερός μου. 595
ΒΛ. καὶ τῶν σπελέθων κοινωνοῦμεν;
ΠΡ.   μὰ Δί᾽, ἀλλ᾽ ἔφθης μ᾽ ὑποκρούσας.
τοῦτο γὰρ ἤμελλον ἐγὼ λέξειν· τὴν γῆν πρώτιστα
  ποιήσω
κοινὴν πάντων καὶ τἀργύριον καὶ τἄλλ᾽ ὁπόσ᾽ ἐστὶν
  ἑκάστῳ.
εἶτ᾽ ἀπὸ τούτων κοινῶν ὄντων ἡμεῖς βοσκήσομεν ὑμᾶς
ταμιευόμεναι καὶ φειδόμεναι καὶ τὴν γνώμην
  προσέχουσαι.   600
ΒΛ. πῶς οὖν ὅστις μὴ κέκτηται γῆν ἡμῶν, ἀργύριον δὲ
καὶ Δαρεικούς, ἀφανῆ πλοῦτον;
ΠΡ.   τοῦτ᾽ ἐς τὸ μέσον καταθήσει.
ΒΛ. κἂν μὴ καταθεὶς, ψευδορκήσῃ; κἀκτήσατο γὰρ
  διὰ τοῦτο.

---

[a] The interruption exasperates P., who retorts, "You shall eat
muck before I do" (595). Blepyrus affects to suppose this to be part
of her scheme, and innocently inquires whether her communistic
system extends to the muck, so that she will share it with him.
"No," she says, "but you interrupted me by asking a question
which my next words would have answered (596)."

And weigh and perpend, till you quite comprehend,
The drift and intent of the scheme I present.
The rule which I dare to enact and declare,
Is that all shall be equal, and equally share
All wealth and enjoyments, nor longer endure
That one should be rich, and another be poor,
That one should have acres, far-stretching and wide,
And another not even enough to provide
Himself with a grave : that this at his call
Should have hundreds of servants, and that none
    at all.
All this I intend to correct and amend :
Now all of all blessings shall freely partake,
One life and one system for all men I make.

BL.   And how will you manage it ?

PR.[a]   First, I'll provide
That the silver, and land, and whatever beside
Each man shall possess, shall be common and free,[b]
One fund for the public ; then out of it we
Will feed and maintain you, like housekeepers true,
Dispensing, and sparing, and caring for you.

BL.   With regard to the land, I can just understand,
But how, if a man have his money in hand,
Not farms, which you see, and he cannot withhold,
But talents of silver and Darics of gold ?

PR.   All this to the stores he must bring.

BL.   But suppose
He choose to retain it, and nobody knows ;
Rank perjury doubtless ; but what if it be ?
'Twas by that he acquired it at first.

---

[b] " This abolition of private property is very prominently put
forward by Plato, though of course in *his* Republic it applies not
to the citizens generally, but only to one particular class, the
φύλακες, or warders of the state " : R.   Plato, *Rep.* 416 D, 464 B.

ΠΡ. ἀλλ' οὐδέν τοι χρήσιμον ἔσται πάντως αὐτῷ.

ΒΛ.   κατὰ δὴ τί;

ΠΡ. οὐδεὶς οὐδὲν πενίᾳ δράσει· πάντα γὰρ ἕξουσιν
        ἅπαντες,   605
      ἄρτους, τεμάχη, μάζας, χλαίνας, οἶνον, στεφάνους,
        ἐρεβίνθους.
      ὥστε τί κέρδος μὴ καταθεῖναι; σὺ γὰρ ἐξευρὼν
        ἀπόδειξον.

ΒΛ. οὔκουν καὶ νῦν οὗτοι μᾶλλον κλέπτουσ', οἷς ταῦτα
        πάρεστι;

ΠΡ. πρότερόν γ', ὦταῖρ', ὅτε τοῖσι νόμοις διεχρώμεθα
        τοῖς προτέροισιν·
      νῦν δ', ἔσται γὰρ βίος ἐκ κοινοῦ, τί τὸ κέρδος μὴ
        καταθεῖναι;   610

ΒΛ. ἢν μείρακ' ἰδὼν ἐπιθυμήσῃ καὶ βούληται σκαλα-
        θῦραι,
      ἕξει τούτων ἀφελὼν δοῦναι· τῶν ἐκ κοινοῦ δὲ μεθέξει
      ξυγκαταδαρθών.

ΠΡ.   ἀλλ' ἐξέσται προῖκ' αὐτῷ ξυγκαταδαρθεῖν.
      καὶ ταύτας γὰρ κοινὰς ποιῶ τοῖς ἀνδράσι συγ-
        κατακεῖσθαι
      καὶ παιδοποιεῖν τῷ βουλομένῳ.

ΒΛ.   πῶς οὖν, εἰ πάντες ἴασιν
      ἐπὶ τὴν ὡραιοτάτην αὐτῶν καὶ ζητήσουσιν ἐρείδειν; 615

ΠΡ. αἱ φαυλότεραι καὶ σιμότεραι παρὰ τὰς σεμνὰς
        καθεδοῦνται·
      κᾆτ' ἢν ταύτης ἐπιθυμήσῃ, τὴν αἰσχρὰν πρῶθ'
        ὑποκρούσει.

ΒΛ. καὶ πῶς ἡμᾶς τοὺς πρεσβύτας, ἢν ταῖς αἰσχραῖσι
        συνῶμεν,
      οὐκ ἐπιλείψει τὸ πέος πρότερον πρὶν ἐκεῖσ' οἷ φῂς
        ἀφικέσθαι;   620

PR.   I agree.
But now 'twill be useless ; he'll need it no more.

BL.   How mean you ?

PR.   All pressure from want will be o'er.
Now each will have all that a man can desire,
Cakes, barley-loaves, chestnuts, abundant attire,
Wine, garlands and fish : then why should he wish
The wealth he has gotten by fraud to retain ?
If you know any reason, I hope you'll explain.

BL.   'Tis those that have most of these goods, I believe,
That are always the worst and the keenest to thieve.

PR.   I grant you, my friend, in the days that are past,
In your old-fashioned system, abolished at last ;
But what he's to gain, though his wealth he retain,
When all things are common, I'd have you explain.

BL.   If a youth to a girl his devotion would show,
He surely must woo her with presents.[a]

PR.   O no.
All women and men will be common and free,
No marriage or other restraint there will be.[b]

BL.   But if all should aspire to the favours of one,
To the girl that is fairest, what then will be done ?

PR.   By the side of the beauty, so stately and grand,
The dwarf, the deformed, and the ugly will stand ;
And before you're entitled the beauty to woo,
Your court you must pay to the hag and the shrew.

---

[a] Lit. "he will take some of his private property (τούτων) to give; but of the things in common, he will have his share when he goes to bed," τὰ ἐκ κοινοῦ having a new meaning.

[b] Plato, *Rep.* vii. 457 c: there will be a law, he says, τὰς γυναῖκας ταύτας τῶν ἀνδρῶν τούτων πάντων πάσας εἶναι κοινάς, ἰδίᾳ δὲ μηδενὶ μηδεμίαν συνοικεῖν· καὶ τοὺς παῖδας αὖ κοινούς, καὶ μήτε γονέα ἔκγονον εἰδέναι τὸν αὑτοῦ μήτε παῖδα γονέα.

ΠΡ. οὐχὶ μαχοῦνται περὶ σοῦ, θάρρει, μὴ δείσῃς.

ΒΛ.   οὐχὶ μαχοῦνται;
περὶ τοῦ;

ΠΡ.   περὶ τοῦ ξυγκαταδαρθεῖν. κοὐ σοὶ τοιοῦτον
ὑπάρξει.

ΒΛ. τὸ μὲν ὑμέτερον γνώμην τιν' ἔχει· προβεβούλευται
γάρ, ὅπως ἂν
μηδεμιᾶς ᾖ τρύπημα κενόν· τὸ δὲ τῶν ἀνδρῶν τί
ποιήσει;
φεύξονται γὰρ τοὺς αἰσχίους, ἐπὶ τοὺς δὲ καλοὺς
βαδιοῦνται.   625

ΠΡ. ἀλλὰ φυλάξουσ' οἱ φαυλότεροι τοὺς καλλίους ἀπ-
ιόντας
ἀπὸ τοῦ δείπνου καὶ τηρήσουσ' ἐπὶ τοῖσιν δημοσίοισιν
[οἱ φαυλότεροι]· κοὐκ ἐξέσται παρὰ τοῖσι καλοῖς
καταδαρθεῖν
ταῖσι γυναιξὶ πρὶν ἂν τοῖς αἰσχροῖς καὶ τοῖς μικροῖς
χαρίσωνται.

ΒΛ. ἡ Λυσικράτους ἄρα νυνὶ ῥὶς ἴσα τοῖσι καλοῖσι
φρονήσει.   630

ΠΡ. νὴ τὸν Ἀπόλλω· καὶ δημοτική γ' ἡ γνώμη καὶ
καταχήνη
τῶν σεμνοτέρων ἔσται πολλὴ καὶ τῶν σφραγῖδας
ἐχόντων,
ὅταν ἐμβάδ' ἔχων εἴπῃ, προτέρῳ παραχώρει, κᾆτ'
ἐπιτήρει,
ὅταν ἤδη 'γὼ διαπραξάμενος παραδῶ σοι δευτε-
ριάζειν.

ΒΛ. πῶς οὖν οὕτω ζώντων ἡμῶν τοὺς αὑτοῦ παῖδας
ἕκαστος   635
ἔσται δυνατὸς διαγιγνώσκειν;

ΠΡ.   τί δὲ δεῖ; πατέρας γὰρ ἅπαντας

BL.   For the ladies you've nicely provided no doubt ;
      No woman will now be a lover without.[a]
      But what of the men ?   For the girls, I suspect,
      The handsome will choose, and the ugly reject.

PR.   No girl will of course be permitted to mate
      Except in accord with the rules of the State.
      By the side of her lover, so handsome and tall,
      Will be stationed the squat, the ungainly and small.
      And before she's entitled the beau to obtain,
      Her love she must grant to the awkward and plain

BL.   O then such a nose as Lysicrates shows
      Will vie with the fairest and best, I suppose.

PR.   O yes, 'tis a nice democratic device,
      A popular system as ever was tried,
      A jape on the swells with their rings and their pride.
      Now, fopling, away, Gaffer Hobnail will say,
      Stand aside : it is I have precedence to-day.

BL.   But how, may I ask, will the children be known ?
      And how can a father distinguish his own ?

PR.   They will never be known : it can never be told ;[b]

---

[a] Lines 619-628 : Blepyrus fears lest a certain disaster should befall him (620) : on which Praxagora says, " You need not be alarmed : you will not be in such request as you anticipate. They won't fight about you."   Blepyrus does not quite catch her meaning. " Won't fight ! " he retorts, " what for ? "   " For the honour of being your bedfellow," she replies.   " No such disaster as you fear will befall you."   He goes on (623) : " Your part has some sense in it ; for it is provided that no woman shall be unoccupied : but what of the men ?   They will flee the ugly, and seek the fair."   Praxagora replies : " But the less comely will watch the more handsome, when they go from dinner ; and no women will be allowed to sleep with the fair until they have granted their favours to the ugly and the dwarf."

[b] Plato, *Rep.* 461 c πατέρας δὲ καὶ θυγατέρας πῶς διαγνώσονται ἀλλήλων; Οὐδαμῶς, ἦν δ' ἐγώ.

ARISTOPHANES

τοὺς πρεσβυτέρους αὐτῶν εἶναι τοῖσι χρόνοισιν
νομιοῦσιν.

ΒΛ. οὐκοῦν ἄγξουσ' εὖ καὶ χρηστῶς ἑξῆς τότε πάντα
γέροντα
διὰ τὴν ἄγνοιαν, ἐπεὶ καὶ νῦν γιγνώσκοντες πατέρ'
ὄντα
ἄγχουσι. τί δῆθ', ὅταν ἀγνὼς ᾖ, πῶς οὐ τότε
κἀπιχεσοῦνται;

ΠΡ. ἀλλ' ὁ παρεστὼς οὐκ ἐπιτρέψει· τότε δ' αὐτοῖς
οὐκ ἔμελ' οὐδὲν   640
τῶν ἀλλοτρίων, ὅστις τύπτοι· νῦν δ' ἢν πληγέντος
ἀκούσῃ,
μὴ τὸν ἐκείνου τύπτῃ δεδιώς, τοῖς δρῶσιν τοῦτο
μαχεῖται.

ΒΛ. τὰ μὲν ἄλλα λέγεις οὐδὲν σκαιῶς· εἰ δὲ προσελθὼν
Ἐπίκουρος,
ἢ Λευκόλοφος, πάππαν με καλεῖ, τοῦτ' ἤδη δεινὸν
ἀκοῦσαι.

ΧΡ. πολὺ μέντοι δεινότερον τούτου τοῦ πράγματός ἐστι

ΒΛ.   τὸ ποῖον; 645

ΧΡ. εἴ σε φιλήσειεν Ἀρίστυλλος, φάσκων αὐτοῦ πατέρ'
εἶναι.

ΒΛ. οἰμώζοι γ' ἂν καὶ κωκύοι.

ΧΡ.   σὺ δέ γ' ὄζοις ἂν καλαμίνθης.

ΠΡ. ἀλλ' οὗτος μὲν πρότερον γέγονεν, πρὶν τὸ ψήφισμα
γενέσθαι,

306

All youths will in common be sons of the old.

BL. If in vain to distinguish our children we seek,
Pray what will become of the agèd and weak ?
At present [a] I own, though a father be known,
Sons throttle and choke him with hearty goodwill ;
But will they not do it more cheerily still,[b]
When the sonship is doubtful ?

PR.   No, certainly not.
For now if a boy should a parent annoy,
The lads who are near will of course interfere ;
For they may themselves be his children, I wot.[c]

BL. In much that you say there is much to admire ;
But what if Leucolophus claim me for sire,
Or vile Epicurus ?   I think you'll agree
That a great and unbearable nuisance 'twould be.

CHR. A nuisance much greater than this might befall you.

BL. How so ?

CHR.   If the skunk Aristyllus should call you
His father, and seize you, a kiss to imprint.

BL. O hang him ! Confound him ! O how I would
pound him !

CHR. I fancy you soon would be smelling of mint.[d]

PR. But this, sir, is nonsense : it never could be.
That whelp was begotten before the Decree.

tainess of the just established γυναικοκρατία, uses νῦν of that
government, and τότε of the pre-existing and now abolished
system. Her νῦν therefore answers to the τότε, and her τότε to
the νῦν, of Blepyrus " : R.

   [b] Quomodo non tunc eum etiam male concacabunt ?

   [c] " μὴ τὸν ἐκεῖνον. Sc. πατέρα, the bystander's father. So
I think we should read for the common μὴ αὐτὸν ἐκεῖνον, which
does not give the sense required " : R.   Plato, *Rep.* v. 465 в τὸ
τῷ πάσχοντι τοὺς ἄλλους βοηθεῖν, τοὺς μὲν ὡς υἱεῖς, τοὺς δὲ ὡς ἀδελφούς,
τοὺς δὲ ὡς πατέρας. Bystanders will protect a man assaulted,
because he may be their own father, etc.

   [d] A play on μίνθος, *dung*, with which A.'s face had on some
occasion been smeared ; *P.* 314.

ὥστ' οὐχὶ δέος μή σε φιλήσῃ.

ΒΛ.   δεινὸν μεντᾶν ἐπεπόνθειν. 650
τὴν γῆν δὲ τίς ἔσθ' ὁ γεωργήσων;

ΠΡ.   οἱ δοῦλοι. σοὶ δὲ μελήσει,
ὅταν ᾖ δεκάπουν τὸ στοιχεῖον, λιπαρῷ χωρεῖν ἐπὶ
δεῖπνον.

ΒΛ. περὶ δ' ἱματίων τίς πόρος ἔσται; καὶ γὰρ τοῦτ'
ἔστιν ἐρέσθαι.

ΠΡ. τὰ μὲν ὄνθ' ὑμῖν πρῶτον ὑπάρξει, τὰ δὲ λοίφ'
ἡμεῖς ὑφανοῦμεν.

ΒΛ. ἓν ἔτι ζητῶ· πῶς, ἤν τις ὄφλῃ παρὰ τοῖς ἄρχουσι
δίκην τῳ,   655
πόθεν ἐκτίσει ταύτην; οὐ γὰρ τῶν κοινῶν γ' ἐστὶ
δίκαιον.

ΠΡ. ἀλλ' οὐδὲ δίκαι πρῶτον ἔσονται.

ΒΛ.   τουτὶ δὲ πόσους ἐπιτρίψει;

ΧΡ. κἀγὼ ταύτῃ γνώμην ἐθέμην.

ΠΡ.   τοῦ γάρ, τάλαν, οὕνεκ' ἔσονται;

ΒΛ. πολλῶν ἕνεκεν νὴ τὸν Ἀπόλλω· πρῶτον δ' ἑνὸς
εἵνεκα δήπου,
ἤν τις ὀφείλων ἐξαρνῆται.

ΠΡ.   πόθεν οὖν ἐδάνεισ' ὁ δανείσας 660

ᵃ " ' When the (shadow of the) gnomon is ten feet long,' that is
to say, rather more than half an hour before sunset. In the primitive
dials of which Aristophanes is speaking the hour was determined
not by the direction, but by the length of the shadow. And
according to the most careful observation which I have been able
to make or procure, an object casts a shadow of " over twenty-
two " times its own height at sunset, and a shadow of ten times its
own height about thirty-one minutes earlier. It is plain therefore
that the gnomon or (as we are accustomed to call it) *index* of an
Athenian dial was one foot in height, rising vertically from the
ground " : R.

His kiss, it is plain, you can never obtain.

BL. The prospect I view with disgust and alarm.
But who will attend to the work of the farm ?

PR. All labour and toil to your slaves you will leave ;
Your business 'twill be, when the shadows of eve
Ten feet on the face of the dial are cast,[a]
To scurry away to your evening repast.

BL. Our clothes, what of them ?

PR.   You have plenty in store,
When these are worn out, we will weave you some
      more.

BL Just one other thing. If an action they bring,
What funds will be mine for discharging the fine ?
You won't pay it out of the stores, I opine.

PR. A fine to be paid when an action they bring !
Why bless you, our people won't know such a thing
As an action.[b]

BL.   No actions ! I feel a misgiving.[c]
Pray what are " our people " to do for a living ?

CHR. You are right : there are many will rue it.

PR.   No doubt.
But what can one then bring an action about ?

BL. There are reasons in plenty ; I'll just mention one.
If a debtor won't pay you, pray what's to be done ?

PR. If a debtor won't pay ! Nay, but tell me, my friend,
How the creditor came by the money to lend ?

---

[b] οὐδὲ δίκαι. Plato, *Rep.* v. 464 D τί δέ ; δίκαι τε καὶ ἐγκλήματα
πρὸς ἀλλήλους οὐκ οἰχήσεται ἐξ αὐτῶν, ὡς ἔπος εἰπεῖν, διὰ τὸ μηδὲν ἴδ:ον
ἐκτῆσθαι πλὴν τὸ σῶμα, τὰ δ' ἄλλα κοινά.

[c] Lines 657-8: PR. " But there will never be any actions to
begin with." BL. " But how many will that ruin?" (*i.e.* by
depriving them of the dicast's fee). CHR. " And I too was thinking
the same."

309

ἐν τῷ κοινῷ πάντων ὄντων; κλέπτων δήπου 'στ'
    ἐπίδηλος.

ΧΡ. νὴ τὴν Δήμητρ' εὖ σε διδάσκει.

ΒΛ.   τουτὶ τοίνυν φρασάτω μοι,
τῆς αἰκείας οἱ τύπτοντες πόθεν ἐκτίσουσιν, ἐπειδὰν
εὐωχηθέντες ὑβρίζωσιν; τοῦτο γὰρ οἶμαί σ' ἀπορή-
    σειν.

ΠΡ. ἀπὸ τῆς μάζης ἧς σιτεῖται· ταύτης γὰρ ὅταν τις
    ἀφαιρῇ,   665
οὐχ ὑβριεῖται φαύλως οὕτως αὖθις τῇ γαστρὶ κο-
    λασθείς.

ΒΛ. οὐδ' αὖ κλέπτης οὐδεὶς ἔσται;

ΠΡ.   πῶς γὰρ κλέψει μετὸν αὐτῷ;

ΒΛ. οὐδ' ἀποδύσουσ' ἄρα τῶν νυκτῶν;

ΠΡ.   οὔκ, ἢν οἴκοι γε καθεύδῃς,
οὐδ' ἤν γε θύραζ', ὥσπερ πρότερον· βίοτος γὰρ
    πᾶσιν ὑπάρξει.
ἢν δ' ἀποδύῃ γ', αὐτὸς δώσει. τί γὰρ αὐτῷ
    πρᾶγμα μάχεσθαι;   670
ἕτερον γὰρ ἰὼν ἐκ τοῦ κοινοῦ κρεῖττον ἐκείνου
    κομιεῖται.

ΒΛ. οὐδὲ κυβεύσουσ' ἆρ' ἄνθρωποι;

ΠΡ.   περὶ τοῦ γὰρ τοῦτο ποιήσει;

ΒΛ. τὴν δὲ δίαιταν τίνα ποιήσεις;

ΠΡ.   κοινὴν πᾶσιν. τὸ γὰρ ἄστυ
μίαν οἴκησίν φημι ποιήσειν συρρήξασ' εἰς ἓν ἅπαντα,
ὥστε βαδίζειν εἰς ἀλλήλους.

ΒΛ.   τὸ δὲ δεῖπνον ποῦ παραθήσεις; 675

ΠΡ. τὰ δικαστήρια καὶ τὰς στοιὰς ἀνδρῶνας πάντα
    ποιήσω.

All money, I thought, to the stores had been brought.
I've got a suspicion, I say it with grief,
Your creditor's surely a bit of a thief.

CHR. Now that is an answer acute and befitting.

BL. But what if a man should be fined for committing
Some common assault, when elated with wine ;
Pray what are his means for discharging that fine ?
I have posed you, I think.

PR.   Why, his victuals and drink
Will be stopped by command for awhile ; and I guess
That he will not again in a hurry transgress,
When he pays with his stomach.

BL.   Will thieves be unknown ?

PR. Why, how should they steal what is partly their own?

BL. No chance then to meet at night in the street
Some highwayman coming our cloaks to abstract ?

PR. No, not if you're sleeping at home ; nor, in fact,
Though you choose to go out. That trade, why
            pursue it ?
There's plenty for all : but suppose him to do it,
Don't fight and resist him ; what need of a pother ?
You can go to the stores, and they'll give you another.

BL. Shall we gambling forsake ?

PR.   Why, what could you stake ?

BL. But what is the style of our living to be ?

PR. One common to all, independent and free,
All bars and partitions for ever undone,
All private establishments fused into one.[a]

BL. Then where, may I ask, will our dinners be laid ?

PR. Each court and arcade of the law shall be made
A banqueting-hall for the citizens.

---

[a] Plato, *Rep.* vii. 45-8 c οἰκίας τε καὶ ξυσσίτια κοινὰ ἔχοντες,
ἰδίᾳ δὲ οὐδενὸς οὐδὲν τοιοῦτο κεκτημένου.

ΒΛ. τὸ δὲ βῆμα τί σοι χρήσιμον ἔσται;

ΠΡ.   τοὺς· κρατῆρας καταθήσω
    καὶ τὰς ὑδρίας, καὶ ῥαψῳδεῖν ἔσται τοῖς παιδα-
       ρίοισιν
    τοὺς ἀνδρείους ἐν τῷ πολέμῳ, κεἴ τις δειλὸς γεγέ-
       νηται,
    ἵνα μὴ δειπνῶσ' αἰσχυνόμενοι.

ΒΛ.   νὴ τὸν Ἀπόλλω χάριέν γε. 680
    τὰ δὲ κληρωτήρια ποῖ τρέψεις;

ΠΡ.   εἰς τὴν ἀγορὰν καταθήσω·
    κᾆτα στήσασα παρ' Ἁρμοδίῳ κληρώσω πάντας,
       ἕως ἂν
    εἰδὼς ὁ λαχὼν ἀπίῃ χαίρων ἐν ὁποίῳ γράμματι
       δειπνεῖ·
    καὶ κηρύξει τοὺς ἐκ τοῦ βῆτ' ἐπὶ τὴν στοιὰν
       ἀκολουθεῖν
    τὴν βασίλειον δειπνήσοντας· τὸ δὲ θῆτ' ἐς τὴν
       παρὰ ταύτην, 685
    τοὺς δ' ἐκ τοῦ κάππ' ἐς τὴν στοιὰν χωρεῖν τὴν
       ἀλφιτόπωλιν.

ΒΛ. ἵνα κάπτωσιν;

ΠΡ.   μὰ Δί', ἀλλ' ἵν' ἐκεῖ δειπνῶσιν.

ΒΛ.   ὅτῳ δὲ τὸ γράμμα
    μὴ 'ξελκυσθῇ καθ' ὃ δειπνήσει, τούτους ἀπελῶσιν
       ἅπαντες.

ΠΡ.   ἀλλ' οὐκ ἔσται τοῦτο παρ' ἡμῖν.
    πᾶσι γὰρ ἄφθονα πάντα παρέξομεν· 690
    ὥστε μεθυσθεὶς αὐτῷ στεφάνῳ

ᵃ Cf. P. 1265-1304.
ᵇ See Aristotle, *Constitution of Athens*, col. 31. 15-18 εἰσὶ δὲ κανονίδες (ticket-grooves) [δέκα ἐ]ν ἑκάστῳ τῶν κληρωτηρίων. It was the custom to affix to each of the halls of justice one of the second ten letters of the alphabet (from Λ onwards): the dicastic sections,

312

BL.   Right.
But what will you do with the desk for the speakers ?

PR. I'll make it a stand for the cups and the beakers ;
And there shall the striplings be ranged to recite *a*
The deeds of the brave, and the joys of the fight,
And the cowards' disgrace ; till out of the place
Each coward shall slink with a very red face,
Not stopping to dine.

BL.   O but that will be fine.
And what of the balloting-booths ? *b*

PR.   They shall go
To the head of the market-place, all in a row,
And there by Harmodius *c* taking my station,
I'll tickets dispense to the whole of the nation,
Till each one has got his particular lot,
And manfully bustles along to the sign
Of the letter whereat he's empanelled to dine.
The man who has 𝔄 shall be ushered away
To the Royal 𝔄rcade ; to the next will go 𝔅 ;
And ℭ to the ℭornmarket.

BL.   Merely to *see* ?

PR. No, fool, but to dine.

BL.   'Tis an excellent plan.
Then he who gets never a letter, poor man,
Gets never a dinner.

PR.   But 'twill not be so.
There'll be plenty for all, and to spare.
No stint and no grudging our system will know,
But each will away from the revelry go,

when formed, drew tickets for their halls in the κληρωτήριον.
Under the new system, the first ten letters, hitherto used for
assorting the dicastic sections, are free for the halls, which have
now become banqueting-halls ; and each citizen draws his letter
at the κληρωτήριον.   *c* See Index, and *L.* 633.

πᾶς τις ἄπεισιν τὴν δᾷδα λαβών.
αἱ δὲ γυναῖκες κατὰ τὰς διόδους
προσπίπτουσαι τοῖς ἀπὸ δείπνου
τάδε λέξουσιν· δεῦρο παρ' ἡμᾶς· 695
ἐνθάδε μεῖράξ ἐσθ' ὡραία.
παρ' ἐμοὶ δ' ἑτέρα,
φήσει τις ἄνωθ' ἐξ ὑπερῴου,
καὶ καλλίστη καὶ λευκοτάτη·
πρότερον μέντοι δεῖ σε καθεύδειν 700
αὐτῆς παρ' ἐμοί.
τοῖς εὐπρεπέσιν δ' ἀκολουθοῦντες
καὶ μειρακίοις οἱ φαυλότεροι
τοιάδ' ἐροῦσιν· ποῖ θεῖς οὗτος;
πάντως οὐδὲν δράσεις ἐλθών·
τοῖς γὰρ σιμοῖς καὶ τοῖς αἰσχροῖς 705
ἐψήφισται προτέροις βινεῖν,
ὑμᾶς δὲ τέως θρῖα λαβόντας
διφόρου συκῆς
ἐν τοῖς προθύροισι δέφεσθαι.
φέρε νυν, φράσον μοι, ταῦτ' ἀρέσκει σφῶν;

ΒΛ.   πάνυ. 710
ΠΡ. βαδιστέον τἄρ' ἐστὶν εἰς ἀγορὰν ἐμοί,
ἵν' ἀποδέχωμαι τὰ προσιόντα χρήματα,
λαβοῦσα κηρύκαιναν εὔφωνόν τινα.
ἐμὲ γὰρ ἀνάγκη ταῦτα δρᾶν ᾑρημένην
ἄρχειν, καταστῆσαί τε τὰ ξυσσίτια, 715
ὅπως ἂν εὐωχῆσθε πρῶτον σήμερον.
ΒΛ. ἤδη γὰρ εὐωχησόμεσθα;
ΠΡ.   φήμ' ἐγώ.
ἔπειτα τὰς πόρνας καταπαῦσαι βούλομαι
ἁπαξαπάσας.
ΒΛ.   ἵνα τί;

Elated and grand, with a torch in his hand
  And a garland of flowers in his hair.
And then through the streets as they wander, a lot
  Of women will round them be creeping,
" O come to my lodging," says one, " I have got
  Such a beautiful girl in my keeping."
" But here is the sweetest and fairest, my boy,"
  From a window another will say,
" But ere you're entitled her love to enjoy
  Your toll to myself you must pay."
Then a sorry companion, flat-visaged and old,
  Will shout to the youngster " Avast !
And where are *you* going, so gallant and bold,
  And where are *you* hieing so fast ?
'Tis in vain ; you must yield to the laws of the State,
  And I shall be courting the fair,
Whilst you must without in the vestibule wait,
  And strive to amuse yourself there, dear boy,
  And strive to amuse yourself there." [a]
There now, what think ye of my scheme ?

BL.   First-rate.

PR. Then now I'll go to the market-place, and there,
Taking some clear-voiced girl as crieress,
Receive the goods as people bring them in.
This must I do, elected chieftainess
To rule the State and start the public feasts ;
That so your banquets may commence to-day.

BL. What, shall we banquet now at once ?

PR.   You shall.
And next I'll make a thorough sweep of all
The flaunting harlots.

BL.   Why ?

---

[a] By *folia biferae fici* he signifies τὸ αἰδοῖον.

315

ARISTOPHANES

ΠΡ.   δῆλον τουτογί·
   ἵνα τῶν νέων ἔχωσιν αὗται τὰς ἀκμάς.   720
   καὶ τάς γε δούλας οὐχὶ δεῖ κοσμουμένας
   τὴν τῶν ἐλευθέρων ὑφαρπάζειν Κύπριν,
   ἀλλὰ παρὰ τοῖς δούλοισι κοιμᾶσθαι μόνον
   κατωνάκην τὸν χοῖρον ἀποτετιλμένας.
ΒΛ. φέρε νυν ἐγώ σοι παρακολουθῶ πλησίον,   725
   ἵν᾽ ἀποβλέπωμαι καὶ λέγωσί μοι ταδί·
   τὸν τῆς στρατηγοῦ τοῦτον οὐ θαυμάζετε;
ΧΡ. ἐγὼ δ᾽, ἵν᾽ εἰς ἀγοράν γε τὰ σκεύη φέρω,
   προχειριοῦμαι κἀξετάσω τὴν οὐσίαν.

(ΧΟΡΟΥ)

ΧΡ. χώρει σὺ δεῦρο, κιναχύρα, καλὴ καλῶς   730
   τῶν χρημάτων θύραζε πρώτη τῶν ἐμῶν,
   ὅπως ἂν ἐντετριμμένη κανηφορῇς,
   πολλοὺς κάτω δὴ θυλάκους στρέψασ᾽ ἐμούς.
   ποῦ ᾽σθ᾽ ἡ διφροφόρος; ἡ χύτρα δεῦρ᾽ ἔξιθι.
   νὴ Δία μέλαινά γ᾽, οὐδ᾽ ἄν, εἰ τὸ φάρμακον   735
   ἕψουσ᾽ ἔτυχες ᾧ Λυσικράτης μελαίνεται.
   ἴστω παρ᾽ αὐτήν· δεῦρ᾽ ἴθ᾽ ἡ κομμώτρια·
   φέρε δεῦρο ταύτην τὴν ὑδρίαν, ὑδριαφόρε,

---

[a] κατωνάκη, servile dress : the construction is like *L.* 1151, *B.* 806, " slave fashion."

[b] *Exeunt Praxagora, Blepyrus, and Chremes.* We hear no more of Blepyrus till the closing scene (1152) when he, with his daughters and the Chorus, go off to join in the festivities. Two farcical scenes are introduced to show how the new system works; the two citizens and the public store (746-876), and the three Hags (877-1111).

[c] " As soon as the song is concluded, Chremes reappears with his goods, and proceeds to marshal them on the stage after the fashion, as Bergler observes, of a great religious procession at a Panathenaic or other festival. One is to be the κανηφόρος, the

PR.   That these free ladies
May have the firstling manhood of our youths.
Those servile hussies shall no longer poach
Upon the true-love manors of the free.
No, let them herd with slaves, and lie with slaves,
In servile fashion, snipped and trimmed to match.[a]

BL. Lead on, my lass.   I'll follow close behind ;
That men may point and whisper as I pass,
There goes the husband of our chieftainess.

CHR. And I will muster and review my goods,
And bring them all, as ordered, to the stores.[b]

(*Here was a choral song, now lost, during which Chremes is
      preparing to bring out his chattels from the house.*)[c]

CHR. My sweet bran-winnower, come you sweetly here.
March out the first of all my household goods,
Powdered and trim, like some young basket-bearer.
Aye, many a sack of mine you have bolted down.
Now where's the chair-girl ?   Come along, dear pot,
(Wow ! but you're black : scarce blacker had you
      chanced
To boil the dye Lysicrates employs)
And stand by *her*.   Come hither, tiring-maid ;
And pitcher-bearer, bear your pitcher here.

Queen of the May, the young and noble maiden who bore the holy
basket (*A.* 242, 253 ; *L.* 646).   Next to her walks the διφροφόρος
carrying her chair (*B.* 1552).   Afterwards come the ὑδριαφόροι and
σκαφηφόροι, the resident aliens and their wives and daughters,
carrying pots of water, and dishes filled with cakes and honey-
combs, κηρίων καὶ ποπάνων πλήρεις.   Nor were the θαλλοφόροι
wanting, the feeble old men who walked in the procession carrying
their branches of olive ; see *W.* 544 and the note there.   And
doubtless if we knew more fully the details of a Panathenaic procession, we should find something to explain all the other directions
which Chremes gives in the passage before us " : R.

317

ἐνταῦθα· σὺ δὲ δεῦρ' ἡ κιθαρῳδὸς ἔξιθι,
πολλάκις ἀναστήσασά μ' εἰς ἐκκλησίαν 740
ἀωρὶ νύκτωρ διὰ τὸν ὄρθριον νόμον.
ὁ τὴν σκάφην λαβὼν προΐτω, τὰ κηρία
κόμιζε, τοὺς θαλλοὺς καθίστη πλησίον,
καὶ τὼ τρίποδ' ἐξένεγκε καὶ τὴν λήκυθον·
τὰ χυτρίδι' ἤδη καὶ τὸν ὄχλον ἀφίετε. 745

AN. ἐγὼ καταθήσω τἀμά; κακοδαίμων ἄρα
ἀνὴρ ἔσομαι καὶ νοῦν ὀλίγον κεκτημένος.
μὰ τὸν Ποσειδῶ οὐδέποτέ γ', ἀλλὰ βασανιῶ
πρώτιστον αὐτὰ πολλάκις καὶ σκέψομαι.
οὐ γὰρ τὸν ἐμὸν ἱδρῶτα καὶ φειδωλίαν 750
οὐδὲν πρὸς ἔπος οὕτως ἀνοήτως ἐκβαλῶ,
πρὶν ἂν ἐκπύθωμαι πᾶν τὸ πρᾶγμ' ὅπως ἔχει.
οὗτος, τί τὰ σκευάρια ταυτὶ βούλεται;
πότερον μετοικιζόμενος ἐξενήνοχας
αὔτ', ἢ φέρεις ἐνέχυρα θήσων;

XP.   οὐδαμῶς. 755

AN. τί δῆτ' ἐπὶ στοίχου 'στὶν οὕτως; οὔ τι μὴ
Ἱέρωνι τῷ κήρυκι πομπὴν πέμπετε;

XP. μὰ Δί', ἀλλ' ἀποφέρειν αὐτὰ μέλλω τῇ πόλει
ἐς τὴν ἀγορὰν κατὰ τοὺς δεδογμένους νόμους.

AN. μέλλεις ἀποφέρειν;

XP.   πάνυ γε.

AN.   κακοδαίμων ἄρ' εἶ 760
νὴ τὸν Δία τὸν σωτῆρα.

XP.   πῶς;

AN.   πῶς; ῥᾳδίως.

---

^a The domestic cock ; but the feminine is used because in the
real procession the musician was a female. Here, as in *W.* 815,
the bird produced on the stage is a model.

You, fair musician,[a] take your station there,
You whose untimely trumpet-call has oft
Roused me, ere daybreak, to attend the Assembly.
Who's got the dish, go forward ; take the combs
Of honey ; set the olive branches nigh ;
Bring out the tripods and the bottles of oil ;
The pannikins and rubbish you can leave.[b]

CIT. I bring my goods to the stores !   That were to be
A hapless greenhorn, ill endowed with brains.
I'll never do it ; by Poseidon, never !
I'll test the thing and scan its bearings first.
I'm not the man to fling my sweat and thrift
So idly and so brainlessly away,
Before I've fathomed how the matter stands.
—You there !   what means this long array of
        chattels ?
Are they brought out because you're changing house,
Or are you going to pawn them ?

CHR.   No.

CIT.   Then why
All in a row ?   Are they, in grand procession,
Marching to Hiero the auctioneer ?

CHR. O no, I am going to bring them to the stores
For the State's use : so run the new-made laws.

CIT. (in shrill surprise) You are going to bring them !

CHR.   Yes.

CIT.   By Zeus the Saviour,
You're an ill-starred one !

CHR.   How ?

CIT.   How ?   Plain enough.

---

[b] *Now another door opens, the door upon which Praxagora
had stealthily scratched, supra 34, and the husband of the second
woman again comes out, as he did supra 327.*

ARISTOPHANES

XP. τί δ'; οὐχὶ πειθαρχεῖν με τοῖς νόμοισι δεῖ;
ΑΝ. ποίοισιν, ὦ δύστηνε;
XP.   τοῖς δεδογμένοις.
ΑΝ. δεδογμένοισιν; ὡς ἀνόητος ἦσθ' ἄρα.
XP. ἀνόητος;
ΑΝ.   οὐ γάρ; ἠλιθιώτατος μὲν οὖν   765
    ἁπαξαπάντων.
XP.   ὅτι τὸ ταττόμενον ποιῶ;
ΑΝ. τὸ ταττόμενον γὰρ δεῖ ποιεῖν τὸν σώφρονα;
XP. μάλιστα πάντων.
ΑΝ.   τὸν μὲν οὖν ἀβέλτερον.
XP. σὺ δ' οὐ καταθεῖναι διανοεῖ;
ΑΝ.   φυλάξομαι,
    πρὶν ἄν γ' ἴδω τὸ πλῆθος ὅ τι βουλεύεται.   770
XP. τί γὰρ ἄλλο γ' ἢ φέρειν παρεσκευασμένοι
    τὰ χρήματ' εἰσίν;
ΑΝ.   ἀλλ' ἰδὼν ἐπειθόμην.
XP. λέγουσι γοῦν ἐν ταῖς ὁδοῖς
ΑΝ.   λέξουσι γάρ.
XP. καί φασιν οἴσειν ἀράμενοι.
ΑΝ.   φήσουσι γάρ.
XP. ἀπολεῖς ἀπιστῶν πάντ'.
ΑΝ.   ἀπιστήσουσι γάρ.   775
XP. ὁ Ζεύς σέ γ' ἐπιτρίψειεν.
ΑΝ.   ἐπιτρίψουσι γάρ.
    οἴσειν δοκεῖς τιν' ὅστις αὐτῶν νοῦν ἔχει;
    οὐ γὰρ πάτριον τοῦτ' ἐστίν, ἀλλὰ λαμβάνειν
    ἡμᾶς μόνον δεῖ νὴ Δία· καὶ γὰρ οἱ θεοί·
    γνώσει δ' ἀπὸ τῶν χειρῶν γε τῶν ἀγαλμάτων,   780
    ὅταν γὰρ εὐχώμεσθα διδόναι τἀγαθά,
    ἕστηκεν ἐκτείνοντα τὴν χεῖρ' ὑπτίαν,

---

^a A proverb, "seeing is believing."

CHR. What, must I not, forsooth, obey the laws?

CIT. The laws, poor wretch! What laws?

CHR.   The new-made laws.

CIT. The new-made laws? O what a fool you are!

CHR. A fool?

CIT.   Well, aren't you? Just the veriest dolt
In all the town!

CHR.   Because I do what's ordered?

CIT. Is it a wise man's part to do what's ordered?

CHR. Of course it is.

CIT.   Of course it is a fool's.

CHR. Then won't you bring yours in?

CIT.   I'll wait awhile,
And watch the people what they're going to do.

CHR. What *should* they do but bring their chattels in
For the State's use?

CIT.   I SAW IT AND BELIEVED.[a]

CHR. Why, in the streets they talk—

CIT.   Ay, talk they will.

CHR. Saying they'll bring their goods—

CIT.   Ay, say they will.

CHR. Zounds! you doubt everything.

CIT.   Ay, doubt they will.

CHR. O, Heaven confound you.

CIT.   Ay, confound they will.
What! think you men of sense will bring their
    goods?
Not they! That's not our custom: we're disposed
Rather to take than give, like the dear gods.
Look at their statues, stretching out their hands!
We pray the powers to give us all things good;
Still they hold forth their hands with hollowed palms,

ARISTOPHANES

<pre>
      οὐχ ὥς τι δώσοντ᾽, ἀλλ᾽ ὅπως τι λήψεται.
ΧΡ. ὦ δαιμόνι᾽ ἀνδρῶν, ἔα με τῶν προὔργου τι δρᾶν.
      ταυτὶ γάρ ἐστι συνδετέα. ποῦ μοῦσθ᾽ ἱμάς;   785
ΑΝ. ὄντως γὰρ οἴσεις;
ΧΡ.   ναὶ μὰ Δία, καὶ δὴ μὲν οὖν
      τωδὶ ξυνάπτω τὼ τρίποδε.
ΑΝ.   τῆς μωρίας,
      τὸ μηδὲ περιμείναντα τοὺς ἄλλους ὅ τι
      δράσουσιν, εἶτα τηνικαῦτ᾽ ἤδη
ΧΡ.   τί δρᾶν;
ΑΝ. ἐπαναμένειν, ἔπειτα διατρίβειν ἔτι.   790
ΧΡ. ἵνα δὴ τί;
ΑΝ.   σεισμὸς εἰ γένοιτο πολλάκις,
      ἢ πῦρ ἀπότροπον, ἢ διάξειεν γαλῆ,
      παύσαιντ᾽ ἂν εἰσφέροντες, ὠμβρόντητε σύ.
ΧΡ. χαρίεντα γοῦν πάθοιμ᾽ ἄν, εἰ μὴ 'χοιμ᾽ ὅποι
      ταῦτα καταθείην.
ΑΝ.   μὴ γὰρ οὐ λάβοις ὅποι.   795
      θάρρει, καταθήσεις, κἂν ἕνης ἔλθῃς.
ΧΡ.   τιή;
ΑΝ. ἐγᾦδα τούτους χειροτονοῦντας μὲν ταχύ,
      ἅττ᾽ ἂν δὲ δόξῃ, ταῦτα πάλιν ἀρνουμένους.
ΧΡ. οἴσουσιν, ὦ τᾶν.
ΑΝ.   ἢν δὲ μὴ κομίσωσι, τί;
ΧΡ. ἀμέλει κομιοῦσιν.
ΑΝ.   ἢν δὲ μὴ κομίσωσι, τί;   800
ΧΡ. μαχούμεθ᾽ αὐτοῖς.
ΑΝ.   ἢν δὲ κρείττους ὦσι, τί;
</pre>

ᵃ " We learn incidentally from *Birds* 518 that a sacrificer was accustomed to put a portion of the sacrificial meat into the outstretched hand of the god " : R.

322

Showing their notion is to take, not give.[a]

CHR. Pray now, good fellow, let me do my work.
Hi! where's the strap? These must be tied
together.

CIT. You are really going?

CHR.   Don't you see I'm tying
These tripods up this instant?

CIT.   O what folly!
Not to delay a little, and observe
What other people do, and then—

CHR.   And then?

CIT. Why then put off, and then delay again.

CHR. Why so?

CIT.   Why, if perchance an earthquake came,
Or lightning fell, or a cat cross the street,
They'll soon cease bringing in, you blockhead you!

CHR. A pleasant jest, if I should find no room
To bring my chattels!

CIT.   To RECEIVE, you mean.[b]
'Twere time to bring them, two days hence.

CHR.   How mean you?

CIT. I know these fellows[c]; voting in hot haste,
And straight ignoring the decree they've passed.

CHR. They'll bring them, friend.

CIT.   But if they don't, what then?

CHR. No fear; they'll bring them.

CIT.   If they don't, what then?

CHR. We'll fight them.

CIT.   If they prove too strong, what then?

---

[b] It is difficult to get any meaning from the text, unless the answer is a nonsensical echo of the question. The citizen, catching up the word ἔχοιμι, retorts: "you mean there is a fear μὴ οὐ λάβοις, that you may not get something," and ὅποι is added without meaning, to echo ἔχοιμ' ὅποι.

[c] *He points to the audience.*

ΧΡ. ἄπειμ᾽ ἐάσας.

ΑΝ.   ἢν δὲ κωλύσωσι, τί;

ΧΡ. διαρραγείης.

ΑΝ.   ἢν διαρραγῶ δέ, τί;

ΧΡ. καλῶς ποιήσεις.

ΑΝ.   σὺ δ᾽ ἐπιθυμήσεις φέρειν;

ΧΡ. ἔγωγε· καὶ γὰρ τοὺς ἐμαυτοῦ γείτονας   805
    ὁρῶ φέροντας.

ΑΝ.   πάνυ γ᾽ ἂν οὖν Ἀντισθένης
    αὔτ᾽ εἰσενέγκοι· πολὺ γὰρ ἐμμελέστερον
    πρότερον χέσαι πλεῖν ἢ τριάκονθ᾽ ἡμέρας.

ΧΡ. οἴμωζε.

ΑΝ.   Καλλίμαχος δ᾽ ὁ χοροδιδάσκαλος
    αὐτοῖσιν εἰσοίσει τί;

ΧΡ.   πλείω Καλλίου.   810

ΑΝ. ἄνθρωπος οὗτος ἀποβαλεῖ τὴν οὐσίαν.

ΧΡ. δεινά γε λέγεις.

ΑΝ.   τί δεινόν; ὥσπερ οὐχ ὁρῶν
    ἀεὶ τοιαῦτα γιγνόμενα ψηφίσματα.
    οὐκ οἶσθ᾽ ἐκεῖν᾽ οὕδοξε, τὸ περὶ τῶν ἁλῶν;

ΧΡ. ἔγωγε.

ΑΝ.   τοὺς χαλκοῦς δ᾽ ἐκείνους ἡνίκα   815
    ἐψηφισάμεσθ᾽, οὐκ οἶσθα;

ΧΡ.   καὶ κακόν γέ μοι
    τὸ κόμμ᾽ ἐγένετ᾽ ἐκεῖνο. πωλῶν γὰρ βότρυς
    μεστὴν ἀπῆρα τὴν γνάθον χαλκῶν ἔχων,
    κἄπειτ᾽ ἐχώρουν εἰς ἀγορὰν ἐπ᾽ ἄλφιτα.
    ἔπειθ᾽ ὑπέχοντος ἄρτι μου τὸν θύλακον,   820
    ἀνέκραγ᾽ ὁ κῆρυξ, μὴ δέχεσθαι μηδένα

---

^a Some niggard.

CHR. I'll leave them.

CIT.   If they won't be left, what then ?

CHR. Go, hang yourself.

CIT.   And if I do, what then ?

CHR. 'Twere a good deed.

CIT.   You are really going to bring them ?

CHR. Yes, that's exactly what I'm going to do.
I see my neighbours bringing theirs.

CIT.   O ay,
Antisthenes *a* for instance. Heavens, he'd liefer
Sit on the stool for thirty days and more.

CHR. Be hanged !

CIT.   Well, but Callimachus *b* the poet,
What, will *he* bring them ?

CHR.   More than Callias can.

CIT. Well, here's a man will throw away his substance.

CHR. That's a hard saying.

CIT.   Hard ? when every day
We see abortive resolutions passed !
That vote about the salt, you mind *that*, don't you ?

CHR. I do.

CIT.   And how we voted, don't you mind,
Those copper coins.*c*

CHR.   And a bad job for me
That coinage proved. I sold my grapes, and stuffed
My cheek with coppers ; then I steered away
And went to purchase barley in the market ;
When just as I was holding out my sack,
The herald cried, *No copper coins allowed !*

b A poor man (Schol.), yet he had more to bring in than
Callias, who had run through a fortune. See *B. 283.*

c Bronze coins were issued in the archonship of Callias, shortly
before the *Frogs* was exhibited, because the Athenians were unable
to get at their silver mines owing to the war ; see *F.* 725. Nothing
is known of the salt and the property tax.

χαλκοῦν τὸ λοιπόν· ἀργύρῳ γὰρ χρώμεθα.
AN. τὸ δ' ἔναγχος οὐχ ἅπαντες ἡμεῖς ὤμνυμεν
τάλαντ' ἔσεσθαι πεντακόσια τῇ πόλει
τῆς τεσσαρακοστῆς, ἣν ἐπόρισ' Εὐριπίδης;   825
κεὐθὺς κατεχρύσου πᾶς ἀνὴρ Εὐριπίδην·
ὅτε δὴ δ' ἀνασκοπουμένοις ἐφαίνετο
ὁ Διὸς Κόρινθος καὶ τὸ πρᾶγμ' οὐκ ἤρκεσεν,
πάλιν κατεπίττου πᾶς ἀνὴρ Εὐριπίδην.
XP. οὐ ταὐτόν, ὦ τᾶν. τότε μὲν ἡμεῖς ἤρχομεν,   830
νῦν δ' αἱ γυναῖκες.
AN.   ἅς γ' ἐγὼ φυλάξομαι
νὴ τὸν Ποσειδῶ μὴ κατουρήσωσί μου.
XP. οὐκ οἶδ' ὅ τι ληρεῖς. φέρε σὺ τἀνάφορον ὁ παῖς.
ΚΗΡΥΞ. ὦ πάντες ἀστοί, νῦν γὰρ οὕτω ταῦτ' ἔχει,
χωρεῖτ', ἐπείγεσθ' εὐθὺ τῆς στρατηγίδος,   835
ὅπως ἂν ὑμῖν ἡ τύχη κληρουμένοις
φράσῃ καθ' ἕκαστον ἄνδρ' ὅποι δειπνήσετε·
ὡς αἱ τράπεζαί γ' εἰσὶν ἐπινενησμέναι
ἀγαθῶν ἁπάντων καὶ παρεσκευασμέναι,
κλῖναί τε σισυρῶν καὶ δαπίδων νενασμέναι.   840
κρατῆρας ἐγκιρνᾶσιν, αἱ μυροπώλιδες
ἑστᾶσ' ἐφεξῆς· τὰ τεμάχη ῥιπίζεται,
λαγῷ ἀναπηγνύασι, πόπανα πέττεται,
στέφανοι πλέκονται, φρύγεται τραγήματα,
χύτρας ἔτνους ἕψουσιν αἱ νεώταται·   845
Σμοῖος δ' ἐν αὐταῖς ἱππικὴν στολὴν ἔχων
τὰ τῶν γυναικῶν διακαθαίρει τρυβλία.
Γέρων δὲ χωρεῖ χλανίδα καὶ κονίποδα

---

[a] Some emergency proposal to raise money by a direct property-tax of 2½ per cent.
[b] A common proverb, applicable either to tedious iteration (F. 439), or to high-flown language with no corresponding results.

Nothing but silver must be paid or taken !

CIT. Then that late tax, the two-and-a-half per cent,[a]
Euripides devised, weren't we all vowing
'Twould yield five hundred talents to the State ?
Then every man would gild Euripides.
But when we reckoned up, and found the thing
A Zeus's Corinth,[b] and no good at all,
Then every man would tar Euripides.

CHR. But times have altered ; then the men bare sway,
'Tis now the women.

CIT.   Who, I'll take good care,
Shan't try on *me* their little piddling ways.

CHR. You're talking nonsense.   Boy, take up the yoke.

CRIER.[c] O all ye citizens (for now 'tis thus),
Come all, come quick, straight to your chieftainess.
There cast your lots ; there fortune shall assign
To every man his destined feasting-place.
Come, for the tables now are all prepared
And laden heavily with all good things :
The couches all with rugs and cushions piled !
They're mixing wine : the perfume-selling girls
Are ranged in order : collops on the fire :
Hares on the spit ; and in the oven, cakes ;
Chaplets are woven : comfits parched and dried.
The youngest girls are boiling pots of broth ;
And there amongst them, in his riding-suit,
The gallant Smoius licks their platters clean.[d]
There Geron too, in dainty robe and pumps,

[c] *Enter a crier to summon all citizens to the banquet.* He adds
"for now 'tis thus," because under the old democracy, only
distinguished citizens were entertained in the Prytaneum.

[d] A double meaning runs through lines 845-847.   *Cf. K.* 1285,
W. 1283 ; ἔτνους χύτρας representing the ζωμόν of a similar allusion
in *P.* 885 ; τρυβλία for γυναικῶν αἰδοῖα ; ἱπ. στολήν, an allusion like
Ἱππίου τυραννίδα, *W.* 502.

ἔχων, καχάζων μεθ' ἑτέρου νεανίου·
ἐμβὰς δὲ κεῖται καὶ τρίβων ἐρριμμένος.　　850
πρὸς ταῦτα χωρεῖθ', ὡς ὁ τὴν μᾶζαν φέρων
ἔστηκεν· ἀλλὰ τὰς γνάθους διοίγνυτε.

ΑΝ. οὐκοῦν βαδιοῦμαι δῆτα. τί γὰρ ἕστηκ' ἔχων
ἐνταῦθ', ἐπειδὴ ταῦτα τῇ πόλει δοκεῖ;

ΧΡ. καὶ ποῖ βαδιεῖ σὺ μὴ καταθεὶς τὴν οὐσίαν;　　855

ΑΝ. ἐπὶ δεῖπνον.

ΧΡ. 　　　　οὐ δῆτ', ἤν γ' ἐκείναις νοῦς ἐνῇ,
πρὶν ἄν γ' ἀπενέγκῃς.

ΑΝ. 　　　　ἀλλ' ἀποίσω.

ΧΡ. 　　　　　　πηνίκα;

ΑΝ. οὐ τοὐμόν, ὦ τᾶν, ἐμποδὼν ἔσται.

ΧΡ. 　　　　　　τί δή;

ΑΝ. ἑτέρους ἀποίσειν φήμ' ἔθ' ὑστέρους ἐμοῦ.

ΧΡ. βαδιεῖ δὲ δειπνήσων ὅμως;

ΑΝ. 　　　　τί γὰρ πάθω;　　860
τὰ δυνατὰ γὰρ δεῖ τῇ πόλει ξυλλαμβάνειν
τοὺς εὖ φρονοῦντας.

ΧΡ. 　　　　ἢν δὲ κωλύσωσι, τί;

ΑΝ. ὁμόσ' εἶμι κύψας.

ΧΡ. 　　　　ἢν δὲ μαστιγῶσι, τί;

ΑΝ. καλούμεθ' αὐτάς.

ΧΡ. 　　　　ἢν δὲ καταγελῶσι, τί;

ΑΝ. ἐπὶ ταῖς θύραις ἑστὼς

ΧΡ. 　　　　τί δράσεις; εἰπέ μοι.　　865

ΑΝ. τῶν εἰσφερόντων ἁρπάσομαι τὰ σιτία.

ΧΡ. βάδιζε τοίνυν ὕστερος· σὺ δ', ὦ Σίκων
καὶ Παρμένων, αἴρεσθε τὴν παμπησίαν.

ΑΝ. φέρε νυν ἐγώ σοι ξυμφέρω.

ΧΡ. 　　　　μή, μηδαμῶς.
δέδοικα γὰρ μὴ καὶ παρὰ τῇ στρατηγίδι,　　870

His threadbare cloak and shoon discarded now,
Struts on, guffawing with another lad.
Come, therefore, come, and quickly : bread in hand
The pantler stands ; and open wide your mouths.

CIT. I'll go, for one.   Why stand I idly here,
When thus the city has declared her will ?

CHR. Where will *you* go ?   You haven't brought your
     goods.

CIT. To supper.

CHR.   Not if they've their wits about them
Until you've brought your goods.

CIT.   I'll bring them.

CHR.   When ?

CIT. My doings won't delay the job.

CHR.   Why not ?

CIT. Others will bring them later still than I.

CHR. You are going to supper ?

CIT.   What am I to do ?
Good citizens must needs support the State
As best they can.

CHR.   If they say no, what then ?

CIT. At them, head foremost.

CHR.   If they strike, what then ?

CIT. Summon the minxes.

CHR.   If they jeer, what then ?

CIT. Why, then I'll stand beside the door, and—

CHR.   What ?

CIT. Seize on the viands as they bear them in.

CHR. Come later then.   Now Parmeno and Sicon
Take up my goods and carry them along.

CIT. I'll help you bring them.

CHR.   Heaven forbid !   I fear
That when I'm there, depositing the goods

ὅταν κατατιθῶ, προσποιῇ τῶν χρημάτων.

AN. νὴ τὸν Δία δεῖ γοῦν μηχανήματός τινος,
ὅπως τὰ μὲν ὄντα χρήμαθ' ἔξω, τοῖσδε δὲ
τῶν ματτομένων κοινῇ μεθέξω πως ἐγώ.
ὀρθῶς ἔμοιγε φαίνεται· βαδιστέον   875
ὁμόσ' ἐστὶ δειπνήσοντα κοὐ μελλητέον.

(ΧΟΡΟΥ)

ΓΡΑΥΣ Α. τί ποθ' ἄνδρες οὐχ ἥκουσιν; ὥρα δ' ἦν πάλαι·
ἐγὼ δὲ καταπεπλασμένη ψιμυθίῳ
ἕστηκα καὶ κροκωτὸν ἠμφιεσμένη,
ἀργός, μινυρομένη τι πρὸς ἐμαυτὴν μέλος,   880
παίζουσ', ὅπως ἂν περιλάβοιμ' αὐτῶν τινα
παριόντα. Μοῦσαι, δεῦρ' ἴτ' ἐπὶ τοὐμὸν στόμα,
μελύδριον εὑροῦσαί τι τῶν Ἰωνικῶν.   .

ΜΕΙΡΑΞ. νῦν μέν με παρακύψασα προὔφθης, ὦ σαπρά.
ᾤου δ' ἐρήμας, οὐ παρούσης ἐνθάδε   885
ἐμοῦ, τρυγήσειν καὶ προσάξεσθαί τινα
ᾄδουσ'· ἐγὼ δ', ἢν τοῦτο δρᾷς, ἀντᾴσομαι.
κεἰ γὰρ δι' ὄχλου τοῦτ' ἐστὶ τοῖς θεωμένοις,
ὅμως ἔχει τερπνόν τι καὶ κωμῳδικόν.

ΓΡ.Α. τούτῳ διαλέγου κἀποχώρησον· σὺ δέ,   890
φιλοττάριον αὐλητά, τοὺς αὐλοὺς λαβὼν
ἄξιον ἐμοῦ καὶ σοῦ προσαύλησον μέλος.

(ᾄδει ἡ γραῦς.)

εἴ τις ἀγαθὸν βούλεται παθεῖν τι, παρ' ἐμοὶ χρὴ καθεύδειν.

---

[a] "The scenery seems to have remained unchanged throughout
the play; and Blepyrus comes out of the central house at 1128
infra, just as he has already done at 311 and 520 supra. But the
houses on either side, hitherto the residences of Chremes and the
Second Woman respectively, have changed their occupants; and
one of them has become the abode of an ancient Hag and a young

Beside the chieftainess, you'll claim them yours.

CIT. (*alone*) Now must I hatch some crafty shrewd device
To keep my goods, and yet secure a part
In all these public banquets, like the rest.
Hah ! Excellent ! 'Twill work. Away ! Away !
On to the banquet-hall without delay.

(*Here again was a choral song, now lost.*)

HAG.[a] Why don't the fellows come ? The hour's long past :
And here I'm standing, ready, with my skin
Plastered with paint, wearing my yellow gown,
Humming an amorous ditty to myself,
Trying, by wanton sportiveness, to catch
Some passer-by. Come, Muses, to my lips,
With some sweet soft Ionian roundelay.

GIRL. This once then, Mother Mouldy, you've forestalled
me,
And peeped out first ; thinking to steal my grapes,
I absent ; aye, and singing to attract
A lover ; sing then, and I'll sing against you.
For this, even though 'tis irksome to the audience,
Has yet a pleasant and a comic flavour.

HAG. Here, talk to this, and vanish :[b] but do you,
Dear honey piper, take the pipes and play
A strain that's worthy you, and worthy me,
(*singing*) Whoever is fain love's bliss to attain,
Let him hasten to me, and be blest ;

girl. It is the case contemplated in Praxagora's speech, supra
693-701, but the proceedings do not exactly follow the lines there
shadowed out. For one thing, both the girl and her young lover
are in full revolt against the regulations of Praxagora. For
another no Gaffer Hobnail, no snub-nosed Lysicrates, comes to
claim precedence over the youth. It is difficult to feel absolute
certainty as to the stage arrangements, but in my judgement the
Hag is peeping out through the half-closed door (*P.* 980, 981),
whilst the girl is looking from the window overhead : " R.

[b] Throwing her a δερμάτινον αἰδοῖον.

331

οὐ γὰρ ἐν νέαις τὸ σοφὸν ἔν- 895
εστιν, ἀλλ' ἐν ταῖς πεπείροις·
οὐδέ τοι στέργειν ἂν ἐθέλοι
μᾶλλον ἢ 'γὼ τὸν φίλον γ' ὧ-
περ ξυνείην·
ἀλλ' ἐφ' ἕτερον ἂν πέτοιτο.

(ἀντᾴδει ἡ νέα τῇ γραΐ.)

ΜΕΙ. μὴ φθόνει ταῖσιν νέαισι.   900
τὸ τρυφερὸν γὰρ ἐμπέφυκε
τοῖς ἁπαλοῖσι μηροῖς,
κἀπὶ τοῖς μήλοις ἐπαν-
θεῖ· σὺ δ', ὦ γραῦ,
παραλέλεξαι κἀντέτριψαι,
τῷ θανάτῳ μέλημα.   905

ΓΡ.Α. ἐκπέσοι γέ σου τὸ τρῆμα,
τό τ' ἐπίκλιντρον ἀποβάλοιο,
βουλομένη σποδεῖσθαι,
κἀπὶ τῆς κλίνης ὄφιν
[ψυχρὸν] εὕροις
καὶ προσελκύσαιο [σαύτῃ]   910
βουλομένη φιλῆσαι.

ΜΕΙ. αἰ αἶ, τί ποτε πείσομαι;
οὐχ ἥκει μοὑταῖρος·
μόνη δ' αὐτοῦ λείπομ'· ἡ
γάρ μοι μήτηρ ἄλλῃ βέβηκε
καὶ τἄλλα μ' οὐδὲν τὰ μετὰ ταῦτα δεῖ λέγειν.
ἀλλ', ὦ μαῖ', ἱκετεύομαι,   915
κάλει τὸν Ὀρθαγόραν, ὅπως
σαυτῆς κατόναι', ἀντιβολῶ σε.

ΓΡ.Α. ἤδη τὸν ἀπ' Ἰωνίας
τρόπον τάλαινα κνησιᾷς·

For knowledge is sure with the ripe and mature,
　　And not with the novice, to rest.
Would *she* be as faithful and true to the end,
　　And constant and loving as I ?
No : she would be flitting away from her friend,
　　And off to another would fly,
　　　　Would fly, would fly, would fly,
　　And off to another would fly.

GIRL (*affettuosamente*). O grudge not the young their enjoyment.

　　　　For beauty the softest and best
　　Is breathed o'er the limbs of a maiden,
　　　　And blooms on the maidenly breast.
You have tweezered your brows, and bedizened your face,
And you look like a darling for—death to embrace.

HAG (*con fuoco*). I hope that the cords of your bedstead will rot,
　　I hope that your tester will break,
And O when you think that a lover you've got,
　　I hope you will find him a snake,
　　　　A snake, a snake, a snake,
　　I hope you will find him a snake ᵃ !

GIRL (*teneramente*). O dear, what will become of me ?
　　Where can my lover be flown ?
Mother is out ; she has gone and deserted me,
　　Mother has left me alone.
Nurse, nurse, pity and comfort me,
　　Fetch me my lover, I pray ;
So may it always be happy and well with thee,
　　O, I beseech thee, obey.

HAG (*fortissimo*). These, these, are the tricks of the harlotry

---

ᵃ " ὄφις is used, both in Greek and Latin erotics, to denote a cold and languid lover " : R.

δοκεῖς δέ μοι καὶ λάβδα κατὰ τοὺς Λεσβίους. 920
ΜΕΙ. ἀλλ' οὐκ ἄν ποθ' ὑφαρπάσαιο
    τἀμὰ παίγνια· τὴν δ' ἐμὴν
    ὥραν οὐκ ἀπολεῖς οὐδ' ἀπολήψει.
ΓΡ.Α. ᾆδ' ὁπόσα βούλει καὶ παράκυφθ' ὥσπερ γαλῆ·
    οὐδεὶς γὰρ ὡς σὲ πρότερον εἴσεισ' ἀντ' ἐμοῦ. 925
ΜΕΙ. οὔκουν ἐπ' ἐκφοράν γε; καινόν γ', ὦ σαπρά;
ΓΡ.Α. οὐ δῆτα.
ΜΕΙ.   τί γὰρ ἂν γραῖ καινά τις λέγοι;
ΓΡ.Α. οὐ τοὐμὸν ὀδυνήσει σε γῆρας.
ΜΕΙ.   ἀλλὰ τί;
    ἤγχουσα μᾶλλον καὶ τὸ σὸν ψιμύθιον;
ΓΡ.Α. τί μοι διαλέγει;
ΜΕΙ.   σὺ δὲ τί διακύπτεις;
ΓΡ.Α.   ἐγώ; 930
    ᾄδω πρὸς ἐμαυτὴν Ἐπιγένει τὠμῷ φίλῳ.
ΜΕΙ. σοὶ γὰρ φίλος τίς ἐστιν ἄλλος ἢ Γέρης;
ΓΡ.Α. δόξει γε καὶ σοί. τάχα γὰρ εἶσιν ὡς ἐμέ.
    ὁδὶ γὰρ αὐτός ἐστιν.
ΜΕΙ.   οὐ σοῦ γ', ὤλεθρε,
    δεόμενος οὐδέν.
ΓΡ.Α.   νὴ Δί', ὦ φθίνυλλα σύ. 935
ΜΕΙ. δείξει τάχ' αὐτός, ὡς ἔγωγ' ἀπέρχομαι.
ΓΡ.Α. κἄγωγ', ἵνα γνῷς ὡς πολύ σου μεῖζον φρονῶ.
ΝΕΑΝΙΑΣ. εἴθ' ἐξῆν παρὰ τῇ νέᾳ καθεύδειν,
    καὶ μὴ 'δει πρότερον διασποδῆσαι
    ἀνάσιμον ἢ πρεσβυτέραν· 940
    οὐ γὰρ ἀνασχετὸν τοῦτό γ' ἐλευθέρῳ.
ΓΡ.Α.   οἰμώζων ἄρα νὴ Δία σποδήσεις.
334

This, the Ionian itch ! [a]

GIRL (*con spirito*). No ! no ! you shall never prevail with me,
Mine are the charms that bewitch.[b]

HAG. Aye, aye, sing on : keep peeping, peering out
Like a young cat. They'll all come first to me.

GIRL. What, to your funeral ? A new joke, hey ?

HAG. No, very old.

GIRL. Old jokes to an old crone.

HAG. My age won't trouble *you*.

GIRL. No ? Then what will ?
Your artificial red and white, perchance.

HAG. Why talk to me ?

GIRL. Why peeping ?

HAG. I ? I'm singing
With bated breath to dear Epigenes.

GIRL. I thought old Geres was your only dear.

HAG. You'll soon think otherwise : he'll come to *me*.
O here he is, himself.[c]

GIRL. Not wanting aught
Of you, Old Plague.

HAG. O yes, Miss Pineaway.

GIRL. His acts will show. I'll slip away unseen.

HAG. And so will I. You'll find I'm right, my beauty.

YOUTH. [d] O that I now might my darling woo !
Nor first be doomed to the foul embrace
Of an ancient hag with a loathsome face ;
To a free-born stripling a dire disgrace !

HAG. That you never, my boy, can do !

---

[a] λάβδα, the first letter of λεσβιάζειν.
[b] Lit. "Never shall you intercept my lovers, or destroy the
charm of my youth."
[c] *Enter youth, bearing a torch.*
[d] The metre is that of the Harmodius scolion. εἴθ' ἐξῆν begins
one almost as well known, Athenaeus, xv. 50.

οὐ γὰρ τἀπὶ Χαριξένης τάδ' ἐστίν.
κατὰ τὸν νόμον ταῦτα ποιεῖν
ἔστι δίκαιον, εἰ δημοκρατούμεθα.   945
ἀλλ' εἶμι τηρήσουσ' ὅ τι καὶ δράσεις ποτέ.

NE. εἶθ', ὦ θεοί, λάβοιμι τὴν καλὴν μόνην,
ἐφ' ἣν πεπωκὼς ἔρχομαι πάλαι ποθῶν.

MEI. ἐξηπάτησα τὸ κατάρατον γρᾴδιον·
φρούδη γάρ ἐστιν οἰομένη μ' ἔνδον μένειν.   950
ἀλλ' οὑτοσὶ γὰρ αὐτὸς οὗ μεμνήμεθα.
    δεῦρο δὴ δεῦρο δή,
    φίλον ἐμόν, δεῦρό μοι
    πρόσελθε καὶ ξύνευνός μοι
    τὴν εὐφρόνην ὅπως ἔσει.
    πάνυ γάρ τις ἔρως με δονεῖ
    τῶνδε τῶν σῶν βοστρύχων.   955
    ἄτοπος δ' ἔγκειταί μοί τις
    πόθος, ὅς με διακναίσας ἔχει.
    μέθες, ἱκνοῦμαί σ', Ἔρως,
    καὶ ποίησον τόνδ' ἐς εὐνὴν
    τὴν ἐμὴν ἱκέσθαι.

NE.   δεῦρο δὴ δεῦρο δή,   960
    καὶ σύ μοι καταδραμοῦ-
    σα τὴν θύραν ἄνοιξον
    τήνδ'· εἰ δὲ μή, καταπεσὼν κείσομαι.
    φίλον, ἀλλ' ἐν τῷ σῷ βούλομαι
    κόλπῳ πληκτίζεσθαι μετὰ
    τῆς σῆς πυγῆς.
    Κύπρι, τί μ' ἐκμαίνεις ἐπὶ ταύτῃ;   965

ᵃ The Scholiasts describe Charixena variously as (1) a fool, or
(2) an erotic poet, but they do not explain the proverb, which
means, " this is something quite different " (Gaisford, *Paroemiogr.*
B. 427).

          'Tis not Charixena's *a* style to-day ;
          Now the laws you must needs obey
          Under our democratical sway.
I'll run and watch what next you are going to do.

YOUTH. O might I catch, dear gods, my fair alone,
        To whom I hasten, flushed with love and wine.

GIRL (*reappearing above*). That vile old Hag, I nicely cozened
     her.
She deems I'm safe within, and off she's gone.
But here's the very lad of whom we spake.
  (*Singing*) This way, this way.
       Hither, my soul's delight !
    O come to my arms, my love, my own,
       O come to my arms this night.
       Dearly I long for my love ;
       My bosom is shaken and whirls,
    My heart is afire with a wild desire
       For my boy with the sunbright curls.
Ah me, what means this strange unrest,
This love which lacerates my breast ?
O God of Love, I cry to thee ;
    Be pitiful, be merciful,
    And send my love to me.

YOUTH (*singing*). Hither, O hither, my love,
       This way, this way.
    Run, run down from above,
       Open the wicket I pray :
       Else I shall swoon, I shall die !
       Dearly I long for thy charms,
    Longing and craving and yearning to lie
       In the bliss of thy snow-soft arms.
    O Cypris, why my bosom stir,
    Making me rage and rave for her ?

μέθες, ἱκνοῦμαί σ᾿, Ἔρως,
καὶ ποίησον τήνδ᾿ ἐς εὐνὴν
τὴν ἐμὴν ἱκέσθαι.
καὶ ταῦτα μέν μοι μετρίως πρὸς τὴν ἐμὴν ἀνάγκην
εἰρημέν᾿ ἐστίν. σὺ δέ μοι, φίλτατον, ὦ ἱκετεύω, 970
ἄνοιξον, ἀσπάζου με·
διά τοι σὲ πόνους ἔχω.
ὦ χρυσοδαίδαλτον ἐμὸν μέλημα, Κύπριδος ἔρνος,
μέλιττα Μούσης, Χαρίτων θρέμμα, Τρυφῆς πρόσ-
ωπον,
ἄνοιξον, ἀσπάζου με· 975
διά τοι σὲ πόνους ἔχω.

ΓΡ.Α. οὗτος, τί κόπτεις; μῶν ἐμὲ ζητεῖς;
ΝΕ. πόθεν;
ΓΡ.Α. καὶ τὴν θύραν γ᾿ ἤραττες.
ΝΕ. ἀποθάνοιμ᾿ ἄρα.
ΓΡ.Α. τοῦ δαὶ δεόμενος δᾷδ᾿ ἔχων ἐλήλυθας;
ΝΕ. Ἀναφλύστιον ζητῶν τιν᾿ ἄνθρωπον.
ΓΡ.Α. τίνα;
ΝΕ. οὐ τὸν Σεβῖνον, ὃν σὺ προσδοκᾷς ἴσως. 980
ΓΡ.Α. νὴ τὴν Ἀφροδίτην, ἤν τε βούλῃ γ᾿ ἤν τε μή.
ΝΕ. ἀλλ᾿ οὐχὶ νυνὶ τὰς ὑπερεξηκοντέτεις
εἰσάγομεν, ἀλλ᾿ εἰσαῦθις ἀναβεβλήμεθα.
τὰς ἐντὸς εἴκοσιν γὰρ ἐκδικάζομεν.
ΓΡ.Α. ἐπὶ τῆς προτέρας ἀρχῆς γε ταῦτ᾿ ἦν, ὦ γλύκων· 985
νυνὶ δὲ πρῶτον εἰσάγειν ἡμᾶς δοκεῖ.
ΝΕ. τῷ βουλομένῳ γε, κατὰ τὸν ἐν Παιτοῖς νόμον.

ᵃ Anaphlystus was an Attic deme, a seaport S.W. of the silver
mines of Laureium; but this is a coarse jest on ἀναφλᾶν (mastur-
bare), and Σεβῖνος on βινεῖν. Cf. F. 427.
ᵇ The Hag tries to drag him into her house.
ᶜ εἰσάγομεν, "bring into court," but with τὰς ὑπ. added, δίκας
or γυναῖκας may be supplied.
ᵈ The Paetians were a Thracian tribe: there must have been

O God of Love, I cry to thee,
   Be pitiful, be merciful,
   And send my love to me.
Enough, I trow, is said to show
         the straits I'm in, my lonely grieving.
Too long I've made my serenade :
      descend, sweet heart, thy chamber leaving,
   Open, true welcome show,
   Sore pangs for thee I undergo.
O Love, bedight with golden light,
               presentment fair of soft embraces,
The Muses' bee, of Love's sweet tree
         the flower, the nursling of the Graces,
   Open, true welcome show,
   Sore pangs for thee I undergo.

HAG.   Hi ! knocking ? seeking ME ?
YOUTH.   A likely joke.
HAG.   You banged against my door.
YOUTH.   Hanged if I did.
HAG.   Then why that lighted torch ? What seek you
           here ?
YOUTH. Some Anaphlystian *a* burgher.
HAG.   What's his name ?
YOUTH. No, not Sebinus *a* ; whom *you* want belike.
HAG.   By Aphrodite, will you, nill you, sir.*b*
YOUTH. Ah, but we're not now taking cases *c* over
           Sixty years old: they've been adjourned till later ;
           We're taking now those under twenty years.
HAG.   Aha, but that was under, darling boy,
           The old régime : now you must take us first.
YOUTH. Aye, if I will : so runs the Paetian law.*d*

some law which might be neglected at will. The Youth says:
" I may take you or not, at my choice." The Hag: "What about
dinner? Had you your choice there, or must you dine where
you were put?"

ΓΡ.Α. ἀλλ' οὐδ' ἐδείπνεις κατὰ τὸν ἐν Παιτοῖς νόμον.

ΝΕ. οὐκ οἶδ' ὅ τι λέγεις· τηνδεδί μοι κρουστέον.

ΓΡ.Α. ὅταν γε κρούσῃς τὴν ἐμὴν πρῶτον θύραν. 990

ΝΕ. ἀλλ' οὐχὶ νυνὶ κρησέραν αἰτούμεθα.

ΓΡ.Α. οἶδ' ὅτι φιλοῦμαι· νῦν δὲ θαυμάζεις ὅτι
θύρασί μ' εὗρες· ἀλλὰ πρόσαγε τὸ στόμα.

ΝΕ. ἀλλ', ὦ μέλ', ὀρρωδῶ τὸν ἐραστήν σου.

ΓΡ.Α.   τίνα;

ΝΕ. τὸν τῶν γραφέων ἄριστον.

ΓΡ.Α.   οὗτος δ' ἔστι τίς; 995

ΝΕ. ὃς τοῖς νεκροῖσι ζωγραφεῖ τὰς ληκύθους.
ἀλλ' ἄπιθ', ὅπως μή σ' ἐπὶ θύραισιν ὄψεται.

ΓΡ.Α. οἶδ' οἶδ' ὅ τι βούλει.

ΝΕ.   καὶ γὰρ ἐγώ σε νὴ Δία.

ΓΡ.Α. μὰ τὴν Ἀφροδίτην, ἥ μ' ἔλαχε κληρουμένη,
μὴ 'γώ σ' ἀφήσω.

ΝΕ.   παραφρονεῖς, ὦ γρᾴδιον. 1000

ΓΡ.Α. ληρεῖς· ἐγὼ δ' ἄξω σ' ἐπὶ τἀμὰ στρώματα.

ΝΕ. τί δῆτα κρεάγρας τοῖς κάδοις ὠνοίμεθ' ἄν,
ἐξὸν καθέντα γρᾴδιον τοιουτονὶ
ἐκ τῶν φρεάτων τοὺς κάδους ξυλλαμβάνειν;

ΓΡ.Α. μὴ σκῶπτέ μ', ὦ τάλαν, ἀλλ' ἕπου δεῦρ' ὡς ἐμέ. 1005

ΝΕ. ἀλλ' οὐκ ἀνάγκη μούστίν, εἰ μὴ τῶν ἐτῶν
τὴν πεντακοσιοστὴν κατέθηκας τῇ πόλει.

ΓΡ.Α. νὴ τὴν Ἀφροδίτην, δεῖ γε μέντοι σ'. ὡς ἐγὼ
τοῖς τηλικούτοις ξυγκαθεύδουσ' ἥδομαι.

ΝΕ. ἐγὼ δὲ ταῖς γε τηλικαύταις ἄχθομαι, 1010
κοὐκ ἂν πιθοίμην οὐδέποτ'.

ΓΡ.Α.   ἀλλὰ νὴ Δία
ἀναγκάσει τουτί σε.

---

^a κρησέρα = the coarse linen casing of a κόφινος or basket: Schol.

^b The Hag speaks as if she were a modest maiden; the Youth replies that her fittest lover is the "undertaker," who paints the

HAG.   You didn't, did you, dine by Paetian law.

YOUTH. Don't understand you : there's the girl I want.

HAG.   Aye, but *me* first : you must, you rogue, you must.

YOUTH. O we don't want a musty pack-cloth *a* now.

HAG.   I know I'm loved : but O you wonder, don't you,
         To see me out of doors : come, buss me, do.

YOUTH. No, no, I dread your lover.

HAG.   Whom do you mean ?

YOUTH. That prince of painters.

HAG.   Who is he, I wonder.

YOUTH. Who paints from life the bottles for the dead.*b*
         Away ! begone ! he'll see you at the door.

HAG.   I know, I know your wishes.

YOUTH.   And I yours.

HAG.   I vow by Aphrodite, whose I am,
         I'll never let you go.

YOUTH.   You're mad, old lady.

HAG.   Nonsense ! I'll drag you recreant to my couch.

YOUTH. Why buy we hooks to raise our buckets then,
         When an old hag like this, let deftly down,
         Could claw up all the buckets from our wells ?

HAG.   No scoffing, honey : come along with me.

YOUTH. You've got no rights, unless you've paid the tax,
         One-fifth per cent on all your wealth—of years.*c*

HAG.   O yes, you must ; O yes, by Aphrodite,
         Because I love to cuddle lads like you.

YOUTH. But I don't love to cuddle hags like you,
         Nor will I : never ! never !

HAG.   O yes, you will,
         This will compel you.

oil bottles to be buried with the dead. She had better not be seen at the door, or the undertaker may think she is a corpse, and carry her out.

    c If she has not paid her taxes, she cannot claim her rights. He substitutes ἐτῶν comically for ὄντων, "goods."

ΝΕ.   τοῦτο δ' ἔστι τί;
ΓΡ.Α. ψήφισμα, καθ' ὅ σε δεῖ βαδίζειν ὡς ἐμέ
ΝΕ. λέγ' αὐτὸ τί ποτε κἄστι.
ΓΡ.Α.   καὶ δή σοι λέγω.
  ἔδοξε ταῖς γυναιξίν, ἢν ἀνὴρ νέος   1015
  νέας ἐπιθυμῇ, μὴ σποδεῖν αὐτὴν πρὶν ἂν
  τὴν γραῦν προκρούσῃ πρῶτον· ἢν δὲ μὴ θέλῃ
  πρότερον προκρούειν, ἀλλ' ἐπιθυμῇ τῆς νέας,
  ταῖς πρεσβυτέραις γυναιξὶν ἔστω τὸν νέον
  ἕλκειν ἀνατὶ λαβομένας τοῦ παττάλου.   1020
ΝΕ. οἴμοι· Προκρούστης τήμερον γενήσομαι.
ΓΡ.Α. τοῖς γὰρ νόμοις τοῖς ἡμετέροισι πειστέον.
ΝΕ. τί δ', ἢν ἀφαιρῆταί μ' ἀνὴρ τῶν δημοτῶν
  ἢ τῶν φίλων ἐλθών τις;
ΓΡ.Α.   ἀλλ' οὐ κύριος
  ὑπὲρ μέδιμνόν ἐστ' ἀνὴρ οὐδεὶς ἔτι.   1025
ΝΕ. ἐξωμοσία δ' οὐκ ἔστιν;
ΓΡ.Α.   οὐ γὰρ δεῖ στροφῆς.
ΝΕ. ἀλλ' ἔμπορος εἶναι σκήψομαι.
ΓΡ.Α.   κλάων γε σύ.
ΝΕ. τί δῆτα χρὴ δρᾶν;
ΓΡ.Α.   δεῦρ' ἀκολουθεῖν ὡς ἐμέ.
ΝΕ. καὶ ταῦτ' ἀνάγκη μοὐστί;
ΓΡ.Α.   Διομήδειά γε.
ΝΕ. ὑποστόρεσαί νυν πρῶτα τῆς ὀριγάνου,   1030
  καὶ κλήμαθ' ὑπόθου συγκλάσασα τέτταρα,
  καὶ ταινίωσαι, καὶ παράθου τὰς ληκύθους,

---

^a παττάλου=πέους: Schol. In 1020 Procrustes is merely introduced as a play on the προκρούειν of 1017-18.

^b No man's credit extends beyond a bushel now. Women's
contracts were restricted to this amount: Schol.

YOUTH.   What in the world is THIS ?

HAG.   THIS is a law which bids you follow me.

YOUTH. Read what it says.

HAG.   O yes, my dear, I will.
Be it enacted, please to listen, you,
By us the ladies : if a youth would woo
A maiden, he must first his duty do
By some old beldame ; if the youth refuse,
Then may the beldames lawful violence use
And drag him in, in any way they choose.[a]

YOUTH. A crusty law ! a Procrustéan law !

HAG.   Well, never mind ; you must obey the law.

YOUTH. What if some Man, a friend or fellow-burgher,
Should come and bail me out ?

HAG.   A Man, forsooth ?
No Man avails beyond a bushel now.[b]

YOUTH. Essoign[c] I'll challenge.

HAG.   Nay, no quillets now.

YOUTH. I'll sham a merchant.[d]

HAG.   You'll repent it then.

YOUTH. And must I come ?

HAG.   You must.

YOUTH.   Is it a stern
Necessity ?

HAG.   Yes, quite Diomedéan.[e]

YOUTH. Then strew the couch with dittany, and set
Four well-crushed branches of the vine beneath ;
Bind on the fillets ; set the oil beside ;

---

[c] An excuse (such as ill-health) sworn to evade some duty.

[d] The merchant could claim exemption from military service.
Cf. *P.* 904.

[e] *i.e.* absolutely irresistible. The phrase is proverbial; *cf.*
Plato, *Rep.* vi. 493 D ἡ Διομήδεια λεγομένη ἀνάγκη. " Διομήδης ὁ
Θρᾷξ, πόρνας ἔχων θυγατέρας, τοὺς παριόντας ξένους ἐβιάζετο αὐταῖς
συνεῖναι ἕως οὗ . . . ἀναλωθῶσιν οἱ ἄνδρες ": Schol.

ὕδατός τε κατάθου τοὔστρακον πρὸ τῆς θύρας.
ΓΡ.Α. ἦ μὴν ἔτ᾽ ὠνήσει σὺ καὶ στεφάνην ἐμοί.
ΝΕ. νὴ τὸν Δί᾽, ἤνπερ ᾖ γέ που τῶν κηρίνων.   1035
οἶμαι γὰρ ἔνδον διαπεσεῖσθαί σ᾽ αὐτίκα.
ΜΕΙ. ποῖ τοῦτον ἕλκεις σύ;
ΓΡ.Α.   τὸν ἐμαυτῆς εἰσάγω.
ΜΕΙ. οὐ σωφρονοῦσά γ᾽. οὐ γὰρ ἡλικίαν ἔχει
παρὰ σοὶ καθεύδειν τηλικοῦτος ὤν, ἐπεὶ
μήτηρ ἂν αὐτῷ μᾶλλον εἴης ἢ γυνή.   1040
ὥστ᾽ εἰ καταστήσεσθε τοῦτον τὸν νόμον,
τὴν γῆν ἅπασαν Οἰδιπόδων ἐμπλήσετε.
ΓΡ.Α. ὦ παμβδελυρά, φθονοῦσα τόνδε τὸν λόγον
ἐξεῦρες· ἀλλ᾽ ἐγώ σε τιμωρήσομαι.
ΝΕ. νὴ τὸν Δία τὸν σωτῆρα, κεχάρισαί γέ μοι,   1045
ὦ γλυκύτατον, τὴν γραῦν ἀπαλλάξασά μου·
ὥστ᾽ ἀντὶ τούτων τῶν ἀγαθῶν εἰς ἑσπέραν
μεγάλην ἀποδώσω καὶ παχεῖάν σοι χάριν.
ΓΡ.Β. αὕτη σύ, ποῖ τονδί, παραβᾶσα τὸν νόμον,
ἕλκεις, παρ᾽ ἐμοὶ τῶν γραμμάτων εἰρηκότων   1050
πρότερον καθεύδειν αὐτόν;
ΝΕ.   οἴμοι δείλαιος.
πόθεν ἐξέκυψας, ὦ κάκιστ᾽ ἀπολουμένη;
τοῦτο γὰρ ἐκείνου τὸ κακὸν ἐξωλέστερον.
ΓΡ.Β. βάδιζε δεῦρο.
ΝΕ.   μηδαμῶς με περιίδῃς
ἑλκόμενον ὑπὸ τῆσδ᾽, ἀντιβολῶ σ᾽.
ΓΡ.Β.   ἀλλ᾽ οὐκ ἐγώ, 1055
ἀλλ᾽ ὁ νόμος ἕλκει σ᾽.
ΝΕ.   οὐκ ἐμέ γ᾽, ἀλλ᾽ ἔμπουσά τις
ἐξ αἵματος φλύκταιναν ἠμφιεσμένη.

ᵃ "'Then prepare a couch,' cries the youth, but under the pre-

	And at the entrance set the water-crock.[a]
HAG.	Now, by my troth, you'll buy me a garland yet.
YOUTH.	A waxen garland. So, by Zeus, I will.
	You'll fall to pieces, I expect, in there.[b]
GIRL.	Where drag you him ?
HAG.	I'm taking home my husband.
GIRL.	Not wisely then : the lad is far too young
	To serve your turn. You're of an age, methinks
	To be his mother rather than his wife.
	If thus ye carry out the law, erelong
	Ye'll have an Oedipus in every house.
HAG.	You nasty spiteful girl, you made that speech
	Out of sheer envy, but I'll pay you out.[c]
YOUTH.	Now by the Saviour Zeus, my sweetest sweet,
	A rare good turn you have done me, scaring off
	That vulturous Hag ; for which, at eventide,
	I'll make you, darling, what return I can.[d]
SECOND H.	Hallo, Miss Break-the-law, where are you dragging
	That gay young stripling, when the writing says
	I'm first to wed him ?
YOUTH.	Miserable me !
	Whence did *you* spring, you evil-destined Hag ?
	She's worse than the other : I protest she is.
S.H.	Come hither.
YOUTH. (*to the Girl*).	O my darling, don't stand by,
	And see this creature drag me !
S.H.	'Tis not I,
	'Tis the LAW drags you.
YOUTH.	'Tis a hellish vampire,
	Clothed all about with blood, and boils, and blisters.

tence of describing a nuptial bed, he is really describing a funeral
bier.   A waterpot, called ἀρδάνιον, was placed at the house door,
that visitors might purify themselves as they passed out " : R.
Cf. Pollux, viii. 65, Eur. *Alcestis*, 98-100.

  [b] *Enter girl.*   [c] *Exit Hag.*   [d] *Enter second Hag.*

ΓΡ.Β. ἕπου, μαλακίων, δεῦρ' ἀνύσας καὶ μὴ λάλει.

ΝΕ. ἴθι νυν ἔασον εἰς ἄφοδον πρώτιστά με
ἐλθόντα θαρρῆσαι πρὸς ἐμαυτόν· εἰ δὲ μή,   1060
αὐτοῦ τι δρῶντα πυρρὸν ὄψει μ' αὐτίκα
ὑπὸ τοῦ δέους.

ΓΡ.Β.   θάρρει, βάδιζ'· ἔνδον χεσεῖ.

ΝΕ. δέδοικα κἀγὼ μὴ πλέον γ' ἢ βούλομαι.
ἀλλ' ἐγγυητάς σοι καταστήσω δύο
ἀξιόχρεως.

ΓΡ.Β.   μή μοι καθίστη.

ΓΡ.Γ.   ποῖ σύ, ποῖ   1065
χωρεῖς μετὰ ταύτης;

ΝΕ.   οὐκ ἔγωγ', ἀλλ' ἕλκομαι.
ἀτὰρ ἥτις εἶ γε, πόλλ' ἀγαθὰ γένοιτό σοι,
ὅτι μ' οὐ περιεῖδες ἐπιτριβέντ'. ὦ Ἡράκλεις,
ὦ Πᾶνες, ὦ Κορύβαντες, ὦ Διοσκόρω,
τοῦτ' αὖ πολὺ τούτου τὸ κακὸν ἐξωλέστερον.   1070
ἀτὰρ τί τὸ πρᾶγμ' ἔστ', ἀντιβολῶ, τουτί ποτε;
πότερον πίθηκος ἀνάπλεως ψιμυθίου,
ἢ γραῦς ἀνεστηκυῖα παρὰ τῶν πλειόνων;

ΓΡ.ᵃ. μὴ σκῶπτέ μ', ἀλλὰ δεῦρ' ἕπου.

ΓΡ.Β.   δευρὶ μὲν οὖν.

ΓΡ.Γ. ὡς οὐκ ἀφήσω σ' οὐδέποτ'.

ΓΡ.Β.   οὐδὲ μὴν ἐγώ.   1075

ΝΕ. διασπάσεσθέ μ', ὦ κακῶς ἀπολούμεναι.

ΓΡ.Β. ἐμοὶ γὰρ ἀκολουθεῖν σ' ἔδει κατὰ τὸν νόμον.

ΓΡ.Γ. οὔκ, ἢν ἑτέρα γε γραῦς ἔτ' αἰσχίων φανῇ.

ΝΕ. ἢν οὖν ὑφ' ὑμῶν πρῶτον ἀπόλωμαι κακῶς,
φέρε, πῶς ἐπ' ἐκείνην τὴν καλὴν ἀφίξομαι;   1080

ΓΡ.Γ. αὐτὸς σκόπει σύ· τάδε δέ σοι ποιητέον.

ᵃ Enter third Hag. A struggle ensues.

s.h.   Come, chickling, follow me: and don't keep
            chattering.

youth.   O let me first, for pity's sake, retire
            Into some draught-house.   I'm in such a fright
            That I shall yellow all about me else.

s.h.   Come, never mind ; you can do that within.

youth.   More than I wish, I fear me.   Come, pray do,
            I'll give you bail with two sufficient sureties.

s.h.   No bail for me ! [a]

third h. (*to Youth*).   Hallo, where are you gadding
            Away with her ?

youth.   Not " gadding " : being dragged.
            But blessings on you, whosoe'er you are,[b]
            Sweet sympathizer.   Ah! Oh! Heracles!
            Ye Pans ! ye Corybants !   Twin sons of Zeus !
            She's worse than the other !   Miserable me !
            What shall I term this monstrous apparition ?
            A monkey smothered up in paint, or else
            A witch ascending from the Greater Number [c] ?

t.h.   No scoffing : come *this* way.

s.h.   *This* way, I tell you.

t.h.   I'll never let you go.

s.h.   No more will I.

youth.   Detested kites, ye'll rend me limb from limb.

s.h.   Obey the law, which bids you follow me.

t.h.   Not if a fouler, filthier, hag appears.

youth.   Now if betwixt you two I am done to death,
            How shall I ever reach the girl I love ?

t.h.   That's *your* look-out ; but this you needs must do.

---

[b] He imagines it to be some fair girl, as before, that helps him.
When he catches sight of the hag, he calls on Heracles, destroyer
of monsters ; on Castor and Polydeuces, helpers of men in distress ;
on Pans and Corybants, authors of those panic fears which now
distract him.

[c] From the dead, the " majority."

ΝΕ. ποτέρας προτέρας οὖν κατελάσας ἀπαλλαγῶ;
ΓΡ.Β. οὐκ οἶσθα; βαδιεῖ δεῦρ'.
ΝΕ.   ἀφέτω νύν μ' αὑτηί.
ΓΡ.Γ. δευρὶ μὲν οὖν ἴθ' ὡς ἔμ'.
ΝΕ.   ἤν μ' ἡδί γ' ἀφῇ.
ΓΡ.Β. ἀλλ' οὐκ ἀφήσω μὰ Δία σ'.
ΓΡ.Γ.   οὐδὲ μὴν ἐγώ.   1085
ΝΕ. χαλεπαί γ' ἂν ἦστε γενόμεναι πορθμῆς.
ΓΡ.Β.   τιή;
ΝΕ. ἕλκοντε τοὺς πλωτῆρας ἂν ἀπεκναίετε.
ΓΡ.Β. σιγῇ βάδιζε δεῦρο.
ΓΡ.Γ.   μὰ Δί' ἀλλ' ὡς ἐμέ.
ΝΕ. τουτὶ τὸ πρᾶγμα κατὰ τὸ Καννώνου σαφῶς
     ψήφισμα, βινεῖν δεῖ με διαλελημμένον.   1090
     πῶς οὖν δικωπεῖν ἀμφοτέρας δυνήσομαι;
ΓΡ.Β. καλῶς, ἐπειδὰν καταφάγῃς βολβῶν χύτραν.
ΝΕ. οἴμοι κακοδαίμων, ἐγγὺς ἤδη τῆς θύρας
     ἑλκόμενός εἰμ'.
ΓΡ.Γ.   ἀλλ' οὐδὲν ἔσται σοι πλέον.
     ξυνεσπεσοῦμαι γὰρ μετὰ σοῦ.
ΝΕ. .   μὴ πρὸς θεῶν.   1095
     ἑνὶ γὰρ ξυνέχεσθαι κρεῖττον ἢ δυοῖν κακοῖν.
ΓΡ.Γ. νὴ τὴν Ἑκάτην, ἐάν τε βούλῃ γ' ἤν τε μή.
ΝΕ. ὦ τρισκακοδαίμων, εἰ γυναῖκα δεῖ σαπρὰν
     βινεῖν ὅλην τὴν νύκτα καὶ τὴν ἡμέραν;
     κἄπειτ', ἐπειδὰν τῆσδ' ἀπαλλαγῶ, πάλιν   1100
     Φρύνην ἔχουσαν λήκυθον πρὸς ταῖς γνάθοις.
     ἆρ' οὐ κακοδαίμων εἰμί; βαρυδαίμων μὲν οὖν

---

^a The psephism of C. enacted that *if anyone shall wrong the
people of Athens, he shall make his defence before the people in
fetters. And if he shall be found guilty, he shall be put to death*

YOUTH. Which shall I tackle first, and so get free ?

S.H. You know ; come hither.

YOUTH. Make *her* let me go.

T.H. No, no, come hither.

YOUTH. If *she*'ll let me go.

S.H. Zeus ! I'll not let you go.

T.H. No more will I.

YOUTH. Rough hands ye'd prove as ferrymen.

S.H. Why so ?

YOUTH. Ye'd tear your passengers to bits by pulling.

S.H. Don't talk, come hither.

T.H. No, *this* way, I tell you.

YOUTH. O this is like Cannonus's decree,[a]
To play the lover, fettered right and left.[b]
How can one oarsman navigate a pair ?

S.H. Tush, eat a pot of truffles,[c] foolish boy.

YOUTH. O me, I'm dragged along till now I've reached
The very door.

T.H. That won't avail you aught ;
I'll tumble in beside you.

YOUTH. Heaven forbid !
Better to struggle with one ill than two.

T.H. O yes, by Hecate, will you, nill you, sir.

YOUTH. Thrice hapless me, who first must play the man
With this old rotten carcase, and when freed
From her, shall find another Phryne [d] there,
A bottle of oil beside her grinning chaps.
Ain't I ill-fated ? Yea, most heavy-fated !

*and thrown into the Deadman's Pit ; and his goods shall be
forfeited to the state, and the tithe thereof shall belong to the goddess.*
Xen. *Hell.* i. 7. 21.

   [b] μέσον εἰλημμένον : Schol. *Cf. K.* 262.

   [c] Considered to be an aphrodisiac.

   [d] Phryne means a toad ; it was a nickname of courtesans.
The famous P. belonged to a later time.

νὴ τὸν Δία τὸν σωτῆρ' ἀνὴρ καὶ δυστυχής,
ὅστις τοιούτοις θηρίοις συνείρξομαι.
ὅμως δ' ἐάν τι πολλὰ πολλάκις πάθω   1105
ὑπὸ ταῖνδε ταῖν κασαλβάδοιν, δεῦρ' ἐσπλέων,
θάψαι μ' ἐπ' αὐτῷ τῷ στόματι τῆς ἐσβολῆς·
καὶ τὴν ἄνωθεν ἐπιπολῆς τοῦ σήματος
ζῶσαν καταπιττώσαντας, εἶτα τὼ πόδε
μολυβδοχοήσαντας κύκλῳ περὶ τὰ σφυρά,   1110
ἄνω 'πιθεῖναι πρόφασιν ἀντὶ ληκύθου.

ΘΕΡΑΠΑΙΝΑ. ὦ μακάριος μὲν δῆμος, εὐδαίμων δ' ἐγώ.
αὐτή τέ μοι δέσποινα μακαριωτάτη,
ὑμεῖς θ' ὅσαι παρέστατ' ἐπὶ ταῖσιν θύραις,
οἱ γείτονές τε πάντες οἵ τε δημόται,   1115
ἐγώ τε πρὸς τούτοισιν ἡ διάκονος,
ἥτις μεμύρωμαι τὴν κεφαλὴν μυρώμασιν
ἀγαθοῖσιν, ὦ Ζεῦ· πολὺ δ' ὑπερπέπαικεν αὖ
τούτων ἁπάντων τὰ Θάσι' ἀμφορείδια.
ἐν τῇ κεφαλῇ γὰρ ἐμμένει πολὺν χρόνον·   1120
τὰ δ' ἄλλ' ἀπανθήσαντα πάντ' ἀπέπτατο·
ὥστ' ἐστὶ πολὺ βέλτιστα, πολὺ δῆτ', ὦ θεοί.
κέρασον ἄκρατον, εὐφρανεῖ τὴν νύχθ' ὅλην
ἐκλεγομένας ὅ τι ἂν μάλιστ' ὀσμὴν ἔχῃ.
ἀλλ', ὦ γυναῖκες, φράσατέ μοι τὸν δεσπότην, 1125
τὸν ἄνδρ', ὅπου 'στί, τῆς ἐμῆς κεκτημένης.
ΧΟ. αὐτοῦ μένουσ' ἡμῖν γ' ἂν ἐξευρεῖν δοκεῖς.
ΘΕ. μάλισθ'· ὁδὶ γὰρ ἐπὶ τὸ δεῖπνον ἔρχεται.
ὦ δέσποτ', ὦ μακάριε καὶ τρισόλβιε.
ΒΛ. ἐγώ;
ΘΕ.   σὺ μέντοι νὴ Δί' ὥς γ' οὐδεὶς ἀνήρ.   1130

---

a See p. 341, note b. *Exeunt. Enter Praxagora's maid*, sent
to fetch Blepyrus and the children; formerly the master would
350

O Zeus the Saviour, what a wretch am I
Yoked with this pair of savage-hearted beasts !
And O should aught befall me, sailing in
To harbour, towed by these detested drabs,
Bury my body by the harbour's mouth ;
And take the upper hag, who still survives,
And tar her well, and round her ankles twain
Pour molten lead, and plant her on my grave,
The staring likeness of a bottle of oil.*

MAID.   O lucky People, and O happy me,
And O my mistress, luckiest of us all,
And ye who now are standing at our door,
And all our neighbours, aye and all our town,
And I'm a lucky waiting-maid, who now
Have had my head with unguents rich and rare
Perfumed and bathed ; but far surpassing all
Are those sweet flagons full of Thasian wine.
Their fragrance long keeps lingering in the head,
Whilst all the rest evaporate and fade.
There's nothing half so good; great gods, not half !
Choose the most fragrant, mix it neat and raw,
'Twill make us merry all the whole night through.
But tell me, ladies, where my master is ;
I mean, the husband of my honoured mistress.*

CH.   If you stay here, methinks you'll find him soon.
MAID.   Aye, here he comes.*   He's off to join the dinner.
O master, O you lucky, lucky man !
BL.   What I ?
MAID.   Yes you, by Zeus, you luckiest man.

have sent the maids to fetch wife and children, but all that has
been changed now.
  b The man is now described by his relationship to the new head
of the house.
  c Enter Blepyrus and the children (τασδί, 1138).

τίς γὰρ γένοιτ' ἂν μᾶλλον ὀλβιώτερος,
ὅστις πολιτῶν πλεῖον ἢ τρισμυρίων
ὄντων τὸ πλῆθος οὐ δεδείπνηκας μόνος;
ΧΟ. εὐδαιμονικόν γ' ἄνθρωπον εἴρηκας σαφῶς.
ΘΕ. ποῖ ποῖ βαδίζεις;
ΒΛ.   ἐπὶ τὸ δεῖπνον ἔρχομαι.   1135
ΘΕ. νὴ τὴν Ἀφροδίτην, πολύ γ' ἁπάντων ὕστατος.
ὅμως δ' ἐκέλευε συλλαβοῦσάν μ' ἡ γυνὴ
ἄγειν σε καὶ τασδὶ μετὰ σοῦ τὰς μείρακας.
οἶνος δὲ Χῖός ἐστι περιλελειμμένος
καὶ τἄλλ' ἀγαθά. πρὸς ταῦτα μὴ βραδύνετε,   1140
καὶ τῶν θεατῶν εἴ τις εὔνους τυγχάνει,
καὶ τῶν κριτῶν εἰ μή τις ἑτέρωσε βλέπει,
ἴτω μεθ' ἡμῶν· πάντα γὰρ παρέξομεν.
ΒΛ. οὔκουν ἅπασι δῆτα γενναίως ἐρεῖς
καὶ μὴ παραλείψεις μηδέν', ἀλλ' ἐλευθέρως   1145
καλεῖν γέροντα, μειράκιον, παιδίσκον; ὡς
τὸ δεῖπνον αὐτοῖς ἔστ' ἐπεσκευασμένον
ἁπαξάπασιν, ἢν ἀπίωσιν οἴκαδε.
ἐγὼ δὲ πρὸς τὸ δεῖπνον ἤδη 'πείξομαι,
ἔχω δέ τοι καὶ δᾷδα ταυτηνὶ καλῶς.   1150
ΧΟ. τί δῆτα διατρίβεις ἔχων, ἀλλ' οὐκ ἄγεις
τασδὶ λαβών; ἐν ὅσῳ δὲ καταβαίνεις, ἐγὼ
ἐπάσομαι μέλος τι μελλοδειπνικόν.
σμικρὸν δ' ὑποθέσθαι τοῖς κριταῖσι βούλομαι·
τοῖς σοφοῖς μέν, τῶν σοφῶν μεμνημένοις κρίνειν
ἐμέ·   1155
τοῖς γελῶσι δ' ἡδέως, διὰ τὸν γέλων κρίνειν ἐμέ·
σχεδὸν ἅπαντας οὖν κελεύω δηλαδὴ κρίνειν ἐμέ.
μηδὲ τὸν κλῆρον γενέσθαι μηδὲν ἡμῖν αἴτιον,

ᵃ The Chorus seem to take the maid's words as a sarcasm;
but she may mean that Blepyrus's joys are still to come.

What greater bliss than yours, who, out of more
Than thrice ten thousand citizens, alone,
Have managed, you alone, to get no dinner ?

CH.   You tell of a happy man, and no mistake.[a]

MAID.   Hi ! Hi ! where now ?

BL.   I'm off to join the dinner.

MAID.   And much the last of all, by Aphrodite.
Well, well, my mistress bade me take you, sir,
You and these little girls and bring you thither.
Aye, and there's store of Chian wine remaining,
And other dainties too ; so don't delay.
And all the audience who are well disposed,
And every judge who looks not otherwards,
Come on with us ; we'll freely give you all.

BL   Nay, no exceptions ; open wide your mouth,
Invite them all in free and generous style,
Boy, stripling, grandsire ; yea, announce that all
Shall find a table all prepared and spread
For their enjoyment, in—their own sweet homes.
But I ! I'll hurry off to join the feast,
And here at least I've got a torch all handy.

CH.   Then why so long keep lingering here, nor take
These little ladies down ? And as you go,
I'll sing a song, a Lay of Lay-the-dinner.
But first, a slight suggestion to the judges.
Let the wise and philosophic
           choose me for my wisdom's sake,
Those who joy in mirth and laughter
           choose me for the jests I make ;
Then with hardly an exception
           every vote I'm bound to win.

ὅτι προείληχ'· ἀλλ' ἅπαντα ταῦτα χρὴ μεμνημένους
μὴ 'πιορκεῖν, ἀλλὰ κρίνειν τοὺς χοροὺς ὀρθῶς ἀεί, 1160
μηδὲ ταῖς κακαῖς ἑταίραις τὸν τρόπον προσεικέναι,
αἳ μόνον μνήμην ἔχουσι τῶν τελευταίων ἀεί.
ὦ ὦ ὥρα δή,
ὦ φίλαι γυναῖκες, εἴπερ μέλλομεν τὸ χρῆμα δρᾶν,
ἐπὶ τὸ δεῖπνον ὑπανακινεῖν. Κρητικῶς οὖν τὼ πόδε 1165
καὶ σὺ κίνει.

ΒΛ.   τοῦτο δρῶ.

ΧΟ. καὶ τάσδε νῦν λαγαρὰς
τοῖν σκελίσκοιν τὸν ῥυθμόν. τάχα γὰρ ἔπεισι
λοπαδοτεμαχοσελαχογαλεο-
κρανιολειψανοδριμυποτριμματο-   1170
σιλφιοπαραομελιτοκατακε-
χυμενοκιχλεπικοσσυφοφαττοπε-
ριστεραλεκτρυονοπτεκεφαλλιο-
κιγκλοπελειολαγῳοσιραιοβα-
φητραγανοπτερύγων. σὺ δὲ ταῦτ' ἀκρο-   1175
ασάμενος [ταχὺ καὶ] ταχέως λαβὲ τρύβλιον.
εἶτα λαβὼν κόνισαι
λέκιθον, ἵν' ἐπιδειπνῇς.

Let it nothing tell against me,
> that my play must first begin ;
See that, through the afterpieces,
> back to me your memory strays ;
Keep your oaths, and well and truly
> judge between the rival plays.
Be not like the wanton women,
> never mindful of the past,
Always for the new admirer,
> always fondest of the last.
> Now 'tis time, 'tis time, 'tis time,
Sisters dear, 'tis time for certain,
> if we mean the thing to do,
To the public feast to hasten.
> Therefore foot it neatly, you,
> First throw up your right leg, so,
> Then the left, and away to go,
> Cretan measure.

BL.   Aye, with pleasure.

CH.   Now must the spindleshanks, lanky and lean,
Trip to the banquet, for soon will, I ween,
High on the table be smoking a dish
Brimming with game and with fowl and with fish,
> All sorts of good things.
Plattero-filleto-mulleto-turboto-
-Cranio-morselo-pickleo-acido-
-Silphio-honeyo-pouredonthe-topothe-
-Ouzelo-throstleo-cushato-culvero-
-Cutleto-roastingo-marrowo-dippero-
-Leveret-syrupo-gibleto-wings.
So now ye have heard these tidings true,
Lay hold of a plate and an omelette too,
And scurry away at your topmost speed,
And so you will have whereon to feed.

ΒΛ. ἀλλὰ λαιμάττουσί που.
ΧΟ. αἴρεσθ' ἄνω, ἰαί, εὐαί.
    δειπνήσομεν, εὐοῖ, εὐαί,   1180
    εὐαί, ὡς ἐπὶ νίκῃ·
    εὐαί, εὐαί, εὐαί, εὐαί.

BL. They're guzzling already, I know, I know.
CH. Then up with your feet and away to go.
  Off, off to the supper we'll run.
With a whoop for the prize, hurrah, hurrah,
With a whoop for the prize, hurrah, hurrah,
  Whoop, whoop, for the victory won !

THE PLUTUS

INTRODUCTION

At the time when this play was exhibited, Athens had made a remarkable recovery from her defeat. Under the leadership of Conon, she had made head against Sparta, and she had already a considerable fleet. Doubtless the Persian gold which Conon had brought was the beginning of her recovery; but the Athenians must have made great sacrifices themselves. " And very welcome to the whole audience must have been the restoration of Wealth, at the close of the Comedy, to his long-deserted home in the Athenian Treasury." [a]

Aristophanes had produced a *Plutus* in 408 B.C.; but it probably had " an entirely different plot carried out in an entirely different manner." [b] The present Comedy was exhibited in the spring of 388. It was the last which he brought out in his own name; but " there seems every reason to believe that he afterwards revised it, and exhibited the revised edition in the name of his son Araros." [c] There was no third *Plutus*, but only a double representation of the second, revised and touched up. The allusions imply the same general situation in politics as those of the *Ecclesiazusae*.

" Everywhere in the play before us we find tokens of the change which is passing over Athenian

[a] Rogers, Introduction, p. vii.   [b] *Ib.*   [c] *Ib.* p. viii.

Comedy. The stately Parabasis is gone; the beautiful lyrics which elevated the whole performance into a higher and purer atmosphere have altogether disappeared; the great historical personages, literary and political, the poets, the philosophers, the demagogues, the generals, who moved through the earlier scenes of the Aristophanic drama, have faded not only from his own satire, but almost from the very recollection of his audience: we are no longer amidst the pomp and glory, the boundless activities of Imperial Athens with her Imperial instincts and her splendid ambitions; comedy has become social instead of political; the performers might almost be treading, so to say, the boards of some provincial theatre." [a]

The idea on which the play turns is that ancient problem, Why do the ungodly prosper, while the righteous are needy and poor? The question is answered with a jest: it must be that Wealth is blind. He is restored to sight, and the tables are turned. The scenes described as taking place in the sanctuary of Asclepius are close enough to the facts, if rather farcical. We know a good deal about what happened at the great shrine in Epidaurus; there are important remains—the temple, the dormitory, a Rotunda, a stadium, a great theatre, and various shrines; above all, a long series of inscriptions describing the cures, which often illustrate the play, as when serpents come out of their holes and lick the patient's sores. At Cos also the remains of a temple and precinct of Asclepius have been found; and the Fourth Mime of Herondas describes a scene in that place.

[a] Rogers, Introduction, p. xiv.

ΤΑ ΤΟΥ ΔΡΑΜΑΤΟΣ ΠΡΟΣΩΠΑ

ΚΑΡΙΩΝ

ΧΡΕΜΥΛΟΣ

ΠΛΟΥΤΟΣ

ΧΟΡΟΣ ΓΕΩΡΓΩΝ

ΒΛΕΨΙΔΗΜΟΣ

ΠΕΝΙΑ

ΓΥΝΗ ΧΡΕΜΥΛΟΥ

ΔΙΚΑΙΟΣ ΑΝΗΡ

ΣΥΚΟΦΑΝΤΗΣ

ΓΡΑΥΣ

ΝΕΑΝΙΑΣ

ΕΡΜΗΣ

ΙΕΡΕΥΣ ΔΙΟΣ

ΠΛΟΥΤΟΣ

ΚΑΡΙΩΝ. Ὡς ἀργαλέον πρᾶγμ' ἐστίν, ὦ Ζεῦ καὶ θεοί,
δοῦλον γενέσθαι παραφρονοῦντος δεσπότου.
ἢν γὰρ τὰ βέλτισθ' ὁ θεράπων λέξας τύχῃ,
δόξῃ δὲ μὴ δρᾶν ταῦτα τῷ κεκτημένῳ,
μετέχειν ἀνάγκη τὸν θεράποντα τῶν κακῶν.   5
τοῦ σώματος γὰρ οὐκ ἐᾷ τὸν κύριον
κρατεῖν ὁ δαίμων, ἀλλὰ τὸν ἐωνημένον.
καὶ ταῦτα μὲν δὴ ταῦτα. τῷ δὲ Λοξίᾳ,
ὃς θεσπιῳδεῖ τρίποδος ἐκ χρυσηλάτου,
μέμψιν δικαίαν μέμφομαι ταύτην, ὅτι   10
ἰατρὸς ὢν καὶ μάντις, ὥς φασιν, σοφός,
μελαγχολῶντ' ἀπέπεμψέ μου τὸν δεσπότην,
ὅστις ἀκολουθεῖ κατόπιν ἀνθρώπου τυφλοῦ,
τοὐναντίον δρῶν ἢ προσῆκ' αὐτῷ ποιεῖν.
οἱ γὰρ βλέποντες τοῖς τυφλοῖς ἡγούμεθα·   15
οὗτος δ' ἀκολουθεῖ, κἀμὲ προσβιάζεται,
καὶ ταῦτ' ἀποκρινομένῳ τὸ παράπαν οὐδὲ γρῦ.
ἐγὼ μὲν οὖν οὐκ ἔσθ' ὅπως σιγήσομαι,
ἢν μὴ φράσῃς ὅ τι τῷδ' ἀκολουθοῦμέν ποτε,
ὦ δέσποτ', ἀλλά σοι παρέξω πράγματα.   20
οὐ γάρ με τυπτήσεις στέφανον ἔχοντά γε.

ᵃ Scene: a street in Athens with the house of Chremylus in the background. Groping along in front is a blind man of sordid

THE PLUTUS[a]

CARIO. How hard it is, O Zeus and all ye Gods,
To be the slave of a demented master !
For though the servant give the best advice,
Yet if his owner otherwise decide,
The servant needs must share the ill results.
For a man's body, such is fate, belongs
Not to himself, but to whoe'er has bought it.
So much for that.   But now with Loxias,
Who from his golden tripod chants his high
Oracular strains, I've got a bone to pick.
A wise Physician-seer they call him, yet
He has sent my master off so moody-mad,
That now he's following a poor blind old man,
Just the reverse of what he ought to do.
For we who see should go *before* the blind,
But he goes *after* (and constrains me too)
One who won't answer even with a gr-r-r.
I won't keep silence, master, no I won't,
Unless you tell me why you're following *him*.
I'll plague you, Sir ; I know you won't chastise me
So long as I've this sacred chaplet on.[b]

---

appearance, followed by Chremylus, an elderly citizen, and a slave
Cario, wearing wreaths of bay.
  [b] So long as he wore this symbol he was inviolate.   He would
" smart the more," if this slight protection were removed.

ΧΡΕΜ. μὰ Δί', ἀλλ' ἀφελὼν τὸν στέφανον, ἢν λυπῇς τί με,
    ἵνα μᾶλλον ἀλγῇς.

ΚΑ.   λῆρος· οὐ γὰρ παύσομαι
    πρὶν ἂν φράσῃς μοι τίς ποτ' ἐστὶν οὑτοσί·
    εὔνους γὰρ ὢν σοι πυνθάνομαι πάνυ σφόδρα. 25

ΧΡ. ἀλλ' οὔ σε κρύψω· τῶν ἐμῶν γὰρ οἰκετῶν
    πιστότατον ἡγοῦμαί σε καὶ κλεπτίστατον.
    ἐγὼ θεοσεβὴς καὶ δίκαιος ὢν ἀνὴρ
    κακῶς ἔπραττον καὶ πένης ἦν.

ΚΑ.   οἶδά τοι.

ΧΡ. ἕτεροι δ' ἐπλούτουν, ἱερόσυλοι, ῥήτορες 30
    καὶ συκοφάνται καὶ πονηροί.

ΚΑ.   πείθομαι.

ΧΡ. ἐπερησόμενος οὖν ᾠχόμην πρὸς τὸν θεόν,
    τὸν ἐμὸν μὲν αὐτοῦ τοῦ ταλαιπώρου σχεδὸν
    ἤδη νομίζων ἐκτετοξεῦσθαι βίον,
    τὸν δ' υἱόν, ὅσπερ ὢν μόνος μοι τυγχάνει, 35
    πευσόμενος εἰ χρὴ μεταβαλόντα τοὺς τρόπους
    εἶναι πανοῦργον, ἄδικον, ὑγιὲς μηδὲ ἕν,
    ὡς τῷ βίῳ τοῦτ' αὐτὸ νομίσας συμφέρειν.

ΚΑ. τί δῆτα Φοῖβος ἔλακεν ἐκ τῶν στεμμάτων;

ΧΡ. πεύσει. σαφῶς γὰρ ὁ θεὸς εἶπέ μοι τοδί· 40
    ὅτῳ ξυναντήσαιμι πρῶτον ἐξιών,
    ἐκέλευε τούτου μὴ μεθίεσθαί μ' ἔτι,
    πείθειν δ' ἐμαυτῷ ξυνακολουθεῖν οἴκαδε.

ΚΑ. καὶ τῷ ξυναντᾷς δῆτα πρώτῳ;

ΧΡ.   τουτῳί.

ΚΑ. εἶτ' οὐ ξυνιεῖς τὴν ἐπίνοιαν τοῦ θεοῦ, 45
    φράζουσαν ὦ σκαιότατέ σοι σαφέστατα
    ἀσκεῖν τὸν υἱὸν τὸν ἐπιχώριον τρόπον;

ᵃ " There is probably a play on the words βίος, life, and βιός,
a bow ; *E.* 563 " : R.

CHREMYLUS. I'll pluck it off, that you may smart the more,
　　　　If you keep bothering.
CA. 　　　　　　　　　　Humbug! I won't stop
　　　　Until you have told me who the fellow is.
　　　　You know I ask it out of love for you.
CHR. I'll tell you, for of all my servants you
　　　　I count the truest and most constant—thief.
　　　　—I've been a virtuous and religious man
　　　　Yet always poor and luckless.
CA. 　　　　　　　　　　So you have.
CHR. While Temple-breakers, orators, informers,
　　　　And knaves grow rich and prosper.
CA. 　　　　　　　　　　So they do.
CHR. So then I went to question of the God—
　　　　Not for myself, the quiver of my life
　　　　Is well-nigh emptied of its arrows now,—[a]
　　　　But for my son, my only son, to ask
　　　　If, changing all his habits, he should turn
　　　　A rogue, dishonest, rotten to the core.
　　　　For such as they, methinks, succeed the best.
CA. And what droned[b] Phoebus from his wreaths of bay?
CHR. He told me plainly that with whomsoe'er
　　　　I first forgathered as I left the shrine,
　　　　Of him I never should leave go again,
　　　　But win him back, in friendship, to my home.[c]
CA. With whom then did you first forgather?
CHR. 　　　　　　　　　　Him.
CA. And can't you see the meaning of the God,
　　　　You ignoramus, who so plainly tells you
　　　　Your son should follow the prevailing fashion?

[b] "'Shrilled' or 'shrieked' would be more accurate": R. The tripods and the priestess were wreathed with bay: Schol.

[c] Possibly a reference to Eur. *Ion*, 534-6, where Apollo tells Xuthus that the first person he meets will be his own son.

ΧΡ. τῷ τοῦτο κρίνεις;

ΚΑ.   δῆλον ὁτιὴ καὶ τυφλῷ
γνῶναι δοκεῖ τοῦθ᾽, ὡς σφόδρ᾽ ἐστὶ συμφέρον
τὸ μηδὲν ἀσκεῖν ὑγιὲς ἐν τῷ νῦν βίῳ.   50

ΧΡ. οὐκ ἔσθ᾽ ὅπως ὁ χρησμὸς εἰς τοῦτο ῥέπει,
ἀλλ᾽ εἰς ἕτερόν τι μεῖζον. ἢν δ᾽ ἡμῖν φράσῃ
ὅστις ποτ᾽ ἐστὶν οὑτοσὶ καὶ τοῦ χάριν
καὶ τοῦ δεόμενος ἦλθε μετὰ νῶν ἐνθαδί,
πυθοίμεθ᾽ ἂν τὸν χρησμὸν ἡμῶν ὅ τι νοεῖ.   55

ΚΑ. ἄγε δή, σὺ πότερον σαυτὸν ὅστις εἶ φράσεις,
ἢ τἀπὶ τούτοις δρῶ; λέγειν χρὴ ταχὺ πάνυ.

ΠΛΟΥΤΟΣ. ἐγὼ μὲν οἰμώζειν λέγω σοι.

ΚΑ.   μανθάνεις
ὅς φησιν εἶναι;

ΧΡ.   σοὶ λέγει τοῦτ᾽, οὐκ ἐμοί.
σκαιῶς γὰρ αὐτοῦ καὶ χαλεπῶς ἐκπυνθάνει.   60
ἀλλ᾽ εἴ τι χαίρεις ἀνδρὸς εὐόρκου τρόποις,
ἐμοὶ φράσον.

ΠΛ.   κλάειν ἔγωγέ σοι λέγω.

ΚΑ. δέχου τὸν ἄνδρα καὶ τὸν ὄρνιν τοῦ θεοῦ.

ΧΡ. οὔ τοι μὰ τὴν Δήμητρα χαιρήσεις ἔτι,
εἰ μὴ φράσεις γάρ, ἀπό σ᾽ ὀλῶ κακὸν κακῶς.   65

ΠΛ. ὦ τᾶν, ἀπαλλάχθητον ἀπ᾽ ἐμοῦ.

ΧΡ.   πώμαλα;

ΚΑ. καὶ μὴν ὃ λέγω βέλτιστόν ἐστι, δέσποτα·
ἀπολῶ τὸν ἄνθρωπον κάκιστα τουτονί.
ἀναθεὶς γὰρ ἐπὶ κρημνόν τιν᾽ αὐτὸν καταλιπὼν
ἄπειμ᾽, ἵν᾽ ἐκεῖθεν ἐκτραχηλισθῇ πεσών.   70

ΧΡ. ἀλλ᾽ αἶρε ταχέως.

ΠΛ.   μηδαμῶς.

ΧΡ.   οὔκουν ἐρεῖς;

ΠΛ. ἀλλ᾽ ἢν πύθησθέ μ᾽ ὅστις εἴμ᾽, εὖ οἶδ᾽ ὅτι

CHR. Why think you that ?

CA.   He means that even the blind
Can see 'tis better for our present life
To be a rascal, rotten to the core.

CHR. 'Tis not that way the oracle inclines,
It cannot be. 'Tis something more than that.
Now if this fellow told us who he is,
And why and wherefore he has come here now,
We'd soon discover what the God intended.

CA. (to Wealth) Hallo, you sirrah, tell me who you are,
Or take the consequence ! Out with it, quick !

WEALTH. Go and be hanged !

CA.   O master, did you hear
The name he gave ?

CHR.   'Twas meant for you, not me.
You ask in such a rude and vulgar way.
  (to Wealth) Friend, if you love an honest gentleman,
Tell me your name.

WE.   Get out, you vagabond !

CA. O ! O ! Accept the omen, and the man.[a]

CHR. O, by Demeter, you shall smart for this.
Answer this instant or you die the death.

WE. Men, men, depart and leave me.

CHR.   Wouldn't you like it ?

CA. O master, what I say is far the best :
I'll make him die a miserable death.
I'll set him on some precipice, and leave him,
So then he'll topple down and break his neck.

CHR. Up with him !

WE.   O pray don't.

CHR.   Do you mean to answer ?

WE. And if I do, I'm absolutely sure

---

[a] Take the man for your friend, and the omen (ὄρνιν means the φωνήν, the man's words) as applicable to yourself.

κακόν τί μ' ἐργάσεσθε κοὐκ ἀφήσετον.
ΧΡ. νὴ τοὺς θεοὺς ἡμεῖς γ', ἐὰν βούλῃ γε σύ.
ΠΛ. μέθεσθέ νύν μου πρῶτον.
ΧΡ.   ἤν, μεθίεμεν.   75
ΠΛ. ἀκούετον δή. δεῖ γὰρ ὡς ἔοικέ με
λέγειν ἃ κρύπτειν ἦν παρεσκευασμένος.
ἐγὼ γάρ εἰμι Πλοῦτος.
ΧΡ.   ὦ μιαρώτατε
ἀνδρῶν ἁπάντων, εἶτ' ἐσίγας Πλοῦτος ὤν;
ΚΑ. σὺ Πλοῦτος, οὕτως ἀθλίως διακείμενος;   80
ΧΡ. ὦ Φοῖβ' Ἄπολλον καὶ θεοὶ καὶ δαίμονες
καὶ Ζεῦ, τί φῄς; ἐκεῖνος ὄντως εἶ σύ;
ΠΛ.   ναί.
ΧΡ. ἐκεῖνος αὐτός;
ΠΛ.   αὐτότατος.
ΧΡ.   πόθεν οὖν, φράσον,
αὐχμῶν βαδίζεις;
ΠΛ.   ἐκ Πατροκλέους ἔρχομαι,
ὃς οὐκ ἐλούσατ' ἐξ ὅτουπερ ἐγένετο.   85
ΧΡ. τουτὶ δὲ τὸ κακὸν πῶς ἔπαθες; κάτειπέ μοι.
ΠΛ. ὁ Ζεύς με ταῦτ' ἔδρασεν ἀνθρώποις φθονῶν.
ἐγὼ γὰρ ὢν μειράκιον ἠπείλησ' ὅτι
ὡς τοὺς δικαίους καὶ σοφοὺς καὶ κοσμίους
μόνους βαδιοίμην· ὁ δέ μ' ἐποίησεν τυφλόν,   90
ἵνα μὴ διαγιγνώσκοιμι τούτων μηδένα.
οὕτως ἐκεῖνος τοῖσι χρηστοῖσι φθονεῖ.
ΧΡ. καὶ μὴν διὰ τοὺς χρηστούς γε τιμᾶται μόνους
καὶ τοὺς δικαίους.
ΠΛ.   ὁμολογῶ σοι.
ΧΡ.   φέρε, τί οὖν;
εἰ πάλιν ἀναβλέψειας ὥσπερ καὶ πρὸ τοῦ,   95
φεύγοις ἂν ἤδη τοὺς πονηρούς;

You'll treat me ill : you'll never let me go.

CHR. I vow we will, at least if you desire it.

WE. Then first unhand me.

CHR. There, we both unhand you.

WE. Then listen, both : for I, it seems, must needs
Reveal the secret I proposed to keep.
Know then, I'm Wealth !

CHR. You most abominable
Of all mankind, you, Wealth, and keep it snug !

CA. You, Wealth, in such a miserable plight !

CHR. O King Apollo ! O ye Gods and daemons !
O Zeus ! what mean you ? are you really HE ?

WE. I am.

CHR. Himself ?

WE. His own self's self.

CHR. Whence come you
So grimed with dirt ?

WE. From Patrocles's *a* house,
A man who never washed in all his life.

CHR. And this, your sad affliction, how came this ?

WE. 'Twas Zeus that caused it, jealous of mankind.
For, when a little chap, I used to brag
I'd visit none except the wise and good
And orderly ; he therefore made me blind,
That I might ne'er distinguish which was which,
So jealous is he always of the good !

CHR. And yet 'tis only from the just and good
His worship comes.

WE. I grant you that.

CHR. Then tell me,
If you could see again as once you could,
Would you avoid the wicked ?

a " Some sordid miser of the day " : R.

ΠΛ.   φήμ' ἐγώ.

ΧΡ. ὡς τοὺς δικαίους δ' ἂν βαδίζοις;

ΠΛ.   πάνυ μὲν οὖν·
πολλοῦ γὰρ αὐτοὺς οὐχ ἑόρακά πω χρόνου.

ΧΡ. καὶ θαῦμά γ' οὐδέν· οὐδ' ἐγὼ γὰρ ὁ βλέπων.

ΠΛ. ἄφετόν με νῦν. ἴστον γὰρ ἤδη τἀπ' ἐμοῦ.   100

ΧΡ. μὰ Δί', ἀλλὰ πολλῷ μᾶλλον ἑξόμεσθά σου.

ΠΛ. οὐκ ἠγόρευον ὅτι παρέξειν πράγματα
ἐμέλλετόν μοι;

ΧΡ.   καὶ σύ γ', ἀντιβολῶ, πιθοῦ,
καὶ μή μ' ἀπολίπῃς· οὐ γὰρ εὑρήσεις ἐμοῦ
ζητῶν ἔτ' ἄνδρα τοὺς τρόπους βελτίονα.   105

ΚΑ. μὰ τὸν Δί'· οὐ γὰρ ἔστιν ἄλλος πλὴν ἐγώ.

ΠΛ. ταυτὶ λέγουσι πάντες· ἡνίκ' ἂν δέ μου
τύχωσ' ἀληθῶς καὶ γένωνται πλούσιοι,
ἀτεχνῶς ὑπερβάλλουσι τῇ μοχθηρίᾳ.

ΧΡ. ἔχει μὲν οὕτως, εἰσὶ δ' οὐ πάντες κακοί.   110

ΠΛ. μὰ Δί', ἀλλ' ἁπαξάπαντες.

ΚΑ.   οἰμώξει μακρά.

ΧΡ. σοὶ δ' ὡς ἂν εἰδῇς ὅσα, παρ' ἡμῖν ἢν μένῃς,
γενήσετ' ἀγαθά, πρόσεχε τὸν νοῦν, ἵνα πύθῃ.
οἶμαι γάρ, οἶμαι, σὺν θεῷ δ' εἰρήσεται,
ταύτης ἀπαλλάξειν σε τῆς ὀφθαλμίας,   115
βλέψαι ποιήσας.

ΠΛ.   μηδαμῶς τοῦτ' ἐργάσῃ.
οὐ βούλομαι γὰρ πάλιν ἀναβλέψαι.

ΧΡ.   τί φής;

ΚΑ. ἄνθρωπος οὗτός ἐστιν ἄθλιος φύσει.

ΠΛ. ὁ Ζεὺς μὲν οὖν οἶδ' ὡς τὰ τούτων μῶρ', ἔμ', εἰ
πύθοιτ', ἂν ἐπιτρίψειε.

ΧΡ.   νῦν δ' οὐ τοῦτο δρᾷ,   120
ὅστις σε προσπταίοντα περινοστεῖν ἐᾷ;

WE.   Yes, I would.

CHR. And visit all the good ?

WE.   Yes ; more by token
    I have not seen the good for many a day.

CHR. No more have I, although I've got my eyes.[a]

WE. Come, let me go ; you know my story now.

CHR. And therefore, truly, hold we on the more.

WE. I told you so : you vowed you'd let me go.
    I knew you wouldn't.

CHR.   O be guided, pray,
    And don't desert me.   Search where'er you will
    You'll never find a better man than I.

CA. No more there is, by Zeus—except myself.

WE. They all say that ; but when in sober earnest
    They find they've got me, and are wealthy men,
    They place no limit on their evil ways.

CHR. Too true !   And yet not every one is bad.

WE. Yes, every single one.

CA. (*aside*)   You'll smart for that.

CHR. Nay, nay, but hear what benefits you'll get
    If you're persuaded to abide with us.
    For well I trust,—I trust, with God to aid,[b]
    That I shall rid you of this eye-disease,
    And make you see.

WE.   For mercy's sake, forbear.
    I do not wish to see again.

CHR.   Eh ? what ?

CA. O why, the man's a born unfortunate !

WE. Let Zeus but hear their follies, and I know
    He'll pay me out.

CHR.   And doesn't he do that now ;
    Letting you wander stumbling through the world ?

---

    [a] He scans the audience as he says this.
    [b] σὺν θ. δ' εἰρ., probably from Eur. *Medea*, 625.

ΠΛ. οὐκ οἶδ᾽· ἐγὼ δ᾽ ἐκεῖνον ὀρρωδῶ πάνυ.
ΧΡ. ἄληθες, ὦ δειλότατε πάντων δαιμόνων;
    οἴει γὰρ εἶναι τὴν Διὸς τυραννίδα
    καὶ τοὺς κεραυνοὺς ἀξίους τριωβόλου,   125
    ἐὰν ἀναβλέψῃς σὺ κἂν μικρὸν χρόνον;
ΠΛ. ἆ, μὴ λέγ᾽, ὦ πόνηρε, ταῦτ᾽.
ΧΡ.   ἔχ᾽ ἥσυχος.
    ἐγὼ γὰρ ἀποδείξω σε τοῦ Διὸς πολὺ
    μεῖζον δυνάμενον.
ΠΛ.   ἐμὲ σύ;
ΧΡ.   νὴ τὸν οὐρανόν.
    αὐτίκα γὰρ ἄρχει διὰ τί ὁ Ζεὺς τῶν θεῶν;   130
ΚΑ. διὰ τἀργύριον· πλεῖστον γάρ ἐστ᾽ αὐτῷ.
ΧΡ.   φέρε,
    τίς οὖν ὁ παρέχων ἐστὶν αὐτῷ τοῦθ᾽;
ΚΑ.   ὁδί.
ΧΡ. θύουσι δ᾽ αὐτῷ διὰ τίν᾽; οὐ διὰ τουτονί;
ΚΑ. καὶ νὴ Δί᾽ εὔχονταί γε πλουτεῖν ἄντικρυς.
ΧΡ. οὔκουν ὅδ᾽ ἐστὶν αἴτιος, καὶ ῥᾳδίως   135
    παύσειεν, εἰ βούλοιτο, ταῦτ᾽ ἄν;
ΠΛ.   ὅτι τί δή;
ΧΡ. ὅτι οὐδ᾽ ἂν εἷς θύσειεν ἀνθρώπων ἔτι,
    οὐ βοῦν ἄν, οὐχὶ ψαιστόν, οὐκ ἄλλ᾽ οὐδὲ ἕν,
    μὴ βουλομένου σοῦ.
ΠΛ.   πῶς;
ΧΡ.   ὅπως; οὐκ ἔσθ᾽ ὅπως
    ὠνήσεται δήπουθεν, ἢν σὺ μὴ παρὼν   140
    αὐτὸς διδῷς τἀργύριον, ὥστε τοῦ Διὸς
    τὴν δύναμιν, ἢν λυπῇ τι, καταλύσεις μόνος.
ΠΛ. τί λέγεις; δι᾽ ἐμὲ θύουσιν αὐτῷ;
ΧΡ.   φήμ᾽ ἐγώ.
    καὶ νὴ Δί᾽ εἴ τί γ᾽ ἔστι λαμπρὸν καὶ καλὸν

WE. Eh, but I'm horribly afraid of Zeus !

CHR. Aye, say you so, you cowardliest God alive ?
What ! do you think the imperial power of Zeus
And all his thunderbolts were worth one farthing,
Could you but see, for ever so short a time ?

WE. Ah, don't say that, you wretches !

CHR.   Don't be frightened !
I'll prove that you're far stronger, mightier far
Than Zeus.

WE.   You'll prove that *I* am ?

CHR.   Easily.
Come, what makes Zeus the Ruler of the Gods ?

CA. His silver. He's the wealthiest of them.

CHR.   Well,
Who gives him all his riches ?

CA.   Our friend here.

CHR. And for whose sake do mortals sacrifice
To Zeus ?

CA.   For *his* : and pray straight out for wealth.

CHR. 'Tis all his doing : and 'tis he can quickly
Undo it if he will.

WE.   How mean you that ?

CHR. I mean that nevermore will mortal man
Bring ox, or cake, or any sacrifice,
If such thy will.

WE.   How so ?

CHR.   How can he buy
A gift to offer, if thy power deny
The needful silver ? Single-handed, thou,
If Zeus prove troublesome, canst crush his power.

WE. Men sacrifice to Zeus for ME ?

CHR.   They do.
And whatsoever in the world is bright,

ἦ χάριεν ἀνθρώποισι, διὰ σὲ γίγνεται. 145
ἅπαντα τῷ πλουτεῖν γάρ ἐσθ' ὑπήκοα.

ΚΑ. ἔγωγέ τοι διὰ μικρὸν ἀργυρίδιον
δοῦλος γεγένημαι, διὰ τὸ μὴ πλουτεῖν ἴσως.

ΧΡ. καὶ τάς γ' ἑταίρας φασὶ τὰς Κορινθίας,
ὅταν μὲν αὐτάς τις πένης πειρῶν τύχῃ, 150
οὐδὲ προσέχειν τὸν νοῦν, ἐὰν δὲ πλούσιος,
τὸν πρωκτὸν αὐτὰς εὐθὺς ἐς τοῦτον τρέπειν.

ΚΑ. καὶ τούς γε παῖδάς φασι ταὐτὸ τοῦτο δρᾶν,
οὐ τῶν ἐραστῶν ἀλλὰ τἀργυρίου χάριν.

ΧΡ. οὐ τούς γε χρηστούς, ἀλλὰ τοὺς πόρνους· ἐπεὶ 155
αἰτοῦσιν οὐκ ἀργύριον οἱ χρηστοί.

ΚΑ.   τί δαί;

ΧΡ. ὁ μὲν ἵππον ἀγαθόν, ὁ δὲ κύνας θηρευτικούς.

ΚΑ. αἰσχυνόμενοι γὰρ ἀργύριον αἰτεῖν ἴσως
ὀνόματι περιπέττουσι τὴν μοχθηρίαν.

ΧΡ. τέχναι δὲ πᾶσαι διὰ σὲ καὶ σοφίσματα 160
ἐν τοῖσιν ἀνθρώποισίν ἐσθ' εὑρημένα.
ὁ μὲν γὰρ αὐτῶν σκυτοτομεῖ καθήμενος,
ἕτερος δὲ χαλκεύει τις, ὁ δὲ τεκταίνεται.
ὁ δὲ χρυσοχοεῖ γε, χρυσίον παρὰ σοῦ λαβών.

ΚΑ. ὁ δὲ λωποδυτεῖ γε νὴ Δί', ὁ δὲ τοιχωρυχεῖ. 165

ΧΡ. ὁ δὲ γναφεύει γ', ὁ δέ γε πλύνει κώδια,
ὁ δὲ βυρσοδεψεῖ γ', ὁ δέ γε πωλεῖ κρόμμυα,
ὁ δ' ἁλούς γε μοιχὸς διὰ σέ που παρατίλλεται.

ΠΛ. οἴμοι τάλας, ταυτί μ' ἐλάνθανεν πάλαι.

ΧΡ. μέγας δὲ βασιλεὺς οὐχὶ διὰ τοῦτον κομᾷ; 170
ἐκκλησία δ' οὐχὶ διὰ τοῦτον γίγνεται;
τί δέ; τὰς τριήρεις οὐ σὺ πληροῖς; εἰπέ μοι.

ᵃ An adulterer " caught " (ἁλούς) by the husband might be put
to death, and R. explains that the husband here is bribed to
content himself with the minor punishment of depilation (οὕτω γὰρ

And fair, and graceful, all is done for thee.
For every mortal thing subserves to Wealth.

CA. Hence for a little filthy lucre I'm
A slave, forsooth, because I've got no wealth.

CHR. And those Corinthian huzzies, so they say,
If he who sues them for their love is poor,
Turn up their noses at the man ; but grant
A wealthy suitor more than he desires.

CA. So too the boy-loves ; just to get some money,
And not at all because they love their lovers.

CHR. Those are the baser, not the nobler sort,
These never ask for money.

CA.   No ? what then ?

CHR. O one a hunter, one a pack of hounds.

CA. Ah, they're ashamed, I warrant, of their vice,
And seek to crust it over with a name.

CHR. And every art existing in the world,
And every craft, was for thy sake invented.
For thee one sits and cobbles all the day,
One works in bronze, another works in wood,
One fuses gold—the gold derived from thee—

CA. One plies the footpad's, one the burglar's trade,

CHR. One is a fuller, one a sheepskin-washer,
One is a tanner, one an onion-seller,
Through thee the nabbed adulterer gets off plucked.[a]

WE. O, and all this I never knew before !

CHR. Aye, 'tis on him the Great King plumes himself ;
And our Assemblies all are held for him ; [b]
Dost thou not man our triremes ?   Answer that.

τοὺς ἁλόντας μοιχοὺς ἤκιζον: Schol. on C. 1083). But more probably
παρατίλλεται is used here metaphorically ; the man is " plucked "
of his money.

[b] The Assembly had been neglected after the Peloponnesian
War ; but when the fee was raised to three obols the meetings
became crowded.

τὸ δ' ἐν Κορίνθῳ ξενικὸν οὐχ οὗτος τρέφει;
ὁ Πάμφιλος δ' οὐχὶ διὰ τοῦτον κλαύσεται;
ΚΑ. ὁ βελονοπώλης δ' οὐχὶ μετὰ τοῦ Παμφίλου;   175
Ἀγύρριος δ' οὐχὶ διὰ τοῦτον πέρδεται;
ΧΡ. Φιλέψιος δ' οὐχ ἕνεκα σοῦ μύθους λέγει;
ἡ ξυμμαχία δ' οὐ διὰ σὲ τοῖς Αἰγυπτίοις;
ἐρᾷ δὲ Λαῒς οὐ διὰ σὲ Φιλωνίδου;
ΚΑ. ὁ Τιμοθέου δὲ πύργος
ΧΡ.   ἐμπέσοι γέ σοι.   180
τὰ δὲ πράγματ' οὐχὶ διὰ σὲ πάντα πράττεται;
μονώτατος γὰρ εἶ σὺ πάντων αἴτιος,
καὶ τῶν κακῶν καὶ τῶν ἀγαθῶν, εὖ ἴσθ' ὅτι.
κρατοῦσι γοῦν κἂν τοῖς πολέμοις ἑκάστοτε
ἐφ' οἷς ἂν οὗτος ἐπικαθέζηται μόνον.   185
ΠΛ. ἐγὼ τοσαῦτα δυνατός εἰμ' εἷς ὢν ποιεῖν;
ΧΡ. καὶ ναὶ μὰ Δία τούτων γε πολλῷ πλείονα·
ὥστ' οὐδὲ μεστὸς σοῦ γέγον' οὐδεὶς πώποτε.
τῶν μὲν γὰρ ἄλλων ἐστὶ πάντων πλησμονή.
ἔρωτος
ΚΑ.   ἄρτων
ΧΡ.   μουσικῆς
ΚΑ.   τραγημάτων   190
ΧΡ. τιμῆς
ΚΑ.   πλακούντων
ΧΡ.   ἀνδραγαθίας
ΚΑ.   ἰσχάδων

---

a " This is the Foreign Legion, the mercenary force established by Conon at Corinth, 393 B.C., in connexion with the Anti-
Spartan League. It had recently distinguished itself, under the
command of Iphicrates, by the sensational destruction of a Spartan
mora " : R.

	Does he not feed the foreign troop [a] at Corinth ?
	Won't Pamphilus be brought to grief for him ?
CA.	Won't Pamphilus and the needle-seller [b] too ?
	Does not Agyrrhius flout us all for him ?
CHR.	Does not Philepsius tell his tales for thee ?
	Dost thou not make the Egyptians our allies ? [c]
	And Laïs love the uncouth Philonides [d] ?
CA.	Timotheus' tower [e]—
CHR.	Pray Heaven it fall and crush you !

Aye, everything that's done is done for thee.
Thou art alone, thyself alone, the source
Of all our fortunes, good and bad alike.
'Tis so in war ; wherever *he* alights,[f]
That side is safe the victory to win.

| WE. | Can I, unaided, do such feats as these ? |
| CHR. | O yes, by Zeus, and many more than these. |

So that none ever has enough of thee.
Of all things else a man may have too much,
Of love,

CA.	Of loaves,
CHR.	Of literature,
CA.	Of sweets,
CHR.	Of honour,
CA.	Cheesecakes,
CHR.	Manliness,
CA.	Dried figs,

[b] Pamphilus and Aristoxenus the needle-seller, a pair of dishonest demagogues whose goods were confiscated.

[c] Reference unknown ; but both Egyptians and Athenians were supporting Euagoras of Cyprus in his contest with the Persian empire.

[d] Philonides, a clumsy blockhead with a voice like the braying of a jackass. But being rich, he became the lover of Laïs the courtesan. *Cf.* 303 below.

[e] T., son of Conon, had lately inherited riches and built a tower.

[f] Sitting on the warrior's helm, like Victory.

ΧΡ. φιλοτιμίας
ΚΑ.   μάζης
ΧΡ.   στρατηγίας
ΚΑ.   φακῆς.
ΧΡ. σοῦ δ' ἐγένετ' οὐδεὶς μεστὸς οὐδεπώποτε.
   ἀλλ' ἢν τάλαντά τις λάβῃ τριακαίδεκα,
   πολὺ μᾶλλον ἐπιθυμεῖ λαβεῖν ἑκκαίδεκα·   195
   κἂν ταῦτ' ἀνύσηται, τετταράκοντα βούλεται,
   ἤ φησιν οὐ βιωτὸν αὑτῷ τὸν βίον.
ΠΛ. εὖ τοι λέγειν ἔμοιγε φαίνεσθον πάνυ·
   πλὴν ἓν μόνον δέδοικα.
ΧΡ.   φράζε τοῦ πέρι.
ΠΛ. ὅπως ἐγὼ τὴν δύναμιν ἣν ὑμεῖς φατὲ   200
   ἔχειν με, ταύτης δεσπότης γενήσομαι.
ΧΡ. νὴ τὸν Δί'· ἀλλὰ καὶ λέγουσι πάντες ὡς
   δειλότατόν ἐσθ' ὁ πλοῦτος.
ΠΛ.   ἥκιστ', ἀλλά με
   τοιχωρύχος τις διέβαλ'. εἰσδὺς γάρ ποτε
   οὐκ εἶχεν εἰς τὴν οἰκίαν οὐδὲν λαβεῖν,   205
   εὑρὼν ἁπαξάπαντα κατακεκλειμένα·
   εἶτ' ὠνόμασέ μου τὴν πρόνοιαν δειλίαν.
ΧΡ. μή νυν μελέτω σοι μηδέν· ὡς, ἐὰν γένῃ
   ἀνὴρ πρόθυμος αὐτὸς εἰς τὰ πράγματα,
   βλέποντ' ἀποδείξω σ' ὀξύτερον τοῦ Λυγκέως.   210
ΠΛ. πῶς οὖν δυνήσει τοῦτο δρᾶσαι θνητὸς ὤν;
ΧΡ. ἔχω τιν' ἀγαθὴν ἐλπίδ' ἐξ ὧν εἶπέ μοι
   ὁ Φοῖβος αὐτὸς Πυθικὴν σείσας δάφνην.
ΠΛ. κἀκεῖνος οὖν σύνοιδε ταῦτα;
ΧΡ.   φήμ' ἐγώ.
ΠΛ. ὁρᾶτε.
ΧΡ.   μὴ φρόντιζε μηδέν, ὠγαθέ.   215

CHR. Ambition,

CA.   Barley-meal,

CHR.   Command,

CA.   Pea soup.

CHR. But no man ever has enough of thee.
    For give a man a sum of thirteen talents,
    And all the more he hungers for sixteen ;
    Give him sixteen, and he must needs have forty
    Or life's not worth his living, so he says.

WE. Ye seem to me to speak extremely well,
    Yet on one point I'm fearful.

CHR.   What is that ?

WE. This mighty power which ye ascribe to me,
    I can't imagine how I'm going to wield it.

CHR. O this it is that all the people say,
    Wealth is the cowardliest thing.[a]

WE.   It is not true.
    That is some burglar's slander ; breaking into
    A wealthy house, he found that everything
    Was under lock and key, and so got nothing :
    Wherefore he called my forethought, cowardliness.

CHR. Well, never mind ; assist us in the work
    And play the man ; and very soon I'll make you
    Of keener sight than ever Lynceus [b] was.

WE. Why, how can you, a mortal man, do that ?

CHR. Good hope have I from that which Phoebus told me,
    Shaking the Pythian laurel as he spoke.

WE. Is Phoebus privy to your plan ?

CHR.   He is.

WE. Take heed !

CHR.   Don't fret yourself, my worthy friend.

---

[a] Eur. *Phoenissae*, 597 δειλὸν δ' ὁ πλοῦτος καὶ φιλόψυχον κακόν.

[b] The keen-eyed Argonaut, who could see into the bowels of the earth : Apoll. Rhod. i. 153 ὀξυτάτοις ἐκέκαστο ὄμμασιν.

ARISTOPHANES

ἐγὼ γάρ, εὖ τοῦτ' ἴσθι, κἄν με δέῃ θανεῖν,
αὐτὸς διαπράξω ταῦτα.

ΚΑ. κἂν βούλῃ γ', ἐγώ.

ΧΡ. πολλοὶ δ' ἔσονται χἄτεροι νῷν ξύμμαχοι,
ὅσοις δικαίοις οὖσιν οὐκ ἦν ἄλφιτα.

ΠΛ. παπαῖ, πονηρούς γ' εἶπας ἡμῖν συμμάχους. 220

ΧΡ. οὔκ, ἤν γε πλουτήσωσιν ἐξ ἀρχῆς πάλιν.
ἀλλ' ἴθι σὺ μὲν ταχέως δραμὼν

ΚΑ. τί δρῶ; λέγε.

ΧΡ. τοὺς ξυγγεώργους κάλεσον, εὑρήσεις δ' ἴσως
ἐν τοῖς ἀγροῖς αὐτοὺς ταλαιπωρουμένους,
ὅπως ἂν ἴσον ἕκαστος ἐνταυθὶ παρὼν 225
ἡμῖν μετάσχῃ τοῦδε τοῦ Πλούτου μέρος.

ΚΑ. καὶ δὴ βαδίζω· τοῦτο δὲ τὸ κρεάδιον
τῶν ἔνδοθέν τις εἰσενεγκάτω λαβών.

ΧΡ. ἐμοὶ μελήσει τοῦτό γ'· ἀλλ' ἀνύσας τρέχε.
σὺ δ', ὦ κράτιστε Πλοῦτε πάντων δαιμόνων, 230
εἴσω μετ' ἐμοῦ δεῦρ' εἴσιθ'· ἡ γὰρ οἰκία
αὕτη 'στὶν ἣν δεῖ χρημάτων σε τήμερον
μεστὴν ποιῆσαι καὶ δικαίως κἀδίκως.

ΠΛ. ἀλλ' ἄχθομαι μὲν εἰσιὼν νὴ τοὺς θεοὺς
εἰς οἰκίαν ἑκάστοτ' ἀλλοτρίαν πάνυ· 235
ἀγαθὸν γὰρ ἀπέλαυσ' οὐδὲν αὐτοῦ πώποτε.
ἢν μὲν γὰρ ὡς φειδωλὸν εἰσελθὼν τύχω,
εὐθὺς κατώρυξέν με κατὰ τῆς γῆς κάτω·
κἄν τις προσέλθῃ χρηστὸς ἄνθρωπος φίλος
αἰτῶν λαβεῖν τι μικρὸν ἀργυρίδιον, 240
ἔξαρνός ἐστι μηδ' ἰδεῖν με πώποτε.
ἢν δ' ὡς παράπληγ' ἄνθρωπον εἰσελθὼν τύχω,
πόρναισι καὶ κύβοισι παραβεβλημένος
γυμνὸς θύραζ' ἐξέπεσον ἐν ἀκαρεῖ χρόνῳ.

I am the man : I'll work the matter through,
Though I should die for it.

CA.   And so will I.

CHR. And many other bold allies will come,
Good virtuous men without a grain of—barley.[a]

WE. Bless me ! a set of rather poor allies.

CHR. Not when you've made them wealthy men once more.
Hi, Cario, run your fastest, and

CA.   Do what ?

CHR. Summon my farm-companions from the fields
(You'll find them there, poor fellows, hard at work),
And fetch them hither ; so that each and all
May have, with me, an equal share in Wealth.

CA. Here goes ! I'm off. Come out there, somebody,
And carry in my little piece of meat.[b]

CHR. I'll see to that : you, run away directly.
But thou, dear Wealth, the mightiest Power of all,
Come underneath my roof. Here stands the house,
Which thou art going evermore to fill
With wealth and plenty, by fair means or foul.

WE. And yet it irks me, I protest it does,
To enter in beneath a stranger's roof.
I never got the slightest good from that.
Was it a miser's house ; the miser straight
Would dig a hole and pop me underground ;
And if some worthy neighbour came to beg
A little silver for his urgent needs,
Would vow he'd never seen me in his life.
Or was it some young madcap's : in a jiffey
Squandered and lost amongst his drabs and dice
I'm bundled, naked, out of house and home.

    [a] *i.e.* possessing nothing. ἄλφιτα is introduced as a surprise;
Chremylus was expected to say " Men who have not a grain of fear."
    [b] " Which he was bringing back from the Delphian sacri-
fice " : R. *Exit Cario.*

ΧΡ. μετρίου γὰρ ἀνδρὸς οὐκ ἐπέτυχες πώποτε.   245
ἐγὼ δὲ τούτου τοῦ τρόπου πώς εἰμ' ἀεί.
χαίρω τε γὰρ φειδόμενος ὡς οὐδεὶς ἀνὴρ
πάλιν τ' ἀναλῶν, ἡνίκ' ἂν τούτου δέῃ.
ἀλλ' εἰσίωμεν, ὡς ἰδεῖν σε βούλομαι
καὶ τὴν γυναῖκα καὶ τὸν υἱὸν τὸν μόνον,   250
ὃν ἐγὼ φιλῶ μάλιστα μετὰ σέ.

ΠΛ.   πείθομαι.

ΧΡ. τί γὰρ ἄν τις οὐχὶ πρὸς σὲ τἀληθῆ λέγοι;

ΚΑ. ὦ πολλὰ δὴ τῷ δεσπότῃ ταὐτὸν θύμον φαγόντες,
ἄνδρες φίλοι καὶ δημόται καὶ τοῦ πονεῖν ἐρασταί,
ἴτ', ἐγκονεῖτε, σπεύδεθ', ὡς ὁ καιρὸς οὐχὶ μέλλειν, 255
ἀλλ' ἔστ' ἐπ' αὐτῆς τῆς ἀκμῆς, ᾗ δεῖ παρόντ' ἀμύνειν.

ΧΟΡΟΣ. οὔκουν ὁρᾷς ὁρμωμένους ἡμᾶς πάλαι προθύμως,
ὡς εἰκός ἐστιν ἀσθενεῖς γέροντας ἄνδρας ἤδη;
σὺ δ' ἀξιοῖς ἴσως με θεῖν, πρὶν ταῦτα καὶ φράσαι μοι
ὅτου χάριν μ' ὁ δεσπότης ὁ σὸς κέκληκε δεῦρο. 260

ΚΑ. οὔκουν πάλαι δήπου λέγω; σὺ δ' αὐτὸς οὐκ ἀκούεις.
ὁ δεσπότης γάρ φησιν ὑμᾶς ἡδέως ἅπαντας
ψυχροῦ βίου καὶ δυσκόλου ζήσειν ἀπαλλαγέντας.

ΧΟ. ἔστιν δὲ δὴ τί καὶ πόθεν τὸ πρᾶγμα τοῦθ' ὅ φησιν;

ᵃ Enter Cario with the chorus of needy agriculturists.

CHR. You never chanced upon a moderate man,
But now you have ; for such a man am I.
For much I joy in saving, no man more,
And much in spending when 'tis right to spend.
So go we in ; I long to introduce
My wife and only son whom most I love—
After yourself of course.

WE.   That I believe.

CHR. Why should one say what is not true to you ? *a*

CA. O ye who many a day have chewed
                          a root of thyme with master,
My labour-loving village-friends,
                          be pleased to step out faster ;
Be staunch and strong, and stride along,
                          let nothing now delay you,
Your fortunes lie upon the die,
                          come save them quick, I pray you.

CHORUS. Now don't you see we're bustling, we,
                          as fast as we can go, sir ?
We're not so young as once we were,
                          and Age is somewhat slow, sir.
You'd think it fun to see us run,
                          and that before you've told us
The reason why your master seems
                          so anxious to behold us.

CA. Why, I've been telling long ago ;
                          'tis you are not attending !
He bade me call and fetch you all
                          that you, for ever ending
This chill ungenial life of yours,
                          might lead a life luxurious.

CH. Explain to me how that can be ;
                          i' faith I'm rather curious

ARISTOPHANES

ΚΑ. ἔχων ἀφῖκται δεῦρο πρεσβύτην τιν’, ὦ πόνηροι,   265
ῥυπῶντα, κυφόν, ἄθλιον, ῥυσόν, μαδῶντα, νωδόν·
οἶμαι δὲ νὴ τὸν οὐρανὸν καὶ ψωλὸν αὐτὸν εἶναι.

ΧΟ. ὦ χρυσὸν ἀγγείλας ἐπῶν, πῶς φῄς; πάλιν φράσον
μοι.
δηλοῖς γὰρ αὐτὸν σωρὸν ἥκειν χρημάτων ἔχοντα.

ΚΑ. πρεσβυτικῶν μὲν οὖν κακῶν ἔγωγ’ ἔχοντα σωρόν.   270

ΧΟ. μῶν ἀξιοῖς φενακίσας ἡμᾶς ἀπαλλαγῆναι
ἀζήμιος, καὶ ταῦτ’ ἐμοῦ βακτηρίαν ἔχοντος;

ΚΑ. πάντως γὰρ ἄνθρωπον φύσει τοιοῦτον εἰς τὰ πάντα
ἡγεῖσθέ μ’ εἶναι κοὐδὲν ἂν νομίζεθ’ ὑγιὲς εἰπεῖν;

ΧΟ. ὡς σεμνὸς οὑπίτριπτος· αἱ κνῆμαι δέ σου βοῶσιν   275
ἰοὺ ἰού, τὰς χοίνικας καὶ τὰς πέδας ποθοῦσαι.

ΚΑ. ἐν τῇ σορῷ νυνὶ λαχὸν τὸ γράμμα σου δικάζειν,
σὺ δ’ οὐ βαδίζεις; ὁ δὲ Χάρων τὸ ξύμβολον δίδωσιν.

ΧΟ. διαρραγείης. ὡς μόθων εἶ καὶ φύσει κόβαλος,
ὅστις φενακίζεις, φράσαι δ’ οὔπω τέτληκας ἡμῖν   280
ὅτου χάριν μ’ ὁ δεσπότης ὁ σὸς κέκληκε δεῦρο·

CA. He's got a man, an ancient man,
      of sorriest form and feature,
Bald, toothless, squalid, wrinkled, bent,
      a very loathsome creature.
I really should not be surprised
     to hear the wretch is circumcised.

CH. O Messenger of golden news,
     you thrill my heart with pleasure.
I do believe the man has come
     with quite a heap of treasure !

CA. O aye, he's got a heap, I guess,
     a heap of woes and wretchedness.

CH. You think, I see, you think you're free
      to gull me with impunity.
No, no ; my stick I've got and quick
      I'll get my opportunity.

CA. What, think you I'm the sort of man
     such things as that to do, sirs ?
Am I the man a tale to tell
     wherein there's nothing true, sirs ?

CH. How absolute the knave has grown !
      your shins, my boy, are bawling
Ah ! Ah ! with all their might and main,
      for gyves and fetters calling.

CA. You've drawn your lot ; *a* the grave you've got
     to judge in ; why delay now ?
Old Charon gives the ticket there ;
     why don't you pass away now ?

CH. Go hang yourself, you peevish elf,
     you born buffoon and scoffer.
You love to tantalize and tease,
      nor condescend to offer
A word of explanation why
     we're summoned here so hurriedly.

ARISTOPHANES

οἳ πολλὰ μοχθήσαντες, οὐκ οὔσης σχολῆς, προθύμως
δεῦρ' ἤλθομεν, πολλῶν θύμων ῥίζας διεκπερῶντες.

ΚΑ. ἀλλ' οὐκέτ' ἂν κρύψαιμι. τὸν Πλοῦτον γάρ, ὦνδρες,
ἥκει
ἄγων ὁ δεσπότης, ὃς ὑμᾶς πλουσίους ποιήσει.   285

ΧΟ. ὄντως γὰρ ἔστι πλουσίοις ἡμῖν ἅπασιν εἶναι;

ΚΑ. νὴ τοὺς θεούς, Μίδαις μὲν οὖν, ἢν ὦτ' ὄνου λάβητε.

ΧΟ. ὡς ἥδομαι καὶ τέρπομαι καὶ βούλομαι χορεῦσαι
ὑφ' ἡδονῆς, εἴπερ λέγεις ὄντως σὺ ταῦτ' ἀληθῆ.

ΚΑ. καὶ μὴν ἐγὼ βουλήσομαι θρεττανελὸ τὸν Κύκλωπα   290
μιμούμενος καὶ τοῖν ποδοῖν ὡδὶ παρενσαλεύων
ὑμᾶς ἄγειν. ἀλλ' εἶα, τέκεα, θαμίν' ἐπαναβοῶντες
βληχώμενοί τε προβατίων
αἰγῶν τε κιναβρώντων μέλη,
ἔπεσθ' ἀπεψωλημένοι· τράγοι δ' ἀκρατιεῖσθε.   295

ΧΟ. ἡμεῖς δέ γ' αὖ ζητήσομεν θρεττανελὸ τὸν Κύκλωπα
βληχώμενοι, σὲ τουτονὶ πινῶντα καταλαβόντες,
πήραν ἔχοντα λάχανά τ' ἄγρια δροσερά, κραι-
παλῶντα,
ἡγούμενον τοῖς προβατίοις,
εἰκῇ δὲ καταδαρθόντα που,   300

---

^a ἀλλ' εἶα . . . ἐπαναβοῶντες and the word, θρεττανελό come
from the *Loves of Galatea and Cyclops* by Philoxenus of Cythera:
Schol. The Cyclops was shown bearing a wallet and herbs
(298). In 299-301, the Chorus promise to treat Cario as Odysseus
did the Cyclops. For the Cyclops dance see Horace, *Sat.* i. 5. 13,
Ep. ii. 2. 124.

^b "The passage may be rendered, 'And verily I, acting the
Cyclops, tralalala, and capering with both my feet, like this, will
go before and lead you on. But hey! my little ones, keeping up
an incessant clamour, and bleating forth the cries of sheep and
malodorous goats, follow after me; and you, ye he-goats, shall
have your breakfast'" : R.

388

I had to shirk some urgent work,
               and here so quickly hasted,
That many a tempting root of thyme
               I passed, and left untasted.

CA. I'll hide it not : 'tis Wealth we've got ;
               the God of wealth we've captured,
You'll all be rich and wealthy now.
               Ha, don't you look enraptured ?

CH. He says we'll all be wealthy now ;
               upon my word this passes, sirs.

CA. O yes, you'll all be Midases,
               if only you've the asses' ears.

CH. O I'm so happy, I'm so glad,
               I needs must dance for jollity,
If what you say is really true,
               and not your own frivolity

CA. And I before your ranks will go,
               Threttanelo ! Threttanelo !
And I, the Cyclops, heel and toe,
               will dance the sailor's hornpipe,—so !
Come up, come up, my little ones all,
               come raise your multitudinous squall,[a]
Come bleating loudly the tuneful notes
Of sheep and of rankly-odorous goats.
Come follow along on your loves intent ;
               come goats, 'tis time to your meal ye went.[b]

CH. And you we'll seek where'er you go,
               Threttanelo ! Threttanelo !
And you, the Cyclops, will we find
               in dirty, drunken sleep reclined,
Your well-stuffed wallet beside you too,
               with many a potherb bathed in dew.
And then from out of the fire we'll take

μέγαν λαβόντες ἠμμένον σφηκίσκον ἐκτυφλῶσαι.

ΚΑ. ἐγὼ δὲ τὴν Κίρκην γε τὴν τὰ φάρμακ' ἀνακυκῶσαν,
ἣ τοὺς ἑταίρους τοῦ Φιλωνίδου ποτ' ἐν Κορίνθῳ
ἔπεισεν ὡς ὄντας κάπρους
μεμαγμένον σκῶρ ἐσθίειν, αὐτὴ δ' ἔματτεν αὐτοῖς, 305
μιμήσομαι πάντας τρόπους·
ὑμεῖς δὲ γρυλίζοντες ὑπὸ φιληδίας
ἕπεσθε μητρὶ χοῖροι.

ΧΟ. οὐκοῦν σὲ τὴν Κίρκην γε τὴν τὰ φάρμακ' ἀνακυκῶσαν
καὶ μαγγανεύουσαν μολύνουσάν τε τοὺς ἑταίρους, 310
λαβόντες ὑπὸ φιληδίας
τὸν Λαρτίου μιμούμενοι τῶν ὄρχεων κρεμῶμεν,
μινθώσομέν θ' ὥσπερ τράγου
τὴν ῥῖνα· σὺ δ' Ἀρίστυλλος ὑποχάσκων ἐρεῖς·
ἕπεσθε μητρὶ χοῖροι. 315

ΚΑ. ἀλλ' εἶα νῦν τῶν σκωμμάτων ἀπαλλαγέντες ἤδη
ὑμεῖς ἐπ' ἄλλ' εἶδος τρέπεσθ',
ἐγὼ δ' ἰὼν ἤδη λάθρα
βουλήσομαι τοῦ δεσπότου
λαβών τιν' ἄρτον καὶ κρέας 320
μασώμενος τὸ λοιπὸν οὕτω τῷ κόπῳ ξυνεῖναι.

---

[a] See above, 179. It was Philonides himself whom Laïs transformed; but Cario speaks of his comrades, because Circe in the story had transformed the comrades of Odysseus.

[b] "Instead of saying we will draw the sword upon you, as Odysseus did with Circe, he transfers to Circe what Odysseus did to Melanthius": Schol. He was hung up, hands and feet made fast to a board behind him. Cf. Homer, Od. xxii. 178.

[c] Cf. E. 647.

[d] Exit Cario to get his bread and meat; enter Chremylus. His speech, and the answer, obviously parody some well-known passage.

A sharply-pointed and burning stake,
And whirling it round till our shoulders ache,
   its flame in your hissing eyeball slake.

CA. And now I'll change to Circe's part,
    who mixed her drugs with baleful art ;
 Who late in Corinth, as I've learned,
    Philonides's comrades turned
 To loathsome swine in a loathsome sty,[a]
And fed them all on kneaded dung
  which, kneading, she amongst them flung.
And turn you all into swine will I.
And then ye'll grunt in your bestial glee
  Wee ! wee ! wee !
Follow your mother, pigs, quoth she.

CH. We'll catch you, Circe dear, we will ;
    who mix your drugs with baleful skill ;
 Who with enchantments strange and vile
    ensnare our comrades and defile ;
 We'll hang you up as you erst were hung
By bold Odysseus,[b] lady fair ;
    and then as if a goat you were
We'll rub your nose in the kneaded dung.
Like Aristyllus[c] you'll gape with glee
  Wee ! wee ! wee !
Follow your mother, pigs, quoth he.

CA. But now, old mates, break off, break off ;
    no longer may we jest and scoff ;
 No longer play the fool to-day.
 And ye must sail on another tack,
 Whilst I, behind my master's back,
 Rummage for meat and bread to eat,
And then, whilst yet the food I chew,
    I'll join the work we are going to do.[d]

ΧΡ. χαίρειν μὲν ὑμᾶς ἐστιν, ὦνδρες δημόται,
ἀρχαῖον ἤδη προσαγορεύειν καὶ σαπρόν·
ἀσπάζομαι δ᾽, ὁτιὴ προθύμως ἤκετε
καὶ συντεταμένως κοὐ κατεβλακευμένως.   325
ὅπως δέ μοι καὶ τἄλλα συμπαραστάται
ἔσεσθε καὶ σωτῆρες ὄντως τοῦ θεοῦ.

ΧΟ. θάρρει· βλέπειν γὰρ ἄντικρυς δόξεις μ᾽ Ἄρη.
δεινὸν γὰρ εἰ τριωβόλου μὲν εἵνεκα
ὠστιζόμεσθ᾽ ἑκάστοτ᾽ ἐν τἠκκλησίᾳ,   330
αὐτὸν δὲ τὸν Πλοῦτον παρείην τῳ λαβεῖν.

ΧΡ. καὶ μὴν ὁρῶ καὶ Βλεψίδημον τουτονὶ
προσιόντα· δῆλος δ᾽ ἐστὶν ὅτι τοῦ πράγματος
ἀκήκοέν τι τῇ βαδίσει καὶ τῷ τάχει.

ΒΛΕΨΙΔ. τί ἂν οὖν τὸ πρᾶγμ᾽ εἴη; πόθεν καὶ τίνι τρόπῳ 335
Χρεμύλος πεπλούτηκ᾽ ἐξαπίνης; οὐ πείθομαι.
καίτοι λόγος γ᾽ ἦν νὴ τὸν Ἡρακλέα πολὺς
ἐπὶ τοῖσι κουρείοισι τῶν καθημένων,
ὡς ἐξαπίνης ἀνὴρ γεγένηται πλούσιος.
ἔστιν δέ μοι τοῦτ᾽ αὐτὸ θαυμάσιον, ὅπως   340
χρηστόν τι πράττων τοὺς φίλους μεταπέμπεται.
οὔκουν ἐπιχώριόν γε πρᾶγμ᾽ ἐργάζεται.

ΧΡ. ἀλλ᾽ οὐδὲν ἀποκρύψας ἐρῶ νὴ τοὺς θεούς.
ὦ Βλεψίδημ᾽, ἄμεινον ἢ χθὲς πράττομεν,
ὥστε μετέχειν ἔξεστιν· εἶ γὰρ τῶν φίλων.   345

ΒΛ. γέγονας δ᾽ ἀληθῶς, ὡς λέγουσι, πλούσιος;

ΧΡ. ἔσομαι μὲν οὖν αὐτίκα μάλ᾽, ἢν θεὸς θέλῃ.
ἔνι γάρ τις, ἔνι κίνδυνος ἐν τῷ πράγματι.

ΒΛ. ποῖός τις;

ΧΡ.   οἷος,

ΒΛ.   λέγ᾽ ἀνύσας ὅ τι φῄς ποτε.

ΧΡ. ἢν μὲν κατορθώσωμεν, εὖ πράττειν ἀεί·   350
ἢν δὲ σφαλῶμεν, ἐπιτετρίφθαι τὸ παράπαν.

392

CHR. To bid you " welcome," fellow-burghers, now
Is old and musty ; so I—" clasp " you all.
Ye who have come in this stout-hearted way,
This strenuous way, this unrelaxing way,
Stand by me now, and prove yourselves to-day
In very truth the Saviours of the God.

CH. Fear not : I'll bear me like the God of War.
What, shall we push and hustle in the Assembly
To gain our three poor obols, and to-day
Let Wealth himself be wrested from our grasp ?

CHR. And here, I see, comes Blepsidemus too.
Look ! by his speed and bearing you can tell
He has heard a rumour of what's happening here.ᵃ

BLEPSIDEMUS. What can it mean ? Old Chremylus grown
wealthy !
Then whence and how ? I don't believe that story.
And yet by Heracles 'twas bruited wide
Amongst the loungers in the barbers' shops
That Chremylus had all at once grown rich.
And if he has, 'tis passing wonderful
That he should call his neighbours in to share.
That's not our country's fashion, anyhow.

CHR. I'll tell him everything. O Blepsidemus,
We're better off to-day than yesterday.
You are my friend, and you shall share in all.

BL. What, are you really wealthy, as men say ?

CHR. Well, if God will, I shall be presently.
But there's some risk, some risk, about it yet.

BL. What sort of risk ?

CHR.   Such as—

BL.   Pray, pray go on.

CHR. If we succeed, we're prosperous all our lives :
But if we fail, we perish utterly.

ᵃ *Enter Blepsidemus.*

393

ΒΛ. τουτὶ πονηρὸν φαίνεται τὸ φορτίον,
    καί μ' οὐκ ἀρέσκει. τό τε γὰρ ἐξαίφνης ἄγαν
    οὕτως ὑπερπλουτεῖν τό τ' αὖ δεδοικέναι
    πρὸς ἀνδρὸς οὐδὲν ὑγιές ἐστ' εἰργασμένου.   **355**
ΧΡ. πῶς οὐδὲν ὑγιές;
ΒΛ.   εἴ τι κεκλοφὼς νὴ Δία
    ἐκεῖθεν ἥκεις ἀργύριον ἢ χρυσίον
    παρὰ τοῦ θεοῦ, κἄπειτ' ἴσως σοι μεταμέλει.
ΧΡ. Ἄπολλον ἀποτρόπαιε, μὰ Δί' ἐγὼ μὲν οὔ.
ΒΛ. παῦσαι φλυαρῶν, ὠγάθ'· οἶδα γὰρ σαφῶς.   **360**
ΧΡ. σὺ μηδὲν εἰς ἔμ' ὑπονόει τοιοῦτο.
ΒΛ.   φεῦ.
    ὡς οὐδὲν ἀτεχνῶς ὑγιές ἐστιν οὐδενός,
    ἀλλ' εἰσὶ τοῦ κέρδους ἅπαντες ἥττονες.
ΧΡ. οὔ τοι μὰ τὴν Δήμητρ' ὑγιαίνειν μοι δοκεῖς.
ΒΛ. ὡς πολὺ μεθέστηχ' ὧν πρότερον εἶχεν τρόπων.   **365**
ΧΡ. μελαγχολᾷς, ὤνθρωπε, νὴ τὸν οὐρανόν.
ΒΛ. ἀλλ' οὐδὲ τὸ βλέμμ' αὐτὸ κατὰ χώραν ἔχει,
    ἀλλ' ἐστὶν ἐπίδηλόν τι πεπανουργηκότος.
ΧΡ. σὺ μὲν οἶδ' ὃ κρώζεις· ὡς ἐμοῦ τι κεκλοφότος
    ζητεῖς μεταλαβεῖν.
ΒΛ.   μεταλαβεῖν ζητῶ; τίνος;   **370**
ΧΡ. τὸ δ' ἐστὶν οὐ τοιοῦτον, ἀλλ' ἑτέρως ἔχον.
ΒΛ. μῶν οὐ κέκλοφας, ἀλλ' ἥρπακας;
ΧΡ.   κακοδαιμονᾷς.
ΒΛ. ἀλλ' οὐδὲ μὴν ἀπεστέρηκάς γ' οὐδένα;
ΧΡ. οὐ δῆτ' ἔγωγ'.
ΒΛ.   ὦ Ἡράκλεις, φέρε, ποῖ τις ἂν
    τράποιτο; τἀληθὲς γὰρ οὐκ ἐθέλεις φράσαι.   **375**

---

[a] Eur. *Danaë*, fr. 325 κρείσσων γὰρ οὐδεὶς χρημάτων πέφυκ' ἀνήρ.
[b] " The three forms of theft here enumerated, κλοπή *furtum*,

BL.   I like not this ; there's something wrong behind,
      Some evil venture. To become, off-hand,
      So over-wealthy, and to fear such risks,
      Smacks of a man who has done some rotten thing.

CHR.   Rotten ! what mean you ?

BL.   If you've stolen aught,
      Or gold or silver, from the God out there,
      And now perchance repent you of your sin,—

CHR.   Apollo shield us ! no, I've not done that.

BL.   O don't tell *me*. I see it plainly now.

CHR.   Pray don't suspect me of such crimes.

BL.   Alas !
      There's nothing sound or honest in the world,
      The love of money overcomes us all.[a]

CHR.   Now by Demeter, friend, you have lost your wits.

BL.   O how unlike the man he used to be !

CHR.   Poor chap, you're moody-mad : I vow you are.

BL.   His very eye's grown shifty : he can't look you
      Straight in the face : I warrant he's turned rogue.

CHR.   I understand. You think I've stolen something,
      And want a share.

BL.   I want a share ? in what ?

CHR.   But 'tis not so : the thing's quite otherwise.

BL.   Not stol'n, but robbed outright ?

CHR.   The man's possessed.

BL.   Have you embezzled someone else's cash ? [b]

CHR.   I haven't : no.

BL.   O Heracles, where now
      Can a man turn ! you won't confess the truth.

simple larceny, ἁρπαγή *latrocinium*, robbery with violence, and
ἀποστέρησις *depositum negare*, embezzlement, are known to all
systems of jurisprudence, though all sometimes comprised under
the generic name *furtum*. ἀποστέρησις differs from the other
two in the circumstance that the money was not *obtained*, but
merely *withheld*, by fraud " : R.

ΧΡ. κατηγορεῖς γὰρ πρὶν μαθεῖν τὸ πρᾶγμά μου.

ΒΛ. ὦ τᾶν, ἐγώ τοι τοῦτ' ἀπὸ σμικροῦ πάνυ
    ἐθέλω διαπρᾶξαι πρὶν πυθέσθαι τὴν πόλιν,
    τὸ στόμ' ἐπιβύσας κέρμασιν τῶν ῥητόρων.

ΧΡ. καὶ μὴν φίλος γ' ἄν μοι δοκεῖς νὴ τοὺς θεοὺς   380
    τρεῖς μνᾶς ἀναλώσας λογίσασθαι δώδεκα.

ΒΛ. ὁρῶ τιν' ἐπὶ τοῦ βήματος καθεδούμενον,
    ἱκετηρίαν ἔχοντα μετὰ τῶν παιδίων
    καὶ τῆς γυναικός, κοὐ διοίσοντ' ἄντικρυς
    τῶν Ἡρακλειδῶν οὐδ' ὁτιοῦν τῶν Παμφίλου.   385

ΧΡ. οὔκ, ὦ κακόδαιμον, ἀλλὰ τοὺς χρηστοὺς μόνους
    ἔγωγε καὶ τοὺς δεξιοὺς καὶ σώφρονας
    ἀπαρτὶ πλουτῆσαι ποιήσω.

ΒΛ.   τί σὺ λέγεις;
    οὕτω πάνυ πολλὰ κέκλοφας;

ΧΡ.   οἴμοι τῶν κακῶν,
    ἀπολεῖς.

ΒΛ.   σὺ μὲν οὖν σεαυτόν, ὥς γ' ἐμοὶ δοκεῖς.   390

ΧΡ. οὐ δῆτ', ἐπεὶ τὸν Πλοῦτον, ὦ μόχθηρε σύ,
    ἔχω.

ΒΛ.   σὺ Πλοῦτον; ποῖον;

ΧΡ.   αὐτὸν τὸν θεόν.

ΒΛ. καὶ ποῦ 'στιν;

ΧΡ.   ἔνδον.

ΒΛ.   ποῦ;

ΧΡ.   παρ' ἐμοί.

ΒΛ.   παρὰ σοί;

---

[a] To pay the speakers three minas, and to declare that he had paid twelve.

[b] "Blepsidemus pretends to see in the near future a culprit (Chremylus) pleading for mercy before a hostile tribunal. He is seated in the raised box set apart for the defendant, and with him are his weeping wife and children brought in to move the pity of

CHR. You bring your charge before you have heard the
    facts.

BL. Now prithee let me hush the matter up
    For a mere trifle, ere it all leaks out.
    A few small coins will stop the speakers' mouths.

CHR. You'd like, I warrant, in your friendly way,
    To spend three minas, and to charge me twelve.[a]

BL.[b] I see an old man pleading for his life
    With olive-branch in hand, and at his side
    His weeping wife and children, shrewdly like
    The suppliant Heracleids of Pamphilus.

CHR. Nay, luckless idiot, 'tis the good alone
    And right- and sober-minded that I'm going
    At once to make so wealthy.

BL.   Heaven and earth !
    What, have you stol'n so largely ?

CHR.   O confound it,
    You'll be my death.

BL.   You'll be your own, I fancy.

CHR. Not so, you reprobate ; 'tis WEALTH I've got.

BL. You, Wealth ! What sort of wealth ?

CHR.   The God himself.

BL. Where ? where ?

CHR.   Within.

BL.   Where ?

CHR.   In my house.

BL.   In yours ?

the Court; see *W.* 568, 976. Probably they all are supposed to be
holding out the olive-branch enwreathed with wool which was the
symbol of supplication ; ἱκετηρία· κλάδος ἐλαίας ἐρίῳ πεπλεγμένος:
Scholiast. The piteous little group which the imagination of
Blepsidemus has conjured up remind him of nothing so much as
the Heracleidae in a painting by Pamphilus. These would doubtless be Iolaus with Alcmena and her grandchildren (the children of
her dead son Heracles) supplicating the King of Athens to protect
them from the emissaries of Eurystheus " : R.

ΧΡ. πάνυ.

ΒΛ. οὐκ ἐς κόρακας; Πλοῦτος παρὰ σοί;

ΧΡ. νὴ τοὺς θεούς.

ΒΛ. λέγεις ἀληθῆ;

ΧΡ. φημί.

ΒΛ. πρὸς τῆς Ἑστίας; 395

ΧΡ. νὴ τὸν Ποσειδῶ.

ΒΛ. τὸν θαλάττιον λέγεις;

ΧΡ. εἰ δ' ἔστιν ἕτερός τις Ποσειδῶν, τὸν ἕτερον.

ΒΛ. εἶτ' οὐ διαπέμπεις καὶ πρὸς ἡμᾶς τοὺς φίλους;

ΧΡ. οὐκ ἔστι πω τὰ πράγματ' ἐν τούτῳ.

ΒΛ. τί φῄς;
οὐ τῷ μεταδοῦναι;

ΧΡ. μὰ Δία. δεῖ γὰρ πρῶτα

ΒΛ. τί; 400

ΧΡ. βλέψαι ποιῆσαι νὼ

ΒΛ. τίνα βλέψαι; φράσον.

ΧΡ. τὸν Πλοῦτον ὥσπερ πρότερον ἑνί γέ τῳ τρόπῳ.

ΒΛ. τυφλὸς γὰρ ὄντως ἐστί;

ΧΡ. νὴ τὸν οὐρανόν.

ΒΛ. οὐκ ἐτὸς ἄρ' ὡς ἔμ' ἦλθεν οὐδεπώποτε.

ΧΡ. ἀλλ' ἢν θεοὶ θέλωσι, νῦν ἀφίξεται. 405

ΒΛ. οὔκουν ἰατρὸν εἰσαγαγεῖν ἐχρῆν τινά;

ΧΡ. τίς δῆτ' ἰατρός ἐστι νῦν ἐν τῇ πόλει;
οὔτε γὰρ ὁ μισθὸς οὐδὲν ἔστ' οὔθ' ἡ τέχνη.

ΒΛ. σκοπῶμεν.

ΧΡ. ἀλλ' οὐκ ἔστιν.

ΒΛ. οὐδ' ἐμοὶ δοκεῖ.

ΧΡ. μὰ Δί', ἀλλ' ὅπερ πάλαι παρεσκευαζόμην 410
ἐγώ, κατακλίνειν αὐτὸν εἰς Ἀσκληπιοῦ
κράτιστόν ἐστι.

CHR. Yes.

BL. You be hanged ! Wealth in your house ?

CHR. I swear it.

BL. Is this the truth ?

CHR. It is.

BL. By Hestia ? [a]

CHR. Aye ; by Poseidon.

BL. Him that rules the sea ?

CHR. If there's another, by that other too.

BL. Then don't you send him round for friends to share ?

CHR. Not yet ; things haven't reached that stage.

BL. What stage ?
The stage of sharing ?

CHR. Aye, we've first to—

BL. What ?

CHR. Restore the sight—

BL. Restore the sight of whom ?

CHR. The sight of Wealth, by any means we can.

BL. What, is he really blind ?

CHR. He really is.

BL. O that is why he never came to me.

CHR. But now he'll come, if such the will of Heaven.

BL. Had we not better call a doctor in ?

CHR. Is there a doctor now in all the town ?
There are no fees, and therefore there's no skill. [b]

BL. Let's think awhile.

CHR. There's none.

BL. No more there is.

CHR. Why then, 'tis best to do what I intended,
To let him lie inside Asclepius' temple [c]
A whole night long.

    [a] *i.e.* I ask you, in Hestia's name, are you telling the truth ?
    [b] Allusion unknown.
    [c] Whether that which was in Athens, at the foot of the Acropolis, or that of Aegina, or another, is not made clear.

399

ARISTOPHANES

ΒΛ.   πολὺ μὲν οὖν νὴ τοὺς θεούς.
μή νυν διάτριβ', ἀλλ' ἄνυε πράττων ἔν γέ τι.

ΧΡ. καὶ δὴ βαδίζω.

ΒΛ.   σπεῦδέ νυν.

ΧΡ.   τοῦτ' αὐτὸ δρῶ.

ΠΕΝΙΑ. ὦ θερμὸν ἔργον κἀνόσιον καὶ παράνομον   **415**
τολμῶντε δρᾶν ἀνθρωπαρίω κακοδαίμονε,
ποῖ ποῖ; τί φεύγετον; οὐ μενεῖτον;

ΒΛ.   Ἡράκλεις.

ΠΕ. ἐγὼ γὰρ ὑμᾶς ἐξολῶ κακοὺς κακῶς·
τόλμημα γὰρ τολμᾶτον οὐκ ἀνασχετόν,
ἀλλ' οἷον οὐδεὶς ἄλλος οὐδεπώποτε   **420**
οὔτε θεὸς οὔτ' ἄνθρωπος· ὥστ' ἀπολώλατον.

ΧΡ. σὺ δ' εἶ τίς; ὠχρὰ μὲν γὰρ εἶναί μοι δοκεῖς.

ΒΛ. ἴσως Ἐρινύς ἐστιν ἐκ τραγῳδίας·
βλέπει γέ τοι μανικόν τι καὶ τραγῳδικόν.

ΧΡ. ἀλλ' οὐκ ἔχει γὰρ δᾷδας.

ΒΛ.   οὐκοῦν κλαύσεται.   **425**

ΠΕ. οἴεσθε δ' εἶναι τίνα με;

ΧΡ.   πανδοκεύτριαν,
ἢ λεκιθόπωλιν. οὐ γὰρ ἂν τοσουτονὶ
ἐνέκραγες ἡμῖν οὐδὲν ἠδικημένη.

ΠΕ. ἄληθες; οὐ γὰρ δεινότατα δεδράκατον,
ζητοῦντες ἐκ πάσης με χώρας ἐκβαλεῖν;   **430**

ᵃ Enter Poverty, a wild-looking woman.

ᵇ " What is the meaning of this ? There has not been a syllable
in the play to justify the charge. No one has thought of expelling
Poverty from Hellas. Yet the men do not deny the charge she
brings. It is admitted ; and becomes the basis of the ensuing
discussion. The fact is that Aristophanes is quietly introducing—
so quietly that it seems to have escaped the notice of every Scholiast
and commentator—an entirely new idea; an idea which dominates

BL.   That's far the best, I swear it.
        So don't be dawdling : quick ; get something done.
CHR.   I'm going.
BL.   Make you haste.
CHR.   I'm doing that.ᵃ
POVERTY. You pair of luckless manikins who dare
        A rash, unholy, lawless deed to do—
        Where ! What ! Why flee ye ? Tarry ?
BL.   Heracles !
POV.   I'll make you die a miserable death.
        For ye have dared a deed intolerable
        Which no one else has ever dared to do,
        Or God or man ! Now therefore ye must die.
CHR.   But who are you that look so pale and wan ?
BL.   Belike some Fury from a tragic play.
        She has a wild and tragic sort of look.
CHR.   No, for she bears no torch.
BL.   The worse for her.
POV.   What do you take me for ?
CHR.   Some pot-house girl
        Or omelette-seller : else you would not bawl
        At us so loudly ere you're harmed at all.
POV.   Not harmed ! Why, is it not a shameful thing
        That you should seek to drive me from the land ? ᵇ

the controversy between Poverty and the two friends, and then
disappears as suddenly as it came, only making its reappearance in
the concluding scene of the play.   He is looking forward to the
second stage of the Revolution he is engineering.   When all good
men are rich, and all bad men are poor, the bad will begin to see
the advantages of virtue, and finding that honesty is the best
policy will themselves become good and, as a consequence,
wealthy.   Thus at length all will be rich (*infra* 1178), and none
will be poor ; and Poverty will be banished out of the land.   *She*
will disappear, because wickedness will disappear, and Wealth will
make πάντας χρηστοὺς καὶ πλουτοῦντας δήπου τά τε θεῖα σέβοντας,
infra 497, a line which furnishes the key to the enigma " : R.

ARISTOPHANES

ΧΡ. οὔκουν ὑπόλοιπον τὸ βάραθρόν σοι γίγνεται;
ἀλλ' ἥτις εἶ λέγειν σ' ἐχρῆν αὐτίκα μάλα.

ΠΕ. ἢ σφὼ ποιήσω τήμερον δοῦναι δίκην
ἀνθ' ὧν ἐμὲ ζητεῖτον ἐνθένδ' ἀφανίσαι.

ΒΛ. ἆρ' ἐστὶν ἡ καπηλὶς ἡ 'κ τῶν γειτόνων,   435
ἢ ταῖς κοτύλαις ἀεί με διαλυμαίνεται;

ΠΕ. Πενία μὲν οὖν, ἢ σφῶν ξυνοικῶ πόλλ' ἔτη.

ΒΛ. ἄναξ Ἄπολλον καὶ θεοί, ποῖ τις φύγῃ;

ΧΡ. οὗτος, τί δρᾷς; ὦ δειλότατον σὺ θηρίον,
οὐ παραμενεῖς;

ΒΛ.   ἥκιστα πάντων.

ΧΡ.   οὐ μενεῖς;   440
ἀλλ' ἄνδρε δύο γυναῖκα φεύγομεν μίαν;

ΒΛ. Πενία γάρ ἐστιν, ὦ πόνηρ', ἧς οὐδαμοῦ
οὐδὲν πέφυκε ζῷον ἐξωλέστερον.

ΧΡ. στῆθ', ἀντιβολῶ σε, στῆθι.

ΒΛ.   μὰ Δί' ἐγὼ μὲν οὔ.

ΧΡ. καὶ μὴν λέγω, δειλότατον ἔργον παρὰ πολὺ   445
ἔργων ἁπάντων ἐργασόμεθ', εἰ τὸν θεὸν
ἔρημον ἀπολιπόντε ποι φευξούμεθα
τηνδὶ δεδιότε, μηδὲ διαμαχούμεθα.

ΒΛ. ποίοις ὅπλοισιν ἢ δυνάμει πεποιθότες;
ποῖον γὰρ οὐ θώρακα, ποίαν δ' ἀσπίδα   450
οὐκ ἐνέχυρον τίθησιν ἡ μιαρωτάτη;

ΧΡ. θάρρει· μόνος γὰρ ὁ θεὸς οὗτος οἶδ' ὅτι
τροπαῖον ἂν στήσαιτο τῶν ταύτης τρόπων.

ΠΕ. γρύζειν δὲ καὶ τολμᾶτον, ὦ καθάρματε,
ἐπ' αὐτοφώρῳ δεινὰ δρῶντ' εἰλημμένω;   455

ΧΡ. σὺ δ', ὦ κάκιστ' ἀπολουμένη, τί λοιδορεῖ

ᵃ A pit or chasm at Athens into which criminals' bodies were
thrown. See F. 574.

ᵇ " The advent of Wealth will at once discomfit Poverty and all

CHR. At all events you've got the Deadman's Pit.[a]
But tell us quickly who and what you are.

POV. One who is going to pay you out to-day
Because ye seek to banish me from hence.

BL. Is it the barmaid from the neighbouring tap
Who always cheats me with her swindling pint-pots?

POV. It's POVERTY, your mate for many a year!

BL. O King Apollo and ye Gods, I'm off.

CHR. Hi! What are you at? Stop, stop, you coward you,
Stop, can't you?

BL.   Anything but that.

CHR.   Pray stop.
What! shall one woman scare away two men?

BL. But this is Poverty herself, you rogue,
The most destructive pest in all the world.

CHR. Stay, I implore you, stay.

BL.   Not I, by Zeus.

CHR. Why, this, I tell you, were the cowardliest deed
That e'er was heard of, did we leave the God
Deserted here, and flee away ourselves
Too scared to strike one blow in his defence.

BL. O, on what arms, what force, can we rely?
Is there a shield, a corslet, anywhere
Which this vile creature has not put in pawn?

CHR. Courage! the God will, single-handed, rear
A trophy o'er this atrophied assailant.[b]

POV. What! dare you mutter, you two outcasts[c] you,
Caught in the act, doing such dreadful deeds?

CHR. O, you accursed jade, why come you here

her ways, τρόπων: not a very apt word but introduced for the sake
of the pun with τροπαῖον": R.

[c] κάθαρμα, "cleansings," that which is thrown away, is "the
designation of the two human victims, doubtless the vilest of the
vile, who were sacrificed at Athens every year, at the festival of
the Thargelia, as scapegoats for the purification of the city": R.

ἡμῖν προσελθοῦσ᾽ οὐδ᾽ ὁτιοῦν ἀδικουμένη;
ΠΕ. οὐδὲν γάρ, ὦ πρὸς τῶν θεῶν, νομίζετε
ἀδικεῖν με τὸν Πλοῦτον ποιεῖν πειρωμένῳ
βλέψαι πάλιν;
ΧΡ.   τί οὖν ἀδικοῦμεν τοῦτό σε,   460
εἰ πᾶσιν ἀνθρώποισιν ἐκπορίζομεν
ἀγαθόν;
ΠΕ.   τί δ᾽ ἂν ὑμεῖς ἀγαθὸν ἐξεύροιθ᾽;
ΧΡ.   ὅ τι;
σὲ πρῶτον ἐκβαλόντες ἐκ τῆς Ἑλλάδος.
ΠΕ. ἔμ᾽ ἐκβαλόντες; καὶ τί ἂν νομίζετον
κακὸν ἐργάσασθαι μεῖζον ἀνθρώποις;
ΧΡ.   ὅ τι;   465
εἰ τοῦτο δρᾶν μέλλοντες ἐπιλαθοίμεθα.
ΠΕ. καὶ μὴν περὶ τούτου σφῷν ἐθέλω δοῦναι λόγον
τὸ πρῶτον αὐτοῦ· κἂν μὲν ἀποφήνω μόνην
ἀγαθῶν ἁπάντων οὖσαν αἰτίαν ἐμὲ
ὑμῖν, δι᾽ ἐμέ τε ζῶντας ὑμᾶς· εἰ δὲ μή,   470
ποιεῖτον ἤδη τοῦθ᾽ ὅ τι ἂν ὑμῖν δοκῇ.
ΧΡ. ταυτὶ σὺ τολμᾷς, ὦ μιαρωτάτη, λέγειν;
ΠΕ. καὶ σύ γε διδάσκου· πάνυ γὰρ οἶμαι ῥᾳδίως
ἅπανθ᾽ ἁμαρτάνοντά σ᾽ ἀποδείξειν ἐγώ,
εἰ τοὺς δικαίους φῂς ποιήσειν πλουσίους.   475
ΒΛ. ὦ τύμπανα καὶ κύφωνες, οὐκ ἀρήξετε;
ΠΕ. οὐ δεῖ σχετλιάζειν καὶ βοᾶν πρὶν ἂν μάθῃς.
ΒΛ. καὶ τίς δύναιτ᾽ ἂν μὴ βοᾶν ἰοὺ ἰοὺ
τοιαῦτ᾽ ἀκούων;
ΠΕ.   ὅστις ἐστὶν εὖ φρονῶν.
ΧΡ. τί δῆτά σοι τίμημ᾽ ἐπιγράψω τῇ δίκῃ,   480
ἐὰν ἁλῷς;
ΠΕ.   ὅ τι σοι δοκεῖ.
ΧΡ.   καλῶς λέγεις.

Abusing us ?   We never did you wrong.

POV. No wrong, forsooth !   O by the heavenly Powers
No wrong to *me*, your trying to restore
Wealth's sight again ?

CHR.   How can it injure *you*,
If we are trying to confer a blessing
On all mankind ?

POV.   Blessing !   what blessing ?

CHR.   What ?
Expelling YOU from Hellas, first of all.

POV. Expelling ME from Hellas !   Could you do
A greater injury to mankind than that ?

CHR. A greater ?   Yes ;   by NOT expelling you.

POV. Now that's a question I am quite prepared
To argue out at once ;   and if I prove
That I'm the source of every good to men,
And that by me ye live— :   but if I fail,
Then do thereafter whatsoe'er ye list.

CHR. You dare to offer this, you vixen you ?

POV. And you, accept it :   easily enough
Methinks I'll show you altogether wrong
Making the good men rich, as you propose.

BL. O clubs and pillories !   To the rescue !   Help !

POV. Don't shout and storm before you have heard the
   facts.

BL. Who can help shouting, when he hears such wild
Extravagant notions ?

POV.   Any man of sense.

CHR. And what's the penalty you'll bear, in case
You lose the day ?

POV.   Whate'er you please.

CHR.   'Tis well.

ΠΕ. τὸ γὰρ αὐτό γ', ἐὰν ἡττᾶσθε, καὶ σφὼ δεῖ παθεῖν.

ΒΛ. ἱκανοὺς νομίζεις δῆτα θανάτους εἴκοσιν;

ΧΡ. ταύτῃ γε· νῷν δὲ δύ' ἀποχρήσουσιν μόνω.

ΠΕ. οὐκ ἂν φθάνοιτε τοῦτο πράττοντ'· ἢ τί γ' ἂν   485
   ἔχοι τις ἂν δίκαιον ἀντειπεῖν ἔτι;

ΧΟ. ἀλλ' ἤδη χρῆν τι λέγειν ὑμᾶς σοφὸν ᾧ νικήσετε τηνδὶ
   ἐν τοῖσι λόγοις ἀντιλέγοντες· μαλακὸν δ' ἐνδώσετε
     μηδέν.

ΧΡ. φανερὸν μὲν ἔγωγ' οἶμαι γνῶναι τοῦτ' εἶναι πᾶσιν
     ὁμοίως,
   ὅτι τοὺς χρηστοὺς τῶν ἀνθρώπων εὖ πράττειν ἐστὶ
     δίκαιον,   490
   τοὺς δὲ πονηροὺς καὶ τοὺς ἀθέους τούτων τἀναντία
     δήπου.
   τοῦτ' οὖν ἡμεῖς ἐπιθυμοῦντες μόλις εὕρομεν ὥστε
     γενέσθαι
   βούλευμα καλὸν καὶ γενναῖον καὶ χρήσιμον εἰς ἅπαν
     ἔργον.
   ἢν γὰρ ὁ Πλοῦτος νυνὶ βλέψῃ καὶ μὴ τυφλὸς ὢν
     περινοστῇ,
   ὡς τοὺς ἀγαθοὺς τῶν ἀνθρώπων βαδιεῖται κοὐκ
     ἀπολείψει,   495
   τοὺς δὲ πονηροὺς καὶ τοὺς ἀθέους φευξεῖται· κᾆτα
     ποιήσει
   πάντας χρηστοὺς καὶ πλουτοῦντας δήπου τά τε
     θεῖα σέβοντας.
   καίτοι τούτου τοῖς ἀνθρώποις τίς ἂν ἐξεύροι ποτ'
     ἄμεινον;

ΒΛ. οὔτις· ἐγώ σοι τούτου μάρτυς· μηδὲν ταύτην γ'
     ἀνερώτα.

ΧΡ. ὡς μὲν γὰρ νῦν ἡμῖν ὁ βίος τοῖς ἀνθρώποις διάκειται,   500

POV. But, if ye are worsted, ye must bear the same.

BL. (*to Chr.*) Think you that twenty deaths are fine enough ?

CHR. Enough for *her* ; but two will do for us.

POV. Well then, be quick about it ; for, indeed,
How can my statements be with truth gainsaid ?

CH. Find something, I pray, philosophic to say,
      whereby you may vanquish and rout her
No thought of retreat ; but her arguments meet
      with arguments stronger and stouter.

CHR All people with me, I am sure, will agree,
      for to all men alike it is clear,
That the honest and true should enjoy, as their due,
      a successful and happy career,
Whilst the lot of the godless and wicked should fall
      in exactly the opposite sphere.
'Twas to compass this end that myself and my friend
      have been thinking as hard as we can,
And have hit on a nice beneficial device,
      a truly magnificent plan.
For if Wealth should attain to his eyesight again,
      nor amongst us so aimlessly roam,
To the dwellings I know of the good he would go,
      nor ever depart from their home.
The unjust and profane with disgust and disdain
      he is certain thereafter to shun,
Till all shall be honest and wealthy at last,
      to virtue and opulence won.
Is there any design more effective than mine
      a blessing on men to confer ?

BL. No, nothing, that's flat ; I will answer for that ;
      so don't be inquiring of *her*.

CHR. For our life of to-day were a man to survey
      and consider its chances aright,

τίς ἂν οὐχ ἡγοῖτ᾽ εἶναι μανίαν, κακοδαιμονίαν τ᾽
   ἔτι μᾶλλον;
πολλοὶ μὲν γὰρ τῶν ἀνθρώπων ὄντες πλουτοῦσι
   πονηροί,
ἀδίκως αὐτὰ ξυλλεξάμενοι· πολλοὶ δ᾽ ὄντες πάνυ
   χρηστοὶ
πράττουσι κακῶς καὶ πεινῶσιν μετὰ σοῦ τε τὰ
   πλεῖστα σύνεισιν.
οὔκουν εἶναί φημ᾽, εἰ παύσει ταύτην βλέψας ποθ᾽ ὁ
   Πλοῦτος,   505
ὁδὸν ἥντιν᾽ ἰὼν τοῖς ἀνθρώποις ἀγάθ᾽ ἂν μείζω
   πορίσειεν.

ΠΕ. ἀλλ᾽ ὦ πάντων ῥᾷστ᾽ ἀνθρώπων ἀναπεισθέντ᾽ οὐχ
   ὑγιαίνειν
δύο πρεσβύτα, ξυνθιασώτα τοῦ ληρεῖν καὶ παρα-
   παίειν,
εἰ τοῦτο γένοιθ᾽ ὃ ποθεῖθ᾽ ὑμεῖς, οὔ φημ᾽ ἂν
   λυσιτελεῖν σφῷν.
εἰ γὰρ ὁ Πλοῦτος βλέψειε πάλιν διανείμειέν τ᾽ ἴσον
   αὑτόν,   510
οὔτε τέχνην ἂν τῶν ἀνθρώπων οὔτ᾽ ἂν σοφίαν
   μελετῴη
οὐδείς· ἀμφοῖν δ᾽ ὑμῖν τούτοιν ἀφανισθέντοιν
   ἐθελήσει
τίς χαλκεύειν ἢ ναυπηγεῖν ἢ ῥάπτειν ἢ τροχοποιεῖν
ἢ σκυτοτομεῖν ἢ πλινθουργεῖν ἢ πλύνειν ἢ σκυλο-
   δεψεῖν
ἢ γῆς ἀρότροις ῥήξας δάπεδον καρπὸν Δηοῦς
   θερίσασθαι,   515
ἢν ἐξῇ ζῆν ἀργοῖς ὑμῖν τούτων πάντων ἀμελοῦσιν;

ΧΡ. λῆρον ληρεῖς. ταῦτα γὰρ ἡμῖν πάνθ᾽ ὅσα νῦν δὴ
   κατέλεξας

He might fancy, I ween, it were madness or e'en
           the sport of some mischievous sprite.
So often the best of the world is possessed
           by the most undeserving of men,
Who have gotten their pile of money by vile
           injustice ; so often again
The righteous are seen to be famished and lean,
           yea, with *thee* as their comrade to dwell.
Now if Wealth were to-night to recover his sight,
           and her from amongst us expel,
Can you tell me, I pray, a more excellent way
           of bestowing a boon on mankind ?

POV. O men on the least provocation prepared
           to be crazy and out of your mind,
Men bearded and old, yet companions enrolled
           in the Order of zanies and fools,
O what is the gain that the world would obtain
           were it governed by you and your rules ?
Why, if Wealth should allot himself equally out
           (assume that his sight ye restore),
Then none would to science his talents devote
           or practise a craft any more.
Yet if science and art from the world should depart,
           pray whom would ye get for the future
To build you a ship, or your leather to snip,
           or to make you a wheel or a suture ?
Do ye think that a man will be likely to tan,
           or a smithy or laundry to keep,
Or to break up the soil with his ploughshare, and toil
           the fruits of Demeter to reap,
If regardless of these he can dwell at his ease,
           a life without labour enjoying ?

CHR. Absurd ! why the troubles and tasks you describe
      we of course shall our servants employ in.

οἱ θεράποντες μοχθήσουσιν.

ΠΕ.   πόθεν οὖν ἕξεις θεράποντας;

ΧΡ. ὠνησόμεθ᾽ ἀργυρίου δήπου.

ΠΕ.   τίς δ᾽ ἔσται πρῶτον ὁ πωλῶν,
ὅταν ἀργύριον κἀκεῖνος ἔχῃ;

ΧΡ.   κερδαίνειν βουλόμενός τις 520
ἔμπορος ἥκων ἐκ Θετταλίας παρὰ πλείστων ἀνδρα-
     ποδιστῶν.

ΠΕ. ἀλλ᾽ οὐδ᾽ ἔσται πρῶτον ἁπάντων οὐδεὶς οὐδ᾽ ἀνδρα-
     ποδιστὴς
κατὰ τὸν λόγον ὃν σὺ λέγεις δήπου. τίς γὰρ
     πλουτῶν ἐθελήσει
κινδυνεύων περὶ τῆς ψυχῆς τῆς αὑτοῦ τοῦτο
     ποιῆσαι;
ὥστ᾽ αὐτὸς ἀροῦν ἐπαναγκασθεὶς καὶ σκάπτειν
τἄλλα τε μοχθεῖν   525
ὀδυνηρότερον τρίψεις βίοτον πολὺ τοῦ νῦν.

ΧΡ.   ἐς κεφαλὴν σοί.

ΠΕ. ἔτι δ᾽ οὐχ ἕξεις οὔτ᾽ ἐν κλίνῃ καταδαρθεῖν· οὐ γὰρ
     ἔσονται·
οὔτ᾽ ἐν δάπισιν· τίς γὰρ ὑφαίνειν ἐθελήσει χρυσίου
     ὄντος;
οὔτε μύροισιν μυρίσαι στακτοῖς, ὁπόταν νύμφην
     ἀγάγησθον·
οὔθ᾽ ἱματίων βαπτῶν δαπάναις κοσμῆσαι ποικιλο-
     μόρφων.   530
καίτοι τί πλέον πλουτεῖν ἐστιν πάντων τούτων
     ἀποροῦντας;
παρ᾽ ἐμοῦ δ᾽ ἔστιν ταῦτ᾽ εὔπορα πάνθ᾽ ὑμῖν ὧν
     δεῖσθον· ἐγὼ γὰρ
τὸν χειροτέχνην ὥσπερ δέσποιν᾽ ἐπαναγκάζουσα
     κάθημαι

POV. Your servants ! But how will ye get any now ?
                    I pray you the secret to tell.
CHR. With the silver we've got we can purchase a lot.
POV.   But who is the man that will sell ?
CHR. Some merchant from Thessaly coming, belike,
            where most of the kidnappers dwell.
Who still, for the sake of the gain he will make,
         with the slaves that we want will provide us.
POV. But first let me say, if we walk in the way
            wherein ye are seeking to guide us,
There'll be never a kidnapper left in the world.
        No merchant of course (can ye doubt it ?)
His life would expose to such perils as those
         had he plenty of money without it.
No, no ; I'm afraid you must handle the spade
         and follow the plough-tail in person,
Your life will have double the toil and the trouble
        it used to.
CHR.   Thyself be thy curse on !
POV. No more on a bed will you pillow your head,
         for there won't be a bed in the land,
Nor carpets ; for whom will you find at the loom,
         when he's plenty of money in hand ?
Rich perfumes no more will ye sprinkle and pour
         as home ye are bringing the bride,
Or apparel the fair in habiliments rare
         so cunningly fashioned and dyed.
Yet of little avail is your wealth if it fail
         such enjoyments as these to procure you.
Ye fools, it is I who alone a supply
         of the goods which ye covet ensure you.
I sit like a Mistress, by Poverty's lash
         constraining the needy mechanic ;

διὰ τὴν χρείαν καὶ τὴν πενίαν ζητεῖν ὁπόθεν βίον
    ἕξει.

ΧΡ. σὺ γὰρ ἂν πορίσαι τί δύναι᾽ ἀγαθόν, πλὴν φῴδων ἐκ
      βαλανείου,   535
     καὶ παιδαρίων ὑποπεινώντων καὶ γραϊδίων κολο-
      συρτοῦ;
     φθειρῶν τ᾽ ἀριθμὸν καὶ κωνώπων καὶ ψυλλῶν οὐδὲ
      λέγω σοι
     ὑπὸ τοῦ πλήθους, αἳ βομβοῦσαι περὶ τὴν κεφαλὴν
      ἀνιῶσιν,
     ἐπεγείρουσαι καὶ φράζουσαι, "πεινήσεις, ἀλλ᾽
      ἐπανίστω."
     πρὸς δέ γε τούτοις ἀνθ᾽ ἱματίου μὲν ἔχειν ῥάκος·
      ἀντὶ δὲ κλίνης   540
     στιβάδα σχοίνων κόρεων μεστήν, ἢ τοὺς εὕδοντας
      ἐγείρει·
     καὶ φορμὸν ἔχειν ἀντὶ τάπητος σαπρόν· ἀντὶ δὲ
      προσκεφαλαίου,
     λίθον εὐμεγέθη πρὸς τῇ κεφαλῇ· σιτεῖσθαι δ᾽ ἀντὶ
      μὲν ἄρτων
     μαλάχης πτόρθους, ἀντὶ δὲ μάζης φυλλεῖ᾽ ἰσχνῶν
      ῥαφανίδων,
     ἀντὶ δὲ θράνου στάμνου κεφαλὴν κατεαγότος, ἀντὶ
      δὲ μάκτρας   545
     πιθάκνης πλευρὰν ἐρρωγυῖαν καὶ ταύτην. ἆρά γε
      πολλῶν
     ἀγαθῶν πᾶσιν τοῖς ἀνθρώποις ἀποφαίνω σ᾽ αἴτιον
      οὖσαν;

ΠΕ. σὺ μὲν οὐ τὸν ἐμὸν βίον εἴρηκας, τὸν τῶν πτωχῶν
      δ᾽ ὑπεκρούσω.

ΧΡ. οὔκουν δήπου τῆς πτωχείας πενίαν φαμὲν εἶναι
      ἀδελφήν.

When I raise it, to earn his living he'll turn,
        and work in a terrible panic.

CHR. Why, what have *you* got to bestow but a lot
        of burns from the bathing-room station [a]
And a hollow-cheeked rabble of destitute hags,
        and brats on the verge of starvation ?
And the lice, if you please, and the gnats and the fleas
        whom I can't even count for their numbers,
Who around you all night will buzz and will bite,
        and arouse you betimes from your slumbers.
Up ! up ! they will shrill, *'tis to hunger, but still*
        up ! up ! to your pain and privation.
For a robe but a rag, for a bed but a bag
        of rushes which harbour a nation
Of bugs whose envenomed and tireless attacks
        would the soundest of sleepers awaken.
And then for a carpet a sodden old mat,
        which is falling to bits, must be taken.
And a jolly hard stone for a pillow you'll own ;
        and, for girdle-cakes barley and wheaten,
Must leaves dry and lean of the radish or e'en
        sour stalks of the mallow be eaten.
And the head of a barrel, stove in, for a chair ;
        and, instead of a trough, for your kneading
A stave of a vat you must borrow, and that
        all broken.   So great and exceeding
Are the blessings which Poverty brings in her train
        on the children of men to bestow !

POV. The life you define with such skill is not mine :
        'tis the life of a beggar, I trow. [b]

CHR. Well, Poverty, Beggary, truly the twain
        to be sisters we always declare.

[a] The poor, crowding round the stove in the public baths, would get blisters and burns.

[b] Lit. "but it is the beggars' life you descanted upon" (ὑπεκρούσω).

413

ΠΕ. ὑμεῖς γ' οἵπερ καὶ Θρασυβούλῳ Διονύσιον εἶναι
  ὅμοιον.   550
  ἀλλ' οὐχ οὑμὸς τοῦτο πέπονθεν βίος οὐ μὰ Δί',
  οὐδέ γε μέλλει.
  πτωχοῦ μὲν γὰρ βίος, ὃν σὺ λέγεις, ζῆν ἐστιν
  μηδὲν ἔχοντα·
  τοῦ δὲ πένητος ζῆν φειδόμενον καὶ τοῖς ἔργοις
  προσέχοντα,
  περιγίγνεσθαι δ' αὐτῷ μηδέν, μὴ μέντοι μηδ'
  ἐπιλείπειν.

ΧΡ. ὡς μακαρίτην, ὦ Δάματερ, τὸν βίον αὐτοῦ κατέλεξας,   555
  εἰ φεισάμενος καὶ μοχθήσας καταλείψει μηδὲ
  ταφῆναι.

ΠΕ. σκώπτειν πειρᾷ καὶ κωμῳδεῖν τοῦ σπουδάζειν
  ἀμελήσας,
  οὐ γιγνώσκων ὅτι τοῦ Πλούτου παρέχω βελτίονας
  ἄνδρας
  καὶ τὴν γνώμην καὶ τὴν ἰδέαν. παρὰ τῷ μὲν γὰρ
  ποδαγρῶντες
  καὶ γαστρώδεις καὶ παχύκνημοι καὶ πιόνές εἰσιν
  ἀσελγῶς,   560
  παρ' ἐμοὶ δ' ἰσχνοὶ καὶ σφηκώδεις καὶ τοῖς ἐχθροῖς
  ἀνιαροί.

ΧΡ. ἀπὸ τοῦ λιμοῦ γὰρ ἴσως αὐτοῖς τὸ σφηκῶδες σὺ
  πορίζεις.

ΠΕ. περὶ σωφροσύνης ἤδη τοίνυν περανῶ σφῷν, κἀνα-
  διδάξω
  ὅτι κοσμιότης οἰκεῖ μετ' ἐμοῦ, τοῦ Πλούτου δ'
  ἐστὶν ὑβρίζειν.

ΧΡ. πάνυ γοῦν κλέπτειν κόσμιόν ἐστιν καὶ τοὺς τοίχους
  διορύττειν.   565

414

POV. Aye YOU ! who to good Thrasybulus forsooth
        Dionysius the Tyrant compare ! [a]
But the life I allot to my people is not,
      nor shall be, so full of distresses.
'Tis a beggar alone who has nought of his own,
       nor even an obol possesses.
My *poor* man, 'tis true, has to scrape and to screw
     and his work he must never be slack in ;
There'll be no superfluity found in his cot ;
      but then there will nothing be lacking.

CHR. Damater ! a life of the Blessed you give :
       for ever to toil and to slave
At Poverty's call, and to leave after all
       not even enough for a grave.

POV. You are all for your jeers and your comedy-sneers,
      and you can't be in earnest a minute
Nor observe that alike in their bodily frame
      and the spirit residing within it.
My people are better than Wealth's ; for by *him*,
      men bloated and gross are presented,
Fat rogues with big bellies and dropsical legs,
      whose toes by the gout are tormented ;
But mine are the lean and the wasplike and keen,
     who strike at their foemen and sting them.

CHR. Ah, yes ; to a wasplike condition, no doubt,
      by the pinch of starvation you bring them.

POV. I can show you besides that Decorum abides
      with those whom I visit ; that mine
Are the modest and orderly folk, and that Wealth's
     are " with insolence flushed and with wine."

CHR. 'Tis an orderly job, then, to thieve and to rob
      and to break into houses by night.

---

[a] The tyrant, to the deliverer from tyrants. Thrasybulus had
delivered Athens from the Thirty Tyrants, yet in his later years
he had been denounced by hireling orators ; *E.* 203.

ARISTOPHANES

ΒΛ. νὴ τὸν Δία γ᾽ εἴ γε λαθεῖν αὐτὸν δεῖ, πῶς οὐ
κόσμιόν ἐστιν;

ΠΕ. σκέψαι τοίνυν ἐν ταῖς πόλεσιν τοὺς ῥήτορας, ὡς
ὁπόταν μὲν
ὦσι πένητες, περὶ τὸν δῆμον καὶ τὴν πόλιν εἰσὶ δίκαιοι,
πλουτήσαντες δ᾽ ἀπὸ τῶν κοινῶν παραχρῆμ᾽ ἄδικοι
γεγένηνται,
ἐπιβουλεύουσί τε τῷ πλήθει καὶ τῷ δήμῳ πολεμοῦσιν. 570

ΧΡ. ἀλλ᾽ οὐ ψεύδει τούτων γ᾽ οὐδέν, καίπερ σφόδρα
βάσκανος οὖσα.
ἀτὰρ οὐχ ἧττόν γ᾽ οὐδὲν κλαύσει, μηδὲν ταύτῃ γε
κομήσῃς,
ὁτιὴ ζητεῖς τοῦτ᾽ ἀναπείθειν ἡμᾶς, ὡς ἔστιν
ἀμείνων
πενία πλούτου.

ΠΕ. καὶ σύ γ᾽ ἐλέγξαι μ᾽ οὔπω δύνασαι περὶ τούτου,
ἀλλὰ φλυαρεῖς καὶ πτερυγίζεις.

ΧΡ. καὶ πῶς φεύγουσί σ᾽ ἅπαντες; 575

ΠΕ. ὅτι βελτίους αὐτοὺς ποιῶ. σκέψασθαι δ᾽ ἔστι
μάλιστα
ἀπὸ τῶν παίδων· τοὺς γὰρ πατέρας φεύγουσι,
φρονοῦντας ἄριστα
αὐτοῖς. οὕτω διαγιγνώσκειν χαλεπὸν πρᾶγμ᾽ ἐστὶ
δίκαιον.

ΧΡ. τὸν Δία φήσεις ἆρ᾽ οὐκ ὀρθῶς διαγιγνώσκειν τὸ
κράτιστον·
κἀκεῖνος γὰρ τὸν πλοῦτον ἔχει.

ΒΛ. ταύτην δ᾽ ἡμῖν ἀποπέμπει. 580

ΠΕ. ἀλλ᾽ ὦ Κρονικαῖς λήμαις ὄντως λημῶντες τὰς φρένας
ἄμφω,
ὁ Ζεὺς δήπου πένεται, καὶ τοῦτ᾽ ἤδη φανερῶς σε
διδάξω.

416

BL.   Such modesty too ! In whatever they do
               they are careful to keep out of sight.

POV. Behold in the cities the Orator tribe ;
               when poor in their early career
How faithful and just to the popular trust,
               how true to the State they appear.
When wealth at the City's expense they have gained,
             they are worsened at once by the pelf,
Intriguing the popular cause to defeat,
             attacking the People itself.

CHR. That is perfectly true though 'tis spoken by you,
             you spiteful malevolent witch !
But still you shall squall for contending that all
           had better be poor than be rich.
So don't be elate ; for a terrible fate
           shall your steps overtake before long.

POV. Why, I haven't yet heard the ghost of a word
           to prove my contention is wrong.
You splutter and try to flutter and fly :
            but of argument never a letter.

CHR. Pray why do all people abhor you and shun ?

POV.   Because I'm for making them better.
So children, we see, from their parents will flee
       who would teach them the way they should go.
So hardly we learn what is right to discern ;
          so few what is best for them know.

CHR. Then Zeus, I suppose, is mistaken, nor knows
        what most for his comfort and bliss is,
Since money and pelf he acquires for himself.

BL.   And *her* to the earth he dismisses.

POV. O dullards and blind ! full of styes is your mind ;
        there are tumours titanic within it.
Zeus wealthy ! Not he : he's as poor as can be :
        and this I can prove in a minute.

417

εἰ γὰρ ἐπλούτει, πῶς ἂν ποιῶν τὸν Ὀλυμπικὸν
αὐτὸς ἀγῶνα,
ἵνα τοὺς Ἕλληνας ἅπαντας ἀεὶ δι' ἔτους πέμπτου
ξυναγείρει,
ἀνεκήρυττεν τῶν ἀσκητῶν τοὺς νικῶντας στεφανώσας 585
κοτίνῳ στεφάνῳ; καίτοι χρυσῷ μᾶλλον ἐχρῆν, εἴπερ
ἐπλούτει.

ΧΡ. οὐκοῦν τούτῳ δήπου δηλοῖ τιμῶν τὸν πλοῦτον
ἐκεῖνος·
φειδόμενος γὰρ καὶ βουλόμενος τούτου μηδὲν
δαπανᾶσθαι,
λήροις ἀναδῶν τοὺς νικῶντας τὸν πλοῦτον ἐᾷ παρ'
ἑαυτῷ.

ΠΕ. πολὺ τῆς πενίας πρᾶγμ' αἴσχιον ζητεῖς αὐτῷ περι-
άψαι,   590
εἰ πλούσιος ὢν ἀνελεύθερός ἐσθ' οὑτωσὶ καὶ φιλο-
κερδής.

ΧΡ. ἀλλὰ σέ γ' ὁ Ζεὺς ἐξολέσειεν κοτίνῳ στεφάνῳ
στεφανώσας.

ΠΕ. τὸ γὰρ ἀντιλέγειν τολμᾶν ὑμᾶς ὡς οὐ πάντ' ἔστ'
ἀγάθ' ὑμῖν
διὰ τὴν Πενίαν.

ΧΡ.   παρὰ τῆς Ἑκάτης ἔξεστιν τοῦτο πυθέσθαι,
εἴτε τὸ πλουτεῖν εἴτε τὸ πεινῆν βέλτιον. φησὶ γὰρ
αὕτη   595
τοὺς μὲν ἔχοντας καὶ πλουτοῦντας δεῖπνον κατὰ
μῆν' ἀποπέμπειν,
τοὺς δὲ πένητας τῶν ἀνθρώπων ἁρπάζειν πρὶν
καταθεῖναι.
ἀλλὰ φθείρου καὶ μὴ γρύξῃς

ᵃ " On the thirtieth day of every month (ταῖς τριακάσι, Athenaeus vii. 126) those who could afford it were accustomed to
418

If Zeus be so wealthy, how came it of yore
        that out of his riches abounding
He could find but a wreath of wild olive for those
        who should win at the games he was founding,
By all the Hellenes in each fourth year
           on Olympia's plains to be holden ?
If Zeus were as wealthy and rich as you say,
        the wreath should at least have been golden.

CHR. It is plain, I should think, 'tis from love of the chink
        that the conduct you mention arises ;
The God is unwilling to lavish a doit
        of the money he loves upon prizes.
The rubbish may go to the victors below ;
        the gold he retains in his coffers.

POV. How dare you produce such a libel on Zeus,
        you couple of ignorant scoffers ?
'Twere better, I'm sure, to be honest and poor,
        than rich and so stingy and screwing.

CHR. Zeus crown you, I pray, with the wild olive spray,
        and send you away to your ruin !

POV. To think that you dare to persist and declare
        that Poverty does not present you
With all that is noblest and best in your lives !

CHR.   Will Hecate's judgement content you ? [a]
If you question her which are the better, the rich
        or the poor, she will say, I opine,
Each month do the wealthy a supper provide,
        to be used in my service divine,
But the poor lie in wait for a snatch at the plate,
        or e'er it is placed on my shrine.
So away, nor retort with a g-r-r, you degraded

send a meal (called Ἑκάτης δεῖπνον) to the little shrines of Hecate
at the cross-roads, ἐν ταῖς τριόδοις. These were intended as offerings to the goddess, but in reality they were soon snapped up by
needy wayfarers " : R.

ἔτι μηδ' ὁτιοῦν.

οὐ γὰρ πείσεις, οὐδ' ἢν πείσῃς. 600

ΠΕ. ὦ πόλις Ἄργους.

ΧΡ. Παύσωνα κάλει τὸν ξύσσιτον.

ΠΕ. τί πάθω τλήμων;

ΧΡ. ἔρρ' ἐς κόρακας θᾶττον ἀφ' ἡμῶν.

ΠΕ. εἶμι δὲ ποῖ γῆς; 605

ΧΡ. ἐς τὸν κύφων'· ἀλλ' οὐ μέλλειν
χρή σ', ἀλλ' ἀνύειν.

ΠΕ. ἦ μὴν ὑμεῖς γ' ἔτι μ' ἐνταυθὶ
μεταπέμψεσθον.

ΧΡ. τότε νοστήσεις· νῦν δὲ φθείρου. 610
κρεῖττον γάρ μοι πλουτεῖν ἐστίν,
σὲ δ' ἐᾶν κλάειν μακρὰ τὴν κεφαλήν.

ΒΛ. νὴ Δί' ἔγωγ' οὖν ἐθέλω πλουτῶν
εὐωχεῖσθαι μετὰ τῶν παίδων
τῆς τε γυναικός, καὶ λουσάμενος 615
λιπαρὸς χωρῶν ἐκ βαλανείου
τῶν χειροτεχνῶν
καὶ τῆς Πενίας καταπαρδεῖν.

ΧΡ. αὕτη μὲν ἡμῖν ἡπίτριπτος οἴχεται.
ἐγὼ δὲ καὶ σύ γ' ὡς τάχιστα τὸν θεὸν 620
ἐγκατακλινοῦντ' ἄγωμεν εἰς Ἀσκληπιοῦ.

ΒΛ. καὶ μὴ διατρίβωμέν γε, μὴ πάλιν τις αὖ
ἐλθὼν διακωλύσῃ τι τῶν προὔργου ποιεῖν.

ΧΡ. παῖ Καρίων, τὰ στρώματ' ἐκφέρειν σ' ἐχρῆν,
αὐτόν τ' ἄγειν τὸν Πλοῦτον, ὡς νομίζεται, 625
καὶ τἆλλ' ὅσ' ἐστὶν ἔνδον εὐτρεπισμένα.

ᵃ From Eur. *Telephus*, fr. 713. The three words, κλύεθ' οἷα
λέγει, which follow in all mss., spoil the metre, and are doubtless
taken from *K.* 813.

ᵇ A painter and a scoundrel.

Importunate scold !
Persuade me you may, but I won't be persuaded.

POV.   O Argos, behold ! ^a

CHR. Nay Pauson,^b your messmate, to aid you invite.

POV.   O woe upon woe !

CHR. Be off to the ravens ; get out of my sight.

POV.   O where shall I go ?

CHR. Go ?   Go to the pillory ; don't be so slack,
Nor longer delay.

POV. Ah me, but ye'll speedily send for me back,
Who scout me to-day !

CHR. When we send for you, come ; not before. So
farewell !
With Wealth as my comrade 'tis better to dwell.
Get you gone, and bemoan your misfortunes alone.

BL.   I too have a mind for an opulent life
Of revel and mirth with my children and wife,
Untroubled by Poverty's panics.
And then as I'm passing, all shiny and bright,
From my bath to my supper, what joy and delight
My fingers to snap in disdain at the sight
Of herself and her frowsy mechanics.

CHR. That cursed witch, thank Heaven, has gone and left
us.
But you and I will take the God at once
To spend the night inside Asclepius' Temple.

BL.   And don't delay one instant, lest there come
Some other hindrance to the work in hand.^c

CHR. Hi ! boy there, Cario, fetch me out the blankets,
And bring the God himself, with due observance,
And whatsoever is prepared within.

---

^c *After 626 they all quit the stage. A whole night is supposed
to pass, and next day Cario suddenly runs in with joyful news.
He addresses the Chorus in the orchestra.*

ΚΑ. ὦ πλεῖστα Θησείοις μεμυστιλημένοι
γέροντες ἄνδρες ἐπ᾽ ὀλιγίστοις ἀλφίτοις,
ὡς εὐτυχεῖθ᾽, ὡς μακαρίως πεπράγατε,
ἄλλοι θ᾽ ὅσοις μέτεστι τοῦ χρηστοῦ τρόπου.　　630

ΧΟ. τί δ᾽ ἐστίν, ὦ βέλτιστε τῶν σαυτοῦ φίλων;
φαίνει γὰρ ἥκειν ἄγγελος χρηστοῦ τινος.

ΚΑ. ὁ δεσπότης πέπραγεν εὐτυχέστατα,
μᾶλλον δ᾽ ὁ Πλοῦτος αὐτός· ἀντὶ γὰρ τυφλοῦ
ἐξωμμάτωται καὶ λελάμπρυνται κόρας,　　635
Ἀσκληπιοῦ παιῶνος εὐμενοῦς τυχών.

ΧΟ. λέγεις μοι χαράν, λέγεις μοι βοάν.

ΚΑ. πάρεστι χαίρειν, ἤν τε βούλησθ᾽ ἤν τε μή.

ΧΟ. ἀναβοάσομαι τὸν εὔπαιδα καὶ
μέγα βροτοῖσι φέγγος Ἀσκληπιόν.　　640

ΓΥΝΗ. τίς ἡ βοή ποτ᾽ ἐστίν; ἆρ᾽ ἀγγέλλεται
χρηστόν τι; τοῦτο γὰρ ποθοῦσ᾽ ἐγὼ πάλαι
ἔνδον κάθημαι περιμένουσα τουτονί.

ΚΑ. ταχέως ταχέως φέρ᾽ οἶνον, ὦ δέσποιν᾽, ἵνα
καὐτὴ πίῃς· φιλεῖς δὲ δρῶσ᾽ αὐτὸ σφόδρα·　　645
ὡς ἀγαθὰ συλλήβδην ἅπαντά σοι φέρω.

ΓΥ. καὶ ποῦ ᾽στιν;

ΚΑ. 　　　　ἐν τοῖς λεγομένοις εἴσει τάχα.

ΓΥ. πέραινε τοίνυν ὅ τι λέγεις ἀνύσας ποτέ.

ΚΑ. ἄκουε τοίνυν, ὡς ἐγὼ τὰ πράγματα
ἐκ τῶν ποδῶν ἐς τὴν κεφαλήν σοι πάντ᾽ ἐρῶ.　　650

ᵃ " At the feasts of Theseus, in token of the unity which he introduced into the Athenian commonwealth, the poorer classes were entertained at a meal, apparently not of a very sumptuous character, provided at the public cost. The meal seems to have consisted of porridge and barley-bread ; and the guests hollowed out bits of the bread as scoops wherewith to eat the porridge. A scoop so made was called μυστίλη, and μεμυστιλημένοι means ' ye who have scooped up your porridge ' ; ἐπ᾽ ὀλιγίστοις ἀλφίτοις, ' on tiniest rations of barley-meal.' These workhouse meals, as we may

CA. Here's joy, here's happiness, old friends, for you
Who, at the feast of Theseus,[a] many a time
Have ladled up small sops of barley-broth !
Here's joy for you and all good folk besides.

CH. How now, you best of all your fellow-knaves ?
You seem to come a messenger of good.

CA. With happiest fortune has my master sped,
Or rather Wealth himself ; no longer blind,
He hath relumed the brightness of his eyes,
So kind a Healer hath Asclepius proved.[b]

CH. (*singing*) Joy for the news you bring.

       Joy ! Joy ! with shouts I sing.

CA. Aye, will you, nill you, it is joy indeed.

CH. (*singing*) Sing we with all our might Asclepius first
and best,
To men a glorious light, Sire in his offspring blest.

WIFE. What means this shouting ? Has good news
arrived ?
For I've been sitting till I'm tired within
Waiting for *him*, and longing for good news.

CA. Bring wine, bring wine, my mistress ; quaff yourself
The flowing bowl ; (you like it passing well).
I bring you here all blessings in a lump.

WIFE. Where ?

CA.   That you'll learn from what I am going to say.

WIFE. Be pleased to tell me with what speed you can.

CA. Listen. I'll tell you all this striking business
Up from the foot on to the very head.

almost deem them, were formerly reckoned luxurious by these
poor old men, but now what a change is impending in their ideas
and prospects " : R.

 [b] Lines 635-6 are from Sophocles, *Phineus* fr. 644. The sons
of Phineus were blinded by him, or by their stepmother ; Phineus
himself, blinded, had to endure the assaults of Harpies until
Asclepius restored sight to his sons. Line 638 is some tragic
fragment or parody : Schol.

ΓΥ. μὴ δῆτ᾽ ἔμοιγ᾽ ἐς τὴν κεφαλήν.

ΚΑ.   μὴ τἀγαθὰ
ἃ νῦν γεγένηται;

ΓΥ.   μὴ μὲν οὖν τὰ πράγματα.

ΚΑ. ὡς γὰρ τάχιστ᾽ ἀφικόμεθα πρὸς τὸν θεὸν
ἄγοντες ἄνδρα τότε μὲν ἀθλιώτατον,
νῦν δ᾽ εἴ τιν᾽ ἄλλον μακάριον κεὐδαίμονα,   655
πρῶτον μὲν αὐτὸν ἐπὶ θάλατταν ἤγομεν,
ἔπειτ᾽ ἐλοῦμεν.

ΓΥ.   νὴ Δί᾽ εὐδαίμων ἄρ᾽ ἦν
ἀνὴρ γέρων ψυχρᾷ θαλάττῃ λούμενος.

ΚΑ. ἔπειτα πρὸς τὸ τέμενος ᾖμεν τοῦ θεοῦ.
ἐπεὶ δὲ βωμῷ πόπανα καὶ προθύματα   660
καθωσιώθη, πέλανος Ἡφαίστου φλογί,
κατεκλίναμεν τὸν Πλοῦτον, ὥσπερ εἰκὸς ἦν·
ἡμῶν δ᾽ ἕκαστος στιβάδα παρεκαττύετο.

ΓΥ. ἦσαν δέ τινες κἄλλοι δεόμενοι τοῦ θεοῦ;

ΚΑ. εἷς μέν γε Νεοκλείδης, ὅς ἐστι μὲν τυφλός,   665
κλέπτων δὲ τοὺς βλέποντας ὑπερηκόντισεν·
ἕτεροί τε πολλοὶ παντοδαπὰ νοσήματα
ἔχοντες· ὡς δὲ τοὺς λύχνους ἀποσβέσας
ἡμῖν παρήγγειλεν καθεύδειν τοῦ θεοῦ
ὁ πρόπολος, εἰπών, ἤν τις αἴσθηται ψόφου,   670
σιγᾶν, ἅπαντες κοσμίως κατεκείμεθα.
κἀγὼ καθεύδειν οὐκ ἐδυνάμην, ἀλλά με
ἀθάρης χύτρα τις ἐξέπληττε κειμένη
ὀλίγον ἄπωθεν τῆς κεφαλῆς του γραδίου,
ἐφ᾽ ἣν ἐπεθύμουν δαιμονίως ἐφερπύσαι.   675
ἔπειτ᾽ ἀναβλέψας ὁρῶ τὸν ἱερέα
τοὺς φθοῖς ἀφαρπάζοντα καὶ τὰς ἰσχάδας
ἀπὸ τῆς τραπέζης τῆς ἱερᾶς. μετὰ τοῦτο δὲ
περιῆλθε τοὺς βωμοὺς ἅπαντας ἐν κύκλῳ,

WIFE. Not on *my* head,[a] I pray you.

CA.   Not the blessings
We have all got ?

WIFE.   Not all that striking business.

CA. Soon as we reached the Temple of the God
Bringing the man, most miserable then,
But who so happy, who so prosperous now ?
Without delay we took him to the sea
And bathed him there.

WIFE.   O what a happy man,
The poor old fellow bathed in the cold sea !

CA. Then to the precincts of the God we went.
There on the altar honey-cakes and bakemeats
Were offered, food for the Hephaestian flame.
There laid we Wealth as custom bids ; and we
Each for himself stitched up a pallet near.

WIFE. Were there no others waiting to be healed ?

CA. Neocleides [b] was, for one ; the purblind man,
Who in his thefts out-shoots the keenest-eyed.
And many others, sick with every form
Of ailment. Soon the Temple servitor
Put out the lights, and bade us fall asleep,
Nor stir, nor speak, whatever noise we heard.
So down we lay in orderly repose.
And I could catch no slumber, not one wink,
Struck by a nice tureen of broth which stood
A little distance from an old wife's head,
Whereto I marvellously longed to creep.
Then, glancing upwards, I behold the priest
Whipping the cheese-cakes and the figs from off
The holy table ; thence he coasted round
To every altar, spying what was left.

   [a] A reference to the common imprecation ἐς κεφαλήν σοι. She misunderstands the words.

   [b] An orator, informer, and thief ; see *E*. 254, 398–407.

εἴ που πόπανον εἴη τι καταλελειμμένον·   680
ἔπειτα ταῦθ' ἥγιζεν εἰς σάκταν τινά.
κἀγὼ νομίσας πολλὴν ὁσίαν τοῦ πράγματος
ἐπὶ τὴν χύτραν τὴν τῆς ἀθάρης ἀνίσταμαι.
ΓΥ. ταλάντατ' ἀνδρῶν, οὐκ ἐδεδοίκεις τὸν θεόν;
ΚΑ. νὴ τοὺς θεοὺς ἔγωγε μὴ φθάσειέ με   685
ἐπὶ τὴν χύτραν ἐλθὼν ἔχων τὰ στέμματα.
ὁ γὰρ ἱερεὺς αὐτοῦ με προυδιδάξατο.
τὸ γρᾴδιον δ' ὡς ᾔσθετο δή μου τὸν ψόφον,
τὴν χεῖρ' ὑφῆκε κᾆτα συρίξας ἐγὼ
ὀδὰξ ἐλαβόμην, ὡς παρείας ὢν ὄφις.   690
ἡ δ' εὐθέως τὴν χεῖρα πάλιν ἀνέσπασε,
κατέκειτο δ' αὑτὴν ἐντυλίξασ' ἡσυχῇ,
ὑπὸ τοῦ δέους βδέουσα δριμύτερον γαλῆς.
κἀγὼ τότ' ἤδη τῆς ἀθάρης πολλὴν ἔφλων·
ἔπειτ' ἐπειδὴ μεστὸς ἦν, ἀνεπαυόμην.   695
ΓΥ. ὁ δὲ θεὸς ὑμῖν οὐ προσῄειν;
ΚΑ.   οὐδέπω,
μετὰ τοῦτο δ' ἤδη· καὶ γελοῖον δῆτά τι
ἐποίησα· προσιόντος γὰρ αὐτοῦ μέγα πάνυ
ἀπέπαρδον· ἡ γαστὴρ γὰρ ἐπεφύσητό μου.
ΓΥ. ἦ πού σε διὰ τοῦτ' εὐθὺς ἐβδελύττετο.   700
ΚΑ. οὔκ, ἀλλ' Ἰασὼ μέν τις ἀκολουθοῦσ' ἅμα
ὑπηρυθρίασε χἠ Πανάκει' ἀπεστράφη
τὴν ῥῖν' ἐπιλαβοῦσ'· οὐ λιβανωτὸν γὰρ βδέω.
ΓΥ. αὐτὸς δ' ἐκεῖνος;
ΚΑ.   οὐ μὰ Δί', οὐδ' ἐφρόντισεν.
ΓΥ. λέγεις ἄγροικον ἄρα σύ γ' εἶναι τὸν θεόν.   705
ΚΑ. μὰ Δί' οὐκ ἔγωγ', ἀλλὰ σκατοφάγον.
ΓΥ.   αἲ τάλαν.

And everything he found he consecrated
Into a sort of sack ; so I, concluding
This was the right and proper thing to do,
Arose at once to tackle that tureen.

WIFE. Unhappy man ! Did you not fear the God ?

CA. Indeed I did, lest he should cut in first,
Garlands and all, and capture my tureen.
For so the priest forewarned me he might do.
Then the old lady when my steps she heard
Reached out a stealthy hand ; I gave a hiss,
And mouthed it gently like a sacred snake.[a]
Back flies her hand ; she draws her coverlets
More tightly round her, and, beneath them, lies
In deadly terror like a frightened cat.
Then of the broth I gobbled down a lot
Till I could eat no more, and then I stopped.

WIFE. Did not the God approach you ?

CA.   Not till later.
And then I did a thing will make you laugh.
For as he neared me, by some dire mishap
My wind exploded like a thunder-clap.

WIFE. I guess the God was awfully disgusted.

CA. No, but Iaso [b] blushed a rosy red
And Panacea turned away her head
Holding her nose : my wind's not frankincense.

WIFE. But he himself ?

CA.   Observed it not, nor cared.

WIFE. O why, you're making out the God a clown !

CA. No, no ; an ordure-taster.[c]

WIFE.   Oh ! you wretch.

---

[a] The παρείας, a harmless yellow snake, many of which were kept in the precinct. See Introd., and below, 733.

[b] Iaso, Panaceia, and Hygieia were daughters of Asclepius.

[c] διότι οἱ ἰατροὶ ἐκ τοῦ τὰ σωμάτων κενώματα βλέπειν καὶ οὖρα τοὺς μισθοὺς λαμβάνουσιν: Schol.

427

ARISTOPHANES

ΚΑ. μετὰ ταῦτ᾽ ἐγὼ μὲν εὐθὺς ἐνεκαλυψάμην
δείσας, ἐκεῖνος δ᾽ ἐν κύκλῳ τὰ νοσήματα
σκοπῶν περιῄει πάντα κοσμίως πάνυ.
ἔπειτα παῖς αὐτῷ λίθινον θυείδιον   710
παρέθηκε καὶ δοίδυκα καὶ κιβώτιον.
ΓΥ. λίθινον;
ΚΑ.   μὰ Δί᾽ οὐ δῆτ᾽, οὐχὶ τό γε κιβώτιον.
ΓΥ. σὺ δὲ πῶς ἑώρας, ὦ κάκιστ᾽ ἀπολούμενε,
ὃς ἐγκεκαλύφθαι φής;
ΚΑ.   διὰ τοῦ τριβωνίου.
ὀπὰς γὰρ εἶχεν οὐκ ὀλίγας μὰ τὸν Δία.   715
πρῶτον δὲ πάντων τῷ Νεοκλείδῃ φάρμακον
καταπλαστὸν ἐνεχείρησε τρίβειν, ἐμβαλὼν
σκορόδων κεφαλὰς τρεῖς Τηνίων. ἔπειτ᾽ ἔφλα
ἐν τῇ θυείᾳ συμπαραμιγνύων ὀπὸν
καὶ σχῖνον· εἶτ᾽ ὄξει διέμενος Σφηττίῳ,   720
κατέπλασεν αὐτοῦ τὰ βλέφαρ᾽ ἐκστρέψας, ἵνα
ὀδυνῷτο μᾶλλον. ὁ δὲ κεκραγὼς καὶ βοῶν
ἔφευγ᾽ ἀνάξας· ὁ δὲ θεὸς γελάσας ἔφη·
ἐνταῦθα νῦν κάθησο καταπεπλασμένος,
ἵν᾽ ὑπομνύμενον παύσω σε τῆς ἐκκλησίας.   725
ΓΥ. ὡς φιλόπολίς τίς ἐσθ᾽ ὁ δαίμων καὶ σοφός.
ΚΑ. μετὰ τοῦτο τῷ Πλούτωνι παρεκαθέζετο,
καὶ πρῶτα μὲν δὴ τῆς κεφαλῆς ἐφήψατο,
ἔπειτα καθαρὸν ἡμιτύβιον λαβὼν
τὰ βλέφαρα περιέψησεν· ἡ Πανάκεια δὲ   730
κατεπέτασ᾽ αὐτοῦ τὴν κεφαλὴν φοινικίδι
καὶ πᾶν τὸ πρόσωπον· εἶθ᾽ ὁ θεὸς ἐπόππυσεν.
ἐξῃξάτην οὖν δύο δράκοντ᾽ ἐκ τοῦ νεὼ
ὑπερφυεῖς τὸ μέγεθος.

CA. So then, alarmed, I muffled up my head,
Whilst *he* went round, with calm and quiet tread,
To every patient, scanning each disease.
Then by his side a servant placed a stone
Pestle and mortar ; and a medicine chest.

WIFE. A stone one ?

CA.   Hang it, not the medicine chest.

WIFE. How saw you this, you villain, when your head,
You said just now, was muffled ?

CA.   Through my cloak.
Full many a peep-hole has that cloak, I trow.
Well, first he set himself to mix a plaster
For Neocleides, throwing in three cloves
Of Tenian garlic ; and with these he mingled
Verjuice and squills ; and brayed them up together
Then drenched the mass with Sphettian vinegar,
And turning up the eyelids of the man
Plastered their inner sides, to make the smart
More painful. Up he springs with yells and roars
In act to flee ; then laughed the God, and said,
Nay, sit thou there, beplastered ; I'll restrain thee,
Thou reckless swearer, from the Assembly now.[a]

WIFE. O what a clever, patriotic God !

CA. Then, after this, he sat him down by Wealth,
And first he felt the patient's head, and next
Taking a linen napkin, clean and white,
Wiped both his lids, and all around them, dry.
Then Panacea with a scarlet cloth
Covered his face and head ; then the God clucked,
And out there issued from the holy shrine
Two great enormous serpents.

[a] Reading and meaning are both uncertain. ὑπομνύμενον, a conjecture for ἐπομν., must imply some sort of obstructive challenging. If he sits poulticed there, he will not be able to obstruct public business.

ΓΥ.   ὦ φίλοι θεοί.

ΚΑ. τούτω δ' ὑπὸ τὴν φοινικίδ' ὑποδύνθ' ἡσυχῇ   735
τὰ βλέφαρα περιέλειχον, ὥς γ' ἐμοὐδόκει·
καὶ πρίν σε κοτύλας ἐκπιεῖν οἴνου δέκα,
ὁ Πλοῦτος, ὦ δέσποιν', ἀνειστήκει βλέπων·
ἐγὼ δὲ τὼ χεῖρ' ἀνεκρότησ' ὑφ' ἡδονῆς,
τὸν δεσπότην τ' ἤγειρον. ὁ θεὸς δ' εὐθέως   740
ἠφάνισεν αὑτὸν οἵ τ' ὄφεις εἰς τὸν νεών.
οἱ δ' ἐγκατακείμενοι παρ' αὐτῷ πῶς δοκεῖς
τὸν Πλοῦτον ἠσπάζοντο καὶ τὴν νύχθ' ὅλην
ἐγρηγόρεσαν, ἕως διέλαμψεν ἡμέρα.
ἐγὼ δ' ἐπήνουν τὸν θεὸν πάνυ σφόδρα,   745
ὅτι βλέπειν ἐποίησε τὸν Πλοῦτον ταχύ,
τὸν δὲ Νεοκλείδην μᾶλλον ἐποίησεν τυφλόν.

ΓΥ. ὅσην ἔχεις τὴν δύναμιν, ὦναξ δέσποτα.
ἀτὰρ φράσον μοι, ποῦ 'σθ' ὁ Πλοῦτος;

ΚΑ.   ἔρχεται.
ἀλλ' ἦν περὶ αὐτὸν ὄχλος ὑπερφυὴς ὅσος.   750
οἱ γὰρ δίκαιοι πρότερον ὄντες καὶ βίον
ἔχοντες ὀλίγον αὐτὸν ἠσπάζοντο καὶ
ἐδεξιοῦνθ' ἅπαντες ὑπὸ τῆς ἡδονῆς·
ὅσοι δ' ἐπλούτουν οὐσίαν τ' εἶχον συχνὴν
οὐκ ἐκ δικαίου τὸν βίον κεκτημένοι,   755
ὀφρῦς συνῆγον ἐσκυθρώπαζόν θ' ἅμα.
οἱ δ' ἠκολούθουν κατόπιν ἐστεφανωμένοι,
γελῶντες, εὐφημοῦντες· ἐκτυπεῖτο δὲ
ἐμβὰς γερόντων εὐρύθμοις προβήμασιν.
ἀλλ' εἶ' ἀπαξάπαντες ἐξ ἑνὸς λόγου   760
ὀρχεῖσθε καὶ σκιρτᾶτε καὶ χορεύετε·
οὐδεὶς γὰρ ὑμῖν εἰσιοῦσιν ἀγγελεῖ
ὡς ἄλφιτ' οὐκ ἔνεστιν ἐν τῷ θυλάκῳ.

ΓΥ. νὴ τὴν Ἑκάτην, κἀγὼ δ' ἀναδῆσαι βούλομαι

WIFE.   O good heavens!
CA.   And underneath the scarlet cloth they crept
       And licked his eyelids, as it seemed to me ;
       And, mistress dear, before you could have drunk
       Of wine ten goblets, Wealth arose and saw.
       O then for joy I clapped my hands together
       And woke my master, and, hey presto ! both
       The God and serpents vanished in the shrine.
       And those who lay by Wealth, imagine how
       They blessed and greeted him, nor closed their eyes
       The whole night long till daylight did appear.
       And I could never praise the God enough
       For both his deeds, enabling Wealth to see,
       And making Neocleides still more blind.
WIFE. O Lord and King, what mighty power is thine !
       But prithee where is Wealth ?
CA.   He's coming here,
       With such a crowd collected at his heels.
       For all the honest fellows, who before
       Had scanty means of living, flocking round,
       Welcomed the God and clasped his hand for joy.
       —Though others, wealthy rascals, who had gained
       Their pile of money by unrighteous means,
       Wore scowling faces, knitted up in frowns,—
       But those went following on, begarlanded,
       With smiles and blessings ; and the old men's shoes
       Rang out in rhythmic progress as they marched.
       Now therefore all, arise with one accord,
       And skip, and bound, and dance the choral dance,
       For nevermore, returning home, ye'll hear
       Those fatal words *No barley in the bin !*
WIFE. By Hecate, for this good news you bring

431

ARISTOPHANES

εὐαγγέλιά σε κριβανωτῶν ὁρμαθῷ,
τοιαῦτ᾽ ἀπαγγείλαντα. 765

ΚΑ. μή νυν μέλλ᾽ ἔτι,
ὡς ἄνδρες ἐγγύς εἰσιν ἤδη τῶν θυρῶν.

ΓΓ. φέρε νυν ἰοῦσ᾽ εἴσω κομίσω καταχύσματα
ὥσπερ νεωνήτοισιν ὀφθαλμοῖς ἐγώ.

ΚΑ. ἐγὼ δ᾽ ὑπαντῆσαί γ᾽ ἐκείνοις βούλομαι. 770

ΠΛ. καὶ προσκυνῶ γε πρῶτα μὲν τὸν Ἥλιον,
ἔπειτα σεμνῆς Παλλάδος κλεινὸν πέδον,
χώραν τε πᾶσαν Κέκροπος, ἥ μ᾽ ἐδέξατο.
αἰσχύνομαι δὲ τὰς ἐμαυτοῦ συμφοράς,
οἵοις ἄρ᾽ ἀνθρώποις ξυνὼν ἐλάνθανον, 775
τοὺς ἀξίους δὲ τῆς ἐμῆς ὁμιλίας
ἔφευγον, εἰδὼς οὐδέν· ὦ τλήμων ἐγώ.
ὡς οὔτ᾽ ἐκεῖν᾽ ἄρ᾽ οὔτε ταῦτ᾽ ὀρθῶς ἔδρων·
ἀλλ᾽ αὐτὰ πάντα πάλιν ἀναστρέψας ἐγὼ
δείξω τὸ λοιπὸν πᾶσιν ἀνθρώποις ὅτι
ἄκων ἐμαυτὸν τοῖς πονηροῖς ἐνεδίδουν.

ΧΡ. βάλλ᾽ ἐς κόρακας· ὡς χαλεπόν εἰσιν οἱ φίλοι
οἱ φαινόμενοι παραχρῆμ᾽ ὅταν πράττῃ τις εὖ.
νύττουσι γὰρ καὶ φλῶσι τἀντικνήμια,
ἐνδεικνύμενος ἕκαστος εὔνοιάν τινα. 785
ἐμὲ γὰρ τίς οὐ προσεῖπε; ποῖος οὐκ ὄχλος
περιεστεφάνωσεν ἐν ἀγορᾷ πρεσβυτικός;

ΓΓ. ὦ φίλτατ᾽ ἀνδρῶν, καὶ σὺ καὶ σὺ χαίρετε.
φέρε νυν, νόμος γάρ ἐστι, τὰ καταχύσματα
ταυτὶ καταχέω σου λαβοῦσα.

ΠΛ. μηδαμῶς. 790

ᵃ καταχύσματα: small articles of confectionery, dried fruit, and
the like (*cf.* 789) which were thrown over a new slave on first
entering his master's house.

432

I've half a mind to crown you with a wreath
Of barley loaves.

CA   Well, don't be loitering now.
The men, by this, are nearly at your gates.

WIFE. Then I will in, and fetch the welcoming-gifts *a*
Wherewith to greet these newly-purchased—eyes.*b*

CA. And I will out, and meet them as they come.*c*

WE. And first I make obeisance to yon sun ;
Then to august Athene's famous plain,
And all this hospitable land of Cecrops.
Shame on my past career ! I blush to think
With whom I long consorted, unawares,
Whilst those who my companionship deserved
I shunned, not knowing. O unhappy me !
In neither this nor that I acted rightly.
But now, reversing all my former ways,
I'll show mankind 'twas through no wish of mine
I used to give myself to rogues and knaves.

CHR. Hang you, be off ! The nuisance these friends are,
Emerging suddenly when fortune smiles.
Tcha ! How they nudge your ribs, and punch your
    shins,
Displaying each some token of goodwill.
What man addressed me not ? What agèd group
Failed to enwreathe me in the market-place ? *d*

WIFE. Dearest of men, O welcome you and you.*e*
Come now, I'll take these welcoming-gifts and pour
    them
O'er *you*, as custom bids.

WE.   Excuse me, no.

         b Exit Wife.
  c Exit Cario. Enter Wealth, alone, to him later Chremylus,
with a crowd at his heels.
       d Enter Wife.   *e Plutus.*

ἐμοῦ γὰρ εἰσιόντος εἰς τὴν οἰκίαν
πρώτιστα καὶ βλέψαντος οὐδὲν ἐκφέρειν
πρεπῶδές ἐστιν, ἀλλὰ μᾶλλον εἰσφέρειν.

ΓΥ. εἶτ᾽ οὐχὶ δέξει δῆτα τὰ καταχύσματα;

ΠΛ. ἔνδον γε παρὰ τὴν ἑστίαν, ὥσπερ νόμος·   795
ἔπειτα καὶ τὸν φόρτον ἐκφύγοιμεν ἄν.
οὐ γὰρ πρεπῶδές ἐστι τῷ διδασκάλῳ
ἰσχάδια καὶ τρωγάλια τοῖς θεωμένοις
προβαλόντ᾽, ἐπὶ τούτοις εἶτ᾽ ἀναγκάζειν γελᾶν.

ΓΥ. εὖ πάνυ λέγεις· ὡς Δεξίνικός γ᾽ οὑτοσὶ   800
ἀνίσταθ᾽ ὡς ἁρπασόμενος τὰς ἰσχάδας.

ΚΑ. ὡς ἡδὺ πράττειν, ὦνδρες, ἔστ᾽ εὐδαιμόνως,
καὶ ταῦτα μηδὲν ἐξενεγκόντ᾽ οἴκοθεν.
ἡμῖν γὰρ ἀγαθῶν σωρὸς εἰς τὴν οἰκίαν
ἐπεισπέπαικεν οὐδὲν ἠδικηκόσιν.   805
[οὕτω τὸ πλουτεῖν ἐστιν ἡδὺ πρᾶγμα δή.]
ἡ μὲν σιπύη μεστή 'στι λευκῶν ἀλφίτων,
οἱ δ᾽ ἀμφορῆς οἴνου μέλανος ἀνθοσμίου.
ἅπαντα δ᾽ ἡμῖν ἀργυρίου καὶ χρυσίου
τὰ σκευάρια πλήρη 'στίν, ὥστε θαυμάσαι.
τὸ φρέαρ δ᾽ ἐλαίου μεστόν· αἱ δὲ λήκυθοι   810
μύρου γέμουσι, τὸ δ᾽ ὑπερῷον ἰσχάδων.
ὀξὶς δὲ πᾶσα καὶ λοπάδιον καὶ χύτρα
χαλκῆ γέγονε· τοὺς δὲ πινακίσκους τοὺς σαπροὺς
τοὺς ἰχθυηροὺς ἀργυροῦς πάρεσθ᾽ ὁρᾶν.
ὁ δ᾽ ἱπνὸς γέγον᾽ ἡμῖν ἐξαπίνης ἐλεφάντινος.   815
στατῆρσι δ᾽ οἱ θεράποντες ἀρτιάζομεν
χρυσοῖς, ἀποψώμεσθα δ᾽ οὐ λίθοις ἔτι,
ἀλλὰ σκοροδίοις ὑπὸ τρυφῆς ἑκάστοτε.

When first I'm entering with my sight restored
Into a house, 'twere meeter far that I
Confer a largess rather than receive.

WIFE. Then won't you take the welcoming-gifts I bring ?

WE. Aye, by the hearth within, as custom bids.
So too we 'scape the vulgar tricks of farce.
It is not meet, with such a Bard as ours,
To fling a shower of figs and comfits out
Amongst the audience, just to make them laugh.

WIFE. Well said indeed : for Dexinicus there
Is rising up, to scramble for the figs.[a]

CA. How pleasant 'tis to lead a prosperous life,
And that, expending nothing of one's own.
Into this house a heap of golden joys
Has hurled itself though nothing wrong we've done.
Truly a sweet and pleasant thing is wealth.
With good white barley is our garner filled
And all our casks with red and fragrant wine.
And every vessel in the house is crammed
With gold and silver, wonderful to see.
The tank o'erflows with oil ; the oil-flasks teem
With precious unguents ; and the loft with figs.
And every cruet, pitcher, pannikin,
Is turned to bronze ; the mouldy trencherlets
That held the fish are all of silver now.
Our lantern, all at once, is ivory-framed.
And we the servants, play at odd-or-even
With golden staters ; and to cleanse us, use
Not stones, but garlic-leaves, so nice we are.

[a] *They all enter the house : henceforth Cario and Chremylus
come out by turns ; they are never on the stage together. Some
interval elapses before Cario's first entrance.* The Schol. says the
scene is modelled on the *Inachus* of Sophocles, where the entry of
Zeus and Wealth brings plenty.

καὶ νῦν ὁ δεσπότης μὲν ἔνδον βουθυτεῖ
ὗν καὶ τράγον καὶ κριὸν ἐστεφανωμένος,   820
ἐμὲ δ᾽ ἐξέπεμψεν ὁ καπνός. οὐχ οἷός τε γὰρ
ἔνδον μένειν ἦν. ἔδακνε γὰρ τὰ βλέφαρά μου.

ΔΙΚΑΙΟΣ. ἕπου μετ᾽ ἐμοῦ παιδάριον, ἵνα πρὸς τὸν θεὸν
ἴωμεν.
ΚΑ.   ἔα, τίς ἔσθ᾽ ὁ προσιὼν οὑτοσί;
ΔΙ. ἀνὴρ πρότερον μὲν ἄθλιος, νῦν δ᾽ εὐτυχής.   825
ΚΑ. δῆλον ὅτι τῶν χρηστῶν τις, ὡς ἔοικας, εἶ.
ΔΙ. μάλιστ᾽.
ΚΑ.   ἔπειτα τοῦ δέει;
ΔΙ.   πρὸς τὸν θεὸν
ἥκω· μεγάλων γάρ μοὖστιν ἀγαθῶν αἴτιος.
ἐγὼ γὰρ ἱκανὴν οὐσίαν παρὰ τοῦ πατρὸς
λαβὼν ἐπήρκουν τοῖς δεομένοις τῶν φίλων,   830
εἶναι νομίζων χρήσιμον πρὸς τὸν βίον.
ΚΑ. ἦ πού σε ταχέως ἐπέλιπεν τὰ χρήματα.
ΔΙ. κομιδῇ μὲν οὖν.
ΚΑ.   οὔκουν μετὰ ταῦτ᾽ ἦσθ᾽ ἄθλιος.
ΔΙ. κομιδῇ μὲν οὖν. κἀγὼ μὲν ᾤμην οὓς τέως
εὐηργέτησα δεομένους ἕξειν φίλους   835
ὄντως βεβαίους, εἰ δεηθείην ποτέ·
οἱ δ᾽ ἐξετρέποντο κοὐκ ἐδόκουν ὁρᾶν μ᾽ ἔτι.
ΚΑ. καὶ κατεγέλων γ᾽, εὖ οἶδ᾽ ὅτι.
ΔΙ.   κομιδῇ μὲν οὖν.
αὐχμὸς γὰρ ὢν τῶν σκευαρίων μ᾽ ἀπώλεσεν.
ΚΑ. ἀλλ᾽ οὐχὶ νῦν.
ΔΙ.   ἀνθ᾽ ὧν ἐγὼ πρὸς τὸν θεὸν   840
προσευξόμενος ἥκω δικαίως ἐνθάδε.
ΚΑ. τὸ τριβώνιον δὲ τί δύναται πρὸς τῶν θεῶν,
ὃ φέρει μετὰ σοῦ τὸ παιδάριον τουτί; φράσον.

And master now, with garlands round his brow,
Is offering up hog, goat, and ram within.
But me the smoke drove out. I could not bear
To stay within ; it bit my eyelids so.[a]

GOOD MAN. Now then, young fellow, come along with me
To find the God.

CA.   Eh ?   Who comes here, I wonder.

G.M. A man once wretched, but so happy now.

CA. One of the honest sort, I dare aver.

G.M. Aye, aye.

CA.   What want you now ?

G.M.   I am come to thank
The God : great blessings hath he wrought for me.
For I, inheriting a fair estate,
Used it to help my comrades in their need,
Esteeming that the wisest thing to do.

CA. I guess your money soon began to fail.

G.M. Aye, that it did !

CA.   And then you came to grief.

G.M. Aye, that I did !   And I supposed that they
Whom I had succoured in their need, would now
Be glad to help me when in need myself.
But all slipped off as though they saw me not.

CA. And jeered you, I'll be bound.

G.M.   Aye, that they did !
The drought in all my vessels proved my ruin.

CA. But not so now.

G.M.   Therefore with right good cause
I come with thankfulness to praise the God.

CA. But what's the meaning, by the Powers, of that,
That ancient gaberdine your boy is bearing ?

---

[a] *Enter a prosperous and well-dressed citizen with an attendant
carrying a tattered gaberdine and a disreputable pair of shoes.*

ARISTOPHANES

ΔΙ. καὶ τοῦτ᾽ ἀναθήσων ἔρχομαι πρὸς τὸν θεόν.

ΚΑ. μῶν ἐνεμυήθης δῆτ᾽ ἐν αὐτῷ τὰ μεγάλα;   845

ΔΙ. οὔκ, ἀλλ᾽ ἐνερρίγωσ᾽ ἔτη τριακαίδεκα.

ΚΑ. τὰ δ᾽ ἐμβάδια;

ΔΙ.   καὶ ταῦτα συνεχειμάζετο.

ΚΑ. καὶ ταῦτ᾽ ἀναθήσων ἔφερες οὖν;

ΔΙ.   νὴ τὸν Δία.

ΚΑ. χαρίεντά γ᾽ ἥκεις δῶρα τῷ θεῷ φέρων.

ΣΥΚΟΦΑΝΤΗΣ. οἴμοι κακοδαίμων, ὡς ἀπόλωλα δείλαιος,   850
   καὶ τρισκακοδαίμων καὶ τετράκις καὶ πεντάκις
   καὶ δωδεκάκις καὶ μυριάκις· ἰοὺ ἰού.
   οὕτω πολυφόρῳ συγκέκραμαι δαίμονι.

ΚΑ. Ἄπολλον ἀποτρόπαιε καὶ θεοὶ φίλοι,
   τί ποτ᾽ ἐστὶν ὅ τι πέπονθεν ἄνθρωπος κακόν;   855

ΣΥ. οὐ γὰρ σχέτλια πέπονθα νυνὶ πράγματα,
   ἀπολωλεκὼς ἅπαντα τἀκ τῆς οἰκίας
   διὰ τὸν θεὸν τοῦτον, τὸν ἐσόμενον τυφλὸν
   πάλιν αὖθις, ἤνπερ μὴ 'λλίπωσιν αἱ δίκαι;

ΔΙ. ἐγὼ σχεδὸν τὸ πρᾶγμα γιγνώσκειν δοκῶ.   860
   προσέρχεται γάρ τις κακῶς πράττων ἀνήρ,
   ἔοικε δ᾽ εἶναι τοῦ πονηροῦ κόμματος.

ΚΑ. νὴ Δία, καλῶς τοίνυν ποιῶν ἀπόλλυται.

ΣΥ. ποῦ ποῦ 'σθ᾽ ὁ μόνος ἅπαντας ἡμᾶς πλουσίους
   ὑποσχόμενος οὗτος ποιήσειν εὐθέως,   865
   εἰ πάλιν ἀναβλέψειεν ἐξ ἀρχῆς; ὁ δὲ
   πολὺ μᾶλλον ἐνίους ἐστὶν ἐξολωλεκώς.

ΚΑ. καὶ τίνα δέδρακε δῆτα τοῦτ᾽;

ΣΥ.   ἐμὲ τουτονί.

ΚΑ. ἦ τῶν πονηρῶν ἦσθα καὶ τοιχωρύχων;

ΣΥ. μὰ Δί᾽, οὐ μὲν οὖν ἔσθ᾽ ὑγιὲς ὑμῶν οὐδὲ ἕν,   870

ᵃ The mystics used to dedicate the fine white garments on their initiation.

438

G.M   This too I bring, an offering to the God.[a]

CA.   That's not the robe you were initiate in ?

G.M. No, but I shivered thirteen years therein.

CA.   Those shoes ?

G.M.   Have weathered many a storm with me.

CA.   And them you bring as votive offerings ?

G.M.   Yes.

CA.   What charming presents to the God you bring ! [b]

INFORMER.   O me unlucky ! O my hard, hard fate !
            O thrice unlucky, four times, five times, yea
            Twelve times, ten thousand times ! O woe is me,
            So strong the spirit of ill-luck that swamps me.[c]

CA.   Apollo shield us and ye gracious Gods,
      What dreadful misery has this poor wretch suffered ?

IN.   What misery quoth'a? Shameful, scandalous wrong.
      Why, all my goods are spirited away
      Through this same God, who shall be blind again
      If any justice can be found in Hellas.

G.M. Methinks I've got a glimmering of the truth.
      This is some wretched fellow, come to grief ;
      Belike he is metal of the baser sort.

CA.   Then well done he to come to wrack and ruin.

IN.   Where, where is he who promised he would make
      All of us wealthy in a trice, if only
      He could regain his sight ?   Some of us truly
      He has brought to ruin rather than to wealth.

CA.   Whom has he brought to ruin ?

IN.   Me, this chap.

CA.   One of the rogues and housebreakers perchance ?

IN.   O aye, by Zeus, and you're quite rotten too.

---

   [b] *Enter Informer with Witness.*
   [c] Lit. "what manifold ill-luck I am mixed up with "; but in
the word πολυφόρῳ he plays on the two meanings of "manifold,"
and wine " that can carry much water " : Schol.

κοὐκ ἔσθ' ὅπως οὐκ ἔχετέ μου τὰ χρήματα.
ΚΑ. ὡς σοβαρός, ὦ Δάματερ, εἰσελήλυθεν
ὁ συκοφάντης. δῆλον ὅτι βουλιμιᾷ.
ΣΥ. σὺ μὲν εἰς ἀγορὰν ἰὼν ταχέως οὐκ ἂν φθάνοις;
ἐπὶ τοῦ τροχοῦ γὰρ δεῖ σ' ἐκεῖ στρεβλούμενον   875
εἰπεῖν ἃ πεπανούργηκας.
ΚΑ.   οἰμώξἄρα σύ.
ΔΙ. νὴ τὸν Δία τὸν σωτῆρα, πολλοῦ γ' ἄξιος
ἅπασι τοῖς Ἕλλησιν ὁ θεὸς οὗτος, εἰ
τοὺς συκοφάντας ἐξολεῖ κακοὺς κακῶς.
ΣΥ. οἴμοι τάλας· μῶν καὶ σὺ μετέχων καταγελᾷς;   880
ἐπεὶ πόθεν θοἰμάτιον εἴληφας τοδί;
ἐχθὲς δ' ἔχοντ' εἶδόν σ' ἐγὼ τριβώνιον.
ΔΙ. οὐδὲν προτιμῶ σου. φορῶ γὰρ πριάμενος
τὸν δακτύλιον τονδὶ παρ' Εὐδάμου δραχμῆς.
ΚΑ. ἀλλ' οὐκ ἔνεστι "συκοφάντου δήγματος."
ΣΥ. ἆρ' οὐχ ὕβρις ταῦτ' ἐστὶ πολλή; σκώπτετον,
ὅ τι δὲ ποιεῖτον ἐνθάδ' οὐκ εἰρήκατον.
οὐκ ἐπ' ἀγαθῷ γὰρ ἐνθάδ' ἐστὸν οὐδενί.
ΚΑ. μὰ τὸν Δί' οὔκουν τῷ γε σῷ, σάφ' ἴσθ' ὅτι.
ΣΥ. ἀπὸ τῶν ἐμῶν γὰρ ναὶ μὰ Δία δειπνήσετον.   890
ΚΑ. ὡς δὴ 'π' ἀληθείᾳ σὺ μετὰ τοῦ μάρτυρος
διαρραγείης, μηδενός γ' ἐμπλήμενος.
ΣΥ. ἀρνεῖσθον; ἔνδον ἐστίν, ὦ μιαρωτάτω,
πολὺ χρῆμα τεμαχῶν καὶ κρεῶν ὠπτημένων.
ὗ ὗ, ὗ ὗ, ὗ ὗ, ὗ ὗ, ὗ ὗ, ὗ ὗ.   895
ΚΑ. κακόδαιμον, ὀσφραίνει τι;
ΔΙ.   τοῦ ψύχους γ' ἴσως,
ἐπεὶ τοιοῦτόν γ' ἀμπέχεται τριβώνιον.
ΣΥ. ταῦτ' οὖν ἀνασχέτ' ἐστίν, ὦ Ζεῦ καὶ θεοί,
τούτους ὑβρίζειν εἰς ἔμ'; οἴμ' ὡς ἄχθομαι
ὅτι χρηστὸς ὢν καὶ φιλόπολις πάσχω κακῶς.   900

'Tis you have got my goods, I do believe.

CA. How bold, Damater, has the Informing rogue
Come blustering in ! 'Tis plain he's hunger-mad.

IN. You, sirrah, come to the market-place at once,
There to be broken on the wheel, and forced
To tell your misdemeanours.

CA.   You be hanged !

G.M. O, if the God would extirpate the whole
Informer-brood, right well would he deserve,
O Saviour Zeus, of all the Hellenic race !

IN. *You* jeer me too ?   Alack, you shared the spoil,
Or whence that brand new cloak ?   I'll take my oath
I saw you yesterday in a gaberdine.

G.M. I fear you not.   I wear an antidote,
A ring Eudemus *a* sold me for a drachma.

CA. 'Tis not inscribed FOR AN INFORMER'S BITE.

IN. Is not this insolence ?   Ye jest and jeer,
And have not told me what you are doing here.
'Tis for no good you two are here, I'm thinking.

CA. Not for *your* good, you may be sure of that.

IN. For off my goods ye are going to dine, I trow.

CA. O that in very truth ye'd burst asunder,
You and your witness, crammed with nothingness.

IN. Dare ye deny it ?   In your house they are cooking
A jolly lot of flesh and fish, you miscreants.

(The Informer gives five double sniffs.)

CA. Smell you aught, lackpurse ?

G.M.   Maybe 'tis the cold,
Look what a wretched gaberdine he's wearing.

IN. O Zeus and Gods, can such affronts be borne
From rogues like these ?   O me, how vexed I am
That I, a virtuous patriot, get such treatment.

---

a Some vendor of charms and amulets; no doubt the purpose
of the charm was inscribed upon it.

ARISTOPHANES

ΚΑ. σὺ φιλόπολις καὶ χρηστός;

ΣΤ. ὡς οὐδείς γ' ἀνήρ.

ΚΑ. καὶ μὴν ἐπερωτηθεὶς ἀπόκριναί μοι,

ΣΤ. τὸ τί;

ΚΑ γεωργὸς εἶ;

ΣΤ. μελαγχολᾶν μ' οὕτως οἴει;

ΚΑ. ἀλλ' ἔμπορος;

ΣΤ. ναί, σκήπτομαί γ', ὅταν τύχω.

ΚΑ. τί δαί; τέχνην τιν' ἔμαθες;

ΣΤ. οὐ μὰ τὸν Δία   905

ΚΑ πῶς οὖν διέζης ἢ πόθεν, μηδὲν ποιῶν;

ΣΤ. τῶν τῆς πόλεώς εἰμ' ἐπιμελητὴς πραγμάτων
καὶ τῶν ἰδίων πάντων.

ΚΑ. σύ; τί μαθών;

ΣΤ. βούλομαι.

ΚΑ. πῶς οὖν ἂν εἴης χρηστός, ὦ τοιχωρύχε,
εἰ σοὶ προσῆκον μηδέν, εἶτ' ἀπεχθάνει;   910

ΣΤ οὐ γὰρ προσήκει τὴν ἐμαυτοῦ μοι πόλιν
εὐεργετεῖν, ὦ κέπφε, καθ' ὅσον ἂν σθένω;

ΚΑ. εὐεργετεῖν οὖν ἐστι τὸ πολυπραγμονεῖν;

ΣΤ. τὸ μὲν οὖν βοηθεῖν τοῖς νόμοις τοῖς κειμένοις
καὶ μὴ 'πιτρέπειν ἐάν τις ἐξαμαρτάνῃ.   915

ΚΑ οὔκουν δικαστὰς ἐξεπίτηδες ἡ πόλις
ἄρχειν καθίστησιν;

ΣΤ. κατηγορεῖ δὲ τίς;

ΚΑ ὁ βουλόμενος.

ΣΤ. οὔκουν ἐκεῖνός εἰμ' ἐγώ.
ὥστ' εἰς ἔμ' ἥκει τῆς πόλεως τὰ πράγματα.

ΚΑ. νὴ Δία, πονηρόν τἄρα προστάτην ἔχει.   920
ἐκεῖνο δ' οὐ βούλοι ἄν, ἡσυχίαν ἔχων

---

^a " I plead this (falsely), when I am wanted for military service,"
from which merchants were exempted.

442

CA. What, YOU a virtuous patriot ?

IN.   No man more so.

CA. Come then, I'll ask you—Answer me.

IN.   Well.

CA.   Are you
A farmer ?

IN.   Do you take me for a fool ?

CA. A merchant ?

IN.   Aye, I feign so, on occasion.[a]

CA. Have you learned ANY trade ?

IN.   No, none by Zeus.

CA. Then how and whence do you earn your livelihood ?

IN. All public matters and all private too
Are in my charge.

CA.   How so ?

IN.   'Tis I WHO WILL.[b]

CA. You virtuous, housebreaker ? When all men hate you
Meddling with matters which concern you not.

IN. What, think you, booby, it concerns me not
To aid the State with all my might and main ?

CA. To aid the State ! Does that mean mischief-making ?

IN. It means upholding the established laws
And punishing the rogues who break the same.

CA. I thought the State appointed Justices
For this one task.

IN.   And who's to prosecute ?

CA. Whoever will.

IN.   I am that MAN WHO WILL.
Therefore, at last, the State depends on me.

CA. 'Fore Zeus, a worthless leader it has got.
Come, WILL you this, to lead a quiet life

---

[b] ὁ βουλόμενος (cf. l. 918) " he who wishes," that is anyone, could in certain cases take action against a wrongdoer. This gave opportunity to the informers.

443

ζῆν ἀργός;

ΣΤ.   ἀλλὰ προβατίου βίον λέγεις,
εἰ μὴ φανεῖται διατριβή τις τῷ βίῳ.

ΚΑ. οὐδ' ἂν μεταμάθοις;

ΣΤ.   οὐδ' ἂν εἰ δοίης γέ μοι
τὸν Πλοῦτον αὐτὸν καὶ τὸ Βάττου σίλφιον.   925

ΚΑ. κατάθου ταχέως θοἰμάτιον.

ΔΙ.   οὗτος, σοὶ λέγει.

ΚΑ. ἔπειθ' ὑπόλυσαι.

ΔΙ.   πάντα ταῦτα σοὶ λέγει.

ΣΤ. καὶ μὴν προσελθέτω πρὸς ἔμ' ὑμῶν ἐνθαδὶ
ὁ βουλόμενος.

ΚΑ.   οὐκοῦν ἐκεῖνός εἰμ' ἐγώ.

ΣΤ. οἴμοι τάλας, ἀποδύομαι μεθ' ἡμέραν.   930

ΚΑ. σὺ γὰρ ἀξιοῖς τἀλλότρια πράττων ἐσθίειν.

ΣΤ. ὁρᾷς ἃ ποιεῖς; ταῦτ' ἐγὼ μαρτύρομαι.

ΚΑ. ἀλλ' οἴχεται φεύγων ὃν εἶχες μάρτυρα.

ΣΤ. οἴμοι περιείλημμαι μόνος.

ΚΑ.   νυνὶ βοᾷς;

ΣΤ. οἴμοι μάλ' αὖθις.

ΚΑ.   δὸς σύ μοι τὸ τριβώνιον,   935
ἵν' ἀμφιέσω τὸν συκοφάντην τουτονί.

ΔΙ. μὴ δῆθ'· ἱερὸν γάρ ἐστι τοῦ Πλούτου πάλαι.

ΚΑ. ἔπειτα ποῦ κάλλιον ἀνατεθήσεται
ἢ περὶ πονηρὸν ἄνδρα καὶ τοιχωρύχον;
Πλοῦτον δὲ κοσμεῖν ἱματίοις σεμνοῖς πρέπει.   940

ΔΙ. τοῖς δ' ἐμβαδίοις τί χρήσεταί τις; εἰπέ μοι.

ΚΑ. καὶ ταῦτα πρὸς τὸ μέτωπον αὐτίκα δὴ μάλα
ὥσπερ κοτίνῳ προσπατταλεύσω τουτῳί.

---

    a Battus led the colony from Thera to Cyrene, and his dynasty reigned there for eight generations. Silphium, a kind of giant

        And peaceful ?
IN.   That's a sheep's life you're describing,
    Living with nothing in the world to do.
CA.   Then you won't change ?
IN.   Not if you gave me all
    Battus's silphium,*ᵃ aye and Wealth to boot.
CA.   Put off your cloak !
G.M.   Fellow, to *you* he's speaking.
CA.   And then your shoes.
G.M.   All this to *you* he's speaking.
IN.   I dare you all. Come on and tackle me
    Whoever will.
CA.   I am that MAN WHO WILL.
IN.   O me, they are stripping me in open day.
CA.   You choose to live by mischief-making, do you ?
IN.   What are you at ? I call you, friend, to witness.
CA.   Methinks the witness that you brought has cut it.
IN.   O me ! I am trapped alone.
CA.   Aye, now you are roaring.
IN.   O me ! once more.
CA. (*to* G. M.)   Hand me your gaberdine,
    I'll wrap this rogue of an Informer in it.
G.M.   Nay, that long since is dedicate to Wealth.
CA.   Where can it then more aptly be suspended ᵇ
    Than on a rogue and housebreaker like this ?
    Wealth we will decorate with nobler robes.
G.M.   How shall we manage with my cast-off shoes ?
CA.   Those on his forehead, as upon the stock
    Of a wild olive, will I nail at once.

fennel, was the wealth of the place, being used for human food,
animals' fodder, and medicine.
  ᵇ As a votive offering, ἀνατίθημι being the technical term for
offering them up. Below, Cario treats the Informer as a tree
growing in the sacred precinct, where offerings were often hung,
and nails or fastens the shoes to the Informer's mask.

ΣΥ. ἄπειμι· γιγνώσκω γὰρ ἥττων ὢν πολὺ
 ὑμῶν· ἐὰν δὲ σύζυγον λάβω τινὰ   945
 καὶ σύκινον, τοῦτον τὸν ἰσχυρὸν θεὸν
 ἐγὼ ποιήσω τήμερον δοῦναι δίκην,
 ὁτιὴ καταλύει περιφανῶς εἷς ὢν μόνος
 τὴν δημοκρατίαν, οὔτε τὴν βουλὴν πιθὼν
 τὴν τῶν πολιτῶν οὔτε τὴν ἐκκλησίαν.   950
ΔΙ. καὶ μὴν ἐπειδὴ τὴν πανοπλίαν τὴν ἐμὴν
 ἔχων βαδίζεις, εἰς τὸ βαλανεῖον τρέχε·
 ἔπειτ᾽ ἐκεῖ κορυφαῖος ἑστηκὼς θέρου.
 κἀγὼ γὰρ εἶχον τὴν στάσιν ταύτην ποτέ.
ΚΑ. ἀλλ᾽ ὁ βαλανεὺς ἕλξει θύραζ᾽ αὐτὸν λαβὼν   955
 τῶν ὀρχιπέδων· ἰδὼν γὰρ αὐτὸν γνώσεται
 ὅτι ἔστ᾽ ἐκείνου τοῦ πονηροῦ κόμματος.
 νὼ δ᾽ εἰσίωμεν, ἵνα προσεύξῃ τὸν θεόν.

ΓΡΑΥΣ. ἆρ᾽, ὦ φίλοι γέροντες, ἐπὶ τὴν οἰκίαν
 ἀφίγμεθ᾽ ὄντως τοῦ νέου τούτου θεοῦ,   960
 ἢ τῆς ὁδοῦ τὸ παράπαν ἡμαρτήκαμεν;
ΧΟ. ἀλλ᾽ ἴσθ᾽ ἐπ᾽ αὐτὰς τὰς θύρας ἀφιγμένη,
 ὦ μειρακίσκη· πυνθάνει γὰρ ὡρικῶς.
ΓΡ. φέρε νυν ἐγὼ τῶν ἔνδοθεν καλέσω τινά.
ΧΡ. μὴ δῆτ᾽· ἐγὼ γὰρ αὐτὸς ἐξελήλυθα.   965
 ἀλλ᾽ ὅ τι μάλιστ᾽ ἐλήλυθας λέγειν σ᾽ ἐχρῆν.
ΓΡ. πέπονθα δεινὰ καὶ παράνομ᾽, ὦ φίλτατε·
 ἀφ᾽ οὗ γὰρ ὁ θεὸς οὗτος ἤρξατο βλέπειν,
 ἀβίωτον εἶναί μοι πεποίηκε τὸν βίον.
ΧΡ. τί δ᾽ ἔστιν; ἦ που καὶ σὺ συκοφάντρια   970
 ἐν ταῖς γυναιξὶν ἦσθα;
ΓΡ.   μὰ Δί᾽ ἐγὼ μὲν οὔ.

ᵃ Lit. "if I get a comrade, even a rotten one." σύκινος, "of

IN.   I'll stay no longer ; for, alone, I am weaker,
     I know, than you ; but give me once a comrade,
     A WILLING *a* one, and ere the day is spent
     I'll bring this lusty God of yours to justice,
     For that, being only one, he is overthrowing
     Our great democracy ; nor seeks to gain
     The Council's sanction, or the Assembly's either.

G.M. Aye run you off, accoutred as you are
     In all my panoply, and take the station
     I held erewhile beside the bath-room fire,
     The Coryphaeus of the starvelings there.

CA.   Nay, but the keeper of the baths will drag him
     Out by the ears ; for he'll at once perceive
     The man is metal of the baser sort.
     But go we in that you may pray the God.*b*

OLD LADY. Pray, have we really reached, you dear old men,
     The very dwelling where this new God dwells ?
     Or have we altogether missed the way ?

CH.   No, you have really reached his very door,
     You dear young girl ; for girl-like is your speech.

O.L.   O, then, I'll summon one of those within.*c*

CHR. Nay, for, unsummoned, I have just come out.
     So tell me freely what has brought you here.

O.L.   O, sad, my dear, and anguished is my lot,
     For ever since this God began to see
     My life's been not worth living ; all through him.

CHR. What, were you too a she-informer then
     Amongst the women ?

O.L.   No indeed, not I.

fig-wood," which usually implies uselessness, is chosen with a play
on συκοφάντης. *Exit Informer.*
  b *The Good Man and Cario enter the house. Enter Old Lady
with attendant, carrying cakes and sweetmeats on a tray.*
  c *Enter Chremylus.*

ΧΡ. ἀλλ' οὐ λαχοῦσ' ἔπινες ἐν τῷ γράμματι;

ΓΡ. σκώπτεις· ἐγὼ δὲ κατακέκνισμαι δειλάκρα.

ΧΡ. οὔκουν ἐρεῖς ἀνύσασα τὸν κνισμὸν τίνα;

ΓΡ. ἄκουέ νυν. ἦν μοί τι μειράκιον φίλον,   975
πενιχρὸν μέν, ἄλλως δ' εὐπρόσωπον καὶ καλὸν
καὶ χρηστόν· εἰ γάρ του δεηθείην ἐγώ,
ἅπαντ' ἐποίει κοσμίως μοι καὶ καλῶς·
ἐγὼ δ' ἐκείνῳ γ' αὖ τὰ πάνθ' ὑπηρέτουν.

ΧΡ. τί δ' ἦν ὅ τι σου μάλιστ' ἐδεῖθ' ἑκάστοτε;   980

ΓΡ. οὐ πολλά· καὶ γὰρ ἐκνομίως μ' ᾐσχύνετο.
ἀλλ' ἀργυρίου δραχμὰς ἂν ᾔτησ' εἴκοσιν
εἰς ἱμάτιον, ὀκτὼ δ' ἂν εἰς ὑποδήματα·
καὶ ταῖς ἀδελφαῖς ἀγοράσαι χιτώνιον
ἐκέλευσεν ἄν, τῇ μητρί θ' ἱματίδιον·   985
πυρῶν τ' ἂν ἐδεήθη μεδίμνων τεττάρων.

ΧΡ. οὐ πολλὰ τοίνυν μὰ τὸν Ἀπόλλω ταῦτά γε
εἴρηκας, ἀλλὰ δῆλον ὅτι σ' ᾐσχύνετο.

ΓΡ. καὶ ταῦτα τοίνυν οὐχ ἕνεκεν μισητίας
αἰτεῖν μ' ἔφασκεν, ἀλλὰ φιλίας οὕνεκα,   990
ἵνα τοὐμὸν ἱμάτιον φορῶν μεμνῇτό μου.

ΧΡ. λέγεις ἐρῶντ' ἄνθρωπον ἐκνομιώτατα.

ΓΡ. ἀλλ' οὐχὶ νῦν ἔθ' ὁ βδελυρὸς τὸν νοῦν ἔχει
τὸν αὐτόν, ἀλλὰ πολὺ μεθέστηκεν πάνυ.
ἐμοῦ γὰρ αὐτῷ τὸν πλακοῦντα τουτονὶ   995
καὶ τἆλλα τἀπὶ τοῦ πίνακος τραγήματα

ᵃ " When all the ten Courts were sitting, each of the ten dicastic
sections would draw at the balloting-booths the letter of the Court-
house in which it was that day to sit. But after the downfall of
the Empire there would rarely be sufficient business to occupy all
the Courts, and therefore some of the sections would draw blanks,
and so would that day hold no sitting, and draw no pay. See
E. 681-3, and 277 *supra.* But some of the poorer citizens would
now, as at the date of the *Wasps* (see lines 304-12 of that play),

CHR. Or, not elected, sat you judging—wine ? [a]

O.L. You jest ; but I, poor soul, am misery-stung.

CHR. What kind of misery stings you ? tell me quick.

O.L. Then listen. I'd a lad that loved me well,
Poor, but so handsome, and so fair to see,
Quite virtuous too ; whate'er I wished, he did
In such a nice and gentlemanly way ;
And what he wanted, I in turn supplied.

CHR. What were the things he asked you to supply ?

O.L. Not many : so prodigious the respect
In which he held me. 'Twould be twenty drachmas
To buy a cloak and, maybe, eight for shoes ; [b]
Then for his sisters he would want a gown,
And just one mantle for his mother's use,
And twice twelve bushels of good wheat perchance.

CHR. Not many truly were the gifts he asked !
'Tis plain he held you in immense respect.

O.L. And these he wanted not for greed, he swore,
But for love's sake, that when my robe he wore,
He might, by that, remember me the more.

CHR. A man prodigiously in love indeed !

O.L. Aye, but the scamp's quite other-minded now.
He's altogether changed from what he was.
So when I sent him this delicious cake,
And all these bon-bons here upon the tray,

depend for their meals on their dicastic pay, and many, it appears, were the fraudulent devices to which they would resort to obtain it. One would attempt to sit in a dicastic section with which he was not really empanelled : that is the meaning of the present passage. Another would contrive to enter his name in more than one list, so as to diminish the chance of a blank : that is the meaning of 1166, 1167 *infra*. Frauds of this kind, if detected, were visited with condign punishment. Women, of course, could take no part in dicastic proceedings " : R.

[b] These sums seem to be considerably above the usual prices.

ἐπόντα πεμψάσης, ὑπειπούσης θ' ὅτι
εἰς ἑσπέραν ἥξοιμι,

ΧΡ.   τί σ' ἔδρασ'; εἰπέ μοι.

ΓΡ. ἄμητα προσαπέπεμψεν ἡμῖν τουτονί,
ἐφ' ᾧ τ' ἐκεῖσε μηδέποτέ μ' ἐλθεῖν ἔτι,   1000
καὶ πρὸς ἐπὶ τούτοις εἶπεν ἀποπέμπων ὅτι
πάλαι ποτ' ἦσαν ἄλκιμοι Μιλήσιοι.

ΧΡ. δῆλον ὅτι τοὺς τρόπους τις οὐ μοχθηρὸς ἦν.
ἔπειτα πλουτῶν οὐκέθ' ἥδεται φακῇ·
πρὸ τοῦ δ' ὑπὸ τῆς πενίας ἅπαντ' ἐπήσθιεν.   1005

ΓΡ. καὶ μὴν πρὸ τοῦ γ' ὁσημέραι νὴ τὼ θεὼ
ἐπὶ τὴν θύραν ἐβάδιζεν ἀεὶ τὴν ἐμήν.

ΧΡ. ἐπ' ἐκφοράν;

ΓΡ.   μὰ Δί', ἀλλὰ τῆς φωνῆς μόνον
ἐρῶν ἀκοῦσαι.

ΧΡ.   τοῦ λαβεῖν μὲν οὖν χάριν.

ΓΡ. καὶ νὴ Δί' εἰ λυπουμένην αἴσθοιτό με,   1010
νηττάριον ἂν καὶ φάττιον ὑπεκορίζετο.

ΧΡ. ἔπειτ' ἴσως ᾔτησ' ἂν εἰς ὑποδήματα.

ΓΡ. μυστηρίοις δὲ τοῖς μεγάλοις ὀχουμένην
ἐπὶ τῆς ἁμάξης ὅτι προσέβλεψέν μέ τις,
ἐτυπτόμην διὰ τοῦθ' ὅλην τὴν ἡμέραν.   1015
οὕτω σφόδρα ζηλότυπος ὁ νεανίσκος ἦν.

ΧΡ. μόνος γὰρ ᾔδεθ', ὡς ἔοικεν, ἐσθίων.

ΓΡ. καὶ τάς γε χεῖρας παγκάλας ἔχειν μ' ἔφη.

ΧΡ. ὁπότε προτείνοιέν γε δραχμὰς εἴκοσιν.

ΓΡ. ὄζειν τε τῆς χροιᾶς ἔφασκεν ἡδύ μου.   1020

ΧΡ. εἰ Θάσιον ἐνέχεις, εἰκότως γε νὴ Δία.

ΓΡ. τὸ βλέμμα θ' ὡς ἔχοιμι μαλακὸν καὶ καλόν.

---

[a] " These are in the nature of wedding presents, sent by the
Old Lady to her lover, as by a bridegroom to the bride. See
Athenaeus xiv. 49, 50 " : R.

Adding a whispered message that I hoped
To come at even—

CHR.   Tell me what he did ?

O.L. He sent them back, and sent this cream-cake too,[a]
Upon condition that I come no more ;
And said withal, *Long since, in war's alarms*
Were the Milesians lusty men-at-arms.[b]

CHR. O, then the lad's not vicious ; now he's rich
He cares for broth no longer, though before,
When he was poor, he snapped up anything.

O.L. O, by the Twain, and every day before,
He used to come, a suppliant, to my door.

CHR. What, for your funeral ?

O.L.   No, he was but fain
My voice to hear.

CHR.   Your bounty to obtain.

O.L. When in the dumps, he'd smother me with love,
Calling me " little duck " and " little dove."

CHR. And then begged something for a pair of shoes.

O.L. And if perchance, when riding in my coach
At the Great Mysteries,[c] some gallant threw
A glance my way, he'd beat me black and blue,
So very jealous had the young man grown.

CHR. Aye, aye, he liked to eat his cake alone.

O.L. He vowed my hands were passing fair and white.

CHR. With twenty drachmas in them—well he might.

O.L. And much he praised the fragrance of my skin.

CHR. No doubt, no doubt, if Thasian you poured in.

O.L. And then he swore my glance was soft and sweet.

---

[b] This proverb, originally a line of Anacreon's, came up after the Milesians had degenerated into luxury. Here it denotes the youth's unwillingness any longer to enter the " lists of love."

[c] In the great procession to Eleusis, described in the *Frogs*: see *F*. 401.

ΧΡ. οὐ σκαιὸς ἦν ἄνθρωπος, ἀλλ' ἠπίστατο
γραὸς καπρώσης τἀφόδια κατεσθίειν.

ΓΡ. ταῦτ' οὖν ὁ θεός, ὦ φίλ' ἄνερ, οὐκ ὀρθῶς ποιεῖ, 1025
φάσκων βοηθεῖν τοῖς ἀδικουμένοις ἀεί.

ΧΡ. τί γὰρ ποιήσει; φράζε, καὶ πεπράξεται.

ΓΡ. ἀναγκάσαι δίκαιόν ἐστι νὴ Δία
τὸν εὖ παθόνθ' ὑπ' ἐμοῦ πάλιν μ' ἀντευποιεῖν·
ἢ μηδ' ὁτιοῦν ἀγαθὸν δίκαιός ἐστ' ἔχειν. 1030

ΧΡ. οὔκουν καθ' ἑκάστην ἀπεδίδου τὴν νύκτα σοι;

ΓΡ. ἀλλ' οὐδέποτέ με ζῶσαν ἀπολείψειν ἔφη.

ΧΡ. ὀρθῶς γε· νῦν δέ γ' οὐκέτι σε ζῆν οἴεται.

ΓΡ. ὑπὸ τοῦ γὰρ ἄλγους κατατέτηκ', ὦ φίλτατε.

ΧΡ. οὔκ, ἀλλὰ κατασέσηπας, ὥς γ' ἐμοὶ δοκεῖς. 1035

ΓΡ. διὰ δακτυλίου μὲν οὖν ἔμεγ' ἂν διελκύσαις.

ΧΡ. εἰ τυγχάνοι γ' ὁ δακτύλιος ὢν τηλία.

ΓΡ. καὶ μὴν τὸ μειράκιον τοδὶ προσέρχεται,
οὗπερ πάλαι κατηγοροῦσα τυγχάνω·
ἔοικε δ' ἐπὶ κῶμον βαδίζειν.

ΧΡ.   φαίνεται. 1040
στεφάνους γέ τοι καὶ δᾷδ' ἔχων πορεύεται.

ΝΕΑΝΙΑΣ. ἀσπάζομαι.

ΓΡ.   τί φησιν;

ΝΕ.   ἀρχαία φίλη,
πολιὰ γεγένησαι ταχύ γε νὴ τὸν οὐρανόν.

ΓΡ. τάλαιν' ἐγὼ τῆς ὕβρεος ἧς ὑβρίζομαι.

ΧΡ. ἔοικε διὰ πολλοῦ χρόνου σ' ἑορακέναι. 1045

ΓΡ. ποίου χρόνου, ταλάνταθ', ὃς παρ' ἐμοὶ χθὲς ἦν;

ΧΡ. τοὐναντίον πέπονθε τοῖς πολλοῖς ἄρα·
μεθύων γάρ, ὡς ἔοικεν, ὀξύτερον βλέπει.

ΓΡ. οὔκ, ἀλλ' ἀκόλαστός ἐστιν ἀεὶ τοὺς τρόπους.

ΝΕ. ὦ Ποντοπόσειδον καὶ θεοὶ πρεσβυτικοί, 1050
ἐν τῷ προσώπῳ τῶν ῥυτίδων ὅσας ἔχει.

CHR. He was no fool : he knew the way to eat
    The goodly substance of a fond old dame.

O.L. O then, my dear, the God is much to blame.
    He said he'd right the injured, every one.

CHR. What shall he do ? speak, and the thing is done.

O.L. He should, by Zeus, this graceless youth compel
    To recompense the love that loved him well ;
    Or no good fortune on the lad should light.

CHR. Did he not then repay you every night ?

O.L. He'd never leave me all my life, he said.

CHR. And rightly too ; but now he counts you dead.

O.L. My dear, with love's fierce pangs I've pined away.

CHR. Nay rather, grown quite rotten, I should say.

O.L. O, you could draw me through a ring, I know.

CHR. A ring ? A hoop that round a sieve could go.

O.L. O, here comes he of whom I've been complaining
    All this long while ; this is that very lad !
    Bound to some revel surely.

CHR.   So it seems.

    At least, he has got the chaplets and the torch.[a]

YOUTH. Friends, I salute you.

O.L.   Eh ?

YOUTH.   Mine ancient flame,
    How very suddenly you've got grey hair.

O.L. O me, the insults I am forced to bear.

CHR. 'Tis years since last he saw you, I dare say.

O.L. What years, you wretch ? He saw me yesterday !

CHR. Why then, his case is different from the rest ;
    When in his cups, methinks, he sees the best.

O.L. No, this is just his naughty, saucy way.

YOUTH. O Gods of eld ! Poseidon of the Main !
    What countless wrinkles does her face contain !

                [a] *Enter Youth.*

ARISTOPHANES

ΓΡ. ἆ ἆ,
    τὴν δᾷδα μή μοι πρόσφερ'.

ΧΡ.   εὖ μέντοι λέγει.
    ἐὰν γὰρ αὐτὴν εἷς μόνος σπινθὴρ λάβῃ,
    ὥσπερ παλαιὰν εἰρεσιώνην καύσεται.

ΝΕ. βούλει διὰ χρόνου πρός με παῖσαι;

ΓΡ.   ποῖ, τάλαν;   1055

ΝΕ. αὐτοῦ, λαβοῦσα κάρυα.

ΓΡ.   παιδιὰν τίνα;

ΝΕ. πόσους ἔχεις ὀδόντας.

ΧΡ.   ἀλλὰ γνώσομαι
    κἄγωγ'· ἔχει γὰρ τρεῖς ἴσως ἢ τέτταρας.

ΝΕ. ἀπότισον· ἕνα γὰρ γόμφιον μόνον φορεῖ.

ΓΡ. ταλάντατ' ἀνδρῶν, οὐχ ὑγιαίνειν μοι δοκεῖς,   1060
    πλυνόν με ποιῶν ἐν τοσούτοις ἀνδράσιν.

ΝΕ. ὄναιο μεντἄν, εἴ τις ἐκπλύνειέ σε.

ΧΡ. οὐ δῆτ', ἐπεὶ νῦν μὲν καπηλικῶς ἔχει,
    εἰ δ' ἐκπλυνεῖται τοῦτο τὸ ψιμύθιον,
    ὄψει κατάδηλα τοῦ προσώπου τὰ ῥάκη.   1065

ΓΡ. γέρων ἀνὴρ ὢν οὐχ ὑγιαίνειν μοι δοκεῖς.

ΝΕ. πειρᾷ μὲν οὖν ἴσως σε καὶ τῶν τιτθίων
    ἐφάπτεταί σου λανθάνειν δοκῶν ἐμέ.

ΓΡ. μὰ τὴν Ἀφροδίτην, οὐκ ἐμοῦ γ', ὦ βδελυρὲ σύ.

ΧΡ. μὰ τὴν Ἑκάτην, οὐ δῆτα· μαινοίμην γὰρ ἄν.   1070
    ἀλλ', ὦ νεανίσκ', οὐκ ἐῶ τὴν μείρακα
    μισεῖν σε ταύτην.

ΝΕ.   ἀλλ' ἔγωγ' ὑπερφιλῶ.

ΧΡ. καὶ μὴν κατηγορεῖ γέ σου.

---

^a εἰρεσιώνη=the harvest wreath, hung up over the house door ; K. 729, W. 399.

454

O.L.	O! O!
	Keep your torch off me, do.
CHR.	In that she's right.
	For if one spark upon her skin should light,
	'Twould set her blazing, like a shrivelled wreath.[a]
YOUTH.	Come, shall we play together?
O.L.	Where? for shame!
YOUTH.	Here with some nuts.
O.L.	And what's your little game?
YOUTH.	How many teeth you've got.[b]
CHR.	How many teeth?
	I'll make a guess at that. She's three, no, four.
YOUTH.	Pay up; you've lost: one grinder, and no more.
O.L.	Wretch, are you crazy that you make your friend
	A washing-pot before so many men? [c]
YOUTH.	Were you well washed, 'twould do you good belike.
CHR.	No, no, she's got up for the market now.
	But if her white-lead paint were washed away,
	Too plain you'd see the tatters of her face.
O.L.	So old and saucy! Are you crazy too?
YOUTH.	What, is he trying to corrupt you, love,
	Toying and fondling you when I'm not looking?
O.L.	By Aphrodite, no, you villain you!
CHR.	No, no, by Hecate, I'm not so daft.[d]
	But come, my boy, I really can't allow you
	To hate the girl.
YOUTH.	Hate her? I love her dearly.
CHR.	Yet she complains of—

---

[b] Instead of "how many nuts": a child's game.

[c] Sousing me with dirty water, that is, abuse.

[d] "The old lady having used a girl's oath, μὰ τὴν Ἀφροδίτην, quite inappropriate to her age and appearance, the old man responds with a woman's oath, μὰ τὴν Ἑκάτην, equally inappropriate to his sex": R.

ARISTOPHANES

NE.   τί κατηγορεῖ;
XP. εἶναί σ' ὑβριστήν φησι καὶ λέγειν ὅτι
    πάλαι ποτ' ἦσαν ἄλκιμοι Μιλήσιοι.   1075
NE. ἐγὼ περὶ ταύτης οὐ μαχοῦμαί σοι,
XP.   τὸ τί;
NE. αἰσχυνόμενος τὴν ἡλικίαν τὴν σήν, ἐπεὶ
    οὐκ ἄν ποτ' ἄλλῳ τοῦτό γ' ἐπέτρεπον ποιεῖν·
    νῦν δ' ἄπιθι χαίρων συλλαβὼν τὴν μείρακα.
XP. οἶδ' οἶδα τὸν νοῦν· οὐκέτ' ἀξιοῖς ἴσως   1080
    εἶναι μετ' αὐτῆς.
ΓΡ.   ὁ δ' ἐπιτρέψων ἐστὶ τίς;
NE. οὐκ ἂν διαλεχθείην διεσπλεκωμένῃ
    ὑπὸ μυρίων ἐτῶν γε καὶ τρισχιλίων.
XP. ὅμως δ' ἐπειδὴ καὶ τὸν οἶνον ἠξίους
    πίνειν, συνεκποτέ' ἐστί σοι καὶ τὴν τρύγα.   1085
NE. ἀλλ' ἔστι κομιδῇ τρὺξ παλαιὰ καὶ σαπρά.
XP. οὐκοῦν τρύγοιπος ταῦτα πάντ' ἰάσεται.
NE. ἀλλ' εἴσιθ' εἴσω· τῷ θεῷ γὰρ βούλομαι
    ἐλθὼν ἀναθεῖναι τοὺς στεφάνους τούσδ' οὓς ἔχω.
ΓΡ. ἐγὼ δέ γ' αὐτῷ καὶ φράσαι τι βούλομαι.   1090
NE. ἐγὼ δέ γ' οὐκ εἴσειμι.
XP.   θάρρει, μὴ φοβοῦ.
    οὐ γὰρ βιάσεται.
NE.   πάνυ καλῶς τοίνυν λέγεις.
    ἱκανὸν γὰρ αὐτὴν πρότερον ὑπεπίττουν χρόνον.
ΓΡ. βάδιζ'· ἐγὼ δέ σου κατόπιν εἰσέρχομαι.
XP. ὡς εὐτόνως, ὦ Ζεῦ βασιλεῦ, τὸ γρᾴδιον   1905
    ὥσπερ λεπὰς τῷ μειρακίῳ προσίσχεται.

---

a " Possibly τίς ὁ ἐπ. was a legal or technical formula of some sort ": R.

b διεσπλεκωμένῃ = συνουσιασμένῃ, διεφθαρμένῃ: Schol. ἐτῶν may be the gen. of either ἔτης "a comrade" or ἔτος "a year."

456

YOUTH.	What ?
CHR.	Your flouts and jeers,

Sending her word *Long since, in war's alarms*
Were the Milesians lusty men-at-arms.

YOUTH. Well, I won't fight you for her sake.

CHR. How mean you ?

YOUTH. For I respect your age, since be you sure
It is not everybody I'd permit
To take my girl. You, take her and begone.

CHR. I know, I know your drift ; no longer now
You'd keep her company.

O.L. Who'll permit *that* ? [a]

YOUTH. I won't have anything to do with one
Who has been the sport of thirteen thousand—
suns.[b]

CHR. But, howsoever, as you drank the wine,
You should, in justice, also drink the dregs.

YOUTH. Pheugh ! they're such very old and fusty dregs !

CHR. Won't a dreg-strainer remedy all that ?

YOUTH. Well, go ye in. I want to dedicate
The wreaths I am wearing to this gracious God.

O.L. Aye then, I want to tell him something too.

YOUTH. Aye then, I'll not go in.

CHR. Come, don't be frightened.
Why, she won't ravish you.

YOUTH. I'm glad to hear it.
I've had enough of her in days gone by.[c]

O.L. Come, go you on ; I'll follow close behind.

CHR. O Zeus and King, the ancient woman sticks
Tight as a limpet to her poor young man.[d]

---

[c] ὑπεπίττουν = ἐσυνουσίαζον : Schol. Properly " to smear ships with pitch."

[d] *They all enter the house, and the door is shut. Hermes enters, knocks, and hides himself. Cario opens, and sees no one : coming out he bears a pot containing tripe, and dirty water.*

ΚΑ. τίς ἔσθ' ὁ κόπτων τὴν θύραν; τουτὶ τί ἦν;
οὐδεὶς ἔοικεν· ἀλλὰ δῆτα τὸ θύριον
φθεγγόμενον ἄλλως κλαυσιᾷ.

ΕΡΜΗΣ.   σέ τοι λέγω,
ὦ Καρίων, ἀνάμεινον.

ΚΑ.   οὗτος, εἰπέ μοι,   1100
σὺ τὴν θύραν ἔκοπτες οὑτωσὶ σφόδρα;

ΕΡ. μὰ Δί', ἀλλ' ἔμελλον· εἶτ' ἀνέῳξάς με φθάσας.
ἀλλ' ἐκκάλει τὸν δεσπότην τρέχων ταχύ,
ἔπειτα τὴν γυναῖκα καὶ τὰ παιδία,
ἔπειτα τοὺς θεράποντας, εἶτα τὴν κύνα,   1105
ἔπειτα σαυτόν, εἶτα τὴν ὗν.

ΚΑ.   εἰπέ μοι,
τί δ' ἔστιν;

ΕΡ.   ὁ Ζεύς, ὦ πόνηρε, βούλεται
ἐς ταὐτὸν ὑμᾶς συγκυκήσας τρυβλίον
ἀπαξάπαντας εἰς τὸ βάραθρον ἐμβαλεῖν.

ΚΑ. ἡ γλῶττα τῷ κήρυκι τούτων τέμνεται.   1110
ἀτὰρ διὰ τί δὴ ταῦτ' ἐπιβουλεύει ποιεῖν
ἡμᾶς;

ΕΡ.   ὁτιὴ δεινότατα πάντων πραγμάτων
εἴργασθ'. ἀφ' οὗ γὰρ ἤρξατ' ἐξ ἀρχῆς βλέπειν
ὁ Πλοῦτος, οὐδεὶς οὐ λιβανωτόν, οὐ δάφνην,
οὐ ψαιστόν, οὐχ ἱερεῖον, οὐκ ἄλλ' οὐδὲ ἕν   1115
ἡμῖν ἔτι θύει τοῖς θεοῖς.

ΚΑ.   μὰ Δί', οὐδέ γε
θύσει. κακῶς γὰρ ἐπεμελεῖσθ' ἡμῶν τότε.

ΕΡ. καὶ τῶν μὲν ἄλλων μοι θεῶν ἧττον μέλει,
ἐγὼ δ' ἀπόλωλα κἀποτέτριμμαι.

---

[a] It would seem that the tongues of the victims were cut out
separately for the Herald Hermes; then wine was poured over

CA. Who's knocking at the door ? Hallo, what's this !
'Twas nobody it seems. The door shall smart,
Making that row for nothing.

HERMES. Hoi, you sir,
Stop, Cario ! don't go in.

CA. Hallo, you fellow,
Was that you banging at the door so loudly ?

HER. No, I was going to when you flung it open.
But run you in and call your master out,
And then his wife, and then his little ones,
And then the serving-men, and then the dog,
And then yourself, and then the sow.

CA. (*severely*) Now tell me
What all this means.

HER. It means that Zeus is going
To mix you up, you rascal, in one dish,
And hurl you all into the Deadman's Pit !

CA. Now for this herald must the tongue be cut.[a]
But what's the reason that he is going to do us
Such a bad turn ?

HER. Because ye have done the basest
And worst of deeds. Since Wealth began to see,
No laurel, meal-cake, victim, frankincense,
Has any man on any altar laid
Or aught beside.

CA. Or ever will ; for scant
Your care for us in the evil days gone by.

HER. And for the other Gods I'm less concerned,
But I myself am smashed and ruined.

the tongues, and they were offered to the God. " Hence
arose the proverb ἡ γλῶττα τῷ Κήρυκι. Hermes in the present
scene has come as the herald of ill tidings ; and Cario, adopting
the proverb, gives a different turn to its meaning ; for on his lips
it signifies ' The herald of this bad news shall have his tongue cut
out ' ; εἴθε ἐκκοπείη, as the Scholiast explains it " : R.

ARISTOPHANES

ΚΑ. σωφρονεῖς.

ΕΡ. πρότερον γὰρ εἶχον μὲν παρὰ ταῖς καπηλίσιν 1120
πάντ' ἀγάθ' ἔωθεν εὐθύς, οἰνοῦτταν, μέλι,
ἰσχάδας, ὅσ' εἰκός ἐστιν Ἑρμῆν ἐσθίειν·
νυνὶ δὲ πεινῶν ἀναβάδην ἀναπαύομαι.

ΚΑ. οὔκουν δικαίως, ὅστις ἐποίεις ζημίαν
ἐνίοτε τοιαῦτ' ἀγάθ' ἔχων;

ΕΡ. οἴμοι τάλας, 1125
οἴμοι πλακοῦντος τοῦ 'ν τετράδι πεπεμμένου.

ΚΑ. ποθεῖς τὸν οὐ παρόντα καὶ μάτην καλεῖς.

ΕΡ. οἴμοι δὲ κωλῆς ἣν ἐγὼ κατήσθιον·

ΚΑ. ἀσκωλίαζ' ἐνταῦθα πρὸς τὴν αἰθρίαν.

ΕΡ. σπλάγχνων τε θερμῶν ὧν ἐγὼ κατήσθιον. 1130

ΚΑ. ὀδύνη σε περὶ τὰ σπλάγχν' ἔοικέ τι στρέφειν.

ΕΡ. οἴμοι δὲ κύλικος ἴσον ἴσῳ κεκραμένης.

ΚΑ. ταύτην ἐπιπιὼν ἀποτρέχων οὐκ ἂν φθάνοις;

ΕΡ. ἆρ' ὠφελήσαις ἄν τι τὸν σαυτοῦ φίλον;

ΚΑ. εἴ του δέει γ' ὧν δυνατός εἰμί σ' ὠφελεῖν. 1135

ΕΡ. εἴ μοι πορίσας ἄρτον τιν' εὖ πεπεμμένον
δοίης καταφαγεῖν καὶ κρέας νεανικὸν
ὧν θύεθ' ὑμεῖς ἔνδον.

ΚΑ. ἀλλ' οὐκ ἔκφορα.

ΕΡ. καὶ μὴν ὁπότε τι σκευάριον τοῦ δεσπότου
ὑφέλοι', ἐγώ σε λανθάνειν ἐποίουν ἀεί. 1140

ΚΑ. ἐφ' ᾧ τε μετέχειν καὐτός, ὦ τοιχωρύχε.
ἧκεν γὰρ ἄν σοι ναστὸς εὖ πεπεμμένος.

ΕΡ. ἔπειτα τοῦτόν γ' αὐτὸς ἂν κατῆσθιες.

ΚΑ. οὐ γὰρ μετεῖχες τὰς ἴσας πληγὰς ἐμοί,
ὁπότε τι ληφθείην πανουργήσας ἐγώ. 1145

---

[a] ἀναβάδην, lit. "with my feet up," *i.e.* reclining. His occupation is gone. [b] Reference uncertain.

[c] Hermes, born on the fourth day of the month (*Hymn to Hermes* 19), received offerings on the fourth day of each month.

460

CA.   Good.

HER. For until now the tavern-wives would bring
From early dawn figs, honey, tipsy-cake,
Titbits for Hermes, such as Hermes loved ;
But now I idly cross my legs *a* and starve.

CA. And rightly too who, though such gifts you got,
Would wrong the givers.*b*

HER.   O, my hapless lot !
O me, the Fourth-day *c* cake in days gone by !

CA. You want the absent ; nought avails your cry.*d*

HER. O me, the gammon which was erst my fare !

CA. Here play your game on bladders, in the air.*e*

HER. O me, the inwards which I ate so hot !

CA. In your own inwards now a pain you've got.

HER. O me, the tankard, brimmed with half and half !

CA. Begone your quickest, taking this to quaff.*f*

HER. Will you not help a fellow-knave to live ?

CA. If anything you want is mine to give.

HER. O, could you get me but one toothsome loaf,
Or from the sacrifice you make within
One slice of lusty meat ?

CA.   No exports here.

HER. O, whenso'er your master's goods you stole,
'Twas I that caused you to escape detection.

CA. Upon condition, ruffian, that you shared
The spoils.   A toothsome cake would go to you.

HER. And then you ate it every bit yourself.

CA. But you, remember, never shared the kicks
Were I perchance detected at my tricks.

---

   d A line from some tragedy, applied to Heracles when searching for his lost favourite Hylas : Schol.

   e Leaping on inflated bladders ; from ἀσκός, with a play on κωλή (1128), a game at the Attic Dionysia. The player hopped on to an inflated bladder, and tried how long he could keep his balance.

   f Offers the dirty water in his pot.

ΕΡ. μὴ μνησικακήσῃς, εἰ σὺ Φυλὴν κατέλαβες.
ἀλλὰ ξύνοικον πρὸς θεῶν δέξασθέ με.

ΚΑ. ἔπειτ᾽ ἀπολιπὼν τοὺς θεοὺς ἐνθάδε μενεῖς;

ΕΡ. τὰ γὰρ παρ᾽ ὑμῖν ἐστι βελτίω πολύ.

ΚΑ. τί δέ; ταὐτομολεῖν ἀστεῖον εἶναί σοι δοκεῖ; 1150

ΕΡ. πατρὶς γάρ ἐστι πᾶσ᾽ ἵν᾽ ἂν πράττῃ τις εὖ.

ΚΑ. τί δῆτ᾽ ἂν εἴης ὄφελος ἡμῖν ἐνθάδ᾽ ὤν;

ΕΡ. παρὰ τὴν θύραν στροφαῖον ἱδρύσασθέ με.

ΚΑ. στροφαῖον; ἀλλ᾽ οὐκ ἔργον ἔστ᾽ οὐδὲν στροφῶν.

ΕΡ. ἀλλ᾽ ἐμπολαῖον.

ΚΑ.   ἀλλὰ πλουτοῦμεν· τί οὖν 1155
Ἑρμῆν παλιγκάπηλον ἡμᾶς δεῖ τρέφειν;

ΕΡ. ἀλλὰ δόλιον τοίνυν.

ΚΑ.   δόλιον; ἥκιστά γε·
οὐ γὰρ δόλου νῦν ἔργον, ἀλλ᾽ ἁπλῶν τρόπων.

ΕΡ. ἀλλ᾽ ἡγεμόνιον.

ΚΑ.   ἀλλ᾽ ὁ θεὸς ἤδη βλέπει,
ὥσθ᾽ ἡγεμόνος οὐδὲν δεησόμεσθ᾽ ἔτι. 1160

ΕΡ. ἐναγώνιος τοίνυν ἔσομαι. καὶ τί ἔτ᾽ ἐρεῖς;
Πλούτῳ γὰρ ἔστι τοῦτο συμφορώτατον,
ποιεῖν ἀγῶνας μουσικοὺς καὶ γυμνικούς.

ΚΑ. ὡς ἀγαθόν ἐστ᾽ ἐπωνυμίας πολλὰς ἔχειν·
οὗτος γὰρ ἐξεύρηκεν αὑτῷ βιότιον. 1165
οὐκ ἐτὸς ἅπαντες οἱ δικάζοντες θαμὰ
σπεύδουσιν ἐν πολλοῖς γεγράφθαι γράμμασιν.

---

a " ' If you have captured Phyle as Thrasybulus did, then grant
an amnesty (μὴ μνησικακήσῃς) as Thrasybulus did.' The capture
of Phyle was the great initial success of Thrasybulus in his campaign to overthrow the Thirty, and restore the democratic constitution of Athens. The Amnesty was the end which crowned
the work of that campaign " : R.

b This is given in the *Corpus Paroemiographorum* (Macarius
ii. 45) ὅπου γὰρ εὖ πράσσει τις, ἐνταυθοῖ πατρίς. It seems to be a

HER. Well, don't bear malice, if you've Phyle got,[a]
But take me in to share your happy lot.

CA. What, leave the Gods, and settle here below ?

HER. For things look better here than there, I trow.

CA. Think you Desertion is a name so grand ?

HER. Where most I prosper, there's my father-land.[b]

CA. How could we use you if we took you in ?

HER. Install me here, the Turn-god[c] by the door.

CA. The Turn-god ?   Turns and twists we want no more.

HER. The God of Commerce ?

CA.   Wealth we've got, nor need
A petty-huckstering Hermes now to feed.

HER. The God of Craft ?

CA.   Craft ? quite the other way.
Not craft, but Honesty, we need to-day.

HER. The God of guidance ?

CA.   Wealth can see, my boy !
A guide no more 'tis needful to employ.

HER. The God of games ?   Aha, I've caught you there.
For Wealth is always highly sympathetic
With literary games, and games athletic.

CA. How lucky 'tis to have a lot of names !
He has gained a living by that " God of games."[c]
Not without cause our Justices contrive
Their names to enter in more lists than one.[d]

cynical version of πᾶσα γῆ πατρίς (Zenobius v. 74) "part of an
oracle given to Meleos the Pelasgian, when inquiring about a
habitation "; Stobaeus, *Flor.* xl. 7 has ἀνδρὶ σοφῷ πᾶσα γῆ βατή.
ψυχῆς γὰρ ἀγαθῆς πατρὶς ὁ σύμπας κόσμος. *Cf.* Cic. *Tusc. Disp.*
v. 37 *patria est ubicumque est bene.*
    [b] H. mentions some of his titles in the hope of favour. Στρο-
φαῖος, the Hinge-God, because his statue was placed by the hinge
(στροφεύς) of the outer door " to keep off other thieves ".: Schol.
    [c] He has gained a living by having a lot of names.
    [d] See note on p. 448.

ΕΡ. οὐκοῦν ἐπὶ τούτοις εἰσίω;

ΚΑ.   καὶ πλῦνέ γε
αὐτὸς προσελθὼν πρὸς τὸ φρέαρ τὰς κοιλίας,
ἵν᾽ εὐθέως διακονικὸς εἶναι δοκῇς.   1170

ΙΕΡΕΥΣ. τίς ἂν φράσειε ποῦ ᾽στι Χρεμύλος μοι σαφῶς;

ΧΡ. τί δ᾽ ἔστιν, ὦ βέλτιστε;

ΙΕ.   τί γὰρ ἀλλ᾽ ἢ κακῶς;
ἀφ᾽ οὗ γὰρ ὁ Πλοῦτος οὗτος ἤρξατο βλέπειν,
ἀπόλωλ᾽ ὑπὸ λιμοῦ.   καταφαγεῖν γὰρ οὐκ ἔχω,
καὶ ταῦτα τοῦ σωτῆρος ἱερεὺς ὢν Διός.   1175

ΧΡ. ἡ δ᾽ αἰτία τίς ἐστιν, ὦ πρὸς τῶν θεῶν;

ΙΕ. θύειν ἔτ᾽ οὐδεὶς ἀξιοῖ.

ΧΡ.   τίνος οὕνεκα;

ΙΕ. ὅτι πάντες εἰσὶ πλούσιοι· καίτοι τότε,
ὅτ᾽ εἶχον οὐδέν, ὁ μὲν ἂν ἥκων ἔμπορος
ἔθυσεν ἱερεῖόν τι σωθείς, ὁ δέ τις ἂν   1180
δίκην ἀποφυγών· ὁ δ᾽ ἂν ἐκαλλιερεῖτό τις,
κἀμέ γ᾽ ἐκάλει τὸν ἱερέα· νῦν δ᾽ οὐδὲ εἷς
θύει τὸ παράπαν οὐδέν, οὐδ᾽ εἰσέρχεται,
πλὴν ἀποπατησόμενοί γε πλεῖν ἢ μυρίοι.

ΧΡ. οὔκουν τὰ νομιζόμενα σὺ τούτων λαμβάνεις;   1185

ΙΕ. τὸν οὖν Δία τὸν σωτῆρα καὐτός μοι δοκῶ
χαίρειν ἐάσας ἐνθάδ᾽ αὐτοῦ καταμενεῖν.

ΧΡ. θάρρει· καλῶς ἔσται γάρ, ἢν θεὸς θέλῃ.
ὁ Ζεὺς ὁ σωτὴρ γὰρ πάρεστιν ἐνθάδε,
αὐτόματος ἥκων.

ΙΕ.   πάντ᾽ ἀγαθὰ τοίνυν λέγεις.   1190

HER. Then on these terms I enter ?

CA.   Aye, come in.
And take these guts, and wash them at the well,
And so, at once, be Hermes Ministrant.[a]

PRIEST. O tell me, where may Chremylus be found ?

CHR. What cheer, my worthy fellow ?

PR.   What but ill ?
For ever since this Wealth began to see,
I'm downright famished, I've got nought to eat,
And that, although I'm Zeus the Saviour's priest.

CHR. O, by the Powers, and what's the cause of that ?

PR. No man will slay a victim now.

CHR.   Why not ?

PR. Because they all are wealthy ; yet before,
When men had nothing, one, a merchant saved
From voyage-perils, one, escaped from law,
Would come and sacrifice ; or else at home
Perform his vows, and summon me, the priest.
But not a soul comes now, or body either,
Except a lot of chaps to do their needs.

CHR. Then don't you take your wonted toll of that ?

PR. So I've myself a mind to cut the service
Of Zeus the Saviour now, and settle here.

CHR. Courage ! God willing, all will yet be well.
For Zeus the Saviour is himself within,[b]
Coming unasked.

PR.   O, excellent good news !

[a] In his character as διάκονος of Zeus (*cf.* Aesch. *Prometheus,* 963 τὸν τοῦ τυράννου τοῦ νέου διάκονον). *Enter the Priest of Zeus Soter, to find Chremylus.*

[b] " In my judgement Chremylus means that the great Zeus himself has followed the example of Hermes ; so that the Priest, thinking to desert his God for the purpose of entering into the service of Wealth, finds that his God has been beforehand with him, and is already himself snugly ensconced within " : R.

ARISTOPHANES

XP. ἱδρυσόμεθ' οὖν αὐτίκα μάλ', ἀλλὰ περίμενε,
τὸν Πλοῦτον, οὗπερ πρότερον ἦν ἱδρυμένος,
τὸν ὀπισθόδομον ἀεὶ φυλάττων τῆς θεοῦ.
ἀλλ' ἐκδότω τις δεῦρο δᾷδας ἡμμένας,
ἵν' ἔχων προηγῇ τῷ θεῷ σύ.

ΙΕ.   πάνυ μὲν οὖν   1195
δρᾶν ταῦτα χρή.

XP.   τὸν Πλοῦτον ἔξω τις κάλει.

ΓΡ. ἐγὼ δὲ τί ποιῶ ;

XP.   τὰς χύτρας, αἷς τὸν θεὸν
ἱδρυσόμεθα, λαβοῦσ' ἐπὶ τῆς κεφαλῆς φέρε
σεμνῶς· ἔχουσα δ' ἦλθες αὐτὴ ποικίλα.

ΓΡ. ὧν δ' οὕνεκ' ἦλθον;

XP.   πάντα σοι πεπράξεται.   1200
ἥξει γὰρ ὁ νεανίσκος ὥς σ' εἰς ἑσπέραν.

ΓΡ. ἀλλ' εἴ γε μέντοι νὴ Δί' ἐγγυᾷ σύ μοι
ἥξειν ἐκεῖνον ὥς ἔμ', οἴσω τὰς χύτρας.

XP. καὶ μὴν πολὺ τῶν ἄλλων χυτρῶν τἀναντία
αὗται ποιοῦσι· ταῖς μὲν ἄλλαις γὰρ χύτραις   1205
ἡ γραῦς ἔπεστ' ἀνωτάτω, ταύτης δὲ νῦν
τῆς γραὸς ἐπιπολῆς ἔπεισιν αἱ χύτραι.

ΧΟ. οὐκ ἔτι τοίνυν εἰκὸς μέλλειν οὐδ' ἡμᾶς, ἀλλ' ἀνα-
χωρεῖν
εἰς τοὔπισθεν· δεῖ γὰρ κατόπιν τούτων ᾄδοντας
ἔπεσθαι.

---

^a " From this point to the close of the play Chremylus is arrang-
ing a great religious procession for the purpose of escorting Wealth
in triumph to his proper home in the Athenian Treasure-house.
There was not much wealth in the Treasury now, owing to the
cessation of the tribute paid by the Allies, and to the enormous
expenditure occasioned by the adhesion of Athens to the anti-
Spartan League " : R.

^b The inner cell of the Parthenon, used as a treasury.

^c *Enter Old Lady from the house.*

466

CHR. So we'll at once install—but bide awhile—
Wealth in the place where he was erst installed,[a]
Guarding the Treasury in Athene's Temple.[b]
Hi ! bring me lighted candles. Take them, you,
And march before the God.

PR. With all my heart.

CHR. Call Wealth out, somebody.[c]

O.L. And I ?

CHR. O, you.
Here, balance me these installation pots [d]
Upon your head, and march along in state.
You've got your festive robes at all events.

O.L. But what I came for ?

CHR. Everything is right.
The lad you love shall visit you to-night.

O.L. O, if you pledge your honour that my boy
Will come to-night, I'll bear the pots with joy.

CHR. These pots are not like other pots at all.
In other pots the mother [e] is atop,
But here the mother's underneath the pot.

CH. 'Tis the end of the Play, and we too must delay
        our departure no longer, but hasten away,
And follow along at the rear of the throng,[f]
        rejoicing and singing our festival song.

---

[d] Pots of boiled pulse were offered at a dedication of altar or temple.

[e] γραῦς means (1) "old woman," (2) "scum" on the surface of milk, boiled vegetables, soup, etc. So "mother" is applied to scum on boiling liquids, mould on fermenting jams, yeast, and the like (*English Dialect Dictionary*, iv. 175).

[f] *In the rear of the actors.* The actors would depart from the *stage*, the Chorus, with dance and song, from the *orchestra* ; but all are supposed to be combining in one great triumphal procession to the Acropolis, there to install Wealth, as a perpetual resident, in a place with which he had once been familiar, but to which he had long been a stranger, viz. in the Treasury of the Athenian Republic at the back of Athene's Temple.

INDEX

INDEX

Cynalopex, nickname of Philostratus, a pander, *L.* 957
Cyprus, *L.* 833
Cythera, an island S. of Greece, where Aphrodite had a temple, *L.* 833

Demostratus, *L.* 391
Dexinicus, *Pl.* 800
Dionysius, tyrant of Syracuse, *Pl.* 550

Echinus, a town on the Melian Gulf, *L.* 1169
Eileithyia, goddess of childbirth, *E.* 369, *L.* 742
Epicrates, a demagogue who took part with Thrasybulus in the overthrow of the Thirty. He afterwards was ambassador to the king of Persia, and accepted bribes from him, *E.* 71
Epicurus, unknown, *E.* 645
Epigonus, an effeminate, *E.* 167
Erinys = Fury, avenger of blood, *Pl.* 423
Euaeon, a pauper, *E.* 408
Eubule, *T.* 808
Eucrates, no doubt the brother of Nicias, put to death under the Thirty, *L.* 103
Eudamus or Eudemus, a vendor of amulets, *Pl.* 884
Euripides, a politician, *E.* 825
Euripides, the poet, *L.* 283, 368
Eurotas, the river of Sparta, *L.* 1308

Gargettus, an Attic deme, *T.* 898
Genetyllis, a title of Aphrodite, or of her attendant love-deities, *L.* 2, *T.* 130
Geres, *E.* 932
Geron, *E.* 848
Geusistrate, *E.* 48
Glaucetes, a glutton, *T.* 1035
Glyce, *E.* 430

Harmodius, statue of, in Agora, *E.* 682
Helen, a play of Euripides, *L.* 155, *T.* 850
Heracleids, children of Heracles, *P.* 385
Heracles, kept waiting for supper in the proverb, *L.* 927
Hiero, an auctioneer, *E.* 757

Hieronymus, an unknown politician, *E.* 201
Hippias, tyrant of Athens, *L.* 617, 1153
Hippocrates, an Athenian general, nephew of Pericles, slain at Delium, *T.* 273
Hyperbolus, a demagogue, *T.* 840

Iaso, daughter of Asclepius, *Pl.* 701
Ibycus of Rhegium, an erotic poet, *T.* 161

King of Persia, the great, *Pl.* 170

Laïs, a courtesan, *Pl.* 178
Lamachus, a distinguished soldier, died at Syracuse 414 b.c., *T.* 841
Lamias, keeper of the public prison, *E.* 77
Leipsydrium, a fortress where the Alcmaeonidae fortified themselves after the death of Hipparchus; probably on Mt. Parnes, *L.* 665
Leonidas, king of Sparta, who fell at Thermopylae, *L.* 1254
Leucolophus, unknown, *E.* 645
Loxias = Apollo, *Pl.* 8
Lycon, husband of Rhodia, *L.* 270
Lycurgia of Aeschylus, the tetralogy containing the *Edonians*, the *Bassarides*, the *Young Men*, and *Lycurgus* (satyric drama), *T.* 135
Lynceus, *Pl.* 210
Lysicrates, an ugly snub-nosed man, *E.* 630, 736

Marathon, *T.* 806
Megarian Walls, *L.* 1169
Melanion, *L.* 785
Melanippe, *T.* 547
Melian Gulf, *L.* 1169
Melistiche, *E.* 46
Menelaus, *L.* 155
Messene, *L.* 1142
Micon, a painter, *L.* 679
Midas, the wealthy king of Phrygia, who had the ears of an ass, *Pl.* 287
Milesian wool, *L.* 729
Miletus, *L.* 108
Myronides, about 457 b.c., led out an army of old men and boys, and defeated the Corinthians near Megara; and in 456 defeated the

470

INDEX